ILIJA GARAŠANIN: BALKAN BISMARCK

by

David MacKenzie

EAST EUROPEAN MONOGRAPHS, BOULDER
DISTRIBUTED BY COLUMBIA UNIVERSITY PRESS, NEW YORK

1985

EAST EUROPEAN MONOGRAPHS, NO. CLXXXI

Copyright © 1985 by David MacKenzie
Library of Congress Catalog Card Number 84-82227
ISBN 0-88033-073-2

Printed in the United States of America

TABLE OF CONTENTS

Ilija Garašanin

PREFACE

During the decade spent in preparing this book, the author received generous cooperation and assistance from many archivists, librarians and scholars in Yugoslavia and the United States. Without their help and support from research and travel grants, this biography could not have been completed. The author wishes to thank the staffs of the National Library (Narodna Biblioteka), the Archive of the Serbian Academy of Sciences and Fine Arts (Arhiv Srpske Akademije Nauke i Umetnosti) and the State Archive of Serbia (Državni Arhiv Srbije) for their courteous assistance. Very helpful at the Historical Institute (Istoriski Institut) in Belgrade were Dr. Liljana Aleksić and Dr. Milorad Radević who went out of their way to provide assistance. Other Yugoslav scholars who provided notable aid were Dr. Vladimir Stojančević and Dr. Vasilije Krestić of the Serbian Academy. Very helpful in numerous ways were my Serbian friends of long standing, Dr. Radoslav Stojanović and his wife, Vera. Warm thanks are due to Dr. Jeffrey Patton of the Geography Department of the University of North Carolina at Greensboro for preparing the map of Serbia under Prince Miloš Obrenović on very short notice.

A research leave from the University of North Carolina at Greensboro in the spring of 1974 enabled me to begin study of the Garašanin papers and research in the Serbian Academy. Summer grants from the Penrose Fund of the American Philosophical Society (1978 and 1979), from Fulbright-Hays (1979) and from the Research Council of the University of North Carolina at Greensboro allowed me to complete my research in Yugoslavia. In the United States the author spent parts of two summers

v

doing research in published materials with the aid of the summer Research Laboratory of the University of Illinois at Champaign-Urbana and its wonderful library staff. Reading the entire manuscript and providing many useful suggestions for its improvement were Dr. Gale Stokes of Rice University and Dr. Ann Saab of the University of North Carolina at Greensboro. Dr. Dimitrije Djordjević of the University of California at Santa Barbara and Dr. Liljana Aleksić-Pejković of the Historical Institute of Belgrade read part of the manuscript and contributed valuable suggestions. Any defects in this work should be attributed to the author, not to his many Yugoslav and American colleagues and friends.

Greensboro, North Carolina
January 1984

PRONOUNCIATION GUIDE FOR SERBIAN NAMES

c — ts as in Cetinje (Tsetinjeh)
ć — ch as in Obrenović (Oh-bren-o-vitch)
č — ch as in Politička (Pol-i-tich-kah)
j — yeh as in Ilija (Il-i-yah)
š — sh as in Garašanin (Gah-RAH-shah-nin)
ž — zh as in Žujović (ZHU-yo--vitch)

IMPORTANT PERSONAGES

Julius (Gyula) ANDRÁSSY (1832-90): Count, Magyar statesman.

Matija BAN (1818-1903): Writer from Dubrovnik, propagandist.

Otto von BISMARCK (1815-98): Prussian premier (1862-70), German statesman.

Milovoje P. BLAZNAVAC (1824-73): Colonel, War Minister, 1865-68, regent, 1868-72.

Jevrem GRUJIĆ (1826-95): Liberal leader, secretary of St. Andrew's Assembly, 1858.

Aleksandar KARADJORDJEVIĆ (1806-85): son of Karadjordje; prince of Serbia, 1842-58.

Stevan P. KNIĆANIN (1807-55): Serbian officer, commander in Vojvodina, 1848-49.

Toma KOVAČEVIĆ (1820-63): native of Bosnia, treasurer of Serbian War Ministry, national activist.

Miloje LEŠJANIN (1830-67): section head in Serbian Foreign Ministry.

Kosta MAGAZINOVIĆ: Serbian envoy in Bucharest, 1863-69, friend of Garašanin.

Stevča MIHAILOVIĆ (1804-88): Liberal leader, Council chairman, 1859-61.

Hippolyte MONDAIN: French major of engineering; Serbian War Minister, 1861-65; close friend of Garašanin.

NIKOLA I (Petrović-Njegoš) (1844-1921): prince then king of Montenegro, 1860-1918.

Anastasije NIKOLIĆ (1803-82): Garašanin's assistant, national activist.

ix

Miloš OBRENOVIĆ (1780-1860): Prince of Serbia, 1815-39, 1858-60.

Mihailo OBRENOVIĆ (1825-68): Prince of Serbia, 1839-42, 1860-68; son of Miloš.

Avram PETRONIJEVIĆ (1791-1852): "Defender" leader, Serbian premier and foreign minister.

Milan PIROĆANAC (1837-97): section chief in Serbian Foreign Ministry, diplomat and politician.

Jovan RISTIĆ (1831-99): Serbian envoy in Constantinople, 1861-67; Regent, 1868-72; later foreign minister and premier; historian.

Nikolai P. SHISHKIN: Russian general consul in Belgrade, 1863-74; friend of Garašanin.

Toma VUČIĆ-PERIŠIĆ (1788-1859): Military chieftain, leader of "Defenders," Interior Minister.

František ZAH (or ZACH) (1807-92): Polish agent in Serbia, 1843-48; commandant of Military Academy.

Other members of Ilija GARAŠANIN'S Family:

Luka (died 1842): Ilija's older brother; killed in Vučić Revolt.

Milutin (Savić) (1762-1842): Father of Ilija.

Milutin (1843-98): Ilija's son, politician and statesman.

Mihailo: Ilija's older brother, livestock merchant.

Sofia (Soka) (Danić): Ilija's wife.

Svetozar (died 1886): Ilija's son, adjutant to Prince Mihailo Obrenović.

LIST OF SOURCE ABBREVIATIONS

AII–Arhiv Istoriskog Instituta (Belgrade)
DAS–Državni Arhiv NR Srbije (Belgrade)
FO PRO–Foreign Office. Public Record Office (London)
GIDBiH–*Godišnjak istoriskog društva Bosne i Hercegovine* (Sarajevo)
GIDUNS–*Godišnjak istoriskog društva u Novom Sadu* (Novi Sad)
GMgrada Beograda–*Godišnjak Muzeja grada Beograda* (Belgrade)
GNĆupića–*Godišnjak Nikole Ćupića*
IG–Fond Ilije Garašanina (in DAS)
ORBL–Otdel rukopisei Biblioteki imeni Lenina (Moscow)
PO–Fond Poklon i Otkupa (in DAS)
Pisma–*Pisma Ilije Garašanina Jovanu Marinoviću* (Belgrade, SKA, 1931, 2 vols.), ed. St. Lovčević
Prepiska–*Prepiska Ilija Garašanina, knjiga I, 1839-1849,* ed. Grgur Jakšić, (Belgrade, SANU, 1950; no further volumes published)
SANU–Srpska Akademija Nauke i Umetnosti (Belgrade)
SKA–Srpska kraljevska akademija (Belgrade)
SKG–*Srpski književni glasnik* (Novi Sad)

Prince Miloš Obrenović

Toma Vučić-Perišić

Ilija Garašanin

CHAPTER I

INTRODUCTION: BISMARCK AND GARAŠANIN

"Politics are not a science based on logic; they are the capacity of always choosing at each instant in constantly changing situations the least harmful, the most useful. . . . A statesman cannot create anything for himself. He must wait and listen until he hears the steps of God sounding through events; then leap up and grasp the hem of his garment."

Otto von Bismarck[1]

Ilija Garašanin (1812-1874) was the leading statesman and bureaucrat of nineteenth century Serbia. Prominent among the "Defenders of the Constitution," the politicians who overturned Prince Mihailo Obrenović in 1842, as Interior Minister of Prince Aleksandar Karadjordjević he organized and directed a competent bureaucracy which maintained order and stability. Responsible for the army, police, communications, and education, as well as civil officialdom, he organized a postal service, established an agricultural school, military academy and arms factory. In manifold ways he promoted Serbia's growth and progress. Very early Garašanin realized that only a stable and progressive Serbia could assume a role of leadership among the South Slavs and Balkan Christians. Even then he evinced deep interest in Serbia's foreign policy. In 1844 with the aid and

1

advice of Polish and Czech émigrés, Garašanin drew up a comprehensive plan for Serbia's foreign and national policies known as "Načertanije" ("Outline") in which he described a three-stage process for the liberation of all Serbs and South Slavs from Turkish and Austrian rule and their unification under the aegis of Serbia's ruling dynasty. Finally, in 1918 this plan was fully achieved with the formation of Yugoslavia.

In the following years, while in power, 1844-53 and 1861-67, Garašanin created a network of agents outside Serbia to gather information and prepare the population of the South Slav lands for an eventual war of national liberation. During 1848-49 he directed a large-scale campaign of assistance from Serbia to the Serbs of the Vojvodina in Hungary, threatened with destruction by the Magyars. As premier and foreign minister of Serbia in 1852-53, while pursuing his national policies, he was removed abruptly from office just before the Crimean War at the insistance of Nicholas I of Russia, the formidable "Iron Tsar." Even while out of power, through his close friend and colleague, Jovan Marinović, he strongly influenced Serbia's foreign policy and helped to keep the country neutral during that war. In the mid-1850s with increasing urgency Garašanin opposed the personal rule of the incompetent and Austrophile Prince Aleksandar Karadjordjević; in 1858 he helped engineer a bloodless coup which removed that ruler and his dynasty from power.

Recalled to service as premier and foreign minister by autocratic but patriotic Prince Mihailo Obrenović (1860-68), Garašanin served him faithfully and intensified the foreign and national policies sketched in "Načertanije." Garašanin and Mihailo organized an alliance of Balkan states and peoples under Russia's aegis and prepared for a general war of national liberation against the Ottoman Empire. Just as preparations neared completion, he was removed suddenly from office by Prince Mihailo in November 1867. In retirement, as Serbia's elder statesman and mentor of the Conservative Party, he was greatly respected in Serbia and throughout Europe.

Why label Garašanin "the Balkan Bismarck"?[2] How does he compare with the great Prussian Junker who achieved German unification between 1864 and 1871, then became Europe's premier statesman for two more decades? There are striking parallels and similarities in their aims, careers and responsibilities which appear to justify such a comparison. Both were born at the end of the Napoleonic era—Bismarck in 1815, Garašanin in

1812—as scions of leading families who grew up in comfortable circumstances and represented the established, landholding interest. Entering
state service in the mid-1830s, they were both affected profoundly by
the European Revolutions of 1848 which broadened their views. From
a common basis of patriotism, conservatism and traditional values, they
became leaders in their respective countries who aimed to enhance their
power and influence, aggrandize them territorially, and make them nuclei
or dominant elements among Germans or South Slavs. For over a generation they exercised preponderant political influence under their monarchs,
sharing the aim of consolidating and strengthening their homelands domestically in order to prepare them to lead the cause of national unification. Both emphasized the need for building national self-reliance and
strength rather than depending unduly upon foreign alliances. Beginning
as patriots whose eyes focused narrowly on Serbia or Prussia, they evolved
after 1848 into statesmen seeking a broader, more comprehensive union.
For both of them Austria comprised the chief obstacle to the attainment
of that goal. They shared a realistic sense of the limitations of national
power. They ended their careers as diplomats enjoying the respect and
admiration of Europe and their countrymen for their intelligence, perceptiveness, and ability to adapt flexibly to changing circumstances. Both
were renowned for the clarity, forcefulness and style of their writing and
speech. As statesmen both were masters of maneuver on the intricate
chessboard of European politics, preferring diplomacy to force. Though
believing firmly in law and order, they were prepared to utilize a variety
of instruments, including war and revolution, to achieve their goals.

But Bismarck and Garašanin differed as significantly as they resembled
one another. Otto von Bismarck was a powerful, robust man inclined to
corpulence; Garašanin, tall, thin and frail, suffered chronically from
numerous ailments and illnesses. Garašanin remained consistently a man
of principle, respected by all for adhering unswervingly to a definite set
of beliefs and values and setting the highest standards of honesty, modesty
and self-sacrificing service. Lacking real vanity or conceit, he never sought
power for its own sake, nor did he seek to hold onto the authority which
came to him. Bismarck, on the other hand, was inordinately vain, powerseeking and arrogant. Very combative and strongwilled, he was unscrupulous in utilizing and exploiting others. Clinging stubbornly to power in
old age, he was miserable in forced retirement, even in comfortable

circumstances, unlike Garašanin who had longed eagerly to cast off the manifold burdens of office and live quietly and modestly. Some of their differences were personal; others reflected the contrast between relatively powerful Prussia, a great European power with a population of roughly eighteen million in 1860 and weak little Serbia with but a million people and still a vassal of the Ottoman Empire. Whereas Bismarck could carry through German unification by combining Prussia's superbly trained civil service, diplomatic corps, and potent army to achieve a German empire, Garašanin, conspicuously lacking such resources, remained a planner, organizer and prophet; of necessity, his work remained incomplete, his dreams unfulfilled. While Bismarck achieved his goals fully on foundations laid by his predecessors, Garašanin had to create laboriously those same foundations for subsequent generations to build upon.

Bismarck understandably has inspired numerous biographies and a tremendous, still growing volume of literature;[3] Garašanin has remained curiously neglected even by his countrymen. No previous published biography of Garašanin exists in any language. This is not because he was unimportant. In American terms he is comparable in significance to Alexander Hamilton or John C. Calhoun. Nor is data about his life sparse —the available materials are abundant. Working in an age before telephone or tape recorder, Garašanin was literally a man of the pen. Sitting for countless hours at his desk or propped up in bed with coffee and cigarettes, he wrote his princely superiors, fellow ministers, district chiefs, friends and acquaintances in Serbia and abroad. Like Bismarck's his correspondence is voluminous and fascinating, and he composed hundreds of memoranda and drafts which indicate his personal views, approach toward government, ideology and morality. Many of them outline Serbia's foreign and domestic policies. Nearly all this has been preserved in his voluminous papers housed in the State Archive of Serbia.[4] His son, Milutin, a major Serbian statesman in his own right, put them in order and copied many of the less legible documents. The author utilized them there in Belgrade in 1974, 1978 and 1979. Garašanin's extensive correspondence with Jovan Marinović—colleague, fellow Conservative leader, and closest friend—has been published in two volumes.[5] His correspondence with other Serbian leaders was collected and issued in Belgrade after World War II.[6]

Using a wide variety of family archives and other source materials, the outstanding Serbian historian, Slobodan Jovanović, assessed Garašanin's foreign policy in a series of articles and his role in Serbian history in a classic history of nineteenth century Serbia.[7] The Serbian scholar who wrote most extensively about Ilija Garašanin and his times was the late Dr. Dragoslav Stranjaković, author of *The Government of the Defenders of the Constitution, 1842-1853*.[8] After writing articles about "Načertanije" and Garašanin's national policies, he gathered extensive materials for a full-length biography, "Ilija Garašanin,"[9] which was never completed. It treats in great detail various aspects of Garašanin's life and career, glorifying him uncritically as a Serbian patriot and advocate of Yugoslav unity. Finding this manuscript in the Archive of the Serbian Academy of Sciences in Belgrade where it has lain since 1949, the author found it an invaluable source although outmoded, one-sided and unduly laudatory. More recently, the late Yugoslav scholar, Vojislav Vučković, also analyzed "Načertanije," the best-known aspect of Garašanin's career, and published some documents from his and other archives.[10] He and Grgur Jakšić later published a detailed monograph based on primary materials, *The Foreign Policy of Serbia during the Rule of Prince Mihailo*,[11] treating among other matters, Garašanin's rule during the 1860s. These accounts, supplemented by memoirs and writings by Garašanin's contemporaries, newspaper articles, and an extensive secondary literature in Serbo-Croatian, provided abundant source materials for this book.

The purpose of this biography is to describe the political and diplomatic role of an outstanding Serbian statesman who has suffered undeserved if unintentional neglect from his countrymen and foreign scholars. This is the attempt of a sympathetic outsider to present an objective picture of Garašanin's life and career. Since most English-speaking readers are unfamilar with Serbia, his life has been set against the background of nineteenth century Serbian and Balkan history.[12] This study of Ilija Garašanin comprises the prelude to an extensive treatment planned by the author of the entire Serbian national movement until the formation of a unified Yugoslavia in 1918.

For almost thirty years the author has studied Serbian and Russian history beginning with a doctoral dissertation for Columbia University: "Serbian-Russian Relations, 1875-1878," revised as *The Serbs and Russian Pan-Slavism, 1875-1878* (Ithaca, New York, 1967). For that work research was required in Vienna and Belgrade in 1955-56, the Soviet Union in 1958-59, and in Belgrade again in 1962. Rewarding secondary tasks included the study of Serbo-Croatian and getting acquainted with the terrain and people of Yugoslavia and Russia. In 1969 the author returned to Vienna and Belgrade for additional materials for a biography of General Cherniaev, commander of Russian and Serbian forces in the Serbo-Turkish War of 1876.[13] In 1974, while studying the Serbian national movement in Belgrade, the author began utilizing the newly opened papers of Ilija Garašanin and decided to prepare this biographical study.

NOTES

1. A. J. P. Taylor, *Bismarck: The Man and the Statesman* (New York, 1955), p. 115.

2. Garašanin could also be compared readily with Count Camillo di Cavour (1810-1861), the Piedmontese statesman and architect of Italian unification. As premier of a relatively minor European power (Piedmont-Sardinia), Cavour confronted situations very similar to those facing Garašanin. Whereas Serbia frequently sought Russian support against Austria and the Ottoman Empire, Cavour relied on external military aid from Napoleon III of France to achieve his goals. Like Bismarck and Garašanin, Cavour was a leading exponent of *Realpolitik;* unlike them he was a political liberal and admirer of British institutions. Cavour, like Garašanin, counted heavily on diplomatic and moral support from the Western powers (Britain and France) against the Habsburg Monarchy. See Denis Mack Smith, *Cavour and Garibaldi, 1860* (Cambridge, England, 1954) and his *Victor Emmanuel, Cavour and the Risorgimento* (London, 1971). On Italo-Serbian relations and the impact of Piedmontese policy on Serbia see Liljana Aleksić-Pejković, *Politika Italije prema Srbiji do 1870 g.* (Belgrade, 1979).

3. See especially Otto Pflanze, *Bismarck and the Development of Germany: The Period of Unification, 1815-1871* (Princeton, N.J.: 1963). A more concise recent treatment is Edward Crankshaw's *Bismarck* (New York, 1981).

4. Državni Arhiv Srbije, Fond Ilije Garašanin, hereafter IG.

5. *Pisma Ilije Garašanina Jovanu Marinoviću* (Belgrade, Srpska kraljevska akademija, 1931, 2 vols.), ed. St. Lovčević, hereafter *Pisma*.

6. *Prepiska Ilije Garašanina*, ed. Grgur Jakšić (Belgrade, Srpska akademija nauka, 1950, 2 vols.), hereafter *Prepiska*.

7. S. Jovanović, "Spoljašnja politika Ilije Garašanin," *SKG,* 1931; *Ustavobranitelji i njihova vlada, 1838-1858* (Belgrade, 1925); *Druga vlada Miloša i Mihaila, 1858-1868* (Belgrade, 1923); and *Vlada Milana Obrenovića, 1868-1889* (Belgrade, 1926-27, 2 vols.).

8. *Vlada Ustavobranitelja, 1842-1853* (Belgrade, 1932).

9. Arhiv SANU (Belgrade), No. 14233, "Ilija Garašanin" (1949).

10. V. Vučković, *Politička aksija Srbija u južnoslovenskim pokrajinama Habsburške Monarhije, 1859-1874* (Belgrade, 1965), henceforth Vučković, *Politička.*

11. G. Jakšić and V. Vučković, *Spoljna politika Srbije za vlade Kneza Mihaila* (Belgrade, 1963), henceforth Jakšić and Vučković, *Spoljna.*

12. For background see Robert L. Wolff, *The Balkans in Our Time* (New York, 1956 and 1974) and Michael B. Petrovich's excellent *A History of Modern Serbia, 1804-1918* (2 vols., New York, 1976), henceforth Petrovich, *History.* For great power diplomacy and relationships see A. J. P. Taylor, *The Struggle for Mastery in Europe, 1848-1918* (Oxford, 1954).

13. David MacKenzie, *The Lion of Tashkent: The Career of General M. G. Cherniaev* (Athens, Georgia, 1974).

Serbia Under Prince Miloš Obrenović

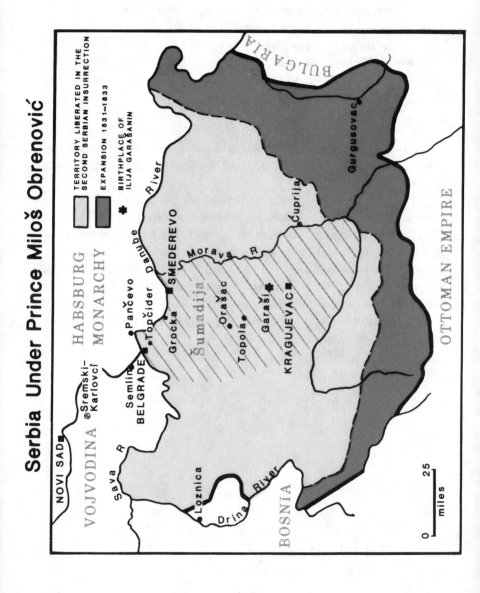

TERRITORY LIBERATED IN THE
SECOND SERBIAN INSURRECTION

EXPANSION 1831-1833

* BIRTHPLACE OF
ILIJA GARAŠANIN

HABSBURG
MONARCHY

VOJVODINA

NOVI SAD

Sremski-
Karlovci

Semlin
BELGRADE

Topčider
Pančevo

Grocka

Smederevo

Danube River

Morava R

Šumadija

Orašac

Topola

Garaši

KRAGUJEVAC

Ćuprija

Gurgusovac

BULGARIA

OTTOMAN EMPIRE

Sava R

Loznica

Drina River

BOSNIA

0 25
miles

CHAPTER II

BEGINNINGS

". . . My son, Ilija, has long desired to be accepted into state
service and be given a post for which he is prepared, provided that Your Highness decides to grant him that honor.
He can envision himself as a clerk. Besides Serbian, he
speaks Greek well and German decently."

—Milutin Garašanin to Prince Miloš Obrenović

—December 17, 1833.

For four centuries the Serbian lands, comprising much of today's
Yugoslavia, were ruled by the Ottoman Turks. Independent in the Middle
Ages and briefly an empire under the warrior king, Stevan Dušan, in the
fourteenth century, Serbia suffered crushing defeat by the Ottoman army
in a great battle in 1389 on the plain of Kosovo. During the following centuries of alien rule, the Serbian language, Greek Orthodox faith, and
memories of ancient glory preserved among Serbian peasants dreams of
freedom and independence. As Turkish control weakened, these dreams
were rekindled in 1804 by Karadjordje ("Black George") Petrović, a
courageous Serbian swine merchant. Facing arrest and probable death at
the hands of Turkish janissary troops, Karadjordje, like other Serbian local
chieftains, fled from his native village of Topola in the heart of Šumadija
("the land of forests") to the nearby hills and became an outlaw (*hajduk*).
He and other chiefs roused the Serbs in the region south of Belgrade in an

9

insurrection against local Turkish overlords. Thus began a nine-year struggle which ended finally with Karadjordje's defeat and flight into neighboring Austria in 1813.

On January 16, 1812 in the midst of this first Serbian uprising, Ilija Garašanin was born in Garaši village, Kragujevac district, near Karadjordje's native village. Late in the seventeenth century the Garašanin family had come there from rugged Montenegro ("The Black Mountain"), a bastion of Slav resistance to the Turks. Sava, a grandson of Prince Vukašin Bošković, settled in Garaši. Milutin Savić (son of Sava)—his son and Ilija's father—was born there about 1762. Until the 1830s he signed his name Milutin Savić, shifting then to Milutin Savić Garašanin (from Garaši), and finally to simply Milutin Garašanin. At first Milutin was a warrior against the Turks and remained a brave and skillful fighter until his death. As a volunteer in the Austrian army, he fought in the same unit as Karadjordje, the so-called Free Corps of Colonel Mihajlević. In 1787 during an Austro-Turkish war, for heroism in battle, Milutin was promoted to corporal and Karadjordje to first sergeant. When the war ended, Milutin returned to Garaši village to become a livestock merchant. Before the first insurrection he married Pauna Lom, sister of a local Serbian chieftain, from Dragolja village in southern Serbia. They raised a large family with at least five children surviving to adulthood; two daughters and three sons: Mihailo, Luka and Ilija, the youngest.[1]

Milutin Garašanin was tall, heavy-set and powerful with a booming voice. He was widely respected for fearfulness, truthfulness and independence of mind. Hating injustice and falsehood, he spoke his mind to everyone regardless of rank. Milutin was serious and taciturn, moderate in food and drink but famous throughout Šumadija region for his warm hospitality. Dynamic, industrious and intelligent, he soon made a fortune in the livestock trade and lived as a gentleman unostentatiously. Though virtually illiterate like nearly everyone then in Serbia, he resolved that his children would be educated. Milutin sought to make his home and family examples for the whole area by their orderliness and discipline, so he taught his children always to speak the truth and respect their elders. He was a benevolent patriarch, a very strict but loving parent on good terms with people of all ranks. Milutin was rewarded by obedience and love from his children and deep respect from his fellow villagers.[2]

Just after Ilija's birth a mysterious fire broke out in Garaši. Karadjordje, hearing reports that Milutin Garašanin had set it, ordered him arrested and punished. Rather than suffer unjust punishment, Milutin grabbed his rifle and rushed off to the hills to become an outlaw in the old Serbian tradition. Karadjordje retaliated by expelling his family from Garaši and orde. · ing his home and livestock destroyed. Thus the infant Ilija with the rest of the Garašanin family took refuge in the Kalemegdan, the formidable Turkish fortress which overlooks the town of Belgrade where the Danube and Sava rivers meet. Fifty-five years later, thanks in part to Ilija's diplomacy, that fortress would finally become Serbian. Soon afterwards Milutin explained his actions to Karadjordje and convinced him of his innocence. Milutin returned with his family to Garaši and Karadjordje, giving him part of his own herd, helped him rebuild his home and business.[3]

Ilija, like his brothers and sisters before him, was formally christened in Garaši and grew up there. With other village youngsters, he and his brothers watched over the livestock and performed farm chores. Unlike the others, Ilija and his siblings were instructed by a series of tutors whom Milutin imported from the Srem in Hungary, giving them room and board, since there were then no public schools in Serbia.[4] Later, since Ilija proved intelligent and adept at learning, Milutin took him across the Danube to Semlin, Austria (now Zemun, a suburb of Belgrade), and inscribed him in the Greek school there. After he had mastered Greek, Ilija attended a German school in Orahović. Spending about four years at the two institutions, Ilija received a sound general education through the secondary level but never attended a university. Instead, in late adolescence he returned home to Garaši to assist his father and older brothers with the family livestock business. His main task was to drive the stock to the ferry where the animals could be sold, then shipped across the Danube to Austria.

At age twenty-one Ilija married Sofia Danić—he called her Soka—in the cathedral church in Belgrade. This match with the daughter of a Belgrade merchant was arranged in traditional fashion by the Garašanin family. Ilija and his Soka were to enjoy a happy and durable marriage. Sofia possessed the loyalty, devotion and solid strength which he needed and appreciated. She entertained his friends and officials but never interfered in political matters. Even marriage did not emancipate Ilija fully from parental controls. Three months after the wedding vows had been exchanged, Milutin Garašanin offered the services of his youngest son to Miloš Obrenović, Prince of Serbia.[5]

There were convincing reasons for Prince Miloš to respond favorably to this request from his faithful comrade and friend. After Karadjordje's flight into Austria in 1813, the Turks had restored full control over Belgrade district and the Šumadija. But their power was now fragile. Only two years later new uprisings erupted. Miloš Obrenović, a warrior from Rudnik district who had fought valiantly under Karadjordje but had refused to flee with him from Serbia, was the main leader of this second major Serbian revolt against Turkish rule.

Milutin Garašanin played a prominent role in preparing the ground for the Second Insurrection. He seems to have been one of the assembled local chieftains beneath the great tree in Takovo in southern Serbia when Miloš raised his banner of revolt. During the insurrection Milutin commanded Serbian detachments in several battles against the Turks and was badly wounded at Dublja. After several victories Miloš, who was a shrewd diplomat and bargainer, managed with some support from the European powers to secure autonomy for his small Principality of Serbia which extended not far beyond Belgrade district. He would rule it as a vassal of the Turkish sultan. In 1817 Miloš had Karadjordje, who had slipped secretly back into Serbia, brutally murdered with an axe and sent his head to the sultan in Constantinople.[6] This terrible crime touched off a blood feud between the two leading families of Serbia; the Karadjordjević and the Obrenović. It would rage for almost a century until the last Obrenović ruler would be killed and thrown out of a palace window in Belgrade in 1903. Prince Miloš ruled henceforth as a patriarchal despot and became unquestionably the wealthiest man in Serbia. So arbitrary and absolute was he that many Serbs considered his regime more cruel and despotic than the Turkish. It was no accident that between 1815 and 1830 his people rose seven times in revolt. The greatest of these popular protests—the so-called Djak Revolt of 1825—was a peasant uprising against princely tyranny, high taxes, and growing bureaucratic oppression. Milutin Garašanin, named elder of Jasenica village by Miloš in 1816, had his home and livestock burned by the rebels who considered him one of the Prince's chief supporters. Milutin took his family to Kragujevac, then the princely capital. After the revolt had been crushed, Prince Miloš out of gratitude did two things: loaned Milutin money to resume his livestock trade and granted him an estate at Grocka near Smederevo which the family retained until after Ilija's death. In November 1829 Milutin, dropping the surname Savić, in a letter to Prince Miloš, first signed his name Milutin Garašanin. He remained on close and friendly terms with Miloš who often corresponded and conferred with him. It is interesting that this bold and outspoken leader occupied various posts under Miloš but never sought high office.[7]

Thus Milutin's letter to Prince Miloš offering him Ilija's services was in response to a princely request. First, Milutin had offered him his second son, Luka, who served as a customs official at Višnjica on the Danube in 1833-1834. When Luka resigned in order to resume his career as a swine merchant, Ilija was suggested in his place. Astute at finding and utilizing men of ability, Miloš was much impressed with young Ilija and assigned him to the Višnjica customs house in 1834. At age twenty-two Ilija Garašanin began his official service to Serbia.

By then Serbia's autonomy under Prince Miloš as hereditary ruler had been confirmed by the Treaties of Akkerman (1826) and Adrianople (1829). Its obligations to the sultan were limited, involving mainly payment of a fixed amount of annual tribute. Russia, which had assisted the Serbs sporadically during the First Insurrection and given them diplomatic support thereafter, acted as Serbia's protector among the European powers. Russia continued to assert an ill-defined right to intervention in behalf of all Christians in the Ottoman Empire which Catherine the Great had first enunciated in 1774. Most Serbs looked to Russia as their natural and benevolent guardian against the Turks partly because Russians were fellow Orthodox and their language resembled Serbian. Inside Serbia the Turks retained control of Kalemegdan fortress in Belgrade and smaller forts in several other Serbian towns. In theory the Serbian people were sovereign and their organ, the Assembly (*Skupština*), constituted the supreme authority. However, without a constitution or the rule of law, all actual power lay in the cruel hands of Prince Miloš. Nonetheless, there was popular agitation beneath the surface for a share of political influence. Agitation was conducted especially by educated Serbs from across the Sava and Danube rivers who became Serbia's leading bureaucrats.

When a country is gradually developing and becoming European as Serbia was in the 1830s, such elements of conflict are virtually inevitable. Still covered almost entirely by dense oak forests penetrated by only an occasional road or trail, Serbia remained economically and politically backward. The first census of 1834 listed the population at 678,192 persons. Most were Orthodox farmers and their families tilling small family farms and overwhelmingly illiterate. The formerly dominant communal system, or *zadruga*, was weakening. Even under Miloš' paternalistic rule, the country began to acquire some attributes of a small European nation. In what had been a homogeneous peasant society without a native aristocracy, differentation was under way: a wealthier upper crust of shopkeepers, bureaucrats, and swine merchants like the Garašanins was emerging. Of Serbia's roughly 15,000 Muslims, mostly Turks, some two-fifths resided in Belgrade, but gradually the Serbs were taking over urban centers which had been predominantly Turkish. However, these towns, little more than overgrown villages, with their narrow, winding, cobbled streets and squat adobe houses, resembled those of the Middle East more than Europe.[8]

After 1830 Prince Miloš faced increasing pressure to grant a constitution and allow other political elements legal organization and status. A revolt of Serbian notables, known as Mileta's Rebellion, frightened him into conceding a constitution and creating a Council (*Sovjet* or *Savet*) which he had promised back in 1830. The democratic-sounding Constitution of 1835 shocked Russia's conservative emperor, Nicholas I, though the assembly it authorized had minimal real power. All the while, Miloš intended to retain actual control. After naming a Council and selecting ministers, he dragged his feet on further reform, then suspended the Constitution with backing from the principal foreign powers concerned: the Porte (Turkey), Russia, and Austria. Curiously, Britain and France, both constitutional monarchies, supported Miloš' absolutism whereas autocratic Austria and Russia sought to curb his power by backing the notables, headed by a bold and popular military man, Toma Vučić-Perišić. Also by 1835 the leading European powers, except for disinterested Prussia, had established consulates in Belgrade or vicinity, enhancing their opportunities to exert influence through Serbian groups which leaned on them for support.

During these years Ilija Garašanin, having launched his official career, achieved high positions very young. After but four years of loyal service in customs houses at Višnjica, then in Belgrade, he was named by Miloš in July 1837 head of the newly established Serbian army. Though Ilija lacked military experience, throughout his career he would rely heavily on a loyal army to support the regime he served. In his letter of appointment

Prince Miloš addressed Ilija, who still called himself Ilija Hadji Milutino-vić,[9] as "Dear nephew." On September 29, 1837 the Prince named Ilija "head of our military-police office" as well as a member of the Council for "excellent services to the country, and your devotion to us," promo-ting the twenty-five year old civilian to full colonel. In response, Ilija promised to execute the Prince's orders precisely and maintain the army's discipline and loyalty.[10]

Why were such honors bestowed on one so young and inexperienced? Partly, because of the Prince's trust and respect for Milutin Garašanin. Also, Miloš was intuitive in selecting men of ability. Very important, too, was the critical shortage of trained and educated Serbs to staff top posi-tions in the infant bureaucracy. With his sound education, two foreign languages, and four years experience in state service, Ilija Garašanin was a scarce commodity in his country. With his roots deep in the soil of peasant Serbia, linked by family ties and a practical outlook to the "Old-sters," Ilija with his Greek education in Semlin was also the harbinger of a new generation of "Parisians," young Serbs who would study at French and German universities, then return to staff important state posts. Ilija Garašanin, despite lacking higher education, readily made friends with these talented youngsters, fostered their careers, and later through foreign travel became increasingly broadminded and cosmopol-itan. He would become an important link between these two groups.[11] A brief note summoning Ilija to the ancient princely capital of Kragu-jevac suggests his value to Prince Miloš: "Dear Ilija: Work here has in-creased, the members of the Council are few and we are falling behind. Thus I urge you to hasten here at once."—Miloš.[12]

Elements in Serbia opposed to Miloš' autocracy encouraged the Porte in December 1838 to proclaim the so-called "Turkish Constitution." While somewhat narrowing Serbian autonomy, it achieved a compromise wel-comed by all groups except Prince Miloš and his entourage. The Constitu-tion stipulated nomination of a seventeen-member Council (*Savet*), to hold office for life, and Miloš found himself compelled to name to it most of his leading opponents. The latter soon called themselves "Defenders of the Constitution" (*Ustavobranitelji*). One of their leaders, Avram Petroni-jević, became premier and foreign minister in Serbia. Marking the virtual end of princely absolutism in Serbia (except for Prince Mihailo's second reign, 1860-1868), this inaugurated a strict separation between the judicial and executive branches. The Council, through which Russia exercised strong influence, opposed nearly everything Miloš proposed. Early in 1839, finding himself impotent under this Constitution, Miloš fled into exile in Austria. However, the Council sent envoys, including Milutin Garašanin, who urged him to return as constitutional ruler. When the Russian and British consuls reinforced this plea, Miloš yielded and in April returned to Belgrade, a chastened instrument of the pro-Russian party. But less than two months later, frustrated and blocked at every turn, Miloš abdicated the throne in favor of his elder son, Milan. With Mihailo, his younger son, Miloš went to live on his estates in Rumania, then still divided and ruled by the Turks.

Prince Milan never actually ruled Serbia, dying less than a month after his accession. The Council then summoned sixteen-year-old Mihailo Obrenović, and the chief "Defender" leaders, Petronijević and Vučić-Perišić—normally called simply Vučić—ruled the country. The bold and demagogic Vučic lost no time and agitated among the people and in the army to build popular support. Visiting an army barracks, Vučić told the assembled soldiers: "I fear no one, neither Prince nor Council, nor ministers nor metropolitan, and no one should fear anyone. We are all equal whether we be prince or swineherd...."[13] Such an attitude boded ill for young Prince Mihailo who after paying his respects to the Sultan, arrived in Belgrade in March 1840. He was received solemnly by the regents, clergy and populace seemingly ending Serbia's political crisis and nine months of struggle between Regent Jevrem Obrenović and the "Defenders."

However, the "Defenders" soon opposed the Obrenović faction openly. Vučić cultivated the army chief, Ilija Garašanin, and both Ilija and his father supported the "Defenders." The latter selected a constitutional commission composed of Ilija Garašanin, Lazar Todorović and Raja Damjanović, which traveled through the interior of Serbia seeking support to restore the rival Karadjordjordjević family to the throne. Upon his return to Belgrade, Ilija participated in a secret night meeting on March 5-6, 1840 at Vučić's home to plot strategy, togehter with Vučic, Petronijević, Stojan Simić and Stefan Stefanović Tenka.[14] When Prince Mihailo started to crack down on the "Defenders," Milutin Garašanin, now seventy-eight, left his Council post in Belgrade for his Grocka estate. Learning of his unauthorized departure, the Prince sent a detachment of men to arrest him, which entered Milutin's home and beat up his daughter-in-law and grandson. Warned in time by another grandson, Milutin had slipped out and followed forest paths back to Belgrade where he sought refuge in the Turkish fortress on Kalemegdan.[15]

As relations between his faction and the "Defenders" deteriorated, Prince Mihailo on May 25th abruptly decreed the return of the government, which had been at Belgrade, to interior Kragujevac. Leading "Defenders" followed the Garašanins' example by taking refuge in the Turkish fortress. The Prince, backed by the Porte, sought to restore public order and accused the "Defenders" of stirring up the populace against Obrenović rule. In July 1840 he convened a handpicked assembly in Belgrade which accused the "Defenders" of fomenting rebellion against Prince Mihailo. The Assembly approved documents accusing Ilija Garašanin of complicty with Vučić and, by fleeing to the Kalemegdan, of abandoning the army and betraying Serbia. Allegedly, he had also ordered two soldiers suspected of stealing army funds brutally beaten without proper trial. Milutin and Luka Garašanin were charged with abetting rebellion and the former with recruiting and bribing people to murder Prince Mihailo.[16] The "Defenders" vehemently denied these charges,[17] but with the Porte supporting the Obrenović regime, there seemed no prospect of their exoneration. When efforts to reconcile the hostile factions failed, thirty-eight leading "Defenders," including Vučić, Petronijević, Milutin Garašanin and his sons, Ilija and Luka, left Belgrade by steamboat for exile in Constantinople. Their followers in Serbia were persecuted and driven from state service. As the Garašanins became avowed enemies of the Obrenović dynasty and young Prince Mihailo, it seemed that Ilija Garašanin's promising career had ended. In June 1841 Prince Mihailo requested the Turkish Grand Vizir to detain the "Defenders" indefinitely so that law and order could be restored in Serbia.[18] Thus the Vučić Revolt of August 1842 which brought the "Defenders" to power in Serbia, would be crucial for Ilija Garašanin's political future.

In Constantinople the exiled "Defender" leaders agitated and sought foreign support for their return to Serbia. Winning the favor of the Porte and of Russian Ambassador Titov, through him they interested the Russian government in their fate. Soon Russia, Turkey and Austria were all exerting pressure on young Prince Mihailo. The Turkish and Austrian governments had been alienated by the Prince's determination to rule

Serbia autocratically while relying on Russia. Austria deplored his hiring of a Russian general to build a Serbian army, and Serbia's aid to Bulgarian insurgents provided the Porte with a pretext. Russia, represented by its Belgrade consul, Gerasim Vashchenko, also favored the "Defenders'" return, and in March 1841 Baron K. A. Liven, a special Russian envoy, came to Kragujevac to persuade Prince Mihailo to authorize it. Russian policy toward Serbia appears confused since later Nicholas I would condemn strongly the "Defenders'" overthrow of Mihailo. Reluctantly, the Prince agreed in the spring of 1841 to the return of all the émigrés except Vučić, Stojan Simić and Milutin Garašanin; officials removed for supporting the "Defenders" would receive pensions. The three leaders were to remain in exile until the Porte decided their return would not provoke disorder. In return, the Turks agreed to have them pledge loyalty to Prince Mihailo.[19]

Thus by the end of 1841 many "Defender" émigrés had been repatriated, but not those whom Mihailo considered his most dangerous opponents. He feared Vučić's popularity and demagogic abilities, and old Garašanin's numerous commercial contacts with people in the interior—both might recruit many adherents. Avram Petronijević was allowed to return since he was merely an able diplomat without a significant personal following. Lacking their top leaders, the Prince realized, the "Defenders" could not seriously threaten his rule. However, faced with persistent foreign pressure, the young prince finally agreed reluctantly to also permit the exiled leaders to come home. In late November 1841 Vučić, Ilija Garašanin and Matija Nenadović arrived in the Austrian town of Semlin just across the Danube from Belgrade, waiting there until late March 1842 for permission to cross the river.[20]

As Prince Mihailo had feared, the return of the "Defender" leaders triggered a revolt encouraged by the Turks and Austrians. Inside Serbia the "Defenders" agitated everywhere and exploited growing internal dissatisfaction with Mihailo's rule. Vučić harangued crowds of peasants, condemning high taxation and official corruption. In the Belgrade region the chief organizers of revolt included Milutin Garašanin. In strategic Kragujevac operated the able military leader, Stevan Knićanin; in Požarevac agitated Stefan Stefanović Tenka. Together they planned and prepared a general insurrection before Prince Mihailo realized what was happening. Only on August 19, 1842 did the Prince, learning of scattered uprisings, alert all the district chiefs. He instructed Jovan Mićić, his chief commander, with his 630 regular troops to march with him to Kragujevac.

It was during that advance that Milutin and Luka Garašanin were killed. Reaching the village of Ripanj at noon August 20th, Prince Mihailo heard that old Milutin Garašanin had come there the previous night, roused the populace to revolt, then gone on to Barajevo village. Mihailo sent a detachment in pursuit which overtook him near the village. Eighty-year-old Milutin defended himself bravely, suffering seven wounds before succumbing. Mihailo ordered his head cut off, put in a sack, and then to deter others, impaled on a stick and placed by the roadside.[21] The very next day Luka Garašanin was captured near Grocka. His head was likewise cut off and with a lighted pipe in his mouth impaled in front of the Garašanins' house in Grocka.[22] Apparently, the two Garašanins were the first prominent victims of the Vučić Revolt. The eldest son, Mihailo, leaving a large family and great wealth, also joined the uprising but survived.

Toma Vučić, a bold and experienced commander and the "Defenders'" principal leader, conducted the decisive military operations against Prince Mihailo. After conferring in Semlin on August 17th with Austrian General Hauer, he went to Pančevo where Militun Garašanin and Raja Damjanović joined him with their men. As Vučić proceeded south toward Kragujevac, amed detachments gathered by Knićanin and others swelled his ranks. On the 20th his army occupied Kragujevac and seized its cannon which would prove decisive. Still professing loyalty to Mihailo, Vučić claimed he was coming to free the Prince from a selfish entourage oppressing the Serbian people. He now commanded some 4,000 men. Prince Mihailo encamped near Kragujevac with his regulars and some 15,000 militia. Vučić then attacked and his cannon caused the Prince's untrained militia to panic. Mihailo refused to authorize his regulars to assault the artillery pieces for fear of spilling too much Serbian blood. The Prince withdrew to Žabara where he was reinforced by his uncle, Jovan Obrenović. Soon the Prince's army swelled to almost 25,000 men and he claimed overwhelming popular support. Denouncing the "Defenders" as traitors, he summoned all good Serbs to rally to the Obrenović banner. Though also being reinforced, Vučić counted mainly on his artillery. Once again his cannon caused the Prince's infantry to flee; with only his cavalry, Mihailo retreated to Belgrade. The Russian consul, Vashchenko, summoned urgently to the Prince's residence in nearby Topčider, advised Mihailo to seek refuge on the Kalemegdan. Spurning a course his cowardly successor would adopt sixteen years later,[23] Prince Mihailo and a few followers crossed the Danube into Austrian exile. "Seeing that I could not quell the revolt, I crossed into Austria rather than expose the populace to a bloody civil war," explained the Prince. He refused to abdicate and appealed to the powers, especially Russia, to restore him as Serbia's legitimate ruler.[24]

The flamboyant Vučić now became Serbia's man of the hour. Rescuing the country from near anarchy, he and Petronijević set up a provisional government which convened a national assembly to elect a new Serbian prince. The Porte approved their actions, and the clever Petronijević likewise secured French support. The "Defenders" simply disregarded protests of the other consuls that Prince Mihailo remained the rightful ruler (August 27th). For the next two months Vučić wielded absolute power in Serbia, repressing all opposition with extreme cruelty. An illiterate but charismatic strongman, Vučić played to his peasant gallery with invariable success. Habitually armed to the teeth, he was a raw, angry and vengeful man. Reported Austrian Consul Atanacković on October 1/13th:

> Yesterday at the archive of a district town hall Vučić discerned a large portrait of [Prince] Miloš. He grabbed his whip, cut out the eyes, sliced up the picture and threw it into the coutyard where his entourage destroyed it completely.[25]

Having prepared and led the insurrection, Vučić made certain the assembly would choose Aleksandar Karadjordjević, unimpressive son of the great Karadjordje, as prince. Promising his supporters money or lucrative posts, Vučić convened the assembly at his camp on Vračar. The deputies, faced menacingly by eight loaded cannon, quickly and unanimously elected Aleksandar ruler of Serbia. After the Sultan confirmed this in writing, a new government was installed with Vučić as Interior Minister and dominant figure, and Avram Petronijević as Foreign Minister. Stojan Simić became chairman of a Council whose members included Matija Nenadović, Stevan Knićanin, and soon young Ilija Garašanin.

The latter had learned of the Vučić Revolt and the tragic deaths of his father and brother while traveling on business. He had returned to Serbia from exile late in March. From Stara Oršava he wrote Stojan Simić August 23rd that he was ill with fever and grief: "Out of suffering and unhappiness at the fate which overtook my father and my dear brother, Luka . . . I cannot write you much." Quickly realizing the significance of political changes in Serbia and the desperate need for capable leaders to restore order, he urged Simić: "Don't wait for the steamship or anything; don't lose a moment but hasten onward day and night [to Belgrade], since you must realize you are needed."[26] So demoralized was Ilija at his family's terrible fate that for the time being he could go nowhere despite urging by Aleksa Simić, Stojan's brother, to return home speedily. In October he finally did so, playing no part in selecting a new prince or government.

However, the "Defenders" did not forget the Garašanins. Vučić and Petronijević wrote Mihailo Garašanin, the family's senior surviving member, praising the family for heroism and heavy sacrifices for Serbia and nominating him to the Council.[27] Mihailo Garašanin, a merchant not a politician, declined that honor, but it was then offered to Ilija who accepted. Soon after his return home, Ilija was also named assistant interior minister under Vučić. For him political power had been purchased at a terrible price.

The "Defenders'" triumph in August 1842 resulted from careful preparation and superior leadership. The prevalent disorder in Serbia after 1838 had played into their hands, giving them support from many peasants, merchants and officials. However, Prince Mihailo's swift defeat was not the product of personal weakness or timidity; he had lacked requisite experience and a decisive man to lead the army and people. When he mounted the Serbian throne eighteen years later, he had learned much from this sad episode and in exile.

NOTES

1. M. D. Milićević, *Pomenik* (Belgrade, 1888), p. 93, 765; Interviews of the author with, Dr. Milutin Garašanin, June 16 and 20, 1978. His

theory is that the Garašanin's came originally from the Bjelopolje region of Montenegro where there is a mountain named Garač.

2. Milićević, op. cit., pp. 765-766; Matija Nenadović, *Karadjordje* (Belgrade, 1860?), p. 228; D. Stranjaković, "Ilija Garašanin," p. 14.

3. Nenadović, op. cit., p. 225.

4. The first tutor was Mihailo Berisavljević, the second Avram Gasparović. Milićević, op. cit., p. 94.

5. See above, p. 9 for his letter. Stranjaković, "Ilija," pp. 17-18.

6. M. Gavrilović, *Miloš Obrenović* (3 vols., Belgrade 1909-1912), I, 346 ff.

7. Stranjaković, "Ilija," pp. 5-6.

8. M. B. Petrovich, *A History of Modern Serbia,* I, 168 ff.

9. Hadji (from Turkish *haci*) in Serbo-Croatian means one who has visited the Holy Places in Jerusalem. Ilija adopted it briefly as a tribute to his father who in 1836 visited Sveta Gora and Christ's grave in Jerusalem. It does not mean that Milutin or Ilija Garašanin became Muslins. Stranjaković, "Ilija," pp. 8-9.

10. IG 17, Miloš Obrenović to Ilija Milutinović (Garašanin), July and September 29, 1837; IG 26, "Zakletva (Oath) Ilije Garašanina" (1838).

11. Slobodan Jovanović, "Ilija Garašanin," in *Portreti iz istorije književnosti* (Novi Sad, 1963), pp. 79-80 and his *Ustavobranitelji i njihova vlada*, pp. 190-192.

12. IG 29, Miloš to Ilija Garašanin in Požarevac, July 4, 1838. Also Miloš' letter of April 10, 1838 in that same collection.

13. Stranjaković, *Vučićeva buna*, p. 23.

14. Ibid., "Ilija," pp. 19-20.

15. Stranjaković, *Vučićeva buna*, pp. 32-33.

16. "Accusatory document submitted to Turkish commissar, Muse-efendi, at the Serbian Assembly," July 23, 1840, in Nil Popov, *Rossiia i Serbiia: istoricheskii ocherk . . .* (Moscow, 1869), pp. 472 ff. This contains separate indictments against all the "Defender" leaders. It accused Ilija Garašanin of "1) participation in a constitutional investigatory commission and collaboration in everything concerning the transfer of rights to the princely office from Mihailo Obrenović to another person; 2) that right after Vučić and Petronijević, he went to the fortress when he heard that the people were demanding an account of their ["Defenders'"] actions, and that as army chief, by abandoning it, betrayed his prince and

country; 3) that he unjustly, when the military treasury was plundered, beat two innocent soldiers who that night were guarding the treasury, without preminary investigation . . . , giving the first one some 800 blows with birth rods and clubs, and the second about 400 blows, and tortured them, not letting them sleep for five days and nights. . . ." Ibid., p. 472.

17. "Replies to the accusatory document: in defense of Ilija Garašanin," ibid., p. 502. This asserts that Garašanin had been slandered and that he had left his post and fled to the fortress to save his life. The army, it affirmed, had repeatedly expressed full confidence in him. As to the military treasury, the guards had not been beaten nearly as much as asserted and there were adequate grounds for suspecting them of the crime which would be borne out by documents in the army offices, and that Garašanin had acted to prevent further similar crimes. Ibid., pp. 510-512 is a similar defense of Milutin and Luka Garašanin.

18. Stranjaković, *Vučićeva buna,* pp. 29-37.

19. Ibid., pp. 46 ff.; Popov, op. cit., pp. 96 ff.; Arhiv SANU, No. 7380/32, "Biografija Anastasije Nikolića," pp. 52-55.

20. Stranjaković, *Vučićeva buna,* pp. 48-50.

21. Mladen Žujovic, *Beleške* (Belgrade, 1902), pp. 65-66. Simić, *Četrdeset drugi,* pp. 7-8. That night a peasant took Milutin's body to Barajevo for burial. Later, he was reburied in the churchyard near his Grocka estate—M. Milićević, *Pomenik,* p. 768.

22. IG 69, S. Herkalović to I. Garašanin, August 27, 1842; Stranjaković, *Vučićeva buna,* pp. 65-66.

23. See below pp. 201-204.

24. Stranjaković, *Vučićeva buna,* pp. 67-75. DAS PO 23 contains much correspondence to and from Mihailo in regard to the Vučić Revolt and the Prince's subsequent efforts to recover the throne, 1842-43. See especially Nos. 26, 28, 35, 40, 44, 54 and 56.

25. Arhiv SANU, No. 9323/2, "Prevrat u Srbiji, 1842-43," Reports of Consul Atanacković to Metternich, September 17/29 and October 1/13, 1842.

26. IG 68, Ilija Garašanin to Stojan Simić, August 23.

27. IG 60, "Ukaz o postavljenju Mihailo Garašanina za člana Sovjeta," October 12, 1842. Wrote Toma Vučić: "The services of your family and yourself, especially recently, deserve the thanks and reward of the country."

CHAPTER III

GOVERNING SERBIA, 1842-1847

"It has not been said in vain that to govern a country is the greatest and most difficult task in the world."
—Garašanin to Marinović, April 3, 1873.

Ilija Garašanin had played a secondary role in the Vučić Revolt which overturned Prince Mihailo in August 1842 but quickly assumed a key position in the regime of the "Defenders." After serving briefly as Vučić's understudy, Garašanin occupied the crucial post of Interior Minister for almost a decade. More than anyone else he was responsible for creating the internal order and stable bureaucracy essential to Serbia's development and prosperity. During his ministry, establishing firm foundations for the modern Serbian state, he remained the chief buttress for the rule of Aleksandar Karadjordjević. The keys to his achievement were a disciplined officialdom, more efficient police force, and a miniscule but obedient regular army. Run by Garašanin's firm and skillful hand, they handled all internal challenges in a faction-ridden turbulent peasant country.

At age thirty Ilija Garašanin, without seeking such authority, became like Bismarck in Prussia after 1862, the indispensable linch-pin of the "Defender" regime. As Interior Minister, besides controlling the army and police, he directed the economy, communications, medical facilities and the infant postal service. Later, these manifold responsibilities would be

24

divided among several ministries. Only a dedicated public servant with immense capacity for work could handle such varied tasks. Prepared to relinquish this key post whenever the Prince desired, Garašanin offered his resignation several times during the 1840s only to have Aleksandar refuse it, realizing that Garašanin was indispensable to the survival of his regime.

Even before his return to Serbia from exile he had been named to the Council (*Savet*), a prestigious body whose other members were all over forty-five years old. Protesting that he lacked the requisite qualifications and experience, he tried to turn down a position greatly coveted by others until finally induced to accept it. Immediately upon his return to Belgrade, he was named assistant interior minister under Vučić, strongman of the "Defenders" but inept as an administrator. Initially, Garašanin's main concern was to restore order, and after Vučić returned to exile, he served for the next year as actual head of the ministry. His task was complicated by the official disapproval of Russia, Serbia's protector, of Aleksandar Karadjordjević's election, accomplished without her participation, and St. Petersburg's consequent insistence on a second election. Nonetheless, Garašanin promptly took firm hold of his job, advising, reminding and scolding officials and insisting they administer Serbia with strict legality. In February 1843 he wrote confidently to his friend, Stevan Knićanin, in Kragujevac:

> Everything is fine with us here. . . . The news from all quarters on the position of Serbia cannot be any better than what we are hearing. All tell us that we are ruling the people well and according to the Constitution. . . . Our enemies are everywhere in disarray.[1]

Garašanin's correspondence during 1843 reveals a man in firm control of a complex and unstable situation.

The triumphant "Defenders" hastened to consolidate their power. Led by the ruthless and autocratic Vučić, they persecuted Obrenovites and drove many foreigners and some Austrian Serbs from the country. Vučić himself, a virtually illiterate peasant and narrowminded Šumadijan, or Serbia-firster, remained distrustful and envious of educated Austrian Serbs whom he wished to expel, then create a pure, patriarchal peasant Serbia. In 1844 he exhibited his draconian policies in crushing with bloodthirsty cruelty the Katanska Revolt in western Serbia. This crude military strongman by his peasant origins and autocratic behavior resembled Prince Miloš, but he lacked Miloš' capacity to govern Serbia in normal times. Tempering his brutal image was the co-leader of the "Defenders," Avram Petronijević, seeking cautiously, reasonably and with rare diplomatic skill peaceful solutions to problems. With his polish and knowledge of foreign languages, he managed to preserve what Vučić had conquered and proved especially valuable in winning foreign recognition and support. Reported the French consul: "Vučić is the force and Petronijević the brains of the 'Defenders'' regime."[2] Except for Ilija Garašanin, most remaining "Defender" leaders, notably Aleksa and Stojan Simić and Metropolitan Petar, were Austrian Serbs. Initially, opposition to the Obrenovites and a common desire for power kept the "Defenders" united.[3]

The "Defenders of the Constitution" had acquired their name and reputation in the struggle with Prince Mihailo by opposing Obrenović absolutism. Comprising Serbia's first political party and reflecting a new spirit in government, they advocated limited monarchy. Ostensibly defending the 1838 Constitution, they were pushed toward political reform by a nascent Belgrade élite of merchants, bureaucrats and intelligentsia. At first mainly Austrian Serbs, this new element sought safeguards and legal protection for their rising prosperity against Miloš' abuse of power. Over Vučić's bitter opposition, this new generation achieved predominant influence in state affairs.

The Constitution of 1838 theoretically had ended monarchical absolutism by creating a seventeen-member Council limited to propertied Serbian citizens thirty-five or older. However, this vaguely worded document failed to describe clearly relations between Prince and Council, merely stipulating that the prince should name prominent men approved by the public. Once appointed, councillors could not be removed unless convicted by a court and unless the Porte approved their dismissal. The Council had exclusive authority to initiate legislation and draw up the state budget. Without its approval, the prince could issue no law, but with his absolute veto power the prince could block passage of any law he opposed. With the Council remaining in permanent session, the prince could not develop independent legislative power. The populace viewed the Council as a gathering of hoary peasant chieftains; educated Austrian Serbs regarded it as a body of administrative leaders.

The Constitution prescribed that the prince should govern through ministers selected from the Council and responsible to it. Would the Council direct state policy or merely observe whether prince and ministers governed constitutionally? The Constitution's imprecision encouraged rivalry between prince and Council for actual control of the government, the outcome depending on the Council's composition and the prince's ability. Repeated quarrels between prince and Council, resembling earlier rivalries between kings and parliaments in Western Europe, stemmed from conflicting interpretations of the Constitution. Supposed to resolve such disputes, the Porte rarely provided clear answers.

When the "Defenders" took power in 1842, the Council had a potent and balanced membership fully capable of asserting its position against weak and ineffective Prince Aleksandar Karadjordjević. Besides Vučić and Petronijević, it included Ilija Garašanin; the military leader, Knićanin; and two men of wealth—Milosav Resavac and Jovan Veljković. Representing the older generation were three popular veterans of the First Insurrection—Matija Nenadović, Luka Lazarević and Stefan Stefanović Tenka.[4]

The new "Defender" regime, which engineered the unanimous election of Prince Aleksandar by a national assembly, secured Turkish recognition and support but faced hostility from Serbia's most powerful neighbors, Russia and Austria. Nicholas I of Russia, opposing revolutions and *coup d'états* in his sphere of influence, refused to recognize the new Serbian regime. He sent Baron Liven to Serbia to investigate, then had him proceed to Constantinople where he persuaded the Sultan to nullify Aleksandar's election. Incongruously, Tsar Nicholas, Europe's most powerful autocratic ruler, then insisted on a genuine popular election of Serbia's prince. To insure this Russia demanded that political prisoners be freed, exiles allowed to return, and that Vučić and Petronijević leave the country along with their Turkish supporter, Governor Kiamil Pasha. The "Defenders" sought to evade or water down these harsh conditions. Émigrés were permitted to return but few chose to do so; Vučić and Petronijević withdrew to interior Kragujevac.

Thus Garašanin became de facto Interior Minister responsible for preserving order and security in the face of Austro-Russian pressure and pro-Obrenovite agitation inside Serbia and from abroad. Reported Jovan Stanković: "In Belgrade there is great concern; already it is said openly

that Karadjordjević [Prince Aleksandar] has been dethroned . . . and that
the Obrenović family will return to the Serbian throne."[5] Austrian Consul
Atanacković was likewise pessimistic about the "Defenders'" chances:

> . . . The mass of the population [in Serbia] is for the Obrenović, or
> more precisely for Prince Miloš. Prince Mihailo enjoys their love
> only as Miloš' son. If Miloš merely came to Semlin . . . , the entire
> country would immediately declare itself for him.[6]

Letters from Belgrade, reported Atanacković in June, described a country
in ferment with open struggle against the "Defenders" already in progress.
In Belgrade people were being arrested in droves. "Every hour there is anti-
cipation of news of a general uprising and terrible bloodshed. The choice
of a prince will not be free. Russian interests . . . will surely bring Serbia
to ruin and to civil war."[7]

Atanasije Nikolić, an Austrian Serb who became one of Garašanin's
closest colleagues, in March 1843 depicted the situation very differently.
Writing Colonel Knićanin on behalf of the extremely busy Garašanin, he
declared: "In the entire countryside prevails peace and order, and there
are no reports of actions against the present government. From all sides
come reports of popular satisfaction."[8] After Obrenovite officials had
fled to Austria with Prince Mihailo, Vučić had named the reluctant Nikolić
to a key post in the Interior Ministry. To Garašanin, then Vučić's assistant, Nikolić explained he was an engineer without administrative experience and would rather teach mathematics. Receiving him warmly, Garašanin responded that to reject the ministerial post, he must first see Vučić.
However, the latter assured him that with Garašanin's aid, he would quickly learn the ropes. "I made my mistakes at first," recalled Nikolić, "which
would have been worse had Garašanin not corrected them." When Garašanin had asked him to write a circular for the office staff, "I wrote it
the best I could: long sentences with the verbs at the end, just as in German." Reading it, Garašanin shook his head in disbelief: "For whom did
you write this, Nikolić? . . . I can barely make it out, so how will my personnel understand it? . . . It should all be brief and clear so the simplest
person can understand it." Garašanin then wrote it out. Perceiving how
simple and intelligibly everything was expressed, Nikolić henceforth read
attentively whatever Garašanin wrote. "That was my schooling in Serbian
language and style."[9]

The reelection of Prince Aleksandar, carefully prepared by Garašanin, was no accident. "Whatever happens," he wrote Knićanin, "the people should be favorably disposed and united, then everything else will be fine."[10] Remaining in constant touch with Knićanin, the army chief, throughout the reelection crisis, Garašanin emphasized how vital it was to maintain national unity in order to block efforts of foreign powers to influence Serbia's affairs.[11] Shortly before the election, he informed Knićanin that the public mood was good and that matters had not been left to chance. "The regular troops and all the cannon are here with us at the assembly."[12] No doubt this was to insure a genuinely free choice by the people! To counter Russian pressure and establish connections with the "Defender" regime, Michal Czajkowski, envoy of Prince Adam Czartoryski's Polish émigré organization,[13] arrived in Belgrade in May 1843 on a French passport. Urging Garašanin and other "Defenders" to resist Russian demands, he advised them to mobilize maximum support at the national assembly before Russia's special envoy, Baron Liven arrived. Garašanin promptly utilized his police to hasten the deputies' arrival so at the assembly's initial session the deputies' loyalty to the "Defenders" was so solid that the Russians found themselves helpless. Even with Baron Liven and Consul Vashchenko present, the assembly, convening June 15, 1843, reelected Aleksandar Karadjordjević unanimously. Congratulating the Prince, Czartoryski proposed to "Defender" leaders that a permanent Polish agency be set up in Belgrade.[14]

Still, the "Defender" regime clung only precariously to power. Before consenting grudgingly to confirm Prince Aleksandar's election, Russia insisted that Vučić and Petronijević be exiled once again from Serbia. Only when that had occurred did Nicholas I in September 1843 finally recognize Aleksandar Karadjordjević as prince of Serbia, apparently believing that without its chief leaders, the "Defender" government would soon succumb to an Obrenovite conspiracy.

The involuntary departure of Vučić and Petronijević left Ilija Garašanin now Interior Minister, as the key to holding regime and country together. As chaos threatened, Colonel Knićanin, the army commander, proposed that the Prince and Treasury come to Kragujevac, which was his headquarters, apparently so he and his staff could act freely without concern for the Council and Constitution. Garašanin immediately vetoed that suggestion showing himself unafraid to cross the formidable Knićanin, next to Vučić Serbia's premier military hero. Soon domestically in Serbia was felt as firm a hand as if Vučić himself were still in charge. To handle persisting domestic turmoil, Garašanin in October 1843, only a month after becoming Interior Minister, proposed a draconian law with sixteen articles to punish all those preparing or executing revolts against the government or who aided rebels. All rebels would be considered traitors to Serbia and suffer the death penalty. Lesser participants and spreaders of slander were to be imprisoned from one week to life depending on the severity of their offenses. Approved by the Council, this severe law came into force just prior to the Rajović Revolt of January 1844.[15]

During their exile Garašanin corresponded with Vučić and Petronijević about his efforts to maintain internal order and to arrange their speedy return to Serbia. The Porte, apparently under Russian pressure, was insisting that they move further from Serbia's frontiers. Garašanin urged them to comply "since otherwise you two will have to remain longer in exile and without you things won't hold together here very long . . . . " Mischief-makers and enemies, he noted, were constantly penetrating Serbia seeking to foment disorder.[16] Although Russian Consul Vashchenko had assured Garašanin that the exiled pair would soon gain the Tsar's favor, he wrote them October 9th:

> I don't know whether you should consider the Turks or the Russians your greater enemies. The Russians have driven you out and are thus your foes, but the Turks, who could defend you from further persecution, refuse to do so.

They must avoid any action which might antagonize Russia, Serbia's offical protector.[17] Soon he informed them that Baron Liven of Russia had promised to aid their repatriation. "I only wish to keep things peaceful until your return." He and the Prince were doing their utmost to insure that.[18]

Garašanin displayed increasing concern over continuing instability and threats of revolt. Obrenovites were agitating in the interior on behalf of Prince Miloš, he wrote the exiles, but whether this portended anything more serious he did not know. So far only a small minority of the people were supporting these enemies; the rest seemed well satisfied with the government and obedient to its orders. Baron Liven had told him that he would work hard in St. Petersburg to arrange the leaders' return. Garašanin was also finding Danilevskii, the new Russian consul in Belgrade, friendly and cooperative.[19]

In December 1843 Garašanin acted to forestall a possible coup camouflaged by supposed public agitation for the exiles' return. "Opponents of popular rights and the Constitution" had plotted to send representatives from all over Serbia to Belgrade ostensibly to urge repatriation of Vučić and Petronijević. While there they planned to organize a mob and overturn the regime. Garašanin instructed Bogdan Djordjević, district chief of Ćuprija in southeastern Serbia, to order his subordinates to prevent such agitation by force if necessary.[20] Informing the exiled leaders of this conspiracy, he noted he had instructed all district chiefs to forbid public gatherings seeking their return and to disperse any unruly crowds. Since pro-Vučić and princely factions were damaging Serbian unity, Garašanin added he had advised, and the Prince had agreed, that Aleksandar declare publicly that he would expel any opponents of Vučić from Serbia. If this were done, Garašanin predicted, "I am convinced that both factions will dissolve."[21]

About New Year's 1844 Garašanin's alert security forces nipped in the bud a potentially serious pro-Obrenović uprising led by Cvetko Rajović, whom Garašanin described to the Czech émigré, Franjo Zah, as "an animal."[22] The conspirators, he informed Knićanin, most of whom favored Prince Mihailo, had been arrested and taken to Kragujevac for interrogation and trial. Under questioning Rajović divulged his intention to lead an uprising; some lesser conspirators admitted receiving Russian support. To avoid antagonizing Russia, the Serbian government ignored that. Consul Danilevskii agreed with Garašanin that the guilty should be punished according to Serbian law, and the latter urged the consul to trust him to handle this delicate affair properly.[23] Garašanin described the problems involved to Zah:

> We are forced to act severely against the *chief* conspirators, but we won't exceed the limits of the law. The verdict will be published in the official newspapers. But some heads will be cut off. God preserve me from rejoicing, but whoever knows the state of Serbia, educated by a tyrant like Miloš, and the spirit of a faction which yields to foreign influence will recognize the need for stern punishment. To

the Serbs leniency would only seem like weakness and cowardice, and six months later they would return to the charge.[24]

The Russian-backed Rajović affair complicated repatriation of the exiles. Garašanin wrote them February 12th that Rajović had sought support by insisting that Russia backed him. "It is certain that all this is a Russian idea" in order to restore Prince Mihailo to the Serbian throne. Russian Ambassador Titov in Constantinople was pressuring the Porte to advise Belgrade not to punish the conspirators. However, Rajović and his followers must be punished severely to deter others: "We have already decided to do so and will stick to this." To eliminate foreign intrigues, stressed Garašanin, the Serbs must be self-reliant. Russia could readily create a faction to promote its policies in Serbia since three Council members—Stefan S. Tenka, Stojan Ćosa and Pavle Stanišić—were "Russomaniacs."

> Those three, I can tell you frankly, serve not Serbia but Russia, and today with the greatest satisfaction would give what is Serbian to Russia merely in order to win more importance for themselves with the Russians. To them Mihailo Obrenović would be much preferable to this Prince [Aleksandar] because Russia desires it and everything that the Russians say is sacred to them.[25]

Not desiring a breach with Russia, Garašanin resolved nonetheless to uphold Serbia's rights and spoke frankly to Consul Danilevskii about the exiles' return. After the Consul asked that a statement by Russian Foreign Minister Nesselrode be published in the Serbian official press, Garašanin retorted: "The reply of Mr. Nesselrode against the return of Vučić and Petronijević cannot be published *as you wish it,* for I know the [Serbian] nation; it would express itself afterwards with a vehemence that would leave no doubts." "But that proves that the Serbs show no deference to the orders of their protector!" objected Danilevskii. "If you believe that I speak too much as a friend of Vučić," replied Garašanin, "then go and ask the Prince . . . , but I as Minister of Interior will never advise him to publish Mr. Nesselrode's reply." Franjo Zah doubted that the Tsar's subordinates would inform Nicholas I how little respect the Serbs really had for him.[26]

Perhaps partly because of Garašanin's resolute stance the Russians agreed to a compromise. Consul Danilevskii pledged that if the Serbs promised not to execute Rajović and his followers, Vučić and Petronijević could return home. Anxious to secure this, Belgrade commuted the conspirators' sentences to life imprisonment.[27] Garašanin denied that the consul was dictating how the conspirators should be treated, but ten days later he noted that the return of the exiled leaders now appeared certain.[28] After Nicholas I had confirmed this to Prince Aleksandar, Garašanin wrote his Loznica district chief that this news had caused general rejoicing in Serbia. In an unusually optimistic statement for a perennial worrier, he exulted: "All factions are destroyed and have suddenly disappeared. Among us now prevail harmony and love."[29]

However, sweetness and light soon faded before new obstacles to the leaders' repatriation. Foreign Minister Nesselrode, writing Prince Aleksandar, attributed the new delay to alleged links between the Serbian exiles and anti-Russian Polish émigré circles.[30] Seeking to explain the frustrating hitch to his district chief, Garašanin warned that Russia might still wish to promote disorder in Serbia. "Our opponents are beginning to raise their heads," he cautioned. And he reacted angrily to scornful remarks about the Serbian people and their leaders by Russian ex-consul Vashchenko. The latter, Garašanin declared, was "a stupid donkey" (the term Vashchenko had attributed to Vučić). The minister feared that Russian pride and the habit of persecuting people might induce them to block the exiles' return.[31] Finally, late in August 1844 Vučić and Petronijević arrived in Belgrade to a heroes' welcome.

Even after their return Garašanin remained Interior Minister and the key figure in maintaining the "Defender" regime as internal frictions and tensions persisted. Factionalism, a political disease endemic in Serbia, soon revived in virulent form. Within months after his return Vučić began distancing himself from his "Defender" colleagues and in 1845 abandoned them wholly to found a pro-Russian faction which relied on the Serbs' traditional popular sympathy for Russia. Other Russophiles included Finance Minister Pavle Stanišić, several councillors, and sometimes the Council's vice-president, Stefan Stefanović Tenka. Often the Simić brothers were also Russophile but pursued chiefly selfish policies. A court camarilla had also developed headed by two Austrian Serbs, Aleksa Janković and the Prince's secretary, Timotej Knežević, and by the

Nenadović clan, relatives of Princess Persida. Soon Avram Petronijević also became the Prince's devoted adherent. This left Garašanin as the principal support of a "Defender" regime which aimed to keep order, consolidate domestic administration and improve economic, legal, and financial conditions in Serbia without subservienace to outside powers. Garašanin faced opposition from an Obrenovite faction divided between pro-Miloš and pro-Mihailo elements. It comprised mainly officials who had served under the Obrenović princes, youths who favored Prince Mihailo's ideas of reform, townsfolk along the Danube, and many dissatisfied for one reason or another with the rule of Prince Aleksandar Karadjordjević.[32]

Deploring this growing self-interested factionalism, Garašanin wrote Laza Teodorović in Constantinople:

> Here one could wish for greater and more sincere activity and for more harmony and love. The Vojvoda [Vučić] and the Prince disagree, complicating the activities of the entire government, since both are important, the one by his position, the other by his services. . . . [33]

Though the Russophile Vučić remained the most powerful individual in Serbia, his popularity declined somewhat after his unnecessarily cruel suppression of the Katanska Revolt of late 1844. Caring little about governing in normal circumstances, Vučić proved more adept at demagogy and organizing uprisings. Lacking political ideas, he tended to oppose now the very system he had brought into power. With Petronijević siding wholly with Prince Aleksandar and the Porte, Garašanin gradually drew away from both former exiles to concentrate upon administration and national issues. However, they all cooperated to prevent the Prince from instituting a personal regime. Everyone, Garašanin believed, shared blame for the personal frictions and backbiting of the "Defender" regime which often made him so pessimistic he could not bear to write about it and even made him contemplate resignation. Deploring the lack of system in state affairs, he noted to his friend, Marinović: "We gyrate back and forth with no idea of our destination."[34]

By 1846 Garašanin was expressing concern about pro-Obrenović agitation in Serbia. Miloš was still intriguing to provoke an uprising on

behalf of his son, Mihailo. Since Miloš declined to act without strong
foreign support, Garašanin intimated that Russia stood behind his plotting which had been uncovered in Constantinople. In August Garašanin
warned his district chief in Ćuprija that Miloš aimed to unleash an insurrection that fall. Constant vigilance was the price Serbia must pay for
physical weakness, factional division, and the lurking presence nearby
of alternative rulers supported by foreign powers.[35] Nonetheless, prior
to 1848 the better aspects of the "Defender" regime predominated over
its shortcomings. To most Serbs their government, although bureaucratic
and illiberal, seemed preferable to Miloš' patriarchal despotism. The
"Defenders" were creating a good system of courts, solid bureaucracy,
schools and the beginnings of social services; its officials governed through
a generally popular and respected Council.

More than anyone else Garašanin kept this regime in power and moving
forward. A man of principle and a stern but just superior, he won the respect of colleagues and subordinates, and through his officials this feeling
was transmitted to the public. Garašanin knew how to issue orders without alienating subordinates and succeeded in having them obeyed more
precisely and fully than previously in Serbia. He allowed no one to interfere in his business, nor did he meddle in matters outside his sphere of
competence. Evenhanded and just, he made no distinctions of rank or
birth, and in state business neither family ties nor friendship could induce
him to disobey his conscience. "I am determined to require obedience from
you," he wrote his friend, Bogdan Djordjević, "and you are duty bound
to give it to me invariably."[36] Garašanin's ideal was that the citizen
tremble before officials and officials before their ministers. However, he
often opposed unduly harsh measures proposed by his district chiefs.
Strongly opposing arbitrariness, petty tyranny and spying on the people,
he admonished Djordjević: "Legal means are much preferable to force."
After inspecting Knjaževac prison and hearing inmate complaints about
excessive severity and finding them justified, Garašanin ordered prisoners
to be allowed to smoke, buy food, and walk about the courtyard. But he
permitted no irregularities by his officials. Learning in 1846 that some
officials in Jagodina district were utilizing police for private purposes, he
issued a severe warning against such behavior to the district chief.[37]

Severity and consistency were hallmarks of Garašanin's administration
of the Interior Ministry. Order, he believed, must be preserved at any

cost; no violation of internal peace, however trivial, could be tolerated. Dealing with his officials Garašanin was invariably serious, even somber, expressing himself tersely, issuing orders clearly, and permitting no objections. He did not hesitate to impose severe punishments. In May 1847 to prevent looting and stealing, which had greatly increased recently, he had a decree issued making theft of livestock and objects valued at over ten talira punishable by death or flogging to the point of death.[38] Like Nicholas I of Russia, his formidable contemporary, he favored flogging as a punishment in the military and also authorized forceful methods in grilling civilian suspects. Such severity was typical of the older Serbian generation, but while employing it neither for personal nor partisan purposes, he believed it essential to promote public welfare.

A sharp letter to the Loznica district chief revealed Garašanin's strict approach even toward trusted subordinates. When Ćvorić neglected to follow instructions to accompany Consul Danilevskii around Serbia, Garašanin admonished him:

> ... Failure to fulfill instructions of the responsible authorities is always regarded as a crime in an official position and may lead to the subordinate's loss of his position, since a subordinate's disobedience in state matters must always be punished severely in order to avert bad consequences.... Thus, in my position, I cannot tolerate a subordinate's disobedience and as long as I retain this post, I must insist that my subordinates... execute my instructions unconditionally. Only thus can I satisfy in full measure the expectations of the Prince and the government.[39]

This letter, added Garašanin, besides reproaching Ćvorić for his oversight, provided him with a guide for future behavior. Ćvorić's reformation was revealed when only a month later Garašanin praised him for exemplary hospitality to a visiting Englishman: "I am happy that even without my instructions you did what a Serb should do for an important foreigner."[40] And Garašanin praised another district chief for receiving Consul Danilevskii so well that the Russian had expressed deep appreciation. "I am happy," wrote the minister, "that you carried out my instructions and even more that I have this opportunity to express my thanks to you and to assure you of my favor."[41]

Despite his formidable bureaucratic image, Garašanin possessed political skills superior to other leading "Defenders." Jovan Ristić, subsequently regent and foreign minister, noted his seemingly magical power to attract and win over people.[42] With those who were not his officials or subordinates, Garašanin would converse in a half-serious, half-jocular manner which created great intimacy. Calculating and resourceful, he spoke rather openly about his immediate plans while keeping silent about what would come afterwards. In critical moments he displayed great courage, decisiveness and heedlessness of personal consequences.

Garašanin found it increasingly difficult and frustrating to serve Prince Aleksandar. While he got along well with the Prince personally, he had a very low opinion of him as ruler and statesman. Indeed, the Prince was less capable and worse prepared than any Serbian ruler of this era. Already in May 1844 Garašanin complained to his exiled colleagues that the Prince refused to authorize constructive measures to benefit Serbia. "He starts out with good will, but because of his instability, he won't discuss matters or much less act. Thus, because of the Prince's indecisiveness, we are in the same old rut."[43] Finding the Prince's arbitrariness and penchant for personal rule intolderable, Garašanin opposed Aleksandar whenever he violated the laws or the Constitution and himself defended the public interest and his subordinates against princely tyranny. Meanwhile the Prince's camarilla was urging him to undertake illegal acts or allow them to be performed in his name. Autocratic by nature and susceptible to external influence, Aleksandar acted just as he pleased often sending friends abroad on personal business at state expense without the Council's permission. When the Prince wished to do something illegal, Garašanin would object openly and sometimes refused to execute his instructions. Aleksandar invariably blamed others when things went wrong while Garašanin believed that all the leaders shared the responsibility. In July 1846 he wrote the Prince it was high time to be honest, admit mistakes, and work hard to remedy them.[44]

Thus even prior to 1848 there were frequent quarrels between the "Defenders" and Prince Aleksandar.[45] Garašanin's first confrontation with him occurred late in 1843 after the Prince promoted Acika Nenadović, his wife's uncle and his adjutant, to the rank of major out of proper turn, angering most army officers. Protesting that decision, Garašanin requested the Prince to remove Nenadović from the army in order to mollify the officers.[46] The following December produced a more serious conflict when the Prince ordered high officers loyal to the "Defenders" removed and replaced with ones devoted to him personally. Garašanin promptly submitted his resignation, but eventually a compromise was worked out. Soon afterwards came another clash and another attempted Garašanin resignation. The Prince wished to remove Garašanin, but Foreign Minister Petronijević told him he could find no one who could run state affairs as well. Finally, Garašanin yielded to his friends' entreaties and withdrew his resignation. In 1845 he again offered to resign and in October 1847 apparently offered his crucial post to Colonel Knićanin.[47] Nonetheless, until 1848 Prince Aleksandar generally proved reasonable and often responsive to his ministers.[48]

As Interior Minister, affirms Slobodan Jovanović, Garašanin was not exactly Serbia's Colbert, doing relatively little to promote its prosperity, but he was a great minister of police.[49] However, his constructive achievements appear to have been greater than Jovanović realized and might well have been still more impressive had he not been saddled with such onerous and manifold responsibilities. During the 1840s stood under his direction the police, the army, the economy, medical services and communications. Garašanin pioneered efforts to establish a postal service and developed a department of construction. He realized that proper roads must be built through Serbia's dense forests before she could develop commercially. At his recommendation Serbia's first agricultural school was founded and economic knowledge spread among its farmers. Garašanin encouraged efforts of his subordinate, Atanasije Nikolić, to found a newspaper devoted chiefly to agrarian affairs, personally purchasing six copies and sending them to teachers in poor village communities. Recognizing the need for a national militia, Garašanin insisted that students at the agricultural school receive military training. He sought to improve Serbia's livestock, obtaining cattle from Austrian Styria and pigs from England. He had work begun on district hospitals and helped organize a more efficient and humane prison system.[50] Thus Garašanin contributed much to Serbia's economic and social growth as he did to its political stability and national prestige.

NOTES

1. *Prepiska Ilije Garašanina,* I, No. 12, p. 20 Garašanin to Knićanin, February 13, 1843.
2. D. Stranjaković, *Vučićeva buna,* p. 132.
3. Ibid., pp. 126 ff; S. Jovanović, *Ustavobranitelji i njihova vlada,* pp. 1-2; M. Petrovich, *A History of Serbia,* I, 223-230.
4. Jovanović, *Ustavobranitelji,* pp. 121-122.
5. DAS PO 27/5, Stanković to (Mihailo?), April 5, 1843.
6. Arhiv SANU, No. 9323/5, May 17, 1843 (Vienna).
7. Ibid., No. 9323/6, June 19/July 1.
8. Ibid., No. 7051/20, Nikolić (Belgrade) to Knićanin (Kragujevac) March 8.
9. Milićević, *Pomenik,* pp. 434-435.
10. *Prepiska,* No. 30, p. 34, Garašanin to Knićanin, May 15.
11. Ibid., No. 33, p. 36, June 5.
12. Ibid., No. 34, pp. 36-37, June 7.
13. See below, pp. 45 ff.
14. Czajkowski to Prince Aleksandar Karadjordjević, June 1843; IG 105, Czartoryski (Paris) to Prince Aleksandar Karadjordjević, September 16, 1843.
15. *Zbornik zakona i uredaba i uredbenik ukaza izdani u Kneževstvu Srbiji* (Belgrade, 1850), II, cited in Stranjaković, "Ilija Garašanin," p. 47.
16. *Prepiska,* No. 36, p. 39, Garašanin to Petronijević (Vidin), September 10.
17. Ibid., No. 40, p. 46, Garašanin to Petronijević and Vučić, October 9.
18. Ibid., No. 42, pp. 49-51, October 15.
19. Ibid., No. 46, pp. 54-55, November 3.
20. Ibid., No. 53, pp. 62-63, Garašanin to B. Djordjević, December 24.
21. Ibid., No. 55, pp. 64-65, Garašanin to Petronijević and Vučić, December 29.
22. Cvetko Rajović became a councillor in 1838 and a minister under Prince Miloš in 1842.
23. *Prepiska,* No. 60, pp. 67-68, Garašanin to Petronijević and Vučić, January 22, 1844.

24. Czartoryski Archive (Krakow), No. 5390, Zah to Czajkowski, January 27.

25. *Prepiska,* No. 64, pp. 72-75, Garašanin to Petronijević and Vučić, February 12.

26. Ibid., pp. 73-74; Czartoryski, No. 5390, Zah to Czajkowski, February 15-24.

27. *Prepiska,* No. 71, pp. 81-82, March 22.

28. Ibid., No. 72, pp. 83-84 and No. 73, p. 84, Garašanin to Knićanin, March 29 and April 8.

29. Ibid., No. 75, p. 88, Garašanin to Ilija Ćvorić, April 9.

30. Ibid., No. 87, pp. 99-100. On these ties see below, pp. 46-47.

31. Ibid., No. 88, pp. 101-102, Garašanin to Laza Teodorović, June 17.

32. Stranjaković, *Vlada ustavobranitelja,* pp. 81-83.

33. *Prepiska,* No. 105, pp. 114-115, Garašanin to Teodorović, May 5, 1845.

34. *Pisma Ilije Garašanina Jovanu Marianoviću,* I, 10, August 22, 1848.

35. *Prepiska,* No. 121, pp. 127-128, August 27, 1846. In a circular of August 6, 1846 to his district chiefs, Garašanin warned that many people in Serbia's interior were in the pay of Miloš. He admonished the chiefs to keep careful watch over such activities. No. 119, p. 126.

36. Ibid., Garašanin to Djordjević, 1845.

37. Stranjaković, "Ilija Garašanin," pp. 81-82.

38. Jovanović, *Ustavobranitelji,* p. 192.

39. *Prepiska,* No. 95, pp. 109-110, Garašanin to Ćvorić, August 12, 1844.

40. Ibid., No. 97, p. 110, September 1.

41. Ibid., No. 96, p. 110, Garašanin to Djordjević, September 1.

42. J. Ristić, *Prepiska,* p. 61.

43. *Prepiska,* No. 84, pp. 95-96, Garašanin to Petronijević and Vučić, May 9, 1844.

44. Ibid., No. 118, pp. 124-126, July 9, 1846, Garašanin to Prince Aleksandar Karadjordjević.

45. For post-1848 conflicts see below, pp. 160 ff.

46. *Prepiska,* No. 49, p. 59, Garašanin to Petronijević, December 8, 1843.

47.   S. Knićanin to Prince Aleksandar, October 8, 1847, cited in Stranjaković, "Ilija Garašanin," p. 37.

48.   "Zabeleške Ilije Garaćanina," cited in ibid., pp. 398-399.

49.   S. Jovanović, *Ustavobranitelji,* pp. 191-192.

50.   Stranjaković, "Ilija Garašanin," pp. 423-424.

CHAPTER IV

FORGING A NATIONAL PROGRAM—NAČERTANIJE

> [Serbia] must realize that she is still small, that she can-
> not remain so, and that she can achieve her future only in
> alliance with other surrounding peoples.
>
> —Načertanije (1844)

Late in 1844 Garašanin drew up an "Outline" ("Načertanije") of Serbian national aims and presented it to Prince Aleksandar Karadjordjević.
It set the goal of uniting all Serbs around Serbia and eventually unifying
all South Slavs. Based on written proposals of Polish and Czech émigrés
anxious to undermine Russian and Austrian influence in the Balkans but
reflecting Serbian conditions and interests, "Načertanije" was destined
to become the most important program for Serbia's foreign policy in the
nineteenth century. This document, long kept secret, became highly controversial. Was this a Greater Serbian or a Yugoslav program?[1] Who was
its principal author: Garašanin himself or Polish and Czech contemporaries
such as Prince Adam Czartoryski and František Zah? Was "Načertanije"
an amalgam of foreign ideas edited and revised by Garašanin, or basically
a product of Serbian conditions and influences? For the past half century
Yugoslav historians have debated these questions without achieving a
consensus.

Rather than continuing this debate, the purpose here is to describe the
origins of "Načertanije," emphasize Garašanin's role and depict the context

in which it developed, including the vital "Polish connection." The complicated historiographical controversy will be examined briefly without its personal polemics.[2] This chapter will delineate the theoretical bases for a Serbian national program; the next one will describe Garašanin's efforts to implement it until 1853. His policies toward the Serbian Vojvodina in 1848-1849 will be discussed separately.

Modern Serbian aspirations for unity and revival of the glory and territories of the Serbian medieval state began with Karadjordje's uprising of 1804. As his successes mounted, Serbs were encouraged to rise in the Srem, eastern Banat and Bosnia. Their hopes focused on Serbia, and Karadjordje in 1809 sought in vain to link up with Montenegro through Sjenica and Novi Pazar. During the Second Uprising of 1815 the practical and realistic Miloš Obrenović confined his concept of Serbia chiefly to the Šumadija while maintaining ties with some other Serbian areas.[3] His acquisition in 1833 of six districts from the Porte reaffirmed his policy of cautious expansion of Šumadijan Serbia and his gradual extension of authority over it. Prince Mihailo, only seventeen when he succeeded his exiled father in 1838, from the start adopted a more catholic view of national liberation of all Serbs and South Slavs under Turkish rule. Already Serbia served as a refuge for Serbs and Bulgars fleeing foreign rule and persecution, and Mihailo and his government received them warmly. Many Austrian Serbs, especially from the Vojvodina, entered his service. However, Mihailo ruled too briefly and insecurely to formulate, much less achieve, a Serbian national program. He could resume such efforts only upon his return to Serbia in 1859.

During their struggle against Prince Mihailo the "Defenders," preoccupied with constitutional and practical political matters, paid little heed to national aspirations of the Serbian people. Nor were their two chief early leaders, Vučić and Petronijević, much interested in broader national unity. Throughout his career Vučić remained a narrow Šumadijan patriot seeking to create a "pure Serbia," undefiled by Austrian Serbs and other "foreigners." Petronijević, the polished diplomat, preferred negotiation and peaceful pressure to nationalist agitation. With his broad, far-reaching political plans and statesmanship, Ilija Garašanin possessed greater dynamism and intellect than other "Defenders." Realizing the irreversible decline of Turkish power, he foresaw eventual Ottoman collapse. Realistically, Garašanin knew it would be far easier to agitate among and attract Serbs of the Ottoman Empire than those of Austria. Ever conscious of Russian and Austrian influence in Serbia, he considered it vital to build greater strength in a larger entity to resist their encroachments and widen Serbia's autonomy. Garašanin also believed that any such undertaking should be based upon a carefully prepared plan and that this was the best time to formulate a general national program of goals for Serbia. Of the South Slav regions only Serbia and tiny Montenegro had their own domestic administrations, and he concluded that Serbia was the destined nucleus for a larger Serbian or South Slav state. Geographical position, resources, history, and power of resistance all seemed to make Serbia far better suited to such a role than barren, impoverished, peripheral Montenegro.

In 1843 Garašanin, unlike Vučić and Petronijević, was already an ardent advocate of Serbian self-reliance. Militant, assertive nationalism set him apart from colleagues who accepted tutelage of strong foreign powers. Prince Aleksandar and Petronijević favored dependence on Austria; Vučić and the Simić brothers preferred Russia. Garašanin was inclined instead rather early to seek backing from France and England which had fewer direct Balkan interests and therefore less desire or incentive to curtail Serbia's autonomy or to dominate her. Unlike his colleagues Garašanin also would display great capacity to grow and expand his horizons and a flexibility contrasting with his severe policies as Interior Minister. Starting as a narrow Serbian patriot, Garašanin steadily extended his gaze until it encompassed all South Slavs and Balkan peoples.

Garašanin's embryonic national views reflected his milieu and the aspirations of the bureaucrats and bourgeoisie to which he belonged. "Načertanije," Serbia's first true program of national and foreign policy, emerged against a background of multi-faceted growth and development. Serbia was experiencing the painful transition from Ottoman feudalism to a developing small European state. Turkish decrees (hatti-šerifs) issued in 1830 and 1833, granting Serbia political autonomy, put a formal end to Turkish feudalism. Miloš' free trade policy, inaugurated reluctantly in 1837 under severe public pressure, contributed to a dynamic commercial growth, especially exportation of livestock to Austria, in which the Garašanin family was involved conspicuously. The livestock trade in particular was linking together town and country in Serbia into a national market. A dramatic increase in applications for trading permits during the 1830s testified to the country's economic development.[4]

Serbian towns, though still small, were growing rapidly from an influx of officials and teachers from Austria. Serbian shopkeepers and artisans were multiplying, gradually taking over from and crowding out the Turks and Serbifying the towns. This growth centered in Belgrade which with a population of perhaps 22,000-25,000 by the early 1840s was by far the largest urban center in Serbia, although considerably smaller than the Vojvodina's Novi Sad.[5] The mercantile and official element in Belgrade sought to lessen Serbia's economic dependence on Austria and political reliance on Turkey and Russia. This could best be achieved by territorial expansion against Turkey and freeing Serbia from economic subservience to Austria by winning access to the Adriatic Sea. The establishment of schools, creation of a national army and development of a Serbian church also fostered Serbia's emerging national consciousness. Anxious to encourage the new bureaucratic and commercial element, Garašanin adapted views from Polish and Czech émigrés so they would correspond with the interests of the Serbian state and bourgeoisie.

Prince Adam Czartoryski was the chief leader of the Polish exiles in Paris. In 1804, as Russia's foreign minister, Czartoryski had become acquainted with Serbian aims from a Belgrade delegation led by Matija Nenadović. He also knew about Metropolitan S. Stratimirović's plan of that year for a great "Slavo-Serbian empire." Prior to the Polish revolt of 1830, Czartoryski had advised the Serbs and other Balkan peoples to unite under Russia's aegis. In 1830, after a vain attempt to win Poland's freedom from Russia, Czartoryski fled into French exile with hundreds of his countrymen. In 1833 this conservative aristocrat and skilled diplomat established at the Hôtel Lambert in Paris the Polish émigrés's chief political and cultural center, serving as an unofficial Polish foreign office.[6] With French diplomatic and financial support, he established a secretariat and an extensive network of agents throughout Europe and the Near East in an effort to undermine Russia internationally and eventually restore an independent Poland. The Near Eastern crisis of 1839-1840 attracted Czartoryski's attention to the Balkans where Russia was deeply involved. In 1841 the Austrian envoy in Constantinople reported that Polish émigrés were arriving under false names and with French passports. Constantinople became a major center of Polish agitation, directed by Ukrainian-born Michal Czajkowski.[7] A close collaborator of Prince Czartoryski, he was in close touch with the French embassy and used its diplomatic pouch. Czajkowski believed that Serbia would play a leading role in combating Russian influence in the Balkans by forming a large South Slav state.

Initial Polish links with the "Defenders" were forged in Constantinople in 1841-1842 during their first exile.[8] Supporting Vučić and Petronijević, Czajkowski warned them against Russian and Austrian influences and urged them with the Porte's aid to make Serbia self-reliant. Upon their return home, the Serbian exiles were accompanied by a Polish agent, Ludwik Zwierkowski, under a pseudonym, Dr. Louis Lenoir, and carrying a French passport.[9] Sent by Czajkowski, Zwierkowski stayed for a time with Petronijević, advised the "Defenders," and helped them prepare Vučić's revolt of 1842. Zwierkowski met Prince Aleksandar Karadjordjević and helped secure his first election. Also in touch with Milutin and Ilija Garašanin, he urged Paris and London to recognize Prince Aleksandar and the "Defender" regime. When Russian pressure forced a second princely election, Czajkowski went to Serbia in May 1843 and spent several weeks directing the campaign in person.[10] Following the Prince's successful reelection, Prince Czartoryski congratulated him: "Serbia and Poland have common interests and common enemies and need the same virtues. Your nation has just provided a noble example of that."[11] At the "Defenders'" request, Prince Czartoryski influenced the Western powers to recognize their regime and defended them against Russian pressure.

As part of this pro-"Defender" diplomatic campaign, Prince Czartory-ski in January 1843 wrote a memorandum, "Advice on conduct to be followed by Serbia," urging the Serbs to reconcile and unify the South Slavs and develop a long-range plan for their future.[12] Czartoryski set only the main guidelines leaving details to his agent in Belgrade and to Serbian leaders. Sent to various Polish agents abroad, this document was com-municated by Zwierkowski in March 1843 to Ilija Garašanin. The main ideas of "Advice" ("Conseils") would later be incorporated in Garašanin's "Načertanije." It assigned to Serbia the leading role in rescuing the Balkan peoples from Russian influence. First, to prevent Russian intereference, the Serbs must strengthen their regime at home and display loyalty and good will toward their suzerain, the Porte. "Serbia should obtain from the Porte without the help of Russia or other powers the hereditary right for its princely family to select princes just as Miloš obtained that right for his family." Once the Ottoman Empire disintegrated, Serbia could develop independently; meanwhile she should conciliate the Turks and prevent Russia from ruining Serbo-Turkish relations. Gradually expanding and strengthening itself, Serbia should seek to unite with Montenegro thus obtaining access to the sea, and negotiate the evacuation of Turkish garrisons from fortresses in Serbia. Acting cautiously toward Russia without antagonizing her needlessly, Serbia should seek Russia's patronage only in case of conflict with the Porte. Serbia, warned Czartoryski, could never trust Austria since Vienna's aims—annexation of Serbia and other Balkan lands—conflicted wholly with Slav interests. To escape Russian or Austrian domination, Belgrade should seek French or English support. With France good relations could be built by improving trade relations, following French advice, and sending Serbian students to Paris. France's national interest required that the South Slav peoples allied with her be free, educated and united. Fostering the spread of education, Belgrade should seek to arouse feelings of nationality and brotherhood among its Turkish and Austrian brethren. At this time Czartoryski's policy was also that of France: to cooperate with the eastern Christians and pending South Slav unity, preserve the Ottoman Empire.

For the Hôtel Lambert Serbia enjoyed special status as the only South Slav state with domestic autonomy recognized by the great powers. Until 1856 close ties persisted between the "Defenders" and Czartoryski's organization. Although a conservative legitimist favoring indefinite preservation of the Ottoman Empire, Czartoryski predicted its eventual demise, perhaps assisted by its own peoples. This approach coincided closely with Garašanin's own view.

Late in 1843 Czajkowski replaced his envoy in Belgrade, Zwierkowski, who had become too conspicuous, with a Czech émigré, František Zah.[13] A remarkable man in his own right, Zah figured prominently in the development of a Serbian national program. Born in Olmouc, Moravia, in 1807, Zah after completing a German classical secondary school, became a Czech nationalist. During legal studies at Vienna University, Zah acquired a liberal bourgeois outlook and enthusiasm for national and political freedom. The Polish insurrection of 1830 spurred him to abandon an excellent law practice and rush to join the Poles' fight for freedom. Arriving after their defeat, he accompanied Polish exiles to Paris, shared their bitter émigré life and participated actively in democratic organizations

such as Young Poland. In 1837 Zah returned to Austria to found secret
organizations of Czech and other Slav students in Vienna against the
Metternich regime. Threatened with exposure, he fled late in 1840 to his
Polish friends in France. Now he interacted with both democratic Polish
elements and Prince Czartoryski's conservatives, vacillating between them.
Repelled by the democrats' factional quarrels, he was attracted to the
conservatives by their able leadership and interest in general Slav problems.

Impressed by Zah's memorandum of April 1843 entitled "Report to
Prince Adam Czartoryski on the mission of a diplomatic agent to Serbia,"[14]
Czartoryski on Czajkowski's recommendation decided to appoint him to
replace Zwierkowski in Belgrade. This memo, determining Zah's subsequent career, was written apparently independently of Czartoryski's
"Conseils," differing from it in content, divisions and minor emphasis on
general Slav policy. It focused on Polish-Serbian relations and Serbia's
relations with Europe. Stressing the Austrian threat to Serbia, Zah urged
the Serbs to cultivate the Austrian Slavs and cooperate with the Porte
against Russia. A disintegrating Turkey would yield to an independent
South Slav state which would stabilize Balkan conditions and block further
Russian or Austrian penetration. A nucleus already existed: Serbia's civil
and military organization. Other South Slavs should follow her example
and seek her friendship. Serbia should lead her South Slav brethren in
Bosnia, Hercegovina, Montenegro and Bulgaria.

By impressing Prince Czartoryski, Zah's April memorandum speeded
his acceptance by the Hôtel Lambert despite objections from some to
employing a foreigner. That August Zah drew up instructions entitled:
"How I understand my mission to the Slav lands of Turkey,"[15] embodying the all-Slav viewpoint to which Zah adhered consistently throughout
his stay in Belgrade:

A harmony of interests exists between the [Slav] peoples of the
west and south. Poles, Austrian Slavs and those in Turkey should
thus act in common; the enemies whom they should fight together
are Russia and Austria.

Above all, the Slavs of European Turkey must unite. "The aim of such unification should be to achieve peacefully the status which Serbia already enjoys or at least giving them a measure of freedom and civil security." After implementing administrative reforms at home, Serbia could lead them and become the focus of their gradual emancipation. Setting Serbo-Montenegran rapprochement as a top priority of his mission, Zah advocated their commercial union which would thus connect Serbia with the Adriatic Sea. Placing herself at the head of Turkish Slavs, Serbia must prevent a fragmentation of European Turkey which would aid Austria or Russia. Belgrade should establish agencies in Bosnia, Hercegovina, Montenegro and Bulgaria to coordinate their policies and watch Russian agents. Belgrade should cooperate closely with the Bulgars and ally itself with the Serbs of Hungary. These were Zah's views before he reached Serbia.

In mid-October 1843 Zah crossed into Serbia, traveling into the interior to ascertain the public mood and the solidity of the "Defender" regime. Although he found Obrenovites intriguing actively, the peasantry seemed largely content. Reaching Belgrade, Zah discovered that Vučić and Petronijević were still in exile, but Prince Aleksandar and Interior Minister Garašanin greeted him warmly.[16] Zah wrote Czajkowski in Constantinople on November 2nd:

> I have just left Mr. Ilija Garašanin. He received me warmly, without embarrassment and confidently. He told me: 'We know very well that it is to Prince Czartoryski that we owe the favorable attitude of the French government toward the changes which have occurred in Serbia.' I confirmed him in that opinion which is so correct. I added that Count Zamoyski [a relative and colleague of Czartoryski] will succeed equally in London and that henceforth one can count on a more independent policy by the English cabinet in all matters concerning Serbia.[17]

Garašanin responded favorably to Zah's assertion that London would replace Thomas Fonblanque with a more friendly English consul. Asked how he would explain an extended stay in Belgrade to the French consul, Zah showed Garašanin his French passport, adding that he would declare that he wished to get to know Serbia and its language better. Cautioning

Zah to avoid the Russian consul, Garašanin regretted that he could not receive Zah at home openly as a friend before everyone. Commented Zah: "This first visit, you see, lets me hope for the closest relations with Mr. Ilija."

This, indeed, soon proved true. Zah reported a few days later that much to his satisfaction he was already beginning to fulfill his mission and had overcome initial suspicion of the Poles by Serbian leaders, including Garašanin. Focusing their attention rather narrowly on Serbia and its immediate vicinity, they failed as yet to appreciate an all-Slav policy, noted Zah. Thus Prince Czartoryski's "Conseils" had been "wholly new for Serbia." He was urging Garašanin to take a stand on the Magyar-Slav quarrel in Hungary as he affirmed prophetically to Czartoryski: "Austria will never agree to the development on her frontiers of a powerful, independent Serbian state [since] it would remove all South Slavs from her."[18]

During December 1843 Zah gradually conveyed to Garašanin his ideas on Slav unity and reform in Serbia while lamenting the absence of the top two "Defenders." "The foreign ministry dares do nothing," he complained "the finance minister is pro-Russian, and the minister of education and justice is a zero. Fortunately, the Prince listens to Garašanin." With the latter Zah had discussed Franco-Serbian relations and criticized vigorously Serbia's inadequate system of public education. Garašanin had welcomed Zah's suggestions to create a model farm and an agricultural school and asked him to draw up plans for these.[19] Then on January 12, 1844, Zah reported to Czajkowski that Garašanin had requested him to compose a plan on the Slav policy of Serbia:

My frequent conservations with Mr. Ilija about the Slavs of Turkey have given me the opportunity to explain to him little by little my views about those peoples. I have just agreed to prepare a plan for him about the manner of acting toward the Slavs, since he realizes it is already time to deal with this formally, or so to speak systematically. I am working conscientiously on this and will communicate to you a translation of my proposal. Let me express to you my joy at the minister's confidence. He told me: 'I am asking the same thing from several of my friends, so that we will be enlightened on this question. Then we will see who will win out [l'emportera].

Now on close terms with Zah, Garašanin confided that the Simić brothers had become anti-Russian: "Aleksa [Simić] detests them more than I do, and Stojan the most capable among us, seeks to deceive them. He pretends to be a friend of Russia in order to learn what she wants."[20] A Zah report from January 1844 revealed that his relationship with Garašanin had grown still closer. On the 13th "he spoke to me so intimately and frankly that my heart beat with joy." Later, Zah urged Garašanin to send an envoy to Montenegro saying: "You don't even know what is going on on your frontiers." However, Zah did not blame Garašanin, already overburdened handling the Interior Ministry, for this. It was Foreign Minister Aleksa Simić who had been remiss in his duties.[21]

Working eagerly on the "Plan" Garašanin had requested, Zah reported to Czajkowski February 24th that it was finished except for a section on Croatia. On this he conferred with Stjepan Car and Pavao Ćavlović, colleagues of Ljudevit Gaj, head of Zagreb's Illyrian circle, who advocated an idealistic, federal Yugoslavism. Desiring Serbo-Croatian agreement over Bosnia, a region containing a mixture of Orthodox Serbs, Catholic Croats and Muslims, Zah concluded it must eventually join with Serbia, the center and nucleus of South Slav unity. Whereas most Serbian leaders remained cold toward the Illyrian movement and the Croats, Garašanin noted Father Laurentius, a Catholic priest, was willing to listen to their viewpoint. Soon Zah informed Czajkowski that his "Plan," based on Czartoryski's views, had been completed. "What I added relates only to execution and details. . . . The original which I wish to submit to Mr. Ilija, is written in my own hand."[22]

The Illyrian idea, he wrote Czajkowski, in its patriotic sentiment resembled Polish views and possessed the same vitality and warlike spirit. Gaj, the Illyrian leader, had accepted Polish policy and Zah's principles: 1) South Slav unity in a constitutional monarchy under the Karadjordjević dynasty; 2) progress toward this goal as European Turkey evolved gradually into a Slav State; 3) Serbia as nucleus and diplomatic representative of the South Slavs; 4) Bosnia to be joined to Serbia; Serbs and Croats would cooperate to achieve Orthodox-Catholic accord, then both groups would seek to win over the Muslims; and 5) independent national action without relying on Austria or Russia, if necessary seeking alliances with France and England. Noted Zah: "I took care to establish well these basic principles." Then he induced Garašanin to mediate between Prince

Aleksandar and the Croatian envoy, young Count Albert Nugent, who came to Belgrade in late March 1844. However, the Prince and most other Belgrade leaders opposed the Illyrian viewpoint.[23]

Unaccountably, only on April 27, 1844 did Zah submit a copy of his "Plan" to Czajkowski and to Garašanin not until late May.[24] He wrote Czajkowski May 31st:

> He [Garašanin] examined it hastily and found it practical. When Mr. Petronijević returns, I will ask Garašanin to give it to him. We shall see how much he will follow it. I explained to Mr. Ilija why I only mention Poland once. I did not wish them to suppose immediately that it came from a Pole so that those who have prejudices about Poland or lack of confidence in her would find no reason to object.

Garašanin had praised both Czartoryski's "Conseils" and Zah's "Plan":

> Mr. Ilija on that occasion told me about the original plan of His Highness [Czartoryski] for Serbia and expressed in words full of respect and amazement that it was a masterpiece. With the basic principles of His Highness' plan before him, he discerned immediately that my proposal ["Plan"] was based on the same principles and congratulated me for adapting it rather well to local [Serbian] circumstances.[25]

Careful perusal confirmed Garašanin's initial favorable impression of Zah's "Plan." In Zah he had found a collaborator of great integrity and value. From the start because of his knowledge, perceptiveness and wide contacts, Zah secured a much more independent position in Belgrade than had Zwierkowski. His main informants about conditions in Serbia were Garašanin himself, Aleksa Janković and T. Kneževic, chief and secretary respectively of Prince Aleksandar's chancellery. Zah had friendly relations with the Illyrian Croats and Franciscan leaders in Bosnia. His chief informant on Bosnian affairs was a native, Toma Kovačević, later a close colleague of Garašanin. These men listened attentively to Zah's views on the need for South Slav rapprochement and unity. However, his relations with Vučić and Petronijević after their return from exile were cooler, and the Simić brothers reacted to him negatively, perhaps because of his pro-

Illyrian sentiments. Zah's all-Slav approach alienated the Serbia-firsters, but he and Garašanin concurred about Serbia's role: he adopted elements of the Greater Serbian approach while Garašanin warmed markedly toward the Croats.[26]

Based on Zah's glowing reports, Czajkowski now lauded Garašanin as the key to the success of Polish policies in Serbia:

> He is a very capable and energetic person,...one of the most active leaders in Serbia, a fine patriot and a person favoring order. Up to now he still does not grasp the full significance of the Slavs' role or of [Serbia's] need for an [hereditary] dynasty, but he has the capacity to grasp that. In talks with Moscow he will certainly be careful, not bow down [to Russia] and will defend the rights and freedoms of his country. He recognizes the need to be shielded by the Porte and to maintain the best possible relations with it.... Ties with him are significant and necessary.[27]

Because Zah's "Plan," like Czartoryski's "Conseils," was crucial in the genesis of Garašanin's "Načertanije," the origins of his ideas are significant. He had brought the Yugoslav and all-Slav aspects with him to Serbia. We find them in his April 1843 memorandum, August instructions, and in "Conseils," comprising the basis for his "Plan." In a sense "Plan" was the practical application of "Conseils" to Serbian conditions. In "Plan," concludes Perović, "The expansionist imperative of the Serbian bourgeoisie and the political aims of the Polish emigration coincided and found common expression."[28] Once in Belgrade Zah included the popular idea of reviving Stevan Dušan's fourteenth century empire. Serbia as nucleus of a Yugoslav state, he believed, would become a reliable instrument of Polish émigré policy. Providing Zah with ideas besides Garašanin were Austroslavs such as Car, Herkalović, Kovačević and A. Nikolić. As a knowledgeable and cultured foreigner, Zah knew his Polish history and conditions in Russia and Austria. Advocating an alliance between southern and western Slavs (Poles and Czechs), he recommended Prague for the education of young Serbs. A native Serb with limited educational background would have possessed neither such knowledge nor views, ruling out a Garašanin assistant as the "Plan's" author.

For over six months after its submission to the Serbian leadership there was little mention of Zah's "Plan." It was being examined carefully by Prince Aleksandar, Garašanin and his close advisers, Aleksa Janković and Atanasije Nikolić. Garašanin found himself caught between Zah and Illyrians advocating South Slav unity and equality. Listening attentively to Zah's enthusiastic vision of Serbia's broad role in the Slav world, he helped the Czech overcome the doubts of other Serbian leaders. Though Garašanin refused to accept all of Zah's ideas and consulted his political colleagues and friends, Zah's influence on him during 1844 was nonetheless great.[29]

The only other reference at this time to Zah's "Plan" in his correspondence was in a report to Czajkowski early in February 1845.[30] From Knežević of the Prince's chancellery he had learned that Aleksandar was delighted with the "Plan" and had also requested a copy of Czartoryski's "Conseils." "You will see," declared Zah, "that we are gradually succeeding and I will try to win the Prince's confidence." However, "Plan" was being criticized by some traditionally minded Serbian leaders for its grandiose Yugoslavism which seemingly exceeded Serbia's limited capacities.[31]

Elaborating a plan for the Slav policy of Serbia and thus shaping Garašanin's "Načertanije" comprised the chief contribution of Zah and conservative Polish émigrés to Serbia's political development. During the next years Zah would be asked to draw up several other proposals, notably his ambitious "Basic Ideas" ("Osnovne misle") of 1847 on Serbia's domestic political system. Studied carefully by Garašanin and other Serbian leaders, it stressed, as had his "Plan," that Serbia should comprise the nucleus for South Slav unification.[32]

A textual comparison reveals that "Načertanije" closely resembles "Plan" and "Conseils" and was derived from them. Zah's "Plan" had made Czartoryski's general principles applicable specifically to the Serbs. "Načertanije" revised and narrowed "Plan" to conform with Serbia's modest strength. Garašanin's changes transformed the Yugoslav-oriented "Plan" into a Serbian national program limited mainly to the Turkish Empire. He omitted everything he disagreed with in "Plan" and added his own conclusions. Realizing that a definite program for Serbia's development and expansion was needed urgently, Garašanin served as an intermediary between Czech and Polish émigrés on the one hand and conservative

Serbian leaders on the other. Thus "Načertanije" deemphasized Serbo-Bulgar collaboration and omitted altogether Zah's section on Croatia composed with Illyrian advice. For Garašanin reviving the traditions of Dušan's empire and Serbian glory were paramount. Therefore throughout the text he replaced the word "Yugoslav" with "Serb" without ever expressly rejecting Zah's assertion that Serbia in its own interest must pursue a Yugoslav policy. Like most Serbian leaders, Garašanin regarded Bosnia and Hercegovina as inherently Serbian lands and directed Serbia's expansion mainly in that direction. His Greater Serbian emphasis was shown by his opposition to the creation of a separate Bosnian dynasty which might hamper or delay Bosnia's unification with Serbia and split the South Slavs. Garašanin proposed to limit Serbia's activity essentially to Bosnia-Hercegovina, Montenegro and northern Albania, that is to Greater Serbia.[33]

As to Serbia's foreign policy, Garašanin adopted many but not all of Czartoryski's and Zah's basic precepts. "Načertanije" ageed that Austria remained Serbia's principal, permanent and most dangerous enemy, and thus that Serbia should seek support from England and specifically France. Concerned about the danger of Austro-Russian partition of European Turkey which would doom Serbian unification, Garašanin agreed that Serbia must act loyally toward the Porte until a new Balkan state led by Serbia could replace it. While agreeing that Serbia and Russia might feud over Bulgaria, Garašanin rejected flatly the negative Czartoryski-Zah view of Russia. Instead, he believed that Serbia could achieve its goals most readily by cooperating with Russia provided the latter abandoned its efforts to subjugate Serbia or interfere in its domestic affairs:

. . . With no one else can Serbia achieve her goal more easily than in agreement with Russia, but only if Russia fully and completely accepts Serbia's conditions, guaranteeing her future in the broadest terms. An alliance between Serbia and Russia would be truly the most natural, but whether it will be achieved depends on Russia, and Serbia would welcome it with open arms, but only if she is convinced that Russia is proposing it sincerely and heartily which can only be the case if she [Russia] renounces her present system [of intervention and realizes] that an alliance with little Serbia is more natural than one with Austria.

Like Nikola Pašić subsequently, Garašanin was a practical, realistic statesman. Without repudiating the Czartoryski-Zah concept of eventual South Slav unification in a greater Yugoslavia in order to discourage external aggression, Garašanin postponed this ambitious goal indefinitely. Instead, in 1844, he focused on building a strong Serbia and expanding it to include the other Serbs of Turkey:

> [Serbia] must realize that she is small, that she cannot remain so, and that she can achieve her future only in alliance with other surrounding peoples. . . . She cannot limit herself to her present frontiers but must seek to attract to herself all the Serbs who surround her. Unless Serbia pursues this policy firmly, . . . , she will be thrown here and there by foreign storms like a small boat until she finally strikes bare rock and is broken up.[34]

While accepting many of Czartoryski's and Zah's ideas of alliance with other South Slav and Balkan peoples, Garašanin considered others premature and beyond Serbia's present strength.

For many years after 1844 Garašanin's "Načertanije" remained secret, known only to a few personal friends of his and Prince Aleksandar, and later to the Obrenović rulers and Garašanin's son, Milutin. Its publication in 1906 in the magazine, Delo,[35] created considerable public furor, but historians remained apathetic. Until 1931 Yugoslav scholars believed that Garašanin had worked out "Načertanije" independently as his own conception and that it advocated South Slav unification. In that year Dr. Dragoslav Stranjaković, a Serbian scholar, on the basis of research by a Polish historian, Marceli Handelsmann, first explained its origins and the close links between the "Defenders" and the Polish emigration. Stranjaković concluded that Czartoryski's "Conseils" had inspired Garašanin to compose "Načertanije." Like previous authors, Stranjakovć interpreted "Načertanije" as Yugoslav in conception but noted that Garašanin for practical reasons of power had limited Serbia's aims to Turkish territories.[36] In subsequent works Stranjaković lauded Garašanin and praised "Načertanije" as a great monument to Yugoslavism. Discovering Zah's "Plan" in Garašanin's papers and realizing that Garašanin had utilized it extensively in composing "Načertanije," Stranjaković published the two texts side by side.[37]

Since the 1930s Stranjaković's "classical" view of "Načertanije" has undergone severe criticism. Reviewing Stranjaković's book, *Serbia from 1833 to 1858*, J. D. Mitrović pointed out that Garašanin had advocated a Greater Serbian, not a Yugoslav, state, omitting Croats, Bulgars and Slovenes from it and considering Bosnia wholly Serbian. The Yugoslav idea in "Načertanije," argued Mitrović, appeared as a vague, undefined concept, not an integral part of Garašanin's program. Uppermost instead was "holy historic right" and Dušan's imperial tradition as bases for annexing other Serb-inhabited areas to Serbia.[38] In 1944 the Croatian nationalist, Šimunjić, pointed out that Garašanin had omitted "Plan's" section on Croatia and everywhere had replaced Zah's "South Slavs" with "Serbs." Denouncing his view of Bosnia and Hercegovina as Serbian lands, Šimunjić concluded that Garašanin's concept was inherently Greater Serbian.[39]

In post-World War II Communist Yugoslavia came further questioning and revision of traditional views of "Načertanije." The Belgrade scholar, Lj. Aleksić, stressed that "Načertanije" reflected the interests of an emerging Serbian bourgeoisie seeking to escape economic dependence on Austria.[40] Vojislav Vučković, the first Yugoslav historian to utilize Zah's reports of 1843-1844, asserted dogmatically that the ideas in Zah's "Plan" were chiefly Garašanin's. "Imbued with the Yugoslav ideal," Garašanin, he affirmed, could have written "Načertanije" without Polish inspiration since the concept of Yugoslav unity had been current among the Serbs since the seventeenth century.[41] Disputing this view and showing Vučković's inconsistences, Radoslav Perović affirmed in 1955 that Stranjaković and Vučković had neglected "the Polish connection," and that "Načertanije" was a virtual copy of Zah's "Plan." Garašanin had merely transformed "Plan's" Yugoslav conception into a Serbian national program, giving it his stamp and that of the Serbian bourgeoisie. Garašanin at age thirty-two, argued Perović, lacked theoretical and political sophistication and thus had borrowed heavily from the cosmopolitan Zah.[42]

As the controversy over "Načertanije" continued, American scholars also became involved. Charles Jelavich aptly compared Garašanin's emphasis on Greater Serbia to contempoary movements in behalf of Greater Croatia, Greater Poland, and Greater Bulgaria.[43] The basic paradox in "Načertanije," noted Michael Petrovich, was the discrepancy between Greater Serbian nationalism and South Slav union. Thus it contained some of the spirit of South Slav brotherhood and mutual acceptance while emphasizing Serbia's role as unifier and as the dominant element in a future Yugoslav state. Garašanin was doubtless influenced by his Serbian colleagues and environment as much as by Czartoryski and Zah. His indisputable achievement was to develop a creative, workable program from disparate ideas and currents.[44] As Vaso Čubrilović, dean of Yugoslav scholars, put it: "Garašanin was not just the copier of Zah's ideas but an independent thinker and interpreter of the concepts and views of the young Serbian bourgeoisie about the state problems of Serbia in the nineteenth century."[45] Critics of Stranjaković's original view have shown convincingly that "Načertanije" represented a Greater Serbian adaptation of the all-Slav and Yugoslav conceptions of Czartoryski and Zah. Garašanin's version, unsurprisingly, reflected Serbia's existing stage of economic and socio-political development. "Načertanije" stamped its author as an ardent Serbian nationalist and a spiritual father of the Yugoslavia of 1918.

NOTES

1. Greater Serbia, besides Serbia proper, would include all areas inhabited primarily by Serbs, i.e., Montenegro, portions of northern Albania and Macedonia ("Old Serbia") as well as Bosnia and Hercegovina (although those provinces were also claimed by the Croats). A Yugoslav, or South Slav, program besides the above-mentioned regions would include the Croats, Slovenes, the Serbian Vojvodina and perhaps Bulgaria.

2. For the best summaries of the controversy see Mirko Valentić, "Koncepcija Garašaninova 'Načertanije' (1844),"*Historijski pregled,* 1961, no. 2, pp. 128-137, and Nikša Stančić, "Problem Načertanije Ilije Garašanina," *Historijski zbornik,* XXI-XXIII, pp. 179-196.

3. For a summary of the First and Second Uprisings see Petrovich, *A History,* I, 27 ff. Already under Prince Miloš existed the concept of a greater Serbian state, notably after the Russo-Turkish war of 1828-1829 when there was discussion of dividing up the Ottoman Empire.

4. Lj. Aleksić, "Šta je dovela do stvaranja 'Načertanije'," *Historijski*

pregled, I (1954), 2, pp. 68-71; Radoslav Perović, "Oko 'Načertanije' iz 1844 godine," *Istoriski glasnik*, I (1963), pp. 71-94. Stated Perović: "Serbia was moving rapidly along the path of economic progress with the gradual growth of agricultural production and trade which united the country into a single market. Capital accumulated in domestic and foreign trade created a new commercial bourgeoisie, anti-feudal and militant, seeking to eliminate obstacles to a new bourgeois society and state...." Ibid., pp. 76-77.

5. On this urban growth see Petrovich, *A History*, I, 167 ff. For example, he notes the growth of interior Kragujevac from 193 houses in 1818 to 639 in 1844 (p. 176). A census of 1837 listed Belgrade's population at 20,000 including 3,000 Muslims. Ibid., p. 172.

6. On the Hôtel Lambert see Robert A. Berry, "Czartoryski and the Balkan Policies of the Hotel Lambert, 1832-1847," Ph. D. dissertation, Indiana University, 1974; Jaroslav Šidak, "L'Hôtel Lambert et les Croates," *Annales de l'institut français de Zagreb*, VI-VII (1942-43), pp. 5-6.

7. On Czajkowski see Berry, op. cit., pp. 56-62. His memoirs ("Zapiski") are in *Russkaia starina*, vols. 94 and 95 (1898).

8. Berry, op. cit., pp. 191 ff.; Šimunjić, *'Načertanije', Tajni spis srpske nacionalne i vanske politike* (Zagreb, 1944), pp. 9 ff. Czartoryski Archive (Krakow) 5410, pp. 502-503.

9. Czartoryski 5410, pp. 544-545, Czajkowski to Czartoryski, December 4, 1841; 5486, same to same, July 24, 1842, p. 31.

10. Ibid., 5486, p. 156, Czajkowski to Czartoryski, June 17, 1843.

11. IG 105, Adam Czartoryski (Paris to Prince Aleksandar Karadjordjević, September 4/16, 1843.

12. Czart. 5405, "Conseils sur la conduite à suivre par la Serbie," January, 1843, also included in D. Stranjaković, "Kako je postalo Garašaninova 'Načertanije'," *Spomenik SAN*, XCI, pp. 63-115. In October 1842 Zwierkowski after studying the situation carefully in Serbia, had urged Czartoryski to send a guide to action to Serbian leaders. Czart. 5410, pp. 733-734, Lenoir (Zwierkowski) to Czartoryski, October 24, 1842, cited in Berry, p. 202. See V. Začek, "Češko i poljsko učešče u postanku Garašaninova 'Načertanije' (1844)," *Historijski zbornik* (1963), pp. 35 ff.

13. On Zah see Začek, op. cit., pp. 37 ff, who has written a recent biography (Prague, 1977). Superficial are J. Z. Zuboric, *General František*

Zach (Prague, 1908), and A. E. Vaska, *V pamet generala Fr. Al. Zacha* (Prague, no date). Zah's reports in French from Serbia, 1843-1848, are in the Czartoryski Archive (Krakow) 5390-5394 (9 vols.). For materials relating to Bosnia-Hercegovina by Zah from the above reports see "Bosna u tajnim političkih izvestija F. Zacha, 1843-1848," ed. Začek, Akademija nauka i umetnosti Bosne i Hercegovine, *Gradja,* knj. XXI, odelenje društvenih nauka, knj. 17. The best general survey of Zah's activities in Serbia is Začek, "Uloga Františeka A. Zaha u Srbiji," *Glas SANU,* CCLXL, Odelenje istoriskih nauka, knj. I (1974), pp. 153-193.

14. Czart. 5390, "Rapport sur la mission d'un agent diplomatique en Serbie," April 2, 1843. Excerpts in Berry, pp. 237-238.

15. Czart. 5390, "Comme j'entends ma mission dans les pays slaves de la Turquie," August 15, 1843, pp. 9-28.

16. Začek, "Uloga Zaha," pp. 159-160.

17. Czart. 5390, pp. 49-52, Zah to Monsieur (Czajkowski), November 2, 1843.

18. Ibid., pp. 69-79, November 8.

19. Ibid., pp. 113-173, reports of December 8, 16, 23 and 30, 1843; p. 183, January 6, 1844.

20. Ibid., p. 205, January 12, 1844.

21. Ibid., January 27 and February 10.

22. Ibid., February 24.

23. Ibid., March 23, 1844, "Rapport sur mes relations avec la Croatie," and regular report of March 23.

24. Začek, "Uloga Zaha," p.1 60.

25. Czart., 5391, May 31, 18, Zah to Czajkowski; Začek, "Bosna u tajnim... ," pp. 110-111.

26. Začek, "Uloga Zaha," pp. 158-161.

27. Začek, "Bosna u tajnim... ," p. 22.

28. R. Perović, "Beograd za vreme Vučićeve bune," *Godišnjak Muzeja grada Beograda,* II (1955), p. 190.

29. Začek, "Poljsko... ," pp. 46-47.

30. Czart. 5392, Zah to Czajkowski, February 7, 1845.

31. Začek, "Poljsko... ," p. 49.

32. On the later work of Zah in Serbia see Začek, "Uloga Zaha," pp. 160 ff.

33. For the textual comparison see Stranjaković, "Kako je postalo... ," pp. 75-102.

34. "Načertanije," published in *Pisma Garašanina Marinoviću*, II, 352-367.

35. *Delo* (Belgrade), XI (March, 1906), knj. 38, ed. M. Vukičević.

36. Stranjaković, "Načertanije Ilije Garašanina," *GIDUNS*, IV (1931). Later he wrote "Uticaj poljskih emigranata na stvaranje Garašaninova "Načertanije," *Pravda* (Belgrade), February 6, 1939, No. 12299.

37. Ibid., "Kako je postalo... ," pp. 75-102.

38. J. D. Mitrović, review of *Srbija od 1833 do 1858* (Belgrade, 1937), *Glasnik Jugoslovenskog profesorskog drustva*, XIX (1938-39), 4, pp. 297-300.

39. Šimunjić, *"Načertanije"*, *Tajni spis*, pp. 3 ff.

40. Aleksić, "Šta je dovela... ," pp. 68-71.

41. V. Vučković, "Učešče Hrvata u pripremi Garašaninova 'Načertanije'," *Jug. revija za medjunarodno pravo*, I (1956), pp. 44-58; "Knez Miloš i osnovna politička misao sadržana u Garašaninova 'Načertanije', ibid., IV (1957), 1, pp. 35-44; "Prilog proučavanju postanka 'Načertanije' (1844) i 'Osnovnih misli' (1847)," ibid., VIII (1961), pp. 49-79.

42. R. Perović, "Beograd za vreme... ," pp. 181-204; "Oko 'Načeranije' iz 1844 godine," *Istoriski glasnik* (1963), I, pp. 71-94.

43. C. Jelavich, "Garašanin's 'Nacertanije'... *Südostforschungen*, XXVII (1968), pp. 131-147.

44. Petrovich, *A History*, I, 230-235.

45. V. Čubrilović, *Istorija političkih misli u Srbije u XIX v.* (Belgrade, 1958), pp. 151-195.

CHAPTER V

IMPLEMENTING A NATIONAL POLICY, 1844-1853

"Without an independent national policy, Serbia can have
no future and must sooner or later belong to some other
power. The present Serbian government has proven that it
is pursuing a national goal full of glory."

František Zah, early 1845

Late in 1844 Garašanin submitted "Načertanije" to Prince Aleksandar
Karadjordjević as the Serbian government's program to achieve its national
goals. Throughout his tenure of office as Serbia's interior and foreign minister, 1844-1853 and 1861-1867, Garašanin utilized it consistently as a
general set of guidelines for action in the national field. Directing a secret
committee in Belgrade, he made vigorous and fruitful efforts during the
1840s to build an organization of agents which would operate primarily
in the Slav provinces of Turkey but also among some Austrian Slavs. Here
we will describe his implementation of this program until his removal in
1853, except for aid to the Vojvodina Serbs in 1848-1849 treated in
Chapter VII. His more intensive efforts to achieve Serbian national goals,
1861-1867, will be described in chapters XIV-XVI.

Supporting the assertion by his Czech colleague quoted above, Garašanin began promptly to carry out his program step by step.[1] He assumed
direction as the chief organizer and head of major propaganda and agita-
tional work conducted systematically in the Ottoman and Habsburg

empires. Since the first task was to obtain precise and detailed information about conditions, popular moods and hostile forces there, Garašanin established close ties with leaders from various South Slav areas during their periodic visits to Belgrade. They brought him valuable information and received instructions there. Already in 1845 Garašanin was sending agents into South Slav regions instructed to report back whatever they saw or heard. By early 1846 he had established close and confidential ties with local leaders in several regions. Meanwhile in Belgrade was created under his direct supervision a central organization for propaganda. His chief co-workers in the national field, recruited over a period of years, included Jovan Marinović, his assistant in conducting propaganda; L. Arsenijević-Batalaka, a native Serb and member of the Council; Matija Ban, a former Franciscan from Dubrovnik; Toma Kovačević from Bosnia; and Atanasije Nikolić and Antonije Orešković, both Austrian Serbs. National activity followed closely on the precepts of "Načertanije;" more detailed and specific plans based upon them were drawn up by Ban and Kovačevic. The Serbian government did its best to conceal its involvement and keep the whole operation secret from the Turks and Austrians.[2]

Garašanin's efforts focused mainly on Bosnia with the aim of preparing the way for its annexation to Serbia, although Serbian activity there had preceded Zah's "Plan" and "Načertanije." Exploiting rising dissatisfaction by Bosnian Catholic Franciscan friars with their Austrophile bishop, Rafael Barišić, Garašanin recruited some of them to direct his propaganda network there. Among those coming to Belgrade late in 1842 to seek moral support and aid was Toma Kovačevic, formerly a Franciscan, who remained permanently in Serbia and became Garašanin's chief agent for Bosnia and main link between the Franciscans and the Serbian government. Kovačević obtained an official position as a clerk in the Interior Ministry. Through him and Stjepan Marjanović, a Catholic priest living in Zemun (Semlin), the Austrian suburb of Belgrade, passed most of the Serbian correspondence with Bosnia. In frontier towns Kovačević met with Franciscans such as Father Blaz Josić who brought him news from Bosnia about local needs and desires.[3]

During 1843-1844 Miloš Popović, editor of Serbia's official newspaper, *Srpske Novine* (*Serbian News*), created a circle in Belgrade and welcomed Bosnian Franciscans and provided a nucleus of dedicated national workers. It included Stevan Herkalović, a Croat residing in Belgrade since 1837;

the Slovak, Janko Šafarik; Kovačević; Pavao Ćavlović, a Croat and colleague of the Illyrian leader, Ljudevit Gaj; Zah, the Czech émigré; and Raja Damjanović, an official of Garašanin's Interior Ministry. Garašanin and Aleksa Simić, Serbia's Interior and Foreign ministers, remained outside the circle but were kept closely informed of its activities and supplied monetary and other assistance from the Serbian government. Reflecting the enthusiasm of visiting Catholic clergymen at the warmth and hospitality provided in Belgrade by Garašanin and other Serbs, Ivan Frano Jukić, a Franciscan, wrote Kovačević June 28, 1843: "From him we understand what love and fire brother Serbs show toward brother Bosnians and other Slavs. . . . In the glorious Garašanin we have a true patriot." A tireless priest-patriot, Jukić strongly advocated South Slav, especially Serbo-Croatian and Catholic-Orthodox cooperation. That fall Kovačević began a lively correspondence with Bosnian Franciscans who had been complaining bitterly of Austrian pressure exerted through Bishop Barišić and sought his aid. This correspondence reveals that already Serbia was attracting significant support from Catholic as well as Orthodox Bosnians. With them national feeling tended to prevail over their religious differences.[4]

During 1844 émigré idealists, including some Illyrians, and some native Serbs created in Belgrade a secret nationalist society of South Slavs which supported the ideas of Czartoryski, Zah and Garašanin. The Society's purpose, explained Matija Ban, one of its leaders, to another native of Dubrovnik, Aleksandar Banović, was to broaden the views of Serbs from Serbia so the latter country could lead South Slav peoples in their struggle for freedom and unity.[5] Ban soon recrutied others including Father Filip Pašalić from Bosnia, young Milivoje Petrović from Serbia,[6] and some Vojvodina Serbs. By May 1845 the Society had twenty-one members, and in June it was further broadened by the inclusion of several Bulgars. Garašanin welcomed the Society and its ideas enthusiastically as coinciding with his "Načertanije"; subsequently many of its members worked with him to spread national propaganda. In December 1845 Ban informed Banović that Garašanin had offered his aid and protection to the Society and that Prince Aleksandar Karadjordjević and the influential Serbian military leader, Stevan Knićanin, favored it.[7] In Belgrade the Society issued a pro-Yugoslav newspaper, *Branislav* (*Defender of the Slavs*) (November 1844 to spring 1845), which was circulated also surreptitiously in South Slav areas of Austria.[8] Society members distributed works of Slav authors in the interior of Serbia and with secret credits provided by Garašanin, books were sent likewise to Bosnia-Hercegovina, "Old Serbia," and western Bulgaria.[9]

A key figure in the Serbian and South Slav national movements emerging under Garašanin was Matija Ban from Dubrovnik in Dalmatia.[10] Poet, publicist, professor and politician, Ban became the preeminent leader of the South Slav club and worked closely with Garašanin. In Constantinople he had become acquainted with Polish émigrés and with Czartoryski's Balkan schemes. Through Polish intercession, he had come to Belgrade in August 1844, ostensibly to teach Prince Aleksandar's daughter.[11] Initially appalled at the narrow political views he encountered in Serbia, he wrote Banović:

> Serbs here limit their patriotism to the Principality, and Serbs from Hungary to Serbdom but in narrow confines. They do not wish to hear of other South Slavs and are not concerned with them, and the same is true in regard to all other Slavs. With such narrow views we will not go far. It is essential to broaden the horizons of national thought and make Serbia the leader of the South Slavs. We few patriots here have sworn to do this and surely we will not break our oath.[12]

Soon after coming to Belgrade with Czajkowski's recommendation, Ban was warmly received by Garašanin whose attitude and speech made a deep and favorable impression upon the Dubrovnik writer. "If other Serbian ministers resemble him," he wrote, "Serbia can be proud to have leading its affairs people worthy of the mission she is destined to fulfill." Believing that the Principality's destiny was to lead the South Slavs, Ban added: "Here one can work better than in any other place for the success of that great idea and I will dedicate may life to it."[13] Ban's pamphlet, *On Yugoslavism,* was translated and distributed inside Bulgaria. Establishing links with Belgrade's student youth, Ban in 1845 helped create the youth organization, "Dušan's Regiment" from which evolved in 1847 the "Society of Serbian Youth" ("Družina Mladeži Srpske"). Through a youth leader at the Belgrade Lycée, Jevrem Grujić (subsequently an important political leader), Ban propagated Yugoslav ideas.

Leaders of the Slav Society, some linked with the Polish emigration, vigorously opposed Russian interference in Serbian affairs and sought to utilize Prince Czartoryski's influence with France, England and the Porte. Responding to Pavao Ćavlović's report from Kragujevac that the Russian consul was busy stirring things up inside Serbia, Ban urged Ćavlović to undercut such intrigues cautiously in every possible way. Garašanin and other Society members read Ćavlović's letter. Russia's incitement of unrest in Serbia in an effort to overturn Prince Aleksandar Karadjordjević conflicted with the Society's aims which Ban summarized to Ćavlović:

> For the achievement of national aims it is essential that Serbia be consolidated once and for all; thus every Serb should be informed about Russian intrigues and should undermine this harmful influence among our people.[14]

Attracting members also from South Slav regions of Austria, the Slav Society favored active Serbo-Croatian cooperation. In the spring of 1846 Ljudevit Gaj, the Illyrian leader, traveled through Serbia and stopped off in Belgrade. Serbian leaders at that time did not know that Gaj had promised to submit a detailed report on Serbia's political situation to the Austrian government.[15] In March 1846 Garašanin confirmed that he had granted Gaj, whose appetite for money seemed insatiable, 392 ducats in gold to defray his expenses. In the summer of 1847 Gaj again visited Belgrade to discuss Serbo-Croatian political cooperation with Serbian leaders, again receiving considerable sums from Garašanin and from Vienna. A warm reception from top Serbian leaders including Garašanin induced Gaj to support the Karadjordjević dynasty over the Obrenović pretenders. Reported Zah: "Gaj expects a large sum which he will use in order to support Prince Aleksandar and the Serbian government in Croatia, Slavonia, Dalmatia and Bosnia."[16] However, Gaj nonetheless returned home disgruntled, complaining that Serbian leaders had failed to fulfill their promises. As his ambitious projects folded, his political influence by 1848 had been virtually dissipated, although some of his colleagues, including Ćavlović, continued to work with the Slav Society and Serbian leaders. One of them, Stevan Herkalović, conferred repeatedly with Garašanin and influenced him considerably.

Frequent contacts with the Illyrian circle broadened Garašanin's horizons and made him more favorable and flexible in his attitudes toward the Croats. This provoked envy and resentment from some Austrian Serbs such as Atanasije Nikolić, and antagonized a group of Serbia-firsters led by Jovan Sterija Popović, the Minister of Education. He and Nikolić sought to undermine the position of the Slav Society throughout Serbia. This induced its persecuted members to seek protection from Garašanin and Knićanin, who supported them and were influential with Prince Aleksandar. Also opposed to the Society was the powerful Vučić who in 1845 went into open opposition to the Prince and Garašanin. Antagonism between Vučić and Garašanin, widening in 1848-1849 over their conflicting attitudes toward the Vojvodina,[17] resulted in part from very different perceptions of Serbia's role in the South Slav national movement.

Among leading Serbian writers from Hungary linked with "Načertanije" were Jovan Hadžić, a native of Novi Sad who lived in Belgrade, and Jakov Ignjatović from Pesth. A Serb leader opposed to Prince Miloš, Hadžić became prominent in 1842, and his name appears in both Zah's "Plan" and "Načertanije." He had been close to young Garašanin, and probably because of his influence and that of other Serbs of Hungary "Načertanije" was not even more strongly anti-Austrian. Garašanin viewed Hadžić as an advocate of Greater Serbia, but seeking Vienna's favor too, Hadžić did not support unreservedly the circle around "Načertanije," continuing instead a dual role as a friend of the Habsburgs and of the Serbian idea until finally he lost Vienna's confidence completely.[18]

Except during 1848-1849, when Belgrade concentrated its efforts on the Vojvodina, Bosnia remained the chief arena of Serbian national activity. During 1847 the Belgrade government, led by Garašanin, through its agents and in cafés fostered a growing anti-Turkish mood which stimulated people in Bosnia and Hercegovina to hope for imminent liberation from Turkish rule. Kovačević asserted that Bosnians were ready to revolt and that Serbia's ties were especially strong in the frontier areas.[19] In May 1848 he reiterated that popular discontent in Bosnia-Hercegovina had increased still further. In Hercegovina, finding everyone armed, he concluded that province was well prepared to rise; Bosnia was less well armed. Kovačević urged that Serbia define and focus its official policy more clearly: "Bosnians and Hercegovinians cannot rise on their own without good and experienced leaders." In October 1848 he urged Prince Aleksandar to encourage people in both provinces to maintain their enthusiasm and protect themselves against harmful external influences. Belgrade needed agents in the interior and on Serbia's frontiers to instruct local leaders and obtain reports from them.[20] When the revolutionary year of 1848 passed without Serbia making war on the Turks, many people in Bosnia and Hercegovina grew discouraged. Kovačević and other agents sought to reassure them by stating that Belgrade had failed to summon them to arms solely because of its preoccupation with aiding the Vojvodina. Once that war ended, Serbia would surely lead them in a war of liberation.[21]

Once he realized that the Vojvodina Serbs could not defeat the Magyars, Garašanin concentrated once again on the Serbs of Turkey among whom Serbia could operate with greater prospects of success. He and his assistants in national work—Marinović, Kovačević and Ban—utilizing several years' experience in agitation, drew up detailed plans of action. Under Garašanin's direction they composed a "Draft of political propaganda to be conducted in Slavo-Turkish lands" of March 1849, approved by him and Prince Aleksandar, which outlined activities to be conducted there from June 1849 to May 1850.[22] The purpose of political propaganda in European Turkey was to prepare and organize "a general and simultaneous armed insurrection lasting until liberation has been achieved with military aid from Serbia and Montenegro." "Načertanije" had indicated that agents conducting this activity should ascertain popular needs and aspirations; discover the military situation in regard to morale, popular armament, enemy troops and supplies; draw up a list of influential local persons; and obtain precise data about what each region thought of Serbia and expected from her. Capable and dedicated people were needed to conduct secret propaganda and agitation throughout South Slav areas of Turkey and in Austrian frontier regions such as Dalmatia and Croatia-Slavonia.[23]

Although burdened with manifold duties in the Interior Ministry, Garašanin himself would act as coordinator of all Serbian political propaganda. Jovan Marinović, his assistant and head of the propaganda division of the ministry, was to examine all reports sent to Garašanin relating to propaganda and submit his views to him for final decisions. The South Slav lands were to be divided into a southern zone including Montenegro, Hercegovina, Dalmatia and northern Albania under Matija Ban, and a northern zone comprising the remaining territories under Kovačević in

Belgrade. These leaders were to travel through their regions at least twice a year, contact agents, give them instructions, and obtain information from them. Through Marinović they would correspond with Garašanin, send him reports, and handle financial matters. For 1849-1850, specified Kovačević's "Draft,"[24] twelve agents were to be chosen, if possible all natives of their area of responsibility, to prevent Turkish or Austrian suspicion. Some patriots would serve gratis, but most agents would have to be paid. Agents were to recruit assistants who would discover reliable people from each locality to report on the public mood, enemy strength and intentions. To minimize danger of betrayal, correspondence would be conducted only between agents or sub-agents and their immediate superiors.

Implementation of Kovačević's "Draft" began in June 1849, and by early 1850 propaganda networks had been set up in both zones. Ban sent Garašanin frequent progress reports about his region. During 1848-1850 the Serbian government paid twenty-nine persons, including Ban, a total of 5,000-6,000 talir for salaries, correspondence and travel.[25] After six months work Ban proposed minor changes including recruitment of sub-agents. Kovačević's "Draft" for 1850-1851, submitted in May 1850, specified that the two regional chiefs should complete military plans by December 1, 1850. By February 1851 agents were to have gathered and reported all necessary information so that a plan for general insurrection could be completed by St. George's Day, 1851. Kovačević emphasized the need for haste: "European conditions are so entangled that there may be an opportunity to put the plan speedily into operation." The general plan was then to be submitted to Petar II Njegoš, prince-bishop of Montenegro, for his approval. In November 1850 Kovačević requested Garašanin to estimate potential contributions in men and supplies by Serbia, Montenegro and the Military Frontiers in the event of war.[26]

Meanwhile Ban worried about Austrian discovery of Serbian propaganda activities in Bosnia-Hercegovina and Dalmatia. The Austrians were already suspicious, he wrote Garašanin in March 1850, but as yet they lacked proof which could compromise the Serbian government. Thus activities begun with such difficulty and so important for Serbia and which in Hercegovina had achieved much success should continue. If people in Hercegovina should lose faith in Serbia, Ban warned, they would turn to Austria or Russia for salvation. Ban wished to remain at his post in Dalmatia because leaders in Hercegovina trusted him. "For them I am a moral force, so if I leave they will fall apart, get discouraged, and our propaganda will soon be reduced to nil." To Garašanin he promised to conduct all business orally to avoid compromising Belgrade.[27] By March 1850 Ban's propaganda network in Dalmatia, Montenegro and parts of Hercegovina was operating, but because of growing Austrian suspicion, he soon had to relinquish his position as southern propaganda chief.

Since becoming assistant interior minister in 1843, Garašanin had considered Bosnia and Hercegovina crucial to Serbia and had established ties there with leaders of all faiths. He regarded those lands as a single entity whose fate was linked indissolubly with Serbia. Well acquainted with conditions and people there by the time he composed "Načertanije," he was prepared to undertake any action consistent with Serbia's interest in order to free them from Turkish rule. Garašanin realized the urgent need for agreement between Orthodox and Catholics there on the basis of equality of faiths and nationalities. Continued collaboration with Catholic friars and ex-divinity students such as Kovačević and Ćavlović served to reinforce this conviction. In 1848 Garašanin wrote confidently to Nikolajević that Serbia had acquired such influence in Bosnia that its populace would rise en masse at a summons from Belgrade.[28] However, the failure of such efforts there during 1848 dampened his optimism and forced him to recognize Austria as a formidable competitor in Bosnia-Hercegovina. He refused to seek any permanent solution for those areas until he could be sure that both provinces would go to Serbia, not Austria. While not indecisive or hesitant in regard to Bosnia-Hercegovina, Garašanin as usual was realistic. An insurrection there, he knew, must be fully prepared, religious differences surmounted and the diplomatic ground prepared abroad before Serbia could undertake decisive action. Beginning in 1850 Austria, after opening a consulate in Sarajevo which provided her with a listening post, agitated actively among Catholics in Bosnia-Hercegovina. "The Germans [Austrians] have cast their eyes on Bosnia," he wrote Knićanin, "and are beginning to speak of its people as their own. They are agitating much there and may succeed among the stupid Turks [Muslims?]."[29] Like most subsequent Serbian statesmen, Garašanin considered Bosnia-Hercegovina the key to Serbia's future.

Tiny Montenegro was also vital for a successful Serbian national policy, and very early Garašanin established good relations with that impoverished and mountainous state. This proved easy during the reign of Prince-Bishop

Petar II Njegoš (1830-1851), a Serbian patriot and an outstanding national poet. Petar thanked Garašanin in May 1845 for securing Prince Aleksandar's permission for poor Montenegrin families to settle in Serbia. In 1846 the Serbian government decided to provide Montenegro with an annual subsidy of 1,000 ducats. Keeping Petar II fully informed of Serbia's propaganda activities, Garašanin sent Matija Ban to Montenegro's village capital of Cetinje in 1848-1849. Furthermore, Garašanin promised Petar II, who headed the Montenegrin church, top clerical rank in a future Serbo-Montenegrin state. Petar and Garašanin thus established a mutual trust and respect rare in nineteenth century relations between the two Serbian states. In July 1850, already gravely ill, Petar wrote Garašanin that he did not wish to die until he had seen real progress "for our whole Serbian people," and pledged to take no action without agreement with Serbia. Unfortunately, he died in 1851 without achieving his wish or meeting Garašanin in person.[30]

Garašanin maintained correct relations with his nephew and successor, Prince Danilo, under whom Montenegro became a secular monarchy, although he did not like him or esteem him highly. Late in 1852 Danilo, siding openly with Hercegovinian insurgents under Luka Vukalović, plunged headlong into an unequal war with the Porte, then blamed Garašanin and Marinović for Serbia's refusal to join the struggle. Regretting the necessity to leave Montenegro to its fate, Garašanin nonetheless realized that European and Balkan conditions did not then favor a general insurrection. Although impressed by the realism of Senator Ivo Radonjić, who headed a Montenegrin delegation to Belgrade in November, Garašanin refused to commit Serbia to premature war. He also opposed the proposed marriage of Prince Aleksandar's daughter, Cleopatra, to Prince Danilo arguing that it might trigger Austrian military action against Serbia. Replying cordially to Danilo's letter, Garašanin wished him success in war in the name of "the holy national cause." However, despite heroic resistance, Montenegro met defeat and only great power intervention saved her from disaster. Garašanin's realistic caution helped spare Serbia from a similar fate. Nonetheless, he recognized that full agreement between Serbia and Montenegro was essential for the triumph of their national cause.[31]

Another area which concerned Garašanin was so-called "Old Serbia," part of Macedonia, a backward, Turkish-ruled region south of Serbia which had belonged to the medieval Serbian state. He created links with "Old

Serbia" primarily through merchants who came from there to Belgrade on business. Visiting Garašanin, they described conditions there and growing popular sympathy for Serbia becoming the first agitators for Serbia in a region later disputed bitterly with Bulgaria. In the later 1840s much pro-Serbian agitation was conducted in Kosovo, Metohija and Novi Pazar regions. A propaganda organization there drew in leaders from Prizren, Djakovo, Peć, and Sjenica. Garašanin dispatched a Serbian agent, Stevan Verković, to Serez in the southernmost portion of "Old Serbia," ostensibly to purchase antiquities, but actually to begin preparing an insurrection, who traveled through most of Serbian Macedonia and contacted its leaders. However, at this time only the first halting steps were taken to prepare "Old Serbia" for revolt.[32]

At that time Bulgaria remained entirely under Turkish rule, lagging far behind the Serbs in national awareness and economic development. Because of their numbers and geographical position, Garašanin regarded the Bulgars as potentially second in importance to the Serbs among South Slav peoples. Already in 1841-1842 while in exile in Constantinople, he had taked with Bulgar leaders there, agreeing with them on the need to create eventually a common Serbo-Bulgarian state. Devoting considerable attention to Bulgaria in "Načertanije," Garačanin predicted that the first clash between Serbian and Russian aims would probably occur there, especially if Russia sought to dominate and utilize the Bulgars as its tool. Realizing that the Bulgars lacked confidence in their own strength, he believed that they would revolt only if organized and incited from without. They then regarded Russia as the sole key to their liberation. Garašanin advocated aiding the Bulgars in ways which would bind Serbs and Bulgars together and frustrate Russian intrigues. These included accepting Bulgars into Serbian secular and theological schools, printing Bularian prayer books, and sending in agents to win over the Bulgars and assure them that Serbia would assist their liberation.[33]

During the 1840s Garašanin sought to propagate in Bulgaria the idea of unification with Serbia after liberation. Bulgarian priests and teachers, armed with religious and secular books published in Belgrade, played a significant part. Joining the secret South Slav society in Belgrade in 1845 were the Bulgar patriot, Ranos, who advocated a common Serbo-Bulgarian literary language, and the clergymen, Nefit, Ilarion and Nikolaj. Father Hrisant, another Bulgar clergyman, translated into Bulgarian Matija Ban's pamphlet, "On the Yugoslavs," and sent it via the monk, Maksim, for distribution in Bulgaria. In Serbia then were many Bulgars who had sought refuge from Turkish prosecution. They were well received and supported materially by the Belgrade government.[34]

During 1848-1849 Garašanin's ties with the Bulgars deepened. Leading Bulgars, believing the time to liberate Bulgaria had come, sought instructions, advice and aid from the Belgrade government. Seeking to counter Russian influence and agitation in Bulgaria, Garašanin warned the Bulgars that Russian rule would prove more onerous and oppressive than Turkish. A leading Bulgar replied that his people would turn to anyone, including Russia, who would remove the Turkish yoke, confirmed Garašanin.[35] He warned the Bulgars not to expect salvation from Russia which would consider only her own interests and make Bulgaria into her Balkan base; soon he managed to extend his propaganda network there: by August 1850 agencies had been set up in most of Bulgaria staffed by respected Bulgarian monks, teachers and priests. While Garašanin remained in office, much attention was paid to the Bulgars, and Serbia remained a haven which welcomed Bulgarian patriots preparing to liberate their homeland and advocating its unification with Serbia.[36]

Garašanin also worked to enlist in Serbia's sphere the primitive tribesmen of northern Albania. "Načertanije" had set the goal of freeing all non-Ottoman Balkan peoples, but Garašanin also had in mind Serbia's commercial and strategic interests in acquiring such Adriatic ports as Ulcinj, Skadar and Medova. Already in 1844 he had sent Stevan Verković on a confidential mission to establish ties with the largely Catholic, anti-Turkish north Albanian tribesmen. In 1846 he enlisted support from Don Karlo Krasnik, a Catholic priest working with the Mirdite tribe. Through him Garašanin contacted chieftain, Bib Doda, who pledged that his Mirdites would revolt in return for autonomy and religious freedom under Serbian rule. To explain Albanian desires, Krasnik visited Belgrade in 1849 and conferred with Garašanin. The Mirdites merely requested powder and flints in order to prepare for struggle against the Turks. After Bib Doda and Petar concluded an anti-Turkish alliance in 1849, Serbo-Albanian relations until the Crimean War were conducted through Montenegro.[37]

Garasanin had deliberately omitted from "Načertanije" Zah's entire section on Croatia believing that only after South Slavs in European Turkey had been freed and joined with Serbia and Montenegro could the South Slavs of Austria be liberated. Since the Croats were ruled mostly by Austria, he tended to postpone their liberation to a later phase of the national struggle. Though "Načertanije" rarely refers to the Croats, Garašanin, through Bosnian friars, conferred repeatedly and fruitfully with Croatian leaders. Especially during 1848-1849 he dealt closely with the Croats and favored common action with them against the Magyars. Thus to depict Garašanin after 1848 as a Greater Serbian chauvinist is a great exaggeration. An important factor in Garašanin's shift away from a narrow Serbian focus apparently was the Austrian weakness revealed during 1848-1849.[38] We have seen that he received warmly the Illyrian leader, Gaj, and repeatedly gave him money. In March 1848 Garašanin sent Matija Ban to confer with Gaj and Josip Jelačić, governor (ban) of Croatia. Later that year he dispatched Pavao Čavlović and Stevan Herkalović to arrange a Serbo-Croat accord against the Magyars. A Croatian delegation from Governor Jelačić headed by Ivan Kukuljević visited Belgrade in May 1848, then conferred with Garašanin and Prince Aleksandar in Kragujevac. The Croats, announced the delegates, desired unification of all South Slavs in a single state, a position shared by the Illyrians. Most Croats appeared to concur, although some leaders wished to exploit the Revolutions of 1848 to unite Bosnia-Hercegovina with Croatia. Welcoming Croatian desires for a common state, Garašanin advised them to abstain from any anti-Turkish actions until the Magyars had been defeated. "The aim is unification of all both here and there," he told them. "First let us finish here, then proceed further." The Croat delegates, seeking support from the powers, requested Garašanin to provide 20,000 ducats to conduct such diplomacy. Although Serbian resources were strained to the limit aiding the Vojvodina, Garašanin nonetheless secured authorization to issue them 5,000 ducats outright.[39] The Croats, he realized, could greatly assist Serbia by blocking moves by Prince Miloš Obrenović and by expelling him from Zagreb.[40] Explaining to the Croats the damage the Obrenović pretender could wreak if allied with the Magyars, Garašanin urged that Miloš be treated severely.

Believing in his ability and good intentions, Garašanin during 1848 remained on good terms with Gaj and his Illyrian circle. He hoped Gaj would foster Serbo-Croat cooperation and promote the idea of a South Slav state. Garašanin became disillusioned when he learned Gaj's intimate ties with Vienna and his unworthy role during Miloš' sojourn in Zagreb. Visiting

Belgrade later in October 1852, Gaj thus met a cool reception and Garašanin refused to see him; he left after only one day. Garašanin wrote
Knićanin: "Recently, Gaj, that well-known Croat apostle, arrived here
from Zagreb to justify himself. . . . But no one believes him any more,
especially his friend, Stevan Herkalović." About Gaj Garašanin declared:
"That man tells a lot of lies."[41] On the other hand, Bishop Juraj Štrosmajer, a leading Croat advocate of South Slav unity, whom he met in
1852, impressed Garašanin greatly and they remained on good terms
thereafter.[42]

Besides drawing up the first Serbian national program, Garašanin had
made a solid beginning in implementing it. Between 1844 and 1853 he
and his colleagues created a widespread network of agents, operated and
controlled from Belgrade, in both the Ottoman and Austrian empires.
Primarily a Serbian nationalist who believed that Serbia should be the
nucleus and leader in South Slav liberation and unification, Garašanin
nonetheless revealed a growing tolerance and breadth of view, influenced
as he was by talking with numerous outside leaders. He contributed much
to overcome the narrow parochialism hitherto prevalent in the Belgrade
regime toward other South Slavs. In combatting Šumadijan prejudices
against Austrian Slavs, he was assisted especially by Zah and Nikolić. At
the same time Garašanin jettisoned much of the idealistic orientation of
the Illyrians and Polish and Czech émigrés for a more restricted but more
practical Greater Serbian approach. His leadership and energy launched an
effective national movement inducing South Slavs under Turkish and
Austrian rule to turn increasingly to Belgrade for support and encouragement. European powers regarded Serbia's enhanced Balkan role with
increasing respect. In March 1853, just before Garašanin's removal from
office, the French consul in Serbia reported: "Belgrade is the political,
moral and almost religious center of the South Slavs of Turkey."[43] Con-
centrating its efforts in the west, that is in Bosnia-Hercegovina, Montenegro and nothern Albania, Garašanin's network served as the cornerstone
of Serbian national agitation until 1875. After his removal from office in
1853 it languished until he returned to power in 1858 and reactivated it;
during the 1860s it would show further impressive growth.

76 ILIJA GARAŠANIN

NOTES

1. See David MacKenzie, "Serbian Nationalist and Military Organizations and the Piedmont Idea, 1844-1914," *EEQ*, XVI, No. 3 (September 1982), pp. 323-326 for additional details.

2. D. Stranjaković, "Politička propaganda Srbije u jugoslovenskim pokrajinama, 1844-1858," *GIDUNS*, XXIV, knj. 9 (1936), sv. 2, pp. 155-179; Stranjaković, "Ilija Garašanin," p. 254.

3. Stranjaković, "Bosanski franjevci u Srbiji, 1843 i 1844," *Pravda* (Belgrade), April 27-30, 1940.

4. Ibid.

5. AII, Ban V/1, Ban to Banović, October 1844.

6. Later, he would call himself Blaznavac after his native village of Blaznava, and subsequently became Serbian War Minister under Prince Mihailo, then regent in 1868. He died suddenly in 1872. See below, pp. 313, 359, 364, 367, 381 ff.

7. AII, Ban V/1, Ban to Banović, December 10, 1845.

8. On that shortlived illegal newspaper see Ljubomir Durković, *Branislav: Prvi Jugoslovenski ilegalni list, 1844-1845* (Belgrade, 1968).

9. IG, R. Damjanović to Garašanin, December 10, 1845.

10. On Matija Ban (1818-1903), whose papers are in Istoriski Institut (Belgrade), see V. Vučković, "Neuspela politička aksija Matije Bana, 1860-1861," *Ist. časopis* (Belgrade), IX-X (1959), pp. 381-407; V. I. Freidzon, "O belgradskom 'Komitete' M. Bana (1860-1861)," *Slavianskii arkhiv* (Moscow), 1963, No. 1, pp. 100-115.

11. Stranjaković, "Politička propaganda," p. 155.

12. AII, Ban V/1, Ban to Banović, December 1845.

13. Ibid., August 1, 1845.

14. Ibid., Ban to Ćavlović, June 23, 1845.

15. V. Ćorović, "Jedan memorandum Ljudevita Gaja o Srbiji u 1846," *Spomenik SAN* LXII.

16. Czart. 5393, Zah to Czajkowski, May 24, July 30, and August 31, 1846; Začek, ""Bosna u tajnim," pp. 154-162.

17. See below, pp. 99, 102-103.

18. Miroš Kićević, *Jovan Hadžić* (Belgrade, 19??).

19. IG 234, Report of Kovačević: "Primečanja sverhu dvižanija narodnog u Bosni," December 12, 1847.

20. IG 269, Kovačević report of October 8, 1848 to Aleksandar Karadjordjević.

21. Stranjaković, "Politička propaganda," p. 163.

22. Ibid., p. 164; Ustav političke propagande imajući se voditi u zemljama Slaveno-turskim," March 1849.

23. Stranjaković, "Politička propaganda," pp. 164-165.

24. "Ustav za 1849/50," cited in ibid., pp. 165-166.

25. Milinković, Godišnjica Nikole Ćupica, XVII, 11; Stranjaković, "Politička propaganda," pp. 171-72.

26. Ibid., pp. 166-170. "Predloženije Tome Kovačevića," to Garašanin, November 24 and 26, 1850.

27. AII Ban V/1, Ban to Garašanin, March 1850.

28. IG, Garašanin to Nikolajević, May 24, 1848.

29. IG 816, Garašanin to Knićanin, November 1852.

30. Stranjaković, "Ilija Garašanin," pp. 257-258.

31. Ibid., pp. 258-259; Stranjaković, Vlada ustavobranitelja, pp. 301-305; IG, Garašanin to Prince Danilo, November 17, 1852.

32. Stranjaković, "Ilija Garašanin," pp. 297A-298.

33. Ibid., pp. 310-311; Stranjaković, Kako je postalo, pp. 82-86.

34. Ibid., "Srbija privlačno," p. 7; "Ilija Garašanin," pp. 311-312.

35. IG, Garašanin to Nikolajević, May 24, 1848.

36. Stranjaković, "Ilija Garašanin," pp. 312-313; Vlada Ustavobranitelja, pp. 314-316.

37. Ibid., "Politička propaganda," pp. 175-176; "Ilija Garašanin," pp. 274-277.

38. See V. Vučković, Politička, No. 118, p. 230, Memoire by Napoleon III.

39. Stranjaković, "Ilija Garašanin," pp. 335-338.

40. See below pp. 80 ff.

41. IG 816, Garašanin to Knićanin, November 4, 1852.

42. Stranjaković, "Ilija Garašanin," p. 339.

43. Ibid., Vlada Ustavobranitelja. The consul wrote March 12: "Belgrade est le centre politique, moral et presque réligieux des pays slaves de la Turquie."

CHAPTER VI

SERBIA AND THE REVOLUTIONS OF 1848: DOMESTIC

"Our people would be sensible if it realized that it already
has what other peoples are seeking and can only improve its
lot further if peace and order are preserved. The people's
trust is being exploited for evil purposes."

Garašanin to Prince Aleksandar, July 1848.[1]

In two days (February 22-24/10-12, 1848) the apparently solidly established French July Monarchy of Louis Philippe was overturned on the
barricades of Paris by a revolution led by republican and socialist intellectuals. Shock waves spread eastward across Europe, soon reaching even
remote Serbia. Only days after the Paris events, in Budapest Louis Kossuth,
a skilled Magyar nationalist agitator, denounced Habsburg absolutism and
demanded a constitutional regime for Hungary. In Vienna demonstrations
led by university students beginning March 1/13th forced Prince Clemens
von Metternich, Austrian foreign minister and the epitomy of European
reaction, to flee to London for his life. By March 19/31st the Austrian
government had yielded to insistent Hungarian demands; soon Emperor
Ferdinand granted the Czechs autonomy. Mass revolts began ominously
in Milan and other Austrian-controlled centers of northern Italy. Nationalism, republicanism, and parliamentarism appeared triumphant as conservative monarchs trembled for their thrones.

News of revolutions in Paris, Vienna and Budapest spread rapidly throughout the Serbian lands. Among students and intellectuals in Belgrade, notably those associated with the South Slav club, reports of the Milan revolt provoked great excitement. As revolution swept inexorably eastward across the European continent, some Serbian leaders hailed it as the long-awaited signal to end Serbia's vassaldom by throwing off the Turkish yoke. On the night of March 24-25, the Illyrian leader, Pavao Ćavlović, spread around Belgrade copies of an "Illyrian-Panslav proclamation" calling on Serbs to free themselves from Turkish servitude. With Austria paralyzed, they should form immediately under Prince Aleksandar Karadjordjević a South Slav (Yugoslav) kingdom including Serbia, Bosnia-Hercegovina, Bulgaria, Croatia, Slavonia, Srem, Dalmatia and southern Hungary. The hopes of liberals and radicals soared that Europe and the Balkans would destroy permanently the stifling conservatism of Metternich,, the Porte and the "Iron Tsar," Nicholas I.[2]

Though rejoicing at Austrian discomfiture, Interior Minister Ilija Garašanin realized that revolution and calls for parliamentary rule also would threaten Serbia's shaky Karadjordjević monarchy. Agitation, revolt and popular demands could play into the hands of Obrenović pretenders and Belgrade radicals. Writing his district chiefs about the revolution in Vienna, Garašanin warned that the constitution grainted reluctantly by Emperor Ferdinand had failed to calm peoples under Habsburg rule; disorder was growing also on Serbia's frontiers. Rather patronizingly he affirmed:

> Our government must turn its attention to these events and seek to maintain the Serbian people in its present peaceful condition so that they will not lose rights which compare favorably with the best in the world. . . . Serbia must exert every effort to remain in peace and order so it can secure its future. . . . The Serbian people does not feel any need so far to indulge in dreams of greater internal freedom since it already enjoys this to the greatest extent.

Serbs must obey the authorities unconditionally. Warning his officials against Obrenović infiltration and intrigue, Garašanin instructed them to exhort the populace to remain calm.[3]

Garašanin had abundant reasons for concern. Ruled by a weak, indecisive prince and wracked by factional strife, Serbia remained politically unstable, susceptible to the blandishments of popular Obrenović pretenders. Thus during the first half of 1848 Garašanin was absorbed primarily with maintaining domestic order and restoring political unity. Only then could Serbia exploit Austrian turmoil and weakness in pursuit of its national goals. By now the "Defenders" had split irrevocably into hostile factions. A disgruntled but popular Vučić, still able by his oratory to rouse the peasant masses against the regime, opposed Prince Aleksandar and Premier Avram Petronijević. Rather than overthrow him, Vučić's aim seemed to be to make Aleksandar his tool and assume chief authority himself. Although premier and foreign minister, Petronijević lacked sufficient popularity and forcefulness to counter Vučić's strident demands for lower taxation and annual popular assemblies. As before, then, the chief responsibility for maintaining the regime and repairing factional rifts fell on Garašanin. Commented Franjo Zah in the spring of 1848 on the uncertain shifting Serbian political scene:

> If Garašanin and Knićanin should leave the government, most probably there would be a crisis. But for now the Prince takes care not to antagonize either one because he fears the [Vučić] opposition. Unfortunately, he [the Prince] is jealous of Garašanin because he is very popular and evil men secretly incite the Prince against him. Knićanin neutralizes Vučić's influence while Garašanin directs internal affairs, the police and the army in a wholly Serbian spirit. The Prince pretends friendship toward Knićanin also. Vučić plots with the Russians and the Obrenović but lacks the courage to negotiate with them.[4]

From Vienna ex-Prince Miloš was seeking a way to recover a Serbian throne he had never formally renounced. Prince Aleksandar's weakness and inconsistency and Vučić's intensified opposition to the Belgrade regime favored Miloš' cause. Although his patron, Prince Metternich, had just fled ignominiously from Austria, Miloš' agents were reporting growing disorder and unrest in Serbia, rekindling his hopes. Miloš distrusted the "Defenders," especially Garašanin, whom he suspected of coveting the premiership or even the throne itself. Milivoje Blaznavac, the Serbian government agent who had won Miloš' confidence, shared this view, writing Knićanin from Vienna:

Mihailo Garašanin [Ilija's brother and a livestock merchant] told me of Ilija's plan to remove Avram [Petronijević] so he will become premier, then to decide the Prince's fate as he wishes. Miloš knows all this. He knows that Ilija is thinking of becoming prince and knows that you are opposed to that. . . . That Ilija's plan is genuine is shown by what Ranko [Alimpić?] told me in Kragujevac: Ilija told him he would do everything to acquire the Prince's trust.[5]

Both Miloš and Blaznavac, themselves power-hungry intriguers, dismissed Ilija Garašanin's protestations of loyalty to Prince Aleksandar as blatant hypocrisy, and interpreted his aims in the light of their own ambitions. But there is no credible evidence that Garašanin, then or later, coveted the premiership or the throne. Nonetheless, growing discord in Serbia raised Miloš' expectations of returning speedily to the Serbian throne. In March he told the Croatian leader, Ljudevit Gaj: within six weeks he would be in Belgrade and could then assist the Croats.[6] His agents, seeking to exploit cool Serbo-Russian relations, asserted that Russia would support his restoration.

However, he failed lamentably to secure significant foreign support. Belgrade learned that Miloš, plotting a return to Serbia, was seeking alliances with the Magyars and Croats. Serbia's official *Srpske Novine* (No. 49) accused Miloš of treasonable ties with the Magyars in order to make himself prince of Serbia and Bosnia.[7] Miloš' intrigues to become military chieftain of the Vojvodina Serbs failed utterly, and he fared poorly with the major powers. Russia and the Porte reiterated their official support for the Karadjordjević regime which likewise received unexpected backing from the new French republic. At this time only England showed real, if Platonic, sympathy for the Obrenović cause.

Even so, Garašanin remained worried. In Belgrade, he wrote Marinović, were appearing slanderous diatribes against Austrian Serbs demanding their expulsion from Serbian service, a favorite Vučić theme. This threatened to become a witchhunt against trans-Sava Serbs until at a cabinet meeting all but two ministers opposed any such persecution of the "Schwaben" ("Germans") as unjust and illegal. "You understand how detrimental it would be under such circumstances," wrote Garašanin, "to allow our people to determine what is good for them." Such arbitrary and unjustified action, he feared, would antagonize the Vojvodina Serbs and cause division in Serbia.[8]

Garašanin acted decisively to prevent any incursion by Miloš. The ex-Prince's supporters in the Vojvodina were extraordinarily active, he informed his district chiefs in April, and were seeking to foster disunity in Serbia. "...Don't let any invaders deceive you. I shall give direct orders to watch them carefully."[9] A month later Garašanin instructed them, in case Miloš invaded, to alert local leaders. "Don't give him time to rouse the populace. Act quietly and secretly to inform your local officials."[10] Although Miloš came closer to Serbia's borders, Garašanin surmised that he would not actually cross the frontier "because he is cowardly," but would instead send others to prepare the way. Without mentioning Miloš officially, Prince Aleksandar should merely describe him as a despicable rebel. Magyar promises to aid him, Garašanin believed, would gravely alienate the Serbian people who sympathized strongly with their Vojvodina brethren fighting those same Magyars.[11] To General Stratimirović, commander of the Vojvodina Serbs, Garašanin wrote in mid-May: "You will perform the greatest service by helping to free us from Miloš, a traitor and enemy to all of Serbdom."[12]

Conferring with the Croatian leaders, Gaj and Herkalović, in Kragujevac, Garašanin promised them financial aid in order to win foreign support provided they would take action against Prince Miloš. On May 21st he told the Croatian delegates that Miloš would pose a great threat to an isolated Karadjordjist Serbia. "I praised Prince Aleksandar Karadjordjević as much as I could," noted Garašanin, "asserting that Serbia was wholly satisfied with him, that he was enthusiastic about the national cause and was always ready to follow the advice of reasonable people."[13] Garašanin knew that he was greatly stretching the truth by such claims! After talking with Garašanin, the Croats sent instructions home to detain Miloš in Zagreb, the Croatian capital, and outlined actions to be taken against his son, Prince Mihailo, should he appear there.

Garašanin prepared a baited trap for Prince Miloš in Zagreb. Blaznavac, Serbia's agent in Vienna, visited Miloš frequently, reporting to Knićanin whatever the exiled prince said or did. Thus he learned from Miloš himself how he intended to return to Serbia and apparently persuaded the Prince to proceed from Vienna to Zagreb. Vučić, drifting toward the Obrenović faction, was corresponding with Miloš and seeking to lure the ex-prince back to Serbia. On May 22nd Blaznavac reported a Miloš agreement with an influential Serbian faction to come to Serbia as prince.[14] After his son, Mihailo, arrived in Vienna from St. Petersburg with intimations of support from official circles in Russia, Miloš and Blaznavac left for Zagreb where, through Gaj's intercession with the Austrian authorities, he was arrested and interned. This scotched the danger of an Obrenović restoration in Serbia in 1848.[15]

However, other serious internal problems soon developed. Stimulated by European revolts and liberal movements, popular agitation, unrest, and criticism of the government grew in Serbia. Demands were voiced, supported by Vučić, for greater political freedom, especially triennial or even annual popular assemblies. Despite some misgivings, Garašanin favored convening an assembly provided it acted according to a preconceived government plan describing what it should accomplish. He refused to yield to pressure by Prince Aleksandar and his entourage to convene an assembly immediately without such a plan. The Serbian people, argued Garašanin, expected important results from an assembly, but without a definite program of action little could be achieved and demagogues such as Vučić could easily seize control and manipulate it for their nefarious purposes. Garašanin would only favor an assembly properly prepared and organized. Guided carefully by the government, it would allow the people through their representatives to state their grievances and desires in an orderly manner.

By June Vučić's increasingly open opposition and effective agitation among the public was causing the government much concern. Garašanin found the picture very bleak. For Vučić, he wrote Nenadović, the Serbian constitution which he had helped to frame, was now meaningless, nor was he any longer loyal to Prince Aleksandar. For him Russia's Consul Danilevskii and the Turkish governor were "the proper authorities."[16] Involving himself with Russia and Miloš, Vučić had incriminated himself and placed the Prince in a difficult and vulnerable position. To counter Vučić's intrigues, Garašanin skillfully pushed forward his friend, Stevan Knićanin, military hero, devoted adherent of the Prince, and bitter enemy of Vučić. The Prince then wrote Vučić and his opponents urging unity, but since the letter failed to exonerate him completely, Vučić spurned this laudable effort at reconciliation.

Appalled by his own courage, Aleksandar soon abandoned this resolute stance and proved wholly unable to resolve the political crisis. In vain Garašanin urged him to stand above the factions as a national figure. "Whether he will take my advice is anybody's guess," he wrote Nenadović.[17]

A few days later Garašanin complained: "The Prince is not decisive in anything. His uncertainty frightens me greatly, but now we will just have
to wait for the Assembly."[18] However, Aleksandar's weakness and Vučić's
successful agitation meant that that body would not be guided by Garašanin or any prepared plan. As Vučić busily lined up support and the
Prince remained apathetic, political conditions deteriorated dangerously.
"We don't expect miracles from him [the Prince]," noted Garašanin,
"but we do ask that he at least show some interest in public affairs."
While Vučić received everyone graciously and gave the impression of deep
concern for public affairs, Aleksandar spent much of his time inspecting
his favorite horses at the stables and ignored officials who came to see
him.[19]

As the Petrovdan (St. Peter's) Assembly approached (its convocation
was delayed until after Miloš had been interned), Garašanin confirmed
that matters seemed to be getting out of hand. "Because of my restless-
ness I can scarcely write you," he informed Nenadović. Vučić and his
supporters appeared to be taking charge. Lamented Garašanin:

> The people is stupid and understands nothing, and thus arbitrariness
> triumphs to the misfortune of the entire people and country to the
> greatest extent. We are at the end of our good fortune and our great
> sacrifices have become playthings of the Vučić faction and the worst
> people who surround him.[20]

Just prior to the Assembly, which met in Kragujevac, Garašanin convened
state officials and explained the entire situation: "I was frank with them
and told them of the consequences . . . if the Assembly is not completed
in orderly fashion." Although many deputies were officials or aligned with
the government, the majority tended to support Vučić's program.[21]

Opening the Petrovdan Assembly on July 1st, Prince Aleksandar explained that its purpose was to maintain peace and order in Serbia, and
protect freedom and the Serbian constitution. When deputies from nearly
all districts loudly supported Vučić's demand for annual or triennial assemblies, the Prince refused to reappear and the assembly was only kept
somewhat in line by Garašanin's firmness and police.[22] Thus the government yielded only slightly, rejecting the idea of frequent assemblies but
allowing Vučić to retain office while his opponents, Knićanin and Aleksa

Janković, were to resign their posts. After the Prince had pledged to submit its petitions to the Council for approval, the Petrovdan Assembly dispersed on July 3rd.[23]

Dismayed at Vučić's partial triumph at the Assembly and the Prince's cowardly surrender to him, Garašanin in anger submitted his resignation declaring that he could no longer continue in office. In an uncharacteristic, if momentary, repudiation of his patriotic duties, he wrote Nenadović: "Nothing will dissuade me from this step, and if someone asks me what will become of Serbia in that case, I will have to say that I don't care about the country." Nenadović should inform Consul Danilevskii that his and the Tsar's sound advice had utterly failed to deter Vučić. Most pessimistically Garašanin continued:

> I wished my country well, served her as its true son should, but in vain; there is so much dishonesty and unpleasantness that a person is bound to be appalled at everything that surrounds him. . . . Thus I must withdraw from all this since I cannot bear to observe such dishonesty any longer.

Let the public criticize his decision to resign if it wished.[24]

Clinging desperately and fearfully to his ablest minister, Prince Aleksandar refused his proferred resignation encouraging Garašanin's friends to seek to reverse what they considered a rash decision. His assistant, Acika Nenadović, exhorted him in the name of his ancestors' blood to remain in office. How could he "with our pitiful prince" abandon the Serbian people in such times? Deploring Garašanin's announced intention to resign, Consul Danilevskii declared that it would deal a major blow to Serbia and its prince. On July 4th Garašanin informed Nenadović that he had convened top officials the previous day to instruct them how to prevent similar trouble with an assembly in the fugure. "Certainly you are condemning me there [in Belgrade], as they do here [in Kragujevac] . . . , but it is useless. I have decided. . .not to remain in service with some of our colleagues. . .I am awaiting my release, then I will leave and do not know where I will go." However, he added, a leading "Defender" must retain office in order to prevent Vučić and his Russian party from seizing total control. Before leaving service, Garašanin promised to inform the district chiefs why he was departing and how they should act. Sounding now a more patriotic note, he declared: "I shall remain true to the Prince as long as I live and while he remains true to his country to which we owe so much." Would Nenadović please proceed to his home in Belgrade and tell his wife, Sofia, that he had left the service? If she wished to accompany him to Kisela Voda, a watering spot, she should proceed to Kragujevac. Otherwise, he did not know where to go since the house at his Grocka estate was not yet ready for occupancy. Garašanin said he had no idea who would replace him.[25]

This all sounded pretty irrevocable, yet the Prince's refusal to accept his resignation left Garašanin once again in limbo. Pressure upon him to remain in office, at least temporarily, mounted steadily. Everyone, including his brother, Mihailo, was condemning his decision to resign. Garašanin began to hesitate: "If I knew there was actual danger [to Serbia], or that bloodshed was imminent, I would remain until matters were resolved . . . ," but no longer. "If danger strikes, I shall also as a private citizen defend legality and thus expose myself to the same danger as I would as an official. . . . But if I continue to serve, honest people would think badly of me. . . . Therefore, my position is very bad and Serbia's is still worse." Meanwhile he continued handling urgent matters. He and Petronijević had agreed that the Prince should issue an explanatory circular to all agencies and the populace about the recent assembly. The issue had also been raised whether the seat of government should be moved from Belgrade where radical intellectuals had much influence to quiet interior Kragujevac. Garašanin opposed this:

> . . . On the basis of the public mood and Vučić's actions, it would not be wise to send all our strength to one corner of Serbia and leave the people at our backs. . . . Thus unless everything changes, we conclude it would be best for the Prince to remain there [Belgrade] and the troops here [Kragujavac], so in case of attack to be able to counter it from there and here.

Garašanin agreed that Stojan Simić, vice-president of the Council, should seek support from Russian Consul Danilevskii who had been friendly and probably would continue to be, but he warned Simić and the rest: "Think only as Serbs and accept from others only what accords with your views."[26]

Soon Garašanin concluded that they were conspiring to keep him in office. Everyone, including his brother, was exerting pressure: "It is as if you have all talked it over." Agreeing to a Compromise, Garašanin asked the Prince to defer his resignation until the political crisis ended. Surely within two months the current troubles would be over and Aleksandar could permit him to leave office. Unless his colleagues insisted, however, he would not remain that long.

> But because of my sense of honor which I value above all else on earth, I had to free myself from all doubt since only because of it am I resigning; otherwise it would give me great pleasure to serve my country. Do not conclude from this that I am renouncing my intention to resign, but I only want to stay on if there is still something dangerous to go through, so people will not say: 'he serves only as long as things are calm and peaceful, then pulls out as soon as he sees danger.'[27]

Appeals to his patriotism and his brother's advice proved decisive: previously Mihailo had advised Ilija repeatedly to resign because of his fragile health; now he urged him to remain in office out of duty.

As Garašanin considered how to master the crisis, ideas of resignation faded. "The Prince's role would be vital," he wrote Stojan Simić: "Only decisiveness and reasonable action by him can overcome the danger and bring order from the present disorder." Soon Garašanin grew more optimistic about that. In the past too he had often encountered obstacles from the Prince, but when he had persisted, "I always induced him to accept whatever I had proposed to him. Thus I grew convinced that one can achieve with him everything positive that needs to be done." The outcome would depend largely on Simić and Tenka, at their best in critical circumstances; his brother and Knićanin had also pledged to help.[28] Thus Garašanin renounced plans of resignation, but this episode demonstrates graphically that far from coveting the premiership, the princely title, or power itself, he was invariably prepared to resign rather than serve under conditions and with colleagues he found unpalatable.

Garašanin's answer to demonstrations and threatened uprisings was severe punishment of troublemakers. After the Petrovdan Assembly's dissolution, Stojan Simić, confronted by an excited Belgrade mob, had humbly asked forgiveness. Garašanin wrote Nenadović that he would never do that:

I have long believed and still do that Belgrade should not be allowed to play with the fate of the Serbian people. The people will curse us for this since everything cooked up in Belgrade since last summer has been to the great disadvantage of the Serbian people.[29]

Next day he added: ". . . If any uprising occurs against the government, it should not hesitate; the rebels must be executed since otherwise the fire may spread among the people. . . . " Naturally, milder measures should be tried first, but if they proved ineffective, tough action must be taken to preserve order. Surely that would be preferable to a Russian or Turkish occupation which might otherwise occur.[30] He wrote the Prince in Belgrade:

Our people would be sensible if it realized that it already has what other people are seeking and can only improve its lot further if peace and order are preserved. The people's trust is being exploited for evil purposes. Your Highness' serious efforts to remove the causes of misfortune in Serbia cause Serbs to hope that you will succeed.[31]

Receiving warnings from his assistant about a possible uprising in Belgrade, Garašanin had ordered chiefs of nearby districts to mobilize troops in order to protect Kragujevac and to increase police forces in other districts. However, he opposed moving the government out of Belgrade except in a dire national emergency since at least 200 buildings would be required which were simply unavailable in little Kragujevac. Also, it "would cost the govenment too much respect among Belgraders when we returned there again. . . . "[32]

Whereas Garašanin successfully opposed having the Council approve the Assembly's demands for annual meetings or expulsion of Austrian Serbs,[33] he believed that Prince Aleksandar must honor his pledge to it on Knićanin's resignation, if it were voluntary. "He pledged his word which cannot honorably be withdrawn and which the Prince should adhere to whatever the cost. There is nothing worse for a ruler than to have it said of him that he does not keep his word." However, no one should be forced to resign in the face of popular pressure. Again Garašanin deplored the episode of the Petrovdan Assembly:

I feel that the position of the people was very disturbed by the actions of the last assembly. Except for party adherents, most people felt abandoned to their fate. . . . Only the Obrenovites rejoice at this. To restore the populace to calm I believe will be very difficult. Lies from Belgrade spread among the people like wildfire and are accepted as truth.[34]

After the Assembly some deputies had insulted cabinet ministers, provoking great public unrest. Now all officials must act to stifle plots and intrigues favoring an Obrenović restoration.[35]

To end domestic turmoil in the Assembly's wake, Garašanin favored a showdown with Vučić. Stojan Simić's resignation following harassment by a Belgrade mob had been shameful for both parties and would be exploited by Vučić and the Obrenovites.[36] Largely because of Vučić's agitation, the Serbian public regarded Belgrade as the source of evil rumors. Only a confrontation with him would scotch intrigues and allow the national work to go forward. "Hold there to the form of government set by the Constitution," he admonished Petronijević from Kragujevac, "and I will do so here. . . . Only from. . . [such] do I expect progress for people and country." With people relying on Petronijević and the Prince, he would do his best to aid them.[37] When the government decided to combat the threat posed by Vučić, Garašanin rejoiced: "The time for dictatorship is past; we must govern constitutionally." Vučić could express his views but not spread dissension nor try to seize power.[38]

Garašanin feared that the internal crisis, which continued to simmer, would distract Serbia from exploiting opportunities created by the Revolutions of 1848 and from aiding its Vojvodina brethren. Won't bickering and complaints ever cease?, he queried Petronijević. "God will punish us for not taking some advantage of present circumstances. Jealousy has always ruined Serbia." He had done his best to change this.[39] If there is civil war in Serbia, he wrote Nenadović, "we will have to neglect everything else, even though the greatest danger to Serbia is external. Somehow, if possible, we must prevent domestic strife."[40] The Prince possessed the authority to achieve beneficial goals, but if he failed to do so, the government would be powerless. "I cannot complain enough about the present situation. Dangers and opportunities confront us on all sides, yet we upset the government and people and split them into factions. I am

powerless to extricate us from this plight."[41] Factionalism and political
bickering would plague the "Defender" regime until its end a decade
later.

By early September Garašanin had grown so pessimistic about his
ability to work with Prince Aleksandar that he again threatened resignation. He wrote his assistant who had quarraled with the Prince on a trivial
constitutional issue:

> If the Prince understood Serbia's situation, he would put aside
> these matters for ordinary times. If the Prince were different,
> Vučić would not be able to damage his position so easily, as oc-
> curred at the last assembly, nor would people abandon him who
> could serve him and Serbia well. . . . He listens to those who cater
> to his passions or agree with his ideas. For six years I have con-
> stantly advised the Prince to adopt a different method of handling
> state affairs, but even when he agreed, it did not last long. We can-
> not impose our views on him. I have decided to resign, but you
> should remain since we need a moderate amidst so many extrem-
> ists. My resignation stems not just from Vučić and his actions but
> just as much from those of the Prince.

Any public denunciation of the Prince and Vučić would only damage
the country. Under such circumstances "I can contribute nothing to
Serbia by my service, so I must withdraw. I will regret the misfortune I
am witnessing to my dying day." Nenadović should retain office at least
until he found a suitable replacement. Aleksa Janković, advised Garašanin, was the only man he knew who could deal properly with Prince
Aleksandar.[42]

However, Garašanin remained in office once more since the Prince
refused his resignation. By October 10th he was advocating a compromise
with Vučić; reconciliation would be in Serbia's best interests.[43] Although
this was not achieved, Garašanin's strenuous efforts gradually restored
order. Obrenovite activities were carefully monitored. Prince Miloš had
hoped that the Prince-Vučić feud would spark an uprising in Serbia. This
had not occurred and became unlikely partly because Vučić displayed
indecisiveness. He was still spreading lies, but many Serbs now concluded
he was merely seeking to promote his selfish interests. Vučić could scream

against the "Germans," the courts, and demand annual assemblies, "but our people will support those who can keep order," concluded Garašanin.[44] Thus the "Defender" regime in Serbia, buttressed by General Knićanin's victories on the battlefields of the Vojvodina, survived precariously the turmoil of 1848. By enhancing the popularity of Knićanin, whom he could supervise, Garašanin could undermine Vučić, whom he could not control.

NOTES

1. Garašanin to Prince Aleksandar, July 16, 1848 (from Kragujevac), *Prepiska Garašanina*, No. 190, pp. 231-232.

2. Ferdo Šišić, "Knez Miloš u Zagrebu 1848," *Jugoslovenska Njiva*, VIII (1924), broj 5, p. 191.

3. Garašanin to District Chiefs, March 18, 1848, *Prepiska*, No. 129, pp. 140-142.

4. Zah to Palacky, (Spring 1848), cided in Začek, "Uloga zaha," p. 175.

5. Arhiv SANU, No. 7051, Knićanin papers, Blaznavac to Knićanin (from Vienna), March 31; Dragoslav Pavlović, *Srbija i srpski pokret u Južnoj Ugarskoj 1848 i 1849* (Belgrade, 1904), pp. 27-28.

6. Ibid., pp. 28-29; Arhiv SANU, No. 7051, Blaznavac to Knićanin, March 9; Šišić, "Knez Miloš," p. 50.

7. Pavlović, p. 32.

8. Garašanin to Nenadović, Spring 1848.

9. Garašanin to District Chiefs, April 11, *Prepiska*, No. 133, p. 144.

10. Ibid. to ibid., May 14, *Prepiska*, No. 141, pp. 151-152.

11. Garašanin to Nenadović, May 15, *Prepiska*, No. 142, p. 152.

12. Garašanin to Djordje Stratimirović, May 17, *Prepiska*, No. 144, p. 157.

13. Garašanin to Stojan Simić, May 21, *Prepiska*, No. 150, pp. 165-167.

14. This group included Stefan S. Tenka, Vučić, Matija Nenadović and Stevča Mihailović.

15. D. Stranjaković, "Odnosi izmedju Zagreba i Beograda 1848,"
Pravda (Belgrade), April 23-26, 1938; Šišić, "Knez Miloš," pp. 50-52.
16. Garašanin to Nenadović, May 20, *Prepiska,* No. 148, pp. 161-162.
17. Ibid. to ibid., June 17, *Prepiska,* No. 168, pp. 199 ff.
18. Ibid. to ibid., June 24, No. 169, p. 203.
19. Ibid. to ibid., end of June, No. 170, pp. 204-205.
20. Ibid. to ibid., June 30, No. 173, pp. 207-208.
21. For a general account of the Petrovdan (St. Peter's) Assembly,
see M. Petrovich, *A History,* I, pp. 241-242.
22. Ibid., p. 241.
23. Pavlović, *Srbija,* pp. 52-55.
24. Garašanin to Nenadović, July 2, *Prepiska,* No. 176, pp. 211-212.
25. Ibid. to ibid., July 4, No. 177, pp. 213-214, from Kragujevac to
Belgrade.
26. Garašanin to Stojan Simić, July 6, No. 178, pp. 214-216, from
Kragujevac to Belgrade.
27. Garašanin to Nenadović, July 8, No. 181, pp. 218-219.
28. Ibid. to ibid., July 11, No. 184, pp. 221-222; Garašanin to Stojan
Simić, July 12, No. 185, pp. 223-224.
29. Garašanin to Nenadović, July 14, No. 188, pp. 227-228.
30. Ibid. to ibid., July 15, No. 189, pp. 229-230.
31. Garašanin to Prince Aleksandar Karadjordjević, July 16, No.
190, pp. 231-232.
32. Garašanin to Nenadović, July 17, No. 191, pp. 233-236.
33. Petrovich, *A History,* I, 242.
34. Garašanin to Nenadović, July 17, No. 191, p. 236.
35. Garašanin to District Chiefs, July 25, No. 194, pp. 242-243.
36. Garašanin to Bogdan Djordjević (Ćuprija district chief), No. 198,
p. 249.
37. Garašanin to Petronijević, August 1, No. 199, pp. 250-252.
38. Ibid. to ibid., August 5, No. 201, pp. 255-257.
39. Ibid. to ibid., August 15, No. 209, pp. 265-266.
40. Garašanin to Nenadović, August 18, No. 212, pp. 269-270.
41. Ibid. to ibid., August 22, No. 213, pp. 271-272. On August 15th
Garašanin wrote Stojan Simić that things were no better. The Prince in
Belgrade was not speaking to Vučić: "I am not optimistic about the outcome," wrote Garašanin. "We should be progressing externally, but our

internal disorder prevents it and may cause our ruin. . . . We must speak more optimistically than the way things really are—no one will blame us for concealing our troubles."—Garašanin to Simić, August 27, No. 216, pp. 276-278.

42.   Garašanin to Nenadović, September 5, No. 221, pp. 290-292.

43.   Ibid. to ibid., October 10, No. 234, pp. 316-317.

44.   Ibid. to ibid., August 1, pp. 252-255; Garašanin to Petronijević, August 5, pp. 255-257.

CHAPTER VII

SERBIA AND THE VOJVODINA, 1848-1849

"We regard the cause of our blood brethen, the Serbs there, as our own and will shrink from no sacrifice, either moral or material, in our efforts to assist you."

Garašanin to Stratimirović, May 17, 1848

In April 1848 the Serbs of Kikinda in southern Hungary revolted against Magyar rule; soon revolts spread throughout Serbian Vojvodina, or "Duchy." Ruled by Hungary, the Vojvodina included the areas of Srem, the Banat, Bačka and Baranja, and a mixed population of Serbs, Magyars and Germans. However, the Serbs had predominated since a mass migration there from European Turkey late in the seventeenth century. Novi Sad, the Vojvodina's chief city, sometimes called "the Serbian Athens," during the eighteenth century became the Serbs' main cultural center. Later, many Vojvodina Serbs crossed the Danube to take service with the Belgrade government.

The Revolutions of 1848 confronted Vojvodina Serbs with opportunities and dangers. During 1848-1849 they fought to protect their rights and lives against the Magyars, but not to dissolve the Kingdom of Hungary.[1] A leading Serbian liberal politician of Novi Sad, Mihailo Polit-Desančić, recalled that prior to 1840 Serbs there were prosperous and secure, life was gay, and cultural activity flourished.[2] Then Magyarization began to threaten this, creating a basis for cooperation with the Croats

94

who likewise feared Magyar pressure. After the Vienna revolution of early March 1848, the Serbs were the first people of the Habsburg Monarchy to seek national rights and freedoms. On March 15th Serbs in Pesth presented a petition, the Sixteen Points. A similar appeal in Novi Sad demanded church freedom and recognition of Serbian as a state language; in return the Serbs pledged to cooperate with the Magyars against Vienna.[3] On March 22nd this petition was presented to the Magyar revolutionary leader, Louis Kossuth, but spurning it angrily, he declared that only the sword would decide such matters. Revealing the Magyar insistence on ruling and assimilating other peoples in Hungary, Kossuth's rejection prevented any Serbo-Magyar cooperation. Eventually, this would doom a Hungarian revolution caught between the Habsburg dynasty and Serbo-Croatian minorities. In a report from Budapest, Serbia's official newspaper, *Srpske Novine,* warned on March 25th: "Our nationality is in danger. The people must gather to declare their grievances and agree on what they seek. . . ."[4]

Vojvodina Serbs of all social groups rallied to a movement against a medieval system imposing severe restrictions on peasants, craftsmen, and merchants. The Orthodox clergy supported it strongly since Catholics and Protestants held most higher clerical posts. At first there was little national antagonism between Serbs and Magyars, but their revolutions conflicted since Magyar revolutionary leaders were noblemen seeking to repress the Serbs. During April 1848 Novi Sad became the center of the Serbian national movement in the Vojvodina as young Svetozar Miletić gave speeches and sounded the alarm. Support grew for holding a Serbian national assembly in Karlovac. Delegates streamed in chanting a new song: "Rise up, rise up Serbs!" This May 1st conclave with deputies from all Serbian lands as well as Croats, Czechs, and Poles, proclaimed restoration of an autonomous Serbian Vojvodina; it elected Colonel Josif Šupljikac from General Radetzky's army in Italy as *vojvoda,*[5] and a Main Committee to coordinate its activities. Simultaneously, a Serbian patriarchate was restored at Karlovac with a conservative, Josif Rajačić, as patriarch. Kossuth's Hungarian revolutionary government promptly denounced these actions, branding as traitors all participants in the May assembly. The Magyar commander, General Hrabovsky, seized the key fortress of Petrovaradin and attacked the Vojvodina Serbs in the hope of crushing their rebellion quickly.

Led by General Djordje Stratimirović, the Serbs repelled Hrabovsky's attack and within days mobilized some 15,000 men and forty cannon. A proclamation of the Main Committee summoned all Serbs to rise in arms against the Magyars. Still in his twenties, Stratimirović was brave, talented and well-educated, popular with his troops and along the Military Frontiers. Inordinately vain and ambitious Stratimirović, opposed by officers senior in rank and age, was suspected justifiably of Obrenovite sympathies. Within the Main Committee was a strong Obrenovite faction including its secretary, Jovan Stanković, and Djordje Protić, formerly Prince Mihailo's righthand man. If that group won control of the Vojvodina movement and selected Miloš or Mihailo as leader, Serbia's Karadjordjević regime across the river would be gravely threatened. However, Prince Miloš' internment in Zagreb in late May and the Obrenovite faction's inactivity in the Vojvodina soon relieved that danger.[6]

Meanwhile Garašanin and the Belgrade government were feeling their way with the Croats and Vojvodina Serbs. Leaving Belgrade March 27th, Matija Ban, Garašanin's envoy, conferred in Karlovac with Bishop Rajačić who gave him a confidential letter to General Josif Jelačić, governor of Croatia. In late April Ban met with Jelačić who asked about Serbia's intentions. "The entire future of Serbia lies in the Balkan peninsula while events in Austria affect her only indirectly," replied Ban. Nonetheless, Prince Aleksandar, opposing Magyar oppression of Austrian Slavs, would support them against any Magyar attack. Belgrade wished to join Serbs and Croats in defense of the legitimate Habsburg Monarchy. In case of war, pledged Ban, under certain circumstances Serbia would provide armed aid to Croatia and Serbs of the Monarchy. Jelačić, Gaj and other Croatian leaders, glimpsing an opportunity to win broader autonomy, welcomed Matija Ban warmly in Zagreb. Other Garašanin envoys—Ćavlović, Herkalović and Kovačević—sent to Croatia, Bosnia and Dalmatia, promoted Serbo-Croat agreement as a basis for common action against the Magyars. Garašanin influenced Governor Jelačić, a loyal servitor of the Habsburgs who viewed the Magyars as destroyers of the Monarchy, to oppose Magyar aspirations decisively. Affirms Ferdo Šišić, a leading Croatian historian:

We see how the policy of Garašanin was the major factor which united Serbs and Croats in 1848 in a common defense against the

Magyars and which deflected the Serbs of Hungary and Srem from the road of agreement with the Magyars, which they had already undertaken in March 1848, and onto the road of alliance with the Croats.[7]

From May 1848 onward the Vojvodina Serbs sought aid from Serbia directly. On May 10th General Stratimirović, head of the Main Committee, appealed to Prince Aleksandar for assistance and urged Colonel Stevan Knićanin to intercede with him. From Zagreb Patriarch Rajačić reinforced these appeals. Patriotic and ambitious, Knićanin was itching to lead Serbian forces in the Vojvodina. Despite public sympathy in Serbia for the Vojvodina Serbs and Knićanin's eagerness, Garašanin informed him that he and the Prince had decided to prohibit his immediate departure:

> You may be needed here at any moment [against a possible Obrenović coup?] . . .and we cannot let you go because of our policy [to prevent a Turco-Magyar agreement] . . .We are obligated to aid the Vojvodina Serbs in every way, but we cannot undertake anything officially.[8]

A strong supporter of Prince Aleksandar and a Council member, Knićanin was too closely involved with the regime and would thus have to wait.

Seeking to overcome the Prince's reluctance to get involved in the Vojvodina, Garašanin wrote encouragingly to General Stratimirović: "We regard the cause of our blood brethren, the Serbs there, as our own, and will make every moral and material sacrifice to help them for the good of the common cause."[9] In his reminiscences Garašanin emphasized that Serbia's participation in the Vojvodina conflict had been his idea and had stemmed largely from his efforts.

Since both Russia and Austria opposed the Magyar insurgents, Garašanin asserted that Prince Aleksandar would please both powers by aiding the Vojvodina Serbs. The Prince yielded, agreeing that Serbia must aid its brethren across the Danube. Belgrade though must tread cautiously, warned Garašanin, and the Vojvodina Serbs should operate independently of Austria and Russia. Sympathizing with the Magyars, the Porte remained neutral fearing that any action might strengthen the Slav element in the

Austrian Empire or provoke Russian intervention in Hungary. The Turks opposed Serbia's aid to the Vojvodina but did not demand its cessation categorically. The Turkish envoy in Serbia, accusing Belgrade of preparing major military intervention in the Vojvodina, protested to Prince Aleksandar. Garašanin realized that Serbia's aid must remain quiet and unofficial.[10] Russia's attitude remained obscure. Never pro-Serbian, Nicholas I feared that Belgrade, pushed forward by the South Slav Club, might become a source of revolutionary contagion. Rumors circulated that 30,000 Russian troops would join Turkish forces in occupying Serbia to eliminate democratic pro-Slav agitation. However, Consul Danilevskii reassured Belgrade that Russia did not support the Obrenović pretenders. As to the Western powers, France supported Serbia lukewarmly whereas pro-Obrenović England waxed indignant over Belgrade's aid to Vojvodina Serbs.

What should Serbia's role be in the Vojvodina?, wondered Garašanin. From Kragujevac he wrote Council chairman, Stojan Simić, in Belgrade:

> We have discussed at length the proposal you made to us on the [Vojvodina] Serbs, concluding that we must aid them since we must admit that we above all pushed them into this dangerous undertaking. But we want everyone [in Serbia] to be agreed about such aid. . . . We should provide serious assistance since the people there have been driven to extremities. Thus we feel we should give them everything we can to satisfy their needs.[11]

Simić, who was closer to the scene, should ascertain the Vojvodina Serbs' true position, offering them whatever Serbia could spare, including reliable volunteer fighters.

Next day Garašanin described for his district chiefs the plight of the Vojvodina Serbs and why Serbia should provide them with secret aid:

> . . .The quarrel between Magyars and Serbs [in Vojvodina] has reached such a point that the Magyars have decided to keep the Serbs in their previous bondage by force of arms; the Serbs are determined to free themselves even if they all perish. The Magyar army is already approaching Karlovac where the Serbs are gathering and arming troops. . . .

The Vojvodina Serbs . . . expect from all of Serbdom a helping hand, so they can triumph over their traditional enemy. Since the Serbs view us as their closest brethren, I need not explain why. . . . But whether we wish to and are able to help them and how—about that we need to decide. Aside from sympathy which as Serbs must attract us to our brethren and compels us as far as possible to assist them. . . , the Magyars, if they defeat the Serbs there, will afterwards attack us and our fatherland. So keeping that circumstance in mind, we cannot remain wholly passive in their quarrel. But because of political factors we cannot aid them publicly; it only remains for us to aid them in secret.

In sending volunteers to the Vojvodina, explained Garašanin, "we cannot let private persons handle this, but neither can we act openly." From Serbia officers would be dispatched to the Srem and Banat to lead volunteers. Later, Belgrade would designate a supreme commander to lead all troops from Serbia against the Magyars. On the Serbo-Vojvodina frontier trained personnel would receive volunteers and send them on under their commanders. To insure that the volunteers were militarily competent and politically loyal, the district chiefs must act secretly through worthy recruiters. To avoid attracting attention volunteers should proceed in twos and threes to frontier points, Smederevo and Požarevac, then cross the Danube into the Vojvodina. Each volunteer was to wear a medallion inscribed: "For Serbdom," to display at mustering centers. Direct official intervention in recruitment must be avoided—the movement must look wholly spontaneous.[12] At first Garašanin encountered apathy in Serbia: "Used to a peaceful life, secure in their work and property, the people were not all desirous of leaving such peaceful activity for war." With Vučić opposing the pro-Vojvodina movement, neither appeals from Patriarch Rajačić nor of Vojvodina Serbs roused sufficient popular enthusiasm in Serbia. However, spurred on by Garašanin, Belgrade started sending money, weapons and troops to the Vojvodina.

Serbia's approach coincided with Illyrian views and those of pro-Habsburg Croats under Governor Jelačić. This created a basis for an unprecedented degree of Serbo-Croat cooperation against the Magyars. Persuaded by Matija Ban to work with the Croats against the common enemy, Patriarch Rajačić wrote the Belgrade government: "Either now or never all South Slav peoples must join to save what is sacred to them;

the Serbs must be delivered from the Magyar yoke."[13] He still hoped Vienna would allow Vojvodina Serbs a separate territory, church, and military command.

From Kragujevac Garašanin carefully fostered the volunteer movement. Volunteers must be picked carefully, he cautioned; they must not discredit the cause by drunkenness or thievery. A massive movement of volunteers from Belgrade must be avoided. He left specific measures to Nenadović: "Issue your orders according to circumstances as you view them there. . . ." Volunteers were to be paid, with larger amounts for cavalry and artillerymen, and be properly equipped. Such unofficial measures, though small in scale, would stimulate and encourage Vojvodina Serbs to fight.[14] After Stratimirović had attacked the Magyars at Feldvar, he wrote Nenadović:

Upon initial success the outcome of the whole affair depends. . . . Over there [Vojvodina] all are discouraged, and a little aid now at the beginning can encourage them and greatly aid the cause. I know that we cannot send enough from here to break Magyar power, but we can send enough to induce the Vojvodina Serbs to enter open struggle, and if so, here and there will be found the manpower to create a great army. . . . We must not lose any time.[15]

Growing enthusiasm in Serbia for the Vojvodina cause was reflected by the behavior of Garašanin's own young servant. Much amused Garašanin wrote: "My Stevan wants to go to fight the Magyars and I don't know whether I can restrain him. If Vučić hears of this, he will die laughing because he knows that dragon's worth. The poor Magyars!"[16]

During June and July 1848 fighting between Serbs and Magyars intensified. After Stratimirović repelled General Hrabovsky's attack on Novi Sad, the Main Committee arranged a short truce until June 10th. Stratimirović utilized that breathing spell to organize a genuine army from local Serbs and volunteers from Serbia which, thanks to Garašanin, remained a secure base and source of men and materiel. Thus the threat by the Magyar leader, Kossuth, to exterminate the Vojvodina Serbs unless they yielded, left them unshaken. Stratimirović, seizing strategeic Pančevo with all its artillery July 11th, appealed to the Vojvodina populace to defy the Magyars and obey only the Main Committee.[17] Garašanin wrote his district chiefs:

The Vojvodina Serbs continue to struggle most courageously against the Magyars. The Magyar victory over them at Vršac because of lack of good leadership, or actually none at all, has been avenged at various points by the Serb army with twofold enemy losses. The war has begun most seriously: will the [the Serbs] free themselves from Magyar slavery or remain in it forever? They are seeking aid from all quarters and most of all cast their glances to us and await aid from their blood brethren here.

There was urgent need for troops, supplies, and small boats. "Thus I urge you to respond to that challenge as soon as possible . . . . They need cavalry especially. Promise each cavalryman two or even three ducats per month and food for himself and his horse."[18]

After the Petrovdan Assembly had dissolved, Belgrade intensified its support for the Vojvodina. No longer fearing disorders in Serbia, the "patron courts" (the Porte and Russia) permitted unofficial aid to continue. Knićanin's removal from the Council by that Assembly freed him to rush off to the Vojvodina, giving the Serbs there an able commander. Despite Vučić's efforts at dissuasion, hundreds of volunteers from Serbia crossed to serve under his banner. When Consul Mayerhofer, at Vienna's instruction, protested to the Serbian foreign office, Belgrade pretended to discourage volunteer bands from crossing the Danube. But Garašanin noted: ". . . We are so involved against the Magyars that we cannot withdraw."[19]

A more favorable international climate now fostered Garašanin's efforts. Confident of Serbia's loyalty, Ali Pasha, Turkish foreign minister, declared that Knićanin and his volunteers could remain in the Vojvodina if aid were provided secretly. Serbian victories over the Magyars at Sentomaš and Tomaševac and Austria's defeat of the Piedmontese at Custozza encouraged Vienna to intervene. In late August Austria proclaimed the Magyars to be rebels and encouraged Governor Jelačić and his Croats to cooperate with Vojvodina Serbs against them. Consul Mayerhofer now supported Belgrade's aid to Vojvodina Serbs who were aiding the Habsburg cause.[20] Russia's Consul Danilevskii likewise backed Serbia's unofficial campaign. Austrian and Russian consuls in Belgrade, noted Garašanin, were supporting Serbia's efforts whereas those in Constantinople opposed them. "We will follow those who are closer," he concluded.

However that may be, we cannot withdraw now no matter what diplomacy does. We have entered this affair and must continue, and if diplomacy attacks us, we must justify ourselves as circumstances require. We will declare maliciously that neither the Poles nor the French have incited us but rather Danilevskii and Mayerhofer.[21]

Discord among its leaders now threatened the Vojvodina cause. Denouncing former Austrian officers in his army as reactionary and pro-Habsburg, General Stratimirović demanded that the Main Committee order all commanders to obey his orders. However, that Committee, still containing many Obrenovites, refused and appealed to Patriarch Rajačić for support. Pending removal of the Obrenovites and settlement of the dispute, S. S. Tenka, Serbia's minister of justice and education, advocated suspending aid to the Vojvodina. Patriarch Rajačić accused Stratimirović of intriguing to become supreme commander (*vojvoda*) and of taking Vojvodina Serbs to destruction with his anti-Habsburg approach. When the Patriarch agreed to remove Obrenovites from the Main Committee, Belgrade backed him and broke with Stratimirović. The latter's enforced submission enhanced General Knićanin's prestige.[22] Stratimirović's foolish behavior, wrote Garašanin, had threatened the Serbian cause. Serbia would not sacrifice for such a selfish, vain individual, and Austria must not be antagonized. Garašanin considered Serbian and Magyar forces about equal militarily, but if Vojvodina Serbs remained disunited, Serbian sacrifices might benefit only the Austrians, who had not yet sanctioned the Vojvodina Serbs' requests for autonomy.[23] On September 27th an assembly at Karlovac under the Patriarch reshaped the leadership of Vojvodina Serbs: overall military authority passed to Vojvoda Šupljikac, Obrenovites were purged from the Main Committee, and Stratimirović was ignored completely.[24]

Over strong opposition at home Garašanin persisted in aiding the Vojvodina Serbs. "The brave Vučić," he wrote Nenadović ironically, was intriguing actively.[25] Anti-government agitation was being spread among the Serbian people, and some Council members had protested assistance to the Vojvodina, he informed Stojan Simić. "All this, I feel, is the work of the patriotic Vučić. . . . How repulsive and low all this is!" Garašanin wanted Serbian troops to remain throughout the winter, then have half return "since we should not remain without troops here."[26] The Vojvodina

Serbs, he wrote Petronijević, were requesting still more aid, "but it seems to me that we cannot provide any more, or at least not as much as they need." Serbia had done its utmost, but where else could the Serbs turn? "It is terrible to consider abandoning them wholly, but it is just impossible to aid them further." Unless the Porte asssted them, "our Serbs will be victims of those wild [Magyar] beasts."[27]

In October 1848 when Patriarch Rajačić appealed to Prince Aleksandar for further aid, Serbian leaders split. Tenka and some others, foreseeing the campaign's eventual failure and fearing public opposition to more aid, advocated its immediate suspension. Garašanin requested Council chairman, Stojan Simić's support to continue assistance. Serbia had aided her brethren generously, but "it would be difficult to look on while so many people perished without the resources we have here."[28]

Garašanin was constantly encouraging Knićanin, congratulating him and his men for heroic efforts. The Serbs, he affirmed, deserved high praise for holding on despite great difficulties and holding the Magyars to a standstill. Do not despair, he urged, resist as long as possible. "You are doing a duty for all of us. If you and the others abandon our brethren, they will succumb and all our sacrifices will be in vain." News of Knićanin's victory of November 23rd had produced general rejoicing in Serbia. Those who had scorned Serbian efforts in the Vojvodina had been hooted down. "We are taking steps to reinforce your army and will do all we can. Your situation there is now our greatest concern." Indeed, Serbia's effort had peaked as 8,000 volunteers were fighting under Knićanin's command.[29] Garašanin exhorted Ćuprija's district chief:

> Our Vojvodina brethren greatly need more volunteers. Since the Magyars are approaching Pančevo, some of its inhabitants came here to plead for volunteers to defend the town. So try hard to collect a maximum number of volunteers and send them straight to Višnjica.[30]

Thus Garašanin was dismayed to learn that Knićanin would have to abandon the Banat and Pančevo: "If your army is exhausted, we must yield to superior force. Many criticize us for not sending you our regular army, but we cannot do so for political reasons." Since Prince Windischgrätz, the top Austrian commander, was attacking the Magyars, could Knićanin fight on until Austrian aid arrived? "I think of nothing but events there and know that you will do your best."[31]

To Loznica's district chief, Garašanin explained Serbia's policy toward the Vojvodina:

> Our government cannot officially and forcibly rouse our people and compel them to go to the aid of the Vojvodina Serbs, but neither can it look on passively while the Magyars crush them when their cause has already been approved by the Vojvoda and Patriarch. And thus it selected a middle course hoping to achieve its goal and preserve the Vojvodina Serbs from the Magyars until the imperial [Austrian] army, moving from all sides against the Magyars, can disperse them and relieve the Serbs from Magyar assaults.

Infantrymen going to the Vojvodina would receive five talir per month, cavalry eight and artillerymen twelve. "I hope you can find well-armed, trained men, especially cavalrymen."[32] Garašanin informed Knićanin that he was urging the district chiefs to send across to the Vojvodina all soldiers they had recruited.[33] Four days later he added:

> By all this I feel that we have responded well to the needs and the desires of the Vojvodina Serbs and could not have done any more, so you and everyone should be satisfied. We have risked and are risking much.

The men now coming to Knićanin were homeowners and taxpayers, reputable and obedient; they should be treated with care.[34] He had never intended, Garašanin wrote Stojan Simić, that Serbian troops comprise the main force in the Vojvodina or conduct major operations; rather they should prevent the Magyars from massacring the Vojvodina Serbs. Some volunteers, he warned, were returning to Serbia complaining of poor treatment by Vojvodina authorities, lack of pay and inadequate food.[35] Soon most had returned home.

In December 1848 Vojvoda Šupljikac, supreme commander in the Vojvodina, died suddenly, reopening the tangled leadership issue. His death, noted Garašanin, came at the worst possible time. To prevent morale from sinking, a new supreme commander must be chosen swiftly. "I rely mostly on you," Garašanin wrote Knićanin. General Stratimirović rushed to Belgrade to push his candidacy. Garašanin found him reckless, selfish and scornful of Austria whose support the Serbs needed badly. Knićanin should receive him cordially but not let him spread an anti-Austrian mood in the army.[36] Denounced by Patriarch Rajačić, Stratimirović offered himself to the Obrenovites which caused Knićanin to break relations with him. The Patriarch then entrusted supreme command in the Vojvodina to Austrian General Mayerhofer from whom it soon passed to General K. Teodorovich who proved indecisive and incompetent. The Patriarch, with Serbia's support, removed Stratimirović's followers from the Main Committee, and assumed quasi-dictatorial civil, military and religious authority himself. Remaining loyal to Vienna, he still believed Austria would grant promised autonomy to Vojvodina Serbs.[37]

In January 1849 as the Magyars pushed General Teodorovich back in the Banat, Patriarch Rajačić secured Vienna's permission for Serbia to renew unofficial intervention. With a small picked force Knićanin returned to the Vojvodina whose forces were dissolving and fleeing into the Srem. In desperation the Patriarch turned to Stratimirović, instructing him to rush to the Šajkaška. Rallying the Serbs brilliantly, Stratimirović and Knićanin defeated Magyar General Pertsel at Vilova and Mosorina and virtually liberated the Bačka and Banat. In the fighting both generals displayed great heroism. These final Serbian victories helped doom the Hungarian revolution and greatly enhanced Serbian self-confidence.[38]

Continuing frequent correspondence with Knićanin, Garašanin wrote that only in collaboration with the Austrian army could the Serbs defeat the Magyars. Knićanin should cooperate with Governor Jelačić who "has the same interest in the Croats as we have in the Serbs...." The Serbs should united with him under Windischgrätz's command and fight the Magyars. "Formerly I opposed this, but not now when the Serbs [of Vojvodina] are so weakened." Praising Knićanin's heroic leadership, Garašanin cautioned: "We will seek to extract ourselves honorably from these troubles."[39] Soon he announced that no more soldiers would cross from Serbia. "We have done all that we could do." Serbia's troops should now come home and let Austrian imperial forces finish off the Magyars. Although suspicious that Austria might not grant autonomy to the Vojvodina, Garašanin nonetheless favored the volunteers' return once the

Vojvodina's frontiers had been secured. Everything now depended on the indecisive and passive Patriarch. The Serbs should quickly occupy the Vojvodina's rightful boundaries without violating the Magyar's legitimate interests.[40]

Pressured by Austria and the Porte, Serbia early in February 1849 recalled Knićanin's volunteers. Garašanin informed Simić of this after a discussion with the Prince, Tenka and Petronijević.[41] Then he wrote Knićanin that he understood his reluctance to return home but that national interest now required such a move:

> You know that the army did not go there wholly voluntarily but largely on orders of its commanders thus opening the way for intrigues in Serbia. Thus I feel that our decision to recall the army is logical in order to prevent these dangers. We have other worries besides our Vojvodina brethren. We decided to help them when they were in extreme need, feeling that we could not watch their destruction, but now we should not be condemned for thinking of ourselves. This does not mean a sudden removal of our troops but when conditions have been prepared to defend the frontiers they have gained.[42]

But Belgrade had to act sooner. On February 9th Garašanin ordered Knićanin to return immediately with his army. Sensitive internal conditions "could be exploited by malicious people," but the real reason for urgency was foreign pressure:

> We were reliably informed that the Porte would demand the return of your army and was strongly supported by other courts. To avoid an attack against us, two days ago we informed the [Belgrade] Pasha that our troops had been recalled and would depart with you for Serbia within a week.[43]

Serbia informed Patriarch Rajačić February 8th that Knićanin was leaving because the Magyar danger was over, which was untrue. On February 16th Knićanin proclaimed to the Vojvodina Serbs:

> Our strength was insufficient to defeat your enemies and those of the Emperor. Serbdom will never forget your sacrifices. With the

happy news that the Serbian Vojvodina has been liberated, I am returning home with all Serbian volunteers.

Persuaded by Austrian Consul Mayerhofer, Knićanin then resolved to plead the Vojvodina's case in person before the Emperor in Vienna. However, Garašanin advised strongly againt this. His mission could not help the Vojvodina Serbs, and it would damage Serbia's honor if he paid homage to a ruler who was reneging on his promises to the Serbs. "Do not separate yourself from your country's policy; let your conscience remain pure," wrote Garašanin. When the Prince also objected, Knićanin abandoned the trip.[44]

When the Magyar threat to the Vojvodina revived, Knićanin in late March again crossed to lead Serbian forces there.[45] "Volunteers are still crossing. We could get many more to cross over if we could pay them, but we lack the resources," wrote Garašanin April 10th. To his dismay Austrian General Teodorovich abruptly withdrew without informing Knićanin. "General Teodorovich only needs to see the enemy in order to retreat." Belgrade's Srpske Novine promptly dubbed him: "General Backwards" ("von Rückwärts"). Soon the entire Banat lay again in Magyar hands. "This insincerity by Austrian officials toward the Vojvodina Serbs," commented Garašanin, "is the greatest cause of the people's misfortune."[46] Fearing an Austrian betrayal, he urged Knićanin if he noticed signs of one, to save himself and his men. "Your forces are too small to fight both treachery and the Magyars." Nonetheless, Knićanin should request Austrian help even though Vienna seemed deliberately to be allowing the Magyars to defeat the weakened Vojvodina Serbs.[47] After the Magyars seized Pančevo, Garašanin informed the district chiefs May 2nd that the Magyars had reconquered much of the Vojvodina wreaking bloody vengeance on the Serbs. The chiefs must watch Magyar troops near the Serbian frontier and if necessary arm frontier villages to defend Serbia.[48] "I realize," Garašanin wrote Knićanin May 6th, "that the Magyars will soon demand that you withdraw and abandon the war against them or they will attack you in great force—[General] Pertsel from Bačka and [General] Bem from the Banat." After Knićanin had twice repelled Pertsel's army, Garašanin could only hope that Governor Jelačić's army would rescue him.[49]

Instead, massive Russian armed intervention in behalf of the Habsburg dynasty transformed the situation in Hungary. Learning from Patriarch Rajačić that an 80,000-man Russian army had invaded Hungary, Garašanin advised Knićanin to disregard Magyar protests and keep his army in Vojvodina until the Russians arrived. Consul Danilevskii gave similar advice.[50] Criticizing Austrian indecisiveness and cowardice, Garašanin wrote Knićanin: "I am amazed the Russians are helping such a bad lot [Austria]. . . . In the entire Vojvodina war you alone remain a true hero."[51]

Made desperate by Russian intervention, the Magyars in April 1849 sought agreement with the Serbs. General Pertsel sent Colonel Bistranowski, a Czartoryski agent, to Knićanin with a peace proposal; Garašanin instructed him to ignore it. The Magyars then threatened that unless Knićanin's army withdrew, Pertsel and Bem would destroy it. Garašanin disregarded this and rejected all Magyar offers of cooperation.[52] As the Russians advanced irresistibly, Garašanin acted to prevent Magyar remnants from seeking refuge in Serbia. He wrote frontier district chiefs to bar Magyar units from Serbia by force if necessary.[53] By August the Russians had crushed Magyar resistance, allowing the Austrian Empire to survive and reassert control over Hungary. Emperor Franz Josef then ended hopes of Vojvodina Serbs for autonomy by removing Patriarch Rajačić and transferring all authority over the Vojvodina to an imperial commissar. "It is the same old policy!" lamented Garašanin.[54] On August 16, 1849 he informed the district chiefs that the Magyar war had ended and with it any threat to Serbia's frontiers.[55]

Indignant over Austria's policy toward the Vojvodina, Garašanin flatly rejected a decoration proffered by the Vienna court. Acceptance would be misinterpreted as inconsistent with his principles and policy toward the Vojvodina Serbs, he explained to Prince Aleksandar.[56] Garašanin wrote Knićanin: "I am indignant if Austria believes that I sought to do anything for her."[57] Early in 1850 when the Austrian consul again offered him the decoration, Garašanin refused it in writing; eventually it went to another Serbian leader. Garašanin did not want his name linked in any way with Austria and refused adamantly to write anything in Vienna's behalf.

Serbia and Garašanin emerged from the Vojvodina campaigns with both pluses and minuses. On the debit side, the Vojvodina Serbs reverted to complete Habsburg control, and under the iron rule of Prince von Schwarzenberg, there was little imminent prospect of freedom. Serbia had expanded much money and energy without apparent benefit to itself or its brethren, letting Vučić and company claim that the campaigns had merely reinforced Austrian reaction. However, intangible gains more than offset all this. In 1848-1849 Serbia escaped the obscurity of Turkish vassaldom to play a considerable role on the European stage. Knićanin's repeated defeats of superior Magyar armies represented a significant moral triumph. Serbia's prestige had been enhanced by its sacrifices of money, materiel and lives for the brethren across the Danube. Increasingly, Serbs of Austria and Turkey regarded Belgrade as the natural center and defender of their interests. Serbia became the eldest brother of a dispersed South Slav family, and strong ties had been forged, at least temporarily, between Serbs and Croats.

Ilija Garašanin, not Prince Aleksandar, deserves the credit for these achievements. From the start he had campaigned vigorously for Serbia's aid to Vojvodina, persuading a timorous and reluctant prince and disregarding opposition from influential leaders like Vučić and Tenka. Championing Knićanin as a hero who could overshadow Vučić, Garašanin had backed him with all the resources and men he could raise from an initially indifferent populace. His energetic actions galvanized his district chiefs to recruit volunteers and send them across the Danube. Garašanin had persisted despite external pressure from Austria and the Porte. Thus he had helped lay a firmer foundation for future efforts to achieve Serbian unity. After the Vojvodina Serbs' defeat in 1849, he realized that Serbia must concentrate its activities first among Serbs of Turkey. Nonetheless, Garašanin's contacts during 1848 with Croatian leaders, and evident Austrian weakness, had broadened his view of South Slav cooperation. During that turbulent revolutionary era he had played the leading role in Serbia's foreign and domestic affairs. The Vojvodina Serbs succumbed not for lack of aid from Serbia but to the overwhelming forces of reaction led by Russia and Austria.

NOTES

1. On the revolution in the Vojvodina in 1848-1849 see Dragoslav Pavlović, *Srbija i srpski pokret u Južnoj Ugarskoj 1848 i 1849* (Belgrade, 1904); Vasa Bogdanov, *Ustanak Srba u Vojvodini i Madjarska Revolucija 1848 i 1849* (Subotica, 1929); Radoslav Perović, *Gradja za istoriju srpskog pokreta u Vojvodini 1848-49* (Belgrade, 1952); A. Lebl, *Revolucionarni pokret u Vojvodini 1848-1849 godine* (Novi Sad, 1960); D. Popović, "Vojvodjanski gradovi u buni," *Zbornik Matice Srpske,* VI (1953), pp. 5-46; and Petrovich, *History,* I, pp. 242-246.

2. M. Polit-Desančić, *Uspomene iz godine 1848-49* (Novi Sad, 1889).

3. Pavlović, *Srbija,* pp. 2 ff.

4. Ibid., p. 8.

5. Military commander. Literally "duke."

6. Pavlović, pp. 17-21, 64-65; Polit-Desančić, pp. 21-25.

7. Šišić, "Knez Miloš u Zagrebu," *Jug. Njiva,* VIII (1924), broj 5, pp. 193-194.

8. Garašanin to Knićanin, May 28, 1848 (from Kragujevac to Belgrade), *Prepiska Ilije Garašanina,* No. 153, pp. 173-174.

9. Garašanin to Stratimirović, May 17, ibid., No. 144, p. 157.

10. Garašanin to Nenadović, June 3, 6 and 13, *Prepiska,* Nos. 161, 164, 167, pp. 185-188, 190-192, 197-198.

11. Garašanin to Stojan Simić, May 28, ibid., No. 152, pp. 170-171.

12. Ibid., No. 154, p. 175, Garašanin to District Chiefs, May 29.

13. SANU, No. 7536, Josip Rajačić to Serbian government, May 28.

14. *Prepiska,* No. 161, pp. 185-186, Garašanin to Nenadović, June 3.

15. Ibid., No. 164, pp. 190-191, Garašanin to Nenadović, June 6.

16. Ibid., No. 165, p. 193, Garašanin to Nenadović, June 7.

17. Pavlović, *Srbija,* pp. 60-62.

18. *Prepiska,* No. 175, pp. 210-211, Garašanin to District Chiefs, July 1.

19. Ibid., No. 192, p. 239, Garašanin to Nenadović, July 20.

20. Pavlović, *Srbija,* pp. 61-63.

21. *Prepiska,* No. 223, p. 295, Garašanin to Petronijević, September 10.

22. Pavlović, *Srbija,* pp. 68-70.

23. *Prepiska*, No. 226, pp. 301-302.
24. Pavlović, *Srbija*, pp. 77-80.
25. *Prepiska*, No. 227, p. 304, Garašanin to Nenadović, September 23.
26. Ibid., No. 231, pp. 312-313, Garašanin to Stojan Simić, October 4.
27. Ibid., No. 230, pp. 310-311, Garašanin to Petronijević, October 3.
28. IG, Garašanin to Stojan Simić, October 8.
29. *Prepiska*, No. 240, pp. 322-324, Garašanin to Knićanin, November 30.
30. Ibid., No. 241, pp. 324-325, Garašanin to Bogdan Djordjević, December 2.
31. Ibid., No. 243, pp. 326-327, Garašanin to Knićanin, December 6.
32. Ibid., No. 245, pp. 328-331, Garašanin to Ilija Ćvorić, December 7.
33. Ibid., No. 246, p. 331, Garašanin to Knićanin, December 11.
34. Ibid., No. 249, pp. 333-335, Garašanin to Knićanin, December 15.
35. Ibid., No. 254, pp. 340-342, Garašanin to Stojan Simić, December 19.
36. Ibid., No. 250, pp. 335-336, Garašanin to Knićanin, December 16.
37. Pavlović, *Srbija*, pp. 110-113.
38. Ibid., pp. 114 ff; Bogdanov, *Ustanak*, pp. 161 ff.; Polit-Desančić, *Uspomene*, pp. 61-62.
39. *Prepiska*, No. 266, pp. 352-353, Garašanin to Knićanin, January 4, 1849.
40. Ibid., No. 269, p. 335, January 9.
41. Ibid., No. 275, p. 362, Garašanin to Stojan Simić, January 25.
42. Ibid., No. 278, p. 365, February 4, Garašanin to Knićanin.
43. Ibid., No. 280, pp. 367-368, Garašanin to Knićanin, February 9.
44. Ibid., No. 282, pp. 369-371, Garašanin to Knićanin, February 26; Pavlović, *Srbija*, pp. 124-133.
45. Ibid., pp. 134 ff.
46. *Prepiska*, Nos. 293, 295, pp. 382-385, Garašanin to Knićanin, April 10 and 17.
47. Ibid., No. 297, pp. 386-387, Garašanin to Knićanin, April 21.

48.   Ibid., No. 300, pp. 393-394, Garašanin to District Chiefs, May 2.
49.   Ibid., No. 302, pp. 395-396, Garašanin to Knićanin, May 6.
50.   Ibid., No. 329, pp. 416-17 and No. 332, pp. 420-421, Garašanin to Knićanin, June 14 and 23.
51.   Ibid., No. 333, pp. 421-423, Garašanin to Knićanin, June 30.
52.   Pavlović, *Srbija,* pp. 164-165.
53.   *Prepiska,* No. 338, pp. 429-430, Garašanin to District Chiefs of Belgrade, Smederevo, Požarevac and Krajina, July 5.
54.   Ibid., No. 345, pp. 436-438, Garašanin to Knićanin, July 22; Pavlović, *Srbija,* pp. 167-174.
55.   *Prepiska,* No. 352, p. 446, Garašanin to District Chiefs, August 16.
56.   Ibid., No. 289, pp. 377-378, Garašanin to Prince Aleksandar Karadjordjević, April 2.
57.   Ibid., No. 319, pp. 409-410, Garašanin to Knićanin, May 22.

CHAPTER VIII

CONFRONTATION WITH RUSSIA, 1850-1853

"I eat bread not with Russian teeth but with my own and those of my forefathers; I am not a servant of Russia. When my father fought for the freedom of my country in the first and second uprisings and shed his blood for it, he truly did not know that the Russians existed."

Garašanin to Marinović, August 28, 1852.

Garašanin's appointment as premier and foreign minister of Serbia in September 1852 provoked an open confrontation with Nicholas I, Russia's "Iron Tsar," triggering his removal from office six months later. Based on Garašanin's independent, nationalistic stance in 1848-1849 and his ties with Polish émigrés and Magyar nationalists, Nicholas and his ministers had long considered him anti-Russian and dangerous. Garašanin's police law of 1850 and "April Circular" of 1852 confirmed their belief that he aimed to undercut their influence in Serbia and destroy Vučić's pro-Russian opposition faction.

Ever since entering the Serbian government in 1842, Garašanin had played a considerable and increasing role in foreign policy.[1] "Načertanije" of 1844 had embodied his basic views on this subject, and he remained quite consistent throughout his career in applying its principles. Garašanin emphasized repeatedly that Serbia must be free and independent,

113

that no foreign power should determine how her policies were formulated or executed. Other Serbs should be liberated and united with Serbia as swiftly as possible. His approach toward foreign powers depended largely upon their attitudes toward his nationalistic goals.

Garašanin generally regarded German Austria as the greatest enemy of Serbdom and the Balkan peoples since it aimed to preserve the Ottoman Empire and maintained control over millions of Serbs and Croats in the Habsburg Empire. Even toward Austria his approach was not intransigent or uncompromisingly hostile, although his usual Austrophobia coincided with Polish émigré views. As to Russia, he was of two minds. On the one hand, he feared Russian domination, highhandedness and interference in Serbian affairs. Deploring the tendency of Russian consuls in Belgrade to act like lords, dictating to Serbian rulers and ministers and acting disdainfully toward the Serbian people, Garašanin soon made it clear he would not tolerate that. Quite consistently during Prince Aleksandar's reign, his relations with Russia and its envoys were therefore cool and hostile. On the other hand, unlike Polish and Czech émigrés, Garašanin believed that the Russians—brethren by blood, language and faith—were of all leading European peoples by nature closest to the Serbs, and that reliance on Russia, but not subservience, was the swiftest means of settling the Eastern Question, provided Russia would tolerate a strong, independent and aggrandized Serbia.

After retirement Garašanin discussed Austrian and Russian influence in Serbia. Austria, lacking popular support there, had threatened to distort Serbia's political life because her influence was exerted through the ruler:

I always feared that influence, partly for its own sake, partly because it seemed to me that behind Austria peeped Russia. Those two powers are natural opponents since both direct their gaze to the same part of Europe. One day they will meet and conflict. . . . Whoever wins, the last days will come, I fear, for the national life of Serbia. Victory by Austria will destroy Serbian political life; victory of Russia will destroy the Serbian people without which one cannot conceive of a Serbian state. If Austria wins, Russia will still remain intact, so to speak, and will await circumstances and prepare to renew the struggle until she attains victory. If Russia wins, the quarrel will be settled definitely. Thus I have always believed that the predominance of Austria in the Balkans will invariably provoke a reaction by Russia. In a life or death struggle between Russia and Austria, in case the latter wins, Serbia would become her province and would remain such for many years even if she did not wholly lose her national identity. This situation would last until Austria cleverly gave the Serbian people some kind of constitutionalism from which it would not much care to emerge.

However, Garašanin believed that a Russian victory was much more probable, and Russia would then regard all Austrian possessions as her own. Thus Garašanin concluded that Austrian influence in Serbia could signify subsequent Russian predominance. "To avoid this danger all of my public work in this country has consisted."[2] What Garašanin and few others could foresee was Serbia's survival and aggrandizement in 1918 with the almost simultaneous defeat and collapse of the Russian, Austro-Hungarian and Ottoman empires!

During Prince Aleksandar's reign, Serbian sympathies for Russia remained strong and widespread. Some Serbian leaders, noted Garašanin, were pro-Russian from emotion or shortsightedness; others after serving or being educated there; still others regarded Russia as Serbia's natural defender and indispensable ally. The latter element emphasized Russian aid to Karadjordje after 1806 ignoring the negative role of Russian envoys such as Rodofinikin and forgetting that in 1812 Russia, facing the French invasion, had abandoned the Serbs. Under the absolute, stubborn and irascible Nicholas I (1825-1855), Garašanin considered Russia a potential menace to Serbia. Seeking aggrandizement and hegemony, Nicholas, he believed, aimed to move into the Balkans, transform its Orthodox Christians into Russians and reach the fabulous imperial city, Tsargrad (Constantinople). Subjugating the eastern Balkans in the process, Russia "would have to go through us first, then if she dared retain Tsargrad in her power, she would not ask us whether or not we liked our position." Even if Russia left Serbia temporarily outside her power sphere, she would remain in perilous limbo "pinned between two powerful neighbors, Russia and Austria." Eventually, Serbia would either have to submit to one or seek aid from France. If Russia achieved her aims in the Balkans, Serbia instead of becoming truly indepedent, would be absorbed into the Russian nationality. To prevent this Garašanin sought to create a Balkan state or federation strong enough to preserve genuine independence.[3]

Other foreign influences, argued Garašanin, were not as important nor as dangerous for the Serbs. They were mild and temporary, manifesting themselves periodically to block Austrian or Russian hegemony in the Balkans. Neither aggressive nor brutal, French and English influences usually took the form of polite advice to Serbia. At times Garašanin relied strongly on a friendly France; at others—notably in the mid- and late 1850s—France intervened more openly. Thus in Paris in 1857 Garašanin protested actions of the French consul in Belgrade: "To dictate and to advise are different matters."[4]

Garašanin, the political realist, knew that great powers were concerned chiefly with their own aims, assisting small Balkan states only if their interests coincided with theirs. His opinion of European diplomacy and its ability to solve complex international problems was rather low. For instance, Europe insisted on maintaining and protecting a moribund Ottoman Empire rather than settling its heritage. In dealing with European powers Garašanin believed that vassal Serbia should adopt a firm, honest and consistent course. He opposed antagonizing any power needlessly, but neither would he approve their policies if he deemed them wrong or harmful for Serbia. Reacting testily to reproaches against Serbia by foreign envoys in Constantinople, he resented European advice to Serbia to await patiently some indefinite future time to secure her interests. Foreign powers should learn that the Serbs knew their interests better than any of them. Small countries must rely chiefly on their own strength and courage, defending their rights vigorously without counting on foreign assistance which could merely facilitate but not determine the outcome.[5] "There is no such thing as political brotherhood but only selfishness," Garašanin wrote Knićanin in 1852. "They [the powers] do not want equality but superiority." Rather than counting on or even expecting foreign help, Serbia must primarily "create herself. Progress and salvation for us depend on our efforts alone." The Serbs must not let others tutor them. "We wish to be the forgers of our own destiny,"[6] he declared in words suggestive of Mazzini's famous phrase: *"Italia fare da se!"* ("Italy will create itself!").[7]

Knowing the Turks and their regime intimately, Garašanin assessed Ottoman rule and future prospects negatively. Despite the Porte's bluster and hauteur, he believed it was crumbling inevitably and fatally, and thus could achieve no beneficial solutions for youthful Serbia. Primarily great power rivalries, antagonisms, and fear of a cataclysmic war over its domains preserved the Ottoman Empire. Understandably, the Turks, he wrote Marinović, think little about the future. Not even all Europe could reform them, nor were they capable of independent policies toward Europe or of reforming themselves.[8] Garašanin thus agreed with Nicholas I that Turkey was the sick man of the East who, having refused to listen to his doctors' advice, was doomed to certain and imminent death. However, England and Austria, fearful lest Russia seize Turkish territories in Europe and become too powerful, would seek to preserve the Ottoman Empire a while longer. While viewing the Porte as an enemy of Serbia and the Balkan peoples, Garašanin preferred that it survive until they were strong and united enough to become its sole heirs in Europe. The Turks, he realized, distrusted the Serbian government, and vice versa, but good relations should be maintained while Serbia extracted maximum possible concessions, avoiding serious conflict until she could lead a Balkan coalition against the Porte.[9]

Among Serbian statesmen Garašanin was the first to advocate close relations with France so as to reduce Serbia's reliance or dependence on Austria and Russia. France under Napoleon III at first supported the Balkan Christian heirs of the Turks in order to block Austro-Russian expansion. During his visit to Paris in May 1852 Garašanin emphasized that of all Balkan Christian regions, Serbia, by geographical and political position was destined to become the nucleus for Balkan unity. French leaders then found that their interests paralleled Serbia's. Austrian and Russian leaders realized, Garašanin wrote Nenadović, that France could block their efforts to dominate the Balkans. Coveting nothing for itself there, France wished to see Serbia's future secured.[10] Replying to an exposé of French policy, Garašanin wrote that he realized that of the powers, only France ever since Karadjordje had regarded Serbia's development sympathetically. Describing Serbia's efforts to strengthen herself, Garašanin noted that if the Porte would trust her, soon "Russian and other plans in this [Balkan] region would disappear quickly and completely." Serbia would leave it to Paris to exert its influence at the Porte in her behalf.

Garašanin's statements produced an excellent impression in Paris. At a breakfast with Napoleon III the Serbian statesman conversed with the French emperor in German (Garašanin knew no French) "so softly that the others could hear scarcely anything." Napoleon told him that Serbia deserved support and that he would assist her to secure her independence.[11] Garašanin could inform Prince Aleksandar that France would play a major role "in behalf of the interests of the Serbian people." When Napoleon queried what aid Serbia needed from France, Garašanin requested diplomatic support against Turkish criticism, prompted by Austro-Russian pressure, of certain Serbian internal measures. Enthusiastic over his reception in Paris, Garašanin rejoiced that France seemed inclined to assist Serbia achieve its political aims. After returning to Serbia, he was widely regarded for the rest of Prince Aleksandar's reign as an ardent Francophile supported and defended by Paris and the Polish émigrés from Austrian or Russian attacks on his policies.

Through his French connection, Garašanin secured sporadic English support and thus was regarded as favoring a western orientation for Serbia. But English backing and protection of Turkey rendered Garašanin's relationship with London merely correct, never one of trust. English consuls in Belgrade, notably Fonblanque, often acted arrogantly and scornfully toward Serbian leaders. Only when Garašanin adopted an apparently anti-Russian stance, as in early 1853, did he obtain open English support. On two occasions during 1850-1851 Belgrade and English consuls conflicted inducing Garašanin to castigate both Fonblanque and the English. Angry at the consul's disparaging reference to the Serbs as "rayahs" (subjects), Garašanin responded: "If we are rayahs, we are not English ones but Turkish. . . . God forbid that we ever become English subjects since we would die of hunger." He considered Fonblanque mentally deranged adding: "The other English diplomats also hate the Slavs and especially the Serbs." Since Serbia had not provoked such hostility, "the devil only knows" why the English were so badly disposed toward her. "With their crazy policy," he wrote Marinović, "the English once attracted Russian influence here and now are seeking to do so again."[12] However, this minor squabble was soon overshadowed by Garašanin's confrontation with Russia.

Garašanin was encountering great difficulty in dealing with Prince Aleksandar's autocratic behavior. Surrounding himself with his wife's relatives and intimates, the Prince in the early 1850s sought zealously and unscrupulously to accumulate personal power. This brought him into frequent conflict with his ministers, especially Garašanin. Serbia's internal situation, the latter confirmed, had deteriorated chiefly because the Prince was denouncing his most loyal and honorable servants.[13] He aspired to unlimited monarchy, believing he was imitating that successful upstart, Napoleon III. However, many Serbs secretly derided the Prince for his vanity and incompetence. As dissatisfaction with Aleksandar grew, Garašanin defended him since he feared that his removal then might threaten Serbia's existence. He wrote his friend, Knićanin:

> I believe that the Prince has made plenty of mistakes, and has many shortcomings, I know these as well as anyone can and I truly wish he did not have them, but when one must choose the lesser evil, it is better to agree with the Prince than endanger the country.

To reach accord with Aleksandar was difficult, he added, but eventually proved feasible. Nonetheless, some accused Garašanin of scorning or neglecting the Prince because he only went to the palace when he had specific business to transact. Others spent many hours at court chatting and drinking coffee, but the ever busy Garašanin considered that a great waste of time.[14]

During the fall of 1852 Garašanin clashed several times eith the Prince but still retained his respect and support. When Garašanin became premier and foreign minister that September,[15] they disagreed sharply as to his successor as Interior Minister. The Prince wished to appoint Garašanin's assistant, Acika Nenadović, the Princess' uncle, which Garašanin opposed categorically. Later, at a cabinet meeting attended by Aleksandar, Garašanin urged that an able, honorable man be appointed to the Appeals Court rather than an unqualified relative of the Prince. Taking offense, Aleksandar told the ministers that they were just managers whose views he did not have to heed. Regarding Garašanin's plan to introduce a definite and permanent system for ministerial work as a device to limit his power, Aleksandar issued threats against Garašanin. Out of patriotism and to save the Prince's dignity, the minister restrained himself and remained silent. But he wrote Knićanin November 30th that in the future he must defend himself against similar attacks. One could please any ruler, noted Garašanin, by bowing to all his wishes, but he refused to follow such a course.[16] Neither could the ministers fight the Prince openly. Facing numerous domestic and foreign foes, Garašanin achieved a reconciliation with the Prince with the aid of the influential Knićanin, thus postponing his downfall for several months.

Garašanin viewed Serbian-Russian relations most pragmatically and was little influenced by sentimental ideas of Panslav solidarity. During Prince Aleksandar's reign his attitude toward Russia remained basically hostile and suspicious. He opposed vigorously though tactfully attempts by Russian envoys to impose their views and interfere in Serbia's internal affairs. Later in Vienna he complained to Russia's Ambassador Meyendorff that Russian consuls in Serbia had treated Serbian leaders habitually with scorn and disdain. Never content with giving advice, they had often commanded the Serbs to do things they could not do or humiliate them and deny them their legitimate rights. Such behavior by consuls Levshin and Tumanskii had chilled Serbian-Russian relations and made it appear that Serbia enjoyed better relations with other countries whose consuls treated the Belgrade government with more respect and courtesy.[17] Resenting such haughteur and unfriendliness by Russian officials, Garašanin emphasized that Serbia should act firmly and unafraid toward Russia:

> We should conduct ourselves as before, not provoking her anywhere or in any way, but also not giving in to her so that if we become reconciled, there will be no greater damage than conciliation on our part.[18]

Russian opposition to Garašanin, apparent from the early 1840s, surfaced first over his police law of 1850.[19] Drawn up and put through by Garašanin, that pioneering statute created and described the strong police power which would persist in Serbia with some amelioration right to 1941. Under its provisions the Serbian police could impose immediate punishment including flogging. Such severity, argued Garašanin, was required by persistent popular disobedience and anarchy fostered by Vučić and the Obrenovites and a consequent decline in police authority. Viewing this measure as directed primarily against Russophile elements in Serbia, Russia protested strongly at the Porte and spitefully urged the Turks to block creation of a Belgrade Military Academy and an arms factory in Kragujevac. Declared General Levshin, the Russian consul: "Why are you taking these steps [police law] when no one will dare do anything to you as long as we are here?"[20] Didn't the tactless consul comprehend the natural Serbian desires for independence?

Russian opposition to Garašanin was increased by his subsequent draconian measures to preserve internal order in Serbia. In late 1851 opposition elements fomented much unrest in the interior. Writing Stojan Simić October 23rd Garašanin noted the arrival of Tumanskii, the new Russian consul, replacing Levshin. "It seems to me that both [Austrian and Russian] courts are protecting the Obrenovites in order to frighten us." Garašanin responded to this disorder with regulations drawn up in agreement with the Prince but without the Council's knowledge, entrusting maintenance of internal security to General Knićanin, commander of the regular army in Kragujevac. Any failure by a police official to obey Knićanin's directives, he warned the district chiefs, would be punishable as treason.[21] The Russians believed this measure was designed to destroy their influence and adherents. After public demonstrations against the Prince and government organized by Vučić's faction, Garašanin in February 1852 drafted a harshly worded circular and after showing it to General Knićanin, sent it on March 26th to all subordinate officials.[22] The seven articles of this "April Circular" described crimes subject to its provisions and punishments to be imposed. In countries where the authorities are respected, Garašanin explained, law and order prevail, citizens are secure, and prosperity can flourish. Anyone slandering authority from evil intent or spreading falsehoods which threatened peace and order, declared the Circular, would be tried in the civil courts. Slander of town or village elders would be punished under the police law of 1850.[23]

The "April Circular" provoked a furor at home and abroad. Garašanin had consulted the Prince, but only afterwards, on April 9th, did he send it to the Council, some of whose members criticized his failure to submit it to them in advance. Council members, retorted Garašanin, were criticizing local authorities without trying to understand their problems. After angry debate, the Council finally approved the Circular, Garašanin informed Knićanin.[24] Opponents of the government reacted indignantly. Not daring attack the Circular directly, they circulated broadsheets in Belgrade and the interior denouncing it. Supporting the Vučić opposition, Russia for the first time demanded Garašanin's removal as Interior Minister and Consul Tumanskii insisted that Belgrade nullify the "April Circular." Prince Aleksandar tried to explain to Baron Liven, another Russian diplomat, that the Circular merely sought to preserve domestic order and would not damage Russian interests in Serbia. He pledged that it would not be enforced with maximum severity.[25] To mollify Russia, the Serbian government issued a new circular on October 14, 1852 omitting any reference to punishing people who denounced the authorities or spread false reports. Only those who acted concretely would be punished. Still dissatisfied, Russia demanded that Belgrade write officially about the circular to St. Petersburg.[26] Garašanin refused, and the struggle lasted until March 1853. The "April Circular" served as Russia's chief pretext for insisting that Garašanin be removed.

Garašanin's trip to France in the spring of 1852 apparently heightened Russia's resolve to force him from office. A month after issuing the "April Circular" he visited France and Switzerland with Jovan Marinović, chief of the Foreign Ministry's staff since 1850. Their evident purpose was to counter Russian pressure by obtaining French support, so Napoleon III's pledges of moral support heartened Garašanin. His trip was partly for treatment and consultation with French and Swiss doctors about his chronic, severe eczema. From Paris he proceeded to Luezh (?), Switzerland, spending over a month in baths which relived the symptoms but did not cure the disease. Writing from Luezh to Marinović, who had returned ahead of him to Serbia, he confirmed that he was bathing most of the day but doubted he would ever recover fully.[27]

As Garašanin left Switzerland, Russia intensified its pressure. Consul Tumanskii and Nil Popov, the consular secretary, showed Assistant Foreign Minister Aleksa Janković a letter from Count K. V. Nesselrode, the Russian Foreign Minister, demanding that the "April Circular" be nullified immediately. Issued without the Council's knowledge, it was despotic and illegal, they asserted. By refusing to void it, Prince Aleksandar would incur Russia's wrath and might even lose his throne. Informed of these ominous developments by Marinović, Garašanin wrote defiantly from Trieste: "Since a Russian official [Nesselrode] has reproached the Serbs and Serbia, I as a Serb and a Serbian official must reproach the Tsar and Russia." Deeply involved personally, he refused to advise Marinović how to act: ". . .Do as you think best."[28]

In a lengthy letter the next day,[29] Garašanin urged Belgrade to respond to the Russian demands before he arrived: "If they are going to swarm at me, it would be better if the issue were resolved without me so they cannot claim later that I made the decision." The situation was most difficult, he realized, partly because Belgrade so far had acted neither firmly nor consistently. Exhorting the government to defend its position vigorously, Garašanin recalled Prince Mihailo's decisive actions in 1840 to save himself:

> It was and is incumbent on us to withstand this torment from Russia, only it would have been easier had we acted differently up to now. You erred in not communicating to me the contents of the [Russian] protest since I could have given you my ideas promptly. . . ; now I don't know what to say.

St. Petersburg was mistaken if it believed that ousting him from office would "make me less dangerous for their bad intentions towards Serbia." In private life too he would oppose all Russian attempts to dominate the country. In no case should the present Serbian government serve Russia's interests; it should inform the Porte of Russia's protest and seek Turkish support. Containing nothing illegal, the Circular should prove easy to defend. If Russia's protest were merely a warning, Belgrade could respond without his help. If the fire was directed at him, a reply should prove even easier since Russia had no legal right to intervene against him. Serbia's response should be prompt; otherwise the Russians would believe they had frightened Belgrade. With Russia through the Vučić faction spreading its protest in Serbia, Belgrade should crack down hard against domestic foes, remain vigilant and instruct the district chiefs to do likewise. "Do not be afraid, but realize that this [confrontation] had to come sooner or later. We must defend ourselves without fear; if we are afraid, we will be destroyed." Consul Tumanskii should be told pleasantly but frankly that "we understand the Russian aim in this action, regret this is happening to us since we did not deserve it, and will defend ourselves as long as we can. . . ." Garašanin stated he would have undertaken this gladly were he not the subject of the Russian demands. To prepare the government for anything, the Prince should proceed to Belgrade while Kničanin, the army chief, remained in Kragujevac.

Again writing Marinović from Trieste,[30] Garašanin noted that his wife, Soka, was reproaching him for failure to write. Thus he was being criticized by Russia, Austria, many groups in Serbia, and now even by his wife! He would happily apologize to Soka for his oversight, but Marinović should justify his actions to the others:

I think that my stay in Paris greatly angered Russia and I feel this is the strongest reason for its new demonstrations. But when [Secretary] Popov told Janković that Russia cannot tolerate me, why was he not given an appropriate reply? And why should I care whether Russia can tolerate me or not? I eat bread not with Russian teeth but with my own and those of my forefathers; I am not a servant of Russia. When my father fought for the freedom of my country in the first and second uprisings and shed his blood for it, he truly did not know that the Russians existed. Those same Russians were the cause of my father's losing his head in an unnatural manner and also caused much misfortune to other Serbs. They would like me to be their slave or servant as many others here have become, but I will not do that. I serve my country and will continue to serve it truly without the least fear of Russia or anyone else.

Only positive Russian deeds could alter his present negative attitude. Marinović should settle the crisis quickly himself so the Russians could not claim that these were only Garašanin's ideas not shared by the rest of the government. Hold on until I arrive, he urged. "Russia would like to destroy everything that fosters the progress of Serbdom. These intentions are obvious, but if she does so, I do not wish it to happen with our help. . . ."

From Vienna on August 31st Garašanin warned Marinović that revoking his "April Circular" would undermine Serbia's policies and internal stability:

[Revocation] would reveal that the Serbian government accepts unconditionally the orders of the Russian consulate in its internal affairs contrary to all the rights it possesses, a circumstance, if it occurs, of great and unfortunate consequence for Serbia's future. But let us leave that to one side since we have people [such as Vučić] who would regard it as good fortune if Russia directed our internal affairs.[31]

Yielding, continued Garašanin, would hearten Belgrade's foes and discourage its supporters. Planning its protest in concert with Vučić, Russia was demanding in effect the resignation of the present government which would produce anarchy in Serbia.

Instead of satisfying the protest, I would in reply formulate an accurate complaint against the [Russian] Ministry and against the
dealings of Russian agents in Serbia with [our] opponents. . . .
Their actions make it essential to issue such circulars. If we don't
pluck up courage to do this, sometime we will have to tell Tumanskii without prevarication that as long as his consulate sympathizes
with opponents of our government, it will have to protect itself
from their bad intentions.

"Here they already regard us as goners (*izgubljene*)," he wrote Marinović a few days later. Austrians wondered how little Serbia, so ob-
stinate toward powerful Russia, could escape its predicament. Why wasn't
Marinović keeping him posted on events there? The previous day he had
exchanged pleasantries with ex-Prince Miloš: there had been "too many
kisses." Miloš might still cause Serbia trouble. While he had been in Paris,
noted Garašanin, the Orthodox priest at the Russian embassy in Vienna,
had spread rumors that he was forging an alliance with France and Polish
émigrés. Such reports must have triggered Russia's démarche.

The miserable [*nesretni*] Russians have really gone crazy. If I had
only four reliable people in the government, they [Russians] would
not threaten Serbia if she followed a course they disliked. Popov
then would not dare to declare that Russia cannot tolerate someone
who serves Serbia honorably. Even so, we can still prevail.[32]

Returning to Belgrade September 10th, Garašanin learned that Avram
Petronijević, Serbian premier and foreign minister, had died a week earlier
in Constantinople of a heart attack. Then Prince Aleksandar, given his
habitual cowardice, made a surprising decision. Three days after Garašanin's return, through he must have realized his Interior Minister was in
disfavor with Russia and over Consul Tumanskii's vehement opposition,
named Garašanin premier and foreign minister,[33] probably because he was
the only Serbian leader who could maintain domestic order in such critical
times.[34] Nicholas I interpreted Garašanin's appointment as an insult to
him and open defiance by Serbia. It brought the simmering quarrel between Garašanin and Russia to a boil. His six months as premier—September 13, 1852 to March 14, 1853—saw constant and escalating tension

between Nicholas and Serbia. At the outset Count Nesselrode warned Prince Aleksandar that Garašanin's appointment could end disastrously for him and his country. Tsar Nicholas' desire to remove from office a man he considered anti-Russian and pro-Polish grew more urgent as a crisis heated up in the Near East which would soon produce the Crimean War. Facing potential hostility from the Porte, Britain and France over alleged Russian expansionism, Nicholas found it intolerable that the "Western-oriented" Garašanin control strategically located Slav Serbia.

Meanwhile Garašanin hastened to crack down hard on Vučić, head of the Russophile opposition. Furious over the "April Circular," Vučić had rushed to Kragujevac, then on to Gruža to campaign against it and Garašanin. But Vučić did not realize that his hour had passed irrevocably. Thanks to Garašanin, the authorities were well-prepared, entrenched and tough. His protests proved ineffective. On November 24th Garašanin announced that Vučić had been removed from all official posts and placed on pension for failure to perform his duties (he almost never attended meetings of the Council). Vučić appealed angrily to the Prince and complained to the Russians. In response Foreign Minister Nesselrode instructed Tumanskii to demand flatly that Garašanin be removed from his posts and Vučić restored to his. Prince Aleksandar responded evasively: the Serbian people were happy with Garašanin's leadership and opposed restoring Vučić to power.[35]

Garašanin's correspondence with his friend, Knićanin, reveals his views on insistent Russian demands for his removal. On January 2, 1853 Garašanin confirmed that Prince Aleksandar had informed him that morning of his conversation with the Russian consul. Tumanskii had declared that he could not help the Prince settle the dispute with St. Petersburg. He offered to show Aleksandar his instructions which confirmed that Russia insisted unconditionally upon Garašanin's removal. Should the Prince spurn his advice, Russia would act unhesitatingly to achieve its goal. In response Aleksandar, praising Garašanin's abilities, told Tumanskii he knew of no fault the minister had committed. General Levshin, the Consul's predecessor, had accused Garašanin of Russophobia. Was Russia condemning his premier because of such old and baseless assertions? Replied Tumanskii: Garašanin can come and say whatever he likes, but I will neither listen nor alter my advice. What should be done now?, the Prince asked Garašanin. The latter, involved personally, refused advice except to urge Aleksandar to consult the Council rather than acting alone on his own responsibility. If the Prince refused to remove Garašanin, he would have to defend him subsequently from Russian attacks; it he did remove him, Aleksandar might face public hostility over such blatant Russian violation of Serbia's treaty rights. The Prince asked Garašanin to send the ministers to him that evening.[36]

At that meeting, from which Garašanin absented himself, they had decided Serbia must reach a friendly agreement with Russia. If Garašanin would renounce his allegedly "Russophobe" policies, the Prince would request Tumanskii to let him retain his posts until April, then retire from state service for health reasons. If by April the Russian consul were satisfied with Garašanin's behavior, the Prince would ask Russia to allow him to remain in office. For Serbia and Garašanin, this solution would save face while yielding to Russian pressure. "I didn't know how to answer such a humiliating communication," wrote Garašanin, "and was angry that the Consul was being given control over my position."[37]

The minister's prompt rejection of such a compromise forced Serbian leaders to debate alternatives. On January 9th Garašanin wrote Knićanin: no reply had yet been made to Russia but one would have to be sent soon. "Nothing remains for us now but to seek to preserve ourselves from Russian badgering by which they seek in their own way to upset conditions in our country." Discussing this with Aleksandar, Garašanin and the Prince agreed on the 8th that the Serbs must watch carefully two areas where Russia could damage them: in Constantinople and Serbia's interior. "We must keep our eyes peeled since you know the tendency of our people to fear the Russians. Our people are used instead to bow to the Russians and accept everything they say rather than being able to defend their rights redeemed with so much Serbian blood." Meanwhile Knićanin should adopt every necessary security measure.[38]

The pressure then relaxed briefly while Russia and Austria sought to prevent Turkish destruction of Montenegro. Its new ruler, Danilo (1851-1860) and its first ruler who was not also bishop, had secured Nicholas I's warm support for his claims as secular ruler. When the Porte refused to recognize his new status, Danilo had instigated an uprising in neighboring Hercegovina which provoked a Turco-Montenegrin war and an invasion of the principality by Omer Pasha. As Montenegro suffered grave defeats, Garašanin emphasized its desperate plight, adding that Austrian troops might be about to enter Bosnia and Hercegovina, keys to Serbia's future:

Then what will we do? This is terrible for us. Pray God that they
remain at peace. I scarcely believe that Austria will enter them
[Bosnia and Hercegovina] to pacify rather than to seize them. Our
people there would be delivered from the Turkish Muslims only to
suffer a much worse rule. The unfortunate Serbian fate! Things are
developing terribly and God knows how it will all turn out.[39]

Later, on January 30th, he wrote Knićanin that a Turkish official had
given him the "happy news," from the Porte's standpoint, that Montenegro had surrendered to Omer Pasha. "I went home," wrote Garašanin,
"and in the greatest desperation began to think about Montenegro's
fate."[40] The Turks were celebrating in their Belgrade fortress. However,
then Austro-Russian diplomatic intervention saved Montenegro from
destruction and restored its prewar boundaries.

Meanwhile Nicholas I had dispatched to Constantinople a high-power-
ed Russian delegation headed by Prince A. S. Menshikov to compel the
Porte to satisfy Orthodox claims at the Holy Places in Jerusalem. For
months Russia and France had contended over the question of the keys
to churches there with Russia backing the Orthodox and France the
Catholics. London provided increasing support to the French position
largely from a belief that Russia was seeking aggrandizement in the Near
East or even the destruction of the Ottoman Empire.

Konstantin Nikolajević, Serbia's experienced envoy in Constantinople,
described these important developments in detailed reports to Garašanin.
Constantinople was boiling with rumors, he wrote January 29, 1853, that
a special Russian delegation would soon arrive and that Russian troops
were massing on Turkey's Danubian frontiers.[41] Lavalette, the French envoy at the Porte, told Nikolajević that Austro-Russian intervention in
behalf of Montenegro aimed partly to erect barriers against Serbia and
transform Montenegro into their client. This would prevent Serbia subsequently from constructing a powerful, unified South Slav state on
Turkey's ruins. The Montenegrins, warned Lavalette, preferred independence and aggrandizement under their own dynasty, but if Montenegro
became a vassal of Russia or Austria, Serbia's future and mission of unifying the South Slavs would be imperilled. Afterwards, those powers would
try the same receipe in Bosnia, Hercegovina and Old Serbia, creating several small, weak states around Serbia inspired by a selfish particularism

and which would gravitate inevitably to Austria or Russia. At Garašanin's suggestion, Nikolajević proposed that Serbia and Montenegro be allowed to federate on the Swiss model under Serbia's leadership, but having just defeated Montenegro, the Turks curtly rebuffed that scheme. As to Menshikov's mission, added Nikolajević, "I have no idea what the Russians propose for us."[42]

This uncertainty ended abruptly and unfavorably for Garašanin. On February 26, 1853 Nikolajević wrote a private letter to "my respected godfather:"[43]

> Bad fortune seems to dog you in your new post. I have just come from the Russian embassy, and this is what I must with great sorrow report from Prince Menshikov: Emperor Nicholas again is demanding your removal from office and issued special instructions to Prince Menshikov to inform Prince [Aleksandar] of this through me with the comment that the Emperor is greatly dissatisfied and amazed that the Prince could disregard and disdain the Tsar's previous warnings and representations through the Belgrade consulate. Menshikov told me this drily and laconically, though not rudely, adding that he had thereby carried out his instructions.

Menshikov had told the envoy to communicate this to Prince Aleksandar "in the most grave and solemn manner." The Serbian prince must choose immediately between retaining the Tsar as his guarantor and savior or arousing his anger and hostility. Continued Nikolajević:

> I sought first of all to justify you with various assertions and proofs noting that from the time you became premier, you could not have deserved such ill-will from the Russian court and that on the contrary both you and the Prince had provided the most positive assurances and guarantees to Consul Tumanskii that in your new post you would conduct the affairs of Serbia in a spirit of the most sincere devotion and respect toward the Imperial court; that if previously you had entertained some negative news toward that court, none of this remained now [sic!] Thus the Emperor would be displaying great favor towards our Prince by accepting these assurances and by abandoning his demand for your removal, and that henceforth you

would seek by every means to justify these guarantees by your actions. I explained to Menshikov that our Prince had retained you in that post only from urgent national need, not from any impudence toward the Imperial court. To all these assurances Menshikov replied briefly and decisively that Russia would make no agreement with you under any conditions which would leave you in your present post.

Menshikov, continued Nikolajević, intimated that fear of the consequences would compel Prince Aleksandar to remove Garašanin. Russia, added Menshikov haughtily, had "higher interests" which overrode particular events or circumstances. He declared:

Garašanin has the reputation and notoriety of being a revolutionary [sic!] and a man oriented towards the West. At the present time when revolutionary leaders are already preparing to set all Europe ablaze, Serbia has been designated among the avenues through which revolution can pass into peaceful and well-ordered lands. How can Russia allow a man to remain at the head of affairs in a country it protects who once stood in league with the revolutionary leaders of the West and upon whom they now rest their hopes? No, Russia cannot have any trust in such a man. She suspects that he still maintains ties with them and merely awaits favorable events with his old acquaintances from the West, and she [Russia] will not suffer him to remain in charge of the affairs of Serbia.

This reflected Nicholas I's continuing paranoia that revolutionary and nationalist currents would surge into the Russian Empire from a liberal West. Surely, he must have known Garašanin himself was scarcely a revolutionary. However, Garašanin's close ties with the French and Poles, and former connections with Kossuth's Hungary which Nicholas' army had crushed so brutally in 1849, made him anathema to the "Iron Tsar." Although an autocrat with awesome power, Nicholas personally was prey to terrible fears and insecurity.

Nikolajević "remained as if petrified" at these words as Menshikov confirmed that their interview was over. The envoy informed Garašanin:

Thus there face us in Serbia new troubles and difficulties, and God knows what serious shifts will occur soon after this. Today I lacked the time and courage to communicate all this to the Prince [Aleksandar] and will leave it up to you to make use of it. If the Prince cannot again repel this Russian persecution of you, the interests of Serbia and the Serbian government require at least that you be restored to the Interior Ministry rather than removing you from service altogether as the Russians now seem to be demanding. If you were willing, it might be best for you to request this from the Prince before anything is decided as the result of Menshikov's demands.

Nikolajević added that he was attempting to find a facesaving formula in order to retain Garašanin in some official capacity.

Garašanin, though, would not hear of any such solution. On March 6th he wrote Nikolajević noting that he had just received his private letter the previous day. He had been surprised that Prince Menshikov had reiterated so forcefully the Tsar's previous demands for his removal from service.

I communicated your letter promptly to the Prince. It upset him greatly since he saw in this Russian demand much more far-reaching aims than just threats by Prince Menshikov which were not at all well-founded. The Prince received this information only for his private knowledge and will take no action until receiving from you, surely by the next mail, a definite communication.

Garašanin then explained to Nikolajević his personal views about the entire question and why he had refused to resign voluntarily or bow to Russia's dictates:

If this demand of the Tsar affected only my own person and did not touch on the rights and future interests of Serbia, you can rest assured that I would at the first declaration of that high though unjust will, resign from my posts without hesitation and would do so happily, but when this demand cuts so deeply into the rights and interests of our people, and when one sees from this the [Russian] intention to transform a protectorate into something which would damage belief in Serbdom and Serbia, then I cannot abet by my resignation foreign intentions so dangerous and destructive without committing a great crime against my country.

You will understand, Sir, how much easier it would be for me to resign from my posts immediately rather than remain in such a terrible and distant struggle with the Russians. . . . No, I cannot ever agree to such a step of voluntary resignation which I would regard as treason. But if it were the desire of the Prince and my colleagues that I resign, then I would bear no responsibility for it. Thinking thus, I know that Russia will not readily abandon its intention; I know that she is great and powerful and realize that she can act forcibly to carry out her intentions in Serbia, and supposing that all this may occur, again comes to my mind the rights of our country and our duty which is imposed on us, and whose rights I prefer to see taken from us by force rather than having us yield them voluntarily. . . .

You know our situation precisely and thus surely you know what an unhappy impression the execution of that Russian demand would have on our Councillors and mny of our officials. Surely you will admit that immediately after the implementation of such a document, Serbia would be transformed into a Russian province, and a poor and unfortunate one at that, resembling Moldavia or Wallachia.[44] Our nationality would be laughed at subsequently by the Russians just as they now make fun of Moldavia and Wallachia, seemingly ignorant that they themselves are the cause of that people's misery and backwardness.

Prince Menshikov in his accusations against me did not wish to take the trouble to examine the true cause of this persecution. On the contrary he sought, alleging different reasons, to cover up the true aim of his cabinet's policy, but from the very way in which he spoke to you, he revealed that he was by-passing completely the Prince and the government and consequently the interests of the Serbian people, and only considered higher Russian interests, naming that country and people as something special. Prince Menshikov would speak better and more genuinely if he stated that Russia and Russian interests could not tolerate Garašanin because he regards Russian patronage in Serbia in a different way than the Russian cabinet wishes that he did. Here, Sir, is the whole Russian effort to run over us, and not in those invented revolutionary chieftains whom he alleges Garašanin was in touch with. The Russians know very well my attitude toward those Western chiefs. Their doubts and miserable assumptions cannot darken or conceal clear and obvious matters. Russia surely knows better how I really reacted toward such chiefs and their revolutions. . . , but she now claims this in order to conceal her trickery and her aspirations which she is naturally ashamed to set forth openly before the world.

Prince Menshikov speaks wholly correctly when he states that Russia does not wish to conclude an agreement with me under which she would leave me in peace in the service, since I, Sir, truly would not wish to serve under any conditions set by Russia, and in such a position I would compare myself to an ordinary soldier and not to a Serbian official, and would never serve at some foreigner's mercy and generosity. You presented abundant reasons to Prince Menshikov with which you sought to alleviate the brutal instructions of his Emperor and he would accept none of them, and I, Sir, would never wish to consent to the conditions which you stated to him, although I approve of your efforts in trying to work out something with that beast [*zverom*].

I send you these views only for your private knowledge and do not wish you to make any other use of them since they are my personal views. Instead, await the Prince's reply which he will send to you after your communication. You must not believe . . . there is the slightest truth in the accusations which Prince Menshikov had delivered so seriously and with such assurance. These are inventions with the intent to subjugate us and Serbia purely to the orders of the Russian consul in Belgrade and make us carry out only Russian policies and that it is unthinkable that in Serbia a Serbian policy can prevail.[45]

In this eloquent letter, found by the author in Garašanin's papers, the minister summed up his views about Serbian policy, Russian bullying, and his approach toward public service.

Responding with a private letter to Garašanin's lengthy missive, Nikolajević wrote:

> I must bow most respectfully before the purity, elevation and consistency of the patriotic principles which you expressed. I would not have proposed such a cowardly idea [having Garašanin return as Interior Minister] had it not been for our situation and need for support. . . . In this I followed the principle: in trouble it is better for us to select the lesser of two evils and that seemed to me to ask the Prince to shift you to another post rather than removing you altogether and agreeing to a blatant violation of our national rights.

While accepting in principle Garašanin's view that it was preferable to have Russia usurp Serbia's rights by force rather than yielding them voluntarily, Nikolajević affirmed: "I have little faith that we can stick to this position and so that our surrender would not be greater and more damaging, I considered a way of reducing it to smaller proportions." He would indeed rejoice if Serbia emerged from "this bitter and unequal struggle with Russia" without substantial damage to its interests.[46]

During the crisis Garašanin expressed similar views to General Knićanin. "If Russia thinks that I will deliver Serbia to her, she is greatly mistaken," he wrote March 10th. "Look at the shameful invention great Russia employs against me. She wishes me to do something evil without blackening her own image." Since he had refused to submit to Consul Tumanskii, the Russians were now associating him with the greatest European revolutionaries in order to hide their intentions. "If I stood in alliance with Kossuth and Mazzini in any revolutionary conspiracy, surely my colleagues and countrymen would know about it." Writing Knićanin March 13th Garašanin still had not received a formal demand for his removal from service, nor had he instructed Nikolajević about Belgrade's policy. Knićanin might criticize his apparent and uncharacteristic extremism in regard to Russia, but hopefully he would approve of it because of the deplorable manner in which the Russians were attacking him:

I cannot bear calmly an injustice which exceeds all bounds of decency. The Russians are persecuting me as if I were under their police, as if I had entered here from some place without a passport. I won't accept that even if it costs me my life. You know how hard it is to budge Garašanin when he is defending a position. I will never make apologies to the Russians nor will I make conditions, nor do I fear them. I would rather die than abandon my rights. Thinking thus I am separating myself completely from the government's policy. Let it examine and conduct its policy as it judges necessary for the state and I will pursue mine as I know best. When the Prince asks me to resign from state affairs, I will readily do so immediately, but when the Russians order me to do so, I won't obey them because they have no right to tell me that.[47]

As Garašanin penned these lines, the Russian government had already issued a twenty-four hour ultimatum to Serbia to remove him from office, threatening otherwise to break relations. Prince Aleksandar promptly caved in to Tumanskii's ultimatum informing the Council March 14, 1853 that he had ordered Garašanin removed as premier and foreign minister and transferred him to the Council. "But since he informed me that his health will not allow him to accept that post, I have placed him on pension pending his recovery. Let me remind the Council of Garašanin's hard and useful work and his sacrifices. The circumstances under which he had to leave are well-known."[48] This last phrase only hinted at the intense Russian pressure which had induced the Prince to capitulate. The Prince's remark about Garašanin's health sought to save a little face.

Garašanin had forced the Prince's hand by refusing to resign voluntarily so that Serbian and foreign opinion would realize that Serbian ministers were being removed without cause at the demand of a foreign power. Garašanin wrote the Prince:

You already know that [my] removal was achieved by forcible means on Russia's part and that it violates Serbia's rights . . . . Russia had no other reason to use against me . . . except that I have defended the internal rights of our country against any [external] influence or orders, as a Serb and a Serbian official was obligated to do.

The ex-premier declared without reference to his health: "Contrary to my will, I am compelled to resign from state service. I have done the best I could for my country."[49] Garašanin's defiant posture was echoed by General Knićanin, the army chief. When Consul Tumanskii delivered his ultimatum on Garašanin's ouster to Aleksandar, Knićanin told the Prince he would rather die honorably defending Serbia than yield. However, Garašanin exhorted him to assist the Prince and government in their hour of peril.[50]

Russia soon followed up its ultimatum with demands that other leading members of the Belgrade regime associated with Garašanin, notably Jovan Marinović and Franjo Zah, likewise be removed from state service. While recognizing that the government was in a bad position, Garašanin deplored this new highhanded move.[51] However, the Serbian Council now drew a firm line. On March 20th its chairman, Stefan S. Tenka, and secretary, Jakov Živanović, wrote Prince Aleksandar that the Council had learned of Garašanin's removal "with the deepest indignation." Initially, the Council had hoped that this sacrifice, which the Prince claimed was necessary, would secure Serbia's future relations with Russia. Now it learned that the Russian consulate had demanded the resignations of Marinović and Zah. This "violated blatantly Serbia's rights and constitution which must therefore produce the most depressing effect on all Serbs." If the government yielded rights upon which the political existence of the country depended, the Serbian people would be deeply offended. The Council strongly urged the Prince to resist these additional Russian demands.[52]

Buttressed by this advice, the Prince rejected these new Russian demands. According to Nil Popov, he then turned to the Turkish pasha in Belgrade and foreign consuls complaining of Russian tyranny and seeking their support. Consul Tumanskii retaliated by cutting off official and personal ties with the Belgrade regime, a move just short of a complete breach in relations. With Obrenovites and Vučićites exploiting this rift to foster popular agitation against the government, Aleksandar knew he could proceed no further in opposing Russia. However, Russia did not wish to push matters to a breach either. Facing increasing danger of war with the Porte and the Western powers, Nicholas I realized that continuance of his embarrassing and unseemly crisis with little Serbia would only damage his position. Consequently, Marinović and Zah retained office, and Serbia salvaged some prestige and self-respect.[53]

Soon afterwards Garašanin blamed the crisis on the Russian envoys' ignorance of conditions in Serbia and the successful Vučićite efforts to mislead them, as well as on Russian expansionism:

> The Russian consul and his secretary, Nil Popov, represent in original form the hatred of Russia for the Serbs. This is based not on my injured feelings but is just a self-evident truth based on their roles and actions. Those people report to Petersburg without ever talking with a Serb. Naturally, I understand very well from what source they derive this information. . . . Vučić remains always the servant of the Russian consulate.[54]

With war apparently imminent between Russia, Turkey and the West, Garašanin wrote Knićanin he had decided to have his illness treated abroad; there seemed little he could accomplish at home.

> A Russian war against Turkey, England and France is likely which I feel Nicholas I would now like to avoid since the prospects are not favorable for Russia. I am going to Switzerland since events here do not depend at all on me now and my illness is severe and unpleasant.[55]

Garašanin's vehement opposition to Russian pressure in 1852-1853 reflected no hatred on his part for Russia generally but merely an objection to its efforts to dominate Serbia which he considered unjustifiable and reprehensible. Subsequently, as we shall see,[56] he cooperated closely with Russia after St. Petersburg had altered its policy toward Serbia to one coinciding with Garašanin's long-term aims. Ironically, when Garašanin was removed by another Serbian prince over policy differences in November 1867, Russia would be his most ardent defender.

NOTES

1. For many of Garašanin's general views on foreign policy I am indebted to Strankaković's "Ilija Garašanin," chapter 4, "Spoljašnja politika," pp. 145 ff.

2. IG 1683, "Moji spomeni," Grocka 1868.

3. Ibid.; Stranjaković, "Ilija," pp. 161-164.

4. Garašanin to Marinović (Paris), November 3, 1857, *Pisma*, 1, 380.

5. Stranjaković, "Ilija," p. 148.

6. Ibid., p. 149; IG 816, Garašanin to Knićanin, May 24, 1852.

7. Giuseppe Mazzini (1805-1872) of Genoa, a cosmopolitan Italian nationalist and founder of "Young Italy," who believed unification could be achieved by armed insurrection against all existing authorities.

8. Garašanin to Marinović, June 18, 1853, *Pisma*, I, 83.

9. Stranjaković, "Ilija," pp. 150-151.

10. IG 814, Garašanin to Nenadović, July 1, 1852.

11. Garašanin to Marinović, June 26, 1852, *Pisma*, I, 29-30; Stranjaković, *Vlada Ustavobranitelja*, pp. 213-214.

12. Garašanin to Marinović, July 23, 1852, *Pisma*, I, 42.

13. IG 988, Garašanin to Knićanin, early 1851; Stranjaković, "Ilija," pp. 117-118.

14. IG 816, Garašanin to Knićanin, May 24, 1852.

15. See below, p. 147.

16. IG 816, Garašanin to Knićanin, November 15, 20 and December 1, 1852. On these quarrels see Stranjaković, *Vlada Ustavobranitelja*, pp. 182-186.

17. Garašanin to Marinović, August 8, 1953, *Pisma*, I, 130-131.

18. IG, 734, Garašanin to Knićanin, 1850; Stranjaković, "Ilija," p. 164.

19. On the police law see ibid., p. 48; *Zbornik zakona i uredaba* (Belgrade, 1853), V, 131.

20. SANU 7380, Autobiografija A. Nikolica.

21. Garašanin's circular to the district chiefs of October 7, 1851, cited in Stranjaković, "Ilija," p. 48; SANU 7391, Knićanin correspondence; Stranjaković, *Vlada Ustavobranitelja*, pp. 136-138.

22. IG 816, Garašanin to Knićanin, April 9, 1852; Stranjaković, "Ilija," p. 48.

23. Ibid., pp. 48-50. This "April Circular" of March 26/April 7, 1852, Stranjaković points out, is neither in the published *Collected Laws and Regulations of Serbia* nor in the State Archive of Serbia because at Russia's demand it was first toned down and finally withdrawn. Stranjaković found a copy of it in the archive of the Rudnik district court at Gornji Milanovac.

24.   IG 816, Garašanin to Knićanin, April 18; Stranjaković, "Ilija," pp. 50-51. The Council adopted the Circular "posle velike vike" at a session held before April 18, 1852.

25.   Prince Aleksandar Karadjordjević to Baron Liven, October 3, 1852, cited in Stranjaković, "Ilija," pp. 50-51.

26.   Ibid., pp. 50-51; Stranjaković, *Vlada,* pp. 178-179.

27.   Garašanin to Marinović, Luezh, July 13, 1852, *Pisma,* I, 36-38.

28.   Garašanin to Marinović, Trieste, August 26, ibid., pp. 58-59. Garašanin mistakenly dated this the 27th as he noted in his letter the following day.

29.   Ibid., pp. 59-61, August 27.

30.   Ibid., pp. 62-63, August 28.

31.   Ibid., pp. 63-65, Vienna, August 31.

32.   Ibid., pp. 65-67, September 3.

33.   According to Nil Popov (*Rossiia i Serbiia,* II, 346-47), the Prince appointed Garašanin after long hesitation despite his pro-Western stance.

34.   Stranjaković, *Vlada,* pp. 179-180.

35.   Ibid., pp. 180-181; S. Jovanović, *Ustavobranitelji,* p. 195.

36.   IG 871, Garašanin to Knićanin, January 2, 1853, No. 1.

37.   Ibid., January 4, No. 2.

38.   Ibid., January 9, No. 4.

39.   Ibid., January 13, No. 5. Radovan Jovanović asserts in *Politički odnosi Crne Gore i Srbije, 1860-1878* (Cetinje, 1977), p. 25, that the shift of Montenegro's status and its apparent strengthening under Danilo had been received hostilely by Belgrade and cites the Garašanin-Marinović correspondence (*Pisma,* I, 66) as his source, but the letter he cites fails to support this.

40.   IG 871, Garašanin to Knićanin, January 30, No. 12.

41.   IG 876, Nikolajević to Garašanin, January 29, 1853.

42.   Ibid., February 23.

43.   Ibid., February 26.

44.   Moldavia and Wallachia, the so-called Danubian Principalities, had been Russian protectorates since the Treaty of Bucharest (1812) while remaining Turkish territories. Subsequently, in 1859 they united and in 1862 became Romania whose independence was recognized by the powers in 1878.

45.   IG 869, Garašanin to Nikolajević, March 6.

46.   Ibid., Nikolajević to Garašanin, March 10.
47.   IG 871, Garašanin to Knićanin, March 10.
48.   IG 902, Prince Aleksandar to the Council, March 14.
49.   IG 1077, Garašanin to Prince Aleksandar, undated draft.
50.   Stranjaković, *Vlada*, pp. 204-205; SANU, No. 7391, "Prepiska Knićanina."
51.   IG 871, Garašanin to Knićanin, March 17.
52.   IG 903, The Council to Prince Aleksandar Karadjordjević, March 20.
53.   Stranjaković, *Vlada*, pp. 204-207; Popov, *Rossiia*, II, 347-349. On Garašanin's fall see also M. Hristić, *Jedan listak iz diplomatske istorije Srbije* (Belgrade, 1893).
54.   IG 877, Garašanin to unknown, April 8, draft.
55.   IG 871, Garašanin to Knićanin, May 19.
56.   See below, Chapters XVI-XVIII.

CHAPTER IX

NEUTRALITY OR WAR (1853-1856)?

"My view is that we should listen to the advice of all European courts, then discuss it ourselves and accept whatever is most helpful for us no matter what the source. If none of it is useful, we should reject it all and do whatever we find good and useful. That is the way I think we should practice a useful Serbian policy, not by obeying orders from outside. . . . "

Garašanin draft of 1855

With the Porte receiving strong Anglo-French support, Prince Menshikov's mission to Constantinople failed to impose Russia's demands over the Holy Places on the Turks. His abrupt departure in May 1853 breached Russo-Turkish relations, and in July followed a Russian occupation of Moldavia and Wallachia. That arbitrary move provoked European protests as, to the dismay of Nicholas I, Austria and Prussia echoed the disapproval of the Western powers. In October 1853 the Porte declared war on Russia and after Admiral P. S. Nakhimov destroyed the Turkish fleet at Sinope and Russia refused to withdraw from the Danubian Principalities, in March 1854 France and Britain joined the war in support of Turkey. The German powers remained neutral but leaned more toward the West than toward Russia.[1]

The Crimean War posed many dangers for little Serbia whose fortresses were still garrisoned with Turkish troops. Despite her small regular army, she was wooed by both sides to join the war. Until July 1854 Russia, counting on the Russophile sentiments of the Serbian populace, exerted strong but intermittent pressure on Belgrade to enter the conflict. The Serbian government, headed by aged, infirm Aleksa Simić and the indecisive Prince Aleksandar, after proclaiming neutrality, pursued a zigzagging, timorous and ineffective policy. Fortunately for vassal Serbia, the Porte accepted her neutrality and allowed her to rearm in self-defense. In a memorandum revealing Garašanin's inspiration, Acting Foreign Minister Jovan Marinović outlined Serbia's neutral posture: were Serbia to be attacked, she could seek aid from any quarter while by fighting alongside Russia, she would risk everything. Marinović and Garašanin doubted Russia would win the war; at best she could defend her present positions, so if allied with her, Serbia would receive nothing. Only armed neutrality, they believed, could avert attack by foreign troops.[2]

Garašanin, initially at Russian insistence, remained out of the government throughout the war but still exercised much influence on its policies. At the outset he helped dissuade Prince Aleksandar from joining Russia for which later a Council member, Živko Davidović, would call Garašanin the savior of Serbia. Indeed, Serbia's neutrality during the Crimean conflict owed much to his advise. In those years he divided his time between Belgrade, his nearby Grocka estate, and trips abroad for medical treatment and diplomatic purposes. Periodically, Prince Aleksandar utilized him as a foreign policy adviser; sometimes he gave unsolicited advice. Although Serbia remained neutral, the government's inconsistent course provoked his misgivings and dismay. At times he found unendurable a regime which became increasingly autocratic and incompetent. But only after the war, when convinced that its subservience to Austria contradicted Serbia's fundamental national interests did he join the opposition to the Karadjordjević dynasty.

To avoid embarrassing the government in the face of Russian and Austrian pressure and to relieve his eczema, in May 1853 Garašanin traveled first to Vienna, then to Luezh, Switzerland. There he met Count A. F. Orlov, adjutant to Nicholas I of Russia and an able diplomat, who asked him why he had opposed Russian policies. Garašanin told Orlov frankly that false or inaccurate reports from Consul Tumanskii and Secretary Nil

Popov to St. Petersburg had caused such a misleading impression and had sparked Russian demands for his removal. While Tumanskii lay gravely ill, Popov, whom Garašanin considered a Serbophobe, had obtained his information from foreigners and opponents of the Serbian government. Expressing his regret, Count Orlov replied that had Garašanin been able to talk directly with Prince Menshikov, he would not have been ousted. Garašanin asked Orlov to inform Russian leaders that those negative reports about him had been groundless.[3]

That interview helped improve official Russian attitudes toward Garašanin. Soon he could write Marinović: "It may turn out that no one knows, not even the Russians, what I was guilty of." If the moribund Tumanskii died, he could be blamed for everything, and Serbia and Russia reconciled. Realizing there had been a serious misunderstanding with Russia, Garašanin now worried chiefly about Austrian hostility:

> Serbia must always regard Austria as bitter poison from which if Serbia is not preserved, she may be poisoned fatally. Austria can never aid Serbia to progress but must rather oppose her as much as possible. That is her natural policy. Having so many Serbs and other Slavs who border on us, Austria is bound to fear Serbia's advancement.[4]

Indeed, the danger of an Austrian military occupation faced Serbia throughout the Crimean War.

Until late summer 1853, St. Petersburg's attitude toward Serbia and its Karadjordjević dynasty remained equivocal. Even before Consul Tumanskii died July 5th and Prince Aleksandar, responding to Russian pressure, removed Marinović from the foreign ministry, Russia had accepted Serbia's probable neutrality in the looming conflict with the West. However former Prince Mihailo Obrenović in a manifesto pledged once back in power to reconcile all Serbian factions. Dissatisfied with the Belgrade's regime Austrophilism, Emperor Nicholas was still considering replacing it with Russophile Prince Mihailo. Any such Russian attempt, Garašanin wrote Marinović, must be resisted forcibly. He favored a frank letter to Foreign Minister Nesselrode describing Serbia's sad plight in the face of Russian hostility. "We must deliver ourselves from this position since further delay would face the country with complications and misfortune."[5]

The opportunity to achieve this came that August. Following Tuman-skii's demise, Chancellor Nesselrode dispatched Felix Fonton, councillor of the Russian embassy in Vienna, to Belgrade with a letter to Prince Aleksandar which attributed disorder in Serbia to previous actions of Belgrade opposed by public opinion. Tsar Nicholas would not allow a Serbia under his protection, warned Nesselrode, to become a haven for rebels and revolutionaries; Serbia must follow Russian advice closely. However, Fonton was to reassure Belgrade that "the patron court" [Russia] did not wish any change in the present ruler in Serbia" and desired her to remain at peace.

Simultaneously, Garašanin held highly important talks with Count Peter Meyendorf, Russian ambassador in Vienna, at the latter's request, which Garašanin reported to Marinović for immediate transmission to Prince Aleksandar.[6] Apparently on behalf of his government, Meyen-dorf declared: "No attack on Serbia [by Austria or Turkey] can occur nor will Russia permit one as long as Serbia remains at peace." Fonton had been sent to Belgrade to clarify matters, eliminate previous mis-understandings, and reassure Belgrade about troop movements and Mi-hailo's manifesto. The Serbs should maintain domestic peace and order and refrain from any military preparations. "Prevously," conceded Meyen-dorf, "our consuls there have been in the habit of giving too many orders, often without any need, but from now on such mistakes will not recur." Without alluding directly to Garašanin's recent removal, the Ambassador stated: "I can only tell you that you are considered [by Russia] to be an honest man." Urged to speak frankly, Garašanin told Meyendorf that Belgrade desired peace. Only the Vučić faction, hitherto supported by the Russian consulate, opposed the government. If Meyendorf were sincere and spoke for St. Petersburg, concluded Garašanin, Serbo-Russian relations could readily be repaired.

Russia was becoming more favorable toward Serbia, Garašanin wrote Marinović the next day,[7] supplying more details of his conversations with Meyendorf. The ambassador had affirmed that Russia did not wish to restore Mihailo nor undermine peace in Serbia: "He has already been prince once," Meyendorf declared, "and Serbia did not enjoy calm under his rule." Vučić and the Belgrade government could never reach agree-ment, warned Garašanin. "He aims to destroy everything that is good and useful and reduce Serbia to a position where everyone will do his evil bidding." Russia formerly had acted hastily toward Garašanin because of biased reports from its Belgrade consulate, Meyendorf admitted, but "from now on I hope everything will go better." Misleading reports had caused St. Petersburg to suspect Garašanin of extreme nationalist and revolutionary views; now it realized its mistake.

His talks with Meyendorf, Orlov, and Fonton's mission, Garašanin informed Marinović a week later,[8] seemingly had dispelled Serbo-Russian suspicions. Fonton had found to be baseless reports about alleged revolutionary spirit in Serbia. Garašanin had told Meyendorf:

> Your Excellency can rest assured that our people will never follow young men and foreign ideas. Our people is not at all revolutionary and only follows leaders it knows well and for a long time and who have done something useful for their country.

While in Belgrade, Fonton had even suggested that Garašanin be restored to state service. On this Garašanin commented to Marinović:

> It is truly too early to speak of that. First of all, I am ill and do not wish to serve. Even if I were healthy, I would need much time to think things over as to whether I ever want to accept another official position.

Garašanin told Meyendorf that he sought no post for himself, nor would he vex anyone. "I do not have much [money], nor do I need much. What I have will be to educate my children as best I can." If Fonton again suggested his return to service, Marinović should say he was ill and could not accept a post. "Better that the Russians know this rather than supposing that I will not serve because I am offended." He would live and let live, let bygones be bygones, remaining in Vienna until Fonton returned there. "I would like to meet someone who has dispelled the troubles which have existed between us for so many years." Garašanin still hoped to change Russia's earlier expressed opposition to Serbia's full independence. If the Serbs worked hard and sensibly, "Russia may sometime approve independence if she sees it will be more beneficial for her than something else." She would need sincere allies, so "let us hold on until she changes her mind. . . . Our best policy is to seek peace and preservation of the status quo."

Garašanin regretted Marinović's resignation under Russian pressure, however. ". . .Do they still condemn you as a youthful extremist with French ideas?" Whatever ideas were not Russian, they tended to consider French even if in fact they were purely Serbian. "With me they [Russians] could hardly wait for me to go to Paris so they could call my ideas French. . . ." How suspicious most Russian envoys remained! Russia had been offended, remarked Meyendorf, that Belgrade had acted more friendly toward the French consul than to Russia's. The Russian consul and his secretary, Garašanin had replied, had scorned and criticized Serbian leaders, while the French envoy had been friendly.

The Fonton mission ended in complete success. On September 2, 1853 Garašanin wrote Marinović he had talked for two hours with the special Russian envoy about everything and everyone.[9] Foreign Minister Nesselrode had approved completely the results of Fonton's mission, noting that Fonton even wanted to send arms to Serbia. Now they must find a capable Russian consul for Belgrade to continue the rapproachement Fonton had begun. Now Garašanin could return home feeling he had contributed to Serbia's reconciliation with Russia, providing her with greater security against Austro-Turkish threats.

Belgrade had been seeking with some success to strengthen Serbia militarily. In February 1853 the Council had authorized money mainly to purchase weapons abroad. By late 1853 Serbia had formed a mainly militia force of 48,000 infantry and 6,000 cavalry. Major Hippolyte Mondain, a French military engineer, who became Garašanin's close friend, aided the Serbian war ministry until Paris recalled him abruptly early in 1854.[10] Franjo Zah drew up plans to create a fortified defensive camp at Požarevac. After the Crimean War began, Zah wrote in March 1854 that Serbia would definitely not fight against Russia and could not fight for Turkey. "I believe that in an extremity, Russia could call on all Turkish Christians to fight Austria." However, Serbian armament, he claimed, was purely defensive and the country was relatively well armed.[11] In the early stages of the war, as long as Russian forces operated in nearby Moldavia and Wallachia, the Serbs appear to have been ready to fight alongside them if Russia gave the signal.

Garašanin, though, was advising Prince Aleksandar not to do so. Russia, he wrote Knićanin in November 1853,[12] was not fighting the Turks to benefit Serbia: "The Russians entered the war on pretext of defending

Orthodoxy, but they attacked into Moldavia and Wallachia which already enjoy the fruits of their benevolence." After failing to lure Serbia to their side, the Russians had advised Serbia to remain neutral and prevent the Turks from entering the country. Garašanin finally induced the Prince to promise "not to follow the Russians no matter what they might promise."

Contrary to fears abroad, Russia did not attempt to provoke a general Balkan insurrection during the Crimean War, although some Russian leaders, and for a time even Nicholas I, appealed for Balkan support at first. During the 1830s and 1840s Russian scholars had laid based for cultural Panslavism, i.e., unification of all Slav peoples, by providing to Russians fuller information about the southern and western Slavs. Professor M. P. Pogodin of Moscow University, a leading Panslav, proclaimed that Russia's destiny was to unite Slavdom and achieve a glorious future. With Austria and Turkey tottering, the first major war would destroy them, he believed. Early in the Crimean conflict, Russian Panslavs appealed to Balkan Slavs to rise against the Turks, and even Nicholas favored this for a time, until Russia's reluctant retirement across the Danube in June 1854 ended such dreams. Earlier, Nicholas had regarded the concept of Slav liberation as seditious and dangerous, commenting in 1849:

> Under the guise of compassion for the supposed oppression of the Slavic peoples there [in Austria] is concealed the idea of rebellion against the legitimate authority of neighboring, and in part, allied states, as well as the idea of a general unification . . . through diorder which would be ruinous for Russia.

The Crimean War had dispelled official Russia's overconfidence by revealing that Russia lacked reliable friends among the European powers. Thus as Russian forces fought the Turks near the Danube, Pogodin bombarded St. Petersburg with Panslav memoranda like this:

> Our only and most helpful and powerful allies in Europe are the Slavs, our kinsmen by blood, tongue, heart, history and faith, and there are ten million in Turkey and twenty million in Austria. . . . Here are our natural allies! Show them the fine, sacred cause of freedom from the intolerable foreign yoke under which they have been groaning for 400 years, be capable of directing their living, mighty,

enthusiastic forces, and you will see the wonders they will perform.[13]

In May 1854 Pogodin proposed that Russia liberate all Slavs and create a Danubian or southeast European union centering in Constantinople. Fifty million Russians would lead the Slav world with the Russian tsar heading a Slav federation in which the various peoples would enjoy autonomy. Nicholas I, however, would only agree to proclaim Russia's traditional role as protector of Orthodoxy and appeal to Turkish Christians to rise and defend their faith, not Slavdom. Fieldmarshal I. F. Paskevich, Nicholas' top commander, even more cautious, disapproved of a Balkan insurrection in any form. In February 1854 he advised Nicholas to evacuate the Danubian Principalities since otherwise Russia would face all of Europe and eventually have to yield. Thus Paskevich opposed any Serbian rising or utilization of Serbian volunteers.[14]

From the outset Garašanin believed that Serbia could not enter the war without risking its entire future. Early in the conflict he outlined to Marinović a complete diplomatic program which had he been in power, he doubtless would have pursued. However, his scheme proved beyond the courage and ability of a weak Belgrade regime which groped desperately for foreign support.[15] Garašanin's thinking on Serbia's policy during the war was expressed in a lengthy draft, apparently from 1855:

> I am accused of being too devoted to a Western policy and therefore an excluded from all the country's affairs, and thus everything is concealed from me in order not to compromise Serbia's policy. They [the leaders] listen to my views but do not follow them. . . . Never hitherto have I preached a Western or any other alien and foreign policy. I have only preached a Serbian policy, but it seems that our leaders regard that as a Western policy.

Indeed, complained Garašanin, the leaders in power were obeying the instructions of either Russia or Austria.

> I don't agree with those gentlemen. My view is that we should listen to the advice of all European courts, then discuss it ourselves and accept whatever is most helpful to us no matter what the source. If

none of it is useful, we should reject it all and do whatever we find good and useful.

Obeying people outside or criticizing Serbs who had shown previously that they were good patriots was no way to pursue a Serbian policy. The leadership instead should seek support from all powers.

We should no longer for a moment deceive ourselves about Russian omnipotence . . . . Events have shown clearly and forecfully that without our own independent policy, we cannot benefit or progress. We should utilize foreign states but rely on ourselves. Only thus can those outside aid us, since only in a pure policy of our own will foreigners find no obstacles and troubles.

Previously, affirmed Garašanin, he had directed national affairs thus, and he was proposing this same course now.[16]

The Belgrade government of Aleksa Simić, painfully unsure what to do, did nothing. Under the circumstances that may have been the wisest course. In the Council were Russophiles led by Stefan S. Tenka, advocating Serbian alliance with Russia. If Russia is defeated, they argued, Serbia, caught between Turkey and Austria, will have no future and must perish. The Prince leaned toward Austria. Others concluded that Serbia, committing itself to neither side, should pursue armed neutrality. Although Garašanin warned that complete neutrality might prove dangerous, Belgrade adopted armed neutrality only to abandon rearmanet in the face of Austrian pressure. If the West won and Serbia remained neutral, cautioned Garašanin, the western powers would leave her to the mercy of Austria and Turkey. If Austria joined the Western powers against Russia, Serbia could not afford to remain neutral since the West would then reward Austria at Serbia's expense. Instead, Garašanin favored promising the West not to let Russia utilize Serbia in return for a Western guarantee of Serbian autonomy. Actually, Western leaders believed Serbia was committed to Russia and by rearming was preparing to enter the war on her side. Depicting Serbia as Russia's secret ally, Austrian diplomacy urged the West to let Vienna act as its gendarme to restrain Serbia. Garašanin criticized Belgrade for cowardly zigzags which lost it Russia's confidence without obtaining Western support. If the West won the war, he feared, Serbia might become an Austrian protectorate.[17]

Until the summer of 1854, as long as Russia's prospects in the war remained favorable, Tenka's Russophiles, basing their influence on majority public sentiment in Serbia, maintained secret ties with Mukhin, the Russian consul in nearby Zemun. Believing in a Russian victory, early in 1854 Tenka drew up a plan for a future Greater Serbia to be achieved with Russia's help.[18] For her part, early in 1854 Russia made some tempting territorial offers to lure Serbia into the conflict,[19] but Garašanin helped dissuade the Prince from swallowing the bait.

European fears of Russian Panslavism would cease, wrote Garašanin in a draft of 1854, if the powers aided the Turkish Slavs. Instead they were accusing Serbia of following blindly behind Russia which had aided Serbia previously and might now exploit that legacy. Thus Serbia must protect itself skillfully from Russian domination. Belgrade had sought, and must continue to seek, support from other powers which seemed not to understand her plight clearly. By leaving suffering Christians under the Porte, Europe was driving them into Russia's embrace. Gleefully observing Europe's foolish behavior, and benefiting therefrom, Russia was saying in effect:

No matter what doubts you [Serbia] may have about Russia . . . the other powers want . . . to restore you as a simple province of Turkey. We will help deliver you from that fate. Their [Western] consuls have been on your necks, attack you every day and would dominate you if Russia did not stand in their way . . . .[20]

Frequently consulted by Prince Aleksandar, Garašanin during 1854 counselled a policy of watchful waiting. "Your Highness asks me to utilize my contacts to avert the danger which threatens us. Although my contacts have disappeared, I have still done my best but have not been able to succeed better than the rest." That summer for several hours Garašanin had hashed things over with French Consul Segur without reaching a solution. The Prince should wait for the West to correct errors it had committed towards Serbia: "Now is not the time to become angry but rather to remain silent. Though we have reason to be angry, that won't help us. We need to sacrifice pride in order to save ourselves from danger, and must bear whatever happens."[21] By June 1854, with Russia on the defensive, Garašanin was expressing general satisfaction with Premier Aleksa Simić's neutrality policy. He advised adhering to it even if the Russians should win some victories or approached Serbia's frontiers with their army. "I parted from them [Serb leaders] wholly satisfied with their wisdom and moderation." Serbia was no longer linked with Russia, Garašanin concluded, and if pressed by her, should act evasively. Belgrade must still watch Austria closely "which constantly reveals its desire to dominate Serbia, causing me great concern." Despite Belgrade's repeated declarations of neutrality, Austria and the West believed Serbia was still obeying orders from Russia.[22]

After Russia that summer retired behind the Danube and renounced active efforts to enlist Serbia's aid, Prince Aleksandar turned toward Austria to Garašanin's disgust:

> The Prince has yielded wholly to the influence of Austria and the Germans [Nemačkara] and with them . . . believes that he can direct the fate of the Serbian people. . . . Through these two foreign sources, the Prince seeks to protect and demonstrate his rights.[23]

Backed by Britain and France, Vienna protested Serbia's rearmament, concentrated troops on its borders and even threatened invasion. Austria itself, noted Garašanin, had provoked these Serbian preparations. If Vienna would stop threatening, Serbia would not need to arm itself. Favoring strong resistance Garašanin argued that yielding supinely to Austria, Serbia would merely insure her eventual destruction. Involvement in a struggle against Austria would be burdensome and dangerous, to be sure, but disarming out of fear would be worse still.[24] Garašanin reacted indignantly to Austria's disdainful dismissal of Serbia as a helpless land of primitive peasants. Thus Count Karl Buol-Schauenstein, Austrian premier and foreign minister, had told Aleksa Janković, Serbia's special envoy: "Your people does not need arms; give them a pickaxe and a hatchet. Those are the proper tools for them, not weapons." As Janković left, Buol added: "Live, pray to God, and till the soil." As if we hadn't been doing that for centuries as rayahs, snorted Garašanin. "The poor stupid aristocrat! He believes that he controls the destiny of the world and can lecture other peoples without seeing that he should follow his own advice."[25]

Austria deeply resented the Marinović-Garašanin memorandum which, intimating Serbia would resist armed incursions, protested Austrian troop

concentrations and threats. The Porte, Garašanin confirmed to Marinović
in April 1854, had welcomed "our memorandum and actions." Count
Buol thundered that Austria would eventually have its way with Serbia
while Teja Radosavljević, the new Austrian consul in Serbia, warned that
Serbia must cease rearming immediately.[26] "She cannot attack us without
cause," Garašanin wrote Marinović June 22nd, "but she can harm us in
other ways." Only the Porte might support Serbia: "If someone must rule
over Serbia, all Serbs agree it should only be the Turks." The French and
English consuls, their governments seeking Austrian support against Russia,
were urging Belgrade to follow Austrian advice, but Garašanin told them
that bowing to Vienna's demands would compromise Serbia's future. "If
we are left alone to face Austria's arbitrariness," he warned, "it will be jsut
as bad as if we were abandoned to Russia's highhandedness." Could not
Austria ally with the West without doing so at Serbia's expense? "We see
from the actions toward us that our very existence bothers Austria which
is most unjust."[27]

Abandoned by the Western powers, which were busily wooing Austria,
and with Russia in retreat, the Serbian government in July 1854 yielded
to Austrian pressure against rearmament. Thereafter Austrian influence in
Serbia became paramount as Prince Aleksandar timidly following his Austrophile entourage. Garašanin confirmed sadly to Marinović that Belgrade
had agreed to halt armaments and military exercises:

> Thus the government will accept this order, and some day we will
> become Vlachs [without arms or troops]. By this act we are ter-
> ribly unhappy. Our people had begun to feel some independence and
> self-confidence, but this is the scythe severing all hope. We cannot
> get help from anywhere, that is certain. . . . We must depend on
> chance and try not to provide any pretext for some kind of evil.[28]

From 1855 Austrian Consul Radosavljević became, next to the Prince, the
most influential man in Serbia; without his approval Belgrade took no
domestic or foreign action. Radosavljević, noted the Prussian consul, was
constantly at court: "The Austrian consul does not let the Prince out of
his sight for a moment and is able to impose his advice on any occasion.
The Prince undertakes almost nothing until he has asked Radosavljević."[29]
He "takes a major part in all affairs," agreed Garašanin, who feared Austria

might destroy Serbia's remaining autonomy. "I am very upset about that," he wrote Marinović. "There is no longer a Serbian government which defends Serbian interests." Rumors were spread, apparently by Austria and his enemies in Serbia, that Garašanin was plotting with Magyar émigrés. "I do not care if Austria repeats such fables, but I am not going to set foot there [Austria]."[30]

Earlier Garašanin had hoped Serbia could rely on France to reduce the danger of domination or occupation by Austria or Russia. As the war progressed, he grew increasingly disillusioned with French policy which turned more and more Austrophile. Seeking Austrian cooperation against Russia, Paris courted Vienna openly. Formerly, French consuls in Belgrade had been tactful, pleasant and helpful, but now Consul Segur, seeking to alienate Serbia from Russia and win favor from Austria and the Porte, advocated policies humilitating to Serbia. Previously when we talked with the French, Garašanin complained to Mondain, they treated us like a regular nation and realized our potential. Now they are saying: "Who are you? You aren't any sort of power, you are dependent . . . on the great powers." The French still suspected that if Russia began winning victories, Serbia would join her. Garašanin emphasized to Mondain that Serbia could fight for neither side:

> What would the Christian peoples think of us if we practiced such a [pro-Turkish] policy? Could we then count at all on them? The Serbian future can be based only on those peoples, not on the Turks who were the cause of their misfortunes. Thus Serbia must at any cost maintain its previous neutral stance and not go over either to Russia against Turkey or vice-versa.[31]

During 1854-1855 Garašanin grew embittered toward France which earlier he had considered Serbia's best friend and chief bulwark. He was indignant when the French foreign minister, because of Austrian opposition, refused to receive Marinović in 1854 or even allow him to remain in Paris as a secret Serbian envoy. Only Marinović's memorandum backed by Serbia's national militia, he claimed, had prevented an Austrian occupation of the country.[32] It would be pointless to send Marinović back to Paris, Garašanin concluded in 1855, since he would not be welcomed there. Vienna now was deciding everything relating to Serbia since Europe had made Austria the arbiter of Serbia's affairs.[33] "It is evident that France has given itself wholly to Austria, its new friend and ally," he had written Marinović earlier. Although Serbia had sacrificed on behalf of the West for twelve years, France was now ready to abandon her completely:

> We have nothing to regret except that we have been deceived by a power [France] from which we expected much and believed in for so long. Eventually, I believe the West will revert to its former policy but where will we be by then?[34]

By July 1854 Garašanin's disillusionment with Western, especially French, policy toward Serbia was complete:

> All the pretty words from the West over the past years have come to naught. We have definitely been sold out. I don't know how to act now. You understand [he wrote Marinović] how much this depresses me. . . . I have never trusted the Russians and had reason not to. Now I don't believe the other side either. . . .[35]

He reacted bitterly to a secret agreement among Austria, Turkey, England and France allowing Austria under certain circumstances to occupy Serbia and contiguous South Slav lands:

> There is no need to state the impact this caused here among all classes of people and officials. I was very angry at this disgusting action. . . . I find the same meanness now on the Western side that I encountered earlier from the Russians. You cannot imagine how slavishly the two Western consuls act toward Radosavljević, so unlike their former hauteur. . . . We have done everything that was asked of us and that we promised to do and what did they do for us? — they told us to obey Austria in whatever she says.

An Austrian occupation would not harm Serbia, Western diplomats were assuring Marinović smugly, and would strengthen legitimate authority there. Exploded Garašanin: "We cannot obey Austria as the West would have us do."[36]

During the final phase of the Crimean War in 1855, as the Allies besieged the Russian naval base at Sevastopol in the Crimea, Serbia pursued a correct neutrality under Austria's watchful eye. Still consulted regularly by Prince Aleksandar, Garašanin generally approved Premier Simić's cautious policy. Russia's influence in Serbia and the Balkans generally was waning. He wrote Marinović:

> The Russians, it appears to me, have already begun to betray their adherents in Serbia. This is truly an amazing way to act, but it pleases me greatly. Won't our blind men now see what the Russians are really like? They are betraying [their Serbian supporters] cruelly. Vučić intends to go to Vienna. . . .[37]

Meanwhile, Premier Simić, anxious to regain French support, was prepared to yield the premiership to Garašanin, but the latter demurred:

> I can help more from private life than in actual service. If I felt that I could improve matters fundamentally here, I would put everything aside, even my illness, and do my duty as long as possible, but since this would only worsen our situation, why press for it? We must correct our relationship with Austria which we can do if she shows us good will. Instead of entering active service, I would gladly take a greater part in affairs from my present position. . . . From the Russians nothing good can be expected now even less than ever. . . .[38]

Garašanin realized clearly that neither Austria nor the Prince wished him to serve in a high post and that he could not turn Serbia's policy around at that time.

In August 1855 the Allies, by capturing Sevastopol, achieved their main objective in the Crimea. An Austrian ultimatum in December finally induced the new Russian tsar, Alexander II, to seek a negotiated settlement. The Treaty of Paris (March 1856), confirming Russia's defeat, ended its protectorate over Serbia and placed her under the protection of all the powers. Garašanin commented on this to Marinović:

> I hear that the Russians rejoice that things are going badly for us and say: 'You see what your new friends are like? You have gotten rid of our tutelage but were immediately sold out to Austria which does harm to you while the West lets her do whatever she wants. Your

situation is onerous, but you will have to bear it and help yourselves as best you can and not rely on anyone.'[39]

That assessment accorded closely with Garašanin's own. At least under Russian domination, he added, conditions in Serbia had been less chaotic.

Under the Paris Treaty all signatory powers were supposed to agree before armed intervention could occur in Serbia. This would prevent unilateral Austrian incursions, but Garašanin had expected that Serbia's correct neutrality would bring full independence or at least evacuation of the Turkish fortresses. Under the new arrangement, he realized, Vienna could interfere frequently in Serbia's internal affairs. He wrote Mondain:[40]

> If the peoples of Turkey had acquired half the benefits which the French armies won in glory during the war, then together they would sing a hallelujah. . . . In the Treaty it states that Serbian rights will be protected, but the Serbs will only be grateful for this when we are sure of it. I can tell you truly that today we are much less secure externally than when Russia alone disturbed us.

By removing Serbia from dependence on Russia, the Paris Treaty would satisfy Europe, Garašanin concluded, but it left major Balkan questions unresolved. "No one any longer finds wisdom in European diplomacy," he wrote Mondain in September, "and even less skill and courage."[41] The bloody Crimean War had ended fruitlessly. Its lesson was that Serbia must become truly self-reliant:

> For us nothing remains expect to pull back from everything and let them [the powers] act as they wish . . . . It is evident from all this that Serbia can never count on anyone's help, and that which she cannot create for herself, she can never expect from another.[42]

Indeed, Serbia had been most fortunate to escape involvement in the war or even foreign occupation.

NOTES

1. On the background and diplomacy of the Crimean War see Ann P. Saab, *The Origins of the Crimean Coalition* (Charlottesville, Va., 1977); J. S. Curtiss, *Russia's Crimean War* (Durham, N.C., 1979); E. V. Tarle, *Krymskaia voina* (Moscow, 1950), 2 vols.; Petrovich, *A History*, I, 248-250. For Serbia on the eve of the war the most complete treatment is Stranjaković, *Vlada Ustravobranitelja*, pp. 223-261 based on French archives. See also Jovan Ristić, *Spoljašnji odnošaji Srbije novijega doba* (Belgrade, 1887), I. On great power relationships see Paul Schroeder, *Austria, Great Britain and the Crimean War* (Ithaca, NY, 1972). On Franco-Serbian relations see the significant article based on French and Serbian documents of Liljana Aleksić, "Francuski uticaj u spoljašnoj i unutrašnjoj politici Srbije za vreme Krimskog rata (1853-1856)," *Ist. čas.* (Belgrade), XI (1960), pp. 55-87.

2. Stranjaković, "Ilija," pp. 151-152; Milivoj Popović, "Borba Srbije za neutralnost u Krimskom ratu," *Politika*, January 6-9, 1940, p. 16. On Garašanin's overall role during the Crimean War see S. Jovanović, "Spoljašnja politika," pp. 426-428.

3. Garašanin to Marinović, June 18, 1853, *Pisma*, I, 79-82.

4. Ibid. to ibid., June 24, *Pisma*, I, 90.

5. Ibid., pp. 88-91.

6. Ibid., pp. 121-128 and note no. 1, p. 117 on Fonton.

7. Garašanin to Marinović, August 8, *Pisma*, I, 128-135.

8. Ibid., August 15, *Pisma*, I, 143-153.

9. Ibid., September 2, *Pisma*, I, 161.

10. Ibid., May 18, 1854, *Pisma*, I, 175-177. Regretting Mondain's departure, Garašanin wrote: "It is felt here [Belgrade] that his recall is not because he is needed there [Paris] but solely because of [Consul] Segur who seeks to persecute Serbia until it renounces its name. Ibid., p. 176.

11. Začek, "Uloga Zaha," pp. 145-146.

12. IG 871, Garašanin to Knićanin, November 1853.

13. Memo to Countess A. Bludova of December 7, 1853, cited in Michael B. Petrovich, *The Emergence of Russian Panslavism, 1856-1870* (New York, 1956), p. 29.

14. Tarle, *Krymskaia voina*, I, 459-462.

15. S. Jovanović, "Spoljašnja politika," p. 427.

16. IG 935, "Beleška Ilije Garašanina o odnosima velikih sila i Rusije po pitanju spasavanja Turske" (1854?).

17. IG 952, "Kritika Spoljne i unutrašnje politike Kneza Aleksandra (1854); IG 932, Draft of Garašanin on Serbo-Austrian relations (1854?); S. Jovanović, "Spoljašnja politika," pp. 426-429.

18. Stranjaković, "Plana Stefana Stefanovića o podeli Evropske Turske 1854 godine," Politika, May 1-3, 1937, pp. 12-13. Under Tenka's plan, Serbia would obtain Macedonia, northern Albania, Bosnia, Hercegovina, southern Serbia, Novi Pazar, Metohija and part of western Bulgaria on national and strategic grounds in return for allying with a victorious Russia.

19. Vilhelm Gabler to František Palacky, 1855, cited in Začek, "Uloga," pp. 147-148.

20. IG 935, "Beleška."

21. IG 965, Garašanin to Prince Aleksandar, draft 1854; Aleksić, "Francuski uticaj."

22. Garašanin to Marinović, June 20, 1854, Pisma, I, 194-199.

23. IG 960, Garašanin draft. "Germans" seemingly refers to Austrian Serbs in Belgrade who favored Serbia's alignment with Austria.

24. Garašanin to Marinović, July 10, 1854, Pisma, I, 217-219.

25. Ibid., July 12, 221.

26. Ibid., April 22, 162-163.

27. Ibid., June 22 and 24, 200-203.

28. Ibid., July 10, 217-218.

29. S. Jovanović, Ustavobranitelji, p. 143.

30. Garašanin to Marinović, November 27, 1854, Pisma, I, 270-272.

31. IG 945, Garašanin to Mondain, June 1.

32. IG 956, Garašanin to Marinović, draft.

33. IG 995, Garašanin to unknown, draft 1855.

34. Garašanin to Marinović, June 4, 1854, Pisma, I, 186-188.

35. Ibid., July 6, 214.

36. Ibid., July (8), 215-216.

37. Ibid., June 17, 1855, 281.

38. Ibid., July 1855; Aleksić, "Francuski uticaj."

39. Garašanin to Marinović, June 10, 1856, Pisma, I, 300-302.

40. IG 1016, Garašanin to Mondain, July 18, 1856.

41. Ibid, September 28.

42. Garašanin to Marinović, July 3, Pisma, I, 307-308.

CHAPTER X

IN OPPOSITION, 1855-1857

"Our affairs truly get worse day by day. This quarrel between the Prince and the Council has so tangled our internal affairs that one can no longer move . . . . Now neither
side thinks of yielding . . . . Seeing how ordinary things
are tending, I would say that everything is going to ruin."

Garašanin to Marinović, August 6, 1857

From private life and inspired by a patriotic desire to prevent foreign
occupation of Serbia, Garašanin during the Crimean conflict had advised
and supported Prince Aleksandar Karadjordjević's fragile regime. After the
war, growing convinced that the Prince was harming Serbia's national
interests, Garašanin gradually passed into the opposition. Deploring bitter
personal rivalries among Serbian leaders, he criticized severely a ruler who,
contrary to Serbia's constitution, sought with Austrian support to erect a
personal despotism.[1]

Various elements were seeking persistently to restore Garašanin to high
office. In the summer of 1854 Marinović, so as not to offend other ministers, proposed that Garašanin become minister without portfolio and
wrote the Serbian envoy in Constantinople, Konstantin Nikolajević, that
Garašanin's return to power was essential for Serbia's welfare. However,
the ex-premier, realizing that his hands would be tied, rebuffed such

efforts. When the Prince, at the urging of Paris, offered him a post, Garašanin objected: "No one [in Serbia] wants me and I do not like the others' policies." What was needed, he noted, was not himself in office, but the willingness by government leaders to work honestly and patriotically for Serbia's welfare. During 1855 the French and English consuls and Turkish pasha in Belgrade, to quiet discord among Serbian leaders, urged the Prince repeatedly to make Garašanin his premier.

Contributing to Garašanin's persistent refusals to serve was his conviction that Prince Alexander's role had become intolerable. Earlier, he and the Prince had quarreled periodically, but by the mid-1850s Garašanin was condemning Aleksandar's illegal actions openly. On the other side, the Prince in November 1854 had slandered him to the Austrians, and late in 1855, accusing Garašanin and Marinović of conspiring with France to become ministers of state, Aleksandar denounced them as traitors. Existing princely despotism which served Austria, affirmed Garašanin in 1855, should yield to a regime which would defend and uphold the national interest. Acting secretly through his agents, the Prince sought to destroy all useful institutions in Serbia and achieve total power. He aimed to remove from office those who were defending national interests and replace them with obedient creatures. Persecuting those who sought order and legality, the Prince proclaimed as traitors persons dedicated to Serbia's welfare. The Council, Garašanin suggested, remained the best potential defender of natinal interests.[3] From Paris he wrote Magazinović in September 1855: "I will not return on any account to become a supporter of present Serbian policy."[4]

While in France in 1855 Garašanin first urged the prompt removal of Prince Aleksandar from the Serbian throne. On behalf of Premier Simić and the Council majority, he wrote confidentially to French Foreign Minister Florien Walewski on September 29, 1855 declaring that Serbia's bad internal situation could only be corrected if the Porte ordered the Prince categorically to respect its laws and constitution. They had asked Garašanin to represent them in resolving the growing internal crisis with French assistance. The Serbian people, he argued, long ruled by semi-educated princes, needed a proper ruler. Some educated Serbs, noting the paucity of outstanding native Serbian candidates, suggested inviting in a foreign prince under Western protection in order to prevent a revival of Russian influence. Members of the Habsburg and Romanov families and those serving their interests would be excluded. The Serbs would accept a Western-selected, Orthodox prince, affirmed Garašanin, as hereditary ruler and vassal of the Porte. An acceptable alternative would be an outstanding Serbian candidate: Serbs at a national assembly could designate three families with the Porte and its Western allies confirming the most deserving.[5]

When this effort failed and Prince Aleksandar's actions became unreasonable, Garašanin in 1856 wrote him a sincere but sharply-worded letter.[6] Having imposed absolutism on Serbia contrary to the 1838 Constitution, the Prince now should follow the laudable example of Belgium's King Leopold I (1830-1865). A conscientious, constitutional monarch, Leopold had established peace and prosperity, becoming thus more secure than any despot. Conditions in Serbia, Garašanin argued, did not favor absolutism. Since the Serbs in revolts against the Turks had restored their country themselves, the ruler should cooperate with them. Instead Aleksandar had grown preoccupied with personal issues while Serbia's survival hung in the balance. Now he alone could save her from disaster. "If you are fated to fall, better to do so while defending the country and the freedom of its people." He must not scorn his subjects for the sake of foreign powers. "Why do you violate the laws and institutions? Do you believe that this will make you happier? You are greatly mistaken and err toward your own people which favored you." Did the Prince believe he could govern Serbia better alone than with ministers and advisers? If he usurped full power, as his coterie advised, Serbia would be ruined and within a year he would be overthrown. The Prince could not govern the country with servile flatterers who at the first critical moment would abandon him. "Once you begin to overturn free institutions," Garašanin warned, "you will likewise overturn popular rights and then yourself." Instead he should rely on his loyal subjects and carry out his prescribed duties. "Even a simple farmer is happiest when he puts his affairs in good order, so can a ruler be less happy when in his country exists good order, and when the land and people he governs are satisfied and happy?" Garašanin cited Prince Miloš whose apparent omnipotence had evaporated in the face of justified public anger. However, this appeal had no apparent effect on Prince Aleksandar.

The chief internal political struggle in Serbia was between Prince and Council.[7] The Constitution of 1838, issued by the Porte, had failed to specify their respective powers clearly. Never smooth, their relations had remained tolerable until Premier Petronijević died in 1852. Devoted to the Prince and dominant in the Council, the tactful Petronijević had prevented sharp clashes. Premier Garašanin continued these conciliatory policies, but under his successor, Aleksa Simić, their quarrels proceeded unchecked. Once the immediate threat of Austrian occupation passed, the old quarrel resumed. The Prince asserted in March 1855 that the Council's composition contradicted the Constitution; the Council resisted his efforts to name its chairman. By now the Council had grown bureaucratic and lacked widespread public support. Since only three members (Janković, Batalaka, and A. Nenadović) had higher education the Council did not represent the rising intelligentsia either. Its strength lay in its members' personal integrity and influence.

Prince Aleksandar's constitutional and personal position was shaky. Not a hereditary prince, he was widely considered a temporary ruler whose prestige derived solely from being the son of the great Karadjordje. Like his Obrenović predecessors, Miloš and Mihailo, one false step could bring his removal. The timorous prince was excessively devoted to his relatives and entourage and tolerated blatant abuses by favorites which increased his unpopularity. With Aleksandar strongly influenced by his wife and several male Nenadovićs in high posts, including two in the Council, many believed that the Nenadović clan ruled Serbia for its own benefit. The Prince, affirmed Zah, was preoccupied with his own wealth and to salvage it was prepared to flee Serbia. In moments of uncontrollable anger Aleksandar said terrible things which his opponents later used against him. Though often stubborn, he quickly lost patience and courage in the face of opposition or obstacles. Once his brittle resistance collapsed, people could manipulate him virtually at will. Lacking political skill, he failed to utilize public opinion in his behalf, and enjoying support only from a narrow court camarilla, as ruler he was neither respected nor feared. Without the prestige of Garašanin, Knićanin, Petronijević, and Vučić—the outstanding Serbs of his time—Aleksandar could not build an effective autocracy.

Despite the Prince's many weaknesses and shortcomings, the struggle against him proved difficult. He had full support from the standing army whose key positions were held by Colonel Jovan Lukavčević and Kosta Nenadović, his wife's relatives. Austria backed him strongly and since the

Crimean War his ties with Consul Radosavljević remained close. Consequently, Russia, France and even the Porte suspected him.

Garašanin grew pessimistic about Serbia's external vulnerability and domestic deterioration under Aleksandar's rule. In a draft, "The Serbian People's Position after the Crimean War,"[8] he affirmed:

> The situation of this country is so damaged in every way as to cause the greatest concern. . . . For several years the people has been abandoned to arbitrariness and speculation. The leaders have lost all public confidence. Instead of supervising precise execution of the laws and regulations, they have been preoccupied by the struggle for power between the Council and the Prince, violating the laws which governed their mutual relations, making any supervision by the executive authorities impossible . . . . As long as Prince and Council themselves observed existing laws, the executive authorities carried out their duties according to them. . . . But for a long time . . . the only concern has been to which faction does an official belong, leading to neglect of the laws and various abuses concealed by disorder in the government. Extraordinary measures by a wise and patriotic government would be needed to overcome this dangerous trend towards anarchy.

As long as the Austrian consul determined policy, declared Garašanin, he could not accept any official post. However, should the government throw off such foreign tutelage, "I will not hesitate to request service and will serve my country with the same desire and energy as previously. Without that condition I could never accept a post since I would merely be exposed to new torments and dishonor."[9]

Garašanin sided mostly with the Council in its struggle with the Prince. He believed the Council's stance was legal and correct, though he criticized its mistakes in defending existing laws and institutions. The Prince, on the other hand, was acting illegally and undermining the country's basic structure. He rejected the Prince's claim that Council members were seeking personal authority; they had a duty to oppose princely despotism. Criticizing the Prince for yielding to Austrian—and the Council to Russian—influence, he believed that both should reject foreign control and work solely for Serbian interests.[10]

Garašanin urged a return to existing constitutional practice. Prince and Council should each regulate and limit the other. Trouble had developed when the Prince began violating laws, accepting Austrian dictation, and frequently shifting ministers and officials. Aleksandar regarded official posts as his personal possessions, handing them out to cronies and removing capable officials at whim.[11] To remedy this problem, Garašanin suggested forming a commission of the four ministers and six councillors to harmonize their relationships. However, the Prince, stung by Garašanin's criticisms, avoided discussing affairs of state with him. When they met in Kragujevac in August 1856, the Prince acted much afraid of him.

The quarrel between Prince and Council, affirmed Garašanin, boiled down to two issues. The Prince, believing the Council was usurping his rightful powers, was acting to prevent it. The Council claimed that in seeking to restrict princely authority it was acting constitutionally and properly. Both sides appealed to existing laws. A new, legal solution was needed in accordance with national interests. "We all bear burdens on our backs," Garašanin concluded, "but when we all load this burden onto one very incapable back [the Prince's], we cannot go forward."[12]

Meanwhile Consul Radosavljević had been reporting to Vienna that Garašanin was opposing the Prince in order to make himself premier or even prince. He claimed in February 1855 that Garašanin was backing the Council and courting England and France in a concerted direve for the princely title. Prince Aleksandar himself believed that Garašanin coveted his throne, reported the consul that December.[13] Such assertions were without foundation. While some Serbian leaders criticized him for not joining the factional struggles, Garašanin held himself aloof from domestic politics explaining that neither faction, one pro-Russian and the other pro-Austrian, was working to benefit Serbia. "Let one of these factions become a national party and I will support it; otherwise I don't wish to get involved."[14]

The Council, denying that the Prince could impose its chairman, demanded that four empty seats be filled with its candidates. Pretending to name ministers only "temporarily," the Prince evaded the constitutional requirement that ministers be drawn from the Council. Summoning representatives of both sides to the Belgrade fortress, the Turkish pasha urged them to end their wrangling and declared that the Porte would itself interpret the Constitution of 1838. Each side then submitted to the Porte a new draft constitution embodying its arguments. The Prince sought Turkish recognition as hereditary Serbian ruler; the Council urged the Sultan to expel Prince Aleksandar forthwith. The Sultan refused to honor these requests. Naming a non-Council member, A. Nenadović, as minister, the Prince prevailed temporarily, then issued a proclamation as to how the Paris Treaty affected Serbia, neglecting to consult his ministers or Council. Garašanin promptly warned that Aleksandar was usurping powers belonging under the Constitution to the Council and the people.[15]

By the summer of 1856 Garašanin and other leaders realized that Serbia urgently needed a more vigorous cabinet since the Prince had no one to help him avert grave external threats. "None of the present leaders understands anything... ," he wrote Marinović. He would refrain from all political activity so no one could suspect him reasonably of seeking power. With the Council rudderless and discouraged, until a new cabinet had been chosen properly, the Prince would continue his non-constitutional course. Suddenly Acika Nenadović, the top princely adviser, asked the amazed Garašanin for advice on selecting a new ministry. The Prince, responded Garašanin evasively, should pick capable men who could handle Vučić and protect the country from disaster. Little could be accomplished, remarked Nenadović, unless the cabinet enjoyed rapport with Garašanin. When Council chairman, Stevan S. Tenka, urged Garašanin on July 2nd to accept the premiership, he refused flatly: "Anyone can run that position now easier than I can."[16]

The Prince deplored Garašanin's severe criticisms of his proclamation about the Paris Treaty, but the ex-minister told Aleksandar's envoy, Matija Ban, that the Prince should have consulted the Council before issuing it.[17] Declining again to serve in any capacity, Garašanin agreed with Ban that younger men such as Filip Hristić and Marinović should form a new ministry. The very next day Nenadović, informing him the Prince would appoint such a cabinet, requested Garašanin to urge Marinović to return promptly to Belgrade. Clearly Aleksandar desired Garašanin's support for the new government. While favoring such a ministry, Garašanin warned that he could back the Prince only if he altered his policies. "I told Acika [Nenadović] that I am no longer such a friend of the Prince as formerly... but would always respond sincerely if he pursued a wise course." Marinović and Nikolajević, whom he believed should occupy the chief posts, could bargain over a new cabinet.[18]

Political negotiations dragged on interminably. A ministry should be formed before a new Russian consul arrived, warned Garašanin, to prevent intrigues by Vučić's Russophiles. The Prince had discussed Russian policy rather sensibly with him recently, he wrote Marinović August 23rd,[19] while avoiding urgent matters of state. The present rotten situation could only be corrected by judicious use of princely authority:

If things in Serbia remain as they are, Europe will have pretexts to prepare new protocols and decisions most unfortunate for her. Men need to be selected who can follow a consistent policy and direct public affairs which are now in disorder. Such a system should then be supported by every good patriot.

Garašanin urged swift creation of a cabinet with Nikolajević as premier, Marinović as interior minister, Nikola Hristić for justice, and "whomever you three want as finance minister." To eliminate pretexts for criticism, no Austrian Serbs should be included.

Finally, on September 16, 1856 the Prince appointed a new cabinet, though not the one Garašanin had recommended. Aleksa Simić became premier, Stevan Marković took over justice, Nikolajević interior, and Marinović finance. Garašanin rejoiced that his friend was in the cabinet but regretted that he held the politically insignificant finance ministry. By naming two non-Council members (Nikolajević and Marinović) as ministers and appointing Acika Nenadović to the Council without its approval, the Prince had doubly violated its prerogatives. Thus his quarrel with the Council persisted. At its meeting of September 21st the Council denounced these princely moves as illegal. The ministers responded reassuringly that the Prince would cooperate with the Council and named a commission of four councillors and the four ministers to study disputed issues. Aleksandar appeared at this juncture to be prevailing over the Council.[20]

But no reconciliation was achieved as Prince and Council continued to quarrel over every issue and minor squabbles became major confrontations. The conviction grew that one side or the other would be destroyed. The Prince's uncharacteristic boldness suggested Austrian prompting. Most Serbian leaders consisered this Austrian tutelage a national misfortune, but the Prince hoped with Vienna's support to obtain the long coveted hereditary title. With the Council full of Russophiles, Aleksandar's pro-Austrian foreign policy complemented his campaign against the Council. However, he needed more domestic support to prevail. Seeking to align Garašanin more firmly with the new cabinet, the court restored him to the Council where he resumed active membership on March 28, 1857. In June the cabinet was reconstructed: Simić yielded the premiership to Stevan Marković, a close friend of the Austrian consul; the other ministers retained their posts in an openly Austrophile cabinet. Acika Nenadović became Aleksandar's "grey eminence" and chief tactician. In pro-Western and Paris-educated Konstantin Nikolajević he found a statesman who advocated restricting the Council's authority and forging close ties with the Porte.

But Prince Aleksandar's efforts to create a personal regime by emasculating the Council foundered on his lack of prestige and popular support. Needing the active backing of either Garašanin or Vučić but disagreeing politically with both, he avoided a true alliance with either. The Prince might win their temporary support against the Council but not for his spineless foreign policy, subservient to Austria. Instead he sought only apparent reconciliation with them in order to utilize their prestige, but that could succeed only while they quarreled. At first each oligarch approached the court out of dislike for the other while politicians of the camarilla exploited their rivalry to erect a princely despotism. But Vučić and Garašanin could be outplayed only temporarily. Once they realized that they were being used, they would combine forces, leaving the Prince support only from his relatives, the army, Austrian Serbs and a few Western-educated leaders. Once the great names sided with the Council, the weakness of the princely regime would be revealed.

The crisis of the "Defenders'" regime, stressed Jovan Milićević,[21] was also socioeconomic, affecting the state organism down to the smallest village. Patriarchal relationships were disintegrating in villages where over ninety percent of Serbia's population still resided and where difficulties were caused by a gradual influx of money into what had been a natural economy. Serbian officials had become under Garašanin's leadership an omnipotent police bureaucracy with a privileged social position whose illegal acts were simply overlooked. While in power Garašanin had punished such malfeasance severely, but now the Prince's nephew, Aleksandar Tripković, as district chief of Zaječar, had exploited the peasantry ruthlessly. The Prince protected him from accusations raised by the Council. The "Defenders" failed to implement basic reforms to remedy such abuses, and the Council itself had become a closed corporation of high privileged officials. During 1857 Prince and Council sparred over Tripković's misdeeds and other issues. In August the Council issued a protest enumerating Prince Aleksandar's illegal actions. Commented Garašanin:

> The greatest offense is that the Prince has shown such a strong desire to wreck the Council as an institution. The doubts which have arisen in the Council as a consequence will not be dispelled until the Prince renounces that intention by some formal document. The Council realizes, as we all do, that the Prince by his violations of law aims to remove all obstalces to his arbitrary rule.

Such an anomalous situation could satisfy few. Fault could also be found with some Council members who advocated giving more power to a prince guilty of gross maladministration. Patriots should induce the Prince to obey the law. Once limits had been set on his authority, the Council could be reformed. To attempt both simultaneously would prove ineffective and produce useless discord.[22]

At the Council's summons, Garašanin, leaving rural Grocka for nearby Belgrade, wrote Marinović July 25th:[23]

> There is nothing new—dead calm prevails. We remain in discord over whether the Prince or Council should predominate; people talk now about nothing else. Unless there are some basic improvements, everything will go to ruin.

Widespread Obrenovite agitation throughout Serbia was worrying the government. Colonel Lukavčević, regular army commander, had rushed to Kragujevac to take precautionary measures. Garašanin believed such reports were exaggerated, but his letter to Marinović of August 6th depicted Serbia in an alarming state of discord:[24]

> Our affairs truly get worse day by day. This quarrel between the Prince and the Council has so tangled our internal affairs that one

can no longer move. As long as there was some give on both sides, once could accomplish something, but now neither side thinks of yielding. . . . I have often criticized the Council for not according more trust to princely authority, but when I consider how unscrupulously that authority acts in everything, I feel I should refrain from such criticism. An intelligent person does not know what to do. Without a new system we cannot survive. . . . Arbitrary action prevails so strongly on every hand that no one takes any account of reason or patriotism. Thus we won't be able to prevent the powers from intervening. . . . Our government has become chaotic. We truly deserve the sharpest condemnation. We have run our affairs so badly that even the powers can do nothing to benefit us.

Drastic action was now imperative to avert collapse of the government. Recently, he wrote Marinović August 11th,[25] even Acika Nenadović had expressed deep concern about the domestic situation, criticized the Prince's behavior sharply and admitted that things seemed hopeless. He wondered who had advised Aleksandar to appoint the blatant Austrophile, Marković, as premier. The Prince had done so, replied Garašanin, after Marinović had refused the premiership. Pessimistically he wrote his friend:

Everyone says let things run their course since they cannot remain as they are. Our government has lost all direction and cannot recapture it. Within it prevails extreme disagreement and anger . . . . One can anticipate only collapse which eventually will occur of itself.[26]

At this critical juncture Garašanin decided reluctantly to travel to Paris. His two friends there, Marinović and Mondain, were urging him to come to join his son, Svetozar, until he entered technical school. For some time Garašanin had worried about Svetozar's deficient self-discipline and unwillingness to work hard. Thus in mid-August 1857 he obtained a two month leave from the Council and remained in Paris until that November. He was thus still abroad when the "Tenka Plot" erupted in Serbia.

From Paris on September 30th he wrote Marinović, who had returned to Belgrade, blaming Vučić largely for the breakdown of law and order in Serbia. If the Prince destroyed the Council opposition, that would merely provoke an even more dangerous one. "Only if the Prince gained victory over himself would all opposition cease and be unable to reform." Council members should draw up a list of the regime's defects and present it to the Prince; if he punished them for so doing, it would be his responsibility. If the Council rejected Garašanin's suggestions, then "let someone propose a better way to correct our miserable situation, and I will speedily endorse it." Vučić's solution of Russian tutelage was, however, "the worst poison for Serbia." Indeed, "that plague of the people," (Vučić) had shifted course recently like a chameleon.

> I propose what I have always proposed to the Prince, the Council and the people. I believe that we should handle our own problems and could do so if we all had enough patriotism, but that is lacking. Neither Prince nor Council will yield to the other, so what else remains to halt our slide into chaos: what do those gentlemen propose? Nothing other than foreign intervention.[27]

Unknown to Garašanin another method of solving them was being planned: murder. Catastrophe overtook the Council in September 1857 with the revelation of "Tenka's Plot" to kill Prince Aleksandar.[28] Involved were its chairman, Stefan S. Tenka, three Council members (Paun Janković, Pavle Stanišić and Raja Damjanović), and the head of the Supreme Court, Cvetko Rajović. After the authorities learned that a hired killer, Milosav Petrović, a peasant, was to murder the Prince at Brestovačka Banja, a spa, the leaders were apprehended and imprisoned. Petrović had blackmailed the conspirators and a relative had informed the authorities. Before the court the conspirators revealed that they had been paid by Prince Miloš through an agent, Dr. Pacek. Linking themselves firmly with the Council opposition, the chief plotters told the investigating commission that the entire Council, except for the Prince's relatives and M. Trifunović, had favored removing Aleksandar. The Council had indeed discussed this, admitted Aleksa Simić, but had not decided to act. Some Serbian leaders had wanted a European Commission to investigate the Prince-Council dispute; others wished to remove the Prince by revolt or a national assembly. The chief conspirators then had decided to kill the Prince, as the Council majority had supposedly desired secretly. To conceal their ties with Prince Miloš, the conspirators depicted the plot at the logical outcome of the Council's opposition. Anxious to compromise and destroy the Council, the investigating commission accepted that view. The government sought to implicate a maximum number of councillors but could merely affirm, not prove, that other disgruntled Council members had wished to remove the Prince.

Effects of the Tenka Plot spread in ever widening circles throughout Serbian political life. Initially, the chief plotters were condemned to death, but the Porte secured commutation of their sentences to life imprisonment at hard labor at Gurgusovac prison. The government threatened six additional councillors with prosecution unless they resigned. Having to choose between prison and sizable state pensions, they all resigned. The government considered three other Council members to have been compromised: Aleksa Simić, Ilija Novaković and Ilija Garašanin. Novaković resigned but his resignation was held in abeyance to insure his compliance. Simić left voluntarily. Only Garašanin resolutely refused to resign, and being in Paris was beyond reach.[29]

Even the regime admitted that Garašanin was not involved directly in the conspiracy, but it considered him nonetheless the Council's ringleader in opposing the Prince. Asserting that Garašanin had known of Tenka's conversation with Miloš, but not that the Prince was to be killed, Tenka's confession implicated him. The cabinet requested Garašanin to resign from the Council or face prosecution.[30]

A letter from Soka first informed Garašanin of Tenka's Plot. "This news amazed and worried me," he wrote Marinović October 4th, "since it will worsen the situation there. Can one believe that they were so reckless as to undertake such a revolting idea which no one can justify?" Might the whole affair have been a police provocation? Marinović surely knew how strongly he deplored crimes like murder.[31]

From Paris on November 2nd Garašanin commented at length to Marinović about the Tenka affair, noting that it should have been separated from the Prince-Council quarrel, which involved neither murder nor revolt. Mere dissatisfaction was not criminal and should not be submitted to Serbian courts which were subject to government control. "The guilty must be punished severely, but the honor of the innocent must also be protected." Garašanin on principle adamantly refused to resign because the Prince was seeking unfairly to implicate him in the conspiracy. The conspirators, he wrote later, had told him nothing about their plans. Fonblanque, the English consul, confirmed in his report of October 22nd:

Garašanin was "free from blame." A letter to Garašanin from the conspirator, D. Janković, confirmed his ignorance of their intentions. Though deeply upset at efforts to drag him into the plot, Garašanin wrote Marinović that he would return home when Svetozar had begun his schooling:

> Surely now my service [in the Council] must cease, but it can occur in only two ways: *either I will resign voluntarily and wholly independently of those events, or the government will accuse me like the others, try, and perhaps imprison me* (Garašanin's italics).

He would act to safeguard his honor and integrity and did not fear imprisonment. He could look any judge in the eye since he knew, as did others, that he had not been involved in the plot.[32]

Next day (November 3rd) Garašanin expressed to Marinović his profound disillusionment at his countrymen's actions:

> Nothing interests men any more that occurs in that unfortunate country [Serbia] or what people say and think about it. I have suffered so much unpleasantness, bitterness and humilitation that except for my childhood, my entire life consists wholly of these . . . , and I suffer these all in vain. When they now accuse me of complicity in the plot and threaten me with trial or removal, what a nice reward for my good will and efforts to create something good for this country!

Apparently realizing he was indulging in excessive self-pity, Garašanin admitted he might have exaggerated and should not write that way. But would not someone who had been injured and humiliated at times go to extremes?

> Thus the Prince awaits my resignation? My resignation from service is truly simple and easy since my wishes agree wholly with his and this may be the only thing we agree upon fully. How well it will suit him when there is no longer a single Garašanin in service; it will be an equally happy day for me. But if I must do so as a participant in attempted murder, I cannot do so. It is a much greater punishment to brand with such a lie someone who never had the intention to remove him from this world.

Some councillors might have discussed revolt or murdering the Prince, but not he. Though dissatisfied with Prince Aleksandar, he had refrained from agitating against him publicly. As to his resignation, only the form and time presented problems. He would not allow his withdrawal to be linked with the plot in any way. If it were separated from it, he would submit his resignation gladly "since we realize that I could not serve either the country or anyone in it any longer." Garašanin would freely tell the courts, the Prince, or the world all that he had done and why. While refusing to obey any foreign consul, he could defend himself unaided.[33]

Actually Garašanin was overdramatizing his case and overestimating his danger. Realizing that he was involved only indirectly, the government wisely decided to leave him alone. Nor did it bother Vučić, though a leading follower, Damjanović, had been a ringleader in the conspiracy. Both men were far too popular at home, and Garašanin also abroad, to prosecute. Initially, revelation of Tenka's Plot had enhanced Prince Aleksandar's popularity, but that changed after reports multiplied of maltreatment of the imprisoned conspirators. The growing scandal at Gurgusovac prison soon destroyed any princely gains.[34] "As a man and a Serb," commented Garašanin, "I would have greatly preferred execution to being exposed to such ridicule . . . . Better death lasting a few moments than lengthy torture from winter and frost." He would resign upon arrival in Belgrade, he wrote Marinović November 12th, unless they tried to link it with the Tenka affair. "In any case I cannot serve with that crowd."[35]

Tenka's Plot devastated the old oppositionist Council: four members were imprisoned, six forced to resign, and one—A. Simić—resigned voluntarily. Of the remaining six, two (Garašanin and Novaković) had been compromised and were prepared to leave office. Only four members remained firmly in place: J. and A. Nenadović, the Prince's relatives; Trifunović, a loyal supporter of the dynasty; and the clever intriguer, Aleksa Janković. But decapitating the Council proved unpopular in Serbia; people knew that resignations had been involuntary. "Resignations don't come in bunches," commented *Srpski Dnevnik*. The Prince, many believed, had no right to persecute Council members just for opposing him; his actions resembled a *coup d'état*. Nonetheless, it looked for a time as if he had succeeded fully. The Council was refilled with princely adherents: relatives, district chiefs, and officials jealous of their careers. But when Aleksandar failed to follow this up by revising the Constitution, opposition resurfaced in the Council.[36]

Resistance to the Prince outside the Council would prove much more formidable. Councillors who had been removed or forced to resign plotted to return to office, and Garašanin conferred with them at his home. Retaining formal Council membership, he never attended meetings, ostensibly from ill health. Garašanin now felt he owed the Prince nothing and was ready to lead the non-Council opposition. Now he viewed the Prince's quarrel with the Council as one between Austrian domination and the national spirit. "The Prince has delivered himself wholly to Austria and the *Nemačkari,* and in alliance with them thinks he can direct the fate of the Serbian people. The Council remains the defender of national rights and thus must surround itself purely with national adherents. . . ."[37]

The opposition's plan of campaign was simple. By firing six Council members the Prince had in fact dissolved the Council, violating the Constitution. The fired members could now appeal to the Porte, guarantor of that document, and to the powers. While in Paris Garašanin had already begun working in that direction. But first the powers must conclude that Aleksandar had truly attempted to overthrow the constitution. Here the Russian and French consuls aided the non-Council opposition. On bad terms with the Prince even before Tenka's Plot, they now gleefully reported his blunders in dealing with the conspiracy, depicting dismissal of the six members as a coup to destroy the Council. French Consul Bernard des Essards, advising the six not to resign, threatened to break relations with the Prince, and persuaded his fellow consuls and the Belgrade pasha to lodge a joint protest with the Serbian government.

By then France and Russia were cooperating against Austria and its influence in Serbia and elsewhere. They viewed increased princely power as enhancing Austrian influence. Thus when St. Petersburg and Paris learned from their Belgrade consuls that the Prince had emasculated the Council and made himself dictator, they decided to intervene. On October 13th the six members resigned. Already on the 21st Baron Edouard Thouvenel, French ambassador to Constantinople, urged the Porte to investigate the affair. The Turks promptly affirmed the right to send a commissar to Serbia, though only on November 10th did the Grand Vizier, demanding explanations from Aleksandar, note that firing Council members without the Porte's consent violated Serbia's consititution.[38]

Believing that France and Russia, not the Porte, were its chief enemies, Aleksandar's regime sought Austrian support. Serbia was "exposed to the blows of Russia and France," Premier Marković explained to Vienna, "because the former finds among the conspirators its most enthusiastic adherents and the latter believes that with the cabinet's removal, it can entrust the government to its friends." Marković denied any need for a Turkish commissar. Curiously, Austria failed to buttress the Belgrade regime. The Porte, concluded Count Buol, had every right to intervene. Not until January 1858 did he instruct his ambassador in Constantinople to oppose the dispatch of a Turkish commissar. By then the Porte had already resolved to send one while remaining secretive about his objectives.[39] Apparently, the Turks dispatched the commissar, Etem Pasha, under Franco-Prussian pressure to preempt the convening of a European commission which would have reduced Turkish authority in vassal Serbia. The coming to Belgrade of Etem Pasha would be fraught with the gravest consequences for Prince Aleksandar Karadjordjević.

NOTES

1. For the final years of Aleksandar Karadjordjević's rule see Petrovich, *A History*, I, 251-259; S. Jovanović, *Ustavobranitelji*, pp. 112-183; J. Milićević, *Jevrem Grujić*, pp. 53-59; *Pisma Garašanina Marinoviću*, I, 272 ff.; and D. Ilić, *Toma Vučić-Perišić*.

2. IG 991, Garašanin to Magazinović, September 12, 1855; L. Aleksić, "Francuski uticaj," pp. 72-73; A. I. Ristić XXV/305, K. Nikolajević to A. Nenadović, July 17, 1854; *Pisma*, I, 234, August 2 and 259, September 2-3.

3. IG 952, "Kritika," (1854).

4. IG 991, Garašanin to Magazinović, September 12, 1855.

5. IG 982, "Kritika vlade Kneza Aleksandra." This proposal of Garašanin of October 1855, apparently remained unknown to Prince Aleksandar.

6. Garašanin to Prince Aleksandar (IG 1026?) (1856?) in Stranjaković, "Ilija," pp. 118-120.

7. On this quarrel see especially S. Jovanović, *Ustavobranitelji*, pp.

129 ff. and IG 1003, "Šta ima uči u dogovaranje Komisije i o čemu je raspra," draft by Garašanin, and IG 1008, "Kritika."

8. IG 1004, "Stanje srbskog naroda posle Krimskog rata," Garašanin draft of 1856.

9. IG 1008, Garašanin draft of 1856.

10. IG 984, Garašanin draft of 1855.

11. IG 1026, Garašanin draft of 1857 on the need for the Prince to change his behavior; IG 982, "Kritika."

12. IG 1003, "Sta ima uči,"

13. Stranjaković, "Ilija," p. 174, citing Radosavljević's reports to Vienna located in HHSA (Vienna).

14. IG 951, Garašanin to unknown (1854).

15. S. Jovanović, Ustavobranitelji, pp. 133-135.

16. Garašanin to Marinović, July 3, 1856, Pisma, I, 307-312.

17. Ibid., July 8, 314-317.

18. Ibid., July 9, 318-319.

19. Ibid., August 23, 327-329.

20. Ibid., late September, 330.

21. J. Miličević, Jevrem Grujić, pp. 53-55.

22. IG 1029, "Najveća uvreda," Garašanin draft of 1857.

23. Garašanin to Marinović, July 25, Pisma, I, 335.

24. Ibid., August 6, 342-343.

25. Ibid., August 11, 346-347.

26. Ibid., August 12, 347-348.

27. Ibid., September 30, 356-357.

28. On Tenka's Plot see S. Jovanović, Ustavobranitelji, pp. 154-161.

29. Ibid., pp. 161 ff.

30. Ibid., pp. 164-165.

31. Garašanin to Marinović, October 4, 1857, Pisma, I, 362.

32. Ibid., November 2, 372-379.

33. Ibid., November 3, 380-386.

34. S. Jovanović, Ustavobranitelji, pp. 162-165.

35. Garašanin to Marinović, November 12, Pisma, I, 395-397.

36. S. Jovanović, pp. 164-167.

37. Ibid., pp. 168-169.

38. Ibid., pp. 170-173.

39. Ibid., pp. 173-174.

CHAPTER XI

BACK IN THE SADDLE (January-October 1858)

"Never has Prince Aleksandar had fewer followers among the people. The latest events and especially his actions against the convicted plotters has made everyone disagree with his intentions. Not only can he not count at all on the support of the new Council, but everything is breaking down and no one believes that the present situation can persist unchanged."

Garašanin to Mondain, January 21, 1858

Plunging into Serbia's political turmoil after returning from Paris in November 1857, Garašanin soon gathered most reins of power in his hands. Achieving reconciliation with the still popular Vučić, he returned to the cabinet in March 1858 as Interior Minister and became preeminent in the Council. Once again he controlled the police, officialdom and the army. As a groundswell of discontent mounted against the regime of Prince Aleksandar, Garašanin exploited this movement skillfully to prepare the way for convening a national assembly. Clearly, such a body would demand removal of the Prince, restoration of the Obrenović dynasty, and rescuing Serbia from dependence on Austria.[1]

Everything happening in Serbia, reported French Consul Segur in December 1857, was prepared and executed by Austria. The Austrian premier,

Count Buol-Schauenstein, delcared confidently to a Serbian envoy, Milivoje Blaznavac:

> Tell Prince Aleksandar not to fear but to continue on as he has been doing and we will support him energetically. But if he renounces this course, we can do nothing for him. The Porte will do everything we wish, and as to the attitudes of the other powers, there is no need to worry.[2]

As late as March 1858 Austrian dominance in Serbia still seemed complete. Meeting almost daily with the Prince, Consul Radosavljević remained confident that all would proceed as he had predicted. The Consul, Garašanin informed Mondain, had intrigued against him and sought to link him with Tenka's Plot. Radosavljević had been genuinely sorry that Garašanin did not suffer the fate of the prisoners at Gurgusovac. "Vučić and I stood like bones in his throat. Mr. Radosavljević wants to eliminate all Serbs of any importance, then he believes that Serbia would be finished." He added: "That consul truly is upsetting our whole country. In short he is clearly directing all our affairs." Premier Marković was spending more time conversing and consulting with the Austrian consul than with the Prince and his fellow ministers. Other consuls realized this and knew that it violated the spirit of the Paris Treaty, but "Europe is silent as if nothing is happening."[3] Such Austrian interference was angering Serbian patriots and the pro-Russian peasantry. Garašanin believed that to end Austrian domination, the Prince must be removed.

To oust the Prince and undercut Austrian influence, Garašanin needed to achieve reconciliation with Vučić who possessed the essential mass support. Both oligarchs opposed princely despotism and Austrian predominance:

> Vučić was in open opposition to Aleksandar Karadjordjević. . . .
> Vučić was a unique phenomenon. . . . I was in constant contact with him but still could not be wholly sure of that unusual man. His popularity in Serbia was not cooked up, nor was it based only on certain segments of the population; it was genuine and general. . . .
> He cultivated his popularity assiduously, always opposed arbitrariness by the rulers. . . . The Serbian people had full confidence in him.[4]

Early in 1858, Garašanin and Vučić, long antagonistic, drew together to destroy a regime which they had helped to create sixteen years earlier.

By 1858 Aleksandar Karadjordjević's regime combined the negative attributes of autocracy: brutality, corruption and delay, with few compensating advantages. Documents piled up, decisions were put off, and corruption was rife. The authorities acted haughtily and roughly toward the peasantry to stifle protests. Abroad, where strong policies were needed to protect Serbia's rights against neighboring powers, Belgrade revealed softness and weakness. Thereby Prince Aleksandar alienated the populace and drove his enemies together in opposition. So isolated had the regime become that it might be overthrown with minimal resistance.

Opposition to the Prince grew daily behind an unofficial triumvirate of Garašanin, Serbia's chief statesman; Vučić, its greatest demagogue; and Miša Anastasijević, one of its wealthiest men. The latter joined the opposition chiefly to rescue his brother-in-law, Raja Damjanović, from Gurgusovac prison. The prisoners' families, many very influential, agitated for the prisoners' release as the public grew increasingly critical of their mistreatment. Joining the opposition were younger educated men friendly with Garašanin such as Jevrem Grujić and Kosta Magazinović.[5]

Leading the opposition, Garašanin had by now renounced all cooperation with the Prince and was committed secretly to his removal. He resolved to utilize the Turkish commissar, Etem Pasha, to foster his aims, though it remained uncertain precisely when the commissar would arrive in order to bring stability into Serbian affairs. Serbia's position would only worsen, Garašanin believed, if Etem merely sought to patch things up. He wrote Mondain January 17, 1858: "Things are so badly torn that patching cannot be considered." The Marković government was foundering: ministers let subordinates run their agencies while they drank coffee with the Prince until dinner time. Mistrusting one another, ministers shared secrets with the Prince while keeping their colleagues in the dark. "There has never been a more disorganized or careless ministry in Serbia. Everyone realizes the situation is bad, but no one . . . tries to correct matters." Premier Marković was being dubbed ironically: "the minister of foreign affairs."[6]

Describing Garašanin's key role in organizing the opposition, Jevrem Grujić found himself drawn irresistibly into a conspiracy against Aleksandar's regime.[7] Born in a village near Garašanin's, Grujić had been studying in Paris on a state scholarship and corresponding with Garašanin.

Strolling along Paris boulevards in 1857, they discussed at length Serbia's political plight. Young Grujić's ability, strong interest in politics, and independent stance had impressed Garašanin. When incautious journalistic activity cost Grujić his state stipend, he obtained a loan from Garašanin after rejecting offers of financial aid from Vučić and Prince Miloš since he did not wish to be obligated to them. Just before Etem Pasha reached Belgrade, Garašanin asked Grujić to draw up a memorandum detailing the Prince's illegal and unconstitutional acts in order to win support from Etem and foreign consuls.[8] The Council opposition, noted Grujić, had resolved to convene a national assembly to remove the Prince in favor of a regency, then have a great national assembly elect a new ruler. Grujić urged Garašanin himself to become a candidate as "the best man to develop [Serbia's] external independence and unify all Serbs," and wished to serve as one of his administrators. Grujić advocated fusing their opposition with that of the Council. With the memorandum, Garašanin counted on winning Etem's support in order to restore the six members to the Council and convene a national assembly which would remove the Prince and set up a three-man regency. The latter, warned Grujić, would be unpopular in Serbia and might be opposed by Austria and Russia. The regency, responded Garašanin, would retain office very briefly and be followed promptly by a great national assembly to elect a new prince.[9] The opposition, recalled Grujić, was agitating among the people, with the Turks and was supported by the Russian and French consuls who shared its dislike of Aleksandar's regime.

However, the liberal Grujić did not remain intimately aligned for long with Garašanin When Etem Pasha arrived in Belgrade March 17th:

> I ceased all political work ... and taking on an independent position, [became] wholly neutral and indifferent except on the national assembly which ... I demanded and defended before all groups as a popular institution. And because of that neutrality, all groups sought me out.

Deliberately, Grujić did not visit Etem and saw little of the preoccupied Garašanin. To Grujić's dismay, by late March Garašanin seemed to have abandoned plans to remove the Prince. Temporarily, Grujić broke off political ties with him believing they could not achieve great national goals together.[10]

Even before Etem's arrival, the Prince and opposition started wooing him. Despite an invitation from the Prince, Etem stayed at the Turkish governor's. The opposition hastened to present its views to him before he could meet with the Prince and the government. At his first audience with the Prince on March 19th, Etem demanded that the Gurgusovac prisoners be released to the Porte's custody along with all documents concerning their trial. Etem gave him twenty-four hours to consult the Council. Talking with the prisoners' relatives and foreign consuls (Radosavljević was unaccountably absent), Etem was converted completely by the opposition. Almost everyone in Serbia, Etem concluded, opposed the Prince who should leave the country. Next day the Prince pardoned the prisoners and his adherents lost heart. Encouraged by financial offers from Anastasijević, the Turkish commissar sought the removal of Prince Aleksandar.

However, Etem's mission ended in compromise. On the eve of his second audience with the Prince on March 25th, rumors spread in Belgrade that Aleksandar's fall was imminent. Apparently, the timorous prince had already composed his letter of abdication when news arrived that Turkish Foreign Minister Fuad had declared that Etem lacked authorization to force the Prince's removal. Nevertheless, the expelled members were readmitted to the Council and Aleksandar pledged to restore Vučić and Garašanin to leading posts if the Council would overlook his illegal actions. For the moment all sides seemed to favor compromise and reconciliation even though the settlement favored the opposition more than the regime. Apparently to supervise the settlement, Etem remained in Belgrade until mid-April.[11]

In late March a new ministry was formed with Garašanin as Interior Minister and dominant figure. "Had I not accepted it," he wrote, "people would have asked: 'What does Garašanin want?'" It was easier to act than withdraw completely while genuine danger threatened Serbia. According to Radosavljević, Garašanin had organized the cabinet which would favor France and oppose the Prince and Austria. Vučić, although made chairman of the Council, had been outplayed, concluded the Consul. In fact Garašanin controlled both domestic and foreign policy, though Stevan Magazinović became premier and foreign minister. The other ministers were D. Crnobarac (justice) and J. Veljković (finance). For the first time in years the cabinet consisted exclusively of Council members, and only one minister, Crnobarac, had not been implicated in some way in Tenka's

Plot. The Prince accepted this government reluctantly being unable to govern longer with Marković's inept, unpopular cabinet. Calling in Garašanin and Vučić, Aleksandar had declared: "Go and act as you feel is best." Everyone expected immediate salvation from the new ministry, Garašanin realized, yet to rescue the country from virtual ruin would be difficult. As Interior Minister, controlling police, army and state power, Garašanin exercised great influence over what would take place whereas Chairman Vučić of the Council held a largely honorary and ceremonial post. Vučić insisted that a special chair be prepared for him and that Council members all stand when he entered the chamber. Despite such trappings, he presided rarely, failed to attend regularly, and when he deigned to appear, let his assistant, Aleksa Janković, direct the meetings. This aging, illiterate peasant oligarch was very ill at ease in an office or Council chamber.[12]

"As soon as I become Interior Minister," recalled Garašanin, ". . . I began immediately to plan to utilize my position to counteract Austria's influence in Serbia." At the Council meeting of April 1st, after the new ministers had been presented, Garašanin stated: "Surely now we must have the firm determination to work in a legal direction." He continued:

Gentlemen, I will not conceal from you that the danger [to Serbia] has not been eliminated but only reduced. It is up to us to destroy it completely. The entire country is upset, the people is uncertain, within it prevails the greatest disorder, and outside they are carefully watching our situation.[13]

Even after the "reconciliation" of late March, hostility and suspicion persisted between the Prince and the oligarchs of the "old opposition" (Vučić and Garašanin). As rumors spread that Aleksandar was plotting to have the oligarchs murdered, both soon concluded that he must be removed. Earlier plans to utilize a European commission or the Porte's authority to do so had been revealed as unworkable. Neither leader wished to organize a plot: Vučić was too old and Garašanin too legalistic. With the abortive Tenka Plot fresh in everyone's mind, the oligarchs acted cautiously. The only other means to remove Aleksandar was by a national assembly, but would the Prince consent to one? Meanwhile Garašanin urged that the Council's position be buttressed with reforms. These would leave the Prince only a suspensive veto and require him to sign any proposed law approved three times by a two-thirds vote of the Council. Ministers were to be selected solely from members nominated by the Council; councillors would no longer be tried without its consent. Garašanin finally overcome the Prince's objections that the Porte might refuse to confirm these changes. If Prince and Council were in accord, affirmed Garašanin, the Porte would go along. After the Council had adopted some minor princely suggestions on revision, Aleksandar meekly accepted the reforms making the Council the dominant legislative and administrative authority in Serbia, resembling the old Venetian Senate. The cabinet then sought popularity by eliminating torture and the stocks and even discussed abolishing censorship. Cloaking itself with liberalism, the Council oligarchy blamed all illegalities and corruption on the former personal regime of Prince Aleksandar.

Nonetheless, the Garašanin government remained vulnerable and unstable since the Council promptly split between pro-Garašanin and princely factions. The six members, returning after the Tenka Plot, normally voted with the government but were outnumbered ten to seven by the Prince's relatives, cronies and newly appointed members. Soon the princely faction recovered its courage and once again Council sessions grew stormy. However, the princely group could not assume power since if it formed a cabinet, four of its members would become ministers and the faction would then command only a minority in the Council. Instead, it kept the Garašanin government on tenterhooks "The reaction has already formed," wrote Grujić May 12th, "and seeks to compromise the government by making demands, such as the evacuation of all Turks from Serbia, in order to induce the Turks to restore predominance to the Prince." Whereas the princely faction, affirmed Grujić July 22nd, aimed to restore the old political situation and retain Aleksandar on the throne, the "old opposition" favored his eventual expulsion, while concealing this aim temporarily.[14]

During the next months whether and on what basis to convene a national assembly (*Skupština*) became the chief political issue in Serbia. On June 4th Grujić noted rising public pressure for one, while Garašanin's district chiefs reported much popular support and agitation for an assembly. Considering this the surest means to remove the Prince, Garašanin moved swiftly to secure support from Vučić and liberal elements for the expected difficult struggle to overcome opposition from the Prince and his entourage, backed by the Porte, England and Austria. Vučić and Garašanin, pledging that an assembly would be convened though not immediately, sought to quiet its more rabid adherents. Naturally, the Council's princely majority, recalling the turbulent events of 1848 when Vučić had roused assemblies against Prince, ministers and Council, feared that such a body would be utilized now to expel Prince Aleksandar. While Vučić lives, argued the princely faction, we dare not convene a national assembly since he will take it over and manipulate it. Meanwhile Garašanin sought to lay foundations for convening such an assembly by asking his district chiefs whether the populace really favored one.[15]

During the summer of 1858 the oligarchic and princely factions were locked in struggle over this issue. On his summer trip to the interior, the Prince wrote Garašanin from Kragujevac that intrigues and disorders were spreading among the people which Garašanin as responsible minister had neglected to report to him; this must be discussed upon his return to Belgrade. Garašanin considered this accusation untrue and insulting. Instead of popular "disorders," he replied, there was public agitation for an assembly about which he had informed the Prince repeatedly. On his trip the Prince made speeches defending himself and attacking the oligarchs. Garašanin responded by sending agents among the people urging them to demand an immediate national assembly. Convening large meetings in Šapac and Loznica, Vučić harangued them in its behalf. Between April and August Garašanin received over one hundred written reports that the Prince had ordered him killed, but he gave these little credence.[16]

Garašanin played a major if somewhat disputed role in convening the St. Andrew Assembly which would remove Prince Aleksandar from the throne of Serbia. Andrija Radenić, a contemporary Yugoslav scholar who has studied that assembly, agrees that Garašanin's part in bringing it into being was vital but not exclusive. He revealed himself as not merely a bureaucrat but an intelligent politician, though his subsequent memoirs exaggerated his personal role. Initiative for the assembly, claims Radenić, came actually from liberal political circles and the people. Confronted by widespread popular agitation for an assembly, Garašanin for tactical reasons, resolved to utilize these sentiments against the Prince.[17]

Thus in a letter in June to the chief of Krajina district,[18] Garašanin warned that unless evident popular desires for an assembly were satisfied promptly, they could become demands gravely threatening the government. He and Vučić both favored convening a national assembly: "Without it the princely government cannot possibly recover public trust." Garašanin had explained this to the Prince who, while agreeing, merely questioned when and where it should be held. "Thus there is no doubt that the holding of an assembly will be approved," continued Garašanin. "It only needs time to be prepared." On June 26th he wrote all his district chiefs: [19]

> From all sides people coming here to see me say that everywhere among the people is evinced the strongest desire for a national assembly. Many affirm that the people, because an assembly has not yet been called, are beginning to lose confidence in the princely government.

However, a letter from the Loznica district chief, stated that people there did not favor an assembly and that he believed that one would prove too costly.[20] Disregarding what he considered isolated notes of opposition, Garašanin wrote Magazinović July 26th that popular desires for an assembly must be heeded: "The reports about an assembly absorb all of my concern."[21] That same day he informed Mondain that "the popular wish for convening an assembly is already becoming a true demand and I do not believe one can avoid satisfying that desire . . . ."[22] His aim was to bring that public agitation into official channels. Through articles in the official press, circulars to subordinates and letters to adherents, he informed the public that his government backed it on convening an assembly. While opposing public demonstrations or mass movements firmly, he instructed the district chiefs:

> The people must be induced to understand clearly that any public action against the government will be considered illegal and improper. The police must prevent any movement originating without orders of the government which might be incited by careless or badly intentioned persons.[23]

Writing Mondain July 26th Garašanin approved popular agitation for convening an assembly as preferable to the likely alternative: open revolt.

He complained to his friend about the government's weakness because of
the factional split in the Council.

> When one adds to that the Prince's bad will and stubbornness in
> rejecting the advice of government leaders, you can realize what
> deep trouble my friends and I are in. The Prince won't agree with us
> and without him we cannot work . . . and are not able to respond
> to popular expectations. The Prince in the interests of his personal
> policy (since he never has any other) claims that Garašanin is in-
> capable of moving national affairs forward.[24]

For a weakling prince like Aleksandar, Garašanin proved to be an over-
powering minister. He and Vučić were the only outstanding Serbian
politicians of that time, and Garašanin clearly overshadowed both Prince
and Council. Since he appeared to be the only man able to run the country,
rumors arose that he coveted the throne, something very far removed
from his thoughts and intentions.[25]

In early August Garašanin pressed the assembly question with both
Prince and Council. "We must deal with the problem of the government's
intentions about an assembly, " he wrote Aleksandar. "I feel it is essential
to communicate to the Council at least orally the evident public desire
for an assembly so it can discuss that important questions. A final decision on whether or not to convene it can be made after your return to
Belgrade." Next day he informed the Prince that the Council would debate the assembly issue immediately.[26] In the Council that day Garašanin
declared:

> Gentlemen . . . , you have surely heard that for some time have
> spread rumors about an assembly. The entire people wants an
> assembly. These desires have now turned into a true demand. . . .
> This voice of the people cannot be left longer unheeded. . . . Either
> we will convene an assembly or we must take extraordinary measures
> to maintain order.

He added: "I don't understand a government which fears its people; that
is a miserable government." To his opponents' angry shouts, recorded
Grujić, the Council's secretary, Garašanin smiled, told jokes, and appeared

indifferent about his proposal, but so self-confident and strong that he disdained his enemies' outbursts. After heated discussion, Garašanin urged the Council to ponder his proposal.[27]

On August 9th Garašanin pressed the Prince to reach a swift decision on the national assembly; any further delay, he warned, would imperil the government's survival. Aleksandar should either return to Belgrade immediately or from Kragujevac authorize the Council to decide the issue. The Prince replied evasively that he would decide on his approach after returning. Seeking to smoke out Aleksandar, Garašanin wrote him August 12th that in the meantime the Council would debate the matter thoroughly and warned:

> The assembly would be the only basis upon which one could begin to improve conditions in Serbia and place the country on a constructive path. I do not believe that the people have been incited to demand an assembly but are truly in real difficulties.[28]

Heeding the Austrian consul's advice not to agree to an assembly, the Prince responded that while he approved of an assembly in principle, one should not be convened now because people were too upset. He suggested, with a degree of truth that Vučić and Garašanin had orchestrated the whole affair artificially.

Garašanin's proposal to the Council argued that since ten years had passed since the last national assembly, the government now should inform the people what had been done in the meantime and ask them about their needs. The Council promptly split and initially rejected his proposal. Then Garašanin, buttonholing each Council member individually, explained the peril to Prince and Council if an assembly were delayed. Such was the public mood, he affirmed, that the regime faced overthrow by popular revolution. By a bare majority the Council then adopted his proposal.

Returning to Belgrade August 23rd Prince Aleksandar was met by his four ministers. Garašanin sought to erode his opposition to the assembly. In case of a bloody revolt, he warned, he would not oppose it since the people's demands for an assembly were justified. Garašanin's arguments, reminiscent of Bismarck's confrontation with King William in 1866,[29] carried the day. The Prince, reluctantly confirming the Council's decision to convene the assembly, believed he could be reconciled there with his people. Also he saw no alternative to a Garašanin cabinet since if his own faction took power, it would lose its Council majority. The Prince lacked the courage to rule contrary to the Council wich would amount to a *coup d'état*. He and his advisers agreed to retain Garašanin in office, convene the Assembly, then insist that it be composed of elements loyal to the Karadjordjević dynasty.[30]

With the Prince's consent, the Council approved unanimously Garašanin's written proposal of September 3rd to convene a national assembly; then it set up a commission to decide how the assembly was to be constituted. Over the commission quarrels between princely and Garašanin factions promptly resumed, almost toppling the cabinet. On the commission itself the two factions were equally represented. The princely group demanded that the law on the assembly be drafted in ordinary Council sessions where it commanded a majority. The Council approved this only to have the Garašanin cabinet threaten to resign. Its fall seemed inevitable until the Prince again yielded and refused to confirm the Council's decisions. That left the drafting process to "large" meetings of the Council, including the four ministers, where Garašanin's group held a majority. Nonetheless, Garašanin had to make concessions to the princely group on points where Vučić sided with the later.[31]

Also on September 3rd arose an unexpected external barrier to convening the assembly: the Grand Vizier telegraphed that the Porte opposed an assembly then; Prince and Council were deemed sufficient to conduct Serbia's affairs. Ths communication almost wrecked Garašanin's intricate plans. However, Russia and France concluded that the Vizier was interfering unduly in Serbia's internal affairs in violation of the Paris Treaty. The Turks quickly backed off: they had not *ordered* Belgrade but had merely *advised* it not to convene an assembly. Garašanin told the Turkish pasha in Belgrade September 14th that the Serbian government would disregard such "advice." Convening a national assembly, he told the Council, was a constitutional right which Serbia must not renounce. If she yielded to the Turks over that, they would make other demands, and then "what would become of our domestic autonomy?"[32]

Garašanin had persuaded the Prince and Council to agree to the assembly by exploiting popular discontent and provoking an irresistible public demand for one. Finally unleashed, Vučić had roused the Serbian peasantry against the Nenadović clain. In his set demagogic speech, at public meetings Vučić repeatedly demanded, as he had in 1848, that officials be dismissed and taxes reduced. Garašanin agitated more circumspectly through his district chiefs, letting the Obrenovites and young Belgrade intellectuals lead the way. As the Prince's prestige declined, a burgeoning Obrenovite movement, anticipating that any nationally elected body would restore the Obrenović dynasty, demanded an assembly in order to judge Prince Aleksandar for his misdeeds. Belgrade intellectuals, such as Jevrem Grujić and Milovan Janković, later dubbed "the Liberals of 1858," campaigned for an assembly which they viewed as a democratic organ of self-administration. Taking Western parliamentarism as their model, they were optimistic about "the people."[33] In Belgrade cafés and in the interior, Jovan Ilić, Janković and Ranko Alimpić orchestrated a popular groundswell for the assembly. Garašanin remained in constant touch with them. As Interior Minister he could readily have halted their agitation but made no effort to do so. Before being authorized by Prince or Council, he had informed the district chiefs of his proposal to convene a national assembly and placed his ministry's full authority behind the agitators. Garašanin believed that liberal agitation would help force an assembly which would surely expel the Prince. "Let the people choose as ruler whomever they wish—if he is a good one, so be it; if not, they cannot blame anyone else."[34]

The Serbian people, affirmed Garašanin in September, alienated by the Karadjordjević regime, now favored the Obrenović cuase almost solidly. "If that [Obrenović] party today had even one capable leader," he wrote Marinović September 11th, "it would succeed in its aims in a moment."[35] Without claiming to have initiated this public dissatisfaction with Prince Aleksandar, Garašanin sought to provide it with a legitimate outlet and prevent foreign domination of Serbia:

... The only thing which I considered it my duty to do was to conduct events so that the removal of the Prince and the selection of a new one would occur in a fully orderly manner, not only because I had always hated disorder and anarchy, but also because I wished thereby to show Austria, and ... to some extent Russia, that the people ... by legal expression of its will was resolutely opposed to all foreign influences in Serbia.

By then he was convinced this would only be possible if the Serbian people were encouraged to remove the incompetent and Austrophile prince because his regime was pursuing policies detrimental to Serbia and allow them to choose a successor. He was quite certain Prince Miloš would thus return to power. "In Serbia's interests [I] preferred that Mihailo Obrenović become prince, but I refused to impose my desire on anyone. . . . " Garašanin exaggerated considerably his role in initiating and shaping the movement to remove Prince Aleksandar, however:

> After I had spread among the people the idea of convening an assembly, people came to me from all parts of Serbia solely to beg me to help get it convened in order to remove Aleksandar Karadjordjević. When I asked them whom they wanted as prince, they replied: Miloš, though many felt he would hand over power immediately to Mihailo. . . .

Actually, it appears that he had adopted and exploited popular demands for an assembly through his officials:

> Among the district chiefs some were devoted to the Obrenović, some served regardless of dynasty, and one or two were adherents of Karadjordjević, but all of them obeyed my orders unconditionally. I knew that Aleksandar Karadjordjević could not get his men elected to the assembly because he lacked popular support and because I was blocking this through the district chiefs. Only Kragujevac district might yield to his pressure, but Vučić thwarted that by his vast influence.[36]

The version quoted above was written long after the events described and gives the impression that Garašanin was in total command of the situation. However, one does not obtain that impression from his letter to Marinović of September 11th written in the midst of the campaign to convene a Serbian national assembly:

> You cannot imagine my present position. . . . Everything lies mostly on my neck and I must contend with the worst people in the world [the Prince's adherents]. But there is not only torment from a bad

government but torment among the entire people . . . , so one cannot know what to do in order to reduce the impending danger. The people has completely lost confidence in the government and its authority. . . . If I emerge from this chaos, I will surely never get involved any more in this game [*kolo*].[37]

This scarcely suggests the confident statesman, nor does it support various allegations that Garašanin coveted the throne for himself. Nonetheless, by late September 1858, partly because of Garašanin's actions, partly because of agitation by others, the momentum in favor of a Serbian national assembly had become irresistible.

NOTES

1. For the events of 1858 prior to St. Andrew's Assembly, see the summary in Petrovich, *A History,* I, 258-261; S. Jovanović, *Ustavobranitelji,* pp. 170-183, 207-220; J. Grujić, *Zapisi,* I; Andrija Radenić, "Svetoandrejska Skupština," *Spomenik SANU,* vol. 113 (Belgrade, 1964); J. Ristić, *Spoljašnji odnosaji,* I, 255-278; D. Ilić, *Toma Vučić-Perišić,* and J. Milićević, *Jevrem Grujić,* pp. 61 ff.

2. Report of Segur to Foreign Ministry, December 7, 1857, quoted in Stranjaković, "Ilija," pp. 92-93.

3. IG 1085, Garašanin to Mondain, March 9, 1858.

4. Garašanin, "Begstvo Knjaza Aleksandra u grad" (1859), published in Radenić, "Svetoandrejska," No. 89, p. 185.

5. Ibid., pp. 39-40.

6. IG 1085, Garašanin to Mondain, January 17, 1858.

7. Milićević, *Jevrem Grujić,* pp. 60 ff.

8. Ibid., pp. 62-63. Thus Grujić was the apparent author of the formidable seventy page indictment of Prince Aleksandar's blunders and illegal acts on assignment from Garašanin. A copy is in Garašanin's papers: IG 1068, "Optužnica protiv Kneza Aleksandra (1858)." It is published in full in J. Grujić's *Zapisi,* I, 179-239.

9. Ibid., I, 78-84.

10. Ibid., pp. 83-84; Milićević, *Grujić*, p. 63.

11. Grujić, *Zapisi*, I, 83; S. Jovanović, *Ustavobranitelji*, pp. 176-181. Jovanović notes (p. 177) that Etem, en route to Belgrade, stopped over in Grocka where he stayed the night with Garašanin's merchant brother, Mihailo.

12. Ibid., pp. 182-183; Grujić, *Zapisi*, I, 84-85.

13. Ibid., I, 86.

14. Ibid., I, 122, 153-154. In the "reaction" Grujić included members of the princely faction: J. Stanojević, A. Majstorović, R. Matejić, Trifunović, Resavac and A. Nenadović.

15. Ibid., I, 131; IG 1061, "O želji naroda da se sazove Skupština," Garašanin draft of 1858.

16. IG 1076, Aleksandar Karadjordjević to Garašanin, 1858; IG 1085, Garašanin to Mondain, May 15 and June 26, 1858, Radenić, "Svetoandrejska," p. 50; Grujić, *Zapisi*, I, 156.

17. Radenić, "Svetoandrejska," pp. 38-39.

18. Ibid., p. 51, No. 8, Garašanin to Kosta Janković, June 14.

19. Ibid., No. 9, p. 52, Interior Ministry to District Chiefs, June 26.

20. Ibid., No. 10, p. 52, D. Milenković (Loznica) to Garašanin, July 3.

21. Ibid., No. 84, p. 175, Garašanin to Magazinović, July 26.

22. IG 1085, Garašanin to Mondain, July 26, Radenić, No. 85, p. 176.

23. Ibid., No. 14, p. 57.

24. IG 1085, Garašanin to Mondain, July 26.

25. Garašanin to Marinović, September 11, *Pisma*, I, 405-407, cited below, p. 191.

26. Radenić, "Svetoandrejska," No. 16, pp. 57-58, Garašanin to Prince Aleksandar, August 7 and 8.

27. Grujić, *Zapisi*, I, 157-160, August 8; Jovanović, *Ustavobranitelji*, pp. 214-215.

28. Radenić, Nos. 18 and 19, pp. 58-59, Garašanin to Prince Aleksandar, August 9 and 12.

29. After the Prussian victory at Königgrätz in Bohemia in July 1866 the King and the military chiefs favored Austria's destruction, but Bismarck eventually dissuaded his sovereign after bitter argument. See Gordon Craig, *The Battle of Königgrätz: Prussia's Victory over Austria, 1866* (Philadelphia, 1964), p. 169.

30. Grujić, *Zapisi,* I, 161-162; Jovanović, *Ustavobranitelji,* p. 215.
31. Ibid., pp. 215-216; Grujić, I, 163-168.
32. Ibid., I, 169-170; Jovanović, p. 216.
33. On early Serbian liberalism see Gale Stokes, *Legitimacy through Liberalism* (Seattle, 1975), pp. 13-18.
34. Radenić, "Svetoandrejska," pp. 38-39 and No. 89, pp. 183 ff.; Jovanović, pp. 217-218.
35. Garašanin to Marinović, September 11, *Pisma,* I, 405-407.
36. Radenić, No. 89, pp. 187 ff.
37. Garašanin to Marinović, September 11, *Pisma,* I, 405.

CHAPTER XII

CHANGE OF DYNASTY, 1858

"The removal of Prince Aleksandar and the return of the Obrenović to Serbia was my doing. . . . I, who carried it through, only did so because I believed it was good and beneficial for the country."

Garašanin, "The Flight of Prince Aleksandar to the Fortress" (1859)

By November 1858 all obstacles to the election of Serbia's first national assembly in a decade had been overcome. Having played a key part in arranging it, Garašanin was confident the assembly would remove Prince Aleksandar Karadjordjević from the throne, an essential step, he believed, for Serbia's national interests. Nonetheless, the St. Andrew's Assembly, so-called because it convened November 30th, or St. Andrew's day, held some unpleasant surprises for him and other Serbian political leaders and soon escaped from his control.[1]

The national elections, held November 15th, produced an overwhelming victory for the anti-Karadjordjević coalition. Thanks to Garašanin's influence, a majority of the sixty-three official deputies, supported the triumvirate of Garašanin, Vučić and Anastasijević. However, among elected delegates, predominately peasants, the Obrenovites prevailed. To the shock and dismay of Prince Aleksandar's camp, two well-known

Obrenovites and the militant liberal, Milovan Janković, were elected. The princely faction in the Council demanded promptly that Janković's election be voided as irregular, but this was not approved.[2] When Kosta Janković, a district chief, questioning the right of one elected deputy to take his seat, sought to nullify his election, Garašanin telegraphed him not to do so. Whomever the people had elected must be allowed to serve in the Assembly—such was the law of the land.[3]

The deputies to the St. Andrew's Assembly streamed into Belgrade from all over Serbia. The peasant, or popular, delegates from each district, led by their district chiefs, rode in mounted under arms. After ten years uninterrupted rule by Prince and Council, this massive influx of popular representatives produced a powerful impression on the Belgrade public. The Prince and his followers deluded themselves with the comforting belief which had wrecked previous autocratic regimes that deputies would not dare attack the ruler or the dynasty. The princely group counted on dissension between militant Obrenovite liberals and conservative deputies loyal to the triumvirate. The Prince relied upon the army whose chief commands were held by his wife's relatives. Furthermore, the Assembly would meet right across from the army's barracks which needed only train its artillery upon the meeting place to squelch any unrest.

After the deputies arrived, Belgrade liberal intellectuals and Obrenovites, in order to exert systematic pressure on the Assembly, fused to form a political caucus of some forty members. Its leaders were Stevča Mihailović, A. Stamenković and Jevrem Grujić, but Jovan Ilić contributed most in bringing the two groups together. Whereas Belgrade intellectuals favored Mihailo as prince, Ilić argued convincingly that peasants supported Miloš almost unanimously. Indeed, peasant Obrenovites—ordinary, simple people—wanted a patriarchal despot rather than political freedoms advocated by the liberals.

Besides the Liberal-Obrenovite coalition, Belgrade boasted three other centers of opposition to Prince Aleksandar. One was the Garašanin-Vučić-Anastasijević triumvirate. With many personal followers in the Assembly, Vučić retained wide popular support, Garašanin controlled most official deputies, while Anastasijević, chosen a deputy from Belgrade, exerted influence through his vast wealth and numerous agents. Already he was being touted as the Assembly's probable chairman. Also opposed to Aleksandar was "Boss" (*gazda*) Filip Stanković, a rich livestock merchant from

Smederevo and Prince Miloš' personal agent. Always armed to the teeth and accompanied by a formidable band of armed men, he distributed Miloš' money, followed his instructions, and remained in touch with the Liberal-Obrenović club. In the streets Stanković roused the mob against Prince Aleksandar. Finally, the Russian consulate had been anti-Karadjordist since Aleksandar had aligned himself with Austria. Thus during the Assembly, Liberals and Obrenovites would assert: Russia is with us. Wherever the Assembly delegates turned, they encountered the Prince's enemies.[4]

Before the Assembly met, official deputies and some popular men were greeted with warm hospitality at Garašanin's house. Presiding over a harmonious combination of village warmth and town sophistication was the generously constructed Soka, Garašanin's spouse. Of her it was said that, better than other wives, she had absorbed the spirit of her husband's family so completely that she seemed to have been born in that house. Charmed at their reception, the deputies and district chiefs henceforth considered Garašanin's home their headquarters. When Božić, district chief of Jagodina, asked how they should react to popular desires, Garašanin replied: accept them. He, Garašanin, would harken to the people's voice even if his own views were different. What the people decided, he added, was fait accompli. His main concern was to insure through his police and army that the Assembly's work would be conducted swiftly, legally, and peacefully.[5]

St. Andrew's Assembly, the hero-worshipping Stranjaković exaggerated, was "purely Garašanin's work."[6] To suggestions during its sessions that he act against the legislature, Garašanin replied: "I cannot complain about an assembly which I created, I and no one else."[7] Against his will it could not have been held, nor could the decisions of December 11-12th have been reached since he controlled the district chiefs, army and police. Without Garašanin's participation, agreed Nil Popov, no coup could have been carried out. During the Assembly and while Prince Aleksandar's fate was debated, Garašanin and Vučić were omnipotent. All factions, affirms Ristić, were prepared to follow the course they recommended.[8] By the time the Assembly convened, Garašanin had nearly completed preparations to remove the Prince. Not a single deputy supported Aleksandar. Instead, they looked to Garašanin and were prepared to execute his instructions promptly. At his home he had instructed the district chiefs what to tell the popular deputies.[9] Garašanin remained determined to make no compromises with the Prince and to remove him quickly. Thus when Milovan Janković, a Liberal leader, asked Garašanin during the Assembly whether Aleksandar might remain on the throne, the minister replied: "The present one [prince] cannot retain his place in any case. Instead let come whomever the people chooses even if he is a black gypsy."[10]

Subsequently, Garašanin denied vehemently having plotted to seize power during the Assembly or after Aleksandar's ouster. "For me to have carried out such a coup," he wrote Marinović, "I would no longer have been the Garašanin you know and who loves his honor more than all the brilliance of court life."[11] Nonetheless, many then considered Garašanin, next to Miloš and Mihailo, the likeliest princely candidate. Next to Vučić, he was the strongest contender, noted Grujić, since France backed him, the Porte and England would not oppose him, and a weakened Russia would remain silent. Serbian leaders who shared this view included Magazinović, Crnobarac, Council members Arsenijević-Batalaka and Jeremić; also many scholars, some clergy, and many officials favored him. The populace would not have opposed his candidacy, concluded Grujić, though neither would it have rejoiced wildly.[12]

Despite a consensus in the Assembly and Belgrade against Prince Aleksandar, the opposition differed over how to proceed and who should succeed him. Whereas the Liberals desired a prompt proclamation of Miloš as prince, the oligarchs wished to establish a regency which would later convene a great national assembly to elect a new prince.[13] The triumvirate of oligarchs had apparently agreed with the Porte to form an interim provisional Serbian government. Allegedly, the Porte favored Anastasijević as a regent after he had bribed some Turkish officials. Garašanin recalls that he refrained from asking Vučić his aims following Aleksandar's ouster for fear they might disagree. Responding to a query by Vučić, Garašanin stated that the choice of the next ruler must be left to the Serbian people. For his part, Anastasijević envisioned his brother-in-law and Aleksandar's relative, Prince Djordje Karadjordje as the next ruler; however, the populace did not consider him a suitable candidate. Liberal intellectuals, such as Grujić and Janković, while valuing Garašanin as a statesman, believed that he coveted the throne.

Was this Liberal belief justified? Affirmed Jevrem Grujić: "Garašanin was just . . . what we needed as prince: his wisdom, strong will, honorable

stock, two worthy sons . . . —all this is what the present and future re-
quires."[14] First raised by his opponents, such as Consul Radosavljević, in
order to discredit him, Garašanin's candidacy was now promoted enthusiastically by followers and admirers. French Consul des Essards spoke
openly of Garašanin as his choice. The public took seriously numerous
rumors that he was seeking the throne. Garašanin's prestige and authority
during 1858 was so great that he easily could have stood as a candidate
and probably won the throne had he desired it. Officials, over whom he
exercised immense authority, regarded him with fear, respect and secret
enthusiasm. At the Assembly the district chiefs backed him solidly, noted
Grujić, and popular deputies tended to follow their lead. Garašanin's
reputation abroad, much enhanced by recent meetings with Napoleon III,
was high; he was the only Serbian leader Europe took seriously. Yet
Grujić for one realized that Garašanin lacked princely ambitions. Throughout 1858, he admitted, the minister's posture was eminently correct.
Garašanin had confided to Grujić that he had awaited eagerly an opportunity to withdraw from politics altogehter. "I arranged the convening of the Assembly," he told Grujić, "so you strengthen it in the
future. Watch well what you do then because afterwards I will stay clear
of everything and live quietly."[15]

In private letters and reminiscences Garašanin, discussing reports that
he sought the throne, wondered why anyone would wish to rule Serbia.
For wealth? "But for thirty years I have occupied the most important
and best paid posts in the country; I was almost unlimited in these posts,
but not only did they not improve my material position, but when I left
service, I was burdened with debts." He had served Serbia long and honorably and had been decently paid. Yet Garašanin never displayed interest
in affluence. For the sake of authority? Under Prince Aleksandar, he had
controlled the chief power levers and could do virtually as he chose: "I
was then unlimited director of internal affairs . . . ." After Aleksandar's
removal, as will be shown, he held briefly unchallengeable power but made
no effort to seize the throne.[16]

Before St. Andrew's Assembly convened, the Liberals devised a plan to
block creation of an oligarchic regency and speed selection of a new
prince. This scheme, chiefly Grujić's work, would let the oligarchs remove Prince Aleksandar only after the Liberals had passed a law guaranteeing regular future meetings of the assembly. Then when the Prince had

been removed, the Liberals would propose the Assembly as temporary regent, and it in turn would transfer power over police and army to the Liberal leader, Stevča Mihailović. Simultaneously with Aleksandar's ouster, the Assembly would proclaim Miloš Obrenović prince of Serbia making unnecessary both a regency of oligarchs and a subsequent great national assembly. Popular sovereignty would be at least partly achieved.[17]

The Assembly convened on St. Andrew's Day, November 30th. The oligarch, Miša Anastasijević, was elected chairman; Stevča Mihailović, a Liberal, vice-chairman; and Grujić and Ilić, both Liberals, assembly secretaries. This choice of officers dealt a grievous blow to Prince Aleksandar's prospects, although discord between oligarchs and Liberals was already becoming evident. A princely dinner held at the hotel, "Srpska Kruna," attracted many official delegates but few popular ones, revealing the extent of public opposition to Aleksandar.[18]

Yet there was no immediate attempt to remove him because the Liberals first sought approval of their radical assembly law providing for annual meetings, full power over the budget and authority to accuse ministers. At the heart of Grujić's proposals lay the concept of popular sovereignty, and they would make the assembly a potent and sovereign legislature. This assembly law was to be issued without consulting Prince or Council, thus disregarding the existing constitution. Since Vučić promptly accepted the Liberal proposal, Garašanin, fearing to break with him until the Prince's removal, merely sought to modify Grujić's scheme. Garašanin believed there would be subsequent opportunities to overhaul a Liberal proposal which he considered ridiculous for a country of illiterate peasants. At Garašanin's request, he and Grujić conferred December 6th, revised the proposal, and the Assembly approved the new text December 8th. Next day Garašanin and Obrenovite leaders met to prepare the ouster of Prince Aleksandar.[19]

Meanwhile the secretaries, Grujić and Ilić, had largely assumed control of the Assembly. Although Prince and Council had not yet approved the new assembly law, the Liberals decided to press ahead. Chairman Anastasijević, unwilling to alienate the Porte which opposed that measure, stayed away. Vučić, to prevent his dominating it, had been barred from the Assembly. Garašanin, still Prince Aleksandar's minister, held himself aloof, leaving his district chiefs without instructions. Not always overly scrupulous, Jovanović feels, Garašanin nevertheless always observed proper form. Believing it would be improper as his minister to oppose the Prince openly, he avoided contact with the Assembly until it had ousted Aleksandar, so that move would appear to reflect the popular will. Thus from November 30th until December 10th, Grujić and Ilić filled the Assembly's leadership void and could easily manipulate its mostly illiterate peasant deputies. Outside the Assembly pro-Obrenović crowds of students, commercial apprentices, and the dissatisfied swelled day by day. While anxious to encourage the Assembly to remove the Prince, Garašanin soon found that ordinary police measures could no longer control the turbulent mob.[20]

On December 10th the Assembly, after Chairman Anastasijević reappeared there to reassert his control, removed Prince Aleksandar from the throne. Mihailo Barlovac, a Belgrade deputy supporting the oligarchs, read accusations against Prince Aleksandar prepared previously by Garašanin and Grujić. Three times Chairman Anastasijević asked the Assembly whether it considered the Prince guilty of Barlovac's charges; three times it thundered: "Yes!" "Do you all want his abdication?" queried Anastasijević. The entire Assembly shouted affirmatively. A document was drawn up demanding that Aleksandar return princely authority to the Assembly, and a delegation was named to take it to him.[21]

Meanwhile Garašanin, insuring that nothing unusual occurred in or near the Assembly, watched the Prince and his entourage, and sought to prevent any pretext for foreign intervention. Subsequently, he realized:

The Prince could have used the army to dissolve the Assembly by force. But I had all the officers in my hands and was confident they would obey my orders, but I feared the Prince might go to the barracks and appeal on his own to the soldiers. I know what an oath means to a soldier when a ruler reminds him of it personally, and I knew the Assembly would not quietly debate Serbia's affairs under cannonfire.

Claiming to have split the Porte from Austria, Garašanin believed that this rift would last until after Aleksandar's removal. He had explained to the Turks that Aleksandar's ouster would strengthen them by undermining Austrian influence in Serbia. Only should the Prince's removal provoke serious violence did he fear Austrian military intervention.[22]

Instead of acting to preserve his power, Aleksandar panicked and played into his opponents' hands. Refusing to hold the document of abdication in his hands, he requested a day to consider it. Conferences with the foreign consuls, the Turkish pasha, and Commissar Kabuli convinced the Prince that he lacked real support. From the palace windows he saw armed bands in the streets and learned of popular demonstrations against him. Summoning Garašanin, Aleksandar asked anxiously whether his life was in danger. Not that night, responded the minister, but the Prince had better sign his abdication by the next morning. Clearly terrified, the Prince refused to spend the night in the palace.[23]

Accounts differ about Prince Aleksandar's sudden flight that night to Kalemegdan fortress. The panicky prince, claims one version, begged Garašanin to take him there; others affirm that Garašanin persuaded or deceived him into seeking Turkish protection. There seems little reason to question Garašanin's version of these events, corroborated by other reliable observers, since he had little reason to conceal or distort the truth. Weak and fear-ridden, abandoned by virtually everyone, Aleksandar even in the palace constituted no great threat to Garašanin or to others.[24]

Garašanin recalls that on the evening of December 10th, when pressed by the Assembly to abdicate, Aleksandar summoned his councillors and the foreign consuls to the palace for advice. Entering the palace, Garašanin passed a room full of armed men, causing him to suspect the Prince's intentions. Uneasy, he decided to remain only while the consuls did. Asked by the Prince for their opinions, the consuls and all Council members except his relatives urged his abdication. Denouncing the Prince, Arsenijević-Batalaka declared the people had chosen him solely because of his father's services. He had betrayed public confidence and now must bow to popular will. Only his wife, Princess Persida, vehemently opposed abdication and urged her husband to fight for his throne. Then Jevrem Nenadović, a relative, rushed in shouting that a revolt had broken out in Belgrade. But Garašanin declared calmly that he had just passed through the entire city finding everything peaceful. Going outside to make sure, he soon confirmed there was no sign of trouble.

As councillors and consuls prepared to leave, the Prince suddenly grabbed Garašanin by the coat, pulled him into a room, and forced him to remain behind. When they were alone, the Prince cried out in panic: "I want to go to the fortress; I am not safe here. They will attack me tonight and kill me. I must take refugre in the fortress." Garašanin assured him he had nothing to fear; energetic measures had been taken to protect him and all was peaceful in the town. He, Garašanin, would vouch for Aleksandar's safety. Refusing to listen, the Prince in abject terror kept repeating: "They want to kill me.... Please take me to the fortress immediately." Trying to dissuade him, Garašanin reminded Aleksandar that flight to the fortress meant abandoning the throne. It would be much worthier to submit his signed abdication to the Assembly. Serbs would regard his flight to the Kalemegdan as treason. "I felt pity and scorn for a man who had fallen so far." The Prince continued to plead: "Mr. Garašanin, I beg you not to abandon me. If you were ever my friend, be one now and take me to the fortress." Realizing the Prince no longer valued his personal dignity, Garašanin finally decided to comply with his wishes. "For me the main thing was that he cease to be prince by common agreement with the Assembly and thus prevent any foreign intervention." Garašanin went out and instructed his servant to bring his carriage to a side entrance. The Prince accompanied him, shivering, since in his panic he had forgotten his overcoat. Garašanin ordered the coat brought and they got into the carriage. The Prince kept urging the coachman to drive faster until Garašanin warned that his decrepit old carriage might collapse. On the way to the fortress, out of habit the horses stopped in front of Garašanin's house. The Prince promptly leaped to the coachman's seat shouting: "Drive on, Živko!" "How he knew my coachman's name," marvelled Garašanin, "I do not know except that the Prince paid much more heed to horses and coachmen than to affairs of state."

They arrived at the fortress gate which was locked for the night. Garašanin called to the guard, identified himself, and requested him to open it. While the key was being brought, the Prince in terrible fear and impatience proposed they jump into a ditch beside the road. Laughing, Garašanin said they would risk nothing by waiting quietly in the carriage, but if they leaped into the ditch, they might break their necks or have the guard fire at them! Finally the gate opened and they drove through. No sooner were they inside the fortress on Turkish soil than the Prince, abandoning his humble, begging tone, became proud and imperious. Garašanin paid him no heed: "I knew that once we were in the fortress Austrian influence had been defeated, but I still had to prevent the Turks from abetting it." Arriving at the Turkish governor's residence, they entered the front room, the Prince first. The pasha, Kabuli Efendi, and the dragoman were playing cards. Seeing the two Serbian leaders, the Turks threw down their cards in astonishment. In alarm the Pasha asked whether something had happened to the Prince in Belgrade. Aleksandar declared that his life was in danger there so he was seeking protection in the fortress. Garašanin countered by stating nothing threatened him in town and that he had come to the Kalemegdan voluntarily. The Turks offered the Prince coffee and freedom of the fortress. Leaving, Garašanin never saw the Prince again.

From the fortress, continued Garašanin, he proceeded directly to the Prince's palace. There a band of the Prince's female relatives rushed at him like angry hornets; no one would listen to his soothing explanations. After finally transmitting the Prince's requests, he went home. No one in town yet knew where the Prince was. Garašanin swiftly convened his district chiefs and related what had occurred. Some expressed concern lest the Prince return with Turkish support. However, the minister reassured them that with the Prince's flight, matters had been rather neatly resolved. In the morning the Assembly need merely declare him removed from office for treason to Serbia.[25]

A markedly different version by Vlada Ljotić, the Prince's loyal supporter, based partly on Aleksandar's statements in exile, intimated Garašanin had abducted the Prince or frightened him into taking refuge in the fortress. The Prince had learned, claimed Ljotić, that the crowd milling around the palace was about to storm it. When Garašanin told him he would be safe at his, Garašanin's, house, the Prince asked to be taken there. Continued Ljotić:

> Garašanin's carriage waited ready below and the Prince, telling nobody, got into the carriage with him and they went off to Garašanin's house. Next to the coachman sat the Prince's young servant. The carriage passed through the great square and when it passed Garašanin's house, the Prince asked in amazement: 'Where are we going Garašanin?' 'To the fortress, Sire,' replied Garašanin. At these words, the Prince's bodyguard, sitting to one side, put his hand on his pistol, looked at the Prince and asked: 'Shall I shoot, Sire?' But the Prince, deeply shaken and morally crushed, merely waved his hand and let Garašanin take him to the fortress.

Meeting Garašanin returning from the fortress at the palace, Mita Ljotic, the chronicler's father, shouted pistol in hand: "Where is the Prince? " The Princess rushed from her room and placed herself between them. Garašanin said: "I hid him in the fortress from the people." Dumbfounded, Mita Ljotić drove to the fortress to retrieve the Prince. Aleksandar allegedly agreed to return, but the Turks compelled him to remain at the Kalemegdan.[26]

Garašanin had no need to persuade the Prince to flee, affirmed Slobodan Jovanović later from a neutral perspective. But Garašanin had not tried very hard to dissuade him. Aleksandar's flight, by discrediting him, promoted realization of Garašanin's plans. Morally, the minister's behavior was not very praiseworthy: the Prince was terribly upset while Garašanin, as usual, remained fully composed. By failing to restrain the Prince from flight, he aided him to commit political suicide. However, from a political standpoint, Garašanin's action was a masterstroke. An attempt to have the Assembly alone remove the Prince would be dangerous since Aleksandar could have ordered the army to disperse it. Once the Prince had fled, that danger dissipated since his control over the army had passed to Garašanin as Interior Minister.[27] Thus Garašanin could claim: "The removal of Prince Aleksandar and the return of the Obrenović to Serbia was my doing." Continued Garašanin:

> Truly many people have ascribed this to themselves, but I who carried it through only did so because I believed this was good and beneficial for the country. . . . Not seeking any special reward in the overthrow of Karadjordjević and the return of the Obrenović, I will merely mention that up til then I had wanted to retain Karadjordjević as long as I found his rule did not damage the country's interests; until then he held on. As long as I desired that the Obrenović not enter the country, they indeed did not enter it. As soon as I perceived that Karadjordjević was sacrificing the country's interests, I abandoned him and he fell.[28]

Again, Garašanin exaggerated somewhat his role in the crisis.

The Prince's flight defused the Liberals' strategy. They had counted on surprising the oligarchs with an immediate Obrenović restoration after removing Prince Aleksandar. Now since Garašanin had accompanied the

Prince to the fortress *before* the Assembly removed him formally, the oligarchs held the initiative. Garašanin had almost twelve hours to create a fait accompli. Had he wished, he could have become dictator or even prince. However, what he wanted was to have the Assembly, in agreement with the Council, designate a provisional government. To obtain popular support, such a government must at least apparently be installed by both Assembly and Council.

Thus Garašanin instructed his district chiefs to engineer the bloodless removal of the Prince next day in the Assembly. As usual, calculating his every move calmly, he planned to prevail with patience and skill and without force. To remove any pretext for foreign intervention, everything must be completed legally. With the Prince's relatives still holding the chief commands, he could not count fully on the army, nor could he control the Belgrade mob. Thus Garašanin required the authority of both Council and Assembly.

Learning swiftly of the Prince's flight, the Liberals prepared through the night. They resolved immediately after the Assembly had removed Aleksandar to proclaim Miloš Obrenović prince of Serbia. Pending his arrival, princely power would be vested in the Assembly, thus blocking a regency by the oligarchs. A vital first step would be to place the army and police under the Assembly's authority. Assuming the regency, the Assembly could name its vice-chairman, Stevča Mihailović, commandant of the garrison and town of Belgrade. Liberal leaders primed a deputy, Sima Protić, to propose restoring the Obrenović to power. They also prepared a proclamation removing Aleksandar and restoring the Obrenović, and a decree placing army and police under Mihailović. Instructions were sent out that night that all Belgraders favoring the Obrenović should gather next morning under arms at the Assembly. Seemingly, nothing had been left to chance.[29]

Next morning (December 11th) matters at first went as the Liberals had planned. Chairman Anastasijević, informing the Assembly of the Prince's flight, sent a delegation to the Council which promptly backed the Assembly fully. Then the Assembly approved Anastasijević's proposal to oust the Prince from office as a traitor. Legally, the Assembly should then have awaited the Council's confirmation of Aleksandar's removal. But at Secretary Grujić's signal, Deputy Protić rose and declared: the people cannot remain without a prince even for an hour. The Assembly must choose a new ruler immediately. At this cue, up jumped the Obrenović deputies shouting: "We want Miloš Obrenović!" A window was thrown open as the crowd outside chorused: "Long live Prince Miloš!" Taking up the shout, the mob proclaimed him prince even before the Assembly completed its actions. Then Protić proposed that pending Miloš' arrival, the Assembly act as regent and entrust control over army and police to Mihailović. The latter was to appoint as his assistants Ranko Alimpić for the army and Jovan Belimarković for the police. Amidst a deafening din, all this was accepted.

These unexpected events dumbfounded Chairman Anastasijević who discovered that in the confusion Secretary Grujić had seized his chair. In vain Anastasijević sought to separate Aleksandar's removal from the Obrenović restoration by having separate documents drawn up. At Grujić's suggestion, approved by the Assembly, they were signed simultaneously. Instead of awaiting Council confirmation of Aleksandar's removal, the Assembly presented it with a fait accompli, thus acting unconstitutionally, as a fully sovereign body. In response the Council dispatched a prestigious deputation to the Assembly headed by Vučić. That proved to be a mistake. Entering the Assembly with Garašanin, Vučić reproached and threatened the deputies and opposed an Obrenović restoration. The Obrenovites, enthusiastic and self-confident, interrupted him and shouted him down. Vučić's hour had passed. Seeking by more peaceful tactics to retrieve the situation, Garašanin, without mentioning the Obrenović, argued that the Assembly was acting illegally. However, his carefully prepared speech was drowned out in the confusion provoked by Vučić. Angry at his inability to manipulate the Assembly, Vučić threatened Mihailović, but the latter retorted: "Enough of you! We will do as the people wishes." Defeated, the deputation left the Assembly and the Council itself dispersed.

In the Assembly's name, Stevča Mihailović sought to take over the Belgrade garrison and police. But Garašanin, controlling them, refused to relinquish authority to him. Grujić and Mihailović then sent a mob of Belgraders which surrounded Garašanin's house and demanded that he hand over army and police to Mihailović. Coming to the window, Garašanin quieted the crowd, then asked whether its members had confidence in him. When they said they did, he promised to do everything legally and properly, pledging his home, life and family as security. The crowd quickly dispersed.[30]

The Liberals then sought to negotiate a transfer of control, but Garašanin declared that the Assembly could not exercise legal authority even temporarily and had violated the Constitution by assuming the regency and issuing proclamations to the people. Instead, a regular regency must be created. That evening agreement was reached: next day a temporary government would be set up headed by Garašanin, Mihailović, and a third regent they could appoint. Only to such a legal provisional government would Garašanin consent to relinquish control over army and police.

The morning of December 12th troops were placed on alert and cannon loaded in the army barracks next to the Assembly. Responding to Mihailović's appeal to protect the Assembly, a large crowd of Obrenovites milled about in front of its chamber. The two officers assigned by the Assembly as Mihailović's assistants, rode before the crowd on horseback as its commanders. As the Assembly and Council convened in their meeting places, some councillors came armed, others brought bodyguards. In the Assembly Chairman Anastasijević again sought to reassert his authority over secretaries Grujić and Ilić by refusing to sign Liberal documents drawn up outside the Assembly. While defending himself, Grujić was interrupted repeatedly and sat down defeated. The Obrenović restoration looked like a secretarial deception; Liberal maneuvers of the previous days appeared to have failed. With the Assembly divided between Obrenovites and their opponents, whichever faction acted boldly would carry the Assembly. The conservatives were prevailing until Secretary Ilić, whipping out his pistol, threatened to shoot Anastasijević. The frightened chairman quickly dropped his accusations against Grujić who urged the Assembly not to yield to force from the army barracks.

Meanwhile the previous evening (December 11th) two conservative supporters of Prince Aleksandar had launched a counterrevolutionary plot. Councillors Majstorović and Matejić conspired with Colonel Lukavčević, commander of the army barracks and the Prince's relative, to have the Council and army restore Aleksandar to the throne. Early on the 12th Lukavčević was to occupy the Council chamber with troops and summon the councillors to the barracks. He carried out the latter task, but did not occupy the Council chamber. Eleven of its seventeen members complied immediately with his demand. Asked by Councillor Gavrilo Jeremić why they had been called to the barracks, Colonel Lukavčević replied: the army wants Aleksandar as prince. The councillors present

agreed. When Vice-Chairman Aleksa Janković urged the troops in the barracks to remain loyal to the Prince, they shouted: "Long live Prince Aleksandar!" The mob before the Assembly responded: "Long live Prince
Miloš!" The Council was in the barracks while the Assembly was ringed
with armed men split between Karadjordjists and Obrenovites. It looked
like the eve of a bloody civil war.

After the barracks proclaimed Aleksandar restored, the councillors
returned to their chambers. There they drew up a document urging Aleksandar to return from the fortress, ordering the Assembly to disperse,
and affirming that Aleksandar's abdication had been engineered "not by
the will of the people, but only by a few hotheads, notably the Assembly's secretaries." The Council thereby repudiated all its earlier decisions! With this document the councillors returned to the barracks for a
military escort so Majstorović and Matejić could take it personally to
Prince Aleksandar. Next the army attempted to disperse the Assembly.
Its artillery commander, Lieutenant Kosta Nenadović, Prince Aleksandar's
relative, was about to order his guns to fire buckshot at the crowd before
the Assembly when Colonel Lukavčević restrained him. Instead about a
hundred infantry and fifteen cavalry issued from the barracks on the hill
and with drums beating and bugles playing descended toward the Assembly in the valley. Then Ranko Alimpić, rushing before the crowd pistol
in hand, stopped the officer leading the infantry; a man in the crowd
trained his pistol on the cavalry officer. The two officers, who had believed they could disperse the crowd without using force, now turned
back with their men. Emboldened, the mob shouted: "Long live the
Obrenović!" As the troops retired into the barracks, Assembly delegates
returned to their seats and resumed business. Under the terms of the
Garašanin-Liberal agreement of the previous evening, the Assembly now
revoked its regency and selected instead as regents Garašanin, Mihailović
and J. Ugrinjić, chairman of the Court of Cassation. The deputies now
realized that until Miloš arrived, this was the proper course since the army
and police would not recognize the Assembly even as interim ruler.

About 160 troops made a second sortie from the back gate of the
barracks, seeking to convey the two councillors to the fortress, but a
crowd mostly of students halted them. Ordered to avoid force, the cavalry returned to the barracks while the infantry surrendered to Alimpić
and were confined temporarily in the Assembly. Thus ended with a

whimper the army's attempt to restore Prince Aleksandar.[31] The Belgrade pasha and the foriegn consuls urged the army and Council to avoid bloodshed while the formation of a provisional government revealed that agreement between the oligarchs and Liberals had been reached. Two regents— Mihailović and Ugrinjić—were already in the Assembly as delegates. Then a delegation went to fetch Garašanin.

The Assembly had chosen him unanimously as the top leader of the provisional government. Its delegation came to him saying: "Now or never; come and help." The situation was "truly dangerous," Garašanin wrote Marinović later, "and it would have been shameful for me not to share those dangers. The people wanted me and summoned me."[32] Garašanin promptly walked back to the Assembly with the delegates. At his entrance, the members of the Assembly took off their hats and cheered: "Long live Garašanin!" He told the expectant Assembly that he was entering the regency only until order had been restored. "The difficult circumstances. . .and danger which was about to shake our whole country and to cause terrible bloodshed," he wrote Mondain, had compelled him to assume temporary power. With Austrian troops concentrated on the frontier, Garašanin believed his action had averted military intervention.[33]

Garašanin then took a seat at the chairman's desk and began issuing instructions. First he ordered the army, through its commander, Colonel Lukavčević, to remain quietly in its barracks. Lukavčević was Prince Aleksandar's nephew but he was also a dedicated soldier and an honorable man. Previously, Garašanin had admonished him to obey his orders and his alone, warning that any disobedience would be punished severely. Lukavčević had replied that he understood his military duties and despite his family ties, would obey Garašanin unconditionally. When the chief of the Interior Ministry's military section, Milivoje Blaznavac, went to the barracks and sought to give commands, Lukavčević adhered loyally to his pledge. Blaznavac, noted his superior, Garašanin, had been intriguing constantly with the Prince and the Austrian and Russian consuls. Unwilling to commit himself fully until he saw which side would win, Blaznavac feared an Obrenović restoration because of his role in Miloš' internment in Zagreb in 1848.

Having ordered the army through Lukavčević to remain quiet and avoid using force, Garašanin waited discreetly at home for the Assembly to inform him that the regency, agreed upon the previous night, had been formed. Apparently, he did not expressly prohibit the army from leaving its barracks. Mihailović's assistant, Belimarković, came to see him twice at home: first, he informed Garašanin that the soldiers intended to move against the Assembly, and the second time that they had left the barracks. Garašanin remained calm, convinced that Lukavčević and the army would not use force without his authorization. After the army's initial sortie, Blaznavac wrote him that with the councillors in the barracks, the army awaited his further orders. Garašanin then reiterated to Lukavčević that the army would remain quiet and take no action without his instructions. When the army detachment moved towards the Assembly, Garašanin had repeated this order. Some Liberals criticized Garašanin for not rushing to the scene when he first learned that army units had left the barracks. However, Garašanin was not a soldier, but a bureaucrat accustomed to handle matters with written notes. After coming to the Assembly and being named to head the provisional government, in order to remove the councillors from the barracks, Garašanin had sat down and written Lukavčević a lengthy letter. Only a true bureaucrat, notes Jovanović, continues in the midst of a revolution to administer calmly and dispatch circulars.[34] Amazingly enough, this procedure proved very effective.

The "victory" of the Obrenovite crowd over the regulars on December 12th resulted from the army's reluctance to employ force, which in turn stemmed from Garašanin's orders to its commanders. The army could use force only if Lukavčević ordered it on his own hook, but he refused to do that. He did authorize, perhaps persuaded by Blaznavac, a sortie against the crowd, but he had ordered his officers and men not to fire on it. The hot-tempered artillery commander, Lieutenant Kosta Nenadović, was about to use cannonfire against the mob when his superior restrained him. Lukavčević saved the situation by jumping in front of the guns. Had they been fired, the crowd would have doubtless have been dispersed, the Assembly dissolved, and Prince Aleksandar restored.[35] Instead, the army had been paralyzed, the Liberal crowd allowed to triumph, and the attempt to restore Aleksandar was doomed.

Precisely what Garašanin intended on December 12th remains somewhat unclear, but he took great pains to act legally and correctly. One might claim he was protecting himself regardless of the outcome. Certainly he opposed Prince Aleksandar's restoration since all his actions during 1858 had been designed to remove him. After the Prince's flight, his chief concern was to prevent an army coup on his behalf. Garašanin also did not intend under any circumstances to seize the throne himself. Because of his family's travail at the hands of Obrenović princes, he remained uneasy about their restoration but did not oppose it. Indeed, apparently he welcomed their proclamation by the Assembly, went there, agreed to enter a regency with Liberal leaders, then persuaded the Council and army to cease resisting the Assembly. Prepared to reach agreement with the Obrenovites, Garašanin still clearly favored Mihailo over Miloš, the Assembly's choice, as prince. Before Prince Aleksandar fell, he had told Nikola Hristić:

> As to the Obrenović, I cannot bear to work in their behalf. If it turned out that Prince Mihailo should come, I would greet him, but if Miloš should come, there would be no place for me here and I would have to leave the country.[36]

Once St. Andrew's Assembly convened, argues Jovanović, Garašanin lost control of events, was outplayed by the Liberals, and suffered a great personal reverse. Although an Obrenović restoration under certain circumstancs fitted his political plans, he allowed others to seize the initiative and win the glory for restoring them, leaving him in an ambiguous and uncomfortable position. Escaping his supervision, the Assembly confronted him with a surprising fait accompli which revealed that the great oligarch and police chief was not a revolutionary leader. The masses moved too swiftly and unpredictably for him. Accustomed to meditate in his office and hampered by adherence to legality, Garašanin did not fit in with the rapid tempo of revolution, nor did he sympathize with mobs or a people in revolt. However, his superb abilities as minister of police enabled him to contain and limit the revolution. By taking the Prince to the fortress, halting the army with his notes, and persuading the Assembly to revoke its usurpation of power, he, more than anyone else, prevented a bloody civil war. Conflict between the Assembly and the army would almost surely have provoked foreign intervention. Unable to direct the revolution, he supervised and restrained it from excesses.[37] Thanks to Garašanin, the dynastic change of 1858 was the most peaceful overturn in modern Serbian history until the Simović coup of March 1941. Believing that no Serbian assembly could govern, least of all one dominated by passions and excitement, he had insisted upon and secured strong, organized legal authority and swift, non-violent completion of the coup d'état.

Thus on December 13th, thanks largely to Garašanin, the army and Assembly were reconciled. Prominent army leaders—Lukavčević, Blaznavac and Kosta Nenadović—all declared that the army had joined with the people. The Assembly's work ended with the Obrenović restoration. Pending Turkish confirmation of the dynastic overturn, a provisional government representing both Liberals and oligarchs exercised authority. That same day the Council revoked all its hasty actions taken while in the army barracks.

Though the entire people favored the Obrenović, the situation remained perilous, Garašanin wrote Marinović. Except for the conviction that without him matters would be still worse, he would not have retained office after Prince Aleksandar's fall. He had merely heeded the insistent summons of the people. Alluding apparently to persistent reports of his princely candidacy, Garašanin added: "Nothing else was prepared, you can rest assured. I was firmly resolved to accept whatever the people decided and made this clear to everyone." Garašanin did not know what would happen next, though he still preferred Prince Mihailo. "Then I would still have hopes for salvation from the evils that afflict us; now I fear we may sink deeper in the mire and even regret that we got rid of Aleksandar." Prince Miloš was old; if he acted as before, he could ruin much. His rule would only turn out well, if he selected able advisers. "With those he is allied with now and who take all the credit, he won't get far," predicted Garašanin. He should hand over the throne immediately to his son, Mihailo, but was most unlikely to do so. Garašanin declared he would leave the government as soon as Miloš arrived:

> As a member of the government and interior minister, I am signing proclamations for Prince Miloš, send them to be made public, write documents and work day and night to preserve order and peace and do everything I can to promote the success of popular desires . . . and despite all that, guards are placed before my house so that I won't betray the national cause.!![38]

After restoring Prince Miloš, the St. Andrew's Assembly had requested the Porte to confirm him as ruler. For over three weeks Serbia remained uncertain whether the Turks would do so and what might happen if they refused. Two hostile groupings observed an uneasy truce which could collapse at any time as the Council under Garašanin and Vučić faced an Assembly faction led by old Obrenovites. Quarrels began immediately between these elements, soon to be called Conservatives and Liberals. The provisional government itself was split also with Garašanin controlling the police and Mihailović the army. "Boss" Filip Stanković's 600-man independent force, paid by Miloš, dominated Belgrade's streets. On December 27th Stanković provoked a major scandal by not allowing Garašanin, still regent and interior minister, to leave Anastasijević's house. Reacting indignantly to what he considered an affront to his honor and dignity, Garašanin demanded that Mihailović rein in Stanković: "Filip is not a policeman and either should be removed or kept under strict control."

Unable to stem the Liberal tide, Garašanin could merely fight a delaying action. He wished to preserve the Karadjordjević regime without Aleksandar and maintain the 1838 Constitution. With public backing, the Liberals advocated basic changes in state administration, purging officialdom, and adding the assembly to Prince and Council as a third factor in legislation. The new assembly law of January 5, 1859 had been altered significantly in the Council by Garašanin. The assembly would meet triennially, not annually; its advice would not be binding on Prince or Council; and rather than controlling the budget, it would merely be consulted on new taxes. Lacking true power of decision, the assembly would only give opinions and express popular wishes. Garašanin had drawn its teeth and also blocked Liberal efforts to purge his beloved bureaucracy. Thus he had inserted in the December 13th proclamation of the temporary regency the passage: "[We] shall respect all existing authorities in the country. . . ." His message was clear: the Obrenović could rule at the people's will but with the old institutions and officials.[39]

However, on January 3, 1859, once the Porte confirmed him as ruler, Prince Miloš promptly dissolved the three-man regency, appointed Stevča Mihailović interim ruler pending his own arrival in Belgrade, then began issuing decrees from abroad in his old autocratic manner. Mihailović's assistant, Jevrem Grujić, now antagonistic toward Garašanin, became actual head of Serbia's diplomatic service. Garašanin's position, he wrote Mondain, had become most difficult and the future was shrouded in uncertainty. Naming Mihailović as Miloš' stand-in was illegal, nor could the Prince under the Constitution, issue binding decrees until he had taken his oath of office.[40] Garašanin noted that he was composing a circular about Miloš' actions which he would distribute among the people before returning to the Council. "I consider this occasion appropriate to withdraw from affairs before I know the new prince's intentions for governing Serbia." Unwilling to serve under the incapable Mihailović, he resigned as Interior Minister January 9th.[41]

Garašanin had played a vital role in the overturn of 1858, if not quite as dominant a part as he himself claimed. Without his leadership and organizational skill in preparing the campaign, it seems doubtful that Prince Aleksandar would have been removed. His restraining hand had prevented disorder and bloodshed which almost surely would have provoked Turkish or Austrian military intervention and consequent loss of Serbian autonomy. Yet, when the smoke cleared, the Liberals had outplayed him and forced him to relinquish the reins of power to his political opponents. About to be enthroned was an old despot he could not serve. Garašanin's political career seemed to be over.

NOTES

1. On the St. Andrew's Day Assembly and the Serbian overturn of 1858 see A. Radenić, "Svetoandrejska Skupština," *Spomenik SANU*, vol. 113 (Belgrade, 1964); Jevrem Grujić, *Zapisi*, II. Summaries in English are found in Petrovich, *A History*, I, 262-269 and G. Stokes, *Legitimacy through Liberalism*, pp. 18-22. See also S. Jovanović, *Ustavobranitelji*, pp. 235-272; Jaša Prodanović, *Istorija političkih stranaka i struja u Srbiji* (Belgrade, 1947), I, 192-207; J. Milićević, *Jevrem Grujić*, pp. 74-91; and Vlada Ljotić, "Sveto-Andrejska Skupština i odvodjenje Kneza Aleksandra u grad Turcima," *Politika*, July 14, 1935.

2. Milićević, *Grujić*, pp. 74-75; Jovanović, *Ustavobranitelji*, p. 221.

3. IG 1045, Kosta Janković to Garašanin, November ? 1858. Vlada Ljotić in "Svetoandrejska," complained that during the election his father, Mita Ljotić, candidate from Smederevo district, had been defeated through pressure exerted by Garašanin's police. Ljotić's complaint, forwarded to the Council by Prince Aleksandar, was rejected.

4. Jovanović, *Ustavobranitelja,* pp. 221-226; Grujić, *Zapisi,* II, 12-18; Milićević, *Grujić,* pp. 74-75.

5. Grujić, *Zapisi,* II, 24-25.

6. Stranjaković, "Ilija," p. 73.

7. Garašanin to Marinović, January 15, 1859, *Pisma,* II, 15.

8. Ristić, *Spoljašnji odnošaji,* I, 286.

9. Grujić, *Zapisi,* II, 35.

10. N. Popov, *Srbija posle Parižskogo mira,* p. 39.

11. Garašanin to Marinović, January 9, 1859, *Pisma,* II, 9.

12. Grujić, *Zapisi,* II, 45-46.

13. Nikola Hristić, *Memoari.* Designed for special situations when a crucial issue such as a change of dynasty was to be decided upon, a great national assembly (*Velika Skupština*) was roughly twice the size of a regular one.

14. Grujić, *Zapisi,* II, 45.

15. Ibid., II, 45-47, 132 ff.

16. IG 1683, "Moji spomeni,"; Garašanin to Marinović, January 9, 1859, *Pisma,* II, 8-9; Radenić, "Svetoandrejska," No. 89, p. 189.

17. Jovanović, *Ustavobranitelji,* pp. 226-227.

18. Grujić, *Zapisi,* II, 31-33; Prodanović, *Istorija,* pp. 191-194; Jovanović, *Ustavobranitelji,* pp. 240-241. Grujić relates that Vučić and Garašanin had warned the Prince that it would be best to cancel the dinner since no one might come to it. Replied the Prince: "That cannot be; they must come if I summon them." *Zapisi,* II, 31. When few delegates came, this was the first significant blow against Aleksandar's rule, Ibid., p. 33.

19. Ibid., II, 88-99; Jovanović, *Ustavobranitelji,* 241-242.

20. Ibid., pp. 243-246.

21. Ibid., pp. 247-248; Grujić, II, 112-118.

22. Radenić, "Svetoandrejska," No. 89, pp. 193-195.

23. Jovanović, *Ustavobranitelji,* pp. 249-250; Grujić, II, 129-130.

24. Ibid., 130-132; Jovanović, pp. 251-252.

25. Radenić, No. 89, pp. 195-197. Kosta Magazinović's *Memoirs* corroborates Garašanin's account in "Begstvo." The minister had assured the Prince that no danger threatened him in his palace whereas to go through the town to the fortress at night without guards would be highly dangerous. But Aleksandar had insisted: "I will get in the carriage with you and

no one will think I am in it but that you are just driving home." When the coachman stopped in front of Garašanin's house, the Prince had cried out in terror: "Take me to the fortress!"—Arhiv SANU, No. 9288, Memoari Koste Magazinovića.

26.   V. Ljotić, "Svetoandrejska," *Politika*, July 14, 1931, p. 9. The account of R. Stefanović, a personal friend of the Prince, takes a similar approach, notes Stranjaković, "Ilija," p. 132.

27.   Jovanović, *Ustavobranitelji*, p. 252.

28.   Radenić, No. 89, p. 186.

29.   Grujić, *Zapisi*, II, 133-136; Jovanović, *Ustavobranitelji*, pp. 253-254; Milićević, *Grujić*, pp. 87-88.

30.   Ibid., II, 150-151; Arhiv SANU, No. 9288, Memoari Magazinovića; Jovanović, *Ustavobranitelji*, pp. 255-256.

31.   Ibid., pp. 261-267; Radenić, No. 87, pp. 197-199; Grujić, *Zapisi*, II, 163 ff.

32.   Garašanin to Marinović, December 31, 1858, *Pisma*, I, 410-413.

33.   IG 1127, Garašanin to Mondain, January 4, 1859.

34.   Jovanović, *Ustavobranitelji*, pp. 267-270.

35.   Radenić, No. 87, p. 199. In his "Begstvo Knjaza Aleksandra," Garašanin claims a significant personal role in averting bloodshed. Following Lukačević's action, irritation increased steadily between the troops on one side of a levee shouting: "Long live Karadjordjević!" and the armed crowd on the other side crying: "Long live the Obrenović!" Garašanin declared that he stood between them trying to calm down both sides. The soldiers were controlled relatively easily because they obeyed their officers who followed Garašanin's orders, but the Liberal mob, fueled by enthusiasm and liquor, insulted and taunted the soldiers. Fights broke out and individual soldiers charged into the crowd with raised fists. Finally, Garašanin persuaded the soldiers to withdraw into the barracks.

36.   *Memoari Nikole Hristića.*

37.   Jovanović, *Ustavobranitelji*, pp. 271-272.

38.   Garašanin to Marinović, December 31, 1858, *Pisma*, I, 410-414.

39.   Jovanović, *Druga Vlada Miloša i Mihaila, 1858-1868* (Belgrade, 1923), pp. 3-8.

40.   IG 1127, Garašanin to Mondain, January 3 and 4, 1859.

41.   Garašanin to Marinović, January 4 and 6, 1859, *Pisma*, II, 1-5.

CHAPTER XIII:

THE OBRENOVIĆ PRINCES RETURN, 1859-1861

"Our old prince [Miloš] is surrounded by the worst and most incompetent people and his health is bad. As long as he lives, there is no hope of improvement."

Garašanin to Mondain, February 5, 1860.

"Then Mihailo greeted me, offered me his hand and embraced me. . . . We spent an hour together in conversation. . . and then he invited me to supper. . . . I found him to be just the prince we have both always wished for and which the country needs."

Garašanin to Marinović, January 27, 1859.

From Prince Miloš' return to Serbia in January 1859 until early 1861 Garašanin remained in retirement. Unwilling to work with the aged prince and believing it would prove impossible in any case, Garašanin awaited his death, counting increasingly on his heir, Mihailo, to restore unity, discipline, and a sense of national purpose to Serbia. Meanwhile, he was much preoccupied with personal woes: illness, debts, and suspicion by the new regime. Inclined to let matters drift, he felt powerless to stop what he viewed as the deterioration of national morality and political standards.[1]

Before stepping down, Garašanin had completed all necessary preparations to welcome the Obrenović princes back to Serbia. His resignation
as Interior Minister was facilitated by Miloš' obvious coolness and failure
to even mention him in his telegrams from abroad. Garašanin wrote
Marinović January 6th: "Whether the Obrenović will want or need me
and whether I can serve them will depend on their intentions for governing the country. . . . " He urged Stevča Mihailović, the interim ruler, to
accept his resignation without referring the matter to Prince Miloš. On the
9th he could inform Marinović that his resignation had been accepted and
that Stojan Lešjanin had replaced him temporarily as Interior Minister.

> I did not resign insulted, God forbid, but circumstances dictated that
> I take that step for the sake of my honor, and I parted with every-
> one, even with Stevča [Mihailović] with the greatest affection and
> agreement. He hesitated to accept my resignation, but I let him
> know precisely what my position was.

Though predicting that the Obrenović princes would encounter many
difficulties, he declared his support: "Although formerly I was an opponent of the Obrenović family, now I want it to succeed in the good
national cause and will promote this as best I can. I will not be in the
opposition."

Garašanin expressed little faith either in Prince Miloš or in interim ruler,
Stevča Mihailović. To Marinović he judged the old Prince severely and
predicted that his rule would pose many problems. To be sure, Miloš had
been a hero who had created an autonomous Serbian state, but Garašanin
feared his despotism and lack of restraint in domestic affairs:

> Prince Miloš is an old man and does not know the new conditions.
> . . . In my view the old man will not give up ruling while he lives. He
> will say in his habitual way: 'Mihailo is a child who doesn't know
> anything yet; I must correct everything that is ruined . . . .'[2]

Meanwhile Mihailović's temporary government, at the Prince's instructions
hastened to oust leaders and officials of the former regime. The Liberals
removed Franjo Zah from the Military Academy, Anastasije Nikolić, Garašanin's former understudy, and other Austrian Serbs and expelled them

from Serbia. Metropolitan Petar, the top church official and an Austrian Serb, was pressured into resignation. Panic spread among other "prečani" officials. Such removals and expulsions, wrote Garašanin, had dampened public enthusiasm for the Obrenović restoration and would weaken Serbia. "Intelligent people, even many of Miloš' friends, are very worried." Everything must be left up to the old Prince, but Stevča Mihailović, though moderate enough, could neither grasp the whole situation or deal adequately with it.[3]

Garašanin's hopes for retention of the older, better-trained officials were dashed by the Assembly resolution of January 19th expressing lack of public confidence in all old ministers and councillors.[4] Extreme Liberals who favored a wholesale housecleaning justified the Assembly's actions arguing that Prince Miloš should be able to choose new colleagues. Moderates such as Mihailović and Grujić favored replacing some councillors and ministers but wished to retain Garašanin in the Council, among others. No longer bearing responsibility, Garašanin decided not to protest the mass firings. On January 20th, before Mihailović accepted the Assembly's decision, he wrote:

> I would like to get out of this false position somehow. If he rejects the Assembly's proposals, I will submit my resignation [from the Council]. If he accepts it, the matter will be settled anyway . . . . The people [Assembly] has said it does not want me and that is sufficient, as if the Prince had told me that.

Friends urged Garašanin to block the removals or organize a protest, but he declined to oppose the Assembly or appeal to the powers: "When my offers to help are rejected on all sides, what is more natural than to remain a simple spectator?" Criticizing the Assembly's decision to oust the 2,000-3,000 peasant elders (*kmetovi*) from office, he predicted that such radical sudden changes would scarcely produce favorable results:

> Good could only result if all the old institutions were changed gradually, corrected and adjusted, but such abrupt actions can achieve nothing that will satisfy the people. These unfortunate political factions have greatly weakened us. . . . I knew that the people was

unprepared for an assembly and feared it, but the situation [under Prince Aleksandar] was so bad that nothing else could be done.[5]

Only Prince Mihailo might carry through true constitutional reforms. The Assembly's resolution gave Miloš a pretext to remove all ministers and councillors if he chose. Meanwhile, shunning the old leaders, Mihailović and Grujić conducted the interim government. Proceeding under the Act of January 19th, the Liberals conducted a campaign against traditional officialdom and deprived all officials of security. The Assembly, clearly exceeding its mandate, had begun acting like a revolutionary body, noted foreign consuls.[6]

On January 20th Dr. Pacek, confidant of Prince Mihailo, wrote Garašan urging him to confer with the Obrenović princes at Požarevac before they returned to Belgrade. Next day Garašanin informed Marinović: "Tomorrow morning Vuk [Karadžić] [7] and I will respond to this summons and we will see what happens."[8] Noting that relations between his father and Garašanin were strained, Mihailo had asked Pacek to write Garašanin. Indeed, the Požarevac meeting greatly improved Garašanin's relations with Miloš, but even more with Mihailo, laying a foundation of trust and mutual friendship. For him, Garašanin wrote Marinović, the meeting with Mihailo was especially difficult because of the major role of Garašanin's family in Mihailo's expulsion in 1842 during which time Garašanin's father and brother had been killed.[9] There had been such a crowd at Mihailo's quarters that Garašanin could not enter:

Then Mihailo greeted me, offered me his hand and embraced me, apparently with full sincerity. He asked me to await his return from seeing his father. We spent an hour together in conversation . . . , then he invited me to supper. He urged me to be frank with him and promised to reciprocate. He urged me to remain the same patriot I had always been and for which he respected me and requested me to aid his father so that his rule could live up to popular expectations and desires. He said that unless good, honorable and capable men surrounded Miloš, since he was old, he could be misled and damage Serbia. He spoke as only an intelligent prince could speak. We discussed all previous and current events, reached conclusions about them, and set forth ideas on what should be done and how to do it. I can state that in this young man I found all the qualities you had described to me. *I found him to be just the prince we have both always wished for and which the country needs.* . . . * Besides a good heart and steady character, he grasps precisely and fully both the duties of a ruler and every public shift.

After this conversation, Garašanin realized that Mihailo was deeply worried about his father's impending rule, as were other intelligent Serbs. In poor health and unable to supervise matters personally, Miloš would have to rely on advisers whose intentions remained obscure. "I very much fear being summoned into some kind of ministry whose principles I do not at all understand," observed Garašanin.[10] Even after a new cabinet was announced January 30th, he feared some post would be offered to him. He wrote Marinović next day: "I do not wish to serve any more."[11]

Relieved, Garašanin could inform his friend February 10th: "Congratulate me that my name is not on the list of new appointments. I need to work but the way things have gone, I truly could not accept anything under Miloš. To go backwards twenty years is incomprehensible to me, but I will keep my views to myself." To Marinović's comment deploring Garašanin's persecution by Miloš' regime, he responded: "Never have I been more insulted than now, but I am determined to remain patient. I will not seek any defense from abroad and will refuse any that is offered." Again he denied he had sought a regency for himself. Officeseekers were spreading such lies to confuse people and dramatize their own services. The Liberal leaders, he concluded, were "the most malicious people ever to appear in Serbia."[12]

Arriving in Belgrade January 25th, Miloš faced the issue of firings of officials. The Constitution prescribed that no official could be removed without court action, and the removal of councillors required the Porte's confirmation. The Liberals argued that Miloš must be free to select new officials; the Porte and foreign consuls agreed. But Miloš went even further. His recall to the throne, he concluded, had nullified a constitution issued originally against his will. Therefore, Miloš argued, the Council, created by that constitution, no longer existed. Approving the Assembly's decision to remove the old councillors, he refused to name new irremovable ones.

---

* Author's italics.

Serbia, declared Miloš, could not have two rulers. Until the Liberals explained that the Assembly and Porte must give their consent, Miloš intended to eliminate the entire structure of 1838 and rule autocratically. While the Constitution remained in force, Miloš would have to work with the Council. He asked the Assembly to propose new councillors, but disliking its choices and heedless of the Constitution, he then named twelve new ones himself.

On January 28, 1859 Prince Miloš proclaimed his return to the throne. Old officials were to retain office temporarily until investigation decided whether they deserved to remain. Serbia became absorbed with who would stay and who would go. The campaign against older officials, as Garašanin had predicted, undermined public authority. Though deluged with requests for jobs from 5,000 officeseekers the first year, Miloš refued to allow the people to select their own officials. Removing some unreliables, he claimed the power to hire and fire officials at his whim. This imperilled the entire bureaucratic mechanism created under the Constitution of 1838. Garašanin and his colleagues, urging Aleksandar's removal, had not intended such an outcome, but the Assembly had escaped their control. A revolutionary movement against officials began eliminating tenure, rank, and even pensions. Conservatives believed Liberals were seeking their jobs; actually the leaders were being driven on by their followers. Grujić, their most moderate leader, got the blame. Of the Conservatives, Liberals feared Garašanin the most, yet when Miloš entered Belgrade, Garašanin rode right behind Prince Mihailo. Fortunately for the Liberals, Miloš had distrusted Garašanin since 1838 and kept him at a distance. At first Miloš worked with the Liberals but misunderstood the new conditions. Detesting the principle of ministerial responsibility, Miloš believed that his personal judgment was enough.[13]

Therefore, after Miloš' return, despite Mihailo's support, Garašanin's position became difficult. Making constant trouble for him, government leaders barred him from court. During interrogation of some councillors, officials suggested he be arrested and questioned until the influential Judge Jovan Mićić urged Prince Miloš personally to let him be. Prince Mihailo, concluded Grujić, had interceded to prevent harassment of Garašanin. One former councillor, Gaja Jeremić, had even been questioned about "what Garašanin thought."[14] Believing it would be unwise to visit the princes under such circumstances, Garašanin shunned the court. He wished to withdraw to rural Grocka but feared trouble if he did. Milivoje Blaznavac was still in chains and Vučić was being interrogated constantly. Regretting now that his own plan had been been realized during 1858, he wrote Marinović:

> I wished to restore the Obrenovićs without having dealings with the factions. I thought of going forward rather than returning to the past. Selfish men ruined the idea: it seemed more beneficial to them to have partisanship, thus creating great difficulties not just for the princes but for the entire country.

Now almost no one dared come to see him, but he would not object as long as the authorities left him alone. "I would like to go somewhere but do not know where."[15]

Then came a reprieve. Garašanin noted March 20th that heeding a princely summons, he had recently discussed internal problems in Topčider with Prince Miloš. "It was nice to hear Miloš discuss Serbia's problems, and I regret not being able to help him solve them." He had found Miloš very busy, seemingly more so than ever. Unwilling to hear the word law, Miloš preferred to handle matters himself rather than relying on others. Garašanin approved Miloš' idea of simplifying administration but felt it needed to be done thoughtfully and skillfully. "I would like to serve Miloš, but to serve a prince who does not listen would be intolerable." At times he believed Serbia might advance under Miloš, but everything remained chaotic. In government "unfortunately capable and honorable people are lacking."[16] Soon after their interview, Garašanin fell severely ill, and Miloš showed his concern by sending adjutants frequently to inquire about him; in July 1859 the Prince assigned him a sizable pension. Mihailović, complaining he could not find competent men to handle state affairs, also came sometimes. To Mondain Garašanin described the unfortunate trends in Serbian domestic policy under Prince Miloš:

> Everything old, whether good or bad, has collapsed or been halted and in its place nothing new and better has been or is being created. The Constitution, laws and regulations are no longer in force. The new orders which are being issued do not contain any of the old principles. Everything is being done for the moment. Many officials

are being replaced, and the new ones, if they are no worse than the old, are also no better.

Only Prince Mihailo, added Garašanin, could respond properly to Serbian needs and desires.[17]

In foreign affairs, affirmed Piroćanac, Miloš pursued a direction wholly different from Prince Aleksandar's, especially toward the Porte. Too old to conceive a great policy, Miloš nonetheless demarcated a more correct, sensible approach toward the Turks and the powers. Serbia would seek their recognition of her right to full autonomy, obtain evacuation of Turks from areas outside Belgrade, and secure hereditary Obrenović title to the throne. Miloš did not resolve these issues but prepared the ground for Mihailo.[18]

In April 1859 Austria went to war against Sardinia and France which sought to expel Habsburg power from northern Italy. Prince Miloš had sent his son, Mihailo, to Western Europe to ascertain what course Serbia should pursue and try to obtain the powers' recognition of his dynasty as hereditary rulers of Serbia.[19] Before the war erupted Mihailo discussed mutual relations with Magyar leaders including the émigré, Louis Kossuth. In Vienna Russian Ambassador Balabin advised: Serbia should remain quiet and provide no pretext for foreign complaints since Russia opposed reopening the Eastern Question at that time. If she complied, Serbia could count on Russia's support later to acquire Bosnia and Hercegovina.[20] From Paris Mihailo wrote his father that Balabin had favored welcoming secretly to Belgrade Bosnians and Bulgars seeking aid. As to national agitation in Bosnia:

> . . . Ilija Garašanin did much in regard to such matters and I believe he would do much now. He could surely find a way to establish ties with Bosnians in Srem and Slavonia and would employ every effort to satisfy Your Highness and direct matters the right way.

The Russians, Mihailo hoped, would aid Serbia financially to achieve its national goals.[21]

Fearful that a general European war might result from the Austro-Sardinian conflict, Garašanin asked Marinović on May 8th to urge Prince Mihailo to hasten home and advise his father. Although he would normally rejoice at a central European war, "now I feel that our incompetence would leave us without benefit and even damage us."[22]

In the same letter Garašanin noted he had recently composed a memorandum on how Belgrade should react to the European situation resulting from the Austro-Sardinian war. Were the conflict limited to Austria, Sardinia and France, Serbia would remain secure. However, if the remaining powers joined in, the Porte would ally itself with England and Prussia. Upset internally and unprepared militarily, Serbia might well be occupied by Turkish and Austrian troops before the Russians arrived. To prevent such a disaster, Belgrade must discover Franco-Russian intentions and reach full accord with those powers. While reassuring Austria and Turkey, Serbia should prepare secretly against possible attack by forging close ties with Montenegro and if possible with Greece. Anticipating his subsequent national program under Mihailo, Garašanin continued:

> We should secretly prepare areas around Serbia for an imminent movement against Turkey, chiefly by gathering them under our leadership and by creating calm. We should send agents to ascertain the status of Turkish forces everywhere around Serbia as far as Sofia.

All means should be employed to protect Serbia against attacks from stronger foes, including utilizing Magyar émigrés to rouse Hungary and thus prevent Austria from invading Serbia. Then if Russian troops approached its frontiers, Serbia could take the offensive against the Turks. "Good preparation and wise behavior will gain us credit among all the powers."

Domestically, continued Garašanin, Serbia must display unity under a strong monarchy. He relied upon Prince Mihailo to end existing domestic disorder and restore calm disturbed by selfish Liberal philosophizing and untimely civil liberties:

> Showing off with assemblies and juries cannot be the fashion under these circumstances—moderation in that regard is essential. Look at what constitutional Sardinia is doing: transferring promptly all power to the king which is the best method for success.

Contingency plans were required for Serbia and for all those areas and peoples she might ally with. The Balkan peoples must not permit Austria or Turkey to attack them in isolation. As Austrian troops concentrated in Zemun and Pančevo on Serbia's northern borders, Garašanin wondered if Vienna was conspiring with the Turks. "We could be attacked in an hour. Thus we must remain on guard. . . . " Agents should be sent out to report daily on Austrian forces on the frontier. The government and treasury should be prepared to shift to interior Kragujevac at a moment's notice with a printing press to issue essential instructions.[23] This memorandum, though apparently unheeded by Belgrade, reflected Garašanin's views and actions once he came to power again.

With an assembly soon to be held in Kragujevac, noted Garašanin, Prince Miloš had urged him to attend it if his health permitted:

> An assembly would prove valuable in correcting many ills produced by the anarchy of the past winter and to restore calm among the populace, but first they need to prepare a plan for it which I doubt has been done since these [Liberals] are the same people who wrecked everything last winter and today unfortunately have total influence over the administration. Thus the assembly will resemble the last one.

He expressed dismay that loyal officials were still being removed without apparent cause.[24] Mihailović's clique, he affirmed to Marinović, tolerates no one of intelligence unless he follows its ideas blindly. Few older, knowledgeable officials would do so, thus it would be better if they were all removed immediately. While the old officials were not unusually able, at least they could run an orderly administration. Miloš' policy seemed purely destructive:

> The Prince's incapable entourage is able to come up with *the most miserable ideas* since they see clearly that they are hampered by whomever is superior and they will exert power over the Prince only when they have removed from the world, or at least from Serbia, anyone better than they.[25]

Thus Garašanin concluded it would be wisest for him to leave Serbia temporarily. But where should he go?

Truly, I am in a devilish position. Where can I live without being
put under guard for saying something in opposition? I would like
to discuss this with Prince Mihailo, but I don't want to bother him
with my personal woes since I see that he also has to bear it like all
the rest of us. I won't say anything to anyone but will watch how
things develop, then if need be, I will obtain a passport and leave
Serbia *for someplace.*[26]

Late that summer, pleading need of medical treatment, Garašanin left for
Rumania and spent about six months there. He was left undisturbed, he
felt, because of his ties with France and warm relations with Prince Mihailo. Not knowing how Miloš really felt toward him, Garašanin wrote
Mondain October 26th, "imposes on me the greatest caution." Inquiring
again after his health, Miloš urged Garašanin to return home if he wished.
However, under Miloš, he wrote Mondain, illegality was bursting all bonds:
"there is more order among the Arnauti [Albanians] than among us in
Serbia."[27]

As his heath deteriorated, Prince Miloš encountered growing problems
in ruling Serbia. At the Assembly of August 1859 he and the Liberal
intelligentsia parted company. Despite official efforts, all the chief Liberals had been elected delegates. Miloš promptly instructed the authorities to nullify their mandates, then ordered new elections. The Prince
wished to rule as before with a purely peasant, non-partisan assembly.
Conservatives sought to widen the split. That fall *Srpske Novine* published a series of anonymous articles, signed mysteriously with the symbol for a ducat, urging a unified administration and claiming Miloš was
surrounded by political speculators. Written by Matija Ban with Mihailo's
approval, these ducat articles created a furor. They expressed Mihailo's
view that party feuds should cease, the intelligentsia should gather around
the throne with state authority embodied by the prince; assembly and
Council would merely assist him. Opposing the Liberals' purge of officials, the firmly conservative Mihailo felt closer to conservative bureaucrats like Garašanin and Marinović. The ducat articles encouraged conservatives, including younger leaders, such as Filip Hristić, Kosta Cukić
and Jovan Ristić, to rally around Mihailo. Complaining to Miloš, the
Liberals secured removal of *Srpske Novine*'s editor, but by the spring of
1860 Miloš' relations with the Liberals had soured. Their leaders were

watched by the police; some lost their state posts. However, Miloš did not break entirely with the Liberals whom he considered loyal to his dynasty, nor did he turn to Garašanin and Marinović for support. Reverting instead to autocracy, he rendered the Council innocuous by removing arbitrarily any members who opposed him. Miloš' ministers became solely his creatures.[28]

Returning home from Rumania in March 1860, Garašanin was warmly received by Miloš, but preferred to sit quietly at home so the Prince would forget about him.[29] Soon he wrote Marinović that Miloš was ill, and though still able to work, could not venture out. Ministerial meetings were being held under Prince Mihailo's chairmanship. Fortunately, Miloš had a capable administrator, Nikola Hristić, "who knows how to act sensibly on all matters." Garašanin found Mihailo patient though out of sorts. He himself remained apathetic toward everything and would have preferred living in rural Grocka. "I have a thousand misfortunes and cannot help myself," he lamented. After the doctors failed to relieve his illness, Garašanin attended Church frequently and prayed for forgiveness: "When the doctors can do nothing, let God help me."[30] He still hoped that Miloš, despite his eccentricities and corruptness, would keep the country from ruin, but his real hopes centered on Mihailo who with good ministers could rescue Serbia from disaster. Reading books and newspapers more eagerly than ever, Garašanin then only forty-eight, denied any desire to reenter political life:

> I used to be different, but events, the years, and illness have made me regard everything that I see or hear with equanimity. I am not upset directly by anyone, but I am still more or less suspect, so I cannot go to Grocka and have not been there for three years.[31]

Garašanin still worried lest exclusive Serbian reliance on Russia ruin Belgrade's relations with other powers and antagonize the Porte. "Serbia," he wrote in a confidential memorandum for his own use, "should never be allowed to become the tool of Russia or of any other power." In order to secure hereditary Obrenović rule, Belgrade badly needed foreign support, although powers should not expect Serbia to be hostile toward Russia just to demonstrate her independence. If Serbia spoke harshly about Russia, that was being directed to European diplomats who generally responded favorably whenever Belgrade denounced Russia. Instead, Serbia should maintain friendly relations with all major powers in order to guarantee herself against Russian machinations. Serbia should be grateful for Russian favor and support, but she must work equally hard to win favor from other powers by emphasizing that she would not follow Russia contrary to Serbian and European interests. Once again he noted Russia's apparent opposition to everything promoting the strengthening of the Serbian people.[32]

To Marinović, Garašanin expressed amazement at recent Russian behavior in Serbia. "I say Russia because I cannot believe that the Russian envoy can do anything without instructions." Russian Consul Miloshevich had been undermining Prince Mihailo's position, telling Garašanin: things will be much worse for Serbia under Mihailo that under Miloš. Serbian Russophiles were spreading similar views among the populace while Miloš pretended ignorance. "He merely gives orders and thus learns of many things belatedly or not at all."[33]

That summer of 1860, while Miloš was sinking, Garašanin was abroad once more. From Lausanne, Switzerland, he cited reports from Belgrade of the Prince's repeated bouts of severe illness.[34] His own salvation, Garašanin ascribed solely now to his connections with France. From Geneva he wrote Mondain: "If at one time it was fortunate for the Serbian people that the old Prince existed, now it would be much more fortunate if the Prince left immediately this world which he has already greatly outlived."[35] In September, while Garašanin was in Paris, Miloš died at eighty of natural causes, bringing Mihailo to power in Serbia.

Prince Mihailo Obrenović mounted the Serbian throne for the second time with a program of reconciliation, amnestying all Karadjordjists and encouraging them to return and reclaim their official posts and pensions. Mihailo sought to promote Liberal-Conservative cooperation, but neither group favored his brand of princely despotism: Conservatives wanted him to share power with a bureaucratic Council, Liberals with a popularly elected assembly. The Prince's efforts to end factionalism by selecting leaders of both groups as ministers and councillors thus ended in failure.[36]

When Jovan Marinović returned to Belgrade, Prince Mihailo proposed he become premier and foreign minister with Jevrem Grujić as Minister of Justice and Gavrilović as Finance Minister. Marinović would agree only provided he could form a cabinet with compatible colleagues. No ministry without internal unity, he believed, would function properly. Although anxious to have Marinović as premier, Mihailo refused to let him name his colleagues. Vuk Karadžić, the writer and the Prince's intermediary, then asked the liberal leader, Grujić, whether he would serve as premier. Agreeing with Marinović about cabinet harmony, Grujić replied that ministers should be selected who possessed public confidence and were well-known in Europe. Stressing Serbia's urgent need of French support, Grujić argued that Garašanin and Marinović were thus prime candidates. If the Prince chose them as ministers, he and his Liberal Party, from respect for the Prince, would accept the posts offered to them. Grujić advised awaiting Garašanin's return from France before appointing a cabinet. However, if Marinović would not serve as minister, noted Vuk, neither would Garašanin since they agreed on everything.[37]

Returning to Serbia soon thereafter, Garašanin was greeted warmly by Prince Mihailo who promptly offered him the premiership. However, Garašanin flatly refused to serve with Grujić, his former protégé, reportedly telling the Prince: "Sire, expel me from the country if you persist in that idea." Thereupon Mihailo angily seized the cabinet list he had just signed and tore it up. To Mondain, Garašanin explained his refusal on the gound that the Prince had designated Grujić as minister of justice. He now regarded Grujić as a "very suspicious and unreliable person to hold a powerful ministry and would thus bring severe weakness into the government." Plainly, he objected to Grujić's liberal views. For similar reasons, Marinović had likewise refused the premiership.[38] Marinović urged Mihailo to break cleanly with the Liberals, whom he castigated as rebels and demagogues, and form a homogeneous Conservative ministry. For several weeks the Prince hesitated: he preferred the Conservatives ideologically but feared to break with the Liberals who were loyal to his dynasty. Finally, Mihailo appointed a non-partisan cabinet of bureaucrats headed by Filip Hristić. But its ministers were on such bad personal terms that they refused to greet one another at the first cabinet meeting; each dealt directly with the Prince. Thus Garašanin remained outside the government while Marinović, named to the Council, was sent abroad to notify European cabinets of Mihailo's accession and ascertain their attitudes toward Serbia.[39]

Garašanin's memorandum of November 1860, utilizing two speeches of Gioberti to the Italians,[40] outlined Serbia's tasks if she were to lead the Balkan peoples. He and Mihailo already regarded Piedmont-Sardinia as their model. Deploring recent confusion in Serbia which had produced widespread distrust of government, Garašanin warned that time and wisdom were required to restore public confidence. A government needed internal calm to develop strength for the great external task of emancipating the Serbs of Turkey. Good administration and closer bonds forged between Prince and people would enhance Serbia's external position. Criticizing Liberal reforms, Garašanin advocated instead strong princely rule. Prince Mihailo's proclamation on assuming power had aroused high hopes, but the Serbian people must learn to follow written as well as oral instructions. Garašanin advised summoning elders and district chiefs and informing them about the Prince's ideas so they could help restore shaken respect for authority.[41]

In January 1861 Garašanin lay ill in Vienna, apparently as far removed as ever from an active role in Serbian affairs. "One misfortune follows another," he wrote Marinović despondently. "I am ill and in despair." Because of his eczema he could scarcely hold a pen; his son, Svetozar, had also been ill. No one was writing him from Belgrade, and the issue of his pension remained unresolved. He urged Marinović to hasten home and assist Prince Mihailo.[42] A week later, much improved, Garašanin prepared to return also. Troubles were still assailing him "so that I am scarcely able to overcome them all. I can scarcely wait to withdraw once and for all from [public] affairs." At least the pension business had been resolved. Credited with nineteen years and five months service, he had been assigned 2,000 talira monthly. He commented bitterly: "Let others await better rewards for serving their country."[43]

From Vienna he wrote Marinović February 2nd combining pessimism with political commentary. Thanking his friend for consoling words, Garašanin added: "Truly a person must be patient and philosophical." He regretted now an earlier promise to Prince Mihailo to serve him if needed. His attitude toward the Prince and the national cause remained constant, but now he felt too feeble to serve: "I am already exhausted mentally and physically (to say nothing of materially). This exhaustion increases day by day and I cannot overcome it, a type of faintheartedness prevails in me more and more." His eczema was increasingly difficult to bear. "Thus if I am able to withdraw honorably from my pledged word (in which only you can help me), it would be a true blessing for me." If not, he would respond as best he could. Garašanin feared that Marinović's mission to Western Europe had failed to improve Serbia's external position:

The situation now is three times worse than at the beginning. Do they intend at least to utilize everything possible with some hope still of salvation? I don't think so. It would be good if he [Prince Mihailo] accepted our views.

He would welcome Marinović's entry into the cabinet, "especially if it were not possible for me and you, at least he [Mihailo] would have one of us with him." Garašanin wondered whether he could serve usefully as other than Interior Minister. With his illness persisting, he would remain in Vienna for another two weeks.[44]

Belgrade had responded sympathetically to the striking successes of Cavour and Garibaldi in achieving Italian national unification. However, with most European courts regarding Garibaldi and his Polish and Magyar émigré allies as dangerous revolutionaries, and since Serbia needed Europe's support against the Porte, Mihailo could not afford to back the Italians openly. Thus in November 1860 when General Türr, a Magyar émigré and Garibaldi's aide, sought at Cavour's initiative to enlist support from Serbia and neighboring lands in case the Austro-Sardinian War resumed, Prince Mihailo refused to receive him. Precautions were taken at frontier posts to bar Magyar émigré agents from Serbia.

Rebuffing Magyar émigrés, Mihailo approached Hungarian political leaders in power through links established by his marriage to Julija Hunyady, a Magyar aristocrat. The Prince proposed his mediation hoping Austria would then improve the status of Vojvodina Serbs. For this mission Mihailo selected Garašanin, then in Vienna as a pensioner. In March 1861 Foreign Minister Jovan Ristić instructed him to seek full agreement between the Vojvodina Serbs and Magyars. Describing their mission as "more of a private than of an official nature," Ristić and Garašanin approached Baron Nikola Vaj, court chancellor in Vienna for Magyar affairs, urging him to arrange convocation of a Serbian assembly in Hungary; he agreed to do so. If Vienna satisfied the Vojvodina Serbs, Prince Mihailo would back Austria, they told him. From Vienna Garašanin informed Mondain:

The Magyars are causing Vienna much concern. The Vojvodina has been wholly eliminated. The Magyars are too selfish and rash, but at least they are active. And the [Vojvodina] Serbs? They are incapable, talk to themselves, and can be utilized by others. We'll see how things turn out, but I hope that Serbia will not repeat the events of 1848.[45]

Then Garašanin went on to Budapest to negotiate with Magyar Liberal leaders about the Vojvodina and Serbo-Hungarian relations. In March he wrote the influential Magyar statesman, Count Julius Andrássy: "We have found the [Vojvodina] Serbs dismayed by their possible return to . . . a despotic system of centralization [the so-called "Bach System"] of the past decade."[46] Suggesting Serbo-Magyar cooperation to Andrássy and other Magyar Liberals, he and Ristić found them receptive. But they refused to discuss restoring a Vojvodina which Serbs there considered the territorial basis for self-rule, instead denouncing it as a "state within a state." Proceeding to Novi Sad, the Serbian envoys informed leading Vojvodina Serbs about their talks with the Magyars. Both Jovan Hadžić and Svetozar Miletić favored accord with the Magyars but quarreled over other issues and Garašanin could not reconcile them. At a March 20th assembly convened at Vaj's intercession in Sremski Karlovci, prevailed an official faction advocating reliance on Austria.[47] Belgrade's efforts to win autonomy for Vojvodina Serbs proved abortive, but Garašanin's first official mission for Prince Mihailo laid a basis for subsequent Serbo-Magyar rapprochement.

The Vojvodina Serbs' attitudes at this assembly distressed Garašanin greatly. Criticizing Serbia for not fighting Turkey, they yielded to Vienna which supported Serbia's enemies.[48] In a draft Garašanin wrote bitterly:

> Our brethren in Novi Sad and Karlovac are deceiving us. Personal interests have swallowed the general cause. Some expect a bishopric, others accept high civil posts and mayorships, others fear to harm their fine lives and around those rotate all their patriotism. Such are you Serbian Cavours and Garibaldis! Hurrah! [*Živeli!*].

However, he was not surprised knowing of the Vojvodina Serbs' incompetence from 1848. Capable only of wearing a yoke, they were betraying themselves and Serbia too. "With Austria who has always deceived you, you have the courage to make agreements, but not to enter into talks with the Magyars."[49]

Garašanin next went to Constantinople as Prince Mihailo's special envoy to resolve Serbo-Turkish disputes over the 1838 Constitution and to arrange evacuation of Turks from portions of Serbia lying outside the Turkish fortresses. A mission sent by Prince Miloš in 1860 had left Constan-

tinople after six months of fruitless talks. Garašanin would spend about an
equal period there with little success. From Constantinople he wrote
Prince Mihailo at the outset: "I will do everything possible to succeed in
the mission you have given me."[50] His letters to Marinović in Belgrade
reveal that his mission was hampered by Serbo-Turkish tension over refugees residing in Serbia and measures adopted by the Preobrazhenski
Assembly.[51]

A draft memorandum in French, designed apparently to justify Garašanin's mission, explained Serbia's views and position.

> In the disire to place before Your Highness [Grand Vizier?] and the
> organs of the Porte the purpose of my arrival here as clearly as pos-
> sible, I am writing these words which are *wholly frank and very con-
> fidential.* It would be impossible to conceal from the Porte the posi-
> tion of Serbia created by recent events.

The memo, playing the Russian card, asserted that during Miloš' reign, the
Russians had sought to discredit Prince Mihailo. After Mihailo became
ruler, he had sent Marinović fruitlessly to Russia to resolve this problem.
Now through Garašanin, Mihailo was seeking Turkish support:

> Indirect aid by the Porte could do much to complement the Prince's
> firm will. . . . We are not seeking to draw the Porte into open con-
> flict with Russia. . . . Thus we have decided on a method which will
> not involve any sacrifices by the Porte, will contribute much to calm
> public excitement, and give the Prince a chance to come before his
> people with an arrangement placing its relations with Serbia on a
> much clearer footing. . . .

Improved relations with Turkey, Garašanin believed, would lessen Serbia's
dependence on Russia.[52] But without strong European pressure on the
Porte, Garašanin's embassy had little actual prospect of success. The Turks
saw no need to yield to Serbia on the evacuation issue. Serbia needed active
Russian diplomatic support, but during 1861 their relations remained cool.

Still Garašanin did his best to reach agreement. "I will withstand the
test and see whether I can settle matters with the Porte," he wrote Marinović. In Serbia much depended on the two of them. "Help the Prince

sincerely in everything, especially since you say he invariably receives you well and graciously. By his unlimited trust, he obligates us to be completely sincere. We are duty-bound to do so anyway."[53] Garašanin complained that his mission was being complicated by Belgrade's welcome to Serbian and Bulgarian refugees from Turkey.[54] Citing this émigré influx into Belgrade, British Ambassador Bulwer accused Serbia of plotting moves against the Porte and Austria and stirring up people in neighboring provinces. Garašanin denied this vehemently as pure slander:

> Austria seeks from Serbia that it do for her what she is incapable of doing in her own lands. We understand Austria well. Her desire to hamper us in everything and thus her decline can no longer seriously concern us ever again.[55]

As for the Porte, it should specify what Serbia was supposedly doing to bother her. The entire refugee issue, concluded Garašanin, had been overblown. Serbia's interests, he wrote Premier Hristić, would not be aided by harboring refugees indiscriminately: "I don't mean Bulgars who wish to till the soil, but others who are being paid and kept without occupations." Those should be repatriated. Incautious journalism, harmful to Serbia, should be stifled by the Belgrade government:

> I see that our newspapers are comparing us to Piedmont, even in articles regarded as moderate. Let us become Piedmont; I approve of that and wish for it if only we are capable, but let us become such in action and leave it to others to say it about us, since it is not proper for us to claim it before we have taken up arms.[56]

Events on the Serbo-Turkish frontiers complicated Garašanin's task. Why had Serbian border guards fired on Turks crossing the Timok River? he queried May 29th. "I am obliged to try to conclude my mission successfully," he wrote Marinović, "because of the great trust which the Prince has given me and which I value highly. There are no sacrifices I would not make in order to be worthy of his trust." To Marinović's complaints about the current Serbian cabinet, Garašanin urged him to by-pass the ministers and go directly to the Prince and tell him about its incompetence. Whether Mihailo accepted his advice or not, at least Marinović would be doing his patriotic duty and the Prince would not condemn him for that. "He will not accept all your advice, but he will accept some and at times everything." They themselves, he added, were partly to blame for Prince Mihailo's inferior ministers. Mihailo had told him: "I am not to blame, Mr. Garašanin, that my choice is so slight, thus I must put pressure on you [to serve]." The Prince was doing his best, so all Serbian patriots, whether ministers or not, should give helpful advice. He urged Marinović to talk with Mihailo even if the ministers disapproved.[57]

Prince Mihailo announced to the Preobrazhenski Assembly August 7, 1861 that Garašanin's special mission aimed to resolve outstanding issues with the Porte. Whatever its outcome, his regime would strive to broaden Serbia's national rights. The Assembly applauded but its actions doomed any Serbo-Turkish accord. A law on a 50,000-man national militia, very popular in Serbia, caused worry in Constantinople. No sooner had the Assembly dispersed than the Porte denounced its decisions and Mihailo's national policies. Echoing Turkish complaints, Vienna and London through their Belgrade consuls admonished Serbia that it should have secured Turkish consent before implementing such fundamental legal changes. Noted Garašanin's final letter to Marinović from Constantinople: "Two things plague me equally here: the Turks and my illness. I hope to overcome both soon and to see you in Belgrade."[58] Garašanin soon after returned home without achieving his mission's formal objectives; Jovan Ristić replaced him in Constantinople. By then Mihailo realized that Filip Hristić's cabinet was too ineffective and disunited to achieve his goals. More than ever he wished to work with Ilija Garašanin who now yielded to his entreaties. Since the recent assembly had given Mihailo the laws he required to pursue his goals, he could now afford to break with the Liberals and organize a homogeneous Conservative cabinet headed by Garašanin.

NOTES

1.   On the history of the second reign of Prince Miloš (1859-1860) see Petrovich, *A History,* I, 288-295. For Miloš and the Liberals then see

Stokes, *Legitimacy*, pp. 22-32, 42-43. A detailed treatment of Miloš' reign is in S. Jovanović, *Druga vlada Miloša i Mihaila, 1858-1868*, pp. 3-86, and in J. Grujić, *Zapisi*, II, 241-315, and III, 1-72. For Garašanin's extensive correspondence with Jovan Marinović for this period see *Pisma*, II, 1-78.

2. Garašanin to Marinović, January 6 and 9, 1859, *Pisma*, II, 4-11.

3. Ibid., January 16, pp. 11-12; Grujić, *Zapisi*, II, 241-256.

4. Ibid., II, 277-279; Jovanović, *Druga vlada*, pp. 11-16.

5. Garašanin to Marinović, January 20, *Pisma*, II, 13-17.

6. On policies and actions of the St. Andrew's Assembly and the interim government headed by Stevča Mihailović after Garašanin's resignation see Grujić, *Zapisi*, II, 259 ff.

7. Vuk Stefanović Karadžić (1787-1864), writer and grammarian, was responsible for the first important Serbo-Croatian grammar and dictionary.

8. Garašanin to Marinović, January 21, *Pisma*, II, 19.

9. See above, p. 19.

10. Garašanin to Marinović, January 27, *Pisma*, II, 19-21.

11. Ibid., January 31, p. 22. Miloš tried to induce J. Grujić to become premier but he refused unless his Liberal colleagues were included in the cabinet. *Zapisi*, II, 306-308.

12. Garašanin to Marinović, February 10, *Pisma*, II, 25-28.

13. Jovanović, *Druga vlada*, pp. 17-19; Grujić, *Zapisi*, II, 286-307. When Grujić on January 29th suggested Garašanin as premier and foreign minister because of his long experience in dealing with the Turks and the powers and his popularity among Serbs, Prince Miloš told him abruptly: "Don't give me lessons about Garašanin. I know that rock [*flintu*], better than you do. It should be sufficient for him that I allow him to remain in the country, but there will be no official post for him." (II, 305-206).

14. Garašanin to Marinović, February 10, *Pisma*, II, 25-28.

15. Ibid., February 17, II, 29-31.

16. Ibid., March 20, pp. 32-34.

17. IG 1129, Garašanin to Mondain, April 17.

18. M. S. Piroćanac, *Knez Mihailo i zajednička radnja Balkanskih naroda* (Belgrade, 1895), pp. 14-16.

19. Mita Dimitrijević, "Jedno značajno i još neobjavljeno pismo Kneza Mihaila," *Politika*, March 4, 1927, pp. 1-2. In his letter to Miloš of April 17/29, 1859 Mihailo reported his very warm welcome by Napoleon III in

Paris. He had been received twice in audience, once wholly privately. Napoleon had pledged to support and defend Serbia in all of its justified requests.

20. DAS PO 76/22 and 28, K. Cukić to M. Lešjanin (Vienna), March 20/April 1, 1859, published in V. Vučković, *Politička aksija Srbije u južnoslovenskim pokrajinama Habsburške Monarhije, 1859-1874*), No. 3, pp. 7-11.

21. Ibid., No. 4, p. 13, Mihailo to Miloš, March 29/April 10.

22. Garašanin to Marinović, May 8, *Pisma*, II, 41.

23. Ibid., April 10, pp. 39-41; IG 1123, "Nekoliko reči o ratu u Italiji." Garašanin noted that this memorandum remained in his desk drawer and there is no evidence that Belgrade then heeded his warnings.

24. Garašanin to Marinović, May 8, *Pisma*, II, 39-41.

25. Ibid., June 23, pp. 42-43.

26. Ibid., June 29, pp. 44-46.

27. IG 1127, Garašanin to Mondain, October 25 and 26, from Mehadiskih Ilića.

28. S. Jovanović, *Druga vlada*, pp. 30-39. The "dukatovački" articles represent a combination of the ideas of Mihailo, Ban and Ristić, all of whom were strong opponents of the Liberals. The articles were carefully timed (August 18-September 5) to influence the Assembly which convened September 8/20th—Stokes, *Legitimacy*, p. 27.

29. IG 1139, Garašanin to Mondain, March 3, 1860.

30. Garašanin to Marinović, April 1, 1860, *Pisma*, II, 48-50.

31. Ibid., April 10 and 27, II, 52-56.

32. IG 1133, "Poveritelan akt za sebe," February 1860, Garašanin draft.

33. Garašanin to Marinović, May 9, *Pisma*, II, 65-69.

34. Ibid., June 24, p. 77.

35. IG 1139, Garašanin to Mondain, August 14.

36. On Mihailo's program and efforts to reconcile factions see Jovanović, *Druga vlada*, pp. 89-100.

37. Grujić, *Zapisi*, III, 75-77.

38. Ibid., pp. 76-77; IG 1139, Garašanin to Mondain, October 11 and 30.

39. Grujić, III, 77-80.

40. Vincenzo Gioberti (1801-1852), a priest who in *The Civil and*

Moral Primacy of the Italians advocated a federation of states under the Pope.

41. IG 1137, "Stanje 24. nojembra 1860 g., " Garašanin draft.

42. Garašanin to Marinović, January 9/21, 1861, *Pisma*, II, 79.

43. Ibid., January 15/27 and January 20/February 1, pp. 81-84.

44. Ibid., February 2, pp. 84-86.

45. Vučković, *Politička*, No. 19, p. 32, Garašanin to Mondain, February 9/21. Garašanin's reference to "elimination" of Vojvodina refers to Hungary's abolition of the Serbian Vojvodina December 15, 1860, annexing it to the Hungarian crown.

46. Ibid., No. 23, pp. 35-37.

47. Serbia's delegates to this Blagoveštenski Assembly were Ristić and Miloš Popović, editor of *Srpske Novine*. Most elected deputies favored accord with the Magyars, but half the delegates were officials, supported by the Austrian commissar, General Filipović, who agitated against such an agreement. Ristić to Garašanin, June 16, 1861 in Vučković, No. 31, pp. 46-48.

48. IG 1197, Garašanin to Ristić, from Bujukdere, July 30.

49. IG 1176, "Kritika vojvodjanskih Srba...," Garašanin draft, 1861.

50. DAS PO 25/6, Garašanin to Mihailo, May 15, from Constantinople.

51. Garašanin to Marinović, May 6, *Pisma*, II, 88-91.

52. IG 1179, Garašanin drafts, "Odgovor Porte."

53. Garašanin to Marinović, April 18, *Pisma*, II, 86-87.

54. On the refugees, Garašanin had a long talk with the Grand Vizier who asked why Serbia did not expel them. Garašanin replied that Serbian opinion supported them. "Whether this view is right or wrong, it represents the feeling of our entire people toward those whom fate has divided by frontiers, but otherwise are considered identical by faith, language and name." Garašanin to F. Hristić, April 12, 1861.

55. Garašanin to Marinović, May 6, *Pisma*, II, 88-89.

56. IG 1204, Garašanin to F. Hristić, May 6 and 15.

57. Garašanin to Marinović, May 29, *Pisma*, II, 92-94.

58. Ibid., September 13, p. 96; Jovanović, *Druga vlada*, 97-98.

CHAPTER XIV

THE REGIME OF MIHAILO AND GARAŠANIN: GOALS AND POLICIES, 1861-1862

"Yes, it is true that Ilija Garašanin by his talent, skill and devotion to state service was for six years a useful colleague of Prince Mihailo, but he was *only a colleague,* and if his work was full of influence, he was neither the leader nor initiator. Prince Mihailo provided the direction and openly and unhesitantly proclaimed this."

Jovan Ristić, *Jedno namesništvo.*

For almost six years under Mihailo Obrenović, Garašanin held the key positions of premier and foreign minister of Serbia, working closing and harmoniously with the Prince. Indeed, their chief policies were developed in such intimate collaboration that it remains unclear who actually initiated them. In the fall of 1861, as dissatisfaction grew with Premier Filip Hristić, Mihailo called in Garašanin whom he had long respected for patriotism and statesmanship. Urged by the Prince to assume office, Garašanin showed him his "Načertanije"; if state policy followed those principles, he would serve. Reading and approving "Načertanije," Mihailo named Garašanin his chief minister.[1] Only with a cabinet headed by

240

Garašanin, a sincere patriot ready to sacrifice himself for the national cause, affirmed Orešković,[2] could Mihailo win Europe's respect and pursue his goals of national liberation.

Mihailo was the first Serbian ruler to grasp his country's potential role as the South Slav Piedmont, or leader in the struggle to unify Yugoslavs. Unlike his predecessors, Mihailo sought to unite not just Serbs but all South Slavs, including Croats and Bulgars. Not the originator of the Yugoslav idea, he was the first Serbian prince to seek to implement it in the form of an independent South Slav state. In that endeavor he found Garašanin an enthusiastic and loyal collaborator.[3]

Prince Mihailo's second reign embodied the precepts of enlightened absolutism. His was a purely personal regime in which the ruler attempted to make all major decisions. Coming to power with a broad, prepared program, he believed that firm autocratic rule was indispensible for success. Mihailo, developing his own domestic and foreign policies, usually decided matters individually with his ministers, so cabinet meetings under his chairmanship were rare. He conducted foreign policy through Garašanin and domestic affairs with his confidants, Interior Minister Nikola Hristić and Kosta Cukić. Though Garašanin lacked the free hand in domestic policy he had exercised under Aleksandar, his influence on foreign policy was decisive. Two hostile cliques surrounded Prince Mihailo. One, composed of Cukić, the Lešjanins and Marinović, predominated at the beginning. The other, including Mihailo's own cousin, Anka Konstantinović, Miloje Blaznavac and Jovan Ristić, enjoyed paramount influence late in his reign. Independent of these factions were Garašanin and Nikola Hristić, the two chief ministers. Mihailo utilized the former group only until order had been fully restored; the latter clique's influence relied on the Prince's trust. As ruler, he never acted out of hatred. Valuing capable people, he employed Garašanin as long as their views on foreign policy coincided.[4]

Mihailo's major aim was to implement the great national policy which had ripened in his mind during long years of exile. Initially, he resolved to overcome all obstacles in its path. In exile Mihailo had told Kossuth, the Hungarian nationalist leader:

> We wish to be an independent state and now that we have our native administration . . . , we are confident that we will soon be able to match the Turks . . . . We must await favorable circumstances—that

Austrian power is nearby is our misfortune. . . . Should we raise the banner of independence, it is certain that Vienna would intervene unless we drew the sword under Russian protection.

But Serbia, warned Mihailo, must not become dependent on Russia. Partly for that reason he supported Kossuth's idea of a Danubian confederation of Hungary, Rumania and Serbia. When Turkey collapsed, which Mihailo believed to be imminent, it lay in their interests to form such a union and forestall Austrian or Russian domination:

[External control] could only be avoided if the Balkan Slavs joined in one compact mass. But I do not believe that the Croats are destined to comprise the nucleus of the future consolidated state. The Croats are on the periphery; we [Serbia] are in the center of the circle.[5]

The Prince believed his absolutism was justified because the Serbian people was ill-prepared for constitutional government. The ruler required full power also to plan a war of liberation against the Turks. Garašanin shared these ideas. Indeed, Franjo Zah claimed that Mihailo had derived his views from "Načertanije." Obsessed by autocracy and secrecy, Mihailo did not realize that national revolutionary struggle could not be conducted without full public support. He named and removed Council members at will until only the four of seventeen with higher education (Marinović, Filip Hristić, Dimitrije Crnobarac and Dj. Cenić) could perform their tasks properly. The sole case of principled opposition in the Council to Mihailo occurred in 1864 when Filip Hristić defended ministerial responsibility there. When Garašanin denounced this, the Council hastily repudiated Hristić, though many members sympathized with him. All opposition to the regime was considered as directed against the Prince and thus illegal. Theoretically limited by Council and Assembly, Mihailo in fact exercised full power and initiative. Intimate with no one outside his closest entourage and mixing little with the people, the Prince saw even important leaders only in formal audiences. At court he received solely ministers, a few of their assistants, and Marinović, the Council's chairman. Mihailo, moving in a narrow circle of ministers and family, usually dined alone. Proud, remote and melancholy, he spent most of his time working alone in his office, a slave like other personal rulers to official documents.

Ministers of state, though considered by Mihailo mere office directors, actually were very influential since he met chiefly with them and obtained through them his impressions of the outside world. This made it difficult for him to disagree with them. By 1862 new ministries of education, communications and defense had been created, leaving the Interior Ministry with shrunken authority. There were no cabinet crises from 1861 to 1867; the same ministers—Garašanin, Nikola Hristić, Kosta Cukić and Rajko Lešjanin—remained firmly in office. Continuity enhanced their prestige and authority. Mihailo became their model in methods of work: like him they were submerged in documents since every trifle came to their desks for decision. They were model bureaucrats: hard-working, precise, writing almost everything themselves and appearing publicly but once every three years to present carefully worded reports of their activities to the Assembly. As the Prince's reticence spread to them, their work remained shrouded in silence and secrecy. All ministers and officials demanded and usually received unconditional obedience from their subordinates. In the districts one official—the district chief—acted similarly as the omnipotent local authority. Under Mihailo, noted the Austrian consul, Benjamin Kállay, Serbia became the most highly centralized country in Europe.[6]

Seemingly monolithic, this regime, notes Jovanović, proved ineffective in practice because the autocratic, inflexible Prince could not make decisions. He drew up lofty, ambitious, often well-conceived plans but spent more time dreaming and planning than actually working. Mihailo wrote incessantly but tore up most of it. Every day reams of shredded paper were removed from his office. Everyone close to him realized his indecisiveness. Dr. Pacek, perhaps his closest confidant, noted that Mihailo showed steadfast purpose in pursuit of domestic autocracy and national liberation only to be halted by indecision, lack of confidence, and ignorance about how best to proceed. Occasionally, from fear he made hasty, mistaken decisions, then adhered to them out of pride. Everything had to be submitted to him, but generally he accepted his ministers' proposals, often too trustingly. Avoiding technical details, Mihailo knew little about military matters. His model as enlightened despot was Frederick II, "the Great," of Prussia, but he lacked Frederick's intellect and decisiveness. His ministers disagreed politically and remained ignorant of what their colleagues were doing. Nikola Hristić and Garašanin were unyielding conservatives; Kosta Cukić and Rajko Lešjanin favored liberal concessions and softening the regime. They often conflicted over current state business.

Resting upon absolute princely and ministerial authority, the regime lacked external support from political parties or groups. The bureaucratic system, allowing no public initiative, severed all ties with popular opinion. In 1860 Mihailo, widely hailed as Serbia's savior, had promised what many Serbs claimed they wanted: legality, reconciliation of factions and unified administration combined with dynamic foreign and national policies. Sacrificed to these were ministerial responsibility, Council independence and press freedom. For seven years the ministers expressed only the official viewpoint and permitted no criticism. Especially after 1864, as Liberal attacks mounted in the émigré press, Mihailo's rigid and repressive system grew increasingly unpopular. In the Council developed a secret opposition supported by much of the intelligentsia. Younger intellectuals began to urge press freedom, ministerial responsibility and greater powers for the Assembly. Popular discontent simmered over economic hardships, increased taxes for the national militia and abuses of authority.

Two ministers—Nikola Hristić and Ilija Garašanin—supported Mihailo's system unconditionally without realizing that a different method of rule might be preferable. Given their preeminence, they were primarily responsible for the regime's operation. With Premier Garašanin conducting a patriotic foreign policy which even many Liberals approved, opposition focused on Hristić's police.

Garašanin desired "a permanent and patriotic government" in which political freedoms were superfluous. Those advocating freedoms for their own sake he considered foolish visionaries. He never understood fully nor valued highly the people's political strength. Later, in retirement, he wrote: "It was never advantageous for any matter of state to be supported by mob enthusiasm since such an affair could suddenly be compromised and lack support." For him the people remained a "senseless multitude" shouting "Long live!" and "Down with!" indiscriminately. Great affairs, he agreed with Bismarck, were handled best in quiet offices by thoughtful, experienced statesmen. As bureaucrat and office politician, noted Jovanović, Garašanin judged state affairs soberly and showed rare skill in issuing orders and instructions. These and his ability to maneuver had sufficed fully under the "Defenders" when politics remained a complex game played without public participation among Prince, Council, the Porte and the Powers. Then, it was generally believed, the "tall thin man" (*"dugački i mršavi"*) with the penetrating mind and dry, sarcastic humor had worked out everything in advance, utilizing and outplaying everyone. But the popular revolution of 1858 had revealed limits to his political mastery: he could not manipulate crowds like a Vučić, and the Liberals preempted his influence over the Assembly. In the new demagogic politics of 1858 the orderly Garašanin found no place, but once Mihailo restored a strict bureaucratic administration, he returned to his element and persuaded the Prince that a patriotic and conservative government was best.[7]

Of all the rulers he served Garašanin got on best with Mihailo, agreeing with his political methods and the main lines of his domestic and foreign policies. During a close collaboration from 1861 to 1867, their personal relations and friendship, based on mutual respect and liking, deepened. "I am proud to serve such a prince," declared Garašanin. In a draft of 1861 he advocated a strong Serbian government to overcome domestic disorder and conduct a dynamic foreign policy. "Such strength is embodied by a cabinet of honorable and capable men, united, patriotic and courageous." Noting the instability Mihailo had inherited, Garašanin warned it would require both time and good will to overcome disorder.[8]

Installing the Conservatives under Garašanin in power, Mihailo aimed to utilize their ability to govern without permitting persecution of the Liberals. However, when the latter promptly opposed the new cabinet, the Conservatives, arguing that the Liberal opposition must be destroyed to maintain the regime, won over the Prince. During Garašanin's ministry, the chief Liberals were removed from state service and some fled the country. Nonetheless, political squabbling persisted and the idea of party reconciliation faded. Mihailo's reign was one of protracted conflict be-between Conservatives and Liberals. For their part, the people were divided between Obrenovites and Karadjordjists, neither of which supported Garašanin strongly. His cabinet hung in the air with little popular backing.

Initially, Garašanin's ministry was greeted favorably in Contantinople where from his recent diplomatic mission, he was considered a moderate. This helped Garašanin, backed by France and Russia, defend enactments of the Serbian Assembly of August 1861 aginst protests from the Porte and Austria. Foreign Ministers Thouvenel and Gorchakov rejected the Porte's assertions decisively. The Serbs, affirmed Gorchakov, had long since acquired the right to an hereditary prince. Russia considered the Assembly's acts as purely internal matters: the militia aimed merely to assure order and security in Serbia. Connecting formation of a Serbian militia with movements in Italy, Vienna nervously envisioned Garibaldi appearing on the Sava. In Constantinople Austria's Baron Prokesch expressed fear that Garašanin was a revolutionary. However, British Ambassador H. L. Bulwer described him as safely conservative while Turkish Foreign Minister Ali Pasha praised his moderation, telling Ristić that the Porte now was angry only with Prince Mihailo.[9]

In an important memorandum to Prince Mihailo of October 1861 Garašanin urged the need to set bold national goals and determine appropriate means while warning that Serbia was weak and had little prospect of effective external support until she became stronger. Deploring a previous tendency for agents and adventurers to impose their views on the government, Garašanin stressed that Belgrade must wholly regulate and control the national movement. The first task was to decide on Serbia's aims and how to achieve them. These, he believed, could only be to destroy Turkey and expand Serbia. Before action could begin, present suspicions and antagonisms among the Balkan peoples must yield to agreement. There were two ways to accomplish that goal: by individual uprisings in various Turkish provinces, or to organize a simultaneous, general insurrection of Balkan Christians. Both methods had advantages, but Serbia must decide on one and follow it consistently. Individual risings, he argued, might weaken Turkey but would dissipate the Christians' strength as much as the Turks.' Isolated revolts, unless Serbia could assist them, would amount to mere guerrilla operations which would compromise Serbia with the powers and trigger war prematurely. Rejecting them as ineffective, Garašanin advocated instead careful preparation of a general insurrection. At present Serbia was unprepared for even a minor war.[10]

Slobodan Jovanović portrayed Garašanin somewhat misleadingly as a militant, bellicose leader during the 1860s, thirsting for action. Actually, he was never reckless and usually proceeded with exemplary caution. Under Mihailo his policy was to arm Serbia rapidly, unite Balkan states and peoples politically and militarily, then strike boldly at Turkey. He expected little aid from shortsighted, selfish, squabbling European powers. Formerly a convinced Francophile, Garašanin had grown disillusioned with France and no longer trusted any power fully. The Balkan states should rely on themselves and prepare for war. No other minister of Mihailo sounded as warlike. Sending both sons to military school, for three years he desired and awaited war with Turkey "in the spring." Garašanin believed

European conditions favored a war of national liberation led by Serbia which Turkey would be unable to defeat. He had never feared Turkey— only Austria and Russia. Sobered by her Crimean defeat and preoccupied at home, Russia could not now expand in the Balkans; instead she pushed Serbia ahead. For a time Garašanin feared that Austria, despite her debacle in the Sardinian War of 1859, might move into Bosnia and Hercegovina. Especially in 1866-67 he urged that Serbia act quickly before Austria recovered its strength. The Balkan peoples, he believed, had a unique opportunity to resolve the Eastern Question without European intervention.[11]

Prince Mihailo also dreamed of rousing the entire Balkans in an anti-Turkish war of national liberation and creating a great South Slav state led by Serbia. The first task was to prepare his people for this; all else was secondary. Mihailo calculated that would require only a few years of systematic work. Then Serbia should strike without even a credible war pretext. First, party quarrels must be ended and all Serbs united in patriotic enthusiasm behind their authoritiative though benevolent ruler. Serbia, asserted Mihailo, could enact all necessary laws without consulting the Porte.[12]

Despite their militance, Mihailo and Garašanin realized Serbia was too weak to exploit Luka Vukalović's revolt of 1861. Apparently seeking to push her into action, Thouvenel of France telegraphed Tastie, his consul in Belgrade, on November 13, 1861 that Vukalović's insurgent movement in Hercegovina was growing, risings were beginning in Bosnia, and 5,000 Montenegrins had crossed to aid the insurgents. However, Prince Mihailo informed the French consul that Serbia was unprepared: "Great matters are not achieved with small resources, and we have only small resources."[13] The national militia, authorized that August by the Serbian assembly, had not yet been organized or armed.

Negotiations between Serbia and the other Balkan states for political and military alliances were just beginning. In Constantinople Belgrade's envoy, Jovan Ristić, had achieved an understanding in principle with Renijeris, the Greek envoy. Belgrade, Garašanin informed Ristić December 28th, regarded the favorable Greek response to its overtures as "the best augury for the success of our cause." But with typical caution, Garašanin opposed binding Balkan alliances at that time:

> [Serbia] has proposed *delay* in signing a Serbo-Greek convention since it did not wish to *enter into solemn engagements* without the hope of being able to fulfill all its obligations. So it believes today that with even more reason, it should propose delaying a move which threatens to endanger the entire enterprise. . . . The advantages which could come from immediate signature of a protocol are not commensurate with the dangers to which we would inevitably expose our holy cause by allowing it to depart now from a narrow and secret circle.

First, non-intervention by the powers must be assured and Balkan military preparations completed. Garašanin opposed overtures then to two other prospective partners—Montenegro and Rumania:

> We feel that it is extremely dangerous and for the beginning of diplomatic action wholly superfluous to make immediate démarches to Bucharest and Cetinje and to make signature of this protocol [with Greece] a condition of this action.

Agreeing to sound out other Balkan states on cooperation, Garašanin noted that Turkish protests to the powers, especially about the Serbian militia, had placed Belgrade in a difficult diplomatic position. Thus it could not act decisively until certain of success. After Ristić had explained matters to Renijeris and if Athens accepted the preliminary protocol, Serbia and Greece could approach Rumania's Prince Cuza gingerly. The Greeks should leave it up to Serbia to woo Montenegro when circumstances permitted.[14] This important letter of Garašanin confirms that he was already planning a four power Balkan alliance but realized the need for extreme caution and secrecy. Earlier that month Ali Pasha of Turkey had asked Ristić: "Is it true that you are preparing to conclude a defensive-offensive alliance with Greece?" Vassal Serbia, he admonished, had no right to do so.[15]

While laying bases for a Balkan alliance, Garašanin guarded Serbia from a premature conflict with Turkey. Renijeris had informed Ristić that with tension rising in the Greek world, an insurrection the following spring (1862) was certain. Commented Ristić: "I hope events will not catch them unprepared and drag us into the maelstrom."[16] Wondering whether Greece was concealing some war preparations, Garašanin warned

Ristić that either it or Montenegro might force Serbia to enter war unprepared or sit on the sideline while they settled the fate of European Turkey. Delaying signature of a protocol with Greece thus proclaimed Serbia's unreadiness, protected her against unilateral Greek action, and should help discourage excessive Greek territorial claims. Until all parties were ready, Garašanin opposed signing a Balkan alliance since if the secret leaked out, the Turks could destroy it in embryo.[17] Finding Serbia and Greece unprepared to fight and faced with discord among the Hercegovina insurgents, Napoleon III renounced plans then to foment a Balkan insurrection. Hercegovina and Montenegro were left to face greatly superior Turkish forces. Serbia's passivity, while inspiring Montenegrin indignation, let Garašanin ignore Turkish protests against the militia bill. Austria and England too ceased their objections once they realized Serbia would not enter the Turco-Montenegrin conflict. Thus although Garašanin's aims were bellicose, he was pursuing at this time a cautious, patient foreign policy.

Meanwhile Russia was giving Serbia unexpectedly strong moral support. Only eight years earlier, St. Petersburg had forced Garašanin from office as a dangerous revolutionary; now he stood on excellent terms with Russia. Since then much water had flowed past the banks of the Neva. The Paris Treaty (1856) appeared to bar Russia from open Balkan intervention. Alexander II's more liberal and flexible regime was absorbed by the monumental tasks of emancipating the serfs and completely revamping the Russian army. A weakened and impoverished Russia had to avoid war with European powers. Nonetheless, Foreign Minister A. M. Gorchakov, cooperating with France, sought to restore Russian prestige in the Balkans. Supporting the Balkan peoples against its traditional foe, Turkey, St. Petersburg found in the Serbia of Mihailo and Garašanin its most reliable diplomatic base. And Garašanin now believed that only with Russia's backing could a Balkan league be organized to liberate the region from the Porte.[18]

Garašanin, with Mihailo's enthusiastic support, was busily reviving the Serbian national movement, chiefly in Turkish-ruled areas. Praising Garašanin's earlier efforts to promote national propaganda and agitation, the Prince told him: "You began this work, and you shall complete it." He authorized major efforts to prepare the liberation of Bosnia, Hercegovina and Old Serbia from Turkish rule. Early in 1862 Garašanin established a secret "Serbian Committee," headed by a Council member, Lazar Arsenijević-Batalaka, assisted by Atanasije Nikolić and Franjo Zah, Garašanin's confidants, to spread propaganda and prepare insurrection. Only a handful of top Serbian officials knew of its existence.[19] Though meeting rarely in a formal sense, the Committee coordinated Serbia's efforts to gather information for the national cause. Instructions flowed to its network of agents all over European Turkey until Mihailo's assassination in May 1868. Under Garašanin's supervision, the Committee drew up plans for insurrections in Bosnia and Bulgaria, formed a detachment in Valjevo, Serbia of 200 volunteers from various Yugoslav lands, and financed a refugee Bulgarian Legion to promote revolt in Bulgaria.[20]

The Committee was concerned lest a general Balkan insurrection erupt before Serbia was prepared militarily and politically. Early in 1862, amidst threatening Turkish troop movements, Belgrade feared a sudden attack on Serbia from Hercegovina and Montenegro. Militants submitted to the Committee several plans to foster uprisings in nearby regions. The Bosnian, Toma Kovačević, now a cashier in the War Ministry and Garašanin's chief colleague in national propaganda, submitted in February a "Plan for instigating an uprising against Turks living in Bosnia, Hercegovina, Old Serbia and the provinces of Niš and Vidin," containing detailed information and advice on how to prepare revolts, utilizing bases in the Military Frontiers and Dalmatia.[21] Nikolić's memorandum in March warned that since the Turks were alarmed by Serbia's military preparations, the principality might be drawn into war. He advised aiding any uprising in Bosnia or Bulgaria with real prospect of success, even if this provoked war with the Porte. A Serbo-Greek alliance, argued Nikolić, by spreading the fighting to Greek areas, would relieve Turkish pressure on Serbia. "To Serbia remains the task of unfurling the flag of freedom in Bulgaria, and . . . to move into Bosnia."[22]

Garašanin was also worried by a rumored scheme of Napoleon III by which Austria would cede Venetia to Italy in exchange for Bosnia and Hercegovina. On February 8, 1862, he wrote Milan Petronijević, assistant minister of justice, whom he had sent to Russia to obtain rifles and a loan:

> The Italian cause, which so strongly appealed to oppressed peoples, threatens to become a danger to our people. To escape the difficulties posed by the Italian question, diplomacy has pursued a path of

amazing inconsistency, i.e. creating a new country [Italy] according
to the principle of nationality, it wishes simultaneously to deliver
the death blow to another people.

Such a territorial exchange, he warned, "would amount to the destruction of any prospects for our future." Though dubious that Russia would
sanction it, Garašanin asked Petronijević to discuss this issue with Foreign
Minister Gorchakov and explain how detrimentally it would affect Serbia
"which actually for its future counts on Russia alone." The Tsar, replied
Petronijević reassuringly, strongly opposed Napoleon's idea.[23] Furthermore, Russia soon agreed to loan Serbia 300,000 ducats and sell her
30,000 flintlocks. Gorchakov told Petronijević that Serbia comprised
"the nucleus which is to be concerned with the affairs of all Slavs in Turkey," and he urged Serbian rapprochement with Montenegro. Expressing
"special sympathy" for Mihailo and his government, Alexander II warned
that Russia could provide only moral support, so Serbia must be cautious
and guard against revolutionaries like Garibaldi, the Magyars and the
Poles.[24]
    In all these preliminary Serbian moves, Garašanin apparently played
the dominant role, despite Jovan Ristić's later assertions to the contrary:

> Yes, it is true that Ilija Garašanin by his talent, skill and devotion to
> state service was for six years a useful colleague of Prince Mihailo,
> but he was *only a colleague* (*suradnik*), and if his work was full of in-
> fluence, he was neither the leader nor initiator. Prince Mihailo pro-
> vided the direction and openly and unhesitatantly proclaimed this.

Seeking to confirm Garašanin's subordinate role, Ristić quoted Prince
Mihailo's letter of January 8, 1868 to Count Shtakelberg, the Russian
ambassador in Vienna:

> . . . I was the one who unhesitatingly established a national army.
> . . . In order to do that, I sought counsel only with my patriotic
> feelings, and did not borrow these feelings from any of my ministers
> (nor was Garašanin even in state service when the militia army was
> established). I showed them [his ministers] the path they needed to
> follow. Harmful external influences ceased completely in the country;

its moral strength acquired momentum and joined with the development of its military strength.[25]

"Ilija Garašanin," commented Ristić facetiously, "remains nonetheless a leading personality in the modern history of Serbia."[26] Ristić clearly sought to deflate Garašanin's role in order to exalt his own. Significantly, Mihailo's letter which he quoted came just two months after he removed Garašanin as premier, while he was cool towards his former minister and sought to assert his independence from him. During 1861-62, however, Mihailo and Garašanin were in full agreement on foreign and national policy, having come independently to virtually identical conclusions. Not merely did Garašanin implement these policies but apparently provided as well much of the necessary impetus, initiative and decisiveness.

NOTES

1. M. D. Milićević, *Pomenik*, p. 96. For the program, institutions and initial period of Prince Mihailo's second reign see Petrovich, *A History*, I, 295-300 which is based on S. Jovanović, *Druga vlada*, pp. 90 ff., and J. Prodanović, *Istorija*, pp. 266-273.

2. A. Orešković, *Malo više svetlosti* (Belgrade, 1895), p. 7.

3. Ibid., p. 10.

4. M. S. Piroćanac, *Knez Mihailo i zajednička radnja balkanskih naroda* (Belgrade, 1895), pp. 5-6, 13.

5. Ibid., pp. 19-21.

6. S. Jovanović, *Druga vlada Miloša i Mihaila*, pp. 149 ff.

7. Ibid., pp. 159-160.

8. IG 1175, "Razna primečanja na politiku Knjaza Mihaila" (1861).

9. Vučković, *Politička aksija*, pp. 45-46.

10. Ibid., pp. 60-62.

11. S. Jovanović, "Spoljašnja politika," pp. 429-431.

12. Jovanović, *Druga vlada*, pp. 89, 203-204, 209 ff.

13. Thouvenel to Tastie, November 13, 1861 and Tastie to Thouvenel,

November 16, 1861, from Archives étrangerès (Paris), cited in Stranjaković, "Ilija Garašanin," p. 185.

14. AII, Ristić XI/272, Garašanin to Ristić, December 28.
15. Ibid., Ristić XI/269, Ristić to Garašanin, December 2.
16. Ibid., Ristić XI/274, ibid. to ibid., January 22, 1862.
17. Ibid., Ristić XI/275, February 8.
18. S. Jovanović, "Spoljašnja politika," pp. 430-431.
19. Arhiv SANU, No. 7380, A. Nikolić, "Avtobiografija."
20. Jakšić and Vučković, Spoljna politika Kneza Mihaila, pp. 130-135.
21. G. Jakšić, "Jedan 'projekat' srpskog ustanka iz godine 1862," Politika, May 1-4, 1937. For the full plan see Vučković, Politička, No. 47, pp. 69-81.
22. Ibid., No. 48, pp. 81-82, "Mogučnost da se Srbija u boj izazvana i uvućena pre nego što je ona tome nadala."
23. Ibid., No. 46, pp. 67-68.
24. IG 1278, Milan Petronijević to Garašanin, February 26, 1862 and no date.
25. J. Ristić, Jedno namesništvo, p. 5.
26. Ibid., p. 5 note.

CHAPTER XV

THE BOMBARDMENT OF BELGRADE AND AFTER
(June 1862-1865)

"The Serbian government cannot consider Belgrade secure as long as the guns of the [Turkish] fortress are trained upon it. And with the other fortresses in a similar state, the peace and security of Serbia are at the mercy of the least incident. . . ."

Garašanin to Ristić, June 1862

Overlooking the Danube and Sava rivers and the town of Belgrade loomed the massive Turkish fortress of Kalemegdan.[1] As the center of residual Turkish authority in Serbia, its gray walls and towers over which fluttered the Ottoman flag, symbolized Serbia's continuing vassaldom and subjection to the sway of the Sultan. For years Serbia and the Porte had wrangled over the future of Muslim residents outside the garrisoned Turkish fortresses.[2] Successive Serbian missions to Constantinople by Ristić and Garašanin to resolve these disputes had been indecisive. During 1861-1862 Serbo-Turkish tension increased following actions by the Assembly, especially the law on a national Serbian militia, claims by Mihailo, and Luka Vukalović's uprising in nearby Hercegovina. Though encouraging the Porte to blame this friction entirely on Belgrade, Austria and England believed at first that Foreign Minister Garašanin was a moderate working to avert a breach of relations.

254

Urgently needed was a Turkish commissar to regulate evacuation of remaining Muslins from Serbian-dominated towns; however, despite dangerous incidents, the Porte had declined to dispatch one to Belgrade. After Mihailo at a ministerial meeting criticized him for inaction, Garašanin urged Jovan Ristić, Serbia's envoy in Constantinople, to take decisive steps. On May 22, 1862, meeting with Turkish Foreign Minister Ali Pasha, Ristić noted that Belgrade and Soko were seething with potential violence and urged that a commissar be sent to Belgrade immediately. When Ali responded with the usual Turkish excuses and prevarications, Ristić warned that unless the Porte acted, Serbia would proclaim jurisdiction over Muslims living outside the fortresses. The Porte, Ali retorted angrily, would regard such action as a grievous insult, but he promised reluctantly to send a commissar by the first steamship. When one still failed to appear, tension in Belgrade grew unbearable. Incidents multiplied between Serbs and Turks as the pasha of Belgrade doubled the guard at the fortress gates leading to the town. After a fracas on May 24th at Stamboul Gate, Belgrade alerted foreign consuls to this perilous situation, but the refusal of the English consul to cooperate, prevented action by the powers. As had occurred so frequently before, European diplomacy let matters take their natural course.

On June 3rd a Serbian youth quarreled with Turkish soldiers (*nizama*) who shot and killed him. When Serbian city police rushed up to reprimand the Turks, Turkish troops fired on them and killed the police sergeant. This triggered a general Serbo-Turkish mélée lasting all night. Next morning Garašanin intervened to arrange a temporary truce. Relates a Serbian document:

> At the moment when Turkish soldiers were about to use force and had fixed their bayonets, Garašanin arrived on the scene, and after having urged them at length and very strongly to return to the fortress, they indicated willingness to retrace their steps if given an escort for their security. For this purpose Mr. Garašanin provided a police officer, Ivo Prokić, with four or five policemen. After they had arrived under his escort in Zerek Street, one of the regulars fired and at their officer's order the rest followed his example. Prokić fell dead and two policemen were badly wounded . . . . This wholly premediated outbreak leads one to suppose that there

existed a preliminary agreement between the regular troops and Turkish citizens against the Serbian populace.[3]

Serious fighting would then surely have broken out in Belgrade had Garašanin not swiftly regained control over Serbian forces and moved to achieve a compromise settlement. He and the Turkish commandant (*muhafiz*) signed an agreement to end the bloodshed. The Turkish guards and Muslim population were to retire from the town into the fortress while Serbian authorities guaranteed the security of Muslim property in the town. Scattered firing continued next day, June 5th, but things seemed to be quieting down, and the Serbian authorities ordered the shops in town reopened. Then without apparent warning or provocation, the artillery of Kalemegdan fortress opened fire, bombarding defenseless Belgrade for four and a half hours. Serbian forces totalling 1,500 men and four cannon, restrained by Garašanin, wisely remained in defensive positions facing the Turkish garrison of 4,000 men and over 200 cannon. Prince Mihailo, returning hastily next day from a trip to the interior of Serbia, assumed plenary powers from the Assembly. Martial law was proclaimed in Belgrade and environs. The Prince issued orders immediately to dispatch militia units from the interior to Belgrade, and by June 18th Serbian strength in the capital had risen to over 13,000 men. In their other fortresses in Serbia the Turks took up siege positions.[4]

As Turkish troops concentrated on Serbia's frontiers, Garašanin telegraphed the Porte on June 11th:

If the Porte does not wish to create complications, it should immediately cease such demonstrations; otherwise, even though we are at peace with our suzerain, we will be compelled to adopt defensive measures at all threatened points.[5]

Ali Pasha reacted angrily to this message but soon lowered his tone and issued calming assurances. Receiving Garašanin at a gate of Kalemegdan fortress, Ahmed Vefik, the Turkish commissar, handed him a written declaration reserving the Porte's rights but leaving a solution to diplomacy. Serbian patriotic circles denounced the government's response to the bombardment as too theoretical and submissive to the mercy of the Porte and Europe. For their part the Turks, complaining about Serbian war preparations and newspaper proclamations, requested the powers for a free hand if the Serbs attacked. Except for Britain, they rejected this Turkish appeal.

Who had been responsible for the bombardment of Belgrade? The Turkish fortress commander had issued the order, but Turkish subordinate officials rarely took such extreme actions on their own. Subsequently, it was revealed that he had been instructed to act by his superiors, the Belgrade pasha and authorities in Constantinople. In any case the bombardment proved a serious miscalculation. Angered by unilateral Turkish violations of the agreement they had just signed, all foreign consuls in Belgrade except Wassitsch, the Austrian vice-consul, issued a statement blaming Ashir, the Belgrade pasha. English Consul Longworth, intimate with Wassitsch, accused him of encouraging the Pasha to order the bombardment. In Constantinople Ristić told Foreign Minister Ali Pasha: the Porte is mistaken if it believes that the destruction of Belgrade will destroy Serbia. "Serbia is not just Belgrade." When most foreign envoys in Constantinople backed the Serbs, the Porte removed Ashir Pasha and dispatched a special commissar to Belgrade to arrange evacuation of Turks living outside the fortress. On June 13th Garašanin informed Ristić that the Serbian government, relying on the Sultan's benevolence, would gladly talk with Ahmed Vefik, the Turkish commissar, in order to restore peace and order. Belgrade meanwhile would await arrangements reached between the Porte and the powers.[6]

The powers' initial near unanimity in condemning the Turkish attack soon dissipated. Already on June 17th the English ambassador, H. L. Bulwer, accused the Serbs of inciting the whole affair:

> In the memorandum of Garašanin one finds not a word of regret or reprobation for the atrocities about which I have just spoken. The struggle which naturally followed their excitations by the populace and I dare say almost on the part of the Serbian government, since Garašanin's Memorandum was more conducive to bring about rather than to avoid a struggle.[7]

Bulwer suggested maintaining the status quo while a Turkish commission went to the scene to investigate.

The Serbian government hoped the bombardment would convince the powers that all Turks should leave Serbia: the two peoples and religions, unable to coexist under unequal conditions, endangered the peace. Meanwhile, Belgrade and other Serbian towns remained exposed to Turkish cannon. Agreeing they should exploit this issue in order to remove Turks from towns and fortresses in Serbia, Mihailo and his ministers differed over means. Even before the bombardment, Mihailo had acted haughtily toward the Porte which considered Garašanin a moderate. Believing that all difficulties and Turkish measures were designed to force him from the throne, Mihailo feared that any return to the previous status would undermine his prestige. If other methods failed, he advocated resort to force though he knew Serbia was unprepared for war. His ministers, though, mostly favored diplomatic measures. Persuaded by Premier Garašanin, they concluded that using force would provoke Austrian intervention and risk Serbia's entire future. Garašanin argued that with Consul Longworth's apparent support and energetic backing from Russia and France, Europe was more favorable to Serbia than ever before. Serbia's lack of military preparedness reinforced his moderate stance. Supporting him too were Marinović and Colonel Mondain, the French officer subsequently to become Serbia's war minister, who opposed any resort to war. To resist the Turks successfully, Serbia required Russia's backing, yet St. Petersburg had warned repeatedly against any premature Serbian military action. Meanwhile in Serbia prevailed a belicose mood with Mihailo leading the war faction.

Mihailo's letter to Ristić of June 18th suggested the discord which prevailed within the Serbian regime:

> . . . The deadlock which exists between us and the Turks can only be cut by the sabre. I am preparing for this possible, even probable, outcome with a glad heart, although I fail to find a response from my closest entourage for my preparations, as there should be under present circumstances. . . . As long as Turkish fortresses exist in Serbia there can be no progress for her nor existence for me.[8]

The Prince's militance was reflected in his "Talk with the Serbian People": "Listen, Serbs!" Ashir Pasha bombards your chief city and the Sultan blames you! We are a free people under a constitution, our rights are guaranteed." Mihailo's message ended: "People, brethren! Forward soldiers! May God be with us!"[9] This certainly sounded like a call to arms.[10]

For his part, opposing any premature war by Serbia, Garašanin set a dispatch to Ristić for communication to the Porte and European envoys in Constantinople, demanding unequivocally the evacuation and destruction of Turkish fortresses in Serbia:

> The recent events in Belgrade, profoundly felt in all Serbia, have seemed to us from the start to be so extraordinary and to contain the germ of such great difficulties that the Serbian government must submit to the Porte and Guarantor Powers and seek measures which will prevent any repetition. . . . The evidence and the enormity of the aggression committed against a defenseless city, the impossibility of restoring peace and confidence as long as the source from which this aggression came is preserved, and . . . our conviction that the Powers wish to obtain peace and security for Serbia. . . .

> If, Sir, the Powers agree . . . that the bombing of Belgrade has been the most flagrant absue of force, an act of contempt for the rights of the people . . . , it is evident that the simplest course is to make disappear the possibility that such misfortunes can recur. . . . We possess the moral strength to remain patient and reply with moderation to these unmotivated and repeated violations. . . . The conduct we have followed heretofore and which the Prince wishes to continue in the future, will only be possible if we can count on justice from the Powers and sufficient guarantees for the future. . . .

> Unfortunately, the bombing occurred in daylight and one cannot reassure people as long as a fortress exists which makes such use of its cannon. . . . The Serbian government cannot consider Belgrade secure as long as the guns of the fortress are trained upon us. And with the other fortresses in a similar state, it shows that Serbia's peace and security are at the mercy of the least incident. . . .

> The Serbian government believes that the best solution in order to restore confidence and insure peace and order is to evacuate and destroy the fortresses. . . . [11]

Once that had been achieved, intimated Garašanin, other issues such as an indemnity and rights of Muslim civilians could easily be resolved.

Jovan Ristić, then Serbia's envoy in Constantinople, in later writings sought to dramatize his own services, intimating that Garašanin was dragging his feet from fear of the Turks. On the other hand, Ristić claims that he had favored energetic action:

> From the time of the bombardment I proposed consistently to my government that the destruction of the fortresses in Serbia should be demanded *formally and publicly,* but Garašanin invariably replied: 'Slowly, we must not hurry anything' and waited on this step until when such a document was composed at Prince Mihailo's insistence, the time had already passed when it could be submitted.[12]

However, Ristić then held a subordinate diplomatic post; it was Garašanin who bore the responsibility for decisionmaking.

Belgrade somewhat reluctantly accepted a French proposal for a European conference in Constantinople to settle the Serbo-Turkish quarrel. In advance of this Kanlice Conference, France and Russia agreed upon a common policy: "the existence of a Turkish fortress in Belgrade represents for Serbia a source of insecurity and danger which should be ended quickly." They would favor destroying the Kalmegdan's external fortifications, razing Turkish forts in the interior and evacuating their garrisons; Turks remaining in Serbia would come under Belgrade's jurisdiction. French and Russian diplomats realized that, faced with Anglo-Austrian opposition, the Conference would not approve all of that, so they did not press the Turks very hard on the Kalemegdan. Anglo-Austrian proposals suggested that the Conference should be convened primarily to blame Serbia for the violence. The Porte knew well how to exploit this familiar great power wrangling to minimize its concessions.

Realizing that England and Austria at Kanlice aimed to preserve the status quo as far as possible, Garašanin on June 30th set forth Serbia's position to the foreign consuls, the Porte, and the Guarantor Powers. Describing recent events in Belgrade, he demanded "that Serbia be freed wholly from the Turks in the fortresses." This diplomatic language was employed so as not to complicate Franco-Russian efforts in Serbia's behalf.[13]

The Conference convened July 10/22, 1862 with no Serbian representation. At the first session the Porte accused Serbia of placing 80,000 men under arms and preparing to attack Turkish fortresses; England and Austria continued to block Franco-Russian efforts to win concessions for Belgrade. The Porte did pledge not to attack or threaten Serbia in return for European warnings through their Belgrade consuls that Serbia must do nothing to worsen the situation and act to restrain the populace.[14] As the Conference dragged on fruitlessly, Prince Mihailo at a cabinet meeting of July 28th threatened to reject Kanlice's decisions if they included too many concessions to the Porte. He would prefer, if need be, to perish in the ruins of his capital. When moderates, including Garašanin, Marinović and Mondain, argued that Serbia must avoid war under present conditions, the Prince suspended the session angrily: "The ministers are here to execute my will. Those who do not wish to submit to it can leave with my thanks."[15]

The Kanlice Conference finally achieved agreement, but Serbia received far less than she had demanded or anticipated. The Porte did guarantee there would be no more bombardments, but only the small and militarily useless interior forts of Soko and Užice were to be destroyed. The rest, including Belgrade, would retain their Turkish garrisons. Muslims living in Serbia outside the fortresses were to be evacuated, but the Serbs considered this merely a confirmation of previous pledges. France urged the Serbs to be satisfied with these gains, but Mihailo reacted most unfavorably to the Kanlice protocol which he received about August 29th. Considering the decision to extend the Kalemegdan's boundaries, an indirect legitimization of the bombardment, Prince Mihailo initially wished to reject the protocol even if that meant keeping Belgrade under martial law. Ultimately, he yielded to Garašanin's arguments:

By rejecting the decisions [of Kanlice Conference] and not entering war, we would still have to remain on an emergency footing which would cost us money and effort and would not leave us the time to prepare as we should [for a Balkan insurrection] or to develop internally.

Furthermore, France and Russia, friendly powers, were urging acceptance, and Serbia, unprepared and isolated, had little prospect of success in war.

Admitting that accepting the protocol might damage Serbia's standing among Balkan Christians who had anticipated deliverance, Garašanin argued that this was insufficient reason to reject it. When the Christians realized that Serbia was continuing to prepare and encourage them, "then they will follow Serbia as they have done previously." Without the efforts of friendly powers, he added, Serbia would have gained nothing and Kanlice would have decided wholly in favor of the Porte. France and Russia had done their best for Serbia and without a war which they could not then face, could achieve no more.[16] Nor could Serbia then count on aid from neighboring Turkish Slavs in a war with Turkey: "With Bulgars and Bosnians, aside from a desire for deliverance, everything is largely lacking."[17] Grudgingly, Prince Mihailo accepted Kanlice, ended the state of emergency, and dispersed the Valjevo volunteer corps and the Bulgarian Legion in Serbia.

After the peaceful resolution of the crisis over the bombardment of Belgrade, Garašanin had his agents explain to other Balkan Christians that preparations for a final reckoning with the Porte had been merely delayed. Serbia, he explained, could not—as Hercegovina and Montenegro had done —plunge lightheartedly into battle and sacrifice many lives in vain. Montenegro's pressure on Serbia to join in her war with Turkey had been "an impudent demand." Was Serbia a mere province which could make war without agreements or calculations how it would be completed? Had Montenegro wished to cooperate, the common cause would have fared much better. The Porte, he cautioned, could not be beaten by guerrilla warfare in the mountains; she must be defeated in the plains. That was Serbia's great task, but to fulfill it, she must prepare well and fully; otherwise, she would merely rush to her destruction. Garašanin hoped that Montenegro, after realizing its error, would discuss common future action with Belgrade. While admiring Montenegrin heroism, the Serbs regretted they had dissipated their strength in premature conflict without real prospects of victory.[18] However, all during 1862 their relations remained strained as Montenegrin leaders denounced Serbia and quarreled with Vukalović, leader of the Hercegovina insurgents.[19]

Providing only cautious moral support to Serbia, the French urged Belgrade to be patient, prepare carefully and rely on Russia. During Kanlice Conference Garašanin had sent Miloje Lešjanin as a special envoy to sound out French attitudes and to seek weapons for Serbia's militia.

Lešjanin, a Garašanin understudy, met repeatedly with French Foreign Minister Thouvenel. Admitting the bombardment had caught Belgrade unawares, Lešjanin added that Serbia's ability to fight later would depend on Austrian neutrality and support from friendly powers. Strongly advising Belgrade to accept Kanlice's decisions, Thouvenel warned that France could provide only moral backing and that Russia was too preoccupied internally for war.[20] Thus the Serbs must accept whatever the Conference gave them. This was no time to risk everything. Continued the French diplomat:

> Prepare as best you can, train your militia, arm yourselves, work on an alliance with Montenegro, and gain for Serbia the support of all Turkish Christians. The Porte believes that Serbia is preparing for war against her; England and Austria agree and thus are aiding Turkey in its accusations against Serbia. If Serbia wishes to fight Turkey, Russia is the one which must help her and do for her what France did for Italy. France cannot aid Serbia with troops. At this moment Russia also can do nothing for the Serbs.

At the French foreign office Lešjanin heard repeatedly: "Russia is destined to be your main support in achieving your aims against Turkey," but "not now."[21] Thus as the Conference ended, Lešjanin advised Garašanin not to insist on further concessions; Serbia had done her best to convince the powers. Now she should prepare, then implement her national goals with other Turkish Christians. "We need close ties with Italy," Lešjanin concluded, in order to prevent Austrian intervention and to secure French neutrality.[22]

Therefore Garašanin authorized Lešjanin, in response to invitations from Italian leaders, to proceed to Turin and sound them out about future common action against Austria and Turkey. Lešjanin should emphasize their mutual anti-Austrian attitudes since that was where their interests coincided most closely. In case they should act against Austria and the Porte, a Serbo-Magyar agreement would likewise prove most beneficial.[23] Earlier, Garašanin had received a letter from Canini, an Italian publicist, with official support, urging Serbo-Magyar cooperation and claiming that a supposed secret army of 120,000 men would rise at Kossuth's order.[24]

Meanwhile Jovan Kumanudi, another Serbian envoy, reported from Athens that Greece was wholly unprepared for war. King Othon had declared that Serbo-Greek interests were identical and Greece would support Serbia morally and materially, but he refused any binding commitments until Greek war preparations were completed. Athens remained evasive during Kanlice Conference, consulting regularly with Paris and Turin. Garašanin informed the Greek government that regardless of the outcome at Kanlice and whether Serbia decided on war or delay, Belgrade wished in any case to cooperate with Greece on the basis of their previous agreement in Constantinople. In mid-August the Greeks strongly advised the Serbs to defer any military action until the spring of 1863.[25]

Nor could the Serbs count on Montenegro which after its defeat by Turkey had accepted onerous peace terms. Abandoned by Paris and with Russia cool, Prince Nikola late in 1862 turned eagerly toward Austria which supplied wheat and cash and pledged diplomatic support.[26] Garašanin's agent, Teodorović, visiting Cetinje that October after Montenegro's defeat, reported serious accusations against Serbia. Garašanin feared that Nikola would hamper any common action since he suspected Serbia of coveting Hercegovina.[27] To avert such suspicions, Garašanin had sent money to Montenegro, asking that some go to Hercegovina, but the insurgents there had received nothing.[28]

Belgrade's efforts to obtain weapons abroad, however, ended in success. Failing to obtain them from France, Garašanin sought them from Russia. On June 5th Garašanin had sent Atanasije Nikolić to Russia with authority to purchase up to 60,000 quality rifles and ship them through Rumania to Serbia. With great difficulty he managed by January 1863 to obtain 39,200 rifles in Russia and transport them to Serbia.[29] The numerous problems involved are reflected in Garašanin's voluminous correspondence during the latter half of 1862 with Dr. Karl Pacek, an intimate of Prince Mihailo, about the rifles.[30] Garašanin wrote him June 18th that Prince Mihailo had enjoined the utmost secrecy on the rifle issue. Dubious about Rumania's Prince Cuza, Garašanin instructed Pacek to conceal from him the origin of the weapons. "The Russians will gladly help us get the weapons, but in a way that won't compromise them." Since the Russians agreed to ship the rifles to the Moldavian frontier, "We must only worry about getting them through Rumania. . . ." On November 1st Garašanin wrote: "We are much worried about the transport of the rifles; it occupies all our thoughts. All else is secondary." On December 29th, much relieved, Garašanin informed Pacek: "We are awaiting the last transport on the Danube shipment. Then the difficult task will be complete. Thank everyone who helped us on this." In a later undated note, he added, "The matter of the rifles, thank God, is successfully completed, though the Porte is still raising questions. To you personally belongs much of the credit with your patriotic zeal and skillful work. We will thank Prince Cuza for his honorable behavior towards Serbia."[31] Meanwhile Prince Mihailo reassured the Grand Vizier: "This purchase of arms was motivated solely by ordinary needs of order and public security; there is no idea of any war preparations on Serbia's part."[32] His assurances were wholly false: purchase of the weapons was a vital part of Serbia's war preparations and the successful transfer likewise improved Serbo-Rumanian relations.

During the bombardment crisis, Garašanin had instructed his agents to intensify their agitation in Bosnia, Hercegovina, and the Military Frontiers. After Kanlice he wrote sadly: "We are frustrated for now at our inability to utilize the readiness of those brave warriors for our intentions . . . to attack Turkey."[33] In Hercegovina Archimandrite S. Perović had established a network of agents, corresponding with Garašanin through the Russian consulate in Mostar. In Belgrade Mico Ljubibratić worked as a paid Serbian agent to prepare an insurrection in Hercegovina. Based on the solid political ties forged then, Garašanin was confident that "Serbia can count reliably on Hercegovina which will be ready to rise whenever Serbia instructs her."[34] After 1861 in Bosnia Garašanin had revived a network based upon his former agents, chiefly merchants and priests. Revolutionary in a national sense, this organization remained socially conservative, seeking to preserve feudal control by Bosnian Muslims and promote their cooperation with Serbia.[35]

By late 1862 therefore the acute crisis sparked by the bombardment of Belgrade had subsided. During the next relatively quiet three years Garašanin strove to lay a sound basis for cooperation among Balkan states and peoples while pressing them to complete their military preparations and awaiting a suitable opportunity to strike at Turkey. Action was deferred from spring to spring with little apparent real progress. Discouraging factors were Serbia's continuing diplomatic isolation and the end of Franco-Russian cooperation. Encouraging was Serbia's improving relations with

Montenegro and Bulgarian exiles. However, even at the end of 1865, with divisions among the Balkan peoples persisting, prospects for a successful Balkan insurrection remained poor.

The Polish Revolt of January 1863 against Russian rule abruptly ended a Franco-Russian entente which had supported national movements in the Balkans during the previous six years. The Western powers—France and Britain—denounced Russian repression in Poland and even threatened to intervene militarily. The resulting danger of war caused concern in Belgrade while inducing it to intensify its diplomatic and political activity. Garašanin wrote Prince Nikola of Montenegro:

> Our interests cannot be involved in a war which the West might fight with the North [Russia] simply over Poland, but from such a war all sorts of circumstances may develop. A war begun for one reason can turn into a wholly different direction. We must be ready for anything. We must pay especial attention to two things: not to be deceived by anyone and not to miss an opportunity if it presents itself.[36]

Concerned lest there be an attempt by Britain or by an Anglo-French coalition to resolve the Eastern Question while Russia was mired in Poland, Garašanin sent Filip Hristić to London to win English public support. This had little result. Through Hristić Lord Palmerston warned Belgrade in March 1863 that England would not permit Serbia to fight the Turks. Serbia, he believed, was not ready for full independence; if she secured nominal independence, she would merely become a Russian tool. "We consider your present agitation [against the Turks] dangerous and cannot support you," he declared. Once Serbia had grown strong enough to protect genuine sovereignty, he stated condescendingly, England would back her gladly.[37]

Meanwhile Garašanin and his staff continued secret preparations for eventual war with Turkey. In January 1863 the former Austrian officer, Antonije Orešković, drew up a war plan which assessed the actual and potential strength of Serbia and the Porte. His gross underestimation of Turkish forces which could be employed against Serbia and his equally great overestimation of Serbia's potential helps to explain Garašanin's subsequent bellicosity and optimism about Serbia's prospects in such a conflict.[38] Already in 1862 Garašanin was laying plans for an eventual Serbo-Bulgarian federation under the Obrenović dynasty as part of his Greater Serbian conception.[39] Serbs and Bulgars should each have separate kingdoms with only their foreign and military policies conducted in common; both would be federated with Greece. This would be the form taken by the subsequent Austro-Hungarian monarchy of 1867. Serbia and the Bulgar émigré committee in Bucharest were to seek an accord to create such a Serbo-Bulgarian kingdom under Prince Mihailo. Setting up a separate Bulgarian dynasty, argued Garašanin, would meet European opposition, but since Serbia's dynasty was already recognized, this would simplify the powers' acceptance of the new federation.

Fear of isolation and the desire to assure Serbia's participation in future territorial arrangements in the Balkans induced Garašanin during 1863 to renew efforts to reach meaningful agreements with other Balkan Christians. Overtures were also made to Italy and the Magyar emigration, both opponents of Austria. For secret missions in Croatia, the Military Frontiers and Bosnia Garašanin employed Orešković who still retained his Austrian citizenship. Receiving reports about Orešković's activities, the Porte accused Serbia of preparing revolts in Bosnia and Hercegovina. Austria's Count Rechberg alleged that Serbia in cooperation with Rumania was preparing an uprising in Bulgaria.[40] Although Garašanin denied these accusations vehemently, they were accurate enough: Belgrade fostered his plans for diplomatic and military preparations throughout the Balkans. Garašanin emphasized the neceesity for alliance with Montenegro and Greece, closer cooperation with Bulgar émigrés, organizing national elements in Bosnia and on the Military Frontiers, and arming Serbia's national militia.[41] Serbo-Rumanian relations improved also after they established permanent diplomatic ties in March 1863. Belgrade sent Kosta Magazinović, a Garašanin loyalist, to Bucharest as its envoy. The Porte suspected that the two had already concluded a military alliance against her, but that was still distant.

These Serbian moves, however, stemmed more from insecurity than any intent to provoke conflict. With its former friends quarreling over Poland, Belgrade felt vulnerable and abandoned and its leaders realized that immediate war would prove disastrous. Except in Montenegro, its attempts during 1863 to forge closer links with the other Balkan states proved abortive. Almost everywhere Garašanin's men met distrust, suspicion, and inability to keep secrets. Thus negotiations with Ali-beg, the Turkish commissar in Belgrade, Garašanin in May 1863 adopted a moderate stance. Serbia, he told the French consul in June, had valid claims to Mali Zvornik and Kastel, but he would not demand them immediately. Later in 1863 the Porte repeatedly denounced Prince Mihailo to the powers's envoys and Belgrade no longer received accustomed support from France and Russia.

There were inherent difficulties in dealing with the Turks, Garašanin informed Marinović, who had violated the Kanlice Protocol repeatedly. To be on good terms with the Porte was virtually impossible, he concluded. The powers were advising him not to make a fuss over Mali Zvornik. "For us this will signify: let the Turks do as they wish because we have Poland to worry about." Garašanin urged Marinović to try to persuade the French to support Serbia on the Mali Zvornik question:

The Porte, I would say, because of the Polish war, is already beginning to bristle at us. England is eagerly promoting such a conflict so she can operate more freely in the East and secure the Porte. Her first effort will be to incite the Porte against the Danubian principalities [Romania] and especially against Serbia.[42]

To Ristić, his envoy in Constantinople, Garašanin denied Turkish charges that Serbia was arming against them. The Porte, reported Ristić, was still depicting Serbia as conducting intensive war preparations such as forcible recruitment of 100,000 soliders and employing 1,500 workers in feverish work at its arsenals. "We have been accused of such things before," responded Garašanin, "yet none of these accusations has turned out to be true." Such charges must be refuted point by point so that Serbia would not be damaged before the powers. "This year we have recruited only 800 men to replace regulars who have served their terms." There had been no further recruitment for a national militia, the number of militiamen trained had been cut by half and their training period reduced from twice to once a week. There had been no forced recruitment nor would such be permitted. Only 350 workers were employed at Kragujevac arsenal, the only one in Serbia, and they were not manufacturing new weapons, nor had any new Serbian fortifications been built.[43] Garašanin's denials may well have been accurate, but the Porte's assertions that Serbia was engaged in "an extraordinary movement" against it were equally valid!

Serbia's relations with Montenegro began to improve early in 1863 after a visit to Belgrade by Princess Darinka, Danilo's widow. That intelligent and patriotic lady grasped intuitively the vital importance of the Serbian states' cooperation. Her conversations with Mihailo and Garašanin impressed her deeply and she became the mediatrix in restoring the countries' friendship. She took back to Vojvoda Mirko, Nikola's autocratic and suspicious father, a letter in which Garašanin emphasized his desire for Serbo-Montenegrin brotherhood,[44] as well as a gift of 18,000 ducats to Prince Nikola "for war preparations." Better relations were restored soon after her return to Cetinje and correspondence increased among Garašanin, Mihailo and Prince Nikola. Writing Nikola, Garašanin regretted the end of Franco-Russian cooperation since both powers had favored the Serbs. A Serbo-Montenegrin agreement was essential and urgent, especially if the powers fought over Poland. Neither Serbian state, continued Garašanin, should make separate agreements with outside states. He hoped Nikola agreed with Belgrade's strong respect for Russia and France.[45]

Nonetheless, some suspicions persisted between Cetinje and Belgrade. Vital letters to Montenegrin leaders during 1863-64 were apparently not even received in Cetinje, Garašanin believed. Concealing his plans from Serbia, Nikola tended to turn to her only when he needed aid badly. As the Turks concentrated troops in Novi Pazar sancak, Garašanin warned Nikola that they must watch this carefully since such moves affected both states.[46] Garašanin praised Princess Darinka as a trailblazer of Serbo-Montenegrin friendship while warning of Austrian intrigues to block an accord between them.[47]

Another significant turning point in Serbo-Montenegrin rapprochement came in December 1864. Responding to Nikola's invitation, Belgrade sent Djosa Milovanović to Cetinje, ostensibly to represent Prince Mihailo at the christening of Prince Nikola's daughter, but chiefly to sound him out on a military alliance.[48] For Milovanović Garašanin prepared detailed instructions which summarized the European situation and how it affected the Serbs. Warning against any premature action, he advocated a Serbo-Montenegrin secret military alliance and common war preparations. In the meantime they must both show restraint toward the Porte. Thus Belgrade was avoiding actions irritating to the Turks while keeping some issues open, such as Mali Zvornik and the fortresses. Garašanin urged Montenegro to adopt this same tactic.[49]

Warmly received in Cetinje, Milovanović found Montenegrin leaders receptive to Garašanin's explanations about Serbian policy. Milovanović's lengthy report to Garašanin described these leaders and their attitudes. Apparently, Prince Nikola, overcoming earlier distrust, now was displaying real interest in ties with Serbia and criticized those in his entourage who had fostered hatred between the two states. While a young and inexperienced ruler, affirmed Milovanović, Prince Nikola had been dominated by Vojvoda Mirko Petrović, his Serbophobe father; now he ruled autocratically and desired Mihailo's friendship. The Prince told Milovanović impulsively:

> Let Mihailo tomorrow raise his banner to fight for the independence and freedom of all Serbdom, and I will immediately retire from ruling Montenegro and will be satisfied if I am given command of a regiment of cavalry, if Prince Mihailo thinks my presence in the country may be beneficial, but if it seems harmful, I would ask him to designate a place abroad for me to live and merely provide me with means proper for my position.

He repeated this with his closest advisers present, although such self-abnegation conflicted sharply with his usual viewpoint. Vojvoda Mirko, confided Petar Vukotić, Nikola's father-in-law, remained a threat to the idea of the unity of Serbdom "since he thinks constantly of Montenegro's aggrandizement" and was avaricious and stubborn. Admitting to Milovanović his former anger at Serbia for not joining Montenegro in its war with the Porte, Mirko declared that he realized now that Serbia, serving as the support of her divided brethren, should move together with Montenegro only when they were fully prepared.[50]

Milovanović's mission improved Serbo-Montenegrin relations dramatically. Hailing the "new kinship tie between two brother peoples and their dynasties," Mihailo pledged maximum efforts to strengthen their friendship and sent Captain Ljubomir Ivanović to inquire about Montenegro's military needs.[51] Several highly placed Montenegrins, such as Archimandrive Nićifor Dučić and Vojvoda Vukotić, had become enthusiastic partisans of friendship and alliance with Serbia and even favored their complete unification. They and Prince Nikola now believed Montenegro's policy must be subject to Serbia's and that Serbdom's salvation lay in

Belgrade.[52] Thanking Nikola for a decoration and a diploma, Garašanin wrote that the two Serbian rulers were wisely bringing their policies and interests into harmony and that he would dedicate his efforts to promote this.[53] During his mission, Milovanović had suggested concluding a military alliance followed by political unification. Garašanin had paved the way for this by a draft military alliance which he had sent to Prince Nikola. However, Montenegro was not yet ready for such a fateful step. With Cetinje short of money, Serbia purchased 8,000 rifles in Hamburg and Vienna for the Montenegrin army and promised to send a six cannon battery from Serbia.[54] Responding to Prince Nikola's request for advisers, Belgrade that summer sent artillery captain, Velimir Stefanović, to Cetinje to ascertain how Serbia could best aid Montenegro in weapons. Prince Nikola's adjutant, Mašo Vrbica, toured the Serbian arsenal at Kragujevac only to learn that transportation problems would prevent dispatch of the cannons the Prince had requested.[55]

Nonetheless, Garašanin still feared that those directing Montenegrin foreign policy, notably Prince Nikola and Vojvoda Mirko, out of narrow-mindedness and suspicion, would insist unrealistically on preserving Montenegro permanently as a separate state. Unworried by serious competition from little Montenegro to Serbia's status as the nucleus of Serbdom, Garašanin was concerned that its sometimes reckless leaders might again imperil Serbia by provoking a premature conflict with the Turks. A war preceding full diplomatic and military preparations would place Serbia in an awkward position and threaten her prestige in the national liberation movement. For its part, the Cetinje court, to some degree justifiably, felt that Belgrade was treating Montenegro as a subordinate to be sacrificed if need be, then liquidated politically in the interests of a Greater Serbia.[56] Alternating brotherhood and suspicion would complicate Serbo-Montenegrin relations for the remaining fifty-odd years of Nikola's rule.

Garašanin's other efforts during 1863-1865 to forge a Balkan alliance met with little success. In the spring of 1863 he sent Rakovski, the Bulgar émigré leader, to assure Greece that Bulgaria could supply 20,000 volunteers at the start of a common struggle. Rakovski met a cool reception since the Greeks envied Belgrade's growing Balkan prestige.[57] Garašanin made little effort to conduct national agitation on the Croatian frontiers, believing that Austria would discover his agents. Austria continued very active in Bosnia through its Sarajevo consulate.[58]

While negotiating sporadically with Italy and Magyar émigrés, Garašanin carefully avoided compromising ties with either. During the crisis over Schleswig-Holstein which produced the Danish-German War of 1864, Italian nationalists and Magyar émigrés revived their plans of revolutionary action against Austria. Garašanin maintained informal contacts with them through Antonije Orešković, representing the Serbian national movement. All these groups aimed in event of a major war in Central Europe to destroy the Austrian monarchy and liberate its subject peoples. Through nationalist organizations in Bosnia and the Military Frontiers, Orešković sought to create "a fiery circle around Austria." Late in 1863 he submitted a plan to the Italians through the omnipresent General Türr and sought Italian financial backing. The Porte, receiving vague reports of such clandestine activity, accused Serbia and Rumania of joining in Garibaldi's revolutionary conspiracies in the Balkans. The influential Turkish military leader, Omer Pasha, advised his government to occupy Serbia while Austria urged the Porte to occupy Rumania. In February 1864, Osman Pasha, Turkish governor of Bosnia, after uncovering Serbian military preparations there, issued orders to his bashi-bazouks[59] to prepare to invade Serbia. Realizing that he was playing with fire, Garašanin urged Prince Nikola to act very cautiously; he noted there were bashi-bazouk concentrations at several key points.[60] Apparently, his concern stemmed also from reports he had received from Ristić about Nikola's ties with Italian revolutionaries. He still feared that a premature rising in Bosnia or Hercegovina might involve Serbia in war before she was adequately prepared.

Later that year Garašanin was much worried about renewed reports of a scheme by Napoleon III to make Bosnia and Hercegovina Austrian in return for Austrian cession of Venetia to Italy. Such rumors had long circulated, noted Garašanin, but now Napoleon was proposing it seriously to Vienna. Seeking to win Turkish support in order to block such an exchange, he sent Ristić a memorandum for submission to the Porte which affirmed:

The results [of such a territorial exchange] for Serbia would be most unfortunate. It is self-evident that Austrian expansion into even one of those provinces would make Serbia's existence difficult if not impossible . . . . In such a case, the Porte and Serbia would find themselves damaged irreparably and their future ruined.[61]

Napoleon's scheme accounts for Garašanin's shortlived "new course" involving Serbian concessions to win the Porte's good will. Faced by possible Austrian acquisition of Bosnia and Hercegovina which would block creation of a Greater Serbia, Garašanin was even prepared to propose a Serbo-Turkish alliance against Austria. However, this effort proved abortive since the Turks suspected Belgrade of plotting with the Italian government and revolutionaries to subvert peace in the Balkans. Indeed, Garašanin was then seeking an alliance with Italy which would guarantee that Serbia would at least secure Bosnia. He calculated that Napoleon, in the face of such an Italian pledge, would have to withdraw his exchange proposal, but Turin failed to respond to Belgrade's overtures.[62] Meanwhile Prince Mihailo's efforts to sound out French attitudes toward Serbia by a state visit to Paris were rebuffed. A Mihailo visit, explained Paris, might complicate Serbo-Turkish relations.[63]

During 1864 and 1865 Garašanin utilized Nikola Krstić, a judicial official knowing Magyar, to negotiate with Hungarian leaders. Sent to Paris to learn French, the chief language of diplomacy, Krstić talked there with General Türr (Garašanin opposed having Türr come to Belgrade for fear of attracting unwelcome Austrian attention).[64] Garašanin twice sent Krstić to Pesth for secret talks with Magyar leaders about possible solutions to the Vojvodina problem and prospects for Serbo-Magyar cooperation. In April 1864 Krstić went to Pesth after outlining Serbian desires. These included recreating an autonomous Vojvodina where Serbian would be the legal language, election of a patriarch, and creation of a Serbian assembly. Garašanin approved this program fully. Although desirous of help from Serbia in resolving the Vojvodina problem, Magyar leaders feared any strengthening or expansion of Serbia and opposed a Serbo-Turkish conflict which might involve Hungary's subject peoples. Thus in 1865 Deak advised Serbia to concentrate on internal development. Some Serbian demands could be met, he indicated, but not creation of an autonomous Vojvodina using the Serbian language.[65] Serbo-Magyar cooperation against Austria or Turkey appeared most unlikely.

By late 1865 Serbia's ties with other Balkan peoples, except the Montenegrins, had been virtually suspended; prospects for a Balkan alliance seemed remote. Consultation with Greece had ceased as Greek leaders succumbed to English-sponsored anti-Slav propaganda. Greek squabbles with Rumania and the Bulgars stymied Balkan cooperation. Serbo-Rumanian relations were limited to a superficial friendship as severe internal problems persisted in Rumania. Talks with Bulgar émigrés for a common Serbo-Bulgarian state had been suspended. Also the Porte was growing increasingly hostile to Garašanin. After Constantinople had received a confidential report on Serbia's national-revolutionary activity in Bosnia,[66] Foreign Minister Ali Pasha told Count Ignat'ev, Russian ambassador to the Porte, that Garašanin, not Prince Mihailo, was the sole source of Serbo-Turkish tension. To an earlier remark by Ignat'ev that only the withdrawal of Turkish garrisons from Serbia would end the tension between them, Ali responded that the Porte would never agree to that, because the Kalemegdan was a vital symbol of Turkish authority whose abandonment would trigger a general Balkan Christian uprising.[67] The Turks, regarding Serbia as their chief Balkan opponent, sought during 1865 to reinforce their positions. Compulsory military service was imposed on Bosnians and Albanians, defenses in Bulgaria were strengthened, and strategic highways were built in Bosnia and Bulgaria. Despite these negative factors and the stagnation of progress toward a Balkan league, Garašanin had induced Serbia's neighbors as well as European statesmen to recognize the concept of a Balkan alliance. The Ottoman Empire's continuing decline provided its European peoples and their neighbors with strong incentives to break its hold completely.

NOTES

1.   On the Kalemegdan, meaing "the castle square" in Turkish, see *Oslobodjenje gradova u Srbije od Turaka, 1862-1867* (Belgrade, 1970) which contains articles and pictures on early Belgrade, the fortresses and their liberation from Turkish occupation. For Serbian foreign relations 1862-65 see Jakšić and Vučković, *Spoljna politika Kneza Mihaila.*

2.   Besides Belgrade's Kalemegdan these included three others on the river frontier: Smederevo, Šabac and Kladovo, and two small interior forts: Užice and Soko, which had long since lost their previous military significance. See *Oslobodjenje gradova,* pp. 535-561.

3. AII Ristić, I/15, "Résumé historique des derniers évenements de Belgrade, basé sur les dépositions oculaires."

4. Ristić, *Bombardovanje Beograda (1862 god)* (Belgrade, 1872), pp. 28-36; Jakšić and Vučković, *Spoljna,* pp. 111-113.

5. IG, Garašanin to Ali Pasha, June 11, 1862; IG 1210 and 1211, Garašanin drafts on his mission and the evacuation of the Turks.

6. AII, Ristić I/15, Garašanin to Ristić, June 13.

7. Ibid., Bulwer to Ristić, June 17, copy.

8. Mihailo to Ristić, June 18, quoted in Ristić, *Bombardovanje,* p. 47.

9. DAS PO 25/30, "Beseda 1862."

10. According to Vladimir Ćorović, Mihailo had prepared a declaration of war, but the powers exerted pressure on both sides to prevent a conflict. Prince Mihailo, "cautious and restrained" (sic!), concluded it was not yet time for open struggle." *Velika Srbija,* pp. 48-50. Actually, it was Garašanin who was then "cautious and restrained."

11. AII, Ristić I/15, Garašanin to Ristić (?) (1862).

12. Ristić, "Spectemur Agendo," excerpt from an unpublished autobiography in B. Petrović, *Jovan Ristić* (Belgrade, 1912), p. 8.

13. Jakšić and Vučković, *Spoljna,* pp. 117-118.

14. Ristić, *Bombardovanje,* pp. 47-51.

15. Jakšić and Vučković, *Spoljna,* pp. 147-148.

16. Ibid., p. 154; IG 1251, undated draft by Garašanin on whether or not to accept the Kanlice protocol.

17. AII, Ristić I/15, Garašanin to Ristić, August 16, 1862.

18. IG 1287, Garašanin to Teodorović in Dubrovnik, October 16.

19. Ibid., 1286, Teodorović to Garašanin, November 7.

20. L. Aleksić-Pejković, "Misija Miloje Lešjanina u Parizu, Londonu i Torinu 1862 godine," *Ist. časopis,* XXI, 1974, 126 ff.

21. IG 1279, Lešjanin to Garašanin, July 9 and 30, August 8, 25 and 29.

22. Ibid.; Vučković, *Politička,* No. 52, pp. 86-87.

23. IG 1279, Garašanin's instructions to Lešjanin, 1862. Lešjanin was instructed to suggest to the Italians that if Serbia were well-prepared and acted reasonably, Serbo-Italian-Magyar action would be supported by France and Russia. Could Italy supply Serbia with needed weapons?

24. Mark A. Canini to Garašanin, August 17, 1862 in Vučković, *Politička,* No. 53, pp. 88-90.

25. Jakšić and Vučković, *Spoljna,* pp. 126-129.

26. V. Ćorović, "Pobliski srpskoj prošlosti—Knez Nikola prilazi Austriji, 1862-1866," *Politika,* No. 5186, October 1, 1922, pp. 1-2.

27. AII, Ristić, Garašanin to Ristić, August 16.

28. IG 1286, Teodorović to Garašanin, August 18, from Dubrovnik.

29. IG 1241, "Punomočije," July 2; R. Perović, "Diplomatski spor o prenosu srpskog oruzja 1862 g. preko Rumunije," *Godišnjak N. Čupića.*

30. IG 1273, Garašanin to Dr. Karl Pacek, June 18-December 29, 1862.

31. Ibid.

32. DAS PO 25/27, Prince Mihailo to Grand Vizier, December 15/27, 1862.

33. IG 1279, Garašanin to M. Lešjanin, no date (1862).

34. A. Nikolić, "Opis radnje," cited in Stranjaković, "Ilija."

35. M. Ekmečić, "Nacionalna politika Srbija," *Godišnjak istorije Bosne i Hercegovine,* X (1959), pp. 206-207.

36. IG 1416, Garašanin to Prince Nikola, November 9, 1863, draft.

37. Jakšić and Vučković, *Spoljna,* p. 170.

38. DAS, Fond Milutin Garašanina, 4, "Ratni i operacioni plan za rat protiv Turske," by Antonije Orešković (Belgrade), January 25, 1863. He listed Serbia's population as 1,200,000, her national income as 4,065,351 ducats, regular army of 5,100 men and 24 cannons; militia first-class: 43,000 infantry, 2,500 cavalry, 1,200 artillerymen with 48 cannon; second-class: 49,960 infantry, 2820 cavalry, 1,570 artillerymen and 72 cannon. Grand total for Serbia: 106,200 infantry, 5,650 cavalry and 144 cannon. Turkey, claimed Orešković, could form an army of 155,600 men with 300 cannon but would require 55,600 men and 100 cannon to guard its Asiatic frontiers and keep internal order, leaving only 100,000 men and 200 cannon for Europe. Of those, 30,000 would be needed for garrisons, the Greeks would tie down 13,000, and subtracting also troops needed for Bosnia-Hercegovina and Bulgaria, the Turks would have only about 40,000 men and 56 cannon for operations against Serbia! Serbia, affirmed Orešković, could raise a total of 160,000 men and 144 cannon and after substracting frontier and garrison troops would still have 125,000 men and 110 cannon for an invasion of Turkey. That such a plan was chiefly fantasy is shown by the actual balance of military forces thirteen years later when Serbia, though aided by several thousand Russian volunteers,

was decisively defeated by Turkey despite a large-scale insurrection in Bosnia and Hercegovina.

39.   IG 1253, "Pripreme za narodni ustanak u unutrasnjosti evropske Turske" (1862) and "Politička delatnost glavnih poverenika." See S. Jovanović, *Država* (Belgrade, 1936), I, 272-284.

40.   IG 1408, A. T. Brlić to Garašanin, February 27, 1863.

41.   Jakšić to Vučković, *Spoljna,* p. 175.

42.   Garašanin to Marinović, June 28, *Pisma,* II, 98-99.

43.   AII, Ristić XXV/151, July 4, 1863.

44.   IG 1415, Garašanin to Mirko, February 25.

45.   IG 1416, Garašanin to Nikola, November 9.

46.   Ibid., Garašanin to Nikola, March 5, 1864.

47.   IG 1414, Garašanin to Darinka, no date.

48.   IG 1415, Nikola to Garašanin, December 11.

49.   IG 1500, Garašanin's instructions to Djosa (Milovanović), December, 1864.

50.   IG 1501, Djosa Milovanović, "Izveštaje o Crnoj Gori" (Belgrade), March 7, 1865; Nikola to Mihailo, January 24, 1865, *Zapisi,* IV (1929), p. 365; Garašanin to Nikola, March 2, *Zapisi,* July-August, 1935.

51.   Ibid., Garašanin to Nikola, March 2; IG 1539.

52.   IG 1501, Milovanović, "Izveštaje."

53.   IG 1539, Garašanin to Nikola, March 7.

54.   IG 1518, Blaznavac to Garašanin, March 7, 1865, from Vienna.

55.   Nikola to Garašanin, July 23, *Zapisi,* August 1935, p. 114.

56.   Radoman Jovanović, "Crna Gora i predaja gradova," in *Oslobodjenje gradova,* pp. 251-261.

57.   Toshev, *Balkanskite voini* (Sofia, 1925), I, 71-75.

58.   IG 1512, Garašanin to Mondain, October 26, 1865. Garašanin remained suspicious of Bishop Juraj Štrosmajer, a leading Croatian nationalist.

59.   Rather wild Turkish irregulars who acquired a sinister reputation for looting and murdering Balkan Christians, which was only partly deserved.

60.   IG 1483, Garašanin to Nikola, March 5, 1864.

61.   Garašanin to Ristić, draft memorandum of November 17, 1864, in Vučković, *Politička,* pp. 122-125.

62.   IG 1481, Ristić to Garašanin, December 21, 1864, Report No. 70.

63.   Jakšić and Vučković, *Spoljna,* pp. 202-204.
64.   Arhiv SANU, No. 7198, Nikola Krstić, "Javan život 1865."
Though Krstić valued Garašanin highly as a statesman, he expressed doubts
about his ability to control the cabinet, citing demoralization among Serbian officials and lack of unity among the ministers which he attributed to
Garašanin. Entry of July 18, 1865.
65.   Ibid., Dnevnik Krstića, entries of April 25-27, 1864; October 30
and November 3, 1865.
66.   Vučković, *Politička,* No. 71, pp. 145-149, "Bosnien betreffender
Bericht" by Aleksandar Vukobratić, a defector from Serbian service, who
revealed many of Garašanin's secret policies to the Turks.
67.   AII, Ristić XXV/281, Ristić to Garašanin, December 15, 1865.

CHAPTER XVI

GARAŠANIN REJECTS AN ANTI-AUSTRIAN COALITION
(January-August 1866)

"Serbia's interests require her to preserve her resources, retain free hands and not expose herself to anyone. The great day of liberation, we feel, is not yet near . . . and Russia would not and could not support a movement which she considers premature. Instead of putting everything at stake by seeking a final solution, it would be better to limit yourself to one step forward, as for example securing the evacuation of the [Turkish] fortresses."

Count Shtakelberg to Prince Mihailo, June 14/26, 1866

In his "Načertanije" Garašanin had described the Austrian Empire as the deadly foe of Serbia and Serbdom. He recognized clearly that as long as the Habsburg Monarchy persisted, unification of the South Slavs—his avowed ultimate goal—would be impossible. During the year 1866 arose a unique opportunity to destroy that empire in coalition with its other more powerful foes: Prussia and Italy. Garašanin's government was pressured by some Serbian officials and by Liberal leaders in the Vojvodina to exploit Austria's crisis in order to achieve a genuine Yugoslav federated state. Some Serbian leaders swallowed bait cast in their direction by Magyar and Italian revolutionaries seeking to mobilize the nationalist forces in central

279

Europe and smash Vienna's shaky grip over that region. Even Prince Mihailo wavered. Garašanin though remained true to his basic premise that the Serbs of Turkey must be liberated and united with Serbia before fighting Austria. Greater Serbia, he affirmed, must precede Yugoslavia and was an indispensable intermediate step towards it. Thus despite tempting proposals during the Austro-Prussian War for a Serbo-Magyar-Italian-Prussian coalition to destroy the Habsburg Monarchy, Garašanin adhered firmly to his course and prevailed with Prince Mihailo.

During the spring of 1866 ominous war clouds gathered over central Europe as Austria and Prussia prepared to fight a long-deferred civil war for the supremacy of the German world. Rivals since the days of Frederick the Great and Maria Theresa for the allegiance of numerous smaller German states, they had discovered, as Prussia's Minister President Otto von Bismarck put it: "Germany is too small for us both."[1] Bismarck realized that his goal of Greater Prussia, resembling Garašanin's vision of Greater Serbia, could only be achieved when Austrian influence had been eliminated from Germany north of the Main River. Their joint occupation of the north German provinces of Schleswig and Holstein after the victorious war of the German states against Denmark in 1864, had created abundant pretexts for conflict between Austria and Prussia. The conclusion of an Italo-Prussian alliance in the spring of 1866 fortified Bismarck's resolve to force the issue. By dividing Austrian forces between two far-flung fronts, it provided Prussia with excellent prospects for victory. If need be, Bismarck calculated, he could secure support also from the Magyars, whose leaders longed for full independence from the Habsburgs, and Serbia whose potential strength failed to escape the Prussian statesman's watchful eyes.

In Belgrade they realized the alluring potential of an anti-Austrian coalition. Antonije Orešković,[2] Garašanin's assistant and a highly respected military man, had been in contact with leading European statesmen, including Bismarck, Garibaldi and Napoleon III. Transferring from Austrian to Serbian service in 1862 and promoted to major, Orešković was valued highly by Prince Mihailo and by foreign officers seeking information about the Serbian army. In Belgrade his encyclopedic knowledge about the Austrian army and the Military Frontiers made him well-nigh indispensable. Remaining loyal to the goal of a genuine Yugoslav federation, Orešković became the chief advocate of a Serbian alliance with

Prussia and Italy against Austria. Already in February 1866, he claimed he had known that Prussia and Italy were about to conclude an alliance. "We always learned of the aims and plans of France, Prussia and Piedmont [Italy] in time to inform the Serbian government. Believing that Austria would be defeated in the imminent war, Orešković wished Serbia to grasp that opportunity to achieve a Yugoslav state.[3]

Orešković had obtained his information about the pending Italo-Prussian alliance from the man largely responsible for its conclusion, General Stefan Türr, a mysterious officer of dubious nationality and loyalties.[4] Entering the Austrian army in 1842, Türr became a lieutenant six years later. In January 1849 he suddenly defected to the Piedmontese and rose to the rank of lieutenant-colonel. An active agent of Magyar revolutionaries, he joined an English unit during the Crimean War and was promoted to colonel. In 1855 Türr was arrested by men from his former Austrian regiment, and only Queen Victoria's intercession saved him from execution. In 1859 he became Garibaldi's adjutant, helped him conquer Sicily and Garibaldi made him a general; the royal Italian army also gave him a general's commission. In the spring of 1866 Türr, now adjutant to King Victor Emanuel II of Italy, sought to draw the Magyars and Serbia into the Italo-Prussian alliance in order to destroy the Austria he hated.

Early in April Bismarck telegraphed Orešković that if Serbia joined the alliance, she could achieve all her aspirations. When Orešković transmitted this message to Garašanin, the latter instructed him to ascertain which gains Prussia would guarantee to Serbia. In rather typical fashion Bismarck replied:

> If we win, you can as third member of the alliance, defend your own interests; if we are defeated, I will not be able to defend us or you either. My special envoy will bring more detailed information and will leave today for Belgrade.

After conferring with this envoy, Orešković asserts he convinced Mihailo that Austria would lose the coming war and that the Prince had instructed him to conclude an alliance with the Prussians and Italians, i.e. to form a triple alliance of Serbia, Prussia and Italy. Orešković told the allied envoys that Serbia would invade the southern fringes of the Austrian Empire, securing support from the Military Frontiers for a move into

Bosnia. If the allies accepted that idea and would guarantee her Bosnia in case of victory, Serbia would join the alliance; the allies agreed.[5]

Then Garašanin intervened to block Serbia's entry into an alliance he considered dangerous. In this crisis he revealed once again his basic caution and sobriety. Far less sanguine about the allies' military prospects than his assistant, Garašanin insisted on binding guarantees which the allies would not give. Contributing to his cautious policy were Marinović's reports from Western Europe. Rumors still abounded that France was encouraging Austria to obtain Bosnia and Hercegovina in exchange for ceding Venetia to Italy. Then the Italians need not fight Austria for that coveted province. Thus Garašanin feared that the allies might utilize Serbia to invade Bosnia and secure it for Vienna.[6] Another Garašanin subordinate, Milan Piroćanac, believed the allies were seeking to insure victory over Austria by encouraging Serbia to attack her southern flank. Refusing guarantees or binding commitments, they could promise Serbia nothing concrete since the territories Belgrade sought belonged to Austria and Turkey. Even then Garašanin knew that Bismarck opposed Austria's destruction and that the allies would not raise the Turkish question for fear of disrupting their alliance. Therefore Garašanin saw danger in the Italo-Prussian offer: if Austria won, even Serbia's existence would be threatened; if the allies triumphed, Serbia might gain nothing or even have to look on helplessly while Bosnia was handed to Austria.[7]

Thus Garašanin remained dubious and unenthusiastic about negotiations with General Türr. He wondered how Serbia could benefit from joining a war against Austria when her vital and primary interests lay in European Turkey. Suspecting Italy of concealing its talks with Greece, he realized that Turin's goals did not coincide fully with those of the Balkan Christians. "Our goal is not the Italian one, nor is theirs ours," he wrote Ristić. If Serbia entered an Austro-Prussian war, the allies might find a pretext to transfer Bosnia to Austria in compensation for Venetia.[8]

When Italian Consul Scovasso asked him why Belgrade hesitated to join the alliance, Garašanin replied that Orešković, by seeking to bind Serbia to conditions she would find it difficult to meet, had exceeded his authority. Playing for time, Orešković, learning of this reply, persuaded the consul to delay reporting this to his government. He then composed a memorandum to dazzle Prince Mihailo with Serbia's brilliant prospects once she joined the alliance, arguing that it would be foolish for her to offend Prussia and Italy. Before submitting this to the Prince, Orešković read it to his superior, Garašanin, who objected:

> You don't know anything! Do you believe that I don't realize that with the aid of the Graničari and Montenegrins, whom we can always count upon, we could defeat the Turks [in Bosnia]? But who can guarantee that we wouldn't be pulling someone else's chestnuts from the fire? The great powers are quarreling now among themselves, but once they become reconciled, they will finish off us little ones. I will never wish to enter a war against Turkey until I have ironclad guarantees that by such a war we will not be conquering Bosnia for Austria.[9]

But Prussia and Italy have guaranteed us Bosnia if we win, objected Orešković. "That means little until Russia signs," retorted Garašanin. "Give me Russia's guarantee and I will be prepared for anything." "But it is your job to secure such a guarantee!" argued Orešković stubbornly. "Don't you think I haven't tried to obtain such a guarantee?" declared Garašanin. "Not only does she [Russia] refuse to give one, but what is more she dissuades us from a war which she believes would have only harmful consequences."[10] Working harmoniously with Consul Shishkin of Russia,[11] Garašanin knew the vital importance for Belgrade to remain in accord with St. Petersburg. But Russia opposed Serbia's involvement in the Italo-Prussian alliance.[12]

Garašanin also knew that Serbia was not ready for war. From Arandjelovac he informed Lešjanin that recently a speical ministerial meeting had been convened to discuss Serbia's military preparations and set a date for a war of liberation. A few ministers had favored action soon, but War Minister Blaznavac, demanding another year to complete preparations, explained how ill-prepared the country was. "His arguments were stronger than those of all of ours taken together, so we decided to wait another year and at the end of that time . . . set a time when and how to begin." That decision would depend upon when Greece agreed to act because:

> To have the entire Turkish strength concentrated against us would be too much for us regardless of how well we are prepared. Thus in view of our decision, do whatever you can so that the Greeks will

have completed their preparations by then. . . . They will have to utilize the time most energetically. They must not lose a single day. . . . [13]

Consul Shishkin, learning from Garašanin of Serbia's unpreparedness, wrote his superior, Ambassador Ignat'ev in Constantinople, that according to its War Minister, Serbia could not fight for two more years because of lack of war materiel, shortage of officers, untrained conscripts, and lack of food reserves.[14] At that time Garašanin and Blaznavac agreed that an inadequately prepared Serbia should not undertake war without agreements with other Balkan states and peoples.[15]

On the other hand, Ristić adopted a hawkish stance, agreeing with Orešković that if Serbia failed to act during the German crisis, her best opportunity might pass. Would Russia two years hence be any better able to solve the Eastern Question? Could one expect a European conference to do so? The powers might even turn over Bosnia and Hercegovina to Austria. Thus Serbia, aided by Montenegro, Greece and other Christians, should hasten to settle the fate of the Balkans by fighting the Porte. Obtaining European pledges of neutrality and agreements with other Balkan peoples argued Ristić, would outweigh completing Serbia's war preparations. Garašanin should inform Russia that Serbia must fight now and needed money, officers and supplies. He should urge St. Petersburg to advise other Christian peoples to join her.[16]

Garašanin considered such advice foolish and unrealistic. Unprepared and largely isolated, Serbia could expect moral and eventually some material aid from Russia, but not for a suicidal war against Turkey then.[17] Instead of war, Garašanin cautiously defused the fortress question and other issues with the Porte until Serbia could complete its military preparations and a Balkan alliance system. That spring Serbo-Turkish relations grew almost friendly as both countries feared an Austrian move into Bosnia and Hercegovina.

The outbreak of war in central Europe between Austria and the Italo-Prussian alliance on June 6-8/18-20, 1866, altered Serbia's situation dramatically. Only two weeks later (June 21/July 3) the Prussians defeated the main Austrian army decisively at Königgrätz in Bohemia. With the road to Vienna forced open, for a time it seemed possible, even probable, that the Austrian Empire would dissolve. Immediately after Königgrätz,

Garašanin believed briefly that this might occur. If so, unless Russia filled the resulting power vacuum, he felt that Serbia must reach prompt agreement with its neighbors: the Magyars, Rumanians and Croats—to create a confederation able to resist external pressures. As rumors spread of an imminent Magyar revolt which would meet the advancing Prussians, total Austrian defeat loomed. If that happened, even an unprepared Serbia might involve itslef with impunity.

However, prior to Königgrätz, the Russians again had made clear to Garašanin that they opposed Serbia's involvement in the conflict. Count Shtakelberg, Russian ambassador in Vienna, wrote Prince Mihailo June 14th: Russia opposed having the Eastern Question reopened while she was reorganizing her army. The Austro-Prussian War, he reassured Mihailo, would remain localized; Austria thus could not secure Bosnia without triggering general European war.

> The interests of Serbia require her to preserve her resources, retain free hands and not expose herself to anyone. The great day of liberation, we feel, is not yet near; agreement between the Slav peoples and Greece is barely in embryo form, material resources are still lacking, and Russia would not and could not support a movement which she considers premature. Instead of putting everything at stake by seeking a final solution, it would be better to limit yourself to one step forward, as for example securing the evacuation of the [Turkish] fortresses.

Russia, hinted Shtakelberg, would support Serbia on the fortress issue and in the future if Belgrade avoided rash action now.[18] Such advice coincided closely with Garašanin's own approach.

Informed that Prince Mihailo because of this Russian advice, hesitated to join the Italo-Prussian alliance, Orešković telegraphed General Türr in Paris: "Come immediately; otherwise our cause is lost." Eight days later Türr arrived in Belgrade and assured the Prince and Garašanin that France also favored the cause of nationalism. Thus if Austria defeated the allies, France would join them to save the national principle. Persuaded by Türr that joining the alliance would not imperil Serbia, Mihailo tentatively agreed on condition that Serbia would enter the war only if the allies specifically summoned her to do so. However, Orešković noted, once

Prussia and Italy realized that Austria for financial reaons could not even mobilize its total forces, they grew certain of victory without Serbia and thus avoided any commitment to secure Bosnia for her.[19]

Probably only Austria's total collapse before a Magyar-Prussian onslaught would have induced Garašanin to agree to the allies' overtures. In late June he had again sent Nikola Krstić to Pesth to ascertain the mood in Hungary. Two weeks later Krstić returned to report: the Magyars will not revolt unless the Prussian army enters Hungary.[20] During the Austro-Prussian truce after Königgrätz, Krstić returned to Pesth with a letter from Prince Mihailo to his relative, Laszlo Hunyady, about possible negotiations for a Serbo-Magyar confederation. But when he reached Pesth, the war had ended and Magyar leaders were supporting an Austro-Hungarian dual monarchy. Count Gyula Andrássy's new Hungarian government did propose an offensive-defensive alliance: Hungary would support Serbia on the issue of the Turkish fortresses if the Serbs placed a brigade of troops at Budapest's disposal.[21] With their position vis-à-vis Vienna greatly strengthened, Magyar leaders refused to pledge to revive an autonomous Serbian Vojvodina. Instead, they soon reached agreement with Vienna under which both parts of the Monarchy would rule their own Slavs.[22]

During 1866 Serbian Liberals in the Vojvodina constantly pressed Belgrade to adopt a vigorous policy to unify Serbdom. Serbia is destined, proclaimed Zastava of Novi Sad in March, "to become the nucleus of our national crystallization."[23] A month later it called on Serbia to free Bosnia and other Serbs under Turkish rule. "Hasn't our hour struck?," it asked.[24] A report to Zastava in early May predicted a European war which would allow the Serbs to unite like Germans and Italians.[25] One look at the map, affirmed the paper June 12th, showed that Serbia, Montenegro, and Bosnia-Hercegovina comprised a geographic unit destined to form a single state.[26]

After Königgrätz the Vojvodina Liberals sought desperately to prod Serbia into action in order to exploit the opportunity allegedly created by that Prussian victory. Criticizing Belgrade for inaction, Zastava's correspondent there asserted: "[War Minister] Blaznavac delays everything from one day to the next. . . . Garašanin, like the late Petronijević, wishes to maintain the status quo for his lifetime, and his subordinate ministers give him no trouble."[27] Queried Zastava a few days later: "Is the Belgrade government doing what must be done at this time . . . ? Does it know that we still have millions of tearful brethren in Bosnia, Hercegovina and Old

Serbia where the sun of freedom is obscured?"[28] Affirmed a report from
Belgrade:

> There are moments in the life of a people when long meditation,
> lack of courage and fearfulness amount to incapacity, weakness and
> treason . . . when a timorous government misses [opportunities].
> . . . If Serbia looks on while her brethren in Turkey are destroyed
> . . . then goodbye Serbdom!

Urgently needed were a Serbian Victor Emanuel and liberal institutions
which had won European favor for Piedmont-Sardinia; there must be
trust between government and people. Serbia should have mobilized its
militia before Königgrätz, but even now true patriots could transform
matters. Instead, Garašanin's Serbian diplomats were waiting for pears to
fall into their laps.[29] At a recent cabinet meeting, affirmed *Zastava,* whereas Prince Mihailo had favored energetic action, Premier Garašanin opposed
any bold move.[30] "When will Serbia awaken from her sleep?", asked a
report from Srem. Diplomats in Belgrade were wallowing in luxury, disregarding the people's will and deaf to the cries of the rayahs.[31] On August
3rd the prominent Serbian Liberal politician, M. Polit-Desančić complained
of pervasive indolence and selfishness in Serbia's state apparatus:

> We would shout with all our might to Serbian statesmen: do some-
> thing quickly for otherwise it will be too late. The catastrophe at
> Königgrätz is the beginning of the solution of the Eastern Question.
> If Serbia, which within its present narrow frontiers can never regen-
> erate itself, does not take the initiative to begin the great work of
> liberating the Serbs . . . then the same fate will overtake her as hap-
> pened to Bosnia and Hercegovina.

Exploiting circumstances, he concluded, achieves more than the best prepparations; good opportunites do not arise every day.[32]

The Vojvodina Liberals concluded correctly that Belgrade was divided
on what course to pursue, but their accusations of passivity and indolence
were surely unjust. On July 17th Garašanin had explained Belgrade's approach to French Consul Botmillian. The Austrian Empire seemed to be
dissolving; in its place would emerge Hungarian, Bohemian and Slav

nationalities linked into a federation. Soon, predicted Garašanin, a Yugoslav state composed of Serbia, Bosnia-Hercegovina, Montenegro, and hopefully Bulgaria, would be formed, perhaps after war with a moribund Ottoman Empire. This Yugoslav state must then either join the abovementioned confederation or succumb to Russian Panslavism. Belgrade, reported Botmillian, counted heavily on France to realize this grandiose scheme.[33] Pro-Yugoslav sentiments, concluded the consul, had surged mightly since Königgrätz.[34] The Belgrade leadership was borne along on a rising tide of nationalism and optimism about disintegration of the Austrian and Ottoman empires.

All during July 1866 Prussia and Italy, through their envoys in Belgrade, sought to induce Serbia to join them against Austria. Garašanin confirmed on July 5 that Pfuhl, Prussian attaché in Paris, bringing a letter from Ambassador Count Goltz, urged the Serbs to aid an allegedly imminent Hungarian revolt. Garašanin had replied that Serbia, facing Turkey, could not fight without a definite agreement with the Magyars. He refused to promise that armed bands could cross Serbia into Hungary, but Belgrade might cooperate informally with the Magyars. Pfuhl and Italian Consul Scovasso pressured the Serbs almost daily to join the allies, but in vain. Garašanin instructed Ristić to admonish General Türr, coming through Constantinople en route to Belgrade, to keep a low and secret profile.[35]

In late July, as an uneasy truce persisted in the Austro-Prussian war, Prussia's renewed efforts to bring Serbia into the conflict provoked intense debate within the Serbian government and a quarrel between Premier Garašanin and War Minister Blaznavac. Arriving in Belgrade in mid-July, General Türr remaned there about two weeks seeking for the allies precise information on Serbian strength and holding out prospects of Serbian gains in Bosnia.[36] Despite Türr's efforts at concealment, his presence was reported to Vienna by the Austrian consul.[37] Since Garašanin and Mihailo were then in interior Arandjelovac, Türr conferred instead with War Minister Blaznavac and Miloje Lešjanin, Garašanin's assistant.[38] On July 27 or 28 Türr received a telegram from Bismarck noting that since the Hungarian Legion was preparing a possible uprising, he should "continue his activity" in Serbia. Showing this to Blaznavac, Türr inquired about Serbia's military strength. In an amazing turnabout, the formerly pacific Blaznavac who had claimed it would take Serbia years to prepare for war, replied: "We have

50,000 first-class militia wholly ready to enter battle, supplied with necessary munitions, clothing and artillery." He merely expressed misgivings that if the Serbs crossed the Danube into Hungary, Turkey might attack Serbia. Seeking to allay those fears, Türr predicted that aided by Serbia and Rumania, a Hungarian uprising would succeed quickly and fully. Türr then telegraphed Bismarck the detailed information about Serbia's strength Blaznavac had so obligingly supplied and inquired whether Prussia would resume the war against Austria. "Three days after the resumption of hostilities," boasted Türr, "we will start from here." The Serbs, he affirmed, would promptly prepare 50,000 second-class militia and provide 15,000 rifles to assist an Hungarian uprising. However, Lešjanin warned that Serbia would act only if Garašanin agreed and the war resumed.[39]

Miloje Lešjanin served as intermediary between Türr and Skovaso on the one hand who were urging Serbia to act, and Serbia's leaders in Arandjelovac. He cautioned Türr that Serbia would only join the alliance if the purpose of the war became "to divide up Austria and rouse its peoples." Another prerequisite would be an all-sided accord on sacrifices and benefits since if Austria dissolved, Prussia and Italy, much stronger than Serbia, would control the Habsburg lands. Türr and Scovasso assured Lešjanin this would present no problem. Serbia, declared Lešjanin, would not cross the old Hungarian frontiers and would allow the Croats to decide freely whether they wished to join the Serbs or the Magyars. Türr remarked that Serbia's cooperation would be sought only if the allies moved, as he expected, to destroy Austria. "If there is peace, then I do not believe we can undertake anything for now." Lešjanin informed his chief that he had convinced the two envoys: "Serbia will not bloody itself until she knows definitely what she is to bleed for."[40]

Prince Mihailo and Garašanin had cogent reasons to reject Türr's offer just as they had turned down previous ones by Magyar and Italian revolutionaries. Though clearly tempted by prospects of securing Bosnia, the Serbian government, to demonstrate its loyalty, was careful to inform Vienna of these offers. The favorable subsequent Austrian attitude on the transfer of the Turkish fortresses to Serbia vindicated the soundness of this approach.[41]

On July 29th Garašanin wrote Lešjanin that he and Prince Mihailo had been appalled at War Minister Blaznavac's revelations and promises to General Türr. Despite their efforts to give Türr the true picture, "now all of a sudden telegrams have been sent to the Prussian and Italian governments with a different content and more promises than even Türr had sought, i.e., *a war of Serbia against Austria,* and Türr sent this to these governments as a sure thing." The War Minister's terrible blunder threatened to compromise Serbia. "He should have said nothing to Türr but sent him to me who alone an authorized to deal with such matters." How to correct this error now without destroying the War Minister's credibility? "We cannot tell Türr to disregard our War Minister's words, but I intend to explain to him the difficulties which now seem to make the success of his scheme impossible." If the German powers made peace, revolution in Hungary would be a pointless failure. Let the Magyars do as they pleased, but "Serbia cannot and will not risk its existence in any way . . . since nothing has been calculated or agreed to in advance." Lešjanin should see Türr immediately, transmit these views, and warn that Blaznavac had merely expressed good wishes without binding Serbia to anything. "The powers' intentions will determine our attitude toward Austria: *whether Austria survives, is not up to us . . . .*"[42]

Garašanin and Blaznavac now quarreled over the War Minister's revelations to Türr, which the Foreign Minister considered improper, and his interference in diplomacy. Wrote Garašanin: "Now Blaznavac will go at me tooth and nail because in one letter I criticized him strongly. He deserved it."[43] "Our War Minister is no longer even supposed to be criticized," added Garašanin next day. "Reading his explanations, one would conclude that he is either a fool or a person with evil intentions." He did not wish to believe the former but would let Lešjanin judge for himself. Türr still adhered to the figure of 50,000 wholly prepared Serbian troops and had reported it to Berlin. The allies, however, had as yet given no guarantees. Belgrade's war preparations would continue, but Serbia's entry into war against Austria must depend "on the prospects events offer us," a seeming reference to Bosnia. Garašanin refused to commit Serbia to more than she could do militarily.[44]

From Belgrade Blaznavac retorted sarcastically but defensively: "I did not expect our diplomacy [Garašanin] would lose its head only because the War Minister in a conversation with an Italian general admitted that the Serbian army possesses only the military strength which he revealed. . . ."[45] Denying making binding promises to Türr, Blaznavac sought refuge behind Prince Mihailo:

Indeed, I did affirm openly to General Türr that the Serbian prince truly possessed a powerful military force and told him what that force was. The Prince of Serbia is no beggar; he cannot beg before a general . . . who stands on close terms with the cabinets of France, Italy and Prussia. I did not dare nor did I wish to pull down the Serbian prince from those heights of military strength where that general perceived him.

He then blamed Garašanin for not warning him about Türr's possible moves.[46]

The next day, August 2nd, Garašanin castigated Blaznavac for making incautious statements to Türr and meddling in diplomacy:

> That our diplomacy has both a head and guiding intelligence is best proven by the fact that it does not wish anyone to interfere with it except authorized persons. When the Prince and I are at Kisela Voda [Arandjelovac], then our diplomacy is there too. . . . Everything ascertained which affects policy is to be delivered here, and appropriate orders will be issued from here.

Garašanin was telling the War Minister bluntly to stay out of his bailiwick. Though Garašanin had carefully avoided making promises and the General could not by himself take Serbia along an unwanted path, Türr must not hear conflicting voices in the Serbian government. Blaznavac had not needed to disclose Serbia's military strength to protect Prince Mihailo from humiliation. "You have agreed with me countless times that our military strength should be kept secret." If Blaznavac believed Serbian diplomats to be incompetent, let him suggest better ones. "As long as I am conducting diplomacy, I shall answer for it to the Prince and my colleagues, but I can only do so while I am directing it." He was prepared in the cabinet to admit any genuine errors and accept his colleagues' suggestions, but their arguments "must be better reasoned than yours which do not relate to the matter at issue." To act against Austria, Serbia required guarantees more binding than the word of General Türr.[47] Garašanin confided to his subordinate, Lešjanin:

The War Minister virtually swore at me and seemingly does not spare
you much either, believing that you should not have communicated
to me what Türr told you. In his letter of today...he finds my
policy weak and incompetent; he is unusually decisive and for him
Austria is so blameworthy that he wants war with her at any price.

Blaznavac, continued Garašanin, had failed conspicuously to justify a
warlike policy. "I tell you he is a madman [*lud čovek*]. Too bad one cannot tell Türr this so he will not be misled by such nonsense. I replied to
him today, refuting all the crazy things [*ludosti*] that he wrote."[48]
Apparently, the profoundly ambitious and unscruplous Blaznavac had
yielded in Garašanin's absence to the temptation to make policy for Serbia.
Morbidly sensitive, he could not forgive, much less ever forget, Garašanin's
blunt and pungent criticisms of his behavior during the July crisis. Ultimately, Prince Mihailo sided completely with Garašanin while the disgruntled, embittered Blaznavac awaited a suitable opportunity for revenge.
This, as we shall see, would arise soon and help trigger Garašanin's downfall the following year.
     Confirming Garašanin's sound judgment on the war issue, Franjo Zah,
a highly informed military man, wrote him August 6th: "I do not see how
you can hope for any military success without troops (Where were Blaznavac's 50,000 stalwart militiamen?). If things remain as they are now,
we would suffer catastrophe like Benedek.[49] If you think of fighting but
bind the hands of the commander, as the Austrians did with Benedek, misfortune is certain." For Serbia, concluded Zah, war now would be both
undesirable and dangerous. For twenty years he had been arguing that a
capital under Turkish cannon could not serve as a nucleus for Serbdom,
but so far in vain.[50]
     In any case, Garašanin refused wisely to involve Serbia in a conflict
with Austria. No Serbo-Magyar agreement existed on dividing Austrian
territorities, he reminded Lešjanin. Would victorious Prussia and Italy
partition Austria or merely take some of her territory? Only with full
partition and firm guarantees could Serbia enter the war. Nor could Belgrade's actions be dependent upon unknown decisions of the Croats.[51]
     By then the crisis had passed. Milan Petronijević informed Garašanin
August 3rd that an Austro-Prussian peace was imminent (The Peace of

Prague was actually signed August 11/23, 1866). Though many Balkan Christians looked to Serbia as a Piedmont which, with Russia's backing, would raise the Eastern Question and liberate them, that opportunity had passed for the time being. The Magyars refused to fight Austria, and the Croats preferred to occupy Bosnia or form a great Yugoslav state around themselves rather than seek to overturn Austria.[52] Also the Prussian consul informed Prince Mihailo that Bismarck now advised Serbia to remain quiet.[53]

The Austro-Prussian War thus ended too quickly to afford Serbia a real opening. Bismarck's policy had prevailed in Berlin of preserving a shrunken Austrian monarchy excluded from central Germany. Nonetheless, the Italo-Prussian victory had weakened Austria, strengthened the national principle and enhanced Serbia's position as the most potent Balkan state. With Russia and Prussia supportive, Britain inactive on the continent, France preoccupied with the German question, and Austria and Hungary undergoing reorganization, conditions favored realization of more of Garašanin's program. At least for another year would coincide Prussia's German drive, Russia's Balkan aspirations, and Serbia's South Slav mission.[54] This combination allowed Mihailo and Garašanin to solve the longstanding fortress question and build the first Balkan League around Serbia.

NOTES

1. In a report from the Frankfurt Diet in April 1856 Bismarck wrote: "The Viennese policy being what it is, Germany is too small for the two of us." *Gesammelte Werke,* II, 142, quoted in O. Pflanze, *Bismarck and the Development of Germany . . . 1815-1871* (Princeton, N. J., 1963), p. 106. On the Austro-Prussian War of 1866 see Gordon Craig, *The Battle of Königgrätz: Prussia's Victory over Austria, 1866* (Philadelphia, 1964). For Bismarck and the South Slavs in 1866 see H. Wendel, *Bismarck und Serbien im Jahre 1866* (Berlin, 1927). On Serbo-Prussian diplomatic relations, see J. A. von Reiswitz, *Belgrad-Berlin, Berlin-Belgrade, 1866-1871* (Munich, 1936). See also on Serbia and the Austro-Prussian War: Vučković, *Politička,* pp. 155-222; Ristić, *Spoljašnji odnošaji,* II.

2. Reiswitz, *Belgrad-Berlin*, p. 217, note 47.

3. A. Orešković, *Malo više svetlosti* (Belgrade, 1895), pp. 31-32.

4. Born in Baja, Bačka in August 1825, Türr described himself as a full-blooded Magyar, but the Wurzbach biographical dictionary of 1883 claimed he was descended from a German family. Lauberau, Prussian consul in Belgrade, reported to Bismarck November 13, 1866: "Türr is a Serb." See Reiswitz, *Belgrad-Berlin*, pp. 215-216, note 30.

5. Orešković, *Malo više*, pp. 31-32. No evidence was discovered to support Orešković's claim.

6. Garašanin to Marinović, April 27, 1866, *Pisma*, II, 165 ff.

7. M. Piroćanac, *Knez Mihailo*, pp. 24-25.

8. IG 1581, Garašanin to Ristić, May 5.

9. Orešković, *Malo više*, pp. 33-34.

10. Ibid., p. 34.

11. Nikolai Pavlovich Shishkin served as Russian consul in Belgrade, 1863-1874, developing relations of friendship and trust with Garašanin.

12. IG 15??, Garašanin to Shishkin, May 20, draft.

13. IG 1597, Garašanin to Lešjanin, May 25, from Arandjelovac.

14. DAS (MID), Ristić to Garašanin, No. 47, May 30.

15. Ibid., Garašanin to Ristić, May 26, telegram.

16. Ibid., M. Khitrovo to Ristić, no date (1866).

17. DAS (MID), Ristić to Garašanin, No. 45, May 24.

18. Shtakelberg to Mihailo, June 14/26, quoted in Piroćanac, *Knez Mihailo*, pp. 23-24.

19. Orešković, *Malo više*, p. 34.

20. Arhiv SANU, No. 7198, Krstić, "Javan Život 1866," entry of June 29.

21. Ibid., July 31.

22. M. Polit-Desančić, *Sve dosadanje besede Dr. Mihail Polit-Desančića* (Novi Sad, 1883), pp. 48-49.

23. *Zastava* (Novi Sad), March 13, 1866, No. 10, "Opredeljenje Srpstva."

24. Ibid., April 24, No. 22, "Djurdjev dan."

25. Ibid., May 5, No. 25, pp. 5-6, "Glas iz Srbije."

26. Ibid., June 12, "Rusija i Srbija, Bosna i Hercegovina."

27. Ibid., July 3, No. 42, report from Belgrade of June 28.

28. Ibid., July 7, No. 43, report from Srem of July 2.

29. Ibid., July 23, No. 48, report of July 13 from Belgrade.

30. Ibid., July 27, No. 49, report of July 18 from Belgrade.

31. Ibid., July 30, No. 50, report from Srem of July 20.

32. Ibid., August 3, No. 51, "Srbija"; Cukić to Garašanin, August 4, in Vučković, *Politička*, No. 113, p. 220.

33. Botmillian (French consul in Belgrade) to Drouyn de Lhuys (French foreign minister), July 18/30, citing an article in *Svetovid* (Belgrade), cited in Vučković, *Politička*, pp. 178-179. This scheme coincides with an undated memorandum by Matija Ban urging replacement of the Ottoman Empire with a Balkan confederation. The Yugoslavs, once unified and confederated with Hungary, Rumania and Greece, would attract Bohemia, Moravia and the Poles. Only thus could the thirty million southern and western Slavs be torn from Russia's grasp and a confederation of 44,000,000 people be established from the Baltic to the Adriatic. Only France, argued Ban, could help achieve this since Russia would probably seek to divide the South Slavs in order to dominate them. AII Ban IV/7 (1866), "Mémoire pour le Consul de France, M. Botmilio."

34. Botmillian to de Lhuys, July 22/August 3 in Vučković, *Politička*, No. 91, pp. 179-180.

35. AII Ristić, Garašanin to Ristić, July 5, 1866.

36. G. Jakšić, "Jedan sukob,"; V. Ćorović, "Pruska i Srbija 1866 godine," *Politika*, May 1, 1925.

37. Ibid.

38. IG 1597, Lešjanin to Garašanin, July 23.

39. Ibid., Lešjanin to Garašanin, July 28-29.

40. Ibid., July 30.

41. Ćorović, "Pruska i Srbija."

42. DAS PO 47/76, "O misiji Generala Tira i želji Srbije da ostane van ratnog sukoba sa Austrijom"; IG 1698, Garašanin to Lešjanin, July 29.

43. Garašanin to Lešjanin in Vučković, *Politička*, No. 102, p. 198.

44. Ibid., July 31, in Vučković, No. 105, p. 204.

45. Blaznavac to Garašanin in ibid., No. 108, p. 208.

46. Jakšić, "Jedan sukob," pp. 139-140.

47. Garašanin to Blaznavac, August 2, in Vučković, *Politička*, No. 109, pp. 210-212.

48. Garašanin to Lešjanin, August 3, in ibid., No. 111, pp. 218-219.

49. General Ludwig August Benedek, the Austrian commander-in-chief at the Battle of Königgrätz.

50. IG 1605, Zah to Garašanin, August 6, from Kragujevac.
51. Garašanin to Lešjanin, August 10, in Vučković, *Politička,* No. 115, pp. 222-223. Bishop Juraj Štrosmajer, the Croatian leader, accepted Garašanin's proposal that Serbia and the Triune Kingdom form an independent Yugoslav state but only after Štrosmajer had lost all hope of escaping Austrian dualism. Orešković to Mihailo, August 25 in Vučković, *Politička,* No. 116, p. 223.
52. Ibid., No. 112, pp. 219-220, Petronijević to Garašanin, August 3.
53. IG 1611, August 18.
54. Reiswitz, *Belgrad-Berlin,* pp. 35-36. Reiswitz extends that period to the end of the Franco-Prussian War of 1870-71, but after Garašanin's removal in November 1867 and certainly after Prince Mihailo's murder in May 1868, Serbia's policy lost its dynamism.

CHAPTER XVII

THE FORTRESSES AND THE BALKAN LEAGUE
(September 1866-June 1867)

"Our aim is the liberation of the Christians groaning under the Turkish yoke in order to create a basis for unification of all Yugoslav peoples into a single federated state. Organization of this state will be left to time and the participating peoples after liberation is achieved."
Garašanin's amendment of Orešković's plan of March 1867.

During the year after the Austro-Prussian War, Garašanin's government finally resolved the fortress issue successfully and began to build the first league of Balkan states and peoples. Garašanin had long considered these major steps as essential preliminaries to the war of national liberation which remained his chief objective. By the summer of 1867 he was satisfied that war preparations were virtually complete. Abandoning his former caution, Garašanin became the most bellicose of Serbian ministers. However, the War Minister, his arguments supported by a team of visiting Russian officers, still claimed that Serbia was not prepared militarily. Only Prince Mihailo could resolve these differences within the Belgrade leadership over the war issue, and there were already indications he would adopt a more pacific course.

Jovan Ristić, Serbia's envoy in Constantinople, encouraged by Ambassador Ignat'ev of Russia, early in 1866 urged Garašanin to demand evacuation of all Turkish fortresses in Serbia. In mid-February Garašanin stated his intention to have the three smaller forts destroyed. Once that had been achieved, Prince Mihailo could travel to Constantinople, pay respects to his nominal overlord, the Sultan, and seek to resolve the main issue: the future of the Kalemegdan. Before making decisive moves, Garašanin sent Marinović to win Western support on the fortress question. He found the British sympathetic and anxious to avoid a Balkan explosion, but he could not win French backing. Marinović argued that evacuation of the fortresses would remove an important source of friction, save the Porte money, and allow Serbia to defend Ottoman territorial integrity.[1] Marinović's mixed reception in the West and worry over a possible Venetia-Bosnia exchange contributed to Belgrade's caution early in 1866.

Austrian reports were already suggesting major potential differences between Prince Mihailo and Garašanin: the latter adhered to a pro-Russian policy and a Balkan war of liberation; the former toyed with an approach to Austria. Former Austrian consul in Belgrade, Radosavljević, reported to Vienna in February: "The leader of all these [South Slav] plots is doubtless the clever Garašanin who is hostile to Austria; Orešković is his right-hand man."[2] Another Austrian report affirmed:

Prince Mihailo is conducting presently in Serbia a dual policy: an official one toward his ministers, the Council, and the people, and a secret one with his sister, Anka Konstantinović . . . . [Mihailo] is no partisan of a rash, eccentric policy, but he is being pushed on powerfully by a dangerous party in the country. He seeks to satisfy it partly and apparently by phrases and promises, but inside he is nonetheless convinced that any aggressive behavior, any action policy . . . would under any circumstances be a dangerous game. Earlier, Mihailo sympathized with Russia, but now he sees the well-being of his country and especially his personal advantage in an honorable agreement [Anschluss] with Austria.[3]

Such a divergence between prince and premier, however, remained hidden for another eighteen months.

During 1866 Garašanin, knowing Christian unity would help resolve the fortress issue, redoubled his efforts to achieve Balkan alliances. Realizing that close ties with Montenegro were indispensible to his policy, in April he sent his trusted subordinate, Piroćanac, to Dalmatia and Cetinje and instructed him to persuade Prince Nikola and his entourage to cooperate fully with Serbia and to ascertain their aims. Piroćanac was to assure Nikola that Serbia would not fight Turkey or involve Montenegro in war until they were both fully prepared. Since Serbs and Montenegrins were "one people," Piroćanac was to advocate their complete unification. "The idea of unification," wrote Garašanin "has become general among Serbs and nothing can hinder this any longer."[4]

Prince Nikola, reported Piroćanac, wished to be named Mihailo's successor if the latter had no direct heirs. Piroćanac had been instructed not to raise this issue but that if the Montenegrins did, he should state: such a declaration must follow unification and significant contributions by Nikola to the common struggle. The two Serbian states agreed to adopt a common policy in case of an Austro-Prussian war and begin negotiations for a military alliance. Serbia would supply Montenegro with arms, money and advisors to speed its war preparations.[5] Garašanin remained dubious about Prince Nikola and some of his entourage, but Belgrade supplied Montenegro with cannon and instructors. The Porte thereupon protested to Ristić that Serbia's aim was to arm gradually all Turkish Slavs.[6]

With the groundwork laid, Serbia and Montenegro then concluded a military alliance. After the birth of Prince Nikola's second child in July 1866, Garašanin despatched Lešjanin to Cetinje with a draft treaty and empowered him to conclude an alliance. If Lešjanin's mission succeeds, Garašanin wrote Ristić, "the whole Serbian cause will be, I hope, much advanced." Prince Nikola would be promised a high position but without any guarantee he would succeed a childless Mihailo. Political instability and selfishness in Cetinje, noted Garašanin, required that Montenegro be bound firmly with a written alliance.[7]

Aided by Russian pressure on Nikola, Lešjanin's mission succeeded fully. On September 23rd he and Petar Vukotić signed the secret alliance. Returning to Belgrade with Lešjanin, Nićifor Dučić, Nikola's envoy, exchanged copies of the treaty with Garašanin, and Prince Mihailo signed it October 14th.[8] Its stated purpose was to "prepare an insurrection in Turkey and unite the entire Serbian people in a single state." If victorious,

Nikola would join Montenegro to Serbia, recognize Mihailo as their ruler and become a prince of the ruling dynasty enjoying first place after the heir. He pledged to take no action toward Turkey without consulting Serbia and to enter war at Serbia's summons.[9] Supposedly to be kept secret except from Russia, the treaty's terms soon leaked to the public. Later that fall Serbia concluded a secret military convention with Montenegro and reinforced their political ties.[10]

During 1866 Garašanin's efforts to link Serbia closely with other Balkan peoples enjoyed less success. Negotiations with Greece had ebbed and flowed since 1861. After King Othon's fall in 1862, Greece came under strong British influence. To achieve a "Greater Greece," Greek Anglophiles counted more on the powers than on Balkan cooperation. Arguing that compromise between their Megali conception and Slav aspirations was impossible, they delcined to negotiate with their Slav neighbors. Of Greek politicians then only Alexander Kumunduros desired to work with Serbia, but his party was out of power. Garašanin could have dealt with Greece through the Russian embassy in Constantinople, but he preferred direct talks not subject to Russian scrutiny. The Cretan revolt which erupted in April 1866, induced Athens to suggest to Belgrade common action against the Turks; Greece sought to lure Serbia into war without even a preliminary agreement. However, Garašanin refused to commit her to act without a binding alliance with Greece.[11] S. Antonopulos, Greek envoy in Constantinople, was instructed to seek the powers' support whereas Garašanin favored a direct Serbo-Greek accord first, and only later an appeal for European backing.[12]

The ensuing Ristić-Antonopulos talks in Constantinople produced a draft Serbo-Greek alliance based on the proposals of 1861.[13] Pro-Serbian elements in Greece led by Kumunduros were to achieve power as soon as possible, then both sides would push preparations for a war of liberation. Avoiding premature revolts, they should set a date for general insurrection and conclude a formal alliance. North Albanian tribesmen, supported by Serbian and Greek volunteers, were to begin the insurrection, then Serbia and Greece would enter the conflict openly and simultaneously. Mihailo and Garašanin accepted this agreement as a basis but awaited King George's signature before undertaking definite obligations.[14] Such heartening progress halted abruptly with the entry into the Athens cabinet in May of the Anglophile, D. Bulgaris. Commented Garašanin sadly: "This eliminates

our agreement and hopes to enter with Greece into the intended action."
Serbia must involve King George so that cabinet changes would not block
an agreement.[15]

New Greek overtures came in August 1866. Noting that Epirus would
probably soon revolt in sympathy with Crete, Renijeris asked Ristić
whether Serbia could fight. Sending Ristić's telegram to his chief, Lešjanin
remarked that the unprepared Greeks "expect us to do their work."[16]
Garašanin avoided any definite Serbian response on Epirus until Athens
provided concrete, detailed plans on its forces and policies, but he considered such an uprising "premature, unprepared and dangerous."[17] If the
Greeks now fought the Turks, that would delay "a simultaneous general
insurrection which is not far off." Ristić should seek to defer such a conflict.[18] War against the Porte should be fought "by general agreement and
insurrection." Was Greece avoiding agreement with Serbia in order to attract European attention and to aggrandize itself?[19] Greece seemed to
have a confused king and Serbia a bungling war minister.[20] In September
Captain Ljubomir Ivanović reported from Athens that Greece was still
wholly unprepared for war.[21]

Nor was Rumania nearly ready to join an anti-Turkish conflict. Prince
Cuza had just been expelled and replaced by Prince Charles of Hohen-
zollern. Deploring the selection of a foreigner as Rumanian prince for fear
the country might become an Austrian or Russian tool, Garašanin opposed any agreement with the unstable Rumanian provisional government.
When it offered Serbia an alliance in late March 1866, he spun out the
negotiations hoping Rumania would develop a more stable regime. Preferring even a foreign prince in Rumania to anarchy, Garašanin favored his
recognition by Serbia.[22] To Dimitri Bratianu, Prince Charles' envoy, Garašanin promised gunpowder but evaded a military alliance.[23] The Serbs
could do no more, he explained, since they are "compelled to prepare the
best they can for future events which are shrouded in complete uncertainty." Still, Garašanin regarded Bratianu's mission as heralding positive
future ties.[24] Sent to Bucharest in July to congratulate Prince Charles on
his accession, Filip Hristić reported that Serbian overtures had been
welcomed there. "We will cultivate carefully such Rumanian dispositions
towards us," wrote Garašanin, "and hope that therefore we can obtain
some support in time of war."[25] He instructed his regular envoy, Kosta
Magazinović, to continue efforts to arrange an alliance and inquired how

things stood.[26] Young Prince Charles believed naively, replied Magazinović, that the Ottoman Empire would collapse without special efforts by
the Balkan states. Hoping the Rumanian prince would abandon such unrealistic notions, Garašanin stressed that the Balkan peoples could not
prevail or achieve their future without unity, preparation and sacrifice.[27]

Not until the summer of 1866 did Belgrade achieve meaningful ties
with the Bulgars. In Bulgaria itself Turkish repression prevented most
national activity while Bulgarian émigrés, concentrated chiefly in Bucharest, remained divided between prosperous, cautious merchants and bold
but impractical warriors and intellectuals. A small group of youths educated in Serbia and abroad gathered around the revolutionary, Georgi
Rakovski, but viewing Mihailo's regime as a threat to future Bulgarian
independence and greatness, they aimed to free Bulgaria without Serbian
aid. At that time Garašanin regarded the Bulgars with a mixture of pity
and contempt. The émigrés' negative stance and apathy for the Turkish-
ruled Bulgarian masses blocked development of a genuine nationalist
movement. Deploring Bulgar inactivity, Garašanin declared: "They are
patriots until they find bread for themselves; once they obtain it they
leave patriotism to others as no longer paying them enough interest."[28]
He could readily abandon a people with so little national awareness, but
that would hinder other peoples prepared to work for their future. "One
could even say that if (̄ ̄ ̄ ̄ ̄ were no Bulgars on European soil, there would
be no more Turks in the Balkans, he exclaimed. Other Christians wished
that the Bulgars would discern their own true interests. "By their stupidity
they harm themselves, and by their stubbornness those who have the misfortune to be near them." They refused to listen and "seek their Bulgaria
everywhere: in Macedonia, Old Serbia, and even lay claims to half of
present-day Serbia . . . ." Here was an oppressed people demanding more
freedom than their liberators! The Bulgars dreamed of an empire achieved
without bloodshed to which peoples with more glorious histories would
be subordinated. Despite their foolish and grandiose aims, concluded Garašanin, Serbia should not sever its ties with them: doors must be left open
until the Bulgars came to their senses. Magazinović should warn Bulgar
émigrés in Bucharest that Balkan Christian discord merely aided Turkish
tyranny and delayed its collapse.[29]

Prospects for Serbo-Bulgarian cooperation brightened somewhat that
summer. A favorable report by Filip Hristić about the Bulgarian Committee

in Bucharest pleased Garašanin. Through it he hoped the Bulgars would be roused to insurrection "especially now when the time for this is approaching."[30] Soon the Bucharest Committee's envoys came to Belgrade and announced it would establish subcommittees throughout Bulgaria and begin organizing a Bulgarian insurrection. However, the Bulgar émigrés in Constantinople submitted a petition to the Sultan pledging loyalty to him and protesting against the Cretan uprising. Revolted by this, Garašanin declared that it confirmed to the world that Bulgars were still mere slaves; they should know that the Turks would merely scorn their stupidity. Forwarding a copy of this petition to Magazinović, he expressed the hope that Bucharest émigrés could counter "that act of treason."[31] The Bulgars thus remained fragmented and manifestly unprepared.

Despite Garašanin's arduous efforts to rouse the Balkan peoples, ally with them and prepare them for general insurrection and war, the day of reckoning with Turkey still seemed distant. Serbian organizations were operating in Bosnia, Hercegovina and Old Serbia, and Bulgar émigrés were beginning to prepare their countrymen for action, but Belgrade had an alliance only with Montenegro. Agreements with Rumania, Greece and Bulgarian exiles were not even close to completion. These factors, combined with Serbia's military unpreparedness, ruled out any immediate resort to war.

Russian attitudes too would influence powerfully Serbian policy toward the Porte. During the years, 1866-67, Garašanin and Russian leaders agreed on the need to form a Balkan league. While St. Petersburg opposed a Balkan war for fear Russia might be drawn into a premature confrontation, Russian diplomats on the spot mostly favored a war of liberation and sought to convert their government. In August 1866 after Austria's defeat, a memorandum by Ambassador Ignat'ev in Constantinople, warning that the Balkan Christians were so aroused they might not await Russia's signal, advised St. Petersburg to back them. His subordinate, Consul A. S. Ionin in Janina, agreed.[32] In October 1866, after receiving Garašanin's letter seeking Russia's support for a forcible solution of the Eastern Question, Ambassador Shtakelberg in Vienna concluded that Prussian victories had triggered it.[33] Consul Shishkin, valuing Garašanin highly as a person and statesman, assured Foreign Minister Gorchakov that Premier Garašanin would cooperate closely with Russia. For his part, Garašanin rejoiced that in Shishkin he had finally discovered a Russian diplomat who understood and supported Serbia's policies.[34]

Late that fall Garašanin sent Marinović to St. Petersburg to ascertain current Russian thinking. Warmly received, he had frank talks with the Tsar and Gorchakov. Alexander II, rejoicing at Serbia's progress, declared that he "worried like a father that she succeed in her aims and assure her future . . . . " While pledging moral and material aid, he warned against precipitate action. A Serbo-Greek alliance and full agreement on future frontiers, emphasized the Russian leaders, must precede a Balkan war with Turkey. After Christian victory, they added, Serbia should limit herself to taking Bosnia-Hercegovina, Old Serbia and part of Albania.[35] Such gains would have delighted Garašanin. Russia clearly sympathized with the Balkan Christians, reported Marinović, but bound by treaties with other powers and unprepared, she could not aid them militarily. Russian leaders had told Marinović that the Christians must first show Europe they could prepare and agree upon their own future. Marinović had responded that the Christians relied on Russia to prevent great power intervention against them. "No matter how our struggle with the Turks goes, long or short, victorious or not," wrote Garašanin, "we must always fear intervention by other strong powers." Serbia, he believed, could seek open Russian support only after achieving total agreement with Monte-negro and Greece on common action.[36]

At this time Garašanin was displeased with Western attitudes toward Serbia. Napoleon III, apparently still supporting Austrian expansion in the Balkans, sought to divide the Balkan peoples. Garašanin told the French consul that French suspicions that Serbia was subservient to Russia were "complete nonsense":

We are far from following anyone's policy . . . . For once they should understand us better. . . . Now we follow our own plans and will consider as friends only those who do not hamper us in them. We will be grateful to those who give us moral support.[37]

Before leaving Belgrade in November 1866, British Consul Longworth declared that the Porte could not yield Belgrade fortress and advised Gar-ašanin to reduce the Serbian army. Garašanin retorted: "[We] believe in our future and that belief is unshakable." Serbia maintained only the troops she required, would not yield her rights or allow outside states to determine the size of her army.[38] Maneuvers by the Serbian militia, he informed Mondain, would be held regardless of Turkish or British objections.[39]

This intimated that Belgrade was about to demand Turkish evacuation of all the fortresses. Taking credit for this demand and for subsequently achieving it, Ristić recalled that early in October 1866 he had returned to Belgrade to discuss the issue at length with Garašanin. Serbia could not now unfurl the flag of national liberation, Garašanin and Blaznavac told him, since Greece could not yet fight. Orešković proposed that Serbia formally demand the fortresses, and if the Porte refused, seize them by force. However, Ristić believed the Turks might now cede them voluntarily, and Prince Mihailo and Marinović agreed. Only Garašanin hesitated, asserted Ristić. "He still remained on the old path and could not readily enter a new one. He did not trust the new methods of utilizing events and usually shut himself off in passive meditation." Garašanin accused Ristić of exploiting this issue in his own behalf and later complained that he was "disturbing policy." Finally, alleges Ristić, he secured authorization to approach the Porte directly without first seeking the powers' support. Returning to Constantinople in late October with Mihailo's letter to the Grand Vizier, he took the first serious step on the fortress issue. To raise that question formally at the Porte, objected Garašanin, might rouse Turkish suspicions about Serbia's war plans and hamper preparations for a subsequent general Balkan war. Like Garašanin, Russia feared that if Serbia secured the fortresses, she might abandon serious efforts to liberate the Christians. Thus the Tsar told Marinović in December that if the Serbs had asked his advice, he would have advised against demanding the fortresses.[40]

Despite Ristić's assertions, acquisition of the fortresses resulted primarily from Garašanin's policies since 1861. Without Serbia's alignment with Russia and significant progress toward a Balkan league, chiefly Garašanin's work, the Porte would scarcely have relinquished them so readily. Ristić's egoistic account, *The Foreign Relations of Serbia in Modern Times* (Piroćanac felt it should be renamed: "Official reminiscences of J. Ristić") stresses his actions in Constantinople as if Serbian policy had originated there, not in Belgrade. Playing down Balkan cooperation, Ristić emphasized acquiring the fortresses as Prince Mihailo's main objective and his own role as paramount.[41] "Only after the Turkish garrisons left Serbia," trumpeted Ristić, "could the Serbian government throw its glance beyond the borders of the Principality." According to Piroćanac, Serbia has assured Europe and the Porte that if the fortresses were evacuated, it would remain at peace; nonetheless, preparations for Balkan alliances and war continued. To avoid war with the Porte, Mihailo would have had to break his pledges to his Balkan allies. Therefore the fortresses, affirms Piroćanac persuasively, never comprised the final goal of Prince Mihailo's policy, but only one step in the greater enterprise of liberation and unification.[42]

Final negotiations at the Porte over the fortresses proceeded more quickly and smoothly than Garašanin had expected. On February 2, 1867 he telegraphed Ristić in Constantinople not to let Turkish conditions and hairsplitting deter him; the main thing was to secure the fortresses now. Garašanin credited Ristić generously for his skillful negotiation:

Let the envoys quarrel as much as they like as to who is to be credited over the fortresses, but the truth remains that it is *your credit* if it truly succeeds. If that credit belongs to you, *I shall look to Bosnia-Hercegovina out of competition* (Ristić's italics).[43]

Garašanin worried that Prince Mihailo's letter to the Porte in late February might cause complications. If only the Prince had not mentioned that he also sought Bosnia-Hercegovina and Old Serbia! "Such a letter would have been welcome after we had received the fortresses."[44] However, that very day the Grand Vizier telegraphed Prince Mihailo that the Porte had accepted his letter on the fortresses.[45] Favorable European conditions undoubtedly contributed to this Serbian success, and the Turks apparently hoped their concession would undermine the embryo Balkan league. Foreign Minister Ali Pasha had said: "We will settle that question [the fortresses] so as to satisfy completely everyone except Greece since we know the Greeks counted enormously on Serbian discontent against Turkey."[46]

Transfer of the fortresses to Serbian sovereignty was carried out formally April 6, 1867 in Belgrade. For the first time in centuries the Serbian flag waved proudly over the Kalemegdan and Serbia was free of Turkish garrisons. The success of that phase of Serbian policy was complete, and Serbia became independent in all but name. From all sides came congratulations to Garašanin and Ristić for their patient work of negotiation. Praising Ristić, Prince Mihailo called it "the happy conclusion of an undertaking in which you were my right hand."[47] Securing the fortresses, affirmed *Srbija,* assured Serbia of full domestic independence.[48] Rejoiced *Narodni list* of Zadar, Croatia: "The crescent has begun to set and the sun of freedom shines above the hills and mountains of our oppressed brethren."[49]

Concern that gaining the fortresses might deflate Belgrade's enthusiasm for freeing the Balkan Christians proved partially justified. This success seems to have encouraged Prince Mihailo later in 1867 to seek *de facto* control of Bosnia-Hercegovina by negotiation and pressure rather than by risking war which he feared instinctively. Serbia's major diplomatic victory roused Prince Nikola's jealousy, loosened Serbo-Montenegrin ties, and may have delayed Serbia's alliance with Greece. Once the fortresses were won, despite Garašanin's efforts to fan Belgrade's warlike ardor, some of the urgency departed from Serbia's campaign.

This peaceful solution, as the Turks had hoped and Russia feared, aroused widespread suspicions that Serbia might have launched a grandiose liberation campaign only for its own benefit. In Cetinje, reported Pirocanac, the news produced confusion. Had Montenegro been exploited? Would the great work of Balkan unity now lapse? Many Slav papers began writing that way. *Zastava* of Novi Sad even dubbed Prince Mihailo a "Turkish policeman" for accepting the fortresses without bloodshed. In a series of articles it accused Mihailo of utilizing the great opportunity of 1866-1867 "only for the benefit of Belgraders and Small Serbia." To *Zastava* Mihailo's trip to Constantinople early in 1867 signified indefinite postponement of the national liberation struggle.[50] To avoid nourishing rumors of a Serbo-Turkish rapprochement, Garašanin worked strenuously to prevent a visit of the Sultan to Belgrade.

Acquiring the fortresses may have influenced Mihailo to alter course, but not Garašanin. During 1867 he continued to advocate Balkan insurrection and Yugoslav unity. In March he and Orešković collaborated on a plan for insurrection in Bosnia and Hercegovina. Orešković drew it up and Garašanin amended it, toning down its emphasis on national and political equality of Serbs and Croats. This insurrection, wrote Orešković, should look like the spontaneous struggle of an oppressed people for freedom and thus an internal Turkish affair. Incursions into these provinces were to be led by partisans of "our principles: the union of all South Slavs around Serbia." The means of accomplishing this must depend on circumstances, but the goal was immutable:

Our aim is state unification of all Yugoslav peoples. A Yugoslav state must become independent as soon as it is formed and enter with Greeks and Rumanians into a defensive alliance. This state will be organized internally on purely Slav bases, i.e. local administrative autonomy combined with a centralized government in which will participate equally leading figures from all peoples.

Crossing out that Orešković formulation, Garašanin replaced it with this somewhat vaguer version:

Our aim is the liberation of the Christians groaning under the Turkish yoke in order to create a basis for unification of all Yugoslav peoples into a single federated state. Organization of this state will be left to time and to the participating peoples after liberation is achieved.

Belgrade and Zagreb would lead the entire movement, continued Orešković, "as the two poles around which will revolve the entire Yugoslav cause." He emphasized the need for permanent agreement and equality between Serbia and Croatia in creating and leading a Yugoslav state.[51] Quarrels between the two Yugoslav centers must be concealed from the public. Orešković's description of the future federation again reflected his strong Yugoslav and egalitarian emphases:

The Croatian and Serbian people is one, *Yugoslav;* religion must not interfere at all with the national cause; the sole basis for the state is nationality [*narodnost*]. Religion divides us three ways and . . . thus can never be the principle for unification into a single state but rather nationality because we are one people; and in the state all churches must be equal.

By omitting Orešković's passage stressing the equality of the two centers, Belgrade and Zagreb, Garašanin intimated he believed Belgrade must predominate. And he retained his assistant's formulation of Serbia's Piedmontese role: "Belgrade, having its independent government and all military resources at its disposal, is the natural center for diplomatic and military activity. Thus it will direct all this work . . . ." Garašanin then deleted the rest of Orešković's sentence: "... always in agreement with Zagreb." However, he left untouched Orešković's statement: "The unification of all Yugoslavs must be the work equally of all Yugoslav peoples. Thus each people must make sacrifices to it in blood and money."

That summer the national insurrection, organized jointly by Serbia and Croatia, was to begin in Bosnia-Hercegovina. Neither organizer was to be involved officially so as to prevent European intervention. Native bands were to cross into those provinces secretly and simultaneously from Serbia, Montenegro, Dalmatia, Croatia and Slavonia and rouse the entire population. After Orešković had specified that an interim regime should be composed of Serbs, Croats and Bosnian Muslims, Garašanin interjected his conservative political views:

> Immediately at the start of the insurrection will be proclaimed a provisional government... composed of persons from the local populace. During the entire period of struggle it will remain a dictatorship [*diktatura*] ... since without firm administration in this transitional stage, the insurrection could not maintain itself.

Once the insurgents controlled a sizable territory, continued Orešković, they would convene a national assembly which, by pledging to respect Turkish sovereignty, would request the Sultan to grant the province autonomy under Serbian administration. To implement this scheme, Orešković added that once the Croats under Bishop Štrosmajer had agreed, they would set up a joint committee in Zagreb to prepare the uprising.[52] Despite amendments reflecting his conservatism and Greater Serbian views, Garašanin approved most of Orešković's Yugoslav approach, revealing his own broadened attitudes.[53]

Long before Prince Mihailo's August 1867 interview with Count Andrássy,[54] Belgrade had been seeking control of Bosnia and Hercegovina through some administrative scheme if armed insurrection proved impractical. The two provinces figured prominently in Serbia's relations with Austria-Hungary, the Croats and the Turks. Late in 1866 his agents informed Garašanin that people in Hercegovina were itching to revolt, but Garašanin urged restraint until Serbia gave the signal.[55] Soon another agent reported that armed bands had formed in Hercegovina causing alarm among the Turks: "The Serbs are more in favor of an insurrection than ever." Guerrillas were gathering in Zeta. Pleading for Serbian aid, the agent noted: "My friends and I with Vojvoda Bogdan are preparing a sudden blow against the Turks."[56] From Grahovo Mico Ljubibratić assured Garašanin that in case of war, Serbia could count on Hercegovina.[57] In Bosnia's capital, Sarajevo, Garašanin's chief agent, Steva Bogdanović, had formed a Main Committee which established subcommittees in larger towns to prepare an insurrection. By mid-1867 in Bosnia-Hercegovina almost everything seemed ready for action.

However, it was clear that Austria-Hungary, reorganized as a dual monarchy, would not permit Serbia to control the two provinces. The Monarchy, argued Austrian Consul Lenk in Belgrade, required them to protect Dalmatia. Austria would intervene in Bosnia-Hercegovina, French Consul Botmillian warned Garašanin, as soon as disorders broke out there.[58] Austria's premier, Count Beust, opposed their obtaining even autonomy from the Porte and warned that if Bosnia and Hercegovina achieved independence, they would surely join with Serbia and that would threaten Austrian interests. Thus they should either remain firmly Turkish or become Austrian. In late February Vienna ordered troops concentrated on its southern frontiers which could enter the two provinces at the first Serbian action. Through an envoy, Eduard Zichy, Vienna warned Prince Mihailo against any armed incursion into Bosnia-Hercegovina; the Prince apparently convinced the naive Zichy he had no intention of attacking the Turks.[59]

Indeed, Belgrade had been making attempts to win control of the provinces through an administrative arrangement with the Porte. Prince Mihailo suggested to Count Zichy that Serbia be allowed to administer them without detriment to Turkish sovereignty.[60] And the Serbian envoy, Nikola Krstić, in mid-February talks with the Hungarian leader, Count Andrássy, warned that a Turkish Christian insurrection could only be restrained if the Porte entrusted Bosnia, Hercegovina and Old Serbia to Serbia's administration. Intimating his support, Andrássy stated Hungary opposed Balkan expansion for the Monarchy and that without Budapest's consent, Austria could not move.[61] Andrássy indicated willingness to cooperate with Serbia and warned of the dangers of Russian expansion and Panslavism; he advised against any Serbian attempt to unite Turkish Serbs by force. Europe could best prevent Russian domination of the Balkans, responded Krstić, by satisfying Serbian desires in Bosnia-Hercegovina.[62]

Thus Garašanin's March proposal to the Croats was part of his effort to secure Bosnia and Hercegovina for Serbia by one means or another. Given Austria's opposition, he knew that to be successful, an insurrection there must have the cooperation of Croatia and the Military Frontiers, and he disregarded warnings from Russia's Count Shtakelberg not to trust Bishop Štrosmajer. Štrosmajer and the Croatian National Party accepted the Orešković-Garašanin proposal of March 1867 that Serbia annex Bosnia as a step toward unification of all South Slav regions.[63] However, pointed Austrian warnings and mobilization induced Belgrade to suspend temporarily prepparations for an insurrection in Bosnia and Hercegovina.

Early in 1867 another Garašanin assistant, Matija Ban of Dubrovnik, composed for his chief memoranda on solutions of the Eastern Question in differing versions in order to accommodate Russian, French and British views.[64] Ban warned Garašanin repeatedly of the dangers to Serbia of Russian Panslavism. Russia, he affirmed, aimed clearly to divide the South Slav peoples.[65] He opposed later the pro-Orthodox idea of the Metropolitan of Serbia as likely to divide South Slavs:

> You know what time and effort it has cost us to inspire Catholic Yugoslavs with confidence in Serbia and convince them that Belgrade aims at a purely national, not a religious, state. By propagating now the concept of an Orthodox state, they will destroy in an hour what it took us years to build, your whole work will collapse, and the gates will open wide first to Russian influence, then domination. If Europe has hitherto regarded our progress with suspicion and that of all eastern Christians, it is because she has considered us fanatical Orthodox and thus subject to Russian influence. Do not let the Russians ruin your life's work. . . . In Belgrade we should not unfurl the flag of Orthodoxy but rather the flag of the Yugoslav peoples; with the former we will be in Russia's grasp, but with the latter we will remain independent.[66]

Garašanin agreed on the need then for a Yugoslav emphasis in order to win over the Croats, but believed that Russian backing was also essential. In his own Memoire of May 1867,[67] he advocated a Balkan alliance, described its main principles, and obstacles to its achievement. The Ottoman Empire still survived only because the powers could see no viable alternative. To dispel Europe's doubts and prevent it from partitioning their region, Balkan peoples must agree now to work together. Once Serbs, Greeks and Bulgars were in accord, the Eastern Question could be solved. Serbia and Greece must shoulder the main burden, but no solution could be final without Bulgar participation. Agreement would be difficult since each people dreamed of recreating past glories and ancient boundaries. To achieve their freedom, Balkan states must make mutual concessions on frontiers, access to the sea and fertile areas, just as Italy had sacrificed Savoy and Prussia had abandoned Luxemburg. The time had now passed when a small people could achieve its goals primarily with the aid of a great power: "Independence is acquired not by foreign generosity, but by reason and sacrifice." Balkan salvation would depend on close agreement, common effort and compromise to assure each state's viability. "Bulgars and Serbs," predicted Garašanin optimistically, "as sons of a common Slav people, will easily reach agreement. They will probably establish a confederation in which each will be master of his own house, while in a common country both will be strong and equal." The Greeks could ally permanently with this Serbo-Bulgaria, and Rumania's vital interests would bring her in also. Such a Balkan league, reinforced by commercial ties, would best replace the rotten Ottoman Empire and guarantee European security. Balkan peoples must hasten to achieve such an accord.

To reach these goals Garašanin counted on Russia to provide moral and financial assistance and to assure European non-intervention. The Balkan peoples themselves could then defeat and expel the Turks. Early in 1867 he had sent Petronijević to St. Petersburg to secure a Russian loan for Serbia. With the loan still doubtful he wrote Marinović:

> We won't speculate on what the Russians want. Our sincerity toward them will not allow that . . . . The affair for is is serious and we cannot be put off with phrases . . . . We will always be open with them, expecting that they will become clearer toward us, but we cannot abandon the cause we have begun while awaiting a decision; it must be continued no matter what sacrifices it entails. We must obtain that loan by all means . . . . [68]

As a Balkan League gradually took shape, Serbia's war preparedness became a key issue. War Minister Blaznavac's optimistic report in March 1867 on its military strength concluded: "All measures have been taken to complete the organization and instruction of the troops by autumn."[69] But this meant no military action at least until the spring of 1868. In May, at Belgrade's invitation, four well-qualified Russian officers came to inspect Serbian forces. When Consul Longworth inquired about their mission in Belgrade, Garašanin replied facetiously that they were "tourists," but as officers they were in touch with the War Ministry. "If they were druggists, they would surely contact other druggists," he added.[70] Soon Consul Shishkin informed Blaznavac that the officers were encountering obstructions from the War Ministry in securing essential information, and that the Ministry tended to view everything rosily. He requested Blaznavac to remedy these deficiencies.[71] Their inspection in Belgrade and the interior revealed that Serbia remained poorly prepared. "The organization of the Serbian War Ministry," affirmed Infantry Colonel Postel'nikov, "is unsatisfactory and cannot do for wartime."[72] Colonel Leer, the senior officer, reported:

> The militia first-class is the main element of the Serbian army in numbers and represents good war material, but at the present time it lacks proper organization. There is no permanent cadre . . . . In all armies which have militia there are cadre . . . . The military is far superior to the other branches.[73]

Captain Snesarev reported from Kragujevac: "By August 10th, I believe, 228 cannon, equivalent to 38 batteries, will be ready. I am not satisfied with their organization. . . .*I don't see organization in anything; the administration is in disorder*" (his italics).[74] Upon completing the inspection, Leer provided this basically negative overall assessment:

> Elements of the army in Serbia are good, but . . . it is as if organization were wholly lacking. . . . For defensive war, the most important points in the war theater . . . are not secured at all, and the roads are in deplorable condition. They have general staff officers but no general staff, and thus there are no precise maps . . . . From the foregoing you can see to what extent Serbia is prepared, or more

correctly *unprepared* to open hostilities. It could be considered prepared only if the enemy were even less ready.

Serbia, he affirmed, had no real prospect of military success in a war against Turkey.[75]

The Russian officers told the Serbs they needed to obtain 200,000 additional rifles and provide some of them to neighboring peoples, especially the Bulgars, for uprisings. How could Serbia get even half that many? wondered Garašanin. Even if she could afford them, where could so many rifles be obtained and brought into Serbia? Russia alone, he concluded, could supply such aid. Serbia could use the loan money and import them as before via Rumania.[76] Mihailo agreed he should ask Bucharest's permission to transfer the weapons. Through Shishkin Garašanin requested 100,000 rifles and agreed to accept St. Petersburg's conditions.[77] Responded Mihailo:

> There is no doubt that for the great undertaking for which we are preparing we have few weapons which would be fully evident when we enter the struggle. But acquiring the necessary weapons will be most difficult for us in any case. For this will go a large sum of money from the line of credit we have opened [Russian loan]. I fear . . . we may exhaust this, so that when money is most essential for us, we won't have any nor will anyone give us any.

Prince Charles would readily let Serbia receive the rifles, Mihailo believed, but Bratianu and the Liberals might try to block their shipment across Rumania. Concluded the Prince: "Let's try it and see what happens."[78] This cast doubt on Serbia's readiness to fight even the following spring.

Meanwhile Garašanin intensified his efforts to achieve a genuine Balkan alliance system, supervising and conducting negotiations with the various states and peoples. Despite their alliance, Serbo-Montenegro relations, despite his best efforts, deteriorated during 1867, victimized by Prince Nikola's vanity and ambition and by narrowminded courtiers. The alliance's implementation depended heavily on Nikola whose attitude remained most equivocal. Until Russia urged him to reach accord with Serbia, wrote Piroćanac, Nikola had aimed to annex Hercegovina and part of Old Serbia.[79] He had only consented to unite Montenegro with Serbia in the belief he would succeed Prince Mihailo as their ruler. To his request for 50,000 ducats and much war material, Belgrade provided only 3,000 ducats and pledged 5,000 rifles. Nikola refused the money angrily and considered abandoning Serbia and relying on Russia directly. When the Russians told him to obtain his weapons from Serbia, he turned to France. Nikola's constant intrigues made Garašanin doubt the value of their alliance, but he strove to retain Nikola's loyalty by describing Western intrigues in the Balkans.[80] Hearing from Dučić, Montenegro's pro-Serbian envoy, that Nikola had instructed him to confer in Pesth with Liberal opponents of his regime, Prince Mihailo became so angry he almost tore up the alliance treaty. Nonetheless, Serbia kept supplying Montenegro with arms and money.

Garašanin kept Prince Nikola fully informed about Serbia's negotiations over the fortresses. However that affair turned out, he wrote, it must not affect our plans to liberate all Serbs.[81] Envious of Serbia's success at the Porte, Nikola did not regard it as a victory for all Serbs. Without consulting Belgrade, he decided to seek extension of Montenegro's frontiers to the Morača River.[82] Learning that a Montenegrin delegation would go to Constantinople to achieve this, Garašanin reassured Cetinje that Serbia would not object.[83] While pessimistic about Montenegro's prospects at the Porte, Garašanin nonetheless encouraged Prince Nikola to go ahead:

> Serbia can only rejoice at any progress by Montenegro however and whenever it occurs. Every success of hers is our success too, just as any success of Serbia is a victory for Montenegro. In this there can no longer be any differences.[84]

Since frankness was essential in their dealings, Garašanin informed Dučić that he had frequently communicated sensitive information to Nikola.[85]

Nikola's attitude provoked increasing Serbo-Montenegrin friction. The young and inexperienced prince put little store in his promises. Jealous, inconsistent and insecure, Nikola was also greedy, vain and ambitious. Though a patriot, he aspired to lead Serbian liberation and unification himself and refused to become an ordinary prince in a Greater Serbia. Realizing he would not become Serbian heir, he intrigued with other powers and decided not to fulfill his commitments to Serbia.[86] He constantly demanded more money and munitions, remained dissatisfied, and blamed Mihailo for Russia's refusal of many of his requests. Jealous of Serbia, after Mihailo's triumphant return from Constantinople, he asked: "And what did Prince Mihailo get for me?" Fearing the loss of Montenegrin influence in Hercegovina and Albania, he demanded that Serbia withdraw its agents from them. His father, Mirko, and French Consul Vijat inciting him against Serbia, denounced those who favored cooperation with Belgrade as "Serbian spies." In March 1867 Nikola quarreled with Dučić who fled into exile and explained to Garašanin that because selfish courtiers put their personal interests above national ones, he would no longer perform "dark work which splits the Serbian people and leads it to obvious disaster."[87]

By then Garašanin had lost all confidence in Prince Nikola and his entourage. Dučić's exile extinguished his hopes for true Serbo-Montenegrin cooperation. Receiving no replies to several of his letters to Nikola, Garašanin ceased to correspond with him. Eventually, predicted Garašanin, Nikola would regret breaking his promises to the national cause; such a small man was to be pitied.[88] After Dučić's June 26 letter, Garašanin castigated Nikola and Mirko as traitors to the Serbian people selfishly opposing and frustrating national policies. "This should not hinder us though because the Serbian people will prove stronger than two gluttons who by working for the general evil will themselves succumb to it." They were "betraying their family and brethren, and nothing can be worse than that." Eventually, people would give them deserved punishment.[89] Welcoming Dučić warmly into Serbian service, Garašanin warned him to avoid Belgrade so as not to provide Nikola with a pretext to break openly with Serbia; Dučić operated from Dubrovnik. Leaving him a free hand, Garašanin urged Dučić to influence Montenegrins in favor of unification with Serbia.[90] Then Nikola, unwisely and despite Princess Darinka's protests, attended the Paris Exposition to seek territory from the visiting Sultan.[91] During more than fifty years as Montenegro's ruler, Nikola would repeatedly block plans to unity his tiny country with Serbia. By mid-1867 Montenegro was the ally of Serbia in name only.

Throughout that year Garašanin labored to conclude a Serbo-Greek military alliance. On February 27th he telegraphed Ristić:

It is most inconvenient that we have not yet cleared things up with Greece since we could decide more easily how to respond to the

Porte's reply [on the fortresses]. If we can achieve agreement with Greece, or if there are prospects of such an agreement, then it is most essential to obtain the fortresses right away, *so that some time will pass between* acceptance and the beginning of the main [war] plan (Piroćanac's italics).[92]

Next day Garašanin instructed his envoy in Bucharest to assure the Greek envoy there that resolving the fortress question would neither slow negotiations with Greece nor alter Serbia's war plans.[93]

Obstacles in Athens to a military alliance with Serbia included grandiose Greek territorial claims, especially at Bulgar expense, an Anglophile government, and military unpreparedness. In December 1866 the newly formed Kumunduros government had informed Ristić it would resume negotiations. However, the Greeks demanded all of Macedonia and Thrace. "In their exaggerated selfishness," commented Garašanin, "they would like to forget us, so they believe they can claim Macedonia as a province in which live only confirmed Greeks." Serbia could not renounce Macedonia which belonged rightfully more to Serbs than Greeks; she must have some of it to survive as a country.[94] Since back in 1861 Renijeris of Greece had agreed to partition Macedonia, how could Greece now logically deny Serbia a share? Serbia required access to the sea there to achieve economic progress. Before concluding an alliance, Garašanin preferred to settle such territorial issues so as to prevent quarrels later. "The purpose is to agree, not to hurt one another."[95]

When the Greeks told Ristić that unless Serbia accepted fully their draft treaty which claimed all of Macedonia they would suspend negotiations, Garašanin refused angrily. At one blow Athens wished to liberate Greeks from Turkish rule and subjugate Bulgars with the same rights to existence as Greeks. Resolutely defending Bulgar interests in Macedonia and Thrace, he denounced Athens' demands as ridiculous: "Such a degree of lunacy . . . puts in question also their justified claims." Wrote Garašanin: "It has long been said that the Greeks were a selfish people with an exaggerated opinion of their worth," but they had been also a wise people. But their latest demands suggested that "the Greeks have retained fully their ancestors' shortcomings but not the virtues of wisdom which distinguished them."[96] Refusing to side with Athens against the helpless Bulgars, he deplored French support for Greek claims, viewing this as an attempt to split Serbia from Greece. "I would say that Mr. Kumunduros wished to imitate Bismarck," declared Garašanin, "but he is wrong in one thing: [Bismarck] attracts his people to his side while our friend [Kumunduros] seeks to do the same with foreigners."[97]

All this imperilled the accord which Greek Foreign Minister Tricoupis had outlined in late January to his envoy in Constantinople.[98] At a cabinet meeting on February 9th Garašanin approved that Greek proposal with minor changes. Success seemed so certain that he had instructed Ristić to let the Porte set its own conditions in regard to the fortresses so as to provide Serbia with pretexts for a subsequent war with Turkey. Serbia and Greece were to be fully prepared for war by July 1, 1867 with the Serbs providing 60,000 men and reserves, Greece 30,000 men and a fleet. Deciding jointly when to enter the conflict, both were to fight even if the Turks attacked only one partner. Montenegro and Rumania were to be recruited for this alliance.[99]

Extravagant Greek territorial claims in Macedonia threatened this accord. Adhering stubbornly to its views, Athens sought Rumania's support and her agreement to partition Bulgarian lands. Angry at this, Garašanin still hoped the Greeks would abandon their excessive claims. He instructed Magazinović to ascertain details about Antonopoulos' mission to Bucharest and to emphasize to the Rumanians how very delicate was the Bulgarian question. If unsatisfactory boundaries were awarded to the Bulgars, argued Garašanin, the entire Christian cause would suffer.[100] In case Athens should seek Montenegrin support, Garašanin explained carefully to Prince Nikola the status of his talks with Greece. Athens, affirmed Garašanin, was trying to create a Greek state half non-Greek in population. "We are explaining our views sincerely. . . .We will not refuse them our aid in war, but we won't obligate ourselves to do to another what we would not allow to have done to us."[101] Answering Serbian sincerity with treachery, the Greeks were seeking gains "contrary to the interests of all Balkan Slavs." Unless Athens reached agreement with the Bulgars, though, its vision of a great Hellenic empire would remain a chimera.[102]

Late in March, unable to secure French support for a Greater Greece, Athens began to soften its stance. In May Russia helped restart Serbo-Greek negotiations. Milan Petronijević, Serbian envoy in St. Petersburg, visited King George of Greece and discussed an alliance based on the 1861 Garašanin-Renijeris accord.[103] A Serbo-Greek agreement, Garašanin wrote Ristić, must not obligate Serbia to act contrary to Bulgar interests. By their numbers and position in the Balkans, the Bulgars should be mentioned in a Serbo-Greek treaty and invited to the negotiations.[104] By June the bases for such an alliance had been laid though neither party was nearly ready to fight the Turks.

Garašanin achieved a significant agreement with Bulgar exiles in Bucharest. In January 1867, disgusted with what he considered Bulgar stupidity and meanness, he had considered leaving them to their fate.[105] His dismay had deepened over the request in March by a Bulgar émigré group in Bucharest to the Sultan seeking religious and political autonomy for Bulgaria. While some Bulgar émigrés sought to ally with Serbia against Turkey, others intrigued with the Rumanians or sent messages to the Porte, while still others demanded a Greater Bulgaria including nearly all Christians under Turkish rule! Garašanin felt this latter demand threatened Serbs and other Balkan peoples.

Such negative elements were overshadowed by the January 1867 program for Serbo-Bulgarian cooperation by the Bulgar "Benevolent Society" in Bucharest. In April a Bulgar assembly there adopted that program which provided for a future Serbo-Bulgarian federated state under Prince Mihailo.[106] Writing Magazinović February 2nd, Garašanin rejoiced at the Bulgars' favorable response "to our aims and those of the eastern Christians." Belgrade accepted this program tentatively pending its approval by a more representative Bulgarian body; Garašanin urged the Committee to circulate its ideas as widely among Bulgars as possible. Once approved by a majority of leading Bulgars, the program could be made binding. Meanwhile preparations for a general Bulgarian uprising should proceed: "On whatever basis we define our union with the Bulgars," wrote Garašanin, "it will be in our mutual interest to cooperate . . . in the common work of liberation."[107] On April 5th a "national assembly" representing various areas of Bulgaria, adopted a slightly revised "Program" and drew up a "Protocol" as a basis for Serbo-Bulgar unification.[108] In May envoys of the Bulgarian Committee came to Belgrade, discussed the "Protocol" with Garašanin and secured Prince Mihailo's approval. Garašanin rejected the stipulation that Serbo-Bulgaria would include all Thrace and Macedonia as conflicting with the draft Serbo-Greek accord, but he accepted the "Protocol's" main ideas. Both sides should prepared an insurrection while deferring formal agreement. All Bulgar factions should fuse in a single movement and form secret subcommittees inside Bulgaria to spread its views and organize the populace.[109] Cautioning the Bulgarian Committee against foreign influence, Garašanin affirmed that Serbs and Bulgars must primarily liberate themselves:

> We will always accept [foreign aid] happily if it does not obligate us. We must judge carefully foreign service offered to us, advice, and promised material aid, accepting only that which in our judgment will not hamper our independent action. . . .

The Committee's preliminary work could be financed by wealthy Bulgars, but to achieve Bulgaria's liberation it would require a foreign loan, preferably from Russia. Garašanin instructed his envoy in Bucharest to suggest this to the Russian consul there.[110]

Once again Belgrade became the enter of Bulgarian nationalist activity. Arriving were Ljuben Karavelov, advocate of Serbo-Bulgar cooperation and federal union; Vasilj Levski, the popular hero; Vojvoda Panajot Hitov and others. Young foreign educated Bulgars came to lead an expected uprising. Garašanin warned that to avoid attracting hostile foreign attention, only individuals should come to Belgrade. Most Bulgars there wanted to reconstitute a Bulgarian Legion, but War Minister Blaznavac failed to take action on this.

Advocating a general Balkan insurrection, Garašanin urged the Bulgars to avoid local or regional uprisings and raids which would not defeat the Turks. Impatient Bulgars under Panajot Hitov invaded Bulgaria at Rushchuk only to be chased back into Serbia.[111] Garašanin denounced such incursions as "very stupid affairs, not at all thought out and very harmful for the general cause." Instead, "bands must be supported by the populace, and the populace by an army equipped to resist any enemy force." Unplanned attacks would only bring death to the insurgents, their sympathizers and innocent people. This had occurred in Hercegovina and Montenegro in 1861-62, had achieved nothing and cost thousands of lives. Telling this to friendly Bulgars, Magazinović should seek to dissuade them from sending armed bands across the frontier. When the Bulgarian Committee persisted in this nonetheless, Garašanin lamented: "We follow the bands rather than the bands following us, endangering the entire undertaking."[112] As the Bucharest Bulgars spurned his advice,

Garašanin wondered whether they would achieve anything. "An unhappy situation!" he exclaimed.[113]

North Albanian tribal leaders, long courted by Garašanin, were equally impatient. The visit of Vezenković, a Serbian agent, to that area in the spring of 1867 sparked premature uprisings. Some 10,000 tribesmen were ready to revolt, he informed Ristić.[114] Back in Belgrade, Vezenković urged the prompt beginning of an Albanian insurrection: "The Arbanasi are hungry now and can hardly wait to fight in order to feed themselves." Once an uprising began, Serbia should send guns and ammunition; with a monthly subsidy, he predicted extravagantly, they could raise 20,000-50,000 men. Several Serbs from northern Albania accompanied Vezenković to Belgrade, talked with Garašanin and proclaimed their readiness to start risings in their localities. Given travel money, they were told to lead uprisings when summoned. However, Vezenković soon left Serbia in order to rouse all Arnauti tribesmen under the banner of Skenderbeg, the legendary fifteenth century Albanian warrior.[115]

By the summer of 1867 progress was finally being made on a Serbo-Rumanian alliance. Earlier, Rumania's complete unpreparedness had forced her to remain passive. Prince Charles feared that a general Balkan insurrection might erupt before Rumania could join in. Thus Bucharest had sought to block an offensive Balkan alliance by intriguing in Athens and Cetinje and informing the French of everything. Seeking to undermine Slav solidarity, the Rumanians had told Bulgar émigrés that Bulgaria's future lay with Rumania. Bucharest's intrigues to divide Bulgarian lands with Greece infuriated Garašanin. Unable to even put its own house in order, Rumania was wooing the émigrés with fantastic schemes. If the Bulgars joined Rumania, he warned, it would ruin both of them:

> What power in Europe could have confidence in the survival of such an unnatural Rumano-Bulgarian union? To seek one's glory in ancient history, then later to hush this up and even conceal the present means either to be crazy or to believe those are crazy to whom one proposes it.

How could the Bulgars possibly take Bucharest as their model? Why free themselves from Turkey only to succumb to corruption and foolishness, Rumania's incurable diseases? The Rumanians, until recently subservient to the Turks, could scarcely rule other peoples. Like France, they were accommodating the Turcophiles and sowing discord among the Balkan peoples. "Rumanian patriotism is as dangerous for other peoples as Turkish rule," concluded Garašanin.[116]

In early April 1867 Prince Mihailo's state visit to Bucharest largely dispelled such Serbo-Rumanian suspicions. Rumania and Serbia, he told Prince Charles, shared an identical interest in ending their vassaldom. Charles agreed that while strengthening themselves militarily, they should maintain correct relations with the Porte. Hailing Mihailo as his friend and brother, Charles called for closer mutual relations.[117] A new Rumanian envoy, Rade Jonesco, went to Belgrade to seek a Serbo-Rumanian alliance and ties with other Balkan states. Renouncing Rumanian intervention in Bulgarian affairs, Foreign Minister Stevan Golesco entrusted the Bulgars to Serbia "as the proper and natural center. . . . The Serbs are of the same race as the Bulgars; to them belongs the right to lead them and form a single country."[118] Exploiting these improved relations, Garašanin secured Prince Charles' permission to ship Russian rifles across Rumania into Serbia, and in July Nikolić went to Russia to arrange this transfer.[119] However, a Serbo-Rumanian alliance was not yet imminent.

By the summer of 1867 serious rifts had appeared in the Serbian regime over the war issue with Garašanin heading a bellicose faction and Blaznavac a pacific element; Prince Mihailo's position remained ambiguous. Ever since 1862 Garašanin had been telling his confidants: "Let's begin in the spring," but spring after spring had passed without any action. Earlier, he had been cautious and some had accused him of excessive calculation and meditation. Thus in 1862 he had restrained the impatient Mihailo after the bombardment of Belgrade because Serbia was weak militarily. In 1866 he had opposed military action favored by the Prince since preparations were incomplete. Now in the summer of 1867 Garašanin considered preparations for a general Balkan insurrection virtually complete. His confidants, enthusiastic, militant, and optimistic, all assured him they were just awaiting his signal to begin. Garašanin's contacts with agents, guerrilla leaders and national revolutionaries made him bold and impatient. As old age and infirmity loomed, he knew his time was running out. Thus he pressed hard for a definte date for war to begin.[120] Furthermore, Garašanin was linked closely with bellicose Russian elements under Consul Shishkin and P. N. Stremoukhov, director of the Asiatic Department. They sought to push Serbia into war as the Russian Panslavs would do in 1876.[121]

The chief obstacle seemed to be the perennially unprepared War Minister Blaznavac. For him something was always lacking in military preparations, inducing him to urge further delay. Commented Prince Mihailo on his pedantic approach: "My Blaznavac wants to have reserves for every nail." Subordinates were telling Garašanin that Blaznavac opposed war and planned never to be ready. In retrospect, Blaznavac's cautious instincts seem correct: it would have been virtually suicidal for Serbia to have fought Turkey in 1867. Even a decade later, aided by a Russian general and thousands of Russian volunteers, a larger and better prepared Serbian army was defeated decisively by the Turks.[122] In any case, Garašanin and Blaznavac feuded over the war issue and on personal grounds. Garašanin demanded the setting of a final date for completing military preparations; Blaznavac refused to be committed to one. Declaring that war could be delayed no longer, Garašanin intimated that Prince Mihailo must choose between them. Over Blaznavac's opposition, the spring of 1868 was selected apparently as the time for insurrection and war with Turkey.[123]

Prince Mihailo seems to have realized that summer, even if Garašanin did not, that European conditions no longer favored a Balkan insurrection and war led by Serbia. Austria and Hungary were now reconciled in a dual monarchy which consolidated Habsburg rule for another half century. France, earlier so sympathetic to Serbia's interests and aspirations, supported Austria diplomatically, viewing her as a potential ally against a powerful and expansionist Prussia. Franco-Austrian rapprochement strengthened the Porte's position, already improved by the timely concession of the fortresses to Serbia. Russia remained still unable and unwilling to supply the Serbs with more than minimal financial and military aid. Russia's top leaders, especially Foreign Minister Gorchakov and War Minister D. A. Miliutin, opposed involvements in the Balkans which might lead to war with a European power or even a coalition while Russia was absorbed by domestic reform. Finally, the Balkan League which Garašanin had worked so hard to build, was an incomplete and ramshackle structure. Misled by sanguine subordinates, Garašanin apparently did not realize that the best opportunity to achieve his ambitious program had already passed.

NOTES

1. AII, Ristić, XI/176, "Mémoire sur les avantages qui résulteraient pour la Turquie de la retraite de ses garnisons de la Serbie," by J. Marinović, May 7, 1866. On this whole period see Petrovich, *A History,* I, 319-329.

2. Radosavljević to Belcredi, March 4, in Vučković, *Politička,* No. 80, pp. 164-165.

3. Novak to Mensdorff-Pouilly, April 12 in ibid., No. 82, pp. 166-167. In a later report Novak reiterated his belief that Prince Mihailo was pursuing a dual policy: seeking everything possible from the Porte by diplomacy while wishing to adhere to Austria in order to escape excessive dependence on Russia. Energetic Austrian support of the Prince's efforts to obtain the fortresses might keep Mihailo from placing himself under Russian auspices as the head of an anti-Turkish Christian movement. And if Serbia remained quiet, so would other South Slavs. Novak urged that Austria work through a confidential intermediary to win over the Prince. Novak to Beust, December 1, 1866, in ibid., No. 123, p. 239.

4. IG 15??, "Gospodinu Milanu Piroćancu, odredjenom za Crnu Goru," Garašanin draft of April 1866. Before Piroćanac reached Cetinje, foreign newspapers reported that Montenegro would aid Austria against Prussia with volunteers. On April 15, Garašanin wrote Prince Nikola: "We do not believe this at all and have strongly denied such reports. In no case, Your Highness, should you enter into such obligations with anyone; better preserve your strength for events which could develop here suddenly. We rely upon Your Highness' wisdom. . . ." IG 1588, Garašanin to Nikola, April 15. Nikola replied May 28: "There was no truth to the rumors. I realize we must retain our strength for ourselves."

5. *Zapisi,* July-August 1935, p. 115.

6. N. P. Ignat'ev's report of March 23/April 3, 1866.

7. IG 1581, Garašanin to Ristić, no date (August or September 1866).

8. *Zapisi,* August 1935, p. 117.

9. Ibid.

10. Dispatching Piroćanac again to Cetinje, Garašanin wrote that he was willing "to bear any labor for harmony between Serbia and Montenegro. . . . Believe me, dear friend, there is nothing we cannot do if we

will only work in the future for common success." IG 1587, Garašanin to Dučić, December 25, 1866. Captain Ljubomir Ivanović, who concluded the military convention, bore a letter to Cetinje nothing that events could lead rapidly to "liberation and unification of the Serbs in the Balkans." IG 1588, Garašanin to Prince Nikola, December 1866.

11. DAS (MID), Garašanin to Ristić, April 30, telegram; draft of May 5.

12. IG 1581, Garašanin to Ristić, May 17.

13. See above, pp. 247-48.

14. IG 1580, Ristić to Garašanin, May 24; IG 15??, "Sa Grcima stu piti u dogovor," Garašanin's draft of early 1866; G. Jakšić, "Prvi srpsko-grčki savez," p. 7; Lascaris, "La première," p. 11-12.

15. IG 1581, Garašanin to Ristić, June 21, Michel Lhéritier, *Histoire diplomatique de la Grèce de 1821 à nos jours* (Paris, 1925), III, 174; Jakšić and Vučković, *Spoljna,* pp. 246-256.

16. IG 1579, Lešjanin to Garašanin, August 11.

17. IG 1598, Garašanin to Lešjanin, August 11.

18. Ibid., August 14, from Kragujevac.

19. IG 1581, Garašanin to Ristić, August 17.

20. IG 1598, Garašanin to Lešjanin, August 10. "Again the confused one [Blaznavac] has muddled something."

21. Ristić, *Spoljašnji odnošaji,* II, 443-446.

22. Garašanin to Marinović, May 18 and May 22, *Pisma,* II, 188, 192.

23. IG 1581, Garašanin to Ristić, June 7; Garašanin to Magazinović, June 14.

24. Ibid., Garašanin to Magazinović, June 13-14; V. Djordjević, *Evropa i Rumunija,* pp. 166-173.

25. IG 1581, Garašanin to Ristić, July 25.

26. IG 1582, Garašanin to Magazinović, November 8.

27. Ibid., December 7.

28. Ibid., March 15.

29. Ibid.

30. Garašanin to Ristić, July 21, from Arandjelovac.

31. Garašanin to Magazinović, December 27, 1866 and January 7, 1867.

32. Jakšić and Vučković, *Spoljna,* p. 303; Petrović, "Austro-ugarska," in *Oslobodjenje gradova,* pp. 277-278.

33.   Ibid., pp. 265-270. Commented Russian Foreign Minister Gorchakov: "I wholly share this manner of viewing things."

34.   Jovanović, *Druga vlada*, p. 220.

35.   IG 1581, Garašanin to Ristić, December 11; Arhiv SANU, No. 7198, Krstić, "Javan život," 1866.

36.   Garašanin to Prince Nikola, February 10, 1867, in *Zapisi*, October 1935, pp. 42-44.

37.   IG 1595, Garašanin to Mondain, September 16, 1866; IG 1587, Garašanin to Dučić, December 15.

38.   Garašanin to Marinović, November 9, *Pisma*, II, 198.

39.   IG 1595, Garašanin to Mondain, September 16.

40.   Piroćanac, *Knez Mihailo*, p. 70.

41.   Ibid., pp. 62-64; Ristić, *Spoljašnji odnošaji*, III, 9 ff.

42.   Piroćanac, *Knez Mihailo*, pp. 62-63.

43.   IG 1637, Garašanin to Ristić, February 15, 1867.

44.   Garašanin to Marinović, March 3, *Pisma*, II, 201-202.

45.   IG 1677, "Prepiska o pitanju oslobodjenje gradova, 1867."

46.   AII, Ristić XI/242.

47.   Petrović, "Austro-ugarska," in *Oslobodjenje gradova*, p. 277.

48.   Arhiv SANU, No. 7198, Krstić, "Javan život, 1867," entry of April 10.

49.   April 24, 1867 in *Antologija jugoslovenske misle*, p. 311.

50.   *Zastava*, "Beograd ili Srpstvo?" May 1867.

51.   Garašanin crossed out Orešković's statement: "Belgrade will enlist the Bulgars for the common idea and Zagreb the Slovenes. Belgrade will refer all Austrian Yugoslavs to Zagreb, and Zagreb all Turkish ones to Belgrade." Jakšić and Vučković, *Spoljna*, p. 495.

52.   "Program jugoslovenske politike predložen od strane Garašanina Štrosmajeru" ("Program of Yugoslav policy proposed by Garašanin to Štrosmajer"), Belgrade, March 1867, in ibid., pp. 494-504. Professor Grgur Jakšić copied this document about 1921 from the original then in the Garašanin family archive but now missing. The text was handwritten by A. Orešković with additions and deletions by Garašanin.

53.   In mid-January 1867 Garašanin had disclosed a similar plan to Consul Shishkin who informed Ignat'ev and Shtakelberg. To achieve it, noted Garašanin, Serbia needed support from the Croats and trans-Sava Serbs. Soon therefore Stremoukhov, director of the Asiatic Department

of the Russian Foreign Ministry, urged the Porte to grant autonomy to Bosnia and Hercegovina under Serbia's administration. However, in late February under French pressure and to calm the other powers, he withdrew this suggestion. Meanwhile in Constantinople, Ignat'ev was commending the same idea to the Turks. Once Russian military preparations were complete, anticipated in 1868, Ignat'ev confided to Ristić, Russia's armed strength would stand in reserve behind the Balkan Christians. DAS (MID), Ristić to Garašanin, No. 5, January 9, 1867.

54. See below, pp. 334-336.

55. DAS (NID), Garašanin to Ristić, December 1866.

56. IG 1660, Janošević to Garašanin, February 14, 1867.

57. Mico Ljubibratić to Garašanin, February 11.

58. Garašanin to Marinović, November 9, 1866 and March 1867, *Pisma*, II, pp. 199, 202.

59. G. Jakšić, "Knez Mihailo i Bosna," *Politika*, April 23-26, 1937, pp. 1-2; Arhiv SANU, Krstić, "Javan život 1867," entry of April 15, 1867.

60. Zichy to Beust, March 4/16, cited in Jakšić and Vučković, *Spoljna*, p. 353, and Mihailo to Zichy, ibid.

61. Arhiv SANU, Krstić, entry of February 19, 1867.

62. Ibid., February 25.

63. "Okružnica centralnog odbora beogradskog za ujedinjenje sviju južnih slavena odborima na strani" (Belgrade, March 1867), in Vučković, *Politička*, No. 145, pp. 283-287.

64. Ban wrote Ristić January 3/15, 1867, explaining he had removed from the memorandum destined for Russia all Yugoslav ideology. For the French he had included the idea of a great Slav confederation excluding Russia, and for England he had espoused the entire minimum Greater Serbian program, i.e. revival of Stevan Dušan's medieval empire. "Basically, I expressed our true final goal in Paris and Petrograd; London would not take that seriously." Added Ban: "If our sons are worthy, they will easily throw the Turks into Asia and win Constantinople for themselves and Slavdom." AII Ban IV/1, "M. le Senateur," January 1867.

65. Ibid., Ban to Garašanin, February 17.

66. Ibid., April 3.

67. IG 16??, Memoire of May 6, 1867. This lacks Garašanin's signature, but Stranjaković notes that the contents clearly indicate it as his

work. Written during the intensive phase of negotiations with Greece, it was apparently sent to the Russian government under whose patronage Garašanin worked out his plans for a Balkan alliance. "Ilija," p. 340.

68. Garašanin to Marinović, April 30, *Pisma*, II, 204.

69. Arhiv SANU, No. 7114, report of War Minister Blaznavac of March 29. He listed first-class militia in eighty battalions of 500-600 men each, totalling some 44,000; second-class militia of the same number; cavalry in 33 squadrons of 120 sabres each; 258 artillery pieces in 43 batteries; 107,000 rifles with an additional 25,000 to be ready by the end of June.

70. IG 1651, Garašanin to Shishkin, June 29.

71. DAS PO 26/186 and 188, no date.

72. Ibid., 26/158, Pestel'nikov to Shishkin, May 17.

73. Ibid., 26/159, Colonel Leer to Shishkin, May 17.

74. Ibid., 26/161, Snesarev to Shishkin, May 24.

75. Ibid., 26/166, Leer to Shishkin, June 2.

76. IG 1644, Garašanin to Mihailo, June 18.

77. IG 1643, Mihailo to Garašanin, June 26, from Gastein; IG 1651, Garašanin to Shishkin, June 29.

78. Ibid., Mihailo to Garašanin, from Gastein, June 25, also in Jakšić and Vučković, *Spoljna,* pp. 507-509.

79. IG 1622, Piroćanac to Garašanin, January 20, 1867.

80. IG 1646, Garašanin to Prince Nikola, February 15.

81. Ibid., February 19; IG 1637, Garašanin to Ristić, February 28.

82. IG 1636, Ristić to Garašanin, April 25.

83. IG 1648, Garašanin to Dučić, March 11.

84. IG 1646, Garašanin to Nikola, May 30.

85. IG 1648, Garašanin to Dučić, March 11.

86. *Zapisi,* August 1935, pp. ?????

87. IG 1647, Dučić to Garašanin, from Dubrovnik, June 26.

88. IG 1648, Garašanin to Dučić, May 5.

89. Ibid., July 15.

90. Ibid.

91. Ibid., Dučić to Garašanin, June 26. Petkovich, the Russian consul in Dubrovnik, urged his government to halt aid to Montenegro since Prince Nikola's father, Mirko, was allegedly placing aid money in his own account in Paris while hundreds starved in Montenegro. Anger and discontent

prevailed there after Nikola and Mirko left for Paris during a cholera epidemic at home.

92. Piroćanac, *Knez Mihailo*, p. 72.

93. Ibid.; IG 1638, Garašanin to Magazinović, February 28, telegram and March 2.

94. AII Ristić XI/8, Garašanin to Ristić, January 26.

95. Ibid., February 15.

96. Ibid., March 16, No. 262.

97. Ibid., March 16, No. 263.

98. That agreement had assigned Bosnia, Hercegovina and part of Old Serbia to Serbia, and Epirus and Thessaly to Greece. Albania would become independent and Macedonia be divided as envisioned in 1861 with the Serbian sphere running from the sea through Drač, Elbasan, Ohrid, Prilep, Velec, Štip, Djuma and Kratovo northward to the Balkan Mountains. The issues of Thrace and Bulgaria were to be deferred. AII Ristić, Ristić to Garašanin, January 18, 1867; Lacaris, "La première."

99. AII Ristić, Ristić to Garašanin, February 19. A revised Garašanin draft went: "If armed success follows, all Christians will be freed. In such case southern Macedonia and the Archipelago will go to Greece; northern Macedonia, including an outlet to the Ionian Sea, will go to Serbia. Ibid., February 19, No. 15, draft.

100. IG 1638, Garašanin to Magazinović, March 28.

101. IG 1646, Garašanin to Nikola, March 1867.

102. Garašanin to Ristić, April 20 and May 11. Ambassador Ignat'ev had urged Garašanin to hold firm against Greek claims to Macedonia. AII Ristić XI/448, Ignatiev to Shishkin, February 6/18.

103. IG 1639 Garašanin to Petronijević, May 20.

104. AII Ristić, Garašanin to Ristić, May 24; IG 1638, Garašanin to Magazinović, June 11.

105. Garašanin to Ristić, January 26.

106. Piroćanac, *Knez Mihailo*, pp. 36-37.

107. Ibid., pp. 39-40.

108. The Serbo-Bulgarian state would be called a "Yugoslav kingdom" and include Serbia, Bulgaria, Macedonia and Thrace with Prince Mihailo as its hereditary ruler. The "Protocol," signed by 22 Bulgar leaders, specified its frontiers more precisely. Serbia was to provide all possible moral and material aid to liberate Bulgaria. Ibid., pp. 36-42; Toshev, *Balkanskite*, pp. 77-81.

109. IG 1638, Garašanin to Magazinović, May 3.

110. Ibid., June 9.

111. Ibid., May 3; August 14, telegram.

112. Ibid., June 9 and 30.

113. Ibid., Magazinović to Garašanin, September 16.

114. IG 1636, M. Ristić to Garašanin, May 2; Nikolić, "Opis radnje," pp. 6-7.

115. Stranjaković, "Ilija," pp. 245-246.

116. IG 1638, Garašanin to Magazinović, March 2 and 23.

117. V. Djordjević, *Evropa i Rumunija,* p. 189; Garašanin to Ristić, March 24.

118. DAS PO 25/76, Stevan Golosco to Garašanin, June 1867. Garašanin instructed his envoy to express his happiness with this letter. Bucharest's attitude now "fully and equally corresponds to the true interests of both principalities." Garašanin to Magazinović, June 30.

119. IG 1638, Garašanin to Magazinović, July 1867; IG 1644, Garašanin to Mihailo in Gastein, July 3.

120. Jovanović, *Druga vlada,* pp. 220-221. In a draft of this time Garašanin wrote: "The Serbian people does not fully realize the necessity of war for its future or it would gladly bear the necessary burdens. To fight solely for ambition would be stupid." IG 1657, "Treba li Srbija da udje u rat ili ne treba? " (1867).

121. Jovanović, *Druga vlada,* pp. 220-221. On 1876 see D. MacKenzie, *The Serbs and Russian Pan-Slavism,* pp. 93 ff.

122. Jovanović, *Druga vlada,* pp. 221-222.

CHAPTER XVIII

PRINCE MIHAILO CHANGES COURSE
(July-October 1867)

"Besides that policy of Mihailo which the whole world knew: warlike Yugoslav and Russophile, he also had another which was not warlike, nor Yugoslav nor Russophile, but simply aimed at the territorial expansion of Serbia by diplomatic means and with the aid of Austria . . . ."

S. Jovanović, *Druga vlada.*

"For several years I have deceived people about the beginning of war from spring to spring, and now there must be an end to this. The Prince will have to choose between me and the war minister, because I believe the time has come when war can no longer be postponed."

Garašanin in Piroćanac, *Knez Mihailo,* p. 84

During the summer and fall of 1867 Prince Mihailo Obrenović shifted his course in foreign policy, undercutting Garašanin's plan to launch a general Balkan insurrection. Never very decisive, Mihailo for years had vacillated between bellicose and pacific currents in his cabinet. As Garašanin built a Balkan league with Russia's support and completed preparations for a general insurrection and war with Turkey, the Prince shied away from this imminent and risky conflict. His search for a peaceful solution made him receptive in August 1867 to offers made at Ivanac by Count Gyula Andrássy, premier of Hungary, at a time when the new Dual Monarchy of Austria-Hungary was taking shape. Apparently, they agreed tentatively that the new Austria-Hungary would support Serbian efforts to obtain administrative control of Bosnia-Hercegovina if Mihailo pledged not to fight the Turks and aligned Serbia with the Dual Monarchy. Kept secret from Garašanin, this accord contradicted his foreign policy and brought him and the Prince into conflict.

That summer Prince Mihailo spent roughly two and a half months abroad. After taking the waters at Gastein spa, he attended the Paris Exposition, then went to his Ivanac estate in northern Hungary. Preceding him to Paris was Sultan Abdul Aziz whom French leaders welcomed warmly. Their greeting to Prince Mihailo, by contrast, was modest and cool. Napoleon III did not even grant Mihailo the Legion of Honor which he had long held in prospect for him. Paris remained aloof toward Serbia and its Balkan aspirations.[1]

Napoleon III's attitude reflected his search for Austro-Hungarian support against Prussia and his belief that Serbia remained an obedient Russian tool. Denying this allegation, Prince Mihailo informed Garašanin that he should tell Italian Consul Scovasso: "If the Russians utilize us for their selfish purposes as people in the West claim, at least we can benefit from it. . . ." Russia had provided Serbia with loans, weapons, and moral support while the West had given her nothing. "It is the fault of the West," concluded Mihailo, "that we can only expect help from Russia."[2]

Meanwhile Austrian leaders, after seizing some Orešković agents and from confidential reports and Serbian press articles, concluded that Serbia under Garašanin headed a dangerous Yugoslav movement directed against them and the Porte.[3] Foreign Minister Friedrich Beust had learned of agitation directed by the Russian embassy in Constantinople to stir up disorders in European Turkey. Serbia's war preparations were considered part of these Russian machinations which included sending money, weapons and officers to Belgrade. Such reports convinced many Western leaders that Russia directed and closely controlled Serbia's policies. Western consuls in Belgrade believed that Garašanin had yield wholly to Russia from the belief that only with her support could he achieve his Yugoslav goals.[4]

On August 6/18, 1867 Emperors Napoleon III and Franz Josef I of Austria-Hungary met at Salzburg. Accompanied by their foreign ministers and Hungary's premier, Count Andrássy, their discussions lasted almost a week. Foreign Minister Beust, having just concluded the Compromise (*Ausgleich*) with Hungary creating the Dual Monarchy of Austria-Hungary, emphasized the reformed Monarchy's urgent need for peace. He sought French support to counter Russian or Balkan Slav moves against Turkey.[5] Hoping to win Austrian support against an aggrandized Prussia, Napoleon III intimated that Bosnia-Hercegovina should go to the Dual Monarchy. Andrássy opposed this fearing to increase the strength of the Slav element in Hungary, but he also opposed expansion by a pro-Russian Serbia into Bosnia-Hercegovina for fear that Slav elements would encircle Hungary. Instead, Andrássy aimed to replace Russian influence in Belgrade with Austrian.[6] This might be achieved if Serbia, with Austrian backing, assumed the administration of Bosnia-Hercegovina. Also embroiling Serbs and Croats would block their common front against the Magyars. Perhaps the Sultan would yield these provinces voluntarily if Prince Mihailo pledged to pursue a conservative, peaceful policy in the Balkans and defend Ottoman integrity.[7]

Late that June Mihailo invited Garašanin to join him at his summer residence at Ivanac. Before leaving Belgrade, Garašanin convened the cabinet in an effort to set a date for war with Turkey. This seemed urgent because the pending Serbo-Greek alliance treaty was supposed to specify a time for common action. Earlier, War Minister Blaznavac, after agreeing to set a date for war, had obtained funds for additional war preparations. But at the cabinet meeting Blaznavac, admitting preparations were still incomplete, refused to stipulate when Serbia would be ready. Declared Garašanin indignantly:

For several years I have deceived people about the beginning of war from spring to spring, and now there must be an end to this. The Prince will have to choose between me and the War Minister, because I believe the time has come when war can no longer be postponed.[8]

With the war issue still unresolved, Garašanin proceeded to Vienna, writing Marinović from there August 6th:

. . . Today I will return to Ivanka. I don't need to tell you how
we'll spend our time in Ivanka. It is truly gentlemanly and very
pretty with its parks. To hunt geese one needs take only a few
steps in any direction and fire. The palace is pretty and we are all
well housed in it.[9]

As Prince Mihailo's beautiful Ivanac estate was held a crucial though
controversial and mysterious meeting between him and Hungarian Premier Andrássy. At Salzburg Count Laszlo Hunyady had informed Mihailo
that Andrássy wished to see him urgently at Ivanac. A visit by such a
prominent leader indicated that a vital matter would be discussed. Immediately after the emperors' parley at Salzburg, Andrássy traveled to
Ivanac and talked alone with Prince Mihailo for almost five hours. Garašanin, though then at the estate, was not invited to join them and saw
Andrássy only at dinner. Although they were old political acquaintances,
the Magyar leader said nothing to Garašanin about politics, and after dinner returned immediately to Vienna.[10] That same day Garašanin returned
to Belgrade with Prince Mihailo, but neither then nor later did the Prince
mention what he and Andrássy had discussed so secretly. For Garašanin,
who was premier and foreign minister, his exclusion was profoundly
humiliating. With no extant first-hand account of the Mihailo-Andrássy
conversation, we must rely on second-hand versions and indirect allusions
to the Ivanac meeting.

Garašanin's version of what transpired was tantalizingly incomplete. In
"My Reminiscences" he confirmed that the discussion had been held without his participation; only subsequently had he learned what had been
said. Unfortunately, Garašanin's account breaks off right at that point
leaving only a hint at the beginning where he described his general view
of Serbo-Magyar relations: "Hungary will never be a sincere ally of Serbia.
No matter what promises she makes to Serbia and no matter what brilliant
prospects she places before her eyes, all that should never be believed."[11]
This suggests that Garašanin had learned of unnamed Andrássy "promises."

Jovan Ristić, then Serbian envoy in Constantinople, asserted later that
Prince Mihailo had often discussed the Ivanac meeting with him. Ristić
had spent the late summer in Belgrade, often talking with the Prince confidentially about domestic and foreign issues. Never had Mihailo even
hinted that he intended to replace Garašanin with Ristić who returned

to his post on September 25th.[12] Subsequently, Ristić asserted: Count Andrássy at Ivanac, like Zichy the previous March, had assured Prince Mihailo that Hungary opposed any eastward expansion of the Monarchy into Bosnia-Hercegovina; at Andrássy's insistence, at Salzburg Emperor Franz Josef had rejected Napoleon III's offer of these provinces. "The Hungarian ship," Andrássy had declared, "is so full that only a slight additional burden [of Slavs] will sink it." Warning that Russia's Panslav aims threatened them both, Andrássy had urged Mihailo to restrain "leading Serbian politicians," notably Garašanin, from adopting a hostile attitude toward Hungary.[13]

That Mihailo confided details about Ivanac to Ristić while withholding them from his own foreign minister suggests he was already contemplating removing Garašanin from office. Would it not be natural for the Prince to confide in the person with whom he planned to launch a new course? Mihailo knew Garašanin would reject that new policy. About to return to his post in Constantinople, Ristić was asked by the Prince without explanation to take an additional week's leave. From this Pirośanac concluded that Mihailo considered replacing Garašanin with Ristić immediately then changed his mind.[14]

Did Andrássy make promises to Mihailo at Ivanac, and did the Prince accept binding commitments? Garašanin's subordinate, Oreśković, affirmed that Andrássy had pledged to support Serbian efforts to acquire peacefully part of Bosnia-Hercegovina.[15] A letter to Mihailo of March 1868 by Laszlo Hunyady, long a trusted intermediary between Mihailo and Andrássy, suggests they discussed a partition of the two provinces.[16] Andrássy sought to persuade Mihailo to jettison his ties with Russia and rely instead on Austria-Hungary, claims Pirośanac. The Prince should "keep peace in the Balkans until the impending Franco-Prussian conflict is resolved. . . ." If Serbia remained neutral in that war, the Dual Monarchy would allow her to obtain Bosnia-Hercegovina. That would require Serbia to abandon its entire program of action with its Balkan allies and Russia, so Andrássy promised in return that France and Austria would assist her to obtain the provinces if France defeated Prussia. However, alleges Piroćanac, Mihailo was unwilling to renounce his Balkan leadership, alienate Russia, and end cooperation with other Balkan peoples solely on the chance of a French victory. And what would guarantee that a victorious Austria would keep its promise? Wasn't there a less risky and expensive way to secure the two provinces? At Ivanac, concluded Piroćanac, Mihailo proved receptive but committed himself to nothing.[17]

Mihailo probably accepted Andrássy's offer to help Serbia acquire part of Bosnia-Hercegovina peacefully. They may also have discussed tightening Serbo-Magyar ties. Distrusting Russia and his Balkan allies, the Prince desired an alternative in case a Balkan insurrection and war proved impractical. Andrássy sought a complete separation of Serbia from Russia, only possible if Serbia became Austria-Hungary's ally. Only a personal agreement between Mihailo and Emperor Franz Josef could achieve that. Yet vassal Serbia could not conclude formal treaties with outside powers, nor could Andrássy, as Hungarian premier, bind the Dual Monarchy. Therefore, a secret Mihailo-Andrássy accord without Vienna's knowledge and consent would have been most difficult. Probably Andrássy "promised" that at least eastern Bosnia-Hercegovina would go to Serbia if she cooperated with the Monarchy.[18] Or, Andrássy might have given his pledge without ever intending to redeem it, merely in order to separate Serbia from Russia and the Balkan states.

Regardless of pledges and agreements made at Ivanac, Prince Mihailo's foreign policy underwent a clear change afterwards. While the Prince did not signal to his ministers any intention to delay a Balkan insurrection and war, this became evident after he returned to Belgrade. Mihailo grew increasingly cool towards Garašanin, who headed the war faction, and warm towards the pacifically inclined Blaznavac. Garašanin detected the Prince's aloofness too toward Russian officers whom previously he had showered with attention. Earlier Mihailo had echoed Garašanin's criticisms of Blaznavac's slowpaced military preparations; now the Prince criticized those pressuring the War Minister to speed up his work. Rumors began to spread in Serbia that at Ivanac Mihailo had abandoned his broad Balkan policies, and had betrayed the Austrian Slavs to the Dual Monarchy.[19]

After Ivanac, affirms Piroćanac, Prince Mihailo vacillated uneasily between his old and new foreign policies unable to make a final choice. To him Balkan cooperation and war appeared more natural but involved incomparably more sacrifice and risk. To rely on Austria would be far easier; Serbia needed to do little yet presumably would be compensated. Later, if need be, the old policy might be resumed. For several months after Ivanac, the Prince apparently favored cooperation with the Dual Monarchy, then early in 1868 reverted to the older course. Though influenced by

Magyar blandishments and fearful of war, Mihailo never repudiated completely his support for national revolutionary action. Since he was an autocratic, secretive ruler, the result was indecision, paralysis of policy and ultimate failure. Garašanin was the chief victim of the Prince's inability to decide.[20]

Despite Garašanin's valiant efforts, there was little progress in late 1867 on Balkan political and military cooperation. To be sure, a Serbo-Greek alliance was signed, but that was counterbalanced by deteriorating Serbo-Montenegrin relations. Mihailo reacted negatively to Prince Nikola's request in mid-September to visit Belgrade. Garašanin warned him that such a rebuff would wound Prince Nikola's pride, weaken their alliance, and endanger the planned general insurrection. Unable to persuade the Prince to let Nikola come, Garašanin went to the Foreign Ministry, threw a telegram on the table and told Piroćanac: "Write a reply to Prince Nikola that there will be no meeting with Mihailo." To Piroćanac's objection that the great policy they had worked on together for years should not be renounced, Garašanin declared nervously: "I did everything I knew how; now, if you can, go and convince the Prince."[21] When all his arguments and efforts had failed, Garašanin telegraphed Nikola to delay his visit ostensibly because of the meeting of the Serbian assembly in Kragujevac scheduled to convene September 29th. When no Serbian invitation followed dispersal of that assembly, Nikola realized that Prince Mihailo did not desire his presence in Belgrade. As suspicion between the two rulers and dynasties persisted, Nikola reverted to his idea of seeking territorial expansion so Montenegro might eventually preempt Serbia's role of Balkan leadership. Even after Mihailo's rebuff, Prince Nikola praised the Serbo-Montenegrin alliance officially, but their relations worsened steadily.[22]

Superficial progress was scored in Serbia's relations with Greece and Rumania. At the Constantinople talks it had been agreed that a Serbo-Greek alliance treaty would be signed in Vienna in late July. After Peter Zanos, the Greek envoy, had met there with Prince Mihailo and several times secretly with Garašanin to settle minor differences, the alliance was signed August 14th and ratified by the two rulers in September.[23] In February 1868 they concluded a military convention in Athens which revealed that Mihailo refused to renounce ties with Greece, potentially the next most important Balkan state militarily. However, no clear date was set for warlike action as they had agreed to do. Meanwhile Rumania's

Prince Charles had been pressing Serbia for a political and military alliance, but Garašanin remained skeptical. Distrusting Rumanian politicians, he knew that disorganized and militarily weak Rumania could merely facilitate transports of weapons and supplies from Russia. To enhance their security, Rumanian leaders sought primarily to escape isolation and establish ties with Balkan states. Receiving reports from his envoy about persistent instability in Bucharest, Garašanin proceeded very warily.[24]

That fall, Garašanin, hampered by the paucity of reliable Albanian agents, tight Turkish surveillance, and competing Italian and French influences, continued efforts to prepare an uprising in nothern Albania. The propaganda of those powers hindered his efforts to induce Albanian tribesmen to accept a general Balkan insurrection, although Garašanin, unlike the French and Italians, could espouse Balkan liberation and independence. In October, when Garašanin believed a Franco-Prussian war to be imminent, he sent a confident of Vezenković, then in Belgrade, "to clear a path" in Albania by conferring with tribal chieftains there. Preparations must be hastened, he urged, even if risky. "It is better to begin now," Garašanin wrote Ristić, "then be overhasty [prenagliti] later."[25] Despite Vezenković's unreliability, Garašanin authorized Nikolić to satisfy his financial requests, then make further payments dependent on his performance.[26] Lacking a true political or military organization in Albania, Garašanin depended solely on the loyalty and skill of a few chiefs.

Until his removal from office, Garašanin adhered firmly to cooperation with the Croats for Yugoslav goals. During September his confidant, Orešković, and the Zagreb Committee agreed to secure Bosnia as part of a future Yugoslav state. Once these plans were squared with Prussia to assure her support, Austria would be unable to oppose revolutionary actions in Bosnia-Hercegovina, Orešković believed.[27] Early in October he informed the Prussian envoy of Serbo-Croatian plans to win Bosnia, but Bismarck failed to approve them. Deputies from the Zagreb Committee, coming to Belgrade to discuss final arrangements, arrived after Garašanin's fall. They were informed: "Serbia does not plan to continue the policy conducted during Ilija Garašanin's ministry."[28]

Though skeptical of the Bulgars' potential role in a Balkan insurrection, Garašanin wished to enlist their aid if possible. Anyway, his conscience was clear since his government the previous two years had striven to rescue the Bulgars from their plight and lead them toward liberation. "Bulgaria," wrote Garašanin, "can only be a true Bulgaria with Serbia and other South Slavs." As the time for decision neared, the Bulgars must opt either for cooperation with the South Slavs or with Turkey. Magazinović was to stand ready to offer them a brotherly hand. "Leave open the doors through which they [the Bulgars] can enter the house of salvation." Garašanin was most critical of Bulgarian merchants (*chorbajis*):

> They are people who believe that God gave them wealth only so they could enjoy its fruits as they wish . . . without obligation to think about liberation of their unfortunate people and fatherland or to make sacrifices to bring it about.

Soft words concealed these émigrés' selfishness and lack of patriotism.[29] To repair relations with Garašanin's government, the Bulgarian Committee in Bucharest decided in September to send two envoys to Belgrade. Arriving only in mid-October, they were still in the Serbian capital when Garašanin fell. Piroćanac claims they had come to confirm final preparations for impending common action.[30] Thus in October 1867 Garašanin's plans for a general Balkan insurrection and war with Turkey seemingly remained intact.

Russia still supported Garašanin's government strongly while opposing a quick resort to war. Turkish leaders asserted that Russia was still pressuring Prince Mihailo to lead the Balkan Slavs against the Porte. The Turks cited Serbia's war preparations, the revival of a Bulgarian Legion in Belgrade, and recent visits there by Russian officers. The Porte asserted that Russian General M. G. Cherniaev, conqueror of Tashkent and Panslav firebrand, then retired, would command the Serbian army.[31] Some Russian diplomats in Balkan posts, like Shishkin in Belgrade, were vigorous advocates of a Balkan war of liberation, and a few military men such as Generals Cherniaev and R. A. Fadeev, wished to exploit one in their own interests. Russian policy in the 1860s, as in the Balkan crisis of the late 1870s, contained elements of duality, but aggressive Panslavs then were unorganized, few in number, and under better control than a decade later. Apparently, Count Ignat'ev, ambassador in Constantinople and the most influential Russian diplomat of Panslav persuasion, did not then favor Russia's open involvement in a Balkan national struggle, and War Minister D. A. Miliutin firmly opposed it. During the 1866-1868 crisis, argues

Nikola Petrović convincingly, Russian diplomacy worked to prevent the outbreak of war or insurrection in the Balkans. The St. Petersburg leadership, notably Alexander II and his foreign, war and finance ministers, realized Russia was too impoverished, involved in domestic reforms and militarily unprepared to fight a Balkan war. Nor did Russia desire a Balkan conflict in which she could not participate, yet if a Serbo-Turkish war erupted, Russia might be dragged into it willy-nilly.[32]

Evidence to the contrary remains unconvincing. M. S. Piroćanac, for instance, states that in August 1867, after the Serbo-Greek alliance was signed, preparations for a war of national liberation were complete. Russia had assisted in these preparations, and leaders such as Consul Shishkin and P. N. Stremoukhov, director of the Foreign Ministry's Asiatic Department, were pressing for war.[33] Apparently corroborating his claim was the conclusion in May 1867 of a second Russian loan to Serbia for military preparations of a million ducats, the first installment of which was handed in July to a Serb envoy at the Russian embassy in Vienna.[34] Also Russia had readily provided rifles for Serbia's army.[35] However, such moves appeared designed to bolster Serbia as a Russian bastion, not to push her into a war for which Russian military leaders knew she was ill-prepared. Captain Snesarev, the visiting Russian officer who had remained in Belgrade after the inspection, reported that whereas Premier Garašanin and public opinion remained bellicose, Prince Mihailo and Blaznavac had changed their minds.[36]

In October 1867 Prussia intimated to the Garašanin government support for its war plans. A new Prussian consul, Georg Rosen, arrived in Belgrade with proposals of cooperation from Bismarck. From Oresković he obtained information about Serbia's war plans for the following spring or summer. Conditions in neighboring Slav provinces, claimed Oresković, were favorable for a national insurrection against Turkey though he complained about Prince Mihailo's hesitancy and urged Rosen to help him overcome it. Presumably on Garašanin's authority, Oresković declared that Prussia would determine when the war of liberation would begin: "As soon as she [Prussia] beats [ukoči] France, Serbia will attack."[37] Rosen would propose that Serbia cooperate with Prussia in case she had to fight both France and Austria, Oresković told Garašanin, and Prussia would then provide Serbia with financial aid.[38] Conferring with Rosen about October 20th, Garašanin stressed to the Prussian envoy that Serbia counted heavily on Berlin's support. However, he warned that Serbia would not attack Austria as part of the bargain since that would mean sudden abandonment of all her preparations for a war of liberation against Turkey, nor could Serbia fight simultaneously on two fronts. However, Garašanin intimated that if Serbia moved into Bosnia, massive defections from regiments on the Military Frontiers would prevent their utilization against Prussia. Whether Rosen then made any concrete offer to Belgrade, we do not know; apparently, it was Bismarck who again refused to commit Prussia to vassal Serbia. Yet Serbian leaders showed much trust in Rosen. To him Garašanin spoke openly about Serbian state plans and aspirations; Blaznavac disclosed the status of Serbian armaments and data about the distribution of weapons in Bosnia and Bulgaria. This frankness occurred partly, affirmed Garašanin, because of Orešković's immoderate statements and "desire to do much, driven by his lively temperament."[39]

Not content with indiscreet revelations to Consul Rosen, Orešković then confided to Italian Consul Scovasso the secret of "Rosen's alliance offer"; Scovasso promptly reported its home. The Italian envoy in Berlin received a copy and sought explanations from Bismarck. This provoked Rosen's recall for consultations and involved Orešković and his superior, Garašanin, in serious difficulties.[40] It convinced Austrian Premier Beust of Garašanin's aggressive intent, while Turkey's Fuad Pasha believed Serbia now would attack the Porte when the expected Franco-Prussian war broke out in Europe.[41]

Garašanin still suspected Vienna of plotting to grab Bosnia-Hercegovina with French support. Emperor Franz Josef had assured Prince Mihailo that Austria would show favor toward Serbia if she did not disturb the Balkan peace. The French warned Belgrade against interfering in Bosnia and Hercegovina which were vital to the Dual Monarchy. Thus Garašanin clearly realized Franco-Austrian hostility to his Balkan plans.[42] In May he had declared that Serbia would sacrifice its last man to prevent the Monarchy from obtaining Bosnia-Hercegovina. That fall Garašanin received reports of heightened Austrian interest in the provinces and rumors that former Serbian Prince Aleksandar Karadjordjević was being touted as Austria's candidate for prince of Bosnia-Hercegovina. Viewing this as an effort to turn people there against Serbia, Garašanin feared a Turco-Austrian agreement on those provinces and instructed Ristić to try to ascertain the facts.[43] Fuad Pasha stated that in case of a Serbian attack on Bosnia, the Porte would seek Austria's assistance: "If we had to choose between two evils, we would much rather have Bosnia fall into Austrian rather than Serbian hands."[44]

Important differences of approach between Garašanin and Prince Mihailo were becoming apparent in Serbia's relations with Turkey which had deteriorated after Mihailo's transparent excuses that summer to avoid meeting the Sultan either in Belgrade or Paris. When Garašanin sought to smooth over this inattention to the suzerain power, the Sultan cancelled his intended stop in Belgrade, rushing by, in Garašanin's words, as if "past a Turkish cemetery," that is without even saying hello.[45] The Porte complained to European envoys about Mihailo's inattentiveness and rudeness.

During July and August incidents involving the Bulgars reversed the roles of Prince and Premier. Small bands of Bulgar partisans from Serbia invaded Turkish Bulgaria. Informed of this at Ivanac, Mihailo ordered responsible Serbian officials fired or punished. Garašanin, while disapproving such raids as premature and unwise, was reluctant to punish Serbian officials for failing to prevent them. On August 8th at Rushchuk, Bulgaria, a Bulgar was killed by Turkish soldiers. Anticipating then the outbreak of a Franco-Prussian war, Garašanin sought to exploit this incident to heighten tension with the Porte and dispatched an unusually sharply worded note to the Turks. It blamed Turkish authorities for the killing and demanded that the officials responsible be removed and the victim's family be compensated.[46] Reflecting Garašanin's hawkish line, the official Serbian newspaper, *Srpske novine,* proclaimed that Serbia would not allow the guilty to go unpunished.[47]

Though shocked by these severe criticisms, the Porte sent no direct reply, circulating instead its previous correspondence with Garašanin to the powers. As usual this provoked a British warning to Belgrade. After his Ivanac meeting, Prince Mihailo had issued instructions to act moderately toward the Porte. Thus he affirmed to British Consul Longworth September 11th that he had no hostile intentions toward Turkey which in case Austria attacked Bosnia could count on Serbian aid. The next day Garašanin, admitting to Longworth unauthorized attacks on Turkish territory by Bulgar bands, retorted sharply when the Consul insinuated that Serbia had become a Russian puppet, exclaiming: "Never! We shall always remain our own masters and masters of the situation inside our country."[48]

The disparity between Mihailo's and Garašanin's policies toward the Porte deepened in late September and October 1867. The Prince, opening the assembly at Kragujevac September 30th, emphasized Serbia's success in acquiring the fortresses peacefully and welcomed the Porte's concessions. However, the assembly's petition to the Prince, drawn up at Garašanin's instructions, stressing complaints of neighboring Christians about their sad plight, asked that their insecurity be ended.[49] Violating Mihailo's instruction that correspondence with the Porte be moderate, Garašanin wrote Fuad Pasha rejecting the response to his note on the Rushchuk incident as wholly unsatisfactory. In a second sharp note of October 8th, Garašanin accused Fuad of defending actions "in flagrant contradiction with the precepts of truth and justice," denying to Serbs and Bulgars "rights which belong to them as a people." He demanded that the complaints noted in his first message be remedied.[50] Interpreting this as a deliberate effort to worsen relations, the Porte complained to the powers about Belgrade's arrogance.[51]

Meanwhile in Constantinople, envoy Jovan Ristić supported Mihailo's conciliatory approach rather than the bellicose stance of Garašanin, his own superior. Returning there from leave in early October, Ristić had discussed with Fuad all outstanding issues. They agreed that no obstacles remained to restoring good mutual relations and parted with the impression that former frictions had been resolved. Thus Fuad concluded that Prince Mihailo favored a conciliatory policy but had yielded temporarily to those in Belgrade advocating Serbian expansion. Fuad told the Austrian envoy that Ristić had given him Mihailo's personal assurances of complete loyalty.[52] Thus Ristić was dumbfounded by this open telegram from Garašanin of October 14th:

> The Assembly in its session unanimously thanked the Prince for all the work of his government, declaring that the national army is always prepared to carry out his will and its duty. The Prince replied that these wishes of the people and his own were identical.

Garašanin had sent this obviously militant message openly, knowing that the Porte would receive a copy.[53] For this approach, Ristić indirectly rebuked his chief: "Yesterday I had a long talk with Fuad Pasha in which I was able to calm the Porte, but your telegram of last night hampered all my efforts. *I do not understand why it was necessary to send me such an open telegram.*" (Ristić's italics.) After Garašanin's removal, Ristić, as his first act as Foreign Minister, settled the Rushchuk affair without insisting on concessions by the Porte.

Such divergence over policy within the Serbian government became plainly intolerable, especially to the autocratic Prince Mihailo. He was not a ruler who allowed his ministers to prescribe his policies or pursue an independent line. Besides diffrences between Garašanin and the Prince over foreign policy, the feud persisted between the Premier and the War Minister over Serbia's preparedness for war. The indiscretions of his subordinate, Orešković, further weakened Garašanin's position. Only a pretext was now needed to justify his removal: it was provided by Garašanin's involvement in Prince Mihailo's marital plans.

NOTES

1. Garašanin to Marinović, August 6/18, 1868 (Vienna), II, 209-211; von Reiswitz, *Belgrad-Berlin,* p. 93. For a more general account of Prince Mihailo's shift of policy see S. Jovanović, *Druga vlada,* pp. 222-224.

2. IG 1643, Mihailo to Garašanin, from Gastein, June 26/July 7.

3. HHSA, Lenk to Beust, reports from Belgrade, April 20 and May 18.

4. IG 1644, Garašanin to Mihailo, June 19, draft; Jakšić and Vučković, *Spoljna,* p. 397, citing French reports from Archives étrangères, Paris.

5. HHSA, Beust's memorandum, "Exposé für seine Majestät den Kaiser," Varia France, 1867. On the Salzburg Meeting see A. J. P. Taylor, *The Struggle for Mastery in Europe, 1848-1918* (Oxford, 1954), pp. 185-186.

6. Eduard von Wertheimer, *Graf Julius Andrassy* (3 vols., Stuttgart, 1910-1913), I, 458-459.

7. Ibid., I, 460 ff. Count Beust's memoirs affirm that Count Zichy had broached this idea to Prince Mihailo in March 1867 during his mission to Belgrade (II, 263).

8. Piroćanac, *Knez Mihailo,* pp. 83-84.
9. Garašanin to Marinović, August 6/18, 1867, *Pisma,* II, 209.
10. IG 1683, "Moji spomeni," Grocka, 1868.
11. Ibid.
12. Petrović, "Knez Mihailo i Jovan Ristić," *Politika,* 1927.
13. J. Ristić, *Poslednje godine Kneza Mihaila,* pp. 61-62.
14. Piroćanac, *Knez Mihailo,* pp. 76-77.
15. AII Ristić XXVI/404, Memorandum of Orešković of July 16/ 28, 1868, submitted to the Serbian Regency.
16. Vučković, *Politička,* p. 348, Hunyady to Mihailo, March 16, 1868.
17. Piroćanac, *Knez Mihailo,* pp. 76 ff.
18. Jakšić and Vučković, *Spoljna,* pp. 401-402. As Wertheimer notes in *Graf Andrassy,* I, 461, based on *Tagebuch des Baron Orczy,* in late 1868 Andrássy drew up for Austrian Premier Beust a plan to "promise" Serbia the portion of Bosnia-Hercegovina east of the Vrbas and Neretva rivers with the western part to go to Austria-Hungary. If Andrássy was prepared to pledge this to a Serbia weakened by Prince Mihailo's murder and lacking real Russian or Balkan support, he had far more reason to do so in August 1867. *Spoljna,* p. 402.
19. Ibid., pp. 396-403; IG 1683, "Moji spomeni."
20. Piroćanac, *Knez Mihailo,* pp. 74, 80-82; Jovanović, *Druga vlada,* pp. 224-225.
21. Piroćanac, *Knez Mihailo,* p. 86.
22. Jakšić and Vučković, *Spoljna,* pp. 403-408; AII Ristić XI/7, Ristić to Garašanin, November 3, 1867. Prince Mihailo's anger at Nikola's deviousness and stubbornness had been revealed already in his letter to Garašanin from Gastein, June 26/July 7, IG 1643.
23. G. Jakšić, "Prvi srpsko-grčki savez," pp. 7-16; Lascaris, "La première," pp. 41-55; Piroćanac, *Naša završna reč,* pp. 13-14.
24. Jakšić and Vučković, *Spoljna,* pp. 408-411; Garašanin to Marinović, *Pisma,* II, 220, February 10, 1868.
25. AII Ristić XI/7, Garašanin to Ristić, October 25.
26. IG 1634, Garašanin to Nikolić, October 4.
27. Reiswitz, *Belgrad-Berlin,* pp. 98-104.
28. Piroćanac, *Knez Mihailo,* p. 90.
29. IG 1638, Garašanin to Magazinović, September 1867.

30.   Ibid., September 20, telegram; Piroćanac, *Knez Mihailo*, p. 90.

31.   Ali Pasha to Garašanin, July 4/16; IG 1644, Garašanin to Mihailo, July 2/14, draft. This latter report proved unfounded but was based on a letter of Cherniaev to Mihailo of March 3, 1867 offering his sword to the Prince and "to devote myself to the great cause which Your Highness represents and defends." A. M. Cherniaeva, "Pis'ma vlastitelei," *Russkii arkhiv*, LII (1914, no. 1), pp. 34-35. See D. MacKenzie, *The Lion of Tashkent*, pp. 96-98. In the Serbo-Turkish War of 1876 Cherniaev actually would be named commander of the eastern Serbian armies against Turkey. See ibid., pp. 122 ff.

32.   Nikola Petrović, "Austro-ugarska nagodba, gradovi i istočno pitanje," in *Oslobodjenje gradova*, pp. 265 ff., citing AVPR, Kantseliariia 1866, d. 164, f. 473-482 and other Russian archival sources.

33.   Piroćanac, *Knez Mihailo*, pp. 82-83.

34.   IG 1644, Garašanin to Mihailo in Paris, July 25, 1867.

35.   A. Nikolić, "Opis radnje," cited in Stranjaković, "Ilija Garašanin." In October 1867, upon Nikolić's departure on his second trip to Russia to arrange the weapons transfer, Garašanin wished him luck and urged caution in this secret venture: "Work wisely, don't perish foolishly" (*"Radi mudro, ne pogini ludo"*). Nikolić proceeded to Odessa only to learn that 12,000 rifles had been delivered to the Russian port of Nikolaev. He returned to Belgrade without them, intending to obtain them the following spring. IG 1634, Garašanin to Nikolić, October 6.

36.   Otdel rukopisei Biblioteki imeni Lenina (Moscow), D. A. Miliutin Papers, fond 169, k. 11, d. 8 (1867), "Dela Serbskie." These papers confirm the Russian War Minister's own opposition to a Serbo-Turkish conflict. On the Russian military mission see also S. A. Nikitin, "Diplomaticheskie otnosheniia Rossii s iuzhnymi slavianami v 60-kh gg.," *Slavianskii sbornik* (Moscow, 1947), pp. 285-287 and MacKenzie, *The Serbs*, p. 12.

37.   Reiswitz, *Belgrad-Berlin*, pp. 96 ff.

38.   AII Ristić XI/7, Garašanin to Ristić, October 25, 1867.

39.   Garašanin to Marinović, May 22, 1872, *Pisma*, II, 302; Reiswitz, *Belgrad-Berlin*, pp. 96-104.

40.   Ibid., p. 105.

41.   Ibid., p. 116.

42.   Garašanin to Marinović, August 6/18, 1867, from Vienna, *Pisma*, II, 209-211.

43. AII Ristić XI/7, Garašanin to Ristić, October 23.

44. N. Bourée to Moustier, December 4, No. 215, AE Constantinople 370, cited in Jakšić and Vučković, *Spoljna.*

45. Garašanin to Marinović, July 19, *Pisma,* II, 208-209.

46. IG 16??, Garašanin to Fuad Pasha, from Belgrade, August 12/24.

47. *Sprske novine,* August 12, No. 103; August 19, No. 106.

48. FO PRO 1794, Longworth to Stanley, September 15/27, 1867, from Belgrade.

49. During the Assembly, recalled Piroćanac, based on talks with Garašanin, Prince Mihailo soon after blocking Prince Nikola's visit to Belgrade, talked at dinner about the coming war with Turkey. Present were Garašanin, Blaznavac and Dj. Milovanović, a Council member. The latter two were strongly opposed to war. Since Mihailo spoke neither for nor against war, Garašanin concluded that he remained undecided whether to continue his previous course or to reverse it. *Knez Mihailo,* p. 86.

50. AE 17, Garašanin to Fuad Pasha, October 8/20, cited in Stranjaković, "Ilija Garašanin"; Ristić XI/7, Garašanin to Ristić, October 9/21.

51. Jakšić and Vučković, *Spoljna,* pp. 421-425.

52. HHSA, Türkei XII/86, Vechera to Beust, from Constantinople, October 3/15.

53. Piroćanac, *Knez Mihailo,* pp. 84-85.

CHAPTER XIX

REMOVAL FROM OFFICE
(November 1867)

"One evening, while I was sitting in my office completing work for the day, the Prince's adjutant came in and gave me his letter. . . . In it I found my dismissal. This, naturally surprised me greatly since nothing previously had indicated this would occur. I was merely amused at the manner in which I was released from service."

IG 1690, Garašanin to his son, Milutin, November 10, 1867.

On November 2, 1867 without warning Ilija Garašanin was removed abruptly from office by Prince Mihailo and placed on pension. The Prince never explained clearly why he had done this, and Garašanin declared that he did not know then or later the precise causes for it. Various rumors and versions circulated which claimed to explain his removal. Was this largely a personal dispute between prince and premier leaving state policy unchanged, or did it signify a basic change in Serbia's orientation and policies? Were domestic or foreign issues uppermost? In removing Garašanin did Prince Mihailo repudiate the Premier's lifelong policy of fighting a Balkan war of national liberation?

Garašanin's ouster resulted seemingly from a combination of elements —personal and political, domestic and foreign—and it remains disputed

348

how greatly each contributed to an event which left Serbs and their friends abroad shaken and uncertain. Certainly one factor was Garašanin's proposal of November 1st, the day before his removal, to the cabinet on resolving uncertainty over the succession to the Serbian throne. A solution to this problem was urgent, argued Garašanin, because Serbia stood close to the war of liberation with Turkey to free fellow Serbs and create a great Yugoslav state:

> Serbia intends to place herself at the head of South Slav states in the Balkans, a position which she hopes to secure for herself forever. No one can doubt this goal, nor will any branch of the South Slavs oppose it since Serbia by the sacrifices which she will make for the general cause, deserves this fully.

The manifold problems which this Yugoslavia would face could only be surmounted by consolidating the Obrenović dynasty's position by naming an heir to the Serbian throne:

> Securing the dynasty which is essential to the interests of Serbia itself as she is today is equally essential for the interests of the other peoples who seek unification with Serbia. Without that we might create what appears to be a pretty building but which would lack foundations, could be destroyed by the slightest unfavorable occurrence, and could not be rebuilt.

Garašanin urged the cabinet to take immediate action.[1]

Garašanin's memorandum linked two vital issues: designating an heir to the throne and his vision of a great Yugoslav state. The problem was acute because Prince Mihailo and Princess Julija had no direct heirs. Serbian law stipulated that the succession should proceed in the male line of Miloš Obrenović's family starting with the eldest son. If the reigning prince lacked competent male heirs, the throne would pass to a collateral branch of the dynasty. This allowed Ristić to assert that Serbia already had a live heir: Milan, son of Miloš Jevrem Obrenović. However, neither Prince Mihailo nor his government recognized his claims. Three times Garašanin and Marinović had sought to induce Prince Mihailo to designate the boy, Milan, heir to the throne. Mihailo had responded first that Milan was such an unknown quantity that he could not impose on the people a youngster who might not rule in their interests. He responded similarly the second time, and on the third occasion, the Prince had turned his back and avoided any reply. Mihailo's reaction, Piroćanac believed, stemmed from his hope that by marrying his niece, Katarina Konstantinović, he would obtain a direct male heir. Thus it would be premature and unwise then to designate an heir. For similar reasons the Prince refused to name an heir in his treaty with Montenegro. With such views Mihailo found Premier Garašanin's proposal both unpleasant and untimely. However, the latter believed that intrigues connected with Mihailo's projected marriage to Katarina must be ended so the Prince could focus on great national goals. Subsequently, Garašanin asserted that he had been removed because of his proposal, whereas Piroćanac viewed that as a mere pretext concealing the Prince's deeper motives from the public. Mihailo was too good and considerate a ruler, he concluded, to dismiss his premier and foreign minister for personal reasons.[2]

During 1865 it had become widely known, or rumored, that Prince Mihailo wished to divorce his first wife, Princess Julija, and marry his pretty sixteen year old Catholic niece, Katarina Konstantinović. Such moves would raise major religious and moral issues of which the Prince appeared oblivious. Originally, he confided his true intentions only to his close friend, Dr. Pacek. However, rumors of this spread widely that summer and by fall the entire country buzzed with reports. When Garašanin involved himself in the controversy raging over this prospective marriage, Ristić affirmed, he became embroiled with the Obrenović family, particularly with Katarina's influential and unscrupulous mother, Anka, who was Mihailo's sister. She was a leading member of an anti-war, anti-Garašanin clique which also included War Minister Blaznavac and Dr. Pacek.

In mid-October 1865 Garašanin, lying ill and sorely disturbed by the swelling rumors, called in his assistant, Miloje Lešjanin. Declaring that the reports were making him worse, he informed Lešjanin of his thinking on the marriage question and asked him to draft a letter for him to Prince Mihailo. Lešjanin inquired whether he would continue to serve as premier if the Prince went ahead with his marriage to Katarina. Replied Garašanin promptly: "Truly I cannot serve him if he wishes to do that. I won't oppose him, but I will leave him and be estranged from him." Next day Lešjanin brought the draft to Garašanin who approved it, copied it, and sent it to Prince Mihailo.[3] Garašanin's letter urged the Prince for reasons of state to renounce any plans to marry Katarina:

> Enjoying your confidence and support and having been given the top post in your government. . . in order to be the careful guardian of your honor, glory and good name. . . , I will not conceal that this letter deals with a sensitive matter, but I am convinced that I am fulfilling one of my primary duties toward you and the country I have sworn to serve truly and honorably. . . . You are a Serb, Sire, and should know what this [marriage] would mean to the Serbian people. . . whose feelings would be greatly hurt; it would violate the beliefs of the people. . . . You are the bearer of the happy future of the Serbs. Popular strength is the main power of all governments.[4]

Right after sending this letter to the Prince, Garašanin conferred with Metropolitan Mihailo, the highest ranking Serbian churchman, and found that they were in full agreement. The Metropolitan declared that he could never approve the Prince's marriage to his Catholic niece because it would be "a godless and unheard of thing" ("*bezbožno i nečuveno delo*"). Certain of the Metropolitan's support, Garašanin on the 16th wrote Katarina's mother, Anka, pleading with her to scotch rumors of an impending marriage which were humiliating for the Obrenović family "and especially for the innocence of your dear child." Garašanin stressed the evil which could result from such a marriage for the Prince and the entire Serbian people. Surely she would not sacrifice country, dynasty and daughter to her selfish interests. She must not remove Prince Mihailo from the heights where God had seated him.[5] Garašanin's letter had no measurable effect on the ambitious Anka, anxious to see her daughter become princess of Serbia. She continued with redoubled energy to press for the marriage and to intrigue against the Premier.

Garašanin received no reply from Mihailo to his letter of October 14th as rumors spread that the marriage was imminent and that the Prince would not even await a formal divorse from Julija or permission from the Orthodox church. Therefore on October 20th the Premier wrote the Prince asking to be received in audience that day. Mihailo replied that he could see him the next day, October 21st; they talked for one and a half hours about the marriage question. Garašanin warned the Prince of serious dangers if he went through with his rumored intention to marry Katarina. Mihailo complained bitterly of his unhappy life with Julija and of her unfaithfulness. Not wishing to go into the divorce question, Garašanin begged the Prince not to descend from the pedestal upon which Serbs had placed him:

> Rest assured, Sire, there is not a Serb who would not be desolated by the misfortune if you married your niece. That would be an unheard of event for the Serbian people. Thereby you would violate church law, civil law and the customs of the Serbian people, in short you would perpetrate something immoral in the eyes of our people and that by Prince Mihailo whom the entire people considers the guardian of all these sacred values.

Knowing Serbia's position well, continued Garašanin, and its instability over the previous thirty years, only since Mihailo had resumed his rule had the country been consolidated and began to move forward; a happy future had opened up before the Serbian people. "Do you, amidst these fine prospects, wish to destroy all our hopes?" Mihailo replied that he could not continue the life of domestic misery he had been leading with Julija. "You know better than anyone how determined I am to sacrifice for the people, but cannot I enjoy the peace at home such as the most ordinary Serb possesses?" Garašanin made it clear that he had no objection to the Prince's divorce and suitable remarriage which might assure continuance of the dynasty, but to marry his niece would doom his dynasty, church, honor, and good name.

> Excuse me, Sire, I have no right to compel you to do anything, and because I speak so freely to you, do not regard me as impudent. . . . In this case I speak to you, Sire, not as your minister but as the friend of a prince in whom I see the entire future of the Serbian people. Thus I decided to tell you everything I felt about your intention. You may condemn me and dismiss me—I understand very well how much I risk by speaking to you this way, but still I must do my duty and let there happen to me whatever you like. I still ask and beg you to renounce your intention.

Finally and most reluctantly, Prince Mihailo promised Garašanin not to marry Katarina and furthermore not to remarry.[6] Henceforth, Anka Konstantinović became Garašanin's deadly and malevolent foe and sought by every means to remove him from office. During the next two years she intrigued constantly against him, poisoning Prince Mihailo's mind against him and gradually undermining his position.[7]

Garašanin, Piroćanac believed, had exaggerated the objections which Serbs would have raised to Mihailo's prospective marriage with Katarina and had largely disregarded the Prince's feelings. At one point Mihailo had declared: "Oh, if only all of you wished to make sacrifices like those you ask of me, our people would be the happiest in the world, but I see that I, as Prince, will never be a happy man." Rulers are also people, commented Piroćanac, and statesmen must take this into proper account. Garašanin seemed to fear that if the marriage went through, Anka and the anti-war coterie would strengthen their hold over the Prince, endangering the Premier's Balkan policies. At least since 1866 Anka had been in contact with Austrian agents and apparently had helped prepare the way for Mihailo's parleys with Austrian and Hungarian leaders during 1867.[8]

Now in November 1867 Mihailo seems to have concluded that with his proposal Garašanin sought to decide on his prospective marriage and heir contrary to his wishes. On November 1st the Premier's proposal was presented to the cabinet at a meeting attended also by Council chairman Marinović. All those attending approved the memorandum, but before it could be presented formally, Prince Mihailo, insisting that the succession question remain open, removed Garašanin from office by letter without explaining why.

Garašanin's own accounts of his dismissal reveal surprise and bewilderment but no bitterness. Although hurt at his abrupt removal and regretful that he therefore could not complete his life's work, Garašanin then and later expressed profound relief that the heavy burdens of office had been removed from his shoulders. A few days later he wrote his son, Milutin:

One evening, while I was sitting in my office and completing work for that day, the Prince's adjutant came in and gave me his [Mihailo's] letter. Instead of finding in the letter, as was customary, instructions from the Prince, I found in it my dismissal. This, naturally, surprised me greatly since nothing previously had indicated that this would occur. I was merely amused at the manner in which I was released from service.[9]

Soon thereafter, Garašanin wrote his friend, Mondain, that he knew little about why he had been removed: "We ourselves are discussing it without being able to solve it." He continued:

> Now I am a free man and am neither minister nor president of the state council and that is all at the will of His Grace. My removal from those high posts occurred, at least for me, wholly unexpectedly. One evening when I was in my office struggling by candlelight with my thoughts as to how I would begin work next day, one brief note from the Prince put an end to all my worries.

What his dismissal meant for the future he did not know:

> Whether it signifies a change of foreign policy or the desire for a more liberal internal administration which I did not favor will only become evident from further moves by the government. . . . And finally the cause could be that Garašanin had grown too old and was no longer capable of dealing with the new world, or at least that it looked as if he could not deal with new ideas.[10]

Perhaps, he added soon after, the Prince had sought a fresh and more youthful talent to run the government.[11] Whatever the reason or reasons, Garašanin accepted dismissal calmly and even joyfully, without recriminations against Prince Mihailo. How differently would Bismarck behave when dismissed in 1890 at a much more advanced age by Emperor William II!

There are several different and in some ways conflicting versions as to why Garašanin was suddenly removed as premier and foreign minister. The most complete account was provided by Nikola Hristić, his minister of interior and replacement as premier. Early one evening, recalled Hristić, he and Council chairman Marinović were in the room of court director, Anastas Jovanović, when the Prince summoned him. In the Prince's antechamber he encountered Moja Gavrilović, a princely confidant, then entered the Prince's room to find Mihailo, gloomy and upset, walking nervously about. Bitterly he declared: "I summoned you to relate an unpleasant bit of news. I can no longer work with Mr. Garašanin." Telling Hristić of negotiations between the Prussian chargé d'affairs and Orešković, the Prince declared he had warned Garašanin repeatedly not to allow his headstrong and garrulous assistant, Orešković, to conduct those talks; he had believed Garašanin understood him. Nonetheless, Garašanin had let them continue, and now the Austrians knew of the entire affair. "Just now Moja [Gavrilović] brought me a report from our agent in Zemun, Stevan Andrijević, that the Zemun general [Ivan von Wagner] had reported to his government in Vienna that we were holding confidential talks with the Prussian government about starting an insurrection in Austria." Had Garašanin conducted these talks personally, continued Mihailo, this would not have occurred. "Since he acted thus, I can no longer work with Mr. Garašanin, and so I have thanked him for his previous services." Mihailo then turned to Hristić:

> I want you to become chairman of the Council of Ministers while remaining interior minister. I will keep the other ministers in their present posts and take as foreign minister Jovan Ristić, envoy in Constantinople. Prepare a decree and bring it in for my signature tomorrow morning. Meanwhile telegraph Ristić in code and summom him home immediately.

The Prince's decision, without consulting the cabinet, shocked Hristić. At the time the government was handling crucial matters, most of them directed by Garašanin personally. His trusted envoy, Colonel Franjo Zah, director of the Military Academy, had gone to Athens to conclude a secret agreement with Greece to complete war preparations within six months and set a date for a Balkan insurrection. Would not Garašanin's departure mean delaying or abandoning all of this?

Stunned by the Prince's pronunciamento, Hristić looked at him in amazement. Mihailo then asked more mildly: "Don't you like this, don't you consider this advisable?" Responded Hristić: "Not only does this seem inappropriate, but it is a great evil." He continued:

> . . . It will destroy our most important policies since now nothing will come of our planned war against Turkey. Greece will draw back,

Montenegro will hesitate . . . , and everything will go into reverse. Even the Russian government will doubt whether our intentions are serious since you are removing the minister through whom it has been working on this crucial matter and removing him at a time when he must be retained in his post even against his will.

Mihailo asked him: "And what would happen if Garašanin had died? " Replied Hristić: "It would be much easier: we would have problems until we had taken over what he held in his hands, but everywhere people would retain firm confidence and conviction about our intentions." The Prince stated reassuringly:

Everything will remain firm as before. I shall not abandon the work which we have undertaken; we shall communicate this to all who are in contact and agreement with us. We will state that Garašanin's removal does not mean at all abandoning the idea of carrying through our task.

Continued the Prince, "Ristić knows about all these matters. Telegraph him this evening in code to come immediately . . ."

Once again Hristić tried to dissuade Mihailo from what he considered an unwise decision, but the Prince declared resolutely: "I don't want to have trouble with Mr. Garašanin. I told him myself . . . that he should speak in person to the Prussian consul. I repeated that to him two or three times, but all in vain . . . , and now the Zemun general has found out. That is simply the cause of Mr. Garašanin's going astray." Hristić merely managed to persuade Mihailo to delay his own nomination as premier until after Ristić's arrival. What further orders did the Prince intend to issue on Garašanin? , queried Hristić. Mihailo replied he would be retired on pension. How large a pension would the Prince award him? Responded the Prince curtly: "As much as he has coming to him by law on the basis of his years of service." Hristić then left without pressing the Prince further since he was obviously still very upset.

On their way to the Foreign Ministry, Hristić related this entire story to the astonished Marinović. As they arrived there about 8 PM, Garašanin was still at the Ministry putting his papers in order. Serenely, he greeted them: "What is this, people. I don't understand it." After reading Mihailo's letter aloud, Marinović declared: ". . . It means that the Prince doesn't want you as his minister any longer." Responded Garašanin calmly:

> I can see that, and the Prince could always count on my consent
> to that, but the sense of the letter indicates I am to blame for some-
> thing, or perhaps the Prince wants to change the direction of his
> policy in which case I am a hindrance. I served him with complete
> sincerity; he must have been wholly sure of that, so if he intended
> to move in a different direction, he could have told me so nicely,
> and I would have resigned voluntarily. He knows that I myself was
> anxious to retire . . . and I believed that our intentions would be
> achieved under Prince Mihailo.

When Hristić informed him he had just come from the Prince and told him
of his instructions, Garašanin declared: "You should accept the premiership, not reject it on any account, so that our present course and general
cause can be continued and completed. I, for my part, will write my friends
not to be discouraged, but to continue to work steadily at their tasks."
Marinović too urged Hristić to become premier but agreed he should wait
until he had achieved agreement with Ristić. After Garašanin gave him the
code for secret correspondence with Constantinople, Hristić informed
Ristić of his nomination as foreign minister and summoned him home.

The next day (November 3rd), continued Hristić, Garašanin expressed
to the Prince his thanks for consideration shown him while in service.
Mihailo received him warmly, explained his action in retiring him without
revealing its causes, thanked him for his efforts, and hoped he might call
upon Garašanin in the future when his expertise was required. The Prince's
attentiveness pleased Garašanin greatly and they parted satisfied and com-
forted. Right afterwards Mihailo called in Hristić to ask what he had done
about Garašanin's pension. When Hristić replied he had done nothing yet,
the Prince declared: "I must be thankful for Mr. Garašanin's labors, so
propose to the State Council that out of recognition of his services to the
state, his present salary be designated as his pension." While this apparent
shift in Mihailo's attitude amazed everyone, two ministers who were close
to Garašanin—Cukić and Rajko Lešjanin—still announced they would
resign.[12]

Hristić's version of Garašanin's removal appears basically accurate except perhaps as to its causes. The Serbian scholar, Dragoslav Stranjaković,
affirmed in 1949 that no extant document explained clearly why he had

been dismissed. Silent and secretive, Mihailo discussed this matter with no one. His letter of dismissal had merely stated that with the Kragujevac assembly of September 1867, one phase of his rule had ended "and with it also the mission for which I placed you in charge six years ago." Garašanin had met the requirements of that initial period, but now the state's needs had changed. Thus he must part with his premier and entrust Serbia's administration to new forces.[13]

Stranjaković concluded that the main problem was to determine the immediate pretext since the reasons for which Garašanin could be dismissed were numerous. Probably closest to the truth, alleged Stranjaković, was that leakage of news about the Orešković-Rosen talks threatened Mihailo's agreements with Andrassy on Bosnia-Hercegovina.[14] At Ivanac Andrassy had probably held out definite hopes to Mihailo that Serbia would acquire part or all of those provinces. Thus when the Prince learned of the revelation to Vienna of Serbo-Prussian talks directed against Austria, he removed Garašanin to prove his non-involvement in them and his loyalty to Andrassy. Other causes of removal, Stranjaković affirmed, were subsidiary. It would have been out of character for the Prince to have dismissed Garašanin for purely personal reasons, nor would that have cleared the way for his marriage to Katarina. Metropolitan Mihailo, an adamant opponent of that marriage, represented another formidable barrier in his path. When he was murdered seven months later, the indecisive prince had still taken no action to marry Katarina. Therefore, Stranjaković concluded that differences over foreign policy, especially Orešković's disclosures, had been foremost in Mihailo's removal of Garašanin.[15]

The talkative Orešković had communicated details of confidential discussions with Prussian envoys to Italian Consul Scovasso, but did Prince Mihailo know about his indiscretions before he dismissed Garašanin? Vladimir Ćorović, a highly reputable Serbian scholar, argued that he did not know. Scovasso's report with this information, written October 21st, was logged in the Italian foreign ministry in Florence October 26th. Prince Mihailo could not have learned about this from the Prussians before Consul Rosen did, yet Rosen could have informed the Prince only *after* returning from Berlin following Garašanin's fall. There is no evidence that Mihailo learned of Orešković's statements from the Austrians. Garašanin surely would have known whether this diplomatic incident had caused his dismissal, argued Ćorović, yet he failed even to mention it. Already angry with Garašanin over his November 1st memorandum, the Prince surely would have accused Garašanin of responsibility for his subordinate's indiscretions. Assertions by Hristić and Blaznavac that the Orešković affair was crucial relied on General Ivan von Wagner's reports from Zemun to Vienna. However, those reveal that von Wagner, not knowing why the Premier had been dismissed, merely cited versions he had heard. He wrote home on November 21st:

> People in Belgrade are still investigating the reasons which could have led in such an abrupt manner to Minister Garašanin's removal. Some claim that he plotted behind the Prince's back about far-reaching political combinations; others believe his fall should be attributed to intrigues by his enemies linked with the Prince's relatives. In any case, Ms. Anka Konstantinović figures prominently and doubtless contributed her share because she now believes she has eliminated the greatest obstacle to the future marriage of her daughter with the Prince.

Ćorović affirms that nothing in this report indicates that von Wagner contributed at all to Garašanin's ouster, and that Scovasso had divulged nothing of importance to him.

Von Wagner's later report of November 30 (December 12) apparently formed the basis for the Hristić-Blaznavac allegations. One of his agents, the General reported, had learned from Jovan Gavrilović of the Prince's staff matters overheard at Anka's house. Allegedly Gavrilović had found the Prince walking angrily around his room and had been shown the letter dismissing Garašanin. When Gavrilović asked why, the Prince replied indignantly that Garašanin and that fool, Orešković, had conspired behind his back to ignite a Bosnian uprising in February 1868 and make Garašanin president of a Bosnian republic. Interior Minister Hristić, added Mihailo, had intercepted an incriminating letter at the frontier. In Gavrilović's presence, the Prince had summoned his secretary, Joksić, stopped Orešković's salary, and ordered Joksić to take the dismissal letter to Garašanin. Vienna did indeed learn of the confidential Orešković-Rosen talks, but the Austrian report on this was dated November 29th, or long after Garašanin's fall. Thus the Hristić-Blaznavac version was chronologically inaccurate. However, since the Orešković-Rosen affair became a diplomatic incident, the Prince's entourage utilized it as a convenient justification for Garašanin's dismissal to deflect attention from the marriage issue. Hristić's own account reinforces this hypothesis by failing to mention the Orešković affair in his conversation with the Prince right after Garašanin's removal. Neither did Garašanin who surely would have defended himself, nor did Pirоćanac, aware of all the Foreign Ministry's dealings.[16]

Milan Milićević's diary buttresses Ćorović's version. Milićević claimed that Rajko Lešjanin, one of Garašanin's ministers, had asserted that Anka Konstantinović and War Minister Blaznavac had invented a false Garašanin-Orešković correspondence implying they had conspired to obtain Bosnia for themselves. Sent from Pesth to Prince Mihailo, this correspondence allegedly had induced him to remove Garašanin.[17]

Jakšić and Vučković's *The Foreign Policy of Serbia during the Rule of Prince Mihailo* is the most recent full account of Garašanin's fall by Yugoslav scholars. Garašanin's November 1st memo and Orešković's revelations, they concluded, had served as convenient pretexts masking deeper personal and political reasons for Garašanin's dismissal. Finding Ćorović's arguments about von Wagner's reports convincing, they added that the alleged report to Mihailo from Zemun may have been only supposition or intrigue but could nonetheless have affected Mihailo's mood. On the marriage issue Mihailo remained torn between his desire for personal happiness and an heir and considerations of state which Garašanin had summarized forcefully. Since such state reasons made it difficult to reject Garašanin's memorandum summarily, Mihailo avoided all discussion of it by simply removing him. Thus Garašanin's explanation of his dismissal seems more convincing than Hristić's about the Orešković affair.

The authors suggest further that Mihailo believed that by changing his foreign policy, he was sparing Serbia potential disaster. In February 1868 Mihailo told English Consul Longworth that Garašanin's removal had been "a purely political act" to save his country. The Prince argued that Garašanin had been wholly under Russian influence. As Russian demands upon Serbia became ever greater and more unreasonable, Mihailo had concluded that accepting them would lead Serbia to destruction. Thus to shake off Russian domination he had dismissed Garašanin and taken personal control of foreign affairs.[18] Reflecting the Prince's concern about Russian influence, that statement grossly exaggerated Garašanin's subservience to Russia but told the consul what he doubtless wish to hear. Clearly shaken by the Russian officers' reports of June 1867 about Serbia's unpreparedness for war,[19] Prince Mihailo questioned the wisdom of starting a Balkan insurrection and war if they would produce "useless bloodshed" and expose Serbia to defeat and loss of her autonomy. His talks in Vienna and Paris had further undermined his confidence in a successful Balkan war. Then had come Andrassy's cleverly conceived offer of Bosnia without the risk of war. Also Mihailo suspected the loyalty and preparedness of Serbia's Balkan allies.[20]

Mihailo's growing disillusionment with bellicose policies was reinforced by a conviction that Serbia must concentrate on economic progress through railway construction. Foreign powers were debating whether a railway link between western Europe and Constantinople should pass through Serbia, Bosnia or Rumania. That issue had profound economic, political and military significance for Serbia's future. Would the Austrians and Turks construct this vital link through an insecure Slav principality? Mihailo concluded that unless a railroad were built through Serbia, she would face ruin. From a Viennese financier, Count Corti, he heard predictions that if a Suez Canal were built and a railway constructed from Salonika through Serbia, soon Belgrade would become a major European commerical center.[21] En route to Paris, the Prince wrote from Switzerland: "When these [Swiss] republicans have crisscrossed their mountainous country with railroads, it would be shameful if Serbia remained the only country in Europe which only talks about railroads."[22] Yet to construct such railways, Serbia would have to link them with the Austrian and Turkish networks and obtain a foreign loan. Neither could be arranged by a country preparing an aggressive war. Mihailo discerned the need to choose between war and peaceful national development. Inclined now toward the latter, he knew this meant abandoning Garašanin's bellicose policy with its ruinous military expenditures.

Contributing to Garašanin's fall may have been Mihailo's desire to obtain administrative control of Bosnia-Hercegovina by cooperating with Austria-Hungary and abandoning his former Russophile course. Since the strongly Austrophobe Garašanin was considered by Vienna as its avowed enemy, the Prince may have believed that an Austrophile policy would not succeed as song as Garašanin remained foreign minister. In itself that is insufficient to explain Mihailo's sudden action, but disclosure of secret Serbo-Prussian talks against Austria provides a motive for it. Indeed, Blaznavac in Mihailo's name informed Consul Shishkin that Garašanin's clumsiness in talks with Prussia had constituted "the chief factor in Garašanin's removal."[23]

Influenced by these various factors, Prince Mihailo after his Ivanac meeting sought to swing Garašanin over to his new way of thinking. Without revealing his true thoughts, he tried to persuade him to pursue a moderate, cautious foreign policy. Either Garašanin failed to grasp Mihailo's wishes or pretended not to and continued on as before. Then came the Orešković indiscretion and Garašanin's November 1st memo affecting the Prince's personal future and happiness. Mihailo probably felt insulted that his premier even in the realm was seeking to impose his will.[24]

Whatever its causes, Garašanin accepted his dismissal calmly, grateful to the Prince for freeing him from burdensome state service. He had emphasized before and reiterated now that he had never coveted a ministerial post and had accepted one only at the Prince's insistence. Given his history of ill health, he had been fortunate to have survived six strenuous years as premier and foreign minister. Garašanin rejoiced at this since his children could now declare proudly that their father had served Prince Mihailo who had performed great services for Serbia. Now the Prince's decision had ended his worries about affairs of state. He wrote Mondain:

> That very evening I became a free man no longer dependent on the entire world, even less *upon the consuls of the Guarantor Powers,* but on myself alone. From that hour my position became enviable since you know how overburdened I was even when you were here and since that time my worries and work had redoubled. . . . I was glad to enter the service of Prince Mihailo when he desired it and I withdrew from it again at his will. He told me he was satisfied with my service; that is enough for me, and I will try to make him satisfied with me in private life too. The Prince is convinced that I have no further ambitions and have had enough of state service.[25]

Garašanin merely regretted that his retirement had not been handled better. The previous day he had offered his resignation to the Prince through Interior Minister Nikola Hristić, but refusing it the Prince had replied: "That isn't necessary now." Garašanin was concerned lest his sudden removal damage the general cause. Thus it would have been preferable to allow him, as he had sought, to resign for reasons of health.[26]

After Garašanin had written out his resignation and was preparing to depart for his Grocka estate, relates Milićević, Anastas Jovanović, the court director, brought him a pouch containing a large sum of money under princely seal and stated that it was a gift from Prince Mihailo. After Garašanin had refused it, the Prince told Jovanović: "Tell Mr. Garašanin that I urge him to accept it. Up to now he has never offended me, but I will take it as an insult if he rejects my gift." When Jovanović returned, Garašanin accepted the pouch but left it unopened until after Mihailo's murder, although in the meantime he had been very short of funds. "And why didn't you open it sooner? " a friend asked Garašanin. He replied: "The Prince might have offended me in some way, and in that case I would have returned the money to him."[27]

To avoid embarrassing questions about his dismissal, Garašanin swiftly left Belgrade for Grocka. To queries of the curious he replied merely that he had grown too old to bear burdens of state. "For simple people this works, but those who know how to think don't believe my words and seek the true cause of my retirement. But that talk will soon cease. I sometimes marvel that it happened this way."[28] He wrote Marinović that he would never return to state service, but nonetheless "I cannot cease to desire the progress of our country which I always sought while in service." He had taken refuge in Grocka to avoid questions. "Naturally *they cannot count on me any more*, my rule is finished and *will not be resumed.*" If he had made mistakes, he regretted he had not performed better. "Despite that, the results of our activities were good." He urged Marinović to give advice to the Prince if asked and to continue in his important post of Council chairman to "do your duty as you have always done it. . .and *don't change your methods at all* which have always been very beneficial to the country."[29]

Garašanin himself ascribed his dismissal to his November 1st memo and his opposition to the Prince's marriage with Katarina. Mihailo had been influenced significantly by Anka Konstantinović and her clique who had been spreading reports that he was intriguing with the Russians against the Prince and leading everyone in Belgrade around by the nose. Blaznavac complained that Garašanin was seeking to undermine his standing with the

Prince. Crnobarac, another clique member, disliked Garašanin's conservative political orientation which he claimed was opposed strongly by the Serbian public. From many sides disgruntled, embittered persons spoke out or intrigued against Garašanin, unsurprising given his power and long tenure of office. All this created an atmosphere which encouraged the hot-tempered Prince, provoked by the November 1st memorandum, to remove Garašanin by letter.

Garašanin's fall produced a profound, essentially negative impact on Serbia. Longworth, the English Consul, reproted November 6th: "The Serbian public appears gloomy and deeply dissatisfied." Serbs were ascribing his dismissal to differences with the Prince over his proposed marriage. The general conclusion there and abroad was that Mihailo thereby had repudiated a warlike policy. Without the leadership of the man who had prepared so long for a Balkan insurrection and war with Turkey, Serbian leaders doubted they could be implemented now despite Mihailo's assurances that nothing had changed.[30]

The sharpest reaction came from Russia. From Consul Shishkin's reports St. Petersburg may have surmised that the Ivanac talks had been important, that their results had been concealed from Russia, and that Garašanin had known little about them. Knowing Serbian affairs intimately, Shishkin realized the growing influence of Anka's clique and its efforts to oust Garašanin. Russian leaders now suspected Prince Mihailo's loyalty and sincerity.[31] St. Petersburg quickly interpreted Garašanin's dismissal as a basic change in Serbia's policy of support for a Balkan league against Turkey. Soon Jovan Ristić, the other Serbian diplomat Russia had confidence in, would likewise be removed. Enhanced was the influence of War Minister Blaznavac, reputed foe of Russia. The visiting Russian officers had criticized strongly his activities as war minister, and he had responded by denouncing Russia's Balkan policies. In early November Blaznavac told the French consul that Serbia would refuse to fight the Turks if Russia sought to impose the cooperation of a single Russian brigade. If her independence were jeopardized, Serbia would resist Russia and even ally with Turkey against her.[32]

Russian dissatisfaction over Garašanin's dismissal was first expressed by withdrawing the remainder of its loan to Serbia. After paying a second installment of 100,000 ducats in mid-December 1867, Russia refused further payments. Learning with regret of this decision, Garašanin wrote:

"Surely, [Russia] did not link her favor with Garašanin, but with Serbia."
Vainly, he urged Marinović to persuade Shishkin to preserve the loan.[33]
Several weeks later Shishkin presented sharply worded messages from St.
Petersburg and from Count Shtakelberg, Russian ambassador in Vienna,
from which Prince Mihailo discerned that Russian indignation stemmed
from Garašanin's removal and inadequate Serbian military preparations.
Shishkin added impudently that Mihailo had disregarded Russian advice
about Serbia's army and had shown disrespect for the tsar. Denying the
latter charge emphatically, the Prince reproached Shishkin for highhanded
behavior. To some Serbian leaders the Consul's arrogance seemed an attempt to return to the times of Aleksandar Karadjordjević. Shtakelberg's
letter condemned Garašanin's dismissal, urged his reinstatement and
continuation of military preparations, but advised delaying any military
action until complications developed in Europe.[34]

Russian protests and advice merely confirmed Mihailo in his new course
and made Garašanin's restoration to office impossible. While able to accept criticism of his war ministry, the Prince refused to respond to Russian
defenses of Garašanin and was offended that Russia ascribed direction of
Serbian foreign policy to Garašanin rather than to him. While Garašanin
had been in power under Aleksandar Karadjordjević, he reminded Shtakelberg, Serbia had been "without strength, both moral and military." Then,
before Garašanin even returned to state service, he, Mihailo, had constructed a national army "which today causes fear in Constantinople and
fills the Serbian people and other Slavs with hope." Affirmed the Prince
proudly: "I indicated the path they should follow." Without denying
Garašanin's great ability as a statesman, the Prince claimed that his policy
"by its unsteadiness and desire to please all parties had turned Belgrade
into an arena where competed the contradictory interests of the Guarantor Powers." Though Garašanin's ability would be missed, Mihailo
intimated that St. Petersburg's commanding tone made his return to
power unthinkable for a long time to come.[35] Whereas Blaznavac denied
Russian assertions that Prince Mihailo had abandoned an active foreign
policy,[36] those claims subsequently proved accurate whereas the Prince's
criticism of Garašanin's policy as "unsteady" appears groundless.

Prince Mihailo's replies to Foreign Minister Gorchakov and Count
Shtakelberg, noted Crnobarac, had been read at a cabinet meeting. The
Russians expressed intense irritation at Garašanin's removal, especially

since Prince Mihailo declined to specify his reasons. Excessive praise of Garašanin by foreign envoys, speculated Crnobarac, may have contributed to his fall by arousing Mihailo's jealousy. Replying to Shtakelberg, the Prince insisted on writing the sharp criticisms of Garašanin in his own hand. Since Mihailo had made no concessions whatsoever in his letters of response, Crnobarac doubted that St. Petersburg would be satisfied with them.[37] Indeed, this exchange of notes left Serbo-Russian relations frigid.

Serbia's Balkan allies likewise interpreted Garašanin's fall as a fundamental change of policy. The Bulgar Committee's delegates, arriving in Belgrade with Garašanin still in office to discuss preparations for insurrection, found neither aid nor encouragement from acting foreign minister Petronijević; they returned home disillusioned.[38] The Rumanian envoy worried that Garašanin's departure would end negotiations for a Serbo-Rumanian alliance, but he was assured they would continue.[39] Garašanin's removal, followed soon by Ristić's, perplexed Greeks and Montenegrins too as the conviction grew that Prince Mihailo had abandoned plans for war with Turkey.

The abrupt removal of Jovan Ristić as foreign minister, in the aftermath of Garašanin's dismissal, resulted from personal not policy differences. When he agreed to become foreign minister, Premier Nikola Hristić believed Ristić would become reconciled with Garašanin's loyal followers, Kosta Cukić and Rajko Lešjanin. Shocked by Garašanin's sudden removal, they had intended to resign, but at Hristić's urging they consented to remain in the cabinet. However, Ristić affirmed coldly that he could not serve with Garašanin's colleagues whom he characterized as ill-intentioned. Conferring with the Prince, Anka, and Metropolitan Mihailo, Ristić sought to get rid of the two ministers. In return, he tempted the Prince, the Metropolitan would let him marry Katarina. The Prince was furious since Cukić and Lešjanin had informed him that Ristić's coolness resulted from their refusal to accept all of his political ideas. While they sought reconciliation, Ristić remained adamant. Thereupon Mihailo told Hristić that Ristić was unworthy to become foreign minister: "I have now discerned in him malice and an evil heart, and become convinced that he cannot remain with me . . . . Thus I am compelled to dismiss him and name Milan Petronijević foreign minister." With others present the Prince denounced Ristić as an intriguer:

Having summoned you and named you my foreign minister, I was
convinced I would find in you the greatest willingness to aid me with
your strength and ease my heavy state burdens. I hoped to find in
you enough patriotism to overcome your personal dislike of some
members of my government. Unfortunately, I was mistaken, and
found instead . . . the greatest stubbornness in you toward all my
advice and good intentions. . . . I found in you an invincible hatred
toward all those persons whom you believe do not share your ideas.

Concluded Mihailo: "You are not for me, nor am I for you. God bless
Serbia if such characters disappear from her service forever."[40] After this
scene, Hristić became premier and Petronijević foreign minister.[41]

Ristić's fate seemed sealed. Pale and shaken, the usually haughtly diplomat begged Hristić abjectly to help rescue him from his disgrace; Hristić
agreed. The efforts of Anka, Blaznavac and Marinović, whom Ristić enlisted to intercede for him, softened Mihailo's wrath. Even then the Prince
criticized Ristić's bad character but agreed to send him back to Constantinople as Serbian envoy.[42] This incident revealed Ristić's pettiness, personal animosities and penchant for intrigue, all of which would soon be
directed against Garašanin in retirement.

Garašanin's fall from office, not Mihailo's assassination in May 1868,
marked Serbia's decisive move away from Russia, Balkan insurrection and
war. Despite the Prince's later second thoughts, there was little prospect
those policies could be revived. Headed by Hristić, a cautious bureaucrat,
the new cabinet, containing the colorless and inexperienced Petronijević
and the Russophobe Blaznavac, was opposed to a bellicose course. In
retrospect this appears to have benefited Serbia. As Prince Mihailo realized,
she could not have fought Turkey successfully in 1868 nor could her
allies have helped much. Thus Mihailo, by dismissing Garašanin, had saved
Serbia from a potentially disastrous conflict.

NOTES

1. IG 1623, "Predlog Ilije Garašanina Ministarskom Savetu," November 1 (13), 1867, published in Vučković, *Politička,* No. 179, pp. 317-319.
On Garašanin's removal see especially Stranjaković, *Mihailo i Julija* (Belgrade

1940), pp. 111 ff.; Jakšić and Vučković, *Spoljna,* pp. 430-436; and V. Ćorović, "Oko pada Ilija Garašanina," *Politika,* April 23-26, 1938.

2. Piroćanac, *Knez Mihailo,* p. 45 ff.

3. Stranjaković, *Mihailo i Julija,* pp. 117-119.

4. IG 1535, Garašanin to Mihailo, October 14, 1865.

5. Stranjaković, *Mihailo i Julija,* pp. 121-123.

6. Ibid., pp. 123-129. However, as Stranjaković notes, the Prince was not being sincere toward Garašanin since he told Katarina and Anka that he still intended to marry Katarina even though Metropolitan Mihailo had made it plain both to Anka and the Prince on October 23 and 24 that the Orthodox Church was flatly opposed to such a marriage. Ibid., pp. 129-132.

7. Ibid., pp. 141-145.

8. Piroćanac, *Knez Mihailo,* pp. 45-46; Ristić, *Poslednja godina;* Jovanović, *Druga vlada,* pp. 224-225.

9. IG 1633, Garašanin to Milutin Garašanin, November 10, 1867.

10. IG 1635, Garašanin to Mondain, November 12, from Grocka.

11. Ibid., November 24.

12. "Iz memoarskih zabeležaka starog državnika, Nikola Hristića," *Politika,* No. 11392, February 16, 1940, pp. 15-16.

13. IG 1643, Mihailo to Garašanin, November 2, 1867; Stranjaković, *Mihailo i Julija,* p. 144.

14. Dr. Fičko to Milutin Garašanin, September 20, 1895, cited by Stranjaković in "Ilija Garašanin," p. 143.

15. Ibid., pp. 138-144.

16. Ćorović, "Oka pada," *Politika,* April 23-26, 1938.

17. Arhiv SANU, No. 9327, Dnevnik Milana Milićevića, entry of March 12, 1869. The diary also cites a statement attributed to a certain Ferenčević, an official in Austria's Belgrade consulate, about a conspiracy by Anka Konstantinović to remove Garašanin after the resolution of the fortress question that spring. "But Garašanin still remained near the Prince, and together they could still invade Turkey. He needed to be removed from the Prince, and that, it was said, could occur thus: it was rumored that the Prince would marry Katarina. . . . Someone was bribed to go to Garašanin and ask him to urge the Prince to renounce this intention which would put him in a bad light before the [Serbian] people." Mihailo then told Garašanin: "I assure you, Garašanin, that [marriage] will

not happen." For days afterwards, the Prince had been depressed and had seen Anka constantly. Reputedly, then Anka had drawn War Minister Blaznavac into the conspiracy to concoct the fake correspondence.

18. PRO FO 2033, Longworth to Stanley, February 3/15, 1868.

19. See above, pp. 313-14. Mihailo had learned of their negative verdict in Gastein about June 20 as was revealed in his letters to Marinović of June 23/July 5th and to Garašanin of June 26/July 8, 1867.

20. Mihailo's doubts on these scores were revealed in his letter to Garašanin of June 26/July 8. See also IG 1639, Garašanin to Petronijević, October 4.

21. IG 1600, Mihailo to Garašanin, June 22, from Gastein.

22. Ibid., June 26, from Zurich.

23. Vučković, *Politička*, pp. 337-338.

24. Jakšić and Vučković, *Spoljna*, p. 434.

25. IG 1635, Garašanin to Mondain, November 12, from Grocka.

26. Garašanin to Marinović, December 6, 1867, *Pisma*, II, 213-215.

27. M. Milićević, *Pomenik*, pp. 96-97.

28. Garašanin to Marinović, November 7, from Grocka, *Pisma*, II, 212; IG, Ilija to Milutin Garašanin, November 9.

29. Garašanin to Marinović, December 6, *Pisma*, II, 213-215.

30. "Iz memoarskih zabeležaka Nikola Hristića," p. 16.

31. Piroćanac, *Knez Mihailo*, pp. 87-88.

32. Jakšić and Vučković, *Spoljna*, p. 438. Blaznavac's statement was made on November 10th.

33. Garašanin to Marinović, December 6, *Pisma*, II, 214. "Rejection of the loan I would regard as the beginning of real trouble. Russia thus would damage our position even more. The withdrawal of her favor would merely aid our enemies."

34. Ristić, *Jedno namesništvo*, p. 10.

35. Ibid., p. 4, excerpt from Prince Mihailo to Shtakelberg (December 25, 1867)/January 6, 1868; PRO FO 2033, Longworth to Stanley, February (4)/16, 1868. Prince Mihailo read the entire letter addressed to Ambassador Shtakelberg to the English consul. See Jakšić and Vučković, *Spoljna*, pp. 439-440.

36. Ibid., p. 440, Blaznavac to Ignat'ev, January 10, 1868.

37. Arhiv SANU, 7889, Memoari D. Crnobaraca, entry of January 2.

38. Piroćanac, *Knez Mihailo,* p. 90.

39. Jakšić and Vučković, *Spoljna,* p. 435.

40. AII Ristić XI/7, Mihailo to Ristić, November 21, 1867.

41. "Zabeleške Hristića: Sukob Jovana Ristića i Kneza Mihaila, 1867," *Politika,* No. 11,395, February 21, 1940.

42. Ibid., No. 11,401, February 27, 1940.

CHAPTER XX

PERSECUTED RETIREMENT
(1868-1874)

"I am now sitting quietly in my little Grocka occupied with minor economic tasks . . . so I do not have to wander around Belgrade and listen to intrigues which in small as well as in great capitals are conducted ceaselessly."

Garašanin to Mondain, November 12, 1867

Following his dismissal, Garašanin withdrew with Soka to his modest estate at Grocka with no idea of attempting a political comeback. Soon they were joined there by their two sons, Svetozar and Milutin. Garašanin in retirement continued to play an important role as the Conservatives' revered elder statesman and followed political affairs closely in Serbia and abroad. Purely by accident he took a key part in the immediate aftermath of the assassination of Prince Mihailo in May 1868 and helped save Serbia from potential civil strife. Resuming immediately afterwards his unobtrusive retirement, he emphasized that he would on no account assume any further political post or responsibility. Nonetheless, the small-minded regents who succeeded Mihailo, fearful of his political reputation, sought to make his life miserable. Garašanin was subjected to continual police surveillance and periodic harassment. For the most part he accepted this philosophically and without response.

371

In Grocka he and Soka at first lived in a small rented house. His father's large home had already been sold to cover family debts. A few days after his arrival he wrote Marinović:

> So here I am at Grocka. I cannot immediately praise my situation here since things are in the greatest disorder. In two or three days I'll leave this nice and roomy house to take up residence in the true sence in a miserable little house [*sirotinjsku*]. I'll do everything possible to get out of this chaos as soon as possible. But rest assured that I am bearing this calmly, since I never sought to accumulate wealth. I am already beginning gradually to get used to this new world.[1]

He resolved to remain in Grocka and avoid the ceaseless intrigues in Belgrade:

> Here, on the other hand, the village mayor [*kmet*] is the highest authority for me, and I take great satisfaction in carrying out his orders more precisely than any other resident of Grocka.[2]

Thought still preoccupied with political affairs, he refused to provide the government with any pretext for dissatisfaction with him. Nonetheless, Garašanin deplored public criticisms of the dynamic national policy he and Marinović had worked on together: "I do not have to justify my work since it was the idea of all of us." It would have been preferable, he felt, to have continued those policies to the end and then judged them by their results. If Prince Mihailo now regretted having summoned him to power, he should have removed him sooner. All that was over now, and no one could persuade him to reenter state service.[3]

Garašanin and Mihailo were soon fully reconciled, and the Prince began to return gradually to his former Premier's policies. In mid-December Mihailo resumed political talks with Garašanin and invited him to join in a hunt near Rušnja. Dismissal had not lessened his liking or respect for the Prince. Mihailo might err, he wrote Marinović, but one should not therefore let him stray into greater mistakes "since with that everything Serbian will suffer and come into confusion."

Since Serbia was grievously short of capable leaders, "by helping the Prince, we help ourselves."[4]

In January 1868 the Prince and his entire suite were Garašanin's guests while they hunted from Topčider, through Grocka and on to Smederevo on the Danube. He had not been able to provide Mihailo with lavish entertainment, Garašanin admitted to Mondain, but their relationship had been most friendly. Garašanin hoped he could soon entertain Mondain similarly; they could eat roast lamb together on his lawn and drink toasts in red Grocka wine.[5] During the hunt he and Mihailo had discussed politics so avidly, recalled a participant, that they ignored choice game nearby. Asked afterwards why they had not fired at the passing hares, Garašanin replied enigmatically: "On that height Serbdom should erect a monument to Prince Mihailo."[6]

As Mihailo's hopes of acquiring Bosnia-Hercegovina peacefully waned, Orešković suggested, his interest revived in the concept of a general Balkan insurrection. Orešković intimated that the Prince had decided to restore Garašanin to office in order to implement their plan.[7] Significantly, Blaznavac, realizing that Garašanin had been restored to princely favor, now sought reconciliation with him. He found this politic, affirmed Piroćanac, because the unsavory activities of Anka Konstantinović's coterie had seriously undermined the War Minister's relations with the Prince. Thus in late April military inspectors went into the interior of Serbia with instructions from Mihailo to report everything there which needed reform. Captain Ljubomir Ivanović, the Prince's aide who accompanied them, believed that Blaznavac's position was highly vulnerable.[8]

Serbian politicians differed sharply as to when Serbia abandoned plans to lead a Balkan war of liberation. Did this occur after Garašanin's removal in November 1867 or following Mihailo's murder in May 1868? Was Prince Mihailo reverting to a warlike policy in the months prior to his assassination, or did he remain undecided between pro- and anti-war factions? The latter explanation reflects best the Prince's proneness to vacillation and indecision. The politicians' debate on the war issue was affected significantly by emotion and self-interest. Milutin Garašanin, citing evidence of continued Serbian efforts to form Balkan alliances and spur war preparations, concluded that Belgrade adhered firmly to a bellicose policy until after

Mihailo's death. The war was to begin either in 1868 or 1869, he affirmed, and Serbia thus remained poised on the threshold of war until the Regency abandoned abruptly his father's and Mihailo's plans.[9] Antonije Orešković and Milan Piroćanac, colleagues of Garašanin and Mihailo, concur.[10] On the other hand, Jovan Ristić, a leader of the subsequent Regency, insisted that already in Mihailo's lifetime, war with Turkey had been postponed indefinitely because the Balkan peoples were unprepared militarily and failed to cooperate politically. French support of Austria after 1866 had compelled Mihailo to abandon Serbia's war plans. Furthermore, the Ottoman Empire remained stronger than the Balkan peoples all together. Concluded Ristić: "...Serbia in the year 1868 was not on the verge of war. Armed action was delayed indefinitely at the moment when Serbia accepted the fortresses."[11]

This debate about the war question rested on contradictory, confusing signals coming from outside. Piroćanac stresses completion of the Serbo-Greek alliance with August or September 1868 set for the beginning of war. Ratifications of the military convention with Greece were exchanged prior to Mihailo's murder, and a Serbo-Rumanian friendship treaty was also concluded. The Balkan states, argued Piroćanac, were cooperating actively and preparing to fight. Dimitrije Crnobarac, a minister aligned with Blaznavac's anti-war faction, agrees that late August 1868 had been designated by Serbia and Greece as the time for action to begin. In January, he claims, he had told Prince Mihailo it would be too dangerous for Serbia to make war unless a general revolt against the Turks was already underway. The Prince had agreed that Serbia must be careful since a people's militia could not fight like a disciplined regular army. At a cabinet meeting of January 17th War Minister Blaznavac had told Crnobarac that Russia was still urging Serbia to enter war as soon as possible and blamed him for delaying its start. Affirming that Garašanin had been naive and credulous, Blaznavac dismissed his "network" in Bosnia as largely illusory. A former Austrian staff captain had informed the War Minister that Garašanin had only five or six agents there instead of 5,000-6,000 warriors armed to the teeth that Garašanin's subordinates had reported. In case of war, affirmed Blaznavac, the Bulgarian populace would side with the Turks, not with Serbia.[12]

During Mihailo's final months of rule, Russia's attitude toward Serbia's war plans grew ambiguous. Count Ignat'ev wrote the Prince in late March that the Tsar still favored his cause, and Foreign Minister Gorchakov provided assurances that Russia would no longer interfere in Serbia's internal affairs.[13] From Vienna Ambassador Shtakelberg advised Serbia in December 1867 to defer action until circumstances grew more favorable and warned that Russia then could provide no assistance. Yet in Belgrade Consul Shishkin, asserted von Reiswitz, was pressuring Prince Mihailo to reinstate Garašanin and intrigued against the Blaznavac faction.[14] Such discordance occurred repeatedly in Russian foreign policy under Alexander II. Contemporary documents testify, asserted Piroćanac, that Russia then remained a strong supporter of a Balkan league, but not a Balkan war. At the end of 1867, he admitted, Serbian war preparations slowed briefly during an interlude of hesitation and rethinking by Mihailo, but no decision was made to abandon Belgrade's war plans. That could not have occurred, he claimed, without consent by Serbia's Balkan partners, but there is no evidence of such action.[15]

Evidence seems lacking to support allegations of von Reiswitz and others that Garašanin was involved in any Russian-sponsored intrigues against Mihailo during the Prince's final months. His renewed friendship with Mihailo at this time implied the contrary, and his letters early in 1868 suggest a man resigned to quiet retirement and keeping a low profile. Thus Garašanin wrote Marinović from Grocka February 2nd:

Although here I hear plenty about political intrigue, of real politics I know and hear nothing. It is true that political leaders were with me recently,[16] . . . but they say nothing to me and I did not, and do not, wish to ask them anything [about politics] . . . .

Referring to the recent opposition expressed by Austria, France and England against warlike action by Serbia and her Balkan allies, Garašanin continued:

I am not at all surprised at the coalition against our course; that was to be expected. It is important to know whether Serbia has decided to do anything since if her resolve is serious . . . it should be pushed ahead. To a coalition of European powers should be opposed a coalition of Balkan peoples. Opposing powers should be conciliated and informed while they are shown that the East is in agreement and that all of us want the same thing. In this I always sought our success. That is what gained us the fortresses and is the only strength against a European coalition which we can expect. One must know what one wants and want it badly enough, then things will look different even against a coalition of powers. When one yields to threats alone, nothing can be accomplished; that is a child's game and our affairs resemble that now. Now we must wait until the proper people seize the initiative, then help them.[17]

This suggests that Garašanin's views remained consistent, but now he was an outsider uncertain what course Serbia would take.

In reminiscences composed at Grocka before his reconciliation with Prince Mihailo, Garašanin summarized the attitude of the European powers toward Serbia. He reaffirmed that Serbia must pursue an independent course and avoid any subservience to Russia:

One should never believe that Russia desires our progress and strengthening for other motives but only because in us she would find an ally if Europe, which greatly fears Russian advances, should attack her. With Russia Serbia can protect her interests for a long time but always watching carefully that she [Russia] never interferes with her interests.

At present, he continued, France was seeking to split the Balkan Christians from Serbia, but once Paris grew convinced of her independence from Russia, it would support the strengthening of Serbia. England too would gladly abandon its support of Turkey if she discerned an element able to protect the Balkans from external, especially Russian, influences. The best way to achieve that goal would be for Balkan peoples to free themselves alone from Turkish control; England would accept such a *fait accompli* and assist them. Austria, with or without Hungary, had always been hostile towards Serbia and would always remain so, whereas Prussia's present interest was to aid Serbia secure itself from Austria.[18]

Garašanin spent about three hours conferring with the Prince about Balkan policy and other matters only days before Mihailo was murdered.[19]

He had planned to leave Belgrade for Vienna May 29th to advise his friend, Mita Anastasijević, in a judicial dispute. By chance he delayed his depature for two days and thus was in the Belgrade area when the assassination occurred. Before the murder Garašanin had told Piroćanac that Mihailo remained loyal to a policy of Balkan cooperation. At the end of their conference, Mihailo had urged Garašanin to remain in Vienna no longer than necessary and to report to him upon his return.[20] This suggests that Prince Mihailo at the time of his death was favorably inclined toward Garašanin and his active Balkan policies.

On May 29, 1868 (June 10 New Style) Prince Mihailo was walking along a wooded path at Košutnjak near Belgrade, accompanied by Anka and Katarina Konstantinović. Anka's aged mother, Tomanija, was being escorted by Captain Svetozar Garašanin, Ilija's elder son and the Prince's only bodyguard. Three men met the party, bowed, then shot and killed the Prince and Anka outright. Katarina was wounded, and Svetozar Garašanin, as he tried to assist the Prince, was shot in the arm and disabled. Only old Tomanija remained unscathed. Ilija Garašanin later gave this brief account of his actions to his other son:

Last Wednesday Sofia and I were for the first time in years in Topčider after dinner between five and six o'clock. We were walking at that fountain. . .below the hill when we saw the Prince pass with four others. . .and without any armed escort. The Prince. . .was talking with Svetozar about various matters concerning the artillery.[21]

This must have been shortly before the Prince had been shot.

The first news of the murder was borne by a policeman from Košutnjak who found Ilija and Sofia Garašanin in adjacent Topčider still walking. Garašanin promptly instructed the policeman to hasten to Belgrade and alert the government. Soon afterwards, Mihailo's servant, young Mita Timarčević, drove up in a court carriage holding one of his hands which was covered in blood and shouting that the Prince had been killed. Among the assassins he had recognized by sight, Djordje Radovanović, a bankrupt merchant.

Ilija Garašanin faced a difficult choice. Fatherly feeling suggested he should proceed immediately to Košutnjak to care for his son, Svetozar, reportedly gravely wounded. However, civic duty, which for him invariably took precedence over private concerns, dictated driving immediately to Belgrade to alert the government and prevent a possible coup. Wasting no time, Garašanin sent Soka to see about Svetozar and ordered his coachman to drive him at top speed to the seat of government in Belgrade. Behind them he soon noticed a carriage overtaking his containing Pavle Radovanović, another of the assassins. Fearing that he was trying to reach the city first, Garašanin urged his coachman to redouble their speed. Soon the other carriage slowed, its horses apparently exhausted, and Garašanin reached Belgrade first.

He arrived at the Interior Ministry before any preventive action had been taken. Finding Marinović, Nikola Hristić and Kosta Cukić in the courtyard of the Prince's palace, Garašanin exhorted them to summon the War Minister immediately and have the army placed on alert. A cabinet meeting should be convened promptly to agree on measures to avert a *coup d'état* or civil war. Garašanin then ordered an officer of the Prince's guard to place his men on the alert and load their rifles. Entering the Interior Ministry and finding its officials milling around in a daze and since the War Minister Blaznavac still had not arrived, Garašanin assumed command:

> Gentlemen, forget the questions, but see to it before all else to secure the authority you have in your hands in order to prevent further trouble from occurring. Have the War Minister order a strong guard placed around the ministry immediately and dispatch a detachment of police.

Finance Minister Cukić rushed obediently to the nearest police station and brought back a number of gendarmes to the ministry. Now secure, the government could continue to function.

The conspirators were soon rounded up and the dimensions of the threat stood revealed. Coded letters intercepted by the authorities confirmed the chief conspirators to be Lazar Marić, Kosta and Djordje Radovanović, and Stanoje Rogić, two of them bankrupt merchants. The man Garašanin had outraced was Pavle Radovanović, a Belgrade lawyer and the conspirators' brother. Their plans called for killing Interior Minister Hristić and War Minister Blaznavac while accomplices slaughtered other leading officials.[22]

Thanks largely to Ilija Garašanin's prompt and decisive leadership in the first hours after Mihailo's murder, further execution of the plot was foiled. Serbian leaders later expressed deep appreciation for his actions. Rejecting any need for special thanks, Garašanin wrote Magazinović:

> Truly I did do things which were required in that unfortunate hour. But I did my duty as any Serb would have done. . . . I acted in order to halt further trouble . . . assisting the proper authorities to protect the country's security. That the moment was seized meant saving the people from anarchy. That it was grasped should be attributed first of all to luck and then to speed. One must compliment most highly the wisdom of the people generally who in response to that terrible event supported the authorities unanimously in order to preserve peace in the country, and we others, had we not done what we did, would have been among the greatest of sinners.[23]

The Austrian consul, Benjamin Kallay, reported that during the crisis immediately following the assassination of Mihailo the ministers in power had been paralyzed with fear. Only Garašanin kept his head, despite reports his son had been killed.[24] Actually, the wounded all recovered including Svetozar, whose injuries had been exaggerated in some newspaper accounts. Ilija Garašanin told Ranko Alimpić: "Look how things turned out! They killed our Prince, but my unfortunate son was spared, to my shame and misfortune and also his."[25] Garašanin was suggesting that as the Prince's bodyguard, his son had been duty bound to perish if need be to save the Prince. Actually, Svetozar had done all he could.

Garašanin asserted that the Porte and ex-prince Aleksandar Karadjordjević, pretender to the Serbian throne, had engineered the murder plot. The Turks, disturbed at Mihailo's apparent resumption of an active Balkan policy, "incited Karadjordjević to do this evil deed." He hoped the Porte's role would be revealed so that Serbo-Turkish relations could never be repaired. Attending the entire trial of the accused, Garašanin was dismayed that "the criminals often looked like judges and judges like criminals." All the conspirators, he believed, should have been sentenced to death. He credited the Prince's page, Mita, with apprehension of the conspirators. "Had Mita not recognized Djoka Radovanović . . . the murderers would have gone right on killing."[26]

Mihailo's murder plunged Garašanin into grief and dispair. He wrote his son, Milutin, June 6th: "I cannot describe the misfortune which occurred last Wednesday evening between six and seven o'clock. We lost our glorious and good Prince Mihailo. This death is an irreparable loss for Serbia. Serbs will not soon see another such prince. . . ."[27] To Kosta Magazinović he wrote sadly:

> There is no misfortune greater than a Serbian misfortune. The extent of this calamity cannot be described. By losing Mihailo it seems to me we have lost everything. May God encourage us to pursue his path, our only guide to a true future.

One needed to be in Serbia, he continued, to see how the Serbian people were mourning their great prince: "There has never been anything like it, nor will there ever be. . . . In the true sense it is everyone—young, old, male, female—all are shedding rivers of tears."[28] Somewhat later, Garašanin assessed for Milutin more fully what Prince Mihailo had meant for Serbia:

> It was easy to serve under Prince Mihailo. He was a great support for us all and one could work without worry for the great future of Serbia. Everyone was convinced. . . that what Prince Mihailo was doing was good, and those surrounding him sought to do what was best, and did not worry about popular support which was always assured. . . . He was a firm pillar upon which the broadest Serbian success could be built, and it seemed to me at least that the brightest future lay ahead.[29]

Bishop Juraj Štrosmajer, the leading Croatian spokesman of Yugoslavism and cooperation with Serbia, was not so uncritically favorable. He wrote to his friend and collaborator, Franjo Rački, about Mihailo's murder: "It was a terrible deed. Mihailo was a fine person but no statesman becuase by his weakness and irresolution he inspired against himself various elements in Serbia." In the final months of his life, commented the late Croatian scholar, Ferdo Šišić, Prince Mihailo had abandoned a Yugoslav policy and gone over to a narrower, Greater Serbian course. Štrosmajer and Rački, who had worked closely with Garašanin and Mihailo to

promote Balkan cooperation and liberation, were left grievously disillusioned.[30]

Meanwhile War Minister Blaznavac had moved swiftly after the assassination to take power. The next day, May 30th, a temporary regency
had been appointed consisting of Jovan Marinović, Rajko Lešjanin, and
Djordje Petrović, head of the Appeals Court. Until it assumed control
Garašanin exercised *de facto* authority. But already on May 30th the political situation shifted rapidly in Blaznavac's favor. An irreconcilable opponent of Garašanin, he acted decisively to prevent any repetition of the
events of 1858. With army backing but without the knowledge of the
temporary regency or the cabinet, Blaznavac proclaimed Milan Obrenović
thirteen-year-old grandson of Jevrem, brother of old Prince Miloš, prince
of Serbia. When the War Minister read his draft proclamation at a cabinet
meeting, there were stormy scenes. Blaznavac had insisted that Garašanin
being neither regent nor minister, be excluded from that meeting. Some of
those present, including Kosta Ćukić and Marinović, opposed this, but
Garašanin, insulted and aggrieved, left immediately and returned to
Grocka. When agitation and objections met his reading of the proclamation, Blaznavac jumped up, pulled out his sabre and bellowed: "Then
this will decide!" The cowed regents and ministers meekly accepted
this *fait accompli.* Blaznavac then designated a Regency headed by himself, blocking the nomination of Garašanin, who most deserved that
honor. And Marinović refused to enter a regency without Garašanin
or to serve alongside Jovan Ristić whom they both detested.[31]

From the start Garašanin and Marinović virtually excluded themselves
from top state posts by arguing they could only serve with people they
could agree with politically and personally. Discord within a regency
or the government, they believed, would "inevitably obstruct the state
machine."[32] St. Petersburg, through Consul Shishkin, advocated strongly
a regency of Garašanin, Marinović and Metropolitan Mihailo; it was most
unhappy when its chief supporters were brushed aside cavalierly by War
Minister Blaznavac, whom it regarded as a Russophobe.[33] Vehemently
opposed to Ristić's inclusion, Garašanin and Marinović had argued for
hours vainly with Blaznavac on the Regency's composition. The War
Minister though bulled ahead to name himself, Ristić, and the colorless
Jovan Gavrilović as regents until Prince Milan's majority.[34]

Probably Garašanin would not have agreed to join the Regency in any
case. On June 6th he wrote Milutin that although there was much talk of

naming him regent, he had already declared he was "firmly determined to refuse." He had borne the burdens of office long enough; now his strength was ebbing, so it would be difficult for him to execute official duties. "Let them try it without me."[35] He would consent to serve as regent, he explained to Milutin, only if there were an indisputable need, that is if no one else agreed to take on such a responsibility.[36]

Under the Regency, some of Garašanin's opponents questioned his rule the day of the assassination. How was it that Garašanin, living then in Grocka, happened to be in Topčider that day? Jovan Ristić, a regent and longtime rival of Garašanin, suggested much later that Garašanin had been involved indirectly in the plot: "Ilija Garašanin watched from a height in Topčider when Mihailo fell in Košutnjak under the assassin's knife." This intimated that Garašanin knew when the murder would occur and had come to watch the fun! Why had Ristić waited twenty-five years before concocting this filthy lie? wondered Milutin Garašanin. During the Regency, his father had been persecuted and spied upon, but no one had accused him of direct involvement in the murder because there was simply no basis for it. Ristić was accusing him belatedly, surmised Milutin, in order to discredit him and support the contention that he, Ristić, was a great man.[37]

Garašanin's enemies also alleged that after the murder he had rushed into Belgrade not to preserve order but to seize power for himself. Garašanin answered these allegations by explaining why he was in Topčider and that he and his wife had been walking there purely by accident. Neither then nor earlier had he sought personal power:

Let the members of the government and Council say whether I ever said or did anything to suggest that I was seeking power for myself. Let them ask my friends and enemies about this and let them state what was my behavior on that unfortunate night and during the two or three days which followed. Never in my time did I covet power, but when I held it in my hands, I always knew how to use it. . . . I always took care to preserve inviolate the dignity of authority, and this was easier for me since, unlike others, I did not seek power through intrigue and probably that is why it remained in my hands so long. I always acted without considering my personal advantage,

exposed myself to the greatest dangers when it was necessary to prevent or reduce exposure of the people to evil and never trumpeted
about my sacrifices so I would be rewarded.

In this type of political testament to his son, Garašanin intimated that
Ristić and Blaznavac especially had utilized intrigue to achieve power, considered their personal interests first, and boasted of imaginary sacrifices
to obtain reward and applause. He continued:

I have never hindered eager and honorable statesmen from utilizing
their great talents in behalf of the people; rather, I have aided and
encouraged them. I have scorned low character and have always
worked conscientiously and without vengeance, without yielding
to intrigues. I can substantiate this brief statement with known
facts.[38]

Those familiar with Garašanin's career, concludes a leading Yugoslav
scholar, Grgur Jakšić, will confirm the accuracy of this statement.[39]

Nonetheless, at the Assembly meeting of October 10, 1868, convened
by the Regency, Ilija and Svetozar Garašanin were accused publicly of
complicity in Mihailo's murder; they were given no opportunity to reply
or confront their accusers. A Kragujevac deputy, Antonije Protić, accused
Ilija Garašanin of indirect responsibility for the murder because that day
he had rejected the Prince's invitation to accompany him to Košutnjak,
allegedly declaring he would not go there because "there are wild animals
in Košutnjak." Then he had hastened to Belgrade in order to seize power.
Protić and a deputy from Valjevo, Nenad Mihailović, criticized Svetozar
for not attempting to defend the Prince. Deputies Antonije Pantić and
Dragutin Riznić from Janička asserted that Ilija Garašanin was suspect in
the murder, had refused to consult with the Prince that day, and had intrigued to prepare the Prince's downfall. Deputy Kasija Stojsić, supporting
these allegations, demanded an investigation. In the meantime, he declared,
Ilija Garašanin's pension should be suspended! The chairman then announced a committee would investigate these charges and report its findings to the Assembly.[40]

However, no such report was ever submitted, suggesting strongly that
even their enemies could find nothing to incriminate the Garašanins. During

the Assembly cession a cabinet minister absolved Hristić and Barlovac of all blame but failed to defend the Garašanins. Regent Jovan Ristić later confirmed that these attacks in the Assembly had been prepared in advance but denied knowing their instigators. The regents and ministers, Ristić admitted, had known that the accusations would be made on October 10th, claiming that he had tried in vain to prevent them. The entire sordid affair, he added, had been undertaken by several deputies seeking to defame former Interior Minister Hristić who indeed had many enemies.[41]

Garašanin reacted bitterly to these unfounded accusations. The current powerholders, he wrote Marinović, regarded the past as a misfortune which they could blacken at will whereas actually it had proved a basis for progress. The hue and cry in the Assembly, he felt, could not destroy his prestige among the Serbian people since his deeds would overcome such calumny.[42] Garašanin characterized the charges contained in the Assembly's published records as "pure nonsense." Incensed that Interior Minister Radivoje Milojković had defended Hristić and Barlovac but not him, he retorted that the Assembly had been a farce where the innocent were defamed with impunity.[43] He wrote one of the regents, probably Blaznavac, that he was remaining silent to prevent further deterioration of the already bad situation in Serbia. Ignoring insults in brochures and newspapers, he could not overlook the Assembly's ridiculous assertions that he had sought to seize power after Mihailo's assassination.[44]

War Minister Blaznavac's jealous fear of Garašanin's prestige had been revealed in his move on June 12, 1868 to exclude him from consideration as a regent by the Great Assembly. The official newspaper, *Srpske novine,* announced that only ministers, Council members aand members of cassation and appellate courts were eligible to become regents.[45] Despite this prohibition, Garašanin received many votes for that post at the Great Assembly, even though it convened June 20th in Topčider in the presence of 1,600 troops loyal to the War Minister.[46]

There was widespread support inside Serbia and abroad for a Garašanin-Marinović regency. Consul Scovasso of Italy favored that combination, reported Austrian Consul Kallay June 13th, because he considered Garašanin the ablest statesman in Serbia and both were true patriots who would guard Serbia's interests. A week later Kallay reiterated that many Serbs still desired such a regency but that Garašanin had renounced any efforts in his behalf and would serve only if drafted by the Great Assembly. By

June 24th Kallay reported that prospects of a Garašanin-Marinović regency were dwindling as Blaznavac consolidated his position.[47] Count Andrássy, writing Kallay June 28th, regretted that Garašanin would not become a regent. Garašanin was not so Russophile, added Andrássy, that one could not work with him.[48] The Magyar leader had asked Orešković: "How is it that you have left out Garašanin? He is a very intelligent and skilled person." Orešković replied: "Against Garašanin himself they would not have had objections, but in political matters he lets himself be led by Marinović (sic!) who is his close friend and mentor. Marinović is strongly inclined towards Russia, and since his influence over Garašanin cannot be eliminated, we must leave Garašanin out also." That explanation seems rather far-fetched. Henceforth when asked about a possible role for Garašanin, Orešković would declare: "He is a man of the old school who would find it difficult to adjust to the more liberal principles represented by Blaznavac and Ristić."[49]

During the crucial period from the Regency's formation therefore, Garašanin had abstained from political agitiation in his and Marinović's behalf and indicated a willingness to support new leaders. Already on June 6th he had written Milutin predicting that Blaznavac and Ristić would be named regents. "I won't refuse them my support if they follow in all ways the path which Prince Mihailo pointed out. Otherwise, if they follow another path, I won't hamper or interfere, but neither will I support policies I do not agree with." However, he did predict political troubles during the four years of Prince Milan's minority.[50] On June 16th he noted that there were honorable men in the government, but they were cautious and unenergetic. Able leaders who could rise above customary petty partisanship had to be found if Serbia was to progress. Prince Mihailo had left them firm internal foundations and a successful foreign policy. Ristić and Blaznavac, he wrote, were selfish; he feared their timidity, disunity and lack of statesmanship.[51] In meetings with Blaznavac, he made it clear that he opposed the liberal reforms the regents advocated. Nonetheless, Blaznavac had declared, reported Kallay July 16th, they would implement these over objections by Garašanin, Marinović, Cukić and Nikola Hristić. Meanwhile Consuls Shishkin and Scovasso, both Garašanin partisans, allegedly were spreading rumors of widespread dissatisfaction with the Regency.[52]

From the beginning the regents, especially Blaznavac, acted hostilely toward Garašanin and began persecuting him. Instead of thanking the former premier for preventing disorder after Mihailo's assassination, he did everything possible to prevent Garašanin's return to any influential position.[53] Worried and insecure, the regents sought to make his life as miserable as possible, subjecting him to continual police surveillance and periodic harassment. In July 1868 Garašanin had withdrawn permanently to Grocka believing it unlikely that the political situation in Serbia would change soon or that he would ever be recalled to state service. Some dissatisfaction with the way conditions in Serbia were evolving is noticeable in a letter to Mondain. He and his family were residing in a:

> small place distant from the storms of Belgrade intrigue, and I will spend my time calmly, since here one still feels the remnants of the rule of our unforgettable Prince Mihailo. Belgrade has become a kind of new Serbia in which we are not at home. If you ask me: is that new Serbia better or worse than the old one which you know, I truly could not answer you![54]

He would remain in this semi-exile until his death.

Partly to undercut Garašanin's prestige and Russian influence in Serbia, the Regency sponsored a series of liberal reforms. While not defending the old order unconditionally nor claiming that these liberal proposals were necessarily undesirable, Garašanin deplored reforms and freedoms which he believed were premature and ill-suited to a largely illiterate populace. To him the regents resembled sons who had inherited great wealth without knowing how to use it constructively.[55] Seeking a quick popularity they could not achieve by constructive methods, they promised instead more and more political freedoms. Prince Mihailo, on the other hand, had insisted that solid foundations must be built before such freedoms could be granted.[56] Garašanin wrote Mondain a bit later that he could not welcome to Serbia foreign principles based more on theory than reality and inappropriate for its people.[57] Excessive preoccupation with liberal ideas "which our stomach cannot digest" meant neglecting more important national tasks such as expanding the country's frontiers.[58]

Thus Garašanin considered the new constitution proposed by the Regency to be premature and the institutions it instituted unsuitable for a peasant country. "We will have a full package of ministerial responsibility, press freedom, and freedom of assembly—in short all that exists anywhere in Europe. Whether we can utilize all this properly, I will leave up to the results to reveal."[59] The Constitution of 1869, he wrote his friend after its adoption, had inspired many hopes which probably could not be fulfilled, and Mihailo's national goals had been abandoned or forgotten. Lofty European principles such as ministerial responsibility and press freedom were a farce; in Belgrade "party politics is being conducted incessantly for selfish purposes and with confused ideas." No honorable person could live there among its politicians.[60]

Garašanin adhered to this starkly conservative viewpoint to the end. Serbian political parties under the new constitution, he wrote in 1874, were based on blatant egoism and lacked any real principles. For this the regents with their nepotism and selfishness were largely to blame, setting as they did a woeful example to officials.[61] What did vaunted press freedom mean, wondered Garašanin, when the police prevented publication of whatever the authorities disapproved? Whoever writes the truth, he declared, should avoid punishment even if he criticizes the regime. Formerly censorship had been implemented by educated officials, but under the Regency it was enforced by the prefect of police, "and this is what is called here freedom of the press."[62] The assembly established by the new constitution would long remain "a fashionable parade" dependent upon the executive. Progress in Serbia in the future, he predicted, would still depend on the prince and his advisers.[63]

Under a facade of liberalism, the Regency represented concealed personal rule. The Interior Ministry summed up that regime's policy succinctly: "Whoever is with us, we will do all we can for. Whoever is neutral can expect nothing from us. Whoever is against us, we will cut off his head."[64] The self-centered Ristić, noted Consul Kallay, filled his government with second-rate people and his relatives. Kallay regarded Garašanin as a notable exception to the predominance of personal interests among Serbian politicians.[65] Under the Regency, lamented Garašanin, Prince Mihailo's foreign policy had been jettisoned and Serbia's prestige in neighboring Slav lands was eroding:

> To go wholly counter to the ideas and plans of Prince Mihailo shows no sincerity toward the people. . . . One must regret that his plans are rejected so brazenly since they cost us great effort and material sacrifice. I would say that none of our alliances exist any longer and

that by our renunciation we have ruined the [national] cause for
a long time precisely when such friends are most needed.[66]

Regent Blaznavac in particular suspected Russia of plotting his overthrow and was hostile toward Consul Shishkin, Garašanin's friend. Serbia,
Blaznavac told Prussian Consul Rosen, needed to round out its domains in
order to assure her peaceful progress and hitherto only Russia had aided her
in this. Thus thankfulness toward Russia was "inextinguishably implanted
in every Serbian heart." In the future also Blaznavac expected Russia's
support, but currently St. Petersburg was being influenced negatively by
Consul Shishkin's "false and hostile" reports and thus had rebuffed the
Regency's overtures. Shishkin, claimed Blaznavac, wanted Garašanin to
rule, forgetting that the Regency had been chosen by a Great Assembly,
that is by the Serbian people (under the War Minister's guns, he should
have added!). The Regent blamed Serbia's external problems and growing
isolation on Russian hostility. However, only the Regency and a few individuals viewed Russia that way, reported Rosen.[67]

Blaznavac and Ristić, the two regents, were Garašanin's personal and
political enemies who persisted, despite all his disclaimers and lack of political activity, in considering him a dangerous rival. To be sure Consul
Shishkin conferred frequently with the ex-premier and urged him repeatedly, but vainly, to oppose the Regency actively.[68] The regents instigated and approved constant efforts to discredit and ruin Garašanin.
Schooled themselves in intrigue, unscrupulous and powerseeking, they
could not imagine that a politician out of power would not seek a high
post, then exploit it for his own benefit, as they did. Garašanin knew they
feared him and were jealous of his reputation; he tried in vain to convince
them that henceforth he would shun the hurly-burly of Serbian politics.
Ilija had written to his son, Milutin, July 27, 1868: "I have not the least
intention ever to interefere further in state affairs of which I am weary."[69]
He merely wanted the current powerholders to leave him alone in peaceful
retirement. He had done his best; let the regents do likewise, and each
could answer for his own policies.[70] Some accused Garašanin of avoiding
the regents during visits to Belgrade, but when he met with Blaznavac in
1871, both regents promptly interpreted this as an intrigue to prepare his
return to power. "How long will these people conceal their wickedness
from others?" wondered Garašanin. "Can anyone be so foolish as to believe

that I would ever want to be a minister again? "[71] Blaznavac urged him to proclaim publicly his support of Milan Obrenović and the *status quo*. He should come more often to Belgrade, and place a son in state service and thus prove his loyalty to the current regime. Rejecting all this as insincere, Garašanin asserted that such behavior would merely make him subservient to a government he opposed and disapproved of.[72]

To Garašanin's sorrow, the Regency sought to compromise his sons in order to wound him. Soon after its formation Svetozar Garašanin, amidst intimations that he had failed to defend Prince Mihailo, resigned his army commission. Regent Blaznavac asserted that Svetozar had deliberately fallen before being wounded during Mihailo's assassination thus casting a black stain upon the Serbian army.[73] Although this charge remained wholly unsubstantiated, Svetozar had virtually been drummed out of military service. Indignant at this, Ilija, then dissuaded Milutin, who soon thereafter returned to Serbia following competion of military studies in Paris, from entering military service under the Regency. When Assembly delegates in 1870 wondered why neither of his sons were serving the state, Garašanin doubted whether "good sons could serve when their father is exposed to various public insults."

> A strange idea of honor! No matter how far perversion has proceeded here, I will see to it that my sons are preserved from it. It will be better for them to remain ordinary farmers rather than in a position of power and experience their father's fate. . . .[74]

Having his sons remain in private life, he wrote Mondain, would be preferable to increasing the number of useless officers. Besides, "my two friends [Blaznavac and Ristić] . . . could compromise my second son Milutin as they did Svetozar."[75]

To provide employment for his sons, who soon joined him at Grocka, Ilija Garašanin decided to have a small steam-powered flour mill constructed on his property near the Danube. He had pondered this move for some time since it meant borrowing a considerable sum of money, but finally had resolved to go ahead. Milutin assumed the main burden of supervising construction with Ilija assisting him. Begun in April 1869, the mill was completed in March 1870.[76] Nearby was built a five room house for his sons while the parents remained temporarily in the small rented house. Later, when he and Sofia moved in with their sons, they became in Garašanin's words, "a mill family."[77] Helping his sons supervise work at the mill, Ilija felt he did not understand its operations very well, but he explained to Marinović: "My mill will be used by nearby farmers to grind their grain; revenue from it will comprise my entire income . . . ."[78]

Even in rural Grocka Garašanin was not permitted to lead an unhindered life of retirement As long as Prince Mihailo lived, his foes limited their actions to secret slander and innuendo. After the Regency took over, Interior Minister Milojković, because of Garašanin's presence there, removed Grocka's police officials and transferred them elsewhere since he believed they were loyal to their ex-chief. Garašanin wrote Marinović:

My district chief [Mateja Radović] is being removed and surely you can guess why. Keep calm, this won't upset or damage me. Grocka is the calmest place for me, no intrigues can touch me here . . . since I cannot talk with anyone for which they can criticize me. I spend most of my time in minor tasks or alone, and that suits me best.[79]

Thereafter the Interior Ministry watched his activities closely, learning through its agents of his every movement and visitor. At Grocka, Garašanin lived virtually under guard, wrote Kosta Magazinović, former Serbian envoy to Bucharest. When he came to visit Ilije, he encountered a guard with a cocked pistol.[80] Rumors spread in Belgrade that Garašanin, plotting a political comebtack, was holding secret meetings, "playing politics in his mill." This amazed Garašanin who had no intention of seeking anyone's position.[81]

Unfounded or fabricated accusations repeatedly were made against him. Early in 1870 the Kragujevac district chief wrote the Interior Minister citing local reports that Garašanin was plotting "to kill Blaznavac and perhaps the Prince [Milan] too." Instructed to investigate this thoroughly, the district chief found it to be malicious gossip.[82] Later, after the Regency had ended, a policeman watching a house where Garašanin was conferring with Interior Minister Aćim Ćumić, explained he was supposed to watch suspicious persons; four years earlier he had been told that Garašanin was under suspicion. Promptly apologizing to Garašanin, Ćumić declared this had occurred without his knowledge and would be stopped. Garašanin should consider it merely "a remnant of the spirit of the former regime [Regency] . . . ."[83]

The Regency also sought to ruin him financially and largely succeeded. First, the authorities prohibited sales to him of dry wood for his mill.[84] Through Marinović's intercession with the authorities, that unfair measure was rescinded. Since the mill's current income was insufficient to pay off debts incurred in construction and operating expenses, in October 1872 the Garašanins purchased 200,000 kilograms (440,000 pounds) of corn and grain, intending to grind it into flour and sell it to bakers and small shopkeepers in Belgrade and the interior. In December the Belgrade police prohibited sale of the flour claiming it was spoiled. Viewing this as a deliberate attempt to bankrupt him, Garašanin wrote Marinović that the Regency might ruin him financially but could not destroy him morally.[85]

In Belgrade and Smederevo people, protesting this prohibition, claimed the flour was excellent and inexpensive. After testing it, the police found that it made excellent bread. The regents, Interior Minister Milojković, and the Belgrade commandant, Garašanin believed, were chiefly responsible for this harassment. Private property in Serbia, Garašanin wrote Milutin, must be protected against such abuses by the authorities.[86]

Facing unpleasantness and hostility in Belgrade, Garašanin rarely went there though it was nearby and he had still many friends there. The realization he would be under close police surveillance also discouraged trips to the capital. Though he did not hate Belgrade, "it is a place full of intrigue and slander."[87] When Garašanin failed to go there in 1872 to celebrate Prince Milan's majority, the regents accused him of disloyalty to the Obrenović dynasty. The sad events of the past four years had induced him to remain in Grocka, he responded. Not wishing to be accused of coming to Belgrade to seize someone's position, Garašanin declared he would pay his respects to Prince Milan later. Indeed, the Prince received him in Belgrade February 6, 1874.[88]

Never enjoying robust health, Garašanin during his lengthy and strenuous state service was rarely free from illness. Numerous incurable ailments kept him bedridden or at least indoors for several months every year. Nonetheless, he nearly always remained cheerful, joked often about his afflictions, and did not let them distract him long from state business. Compensating for his delicate physiquie was a healthy spirit and an indomitable will. Throughout life he suffered periodically from eczema over his entire body, diarrhea, gout, hemorhoids, gallstones, asthma, frequent and severe dizziness, and various fevers. Of all these the eczema was the most severe and unbearable, appearing sometimes at isolated spots, sometimes all over his body. Beginning during his twenties, the eczema left him briefly during his emigration in Constantinople in 1841-42, but recurred when he returned to Belgrade. Despite repeated treatments in Serbia and abroad with baths, up to several hours long, and medication, it persisted sometimes for years on end, at others appearing in spring and fall. Sometimes Garašanin managed to continue fairly normal activity, but often he would have to spend long periods in bed. For weeks the large pox would prevent him from writing or wearing glasses. Realizing that the disease, inherited from his mother, was incurable, he knew he just had to bear it.[89]

Beginning in 1849 Garašanin suffered from diarrhoea and spent seven weeks in bed that fall.[90] He treated it at various baths, ate yogurt and drank Karlsbad water but suffered from it periodically the rest of his life. In 1854 he suffered such severe gout that he could neither dress nor wear shoes; in 1871 gout combined with severe stomach cramps confined him to bed. Dizziness overtook him in 1853, while severe fevers troubled him in Paris in 1857 and later at Grocka. Fighting these numerous ailments manfully, Garašanin, once he had recovered, tended to ignore his health and act as if he were wholly well. "Because to live by taking precautions means for me not living but acting as if it were the beginning of death. Why do that prematurely?"[91]

From 1870 onwards Garašanin became ill ever more frequently, leaving him increasingly debilitated and unable to fight back. He and his wife, he wrote Mondain in November 1871, "have grown rather old and weak, more than our years would suggest." During the winter of 1872-1873 he still hunted periodically but noted: "The years are taking away more and more of the old strength in my legs." In early morning he would go out alone or with his sons, returning after dark. Awaiting supper, he would often be lectured sharply by Sofia for being overtired, mudspattered and for ruining his clothes. "I always readily admitted my mistakes to my wife, so we never quarrel no matter how many times I repeat the same error." Wandering through streams until his dogs flushed out hare or fox, he would then have one of his sons barbecue some meat, then continued hunting until sundown.[92] Garašanin also derived great pleasure from visits by old friends such as Marinović or Mondain to Grocka, generally in autumn. Abandoning his daily routine, he would devote full time to his guests, showing them around the estate and telling them all about life there.[93]

"Old age is a hospital in which various illnesses gather," wrote Ljubomir Nenadović in *Šumadija*. From early spring 1873 until his death over a year later Garašanin was ill almost constantly and could no longer enjoy either tobacco or coffee, two lifelong pleasures to which he was hopelessly addicted. In September he wrote Milutin from Grocka: "I am ailing like an old man of eighty-five who does not think of recovery."[94] When his eczema returned, Garašanin went to Belgrade, and severe winter weather prevented him returning to spend Christmas with his family at Grocka. Until February 1874, he remained in the capital, rarely able to go out. He was visited by M. Milićević, a well-known Serbian writer:

> I returned to see old Garašanin. He is ill. He remains the only representative of . . . a time which has already passed, but a marvelously intelligent person. He judges things soundly, looks at things correctly, and speaks a direct and beautiful Serbian which is a joy to hear.[95]

Returning finally to Grocka for the last time, he wrote Mondain about his family, the mill, Marinović's relations with Prince Milan, and railway construction in Serbia. To the very end he retained a vital and consuming interest in public affairs.[96] Finally, at 3 A.M. on June 10, 1874 Garašanin died peacefully at Grocka.

A court ball had been scheduled for the very day of Garašanin's death. Premier Marinović tried to have it postponed, but the court and Prince Milan's entourage ignored his entreaties. When the ball was held anyway, there was much indignation and protests at the Belgrade market. On June 11th the official newspaper, *Srpske novine,* carried a full report of the glittering ball which had ended only at 5 A.M. Beneath that article was a brief account of Garašanin's death. In the procession to the cathedral church in Belgrade, noted that paper, the Metropolitan and many priests were present.[97] The burial ceremony revealed deep public respect for Garašanin, noted *Vidovdan.* Numerous persons of all classes and professions had gathered to honor him in a steady rain, including many high dignitaries. During the funeral all markets, cafés and bars were closed in streets through which the procession passed. The diplomatic corps turned out, and Prince Milan was represented by an adjutant. To general amazement, no clergyman was found to deliver the eulogy at his bier. The corpse was placed in a carriage and borne to Grocka for burial in the family plot.[98] "The Serbian people," Prince Julija wrote Sofia Garašanin, "has lost in Garašanin a great patriot and man of great ability." In Grocka almost everyone came out to honor him, and its most distinguished citizens and farmers took turns carrying his coffin. "This is the way great men are honored . . . ,"[99] concluded *Vidovdan*.

NOTES

1. Garašanin to Marinović, November 7, 1867, *Pisma,* II, 212.
2. IG 1635, Garašanin to Mondain, November 12.
3. Garašanin to Marinović, December 15, *Pisma,* II, 245. People in Serbia and abroad, his friend, Kosta Magazinović, learned, were still talking about Garašanin's retirement. IG 1700, Unknown to K. Magazinović in Vienna, January 1/13, 1868.
4. Garašanin to Marinović, December 6, 1867, *Pisma,* II, 213.
5. IG 1686, Garašanin to Mondain, February 15/27, 1868.
6. Piroćanac, *Knez Mihailo,* pp. 90-91 and *Završna reč,* pp. 10-11. This princely hunt had been announced in the official newspaper, *Srpske novine,* No. 13, 1868.
7. A. Orešković, *Malo više svetlosti,* p. 63.
8. Piroćanac, *Knez Mihailo,* p. 91.
9. Milutin Garašanin, *Jedno Namesnikovanje* (Belgrade, 1900).
10. Piroćanac, *Knez Mihailo,* pp. 90 ff.; A. Orešković, "Malo odgovora," *Dnevni list,* October 25, 1895, No. 233.
11. J. Ristić, *Spolijašnji odnošaji,* II.
12. Archiv SANU, 7889, Memoari Crnobarca, entries of January 5 and 17, 1868.
13. AII Ristić XI/7, Ignat'ev to Mihailo, March 28, 1868, copy; Ristić, *Poslednja godina,* p. 57; Jakšić and Vučković, *Spoljna,* p. 442, citing Ignat'ev to Mihailo, March 26, 1868.
14. Von Reiswitz, pp. 121 ff. Reiswitz viewed Mihailo's removal of Garašanin as an act of self-defense against Russian Panslavism and in order

to preserve Serbia's independence. Mihailo's death therefore was not much regretted in St. Petersburg, he affirms.

15. Piroćanać, *Knez Mihailo*, pp. 86 ff.

16. Garašanin is alluding to his hunt with Prince Mihailo on January 22, 1868, which ended up at Grocka. Garašanin met also with Consul Skovaso, Milan Piroćanac, Kosta Ćukić and several Council members.

17. Garašanin to Marinović, February 2, 1868, *Pisma*, II, 218-219.

18. IG 1683, "Moji spomeni" (1868), also in Vučković, *Politička*, pp. 322-324.

19. Orešković in *Malo više svetlosti* (p. 63) claims that their conference was held on May 24 while Piroćanac in *Knez Mihailo* (pp. 90-91) affirms it was on May 27th, two days before the murder.

20. Ibid., pp. 90-91.

21. IG 1690, Ilija to Milutin Garašanin, June 6, 1868, No. 1.

22. Stranjaković, *Mihailo i Julija,* pp. 160-163; D. Marinković, *Uspomene i doživljaji,* pp. 195-198; IG 1690, Ilija to Milutin Garašanin, June 6, 10, and 17, 1868.

23. IG 1688, Garašanin to Magazinović, June 21.

24. *Dnevnik Kalaja,* p. 29, entry of June 10, 1868.

25. Mileva Alimpić, *Život i rad generala Ranke Alimpića* (Belgrade, 1892), p. 419.

26. Garašanin to Marinović, June 14, 1868, *Pisma,* II, 223; IG 1690, Ilija to Milutin Garašanin, June 6 and 17; IG 1686, August 16.

27. IG 1690, Ilija to Milutin Garašanin, June 6, No. 1.

28. IG 1688, Garašanin to Magazinović, June 21. The retired cabinet minister, N. S., later heard Garašanin saying: "We lost everything when we lost him [Mihailo].! Today we would have Bosnia and Hercegovina and certainly Old Serbia." "Knez Mihailo . . . iz uspomena Ilija Garašanina," *Depeša,* No. 1, January 1, 1911.

29. IG 1690, Ilija to Milutin Garašanin, June 19.

30. Ferdo Šišić, "Knez Mihailo i Bugari," *Politika,* August 8, 1937, p. 6.

31. D. Marinković, *Uspomene,* pp. 204-206; S. Jovanović, *Druga vlada,* pp. 264-272.

32. IG 1686, Garašanin to Mondain, August 16, 1868.

33. *Celokupna dela Svetozara Markovića,* sv. 7 (Belgrade, 1893), p. 101.

34.   Piroćanac, *Naša završna reč*, p. 17.

35.   IG 1690, Ilija to Milutin Garašanin, June 6, 1868. He repeated
this refrain in his letter of June 10th to his son.

36.   IG 1690, ibid. to ibid., June 28.

37.   Milutin Garašanin, "Drugi odskok," and "Poslednji odskok,"
Videlo, April 17 and 24, 1894.

38.   IG 1690, Ilija to Milutin Garašanin, June 6, 1868, No. 1.

39.   G. Jakšić, "Tragičan svršetak Kneza Mihaila," *Politika*, January
6-9, 1937.

40.   *Protokol Narodne Skupštine držane u Kragujevcu* (Belgrade,
1870), pp. 189-190; IG 1684, "Beleška Garašanina (1870?): O ubistvu
Kneza Mihaila i pokušaji prevratnika da preuzmu vlast u Srbiji." Nikola
Hristić and Mihailo Barlovac, former Belgrade commandant, were also accused of knowing about the murder plot. There are slight discrepancies
between the Assembly's official record and Garašanin's version. Thus in
the former, Riznić is described as a deputy from Kragujevac; in the latter
as from Janička. The Garašanin memorandum is dated in his papers as
1868 but clearly could not have been written prior to 1870 because of its
references to these accusations.

41.   J. Ristić to F. Hristić, November 17, 1870 in *Pisma Jovana Ristića Filipu Hristiću* (Belgrade, 1931), p. 8. Ristić added that these attacks
"on members of the previous government and on Garašanin are most inconvenient for us." He added that Marinović, whose salary had been reduced, regarded this as a personal affront.

42.   Garašanin to Marinović, October 23, 1870, *Pisma*, II, 276.

43.   Ibid., November 30, II, 280-282.

44.   IG 1700, Garašanin to a Regent, unfinished draft, no date.

45.   Stranjaković, "Kako je postalo namesništvo 1868 g.," *Pravda*
(Belgrade), January 6-9, 1939.

46.   Alimpić, *Život i rad*, pp. 423-424.

47.   *Dnevnik Kalaja*, pp. 35-36, 42, entries of June 13, 20, and 24,
1868.

48.   Ibid., p. 667.

49.   Orešković's memorandum to the Regency, July 16/28, 1868, in
Vučković, *Politička*, No. 198, p. 370. Much later however, Orešković
sounded a different theme. Why, he asked, did Serbia after Mihailo fall
backward in every respect? How could it be avoided, he responded, with

leaders like Alimpije Vasiljević (Liberal leader and professor at the Belgrade Lycée) who called Prince Mihailo a Turkish policeman (*pandur*) and Garašanin a murderer? Ristić then had declined to work with Serbian patriots like Garašanin and Serbia had become isolated and discredited as the center of the South Slavs. "Malo odgovora," *Dnevnik list,* October 25, 1895, No. 233.

50. IG 1690, Ilija to Milutin Garašanin, June 6, 1868, No. 2.

51. Ibid., June 16, No. 5.

52. *Dnevnik Kalaja,* pp. 53, 55-57, entries of July 11 and 16.

53. G. Jakšić, "Jedan sukob," *Arhiv za pravne,* p. 139.

54. IG 1686, Garašanin to Mondain, November 29, 1868, from Grocka. In June 1868 Kallay reported that Garašanin remained "doubtless the cleverest and most experienced Serbian statesman. He has been living quietly on his estate since his sudden removal. . . . Garašanin still enjoys great popularity in the entire country." Since his removal, added Kallay, the Serbian government had been going downhill with little being accomplished. *Dnevnik Kalaja,* p. 35.

55. Garašanin to Marinović, December 22, 1868, *Pisma,* II, 237-238.

56. IG 1686, Garašanin to Mondain, August 14. He concluded his letter: "May God protect Serbia!"

57. IG 1686, ibid., November 20.

58. IG, Garašanin draft, no date.

59. IG 1686, Garašanin to Mondain, November 29.

60. IG 1715, ibid., April 24, 1870.

61. IG 1744, ibid., March 2, 1874. Nikola Krstić likewise deplored the nepotism prevalent under the Regency. Filip Hristić, Ristić's nephew, became Serbia's envoy in Constantinople, and Interior Minister R. Milojković was also related to Ristić. Arhiv SANU, No. 7199, N. Krstić, "Javan Život," August 30, 1870.

62. IG 1728, Garašanin to Mondain, January 29, 1872.

63. IG 1744, ibid., March 3, 1874.

64. Stranjaković, "Ilija Garašanin," pp. 353-354.

65. *Dnevnik Kalaja,* April 8, 1873. Franjo Zah, director of the Military Academy, was highly critical of Blaznavac for his excessive ambition, vanity and corruption: "The whole system of Mr. Blaznavac is swindle, deceit and lies." Zah to Gabler, November 10, 1872.

66. Garašanin to Marinović, December 22, 1868, *Pisma,* II, 237-238.

67. Von Reiswitz, pp. 146-147, 151, 173.

68. *Dnevnik Kalaja,* June 24, 1873, p. 543.

69. IG 1690, Ilija to Milutin Garašanin, July 27, 1868.

70. IG, Garašanin to Piroćanac, draft, no date (1868?).

71. Garašanin to Marinović, April 29, 1871, *Pisma,* II, 284.

72. IG 1704, Garašanin to Blaznavac, drafts (1870).

73. Garašanin to Marinović, September 16, 1868, *Pisma,* II, 227. However, the trial of the assassins produced not a shred of evidence against Svetozar Garašanin.

74. Ibid. to ibid., October 23, 1870, *Pisma,* II, 277.

75. IG 1739, Garašanin to Mondain, January 29, 1873.

76. Garašanin to Marinović, November 12 and December 24, 1869, *Pisma,* II, 259-262; IG 1715, Garašanin to Mondain, April 24, 1870.

77. IG 1715, ibid. to ibid.

78. Garašanin to Marinović, April 1, 1869, *Pisma,* II, 243-244; August 27, 1873, II, 333.

79. Ibid. to ibid., September 16, 1868, *Pisma,* II, 225.

80. Arhiv SANU, No. 9288, Memoari K. Magazinovića.

81. Garašanin to Marinović, December 15, 1867, *Pisma,* II, 216.

82. IG 1721, Atanacković to Interior Minister (Milojković) and his reply, February 6 and 7, 1870.

83. A. Ćumić to Garašanin, no date (1873-74), cited in Stranjaković, "Ilija," pp. 356-357.

84. Garašanin to Marinović, November 5, 1871, *Pisma,* II, 289-290.

85. IG, Ilija to Milutin Garašanin, October 26, 1872; Ilija to Svetozar Garašanin, December 20; Garašanin to Marinović, December 21, *Pisma,* II, 310-312.

86. Ibid. to ibid., February 20, 1873, *Pisma,* II, 316; IG 1749, Garašanin to Milutin Garašanin, February 8, 1874.

87. IG 1739, Garašanin to Mondain, January 29, 1873.

88. Garašanin to Marinović, August 16, 1872, *Pisma,* II, 304; IG 1745, Tihomir Nikolić to Garašanin, February 5, 1874.

89. Dr. Lindenmaier, "Opisanje bolesti Ilije Garašanina," Belgrade, February 12, 1852; Garašanin to Marinović, November 9, 1870, *Pisma,* II, 278-280.

90. Garašanin to Knićanin, November 25, 1849, cited in Stranjaković, "Ilija," p. 366.

91. Ibid., p. 367.
92. IG 1739, Garašanin to Mondain, January 29, 1873.
93. Stranjaković, "Ilija," pp. 351-352.
94. IG 17? ? , Ilija to Milutin Garašanin, September 12, 1873.
95. Arhiv SANU, No. 9327, Dnevnik Milićevića, February 4, 1874.
96. IG 1744, Garašanin to Mondain, March 2, 1874.
97. Kosta Hristić, *Zapisi starog Beogradjanina,* p. 460; *Srpske novine,*
June 11, 1874, No. 128, p. 1.
98. *Vidovdan* (Belgrade), June 12, 1874, No. 115, p. 1, "Beogradski
novosti," Svetozar Garašanin died in 1886 and was buried with his father,
Ilija, in the yard of Paliluske Church in Belgrade. Milićević, *Pomenik,*
p. 98.
99. *Vidovdan,* June 15, No. 117, p. 2, "Beogradske novosti."

CHAPTER XXI

GARAŠANIN AND HISTORY

"By his educational preparation, learning, broad cultural background and calling as a ruler Prince Mihailo stood above Garašanin, but by his wisdom, knowledge, feeling for national instincts and understanding of our people Garašanin stood above Prince Mihailo."

D. Stranjaković, "Ilija Garašanin," p. 416

"The time will come, if it has not arrived already, when everyone will see with regret the great void which [Garašanin] has left behind him. . . . His good character and great intelligence placed him so far above all his compatriots without exception."

H. Mondain to Svetozar Garašanin, December 6, 1874.

Where does Ilija Garašanin deserve to rank in Serbian and Balkan history? Was he Serbia's Bismarck in achievement as well as in aims and aspirations? Certainly, few nineteenth century European statesmen were so well thought of by their contemporaries or fondly remembered by their descendants and countrymen. In domestic affairs Garašanin scored significant achievements: by creating and consolidating Serbia's police, army and bureaucracy, setting with his own example the highest standard of integrity

400

and devotion to duty for its officials, he established the discipline and order required for the erection of a modern Serbian state. In foreign and national affairs, his innovative, far-reaching ideas and plans, influenced strongly by Polish and Czech émigrés, led eventually in 1918 to the creation of a Yugoslavia dominated by his beloved Serbia with Belgrade as its political and intellectual center. Garašanin did much to enhance Serbia's prestige and influence in the South Slav world and in Europe. His consistent and lofty purpose made Serbia a serious factor in Balkan and European power politics.

Unlike Bismarck and Cavour, Ilija Garašanin did not live to see his aim of national unity under Serbia's leadership realized, yet he made a clearer and more comprehensive plan for it than either of his European counterparts. Serving Prince Mihailo with loyalty and devotion, he found in him, as Bismarck did in William I and Cavour in Victor Emanuel II, a ruler sharing many of his aims and willing to grant him wide latitude to implement them. However, Garašanin, unlike the Prussian and Piedmontese statesmen, was removed from office by his prince before he could launch a decisive drive to achieve liberation and unity for Serbs and South Slavs. In retrospect that seems fortunate since Serbia in 1867 was too weak to achieve his goals without major Russian aid, yet Russia could not then provide significant military and political support such as France had given Piedmont-Sardinia in 1859. Therefore Garašanin and Mihailo failed to achieve any territorial increase for a Serbia which remained too small and feeble to stand fully on her own. Their major accomplishment instead, with the aid of Jovan Ristić's diplomatic skill, was to remove Turkish fortresses and garrisons from Serbian soil, an essential prelude to more ambitious undertakings. Nonetheless, the foundations for the Serbian national movement laid by Garašanin and Mihailo eventually proved as sound as those built by Bismarck and Cavour.

It was rare indeed, notes Stranjaković, to find a Serbian leader so universally respected by his contemporaries, both Serbian and foreign. Their assessments of his intellectual, moral and spiritual qualities were almost unanimously favorable. Even his political opponents were often compelled, willy-nilly, to recognize his unselfishness, firmness, political acumen, diligence, and integrity.[1]

Serbian newspaper obituaries of Garašanin generally support this contention. Though the official *Srpske novine* delcared cautiously that only history could judge Garašanin's public activity properly, it praised his "openness, great energy in official work, deep love of country, conscientiousness, and good will in promoting the national cause."[2] The leading Conservative organ in Serbia, *Vidovdan,* was less restrained:

> With the death last night of Ilija Garašanin, Serbia has lost a man who served her welfare and dignity. Our young, stormy but not insignificant history has thrust to the surface several capable and noble statesmen; among them Garašanin occupies first place in several respects. First and foremost, he was a pure and great patriot. . . . Many attribute such descriptions to themselves, but few really deserve them. . . . As a statesmen he was always distinguished by caution, sobriety and solidity. He scorned the dubious means by which . . . people [in Serbia] have often acquired an easy popularity.

In power he pursued what he viewed as Serbia's national interests, sacrificing unhesitatingly in the process an ephemeral personal popularity.

Whoever writes future Serbian histories, continued *Vidovdan,* cannot overlook Garašanin's role. Especially in internal administration will long persist many traces of his hard, pioneering work. The building of roads, organizing a postal service, army and police force, and developing a competent officialdom reflect his industrious and constructive spirit. His contributions to realizing Serbia's national mission were equally significant if not as immediately obvious. His final years were unhappy coinciding as they did with the disintegration of the Balkan league he had been building and a decline in Serbia's external prestige. Self-styled "heroes"—an apparent reference to Regents Blaznavac and Ristić—sought to ruin and humiliate him and deny his achievements. Nonetheless, Garašanin retained his fine name and reputation and numerous friends in national public life. "Today we all feel we have lost a sincere patriot, wise statesman, excellent administrator and a most honorable man."[3]

Another sympathetic newspaper, *Budućnost,* affirmed next day that Garašanin's reputation would proudly stand the test of time. During his lifetime his popularity had been genuine and deeply rooted, he was respected and admired throughout European political circles, enhancing Serbia's prestige. Testimony to this was that his funeral had been attended by all foreign envoys in Serbia.

With Garašanin has disappeared from the Serbian stage the most remarkable political leader in modern Serbian history short of the
throne. His name is intimately connected with that history for an
entire quarter century during which, either as the chief or one of the
chief figures of our national rebirth, he was the soul of all public
activities. Until 1859 he was the omnipotent minister without whose
will nothing in the country was or could be done. He was the nucleus
around which revolved the entire healthy Serbian intelligentsia, and
prior to Prince Mihailo, he was the hinge of the Yugoslav world. He
was as distinguished in character as in statesmanship—in him the two
were happily combined making him an exceptional phenomenon
among us.

Inherent in Garašanin's character, continued *Budućnost,* and a trait unusual in Serbian politics, was unselfishness. For thirteen years as Interior
Minister he had controlled most of the state administration, subsequently
divided among the ministries of Interior, War and Public Works. Although
in Serbia and elsewhere such powerful ministers often became millionaires,
Garašanin in old age, to settle his debts honorably, had to sell his home in
Belgrade and his father's house in Grocka. Oblivious to personal gain, he
died almost penniless. Garašanin's conscientious refusal to exploit official
positions for personal benefit went so far that he refused to seek state
stipends in order to educate his sons in Europe, instead paying all their
expenses out of his own pocket. Then while living modestly in retirement
in Grocka, Garašanin had seen his earlier public activities misrepresented
by political and personal opponents. He answered their distortions, lies
and defamation of his character only with the silence of a great man whose
conscience was wholly clear. Following a life spent in political storms and
struggle, he had ended his earthly existence in great physical suffering
borne heroically. Glory and thanks to him![4]
    Understandably *Istok,* a Liberal paper associated closely with Jovan
Ristić, a leading rival of Garašanin, was less flattering:

Yesterday, was buried the veteran and "great" Serbian statesman,
Ilija Garašanin. The burial was magnificent, and even the Jews turned out in large numbers which, claims *Vidovdan,* showed special
respect toward Serbia and the deceased.

Content with this sarcastic statement and avoiding any overall assessment, *Istok* declared enigmatically that the public had already reached its verdict.[5] Ristić's paper, refraining under a Conservative ministry from attacking the still popular Garašanin, instead damned him with faint praise, then criticized laudatory obituaries in Conservative newspapers:

> We understand what it means to praise the services of a man on the basis of fact, but the praise given by *Vidovdan* and *Budućnost,* in which not a single weakness of Garašanin is mentioned, is not only illogical but looks to everyone as if they are saying: 'I sing to my god for ready cash.' That is what those journalists did which fails to honor the deceased.

To make a giant out of Garašanin, argued *Istok,* and dwarves out of others without supporting evidence was both ridiculous and unjust. Can one call giants those who undermined the dignity of Serbia's ruler before the Turkish pasha, and dwarves those who achieved an hereditary Serbian princely title?[6] After continuing in this vein at great length, *Istok* appealed rather incongruously for Serbs to bury party passions in favor of patriotism.[7] Praise of Garašanin in the Conservative press seemingly had struck Ristić partisans in a sensitive spot. *Istok*'s article appeared to be a devious attempt, not readily traceable to Ristić personally, to denigrate Garašanin's achievements and enhance his own contributions.

The two Serbian historians who wrote most extensively about Ilija Garašanin's career—Dragoslav Stranjaković and Slobodan Jovanović—provided laudatory assessments of his work, the former uncritically, the latter with more balance. Devoting about equal attention to Garašanin as European diplomat and builder of the Serbian state, Stranjaković, for whom Garašanin was the heroic and unblemished Serbian patriot, emphasized his high standing in European chancelleries which benefited Serbia and its national cause. During widespread travel in Europe, Garašanin had conferred with most mid-century premiers and foreign ministers of Austria, France, Italy, Rumania and the Ottoman Empire. In 1843, offered the premiership and foreign ministry while only thirty-one, Garašanin had refused them, declaring modestly that others were more capable and deserving. Under Aleksandar Karadjordjević he became the indispensable Serbian statesman holding almost everything in his hands. As Interior

Minister he had constructed for little Serbia and organized the competent non-party bureaucracy which fostered its emergence as a semi-independent country. Even before Mihailo resumed power in 1860, Garašanin had become the chief leader of the South Slav world. To be sure, Prince Mihailo acted as supreme patron of a national policy which Garašanin designed and implemented. If Serbia were the South Slav Piedmont, concluded Stranjaković, then Garašanin was her Cavour.[8] Prophesying the unification of Serbs and South Slavs, he urged Serbia to acquire a commercial route to the south, thus freeing itself from economic dependence on Austria-Hungary. Under Mihailo he had helped remove the Turks from the fortresses and concluded alliances with Montenegro and Greece. Garašanin had reached agreements with the Croats, Bulgars and Albanians and cleared the way for a treaty of friendship with Rumania. Results achieved in Serbian domestic and foreign policy, concluded Stranjaković, entitle Garašanin to a top place in the pantheon of modern Serbian leaders alongside Karadjordje, Miloš, Mihailo and Nikola Pašić. His exceptional moral and spiritual qualities would inspire future generations of Serbs.[9]

Garašanin as foreign minister, affirmed Slobodan Jovanović, achieved one major success: liberation of the fortresses. He could not foment a general war which would bring about Turkey's collapse and create a Yugoslavia. So closely was he identified with the first Balkan league that when he was removed, Russia promptly interpreted that as Mihailo's repudiation of that policy. Mihailo insisted that he—the prince—was the prime policy-maker, but Russian leaders concluded that Garašanin's authority, skill and enthusiasm were indispensable to achieve Balkan unity. In foreign affairs, concluded Jovanović, Garašanin was more a man of great ideas than of practical successes. More than for any diplomatic success he is remembered for "Načertanije," proclaiming South Slav solidarity and the Balkan league. He was the first Serbian statesman to break out of the narrow confines of Šumadijan patriotism and summon together all South Slavs under the slogan, "The Balkans for the Balkan peoples."[10]

His Serbian contemporaries agreed that Garašanin had been an outstanding and gifted politician and statesman. Those who believed themselves injured or insulted by his policies displayed momentary dissatisfaction with them, and political opponents often criticized his course and exposed his shortcomings. But such sniping was relatively rare and insignificant.

When Lazar Todorović, alarmed by the Katanska Revolt of 1844, realized that Garašanin, "long known by all true Serbs as the reliable pillar of Serbia," commanded the domestic front, his fears dissipated "like fog before the sun."[11] Jevrem Grujić, a Garašanin protégé and subsequently a major Liberal leader, concluded that the St. Andrew's Assembly should have named him prince of Serbia:

> With what majesty Garašanin appears before the people, with what dignity he issues orders, and his aptitude and speech so impress us that I thought repeatedly: God has created that man to be the ruler of this country.

Earlier, Grujić had explained: "His wisdom, firm will, fine family, two worthy sons . . . all that was what the present and the future demands."[12]

Leading Serbs outside Serbia likewise valued Garašanin's dedication and patriotism. Vuk Karadžić, founder of the modern Serbo-Croatian language, recommended him to the great German historian, Leopold von Ranke, as "a man about whom it was said that because of his sound thinking and character, he was the leading personality of Serbia." Well-informed about other Balkan lands, Garašanin could discuss with him everything relating to the Serbs.[13] Petar II Njegoš, venerated prince-bishop and epic writer of Montenegro, becoming Garašanin's true friend, affirmed that no Serb had worked harder for Serbdom or loved and respected the Serbian people more. Shortly before his death, Njegoš characterized Garašanin as "an honorable and dear Serb."[14] The Montenegrin patriot, Nićifor Dučić, affirmed that Garašanin had worked day and night for the Serbs' liberation and unification, and for their happiness and progress; he was the prime mover and inspirer of the entire cause. If all true Serbs supported him, Garašanin's "holy and national" work would necessarily succeed.[15] Much later, another Montenegrin leader, V. M. Vrbica, wrote Milutin Garašanin that his father had been a most conscientious, patriotic Serbian diplomat who had forseen the future of the Balkan peoples.[16]

The opinions of most foreign contemporaries paralleled closely the Serbs' own favorable verdict. Praising Garašanin's role in 1844 were Austrian General Ungerhofer, Eugen von Filipović, and the French consul.[17] Franjo Zah, the Czech partisan of the Slav cause, in close touch with Garašanin for many years, praised his abilities and role most highly.[18] Among

Serbian leaders, affirmed Ljudevit Gaj, Croatian leader of the Illyrian movement, Garašanin ranked next after Prince Aleksandar Karadjordjević and for his pure convictions and tireless work enjoyed wide popularity in Serbia.[19] In June 1853 General Mayerhofer, former Austrian consul in Serbia, described Garašanin as "a man full of character and patriotism."[20] The Russian diplomat, A. Vlangali, regarded him as a remarkable person and statesman and hoped some Serb would write his biography. The Regency had maltreated him, but such men were appreciated not in their own time but only by posterity.[21]

The shrewd and able Magyar, Benjamin Kállay, Austrian consul in Serbia, 1868-1874, had no particular reason to favor Garašanin, but he extolled him as a great man, politician and statesman. The Regency feared him even in retirement as its most dangerous rival because he was "a popular, clever, energetic and capable man." Throughout Serbia he was remembered as an exceptionally honest and scrupulous politician. "He died, as he had lived, a poor man in a country where usually every political post was exploited to advance one's self-interest." With Garašanin's death, predicted Kállay correctly, Marinović's weak government could scarcely maintain itself for long since Garašanin had been his chief adviser and friend.[22]

Finally, Hippolyte Mondain, the French officer who had served as Prince Mihailo's war minister, wrote Svetozar Garašanin with compassion and affection abut his great and recently deceased father: "The time will come, if it has not arrived already, when everyone will see with regret the great void which [Garašanin] has left behind him . . . . His good character and great intelligence placed him so far above all his compatriots without exception."[23]

Garašanin's critics were generally personal or political opponents, often highly inconsistent in their assessments. Thus Councillor Lazar Arsenijević-Batalaka in 1845 recommended Garašanin to Prince Aleksandar as "in every way an honorable man, an excellent Serb devoted sincerely and without self-interest to you and his country." Yet only a year later he complained to the same prince that Garašanin was indecisive, meditated excessively, and failed to consider others' rights and honor.[24] A blind partisan of Aleksandar, Arsenijević blamed excessive ambition for Garašanin's frequent quarrels with the Prince. Ranko Alimpić, an officer who praised Garašanin's role at the St. Andrew's Assembly, asserted later that he was ambitious, vengeful and powerhungry,[25] characteristics which no objective observer would ascribe to Garašanin. Milivoje Blaznavac, probably his bitterest foe, accused Garašanin of frivolity (sic!) and building his national revolutionary organization on sand, assertions stemming from enmity and bitter jealousy.

Jovan Ristić, eventually Garašanin's most formidable and forceful critic, earlier had praised him highly. While in power under Aleksandar Karadjordjević, Garašanin had repeatedly protected Ristić and fostered his career. Later, Ristić repaid his former chief and mentor with intrigues designed to embroil him with Prince Mihailo, then permitted Garašanin's persecution in retirement. Earlier, Ristić had lauded Garašanin as an able writer and skillful politician who knew how to act forcefully in critical situations. In 1858, Garašanin had been "the intellectual leader of the entire movement" against Prince Aleksandar. Later, Ristić harped on Garašanin's alleged shortcomings and disputed his services to Serbia. Seeking full power as regent, Ristić even intimated that Garašanin had been involved in Mihailo's murder, which he must have known to be untrue.[26]

In the heated polemic of the 1890s with Ristić opposing both Milan Piroćanac and Milutin Garašanin over Ilija Garašanin's role in Serbian politics, Ristić questioned some of his qualities and achievements while admitting that Garašanin had been "for many years a good and thoughtful chief" and recalling "those pleasant moments I had spent in his company." Towards Garašanin then he had only "feelings of respect," and agreed that he "had a kind of magical power to win people over."[27] However, Ristić claimed that Garašanin, allegedly miffed at Mihailo's letter praising Ristić as his right-hand man in obtaining the fortresses, had acted to clip his wings.[28] Later, although to some Serbian leaders he still praised Garašanin, Ristić began to make sniping criticisms of him. While admitting his loyalty toward Prince Mihailo, Ristić intimated that Garašanin was disloyal to the Obrenović dynasty and sought to satisfy Russia at any price. Ristić attributed Garašanin's opposition to Prince Mihailo's projected marriage to Katarina partly to fear that his influence would be eclipsed. He accused Garašanin of yielding excessively to the Porte in the fortress negotiations where "his caution bordered on weakness." Garašanin's place in Serbian history, Ristić concluded, should not be exaggerated: Mihailo had been the prime mover and initiator of policy: Garašanin had only executed his orders. "By his talent, experience and dedication to state service, Ilija Garašanin for six years was a valuable collaborator of Prince Mihailo," but the Prince had provided all the basic policy directions. Mihailo could rule effectively without Garašanin, but Garašanin could not conduct diplomacy without the Prince's instructions.[29]

Claiming equality with him as Prince Mihailo's collaborator, Ristić minimized Garašanin's diplomatic role. Later, he assumed the role of Serbia's greatest statesman. Piroćanac agrees that Garašanin did not initiate foreign policy under Mihailo, but Garašanin still contributed his own ideas in implementing the Prince's overall policies which happened to coincide with his own. Garašanin had worked according to his convictions without dependence on anyone.[30] Under Prince Aleksandar, and without Mihailo, Garašanin had laid foundations for Serbia's national policy, continuing these same policies under Prince Mihailo. Even in the 1840s Garašanin had approached Bulgars, Albanians and Croats; Vojvodina Serbs and leaders in Bosnia-Hercegovina and Montenegro were in close touch with him. Before entering Mihailo's cabinet in 1861, Garašanin in Constantinople had established bases for a Serbo-Greek alliance. Precisely when Garašanin had held office, Serbian national policy had progressed the most. On the other hand, his removal as foreign minister in 1853 and 1867 had caused that policy to languish with work on it reduced to a minimum. Although Ristić cites the Serbo-Rumanian treaty of early 1868 to demonstrate that Prince Mihailo had continued his national policy after removing Garašanin,[31] the latter had done all the preparatory work on a treaty which merely needed to be concluded formally.

In conclusion, Garašanin's contributions to Serbia's internal and external development were important and manifold, though somewhat less than Stranjaković has claimed. An ardent Greater Serbian patriot, he promoted cooperation with other South Slavs and Balkan peoples, notably in the 1860s, but should not be considered a genuine advocate of Yugoslavism, as do Vučković and Stranjaković. The coincidence of Garašanin and Mihailo in the Serbian leadership, 1861-1867, greatly enhanced the country's strength and prestige but did not produce the territorial increases they sought and believed were essential for Serbia's political and economic future. Their most serious shortcomings were an unwillingness to allow and foster civil freedoms at home and their insistence on maintaining tightfisted police rule. Prince Mihailo's authoritarian regime, whose principles Garašanin endorsed fully and promoted zealously in cracking down on liberal opposition in Serbia, alienated an increasingly liberal Serbian opinion, especially in the Vojvodina.[32] Only a progressive Serbia with free institutions, such as those of the liberal constitutional monarchy of King Petar of 1903-1914, as it turned out, would prove a truly attractive beacon for other Serbs and South Slavs and lead the way to unification. Nonetheless, by his work at home and in national policy, and by skillful diplomacy, Ilija Garašanin built sound if incomplete foundations upon which a free and dynamic Serbia and a greater Yugoslav union could later be erected.

NOTES

1. Stranjaković, "Ilija Garašanin," pp. 416 ff.
2. *Srpske novine,* June 11, 1874, No. 128, p. 1.
3. *Vidovdan,* June 11, No. 114, p. 1.
4. *Budućnost,* June 12, No. 49, p. 1, Belgrade, June 12.
5. *Istok,* June 13, No. 57, p. 4.
6. Ristić appears to be intimating that Mihailo's trip to Constantinople early in 1867 to pay homage to his suzerain, the Sultan, was a humiliating "trip to Canossa" and that Ristić, as envoy in Constantinople, had obtained for the Prince his hereditary title.
7. *Istok,* June 27, No. 62, p. 3, "Glas iz Šumadije."
8. Stranjaković apparently derived this idea from *Vidovdan* of July 11, 1874. Again, Stranjaković appears to have exaggerated Garašanin's Yugoslavism.
9. Stranjaković, "Ilija," pp. 427-428.
10. Jovanović, "Spoljna politika Ilije Garašanina," pp. 430-431. Jovanović, too, overstresses Garašanin's Yugoslav views.
11. IG 141, Teodorović to Garašanin, October 11, 1844.
12. J. Grujić, *Zapisi,* II, 182, 45-46.
13. *Vukova prepiska,* V (Belgrade, 1910), p. 672.
14. IG, Petar II Njegoš to Garašanin, July 5 and November 11, 1850.

15. IG 1647, Dučić to Garašanin, June 26, 1867, from Dubrovnik.

16. Vrbica to Milutin Garašanin, May 9, 1892, cited in Stranjaković, "Ilija," p. 411.

17. Ibid., p. 417.

18. Czartoryski Archive (Krakow), Nos. 5390-5392, Zah's reports from Serbia, 1843-1845.

19. G. Jakšić, "Ljudevit Gaj o Srbiji, 1846," *SKG,* XI (1924), p. 373.

20. Stranjaković, "Ilija," p. 417. However, his colleague, Consul Teja Radosavljević, disgruntled at his inability to influence Garašanin, called him: "cunning and arrogant," in his report from Belgrade, February 28, 1855. Ibid.

21. Arhiv SANU, No. 8823, A. Vlangali to J. Marinović, August 12, 1874.

22. *Dnevnik Kalaja,* report No. 45, June 24, 1874, p. 797.

23. IG 1750, Mondain to Svetozar Garašanin, December 6, 1874.

24. "Rasmišlanje . . . Arsenijević-Batalaka to Prince Aleksandar, June 1846, cited in Stranjaković, "Ilija," p. 409.

25. Ibid., p. 411; Alimpić, *Život i rad,* pp. 144, 230, 408 and 423.

26. J. Ristić, *Spoljašnji odnošaji,* I, 267; II, 236-237. On Ristić's assessments of Garašanin see Stranjaković, "Ilija," pp. 4123-416.

27. Ristić, *Prepiska,* pp. 33, 61, 65-66; *Da kažemo još koju,* p. 28.

28. Ristić, *Prepiska,* pp. 58-60; *Poslednja godina,* p. 48.

29. Ibid., pp. 50, 56-57; *Prepiska,* vii; *Jedno namesništvo,* p. 4. Commented M. Milićević on Ristić: "He constantly feared that someone would eclipse his fame." Arhiv SANU, No. 9327, Dnevnik Milićevića, entry of February 13, 1887.

30. Piroćanac, *Knez Mihailo,* p. 12; *Naša završna reč,* pp. 22-24.

31. Ristić, *Poslednje godina,* p. 57.

32. On Serbian Liberals against Mihailo's regime after 1864 see especially Stokes, *Legitimacy,* pp. 69 ff. The chief leaders in that movement were Vladimir Jovanović, who was removed from his post as professor at the Belgrade Lycee in 1864 and exiled from Serbia, and Svetozar Miletić of Novi Sad who began publishing the liberal newspaper, *Zastava,* in Pesth in 1866. See also Jovanović, *Druga vlada,* pp. 203 ff.

BIBLIOGRAPHY

I. ARCHIVES
A. State Archive of Serbia (Državni Arhiv NR Srbije–DAS) (Belgrade):

1. *Papers of Ilija Garašanin* (Fond Ilije Garašanina–IG)
Listed below are the more significant items from these papers, one of the most important and largest private Serbian collections, housed at the State Archive of Serbia (DAS). Originally, the papers were put in order by his son, Milutin Garašanin, who copied many of the important letters in his own hand. After the Garašanin family turned the papers over to the Serbian Archive after World War II, archivists assigned numbers based on a chronological system up through item 1751. Some items consist of lengthy documents or over 100 pages of correspondence; others comprise only a single scrap of paper. Some are damaged (torn or burned), others are faint or virtually illegible, but most are excellently preserved. After preparing a catalog with numbers and and descriptions for each item, the archive opened this collection to scholars in 1974. A catalogue of these papers: "Ilija Garašanin: Lični Fond," was prepared in 1974 by Momčilo Zeravčić.

11:   Kabinetska zamečanije (Office comments), no date.
17:   Prince Miloš to Garašanin, July 10-December 9, 1837.
26:   Zakletva (Oath) of Ilija Garašanin (1838?).
28:   Garašanin to Miloš, 1838.
29:   Miloš to Garašanin, April 10-September 16, 1838 (6 brief notes).
48:   Konstantin Nikolajević to Garašanin, May 29, 1840.

53: Garašanin to A. Petronijević, October 19, 1841.

54: Garašanin to Stojan Simić, April 5, 1841.

60: Decree on naming of Mihailo Garašanin as a member of Savet (Council), October 12, 1842.

66: Request of "Defenders" to return to Serbia, 1842.

68: Garašanin to Stojan Simić, March 26-September 13, 1842.

69. Stevan Herkalović to Garašanin, August 27, 1842.

85. A. Petronijević to Garašanin, December 24, 1843.

86: Garašanin to Petronijević and Toma Vučić-Perišić, September-December 1843.

87: Prince A. Karadjordjević to Garašanin, January 16 and July 29, 1843.

88: Garašanin and S. Simić to A. Karadjordjević, April 30, 1843.

102: Garašanin to S. Simić, July 12, 1843.

105: Prince Adam Czartoryski (Paris) to Prince A. Karadjordjević, September 4/16, 1843 (French).

116: Memoire of Serbian government on Serbo-Polish relations, February 12, 1844.

123: Zah's proposal on state policy of Serbia, 1844 (Zah's famous "Plan").

127: Instructions of Garašanin on measures against actions by Prince Miloš (1844).

136: A. Petronijević to Garašanin, 1844 (several letters).

137: Garašanin to A. Petronijević, January-July 1844.

139: Garašanin to B. Djordjević (Ćuprija district chief), January-September 1844.

143: M. Z. Resavac to Garašanin, February 1-25, 1844.

144: Garašanin to Resavac, March 18, 1844.

145: Stevan Knićanin to Garašanin, January-February 1844.

173: Secret letter to Prince Miloš, January 1, 1844.

176: Garašanin on situation in Serbia (1844?).

182: Materials on ending actions of Obrenović partisans (1844).

184: Garašanin to Djordjević, January 17-December 4, 1845.

200: Garašanin on "Situation in Serbia," February 1, 1846.

234: Toma Kovačević's report "On the situation in Bosnia," December 28, 1847.

240: Prince A. Karadjordjević to Garašanin, June 16 and August 26, 1847.

247: Jovan Marinović to Garašanin, November 24, 1847.

252: P. Knežević to Garašanin, August 12, 1847.

263: "Reports and comments on Bosnia," by Toma Kovačević, May 15, 1848.

266: "Survey of political conditions of Europe," by Garašanin, August 11, 1848.

269: Kovačević, October 8, 1848: national propaganda.

270: Garašanin: "Serbia's situation in case of a Russo-Turkish war," October 8, 1848.

284: Garašanin: "The latest from England," (1848?).

309: A. Petronijević to Garašanin, May 14-December 18, 1848.

311: Prince A. Karadjordjević to Garašanin, 1848 and 1850.

312: Garašanin to Prince A. Karadjordjević, September-December 1848.

319: A. Nikolić to Garašanin, March 30-October 16, 1848.

340: J. Marinović to Garašanin, January 26-December 24, 1848 (122 pages).

349: Josif Rajačić, Serbian Patriarch, to Garašanin, 1848.

381: S. Knićanin to Garašanin, 1848.

394: T. Knežević to Garašanin, September 1848.

385: S. Simić to Garašanin, 1848.

418: Patriarch Rajačić to Prince A. Karadjordjević, September-October 1848.

448: Garašanin to district and county chiefs, 1849.

465: Memoire of Serbian government to the Porte, 1849.

477: Prince A. Karadjordjević to Garašanin, June-July 1849.

479: A.Nenadović to Garašanin, June-August 1849.

491: Patriarch Rajačić to Garašanin, 1849.

495: Garašanin to Magazinović, February-August 1849.

496: M. Blaznavac to Garašanin, November-December 1849.

497: Knićanin to Garašanin, January-August 1849 (150 pages).

516: Garašanin to unknown, 1849: on nefarious Austrian policy.

530: Garašanin draft on forthcoming decisive battle of Magyars vs. Austro-Russian forces, 1849.

555: Marinović to Garašanin, January 8, 1849.

588: Kovačević to Garašanin, January-February 1849.

618: Michal Czajkowski to Dr. L. Zwierkowski, May 21, 1849.

649: Annual report of Kovačević on conduct of political propaganda in Slav areas of Turkey, May 26, 1850.

645: Two reports from Hercegovina, March 1850.

647: Document on propaganda to be conducted in Slav lands of Turkey, May 1850.

654: Proposals of Toma Kovačević on agents' activities, November 24, 1850.

656: "Political rights of Principality of Serbia" (1850?).

672: Garašanin to A. Nenadović, January-July 1850.

679: Garašanin to K. Magazinović, April-November 1850.

682: Garašanin to S. Simić, May-August 1850.

690: Garašanin's instructions to district chiefs (1850).

724: Matija Ban to Garašanin, 1850.

733: Knićanin to Garašanin, August 22, 1850.

756: "Proposal for organization of Interior Ministry" (1851).

767: Garašanin to S. S. Tenka, August 12, 1851.

768: S. Simić to Garašanin, January-October 1851.

769: Garašanin to S. Simić, October 9-30, 1851.

790: J. Marinović to Toma Kovačević, September-October 1851.

805: Views on Serbia's role in solving Eastern Question, October 1852.

810: Garašanin to A. Simić, February-November 1852.

815: Knićanin to Garašanin, January-November 1852.

816: Garašanin to Knićanin, December 16, 1852.

817: Garašanin to S. S. Tenka, June-August 1852.

831: K. Magazinović to Garašanin, April-September 1852.

850: Lajos Kossuth (1852): military measures and preparations.

855: Memoranda of Garašanin 1852/53 on Serbia's relationship to the outside world.

864: Memoranda of Garašanin on Military Frontiers and structure of Serbia, 1853.

868: K. Nikolajević to Garašanin (from Constantinople), January-March 1853.

869: Garašanin to Nikolajević, March 6, 1853.

870: Knićanin to Garašanin, January-April 1853. (45 pages.)

871: Garašanin to Knićanin, January-May 1853 (70 pages).

876: Garašanin to unknown, March 6, 1853: Russia demands his removal.

877: Garašanin to Unknown, April 8, 1853: Russian attitudes toward him and Serbia.

883: Garašanin to Unknown (1853): draft on Russian policy toward Serbia.

889: Garašanin (1853?) on Serbian policy and Russia.

901:    Knićanin to Simić, February-May 1853.
902:    Prince A. Karadjordjević to the Council, March 14, 1853.
903:    The Council to Prince A. Karadjordjević, March 1853.
911:    K. V. Nesselrode to Prince A. Karadjordjević, July 17, 1853:
        Fonton mission.
917:    Blaznavac to Knićanin, April 1 and 24, 1853: on Garašanin's re-
        moval.
930:    "Memorandum on Serbo-Turkish relations in light of previous
        treaties" (1854, by Garašanin, draft on treaties of 1812 and
        1826).
932:    Garašanin memorandum "On Austro-Serbian relations" (1854).
933:    Memorandum from "Slavenske zapiske" (1854) on Serbia and
        Crimean War.
934:    Garašanin memorandum on destruction of Turkey (1854).
935:    Garašanin memorandum on great powers and Turkey, Panslavism
        and Serbo-Russian relations (1854).
952:    Garašanin memorandum: "Critique of foreign and domestic policy
        of Prince Aleksandar (1854).
956:    Garašanin draft to Marinović on French demand (1854).
957:    Garašanin excerpt: "On autocracy of the Prince" (1854).
958:    Garašanin draft on Serbia and Turkey (1854).
960:    Garašanin draft to Austrian consul (1854).
965:    Garašanin draft to Prince A. Karadjordjević: conversation with
        Segur, 1854.
982:    Garašanin memorandum on Serbian policy: "A few words"(1855).
983:    Garašanin memorandum: "A few words on inheritance of princely
        dignity in Serbia." (1855).
984:    Garašanin excerpt on Prince Aleksandar's rule (1855).
988:    Garašanin draft: "Bad situation of Serbia." (1855).
995:    Garašanin to Unknown, draft: Europe's attitude toward Serbia
        (1855).
1003:   Garašanin draft: Prince vs. Council (1856).
1008:   Garašanin draft (1856?): "As far as I see" (denounced foreign
        influences).
1009:   Garašanin draft on Prince vs. Council (1856).
1010:   Garašanin draft: "On the country's situation" (1856).
1011:   Portion of Garašanin draft: "On defense of Serbia's rights"(1856).

1024:   Garašanin draft on Austrian intrigues and Radosavljević (1857?).
1029:   Garašanin draft: to prevent powers' intervention in Serbia's affairs (1857).
1036:   Garašanin to Mondain, January-December 1857 (62 pages).
1061:   Garašanin draft (1858): "On people's desire to convene Skupština."
1068:   Indictment against Prince Aleksandar (1858) (by J. Grujić, 71 pages).
1072:   Garašanin memorandum: "Plan of work for this year, 1858."
1076:   Prince A. Karadjordjević to Garašanin, May 27, 1858.
1077:   Garašanin to Prince A. Karadjordjević, May-August 1858 (17 pages).
1091:   Garašanin to Unknown (1858): "Serbia is in a terrible plight."
1123:   Garašanin memorandum: "On war in Italy," April 19, 1859.
1127:   Garašanin to Mondain, January-November 1859 (10 pages).
1133:   Garašanin memorandum: issues in Serbian foreign policy, February 1, 1859.
1137:   Garašanin memorandum on situation of Serbia, 1860/61.
1150:   "One opinion" (that Prince expel foreign influences) (1860?).
1155:   Garašanin draft: duty to promptly end Serbia's uncertain position.
1157:   Garašanin draft on talk with Car on Serbia's demands (1861).
1158:   Garašanin plan: "What should be done among Balkan peoples" (1861).
1163:   Memorandum on Garašanin's mission to Constantinople (1861).
1165:   Garašanin draft on party struggles (1861?).
1174:   Garašanin draft on agreement with the Greeks, 1861.
1175:   Garašanin memorandum on need for strong government in Serbia (1861?).
1176:   Garašanin draft: "Critique of Vojvodina Serbs' unpatriotic policy" (1861).
1177:   Garašanin views on evacuation of Turks from Serbian towns (1861).
1180:   Garašanin reply to Porte on evacuation of Turks, August 1, 1861.
1187:   Garašanin memorandum: "Various comments on policy of Prince Mihailo" (1861).
1196:   Jovan Ristić to Garašanin, 1861, June 16 and December 13.
1203:   Filip Hristić to Garašanin, March-October 1861 (125 pages).

1204:   Garašanin to Hristić (from Contantinople, 1861) (156 pages).
1210:   Garašanin draft on evacuation of Turks, his mission (1861).
1245:   Garašanin draft on decisions at Kanlice Conference (1862).
1251:   Garašanin draft on military and other measures to be taken (1862).
1252:   Garašanin draft on question of ministerial responsibility (1862).
1257:   On Serb loan from Russia and war preparations (1862).
1259:   A. Nikolić: "Plan on national policy of Serbia" (46 pages, 1862).
1272:   Garašanin to Ristić, June-August 1862 (On bombardment of Belgrade).
1273:   Garašanin to Dr. Karl Pacek, June-December 1862: on acquiring rifles.
1279:   M. Lešjanin to Garašanin, July-September 1862 (from Paris).
1282:   Garašanin to Prince Mihailo Obrenović, September 30, 1862.
1283:   Garašanin to Prince Mihailo, draft: government and the opposition (1862).
1311:   Garašanin to Pacek, 1862: on weapons' transfer.
1319:   A. Nikolić to Garašanin, October-December 1862 (on weapons' transfer).
1390:   Andra Andrić, February 27, 1863, "Situation in Bosnia."
1399:   Garašanin draft: "One must understand Serbia's conduct" (1863).
1402:   "Memoire on the fortresses" (1863).
1410:   Garašanin to Ristić, January-November 1863 (36 pages).
1423:   Garašanin to Prince Mihailo, 1863: Turkish military preparations.
1437:   Marinović to Garašanin (from Paris), June-July 1863 (58 pages).
1440:   Blaznavac to Garašanin, March-December 1863 (74 pages).
1481:   Ristić to Garašanin, 1864 (3 letters).
1482:   Garašanin to Ristić, March-December 1864 (37 pages).
1483:   Garašanin to Prince Nikola, March-November 1864 (9 pages).
1491:   Blaznavac to Garašanin, January-December 1864 (28 pages).
1501:   Djosa Milovanović, "Report on Montenegro," March 7, 1865.
1502:   A. Orešković, "Proposal on organization of the army," April 9, 1865.
1509:   Garašanin to Foreign Minister Gorchakov, drafts, June 1865.
1512:   Garašanin to Mondain, September-December 1865.
1514:   Garašanin to Ristić, February-December 1865 (58 pages).
1517:   Kosta Cukić to Garašanin, July 6-30, 1865 (45 pages).
1518:   Blaznavac to Garašanin, January-July 1865 (55 pages).

1520:   M. Lešjanin to Garašanin, July-August 1865 (40 pages).
1521:   Garašanin to Lešjanin, August-October 1865 (19 pages).
1535:   Garašanin to Prince Mihailo, October 14-20, 1865.
1538:   Prince Nikola to Garašanin, January 18 and August 17, 1865.
1539:   Garašanin to Prince Nikola, March-November 1865 (6 pages).
1548:   A. Orešković to Garašanin, February-December 1865 (20 pages).
1552:   Shishkin to Garašanin, April 17 and August 2, 1865.
1568:   Garašanin draft on various events in Serbia and Europe (1866)
        (5 pages).
1580:   Ristić to Garašanin, January-December 1866.
1581:   Garašanin to Ristić, 1866 (142 pages).
1582:   Garašanin to Magazinović, 1866 (54 pages).
1584:   Garašanin to Blaznavac, August 2, 1866 (draft): on Blaznavac's
        conversation with General Turr (many corrections).
1587:   Garašanin to Dučić, November 25 and December 15, 1866.
1588:   Garašanin to Prince Nikola, 1866 (11 pages); Nikola to Garašanin,
        May 28.
1590:   "O politici Rusije . . ." (Garašanin), October 1866.
1591:   "O politici i stavu Turske . . ," 1866.
1592:   V. Pelagić to Garašanin, July 21, 1866.
1594:   H. Mondain to Garašanin, 1866.
1597:   M. Lešjanin to Garašanin, May 16-August 4, 1866.
1598:   M. Petronijević to Garašanin, September 29, 1866.
1600:   Nikola Krstić to Garašanin, July 27-31, 1866.
1602:   Orešković to Garašanin, October 8, 1866.
1603:   Pfuhl to Garašanin, July 11, 1866.
1605:   F. Zah to Garašanin, August 6, 1866.
1608:   Prince Mihailo to K. Magazinović, July 19, 1866.
1610:   Blaznavac to Mihailo, July 25-August 5, 1866.
1611:   Laubereau to Prince Mihailo, 1866.
1621:   On strength of Serbia and Turkey, January 1867 by Russian mili-
        tary attache (63 pages).
1623:   "Proposal to cabinet on inheritance of the throne," November 1,
        1867.
1634:   Garašanin to A. Nikolić, February-October 1867.
1635:   Garašanin to Mondain, November 12-24, 1867.
1636:   Ristić to Garašanin, January-May 1867 (44 pages).

1637:   Garašanin to Ristić, January-October 1867 (61 pages).

1638:   Garašanin to Magazinović, 1867, drafts (31 pages).

1639:   Garašanin to M. A. Petronijević, May 20, 1867 (Serbo-Greek talks).

1643:   Prince Miahilo to Garašanin, June 26-November 2, 1867 (28 pages).

1644:   Garašanin to Prince Mihailo, June-September 1867, drafts (22 pages).

1646:   Garašanin to Prince Nikola, February-September 1867 (31 pages, drafts).

1647:   Dučić to Garašanin, June 26, 1867 (from Dubrovnik).

1648:   Garašanin to Dučić, March-July 1867 (8 pages).

1657:   Garašanin memo: "Should Serbia enter war or not?" (1867).

1661:   Marinović to Garašanin, July 19, 1867.

1662:   Pacek to Garašanin, December 29, 1867.

1666:   M. G. Cherniaev to Garašanin, March 20, 1867.

1669:   F. Zah to Garašanin, January 1867.

1677:   Correspondence on issue of freeing the fortresses, March 1867 (23 pages).

1679:   Memoranda of Garašanin on Skupština, press, ministerial responsibility.

1680:   Memorandum of Garašanin on ideas of Prince Mihailo and reform (1868?).

1682:   Garašanin memoranda on draft constitution, Council and Skupština (1868).

1683:   Garašanin, "My Reminiscences" ("Moji spomeni" early 1868).

1684:   Garašanin memo: "On murder of Prince Mihailo" (1868).

1685:   Mondain to Garašanin, 1868 (5 pages).

1686:   Garašanin to Mondain, 1868 (4 letters).

1688:   Garašanin to Magazinović, June 21, 1868: on death of Mihailo.

1690:   Ilija to Milutin Garašanin, June 6-27, 1868 (36 pages, damaged).

1702:   Garašanin memo: "My Thoughts" (1869).

1704:   Garašanin to Blaznavac, February-June 1869 (8 pages).

1710:   Garašanin memo: "On success of rule of Prince Mihailo."

1721:   N. Atanacković to R. Milojković (1870): on plot to kill Blaznavac.

1731:   Garašanin to Mondain, November 15/27, 1871.

1739:   Garašanin to Mondain, January 29, 1873.

1743: Mondain to Garašanin, March 31/April 12, 1874.
1744: Garašanin to Mondain, March 2/14, 1874.
1750: Mondain to Svetozar Garašanin, December 6, 1874: on greatness of Garašanin.

2. Papers of Milutin Garašanin: 4: "War and operational plan for war against Turkey," January 25, 1863 (37 pages) (by A. Orešković?).

3. Poklon i otkupa (PO); 23, 24, 25, 26, 27, 28, 47/76.

4. Ministry of Foreign Affairs (MID) (Poverljiva arhiva): "Izveštaji srpskih agenata iz Carigrada, 1866-1868" ("Reports of Serbian representatives from Constantinople"), Reports Nos. 1, 2 and 6 (January 1866, Ristić to Garašanin.

B. *Archive of the Historical Institute (Arhiv Istoriskog Instituta—AII)* (Belgrade).
   1. Papers of Matija Ban (Hartije Matije Bana):
      I: 15, 21, 22, 23, 24, 31, 33, 34, 47, 57, 68, 75, 80, 87, 89, 90.
      VI: 1, 3, 4, 7, 11, 13.
      V: 1, "Prepiska u godinama, 1839-1851"; 23, "Spisi, 1867."
      VI: 4, 8.
      VII: 8.
      VIII: 6.
      XVII: 1, 3, 5, 6, 7-10, 12-14, 17, 19, 23, 24, 27, 28, 32, 37, 38.
      XVIII: 1-10.

   2. Papers of Jovan Ristić (Hartije Jovana Ristića):
      I/15: Papers relating to the bombardment of Belgrade, 1862.
      XI/31, 32, 175, 176, 178, 180-206 (Ristić drafts and reports to Garašanin, 1866-1867); 215-236 (drafts), 240, 242, 244, 269-277 (Ristić to Garašanin, 1862, 1864); 279-281 (Ristić reports to Garašanin, 1865); 282-316 (drafts of Ristić to Garašanin, 1866; 448, excerpt of Ignat'ev to (Ristić), February 6/18, 1867); 472, Ristić to Garašanin, telegrams, 1866-1867; 350, excerpt of Garašanin to (Ristić), January 25, 1866; 440, Garašanin to Ristić, May 25, 1866.

XXIV/161-162, Shtakelberg to Prince Mihailo, December 18/30, 1867 and January 6/18, 1868.

XXV/13, "Raspis" (circular), Garašanin to District Chiefs, n.d.,; 151, Garašanin to Ristić, July 4/16, 1863; 196, Vlangali to "Mon Prince," February 1/13, 1865; 197, Garašanin on negotiations with Greece, February 2/14, 1867; 514, Ignat'ev to Nikolai Pavlovich, September 27, 1868, No. 677.

C. *Archive of the Academy of Sciences and Fine Arts*
(Arhiv Srpske Akademije i Umetnosti (Belgrade) (SANU):

No. 741, "O Patriarhu Rajačiću i dogadjajima (1848)."

No. 1405, "Obraz Kniaza Miloša i njegovog vladanje" (Djordje Protić?).

No. 7051, "Prepiska Stevana Knićanina (1843-49)."

No. 7075, "Odbrana vlade knjaza Mihaila Obrenovića od ministra Stevana Radičevića od 1842" (Zemun, February 5, 1842).

No. 7088, Prince Mihailo to Prince Miloš, March 5, 1841.

No. 7089, "Protestation des Fürsten Michael Obrenowitsch an den k. k. Österreichischen Consul überhandet," August 26, 1842 (Semlin).

No. 7114, "Izveštaj Blaznavaca," April 29/May 10, 1867 (War Minister's report on Serbia's military strength).

No. 7078, (Djordje Protić?) to Stojan Simić, February 2, 1846 (Deals with Vučić Revolt).

Nos. 7194-7200, "Dnevnik Nikola Krstića," ("Javan život"), 1860-1873.

No. 7380, "Biografija Anastasije Nikolića" (written 1874-75).

Nos. 7391-7419, "Prepiska Stevana Knićaninova."

Nos. 7474-7501, "Prepiska Ilije Garašanina i J. Šljivić, 1849."

No. 7134, H. Mondain to Stojan Movaković, August 1, 1899 (On Prince Mihailo).

Nos. 7503-7509, "Prepiska J. Šljivića i Ilija Garašanina," etc. (1849).

No. 7515, "Memorandum of April 5/17, 1854 on mobilization of Austrian toops on the Serbian frontier."

Nos. 7536-7550, "Gradja o madjarskoj buni" (materials relating to Vojvodina revolt, Patriarch Rajačić, Knićanin and Jelačić).

No. 7940, "Ispisi iz Bečkih arhiva, 1830-1914," (Documents from HHSA, Vienna).

Nos. 7942-7964, "Prepiska Ilije Garašanina," (Garašanin's letters to Marinović, 1858-1860, published in *Pisma*, II).

Nos. 8807-8861, "Prepiska Jovana Marinovića," especially 8819, N. Shishkin to Marinović, June 6, 1869 (Vienna); 8823, Vlangali to Marinović, November 10, 1874; 8824, F. Huet to Marinović, November 18, 1863 and November 28 (On Prince Milan), June 11, 1868; 8835, Knoring to Marinović, March 23, 1867 (Baden-Baden).

No. 8797, "Dejanija srpskog naroda i Patriarh J. Rajačića, 1848-49."

No. 9023, K. V. Nesselrode (Russian Foreign Minister) to Mihailo Obrenović, July 4, 1853 (from Petrograd).

No. 9094, "Ilija Garašanin" (German translation of an article in *Zastava*).

No. 9203, Djordje Protić, "Istorisko opisanije najnovih u Srbiji dogadjaja" (1842) (anti-Vučić account by close associate of Mihailo).

No. 9288, Kosta Magazinović, "Memoari."

No. 9321, Patriarch J. Rajačić, "Proglas srpskom narodu" (1849).

No. 9323, "Prevrat u Srbiji, 1842-43" (Copies of Austrian documents from HHSA, Vienna, especially reports of Consul Atanacković from Belgrade).

No. 9327, "Dnevnik Milana Milićevića," 1869-70, 1874.

No. 9525, "Ilija Garašanin to Army chief of staff" (1845).

No. 9736, Dragoslav Ilić, "O Jovanu Ristiću, 1858 god" (written 1902).

Nos. 9985-9988, Zaostavština Milana Piroćanca: 9985, Memoir for Garašanin, March 5, 1867. Cetinje; 9986: "O Crnogori" ("About Montenegro").

Nos. 10,025-10,032: Ostavština Jevrema Grujića.

No. 10,514, M. Blaznavac to Ilija Garašanin, 1864.

No. 14,233, Dragoslav Stranjaković, "Ilija Garašanin," and correspondence.

No. 7889, Dnevnik Crnobarca, especially 1868.

D. *Czartoryski Archive (Krakow, Poland):*

1. 5390-5394: Reports of Franjo Zah from Serbia, 1843-1848. 5 vols. (French).

2. 5405, 5410, 5411: Correspondence of A. Czartoryski, M. Czajkowski and L. Zwierkowski.

3. 5387: Slawianszczyzna 1848. Instructions to Lenoir-Zwierkowski. List of agents sent to Garašanin; report of Lenoir of May 17, 1848.

E. *Foreign Office. Public Record Office* (London) (FO PRO).
1. Accounts and Papers (37), LXXV. Correspondence respecting affairs on Serbia, 1867.

F. *Manuscript Division of Lenin Library* (Otdel rukopisei biblioteki imeni Lenina–ORBL) (Moscow).
1. Fond D. A. Miliutina (f. 169), "Dela serbskie."

II. NEWSPAPERS:
Budućnost (Belgrade) (1874)
Depeša (1911)
Dnevni list (Belgrade) (1895)
Istok (Belgrade) (1874)
Politika (Belgrade) (1925, 1927, 1935, 1937, 1940)
Pravda (Belgrade) (1938, 1939, 1940)
Srpske novine (Belgrade) (various)
Videlo (1894, 1895)
Vidovdan (Belgrade) (1874)
Zastava (Novi Sad) (1866-68, 1874)

III. Ph.D. DISSERATIONS
Berry, Robert A. "Czartoryski and the Balkan Policies of the Hotel Lambert, 1832-1847," Indiana University, 1974 (Extremely useful).
Cerick, S. "The Foreign Relations of Serbia, 1868-1903," Georgetown University, 1956.
Hehn, P. "The Constitutional and Party Struggle in Serbia, 1804-1878," New York University, 1962.

IV. WORKS IN ENGLISH
CRAIG, Gordon. *The Battle of Königgrätz: Prussia's Victory over Austria, 1866.* Philadelphia, 1964.
CURTISS, John S. *Russia's Crimean War.* Durham, NC, 1979.
DESPALATOVIĆ, Elinor M. *Ljudevit Gaj and the Illyrian Movement.* New York, 1975.
DJORDJEVIĆ, Dimitrije. "Prospects for the Federation of South-East Europe in the 1860's and 1870's," *Balcanica,* I (1970), pp. 119-146.
—————. "The Serbs as an Integrating Factor," *Austrian History Yearbook,* II (1967), pp. 48-63.

HEHN, P. "The Origins of Modern Pan-Serbism: The 1844 Načertanije," *East European Quarterly,* IX, No. 2 (1975), pp. 153-171.

JELAVICH, Charles. "Serbian Nationalism and the Question of Union with Croatia in the Nineteenth Century," *Balkan Studies,* III (1962), pp. 29-42.

JELAVICH, Barbara. *History of the Balkans.* 2 vols., Cambridge, England, 1983.

JOVANOVIĆ, Vladimir. *The Serbian Nation and the Eastern Question.* London, 1863.

MACKENZIE, David. *The Serbs and Russian Pan-Slavism, 1875-1878.* Ithaca, NY, 1967.

————. "Serbian Nationalist and Military Organizations and the Piedmont Idea, 1844-1914," *East European Quarterly,* XVI, No. 3 (September, 1982), pp. 323-344.

NOVAK, Viktor. "Vuk and the Croats," summary of *Vuk i Hrvati,* pp. 601-635, Belgrade, 1967.

PAVLOWITCH, Stevan K. *Anglo-Russian Rivalry in Serbia, 1837-1839.* The Hague, 1961.

PAXTON, Roger V. "Nationalism and Revolution: A Re-Examination of the Origins of the First Serbian Insurrection, 1804-1807," *East European Quarterly,* VI, No. 3 (September 1972), pp. 337-362.

PETROVICH, Michael B. *The Emergence of Russian Panslavism, 1856-1870.* New York, 1957.

————. *A History of Modern Serbia, 1804-1918.* 2 vols., New York, 1976.

PFLANZE, Otto. *Bismarck and the Development of Germany: The Period of Unification, 1815-1871.* Princeton, NJ, 1963.

SAAB, Ann P. *The Origins of the Crimean Coalition.* Charlottesville, VA, 1977.

SCHROEDER, Paul. *Austria, Great Britain and the Crimean War.* Ithaca, NY, 1972.

STAVRIANOS, Leften S. *Balkan Federation.* Hamden, CT, 1942.

STOKES, Gale. "European Sources of Nineteenth Century Thought and the National Liberation Movement in Serbia," in *American Contributions to the Seventh Congress of Slavists,* vol. III, *History,* pp. 125-141. The Hague, 1973.

————. *Legitimacy through Liberalism: Vladimir Jovanović and the Transformation of Serbian Politics.* Seattle, WS, 1975.

————. "Yugoslavism in the 1860's?," *Southeastern Europe,* I, (1974), pp. 126-135.

TAYLOR, A. J. P. *Bismarck: The Man and the Statesman.* New York, 1955.

————. *The Struggle for Mastery in Europe, 1848-1918.* Oxford, 1954.

TRIVANOVITCH, V. "Serbia, Russia and Austria-Hungary during the Reign of Milan Obrenovich, 1868-1878," *Journal of Modern History,* III (1931).

WILSON, Duncan. *The Life and Times of Vuk Stefanović Karadžić, 1787-1864.* Oxford, England, 1970.

V. BOOKS

ALEKSIĆ, Liljana. *Stav Francuske prema Srbiji za vreme druge vlada Kneza Miloša i Mihaila, 1858-1868.* SAN, Pos. izdanja, knj. 298. Istoriski institut, knj. 8. Belgrade, 1957.

ALEKSIĆ-PEJKOVIĆ, L. *Politika Italije prema Srbiji do 1870 g.* Belgrade, 1979.

ALIMPIĆ, Mileva. *Život i rad generala Ranka Alimpića u svezi sa dogadjajima iz najnovije srpske istorije.* Belgrade, 1892.

ANTOLOGIJA Jugoslovenske misli i narodnog jedinstva, 1390-1930, ed. V. Novak. Belgrade, 1930.

BAN, Matija. *Osnovi ratni.* Belgrade, 1848.

BJELICA, Mihailo. *Politička štampa u Srbiji, 1834-1872.* Belgrade, 1975.

BOGDANOV, Vasa. *Ustanak Srba u Vojvodini i Madjarska Revolucija 1848-49.* Subotica, 1929.

CHARLES-ROUX, F. *Alexandre II, Gortschakoff et Napoléon III.* Paris, 1913.

ĆOROVIĆ, Vladimir. *Velika Srbija.* Belgrade, 1924.

ČUBRILOVIĆ, Vasa. *Istorija političke misli u Srbiji XIX veka.* Belgrade, 1958 (On "Načertanije," pp. 151-195).

DJORDJEVIĆ, Dimitrije. *Révolutions nationales des peuples balkaniques, 1804-1914,* ed. J. Tadic. Belgrade, 1965.

DJORDJEVIĆ, Miroslav R. *Razvitak političkih i državnopravnih ustanova Srbije od kraja XVIII do početka XX veka.* Belgrade, 1970.

DJORDJEVIĆ, Vladan. *Crna Gora i Austrija, 1814-1894.* Belgrade, 1922.

————. *Evropa i Rumunija*. Belgrade, 1911.

DJUKANOVIĆ, Ilija N. *Ubistvo Kneza Mihaila i dogadjaji o kojima se nije smelo govoriti*. 2 vols., Belgrade, 1935-36.

DUČIĆ, Arhimandrit Nićifor. "Odgovor g. M. S. Piroćancu na njegove napomene u 193 br. 'Odjeka,' " *Odjek*, October 17, 1895.

DURKOVIĆ, Ljubomir. *Branislav. Prvi Jugoslovenski illegalni list, 1844-1845*. Belgrade, 1968.

DURKOVIĆ-JAKŠIĆ, Ljubomir. *Jugoslovensko poljska saradnja, 1772-1840*. Novi Sad, Matica srpska, 1971.

GARAŠANIN, Ilija. *Pisma Ilije Garašanina Jovanu Marinoviću*. ed. St. Lovčević. Belgrade, 1931. Srpske Kraljevska Akademija.

————. *Prepiska Ilije Garašanina*, ed. G. Jakšić, knj. I, 1839-1849. Belgrade, 1950 (no further volumes were published).

GARAŠANIN, Milutin. *Dva namesništva*. Belgrade, 1892.

————. *Jedno namesnikovanje*. Belgrade, 1890 (?).

GAVRANOVIĆ, Berislav. *Bosna i Hercegovina od 1853 do 1870 godine*. Sarajevo, 1956. Akademija nauk i umetnosti Bosne i Hercegovine. Gradja, knj. IV, odeljenje istoriko-filososkih nauka, knj. 2 (Archival documents).

GAVRILOVIĆ, Mihail. *Miloš Obrenović*. 3 vols., Belgrade, 1909-1912.

GRADJA za istoriju srpskog pokreta u Vojvodini, 1848-1849, ed. Radoslav Perović. Belgrade, 1952. SANU, Gradja, knj. VIII, Istoriski institut, knj. 7. Serija I, knj. 1 (March-June 1848). (Remainder is in manuscript in SANU).

GRUJIĆ, Jevrem. *Zapisi Jevrem Grujića*. 3 vols., Belgrade, 1922-23, SKA.

HANDELSMANN, Marceli. *Adam Czartoryski*. 3 vols in 4, Warsaw, 1948-1950.

————. *La question d'Orient et la politique yougoslave du Prince Czartoryski après 1840*. Paris, 1929.

————. *Nicolas Ier et la Question du Proche Orient*. Paris, 1934.

HRISTIĆ, Filip. *Pisma Filipa Hristića Jovanu Ristiću, 1868-1880*, ed. G. Jakšić. Belgrade, 1953. SAN, Pos. izdanja, knj, 206, odeljenje društvenih nauka, knj. 8.

HRISTIĆ, M. *Jedan listak iz diplomatske istorije Srbije*. Belgrade, 1893.

HRISTIĆ, M. F. *Srbija i Engleska pre pola veka. Misija Filipa Hristića u Londonu 1863 godine*. Belgrade, 1910.

IGNJATOVIĆ, Jakov. *Memoari*. Belgrade, 1966. Srpska književna zadruga, vol. 399.

ILIĆ, Dragoslav. *Toma Vučić-Perišić.* Belgrade, 1956.

IORGA, Nicolae. *Correspondance diplomatique roumaine sous le Rei Charles Ier.* Bucharest, 1938.

JAKŠIĆ, Grgur. *Evropa i vaskrs Srbije, 1804-1834.* Belgrade, 1927.

JAKŠIĆ, G. and V. VUČKOVIĆ. *Spoljna politika Srbije za vlade Kneza Mihaila.* Belgrade, 1963. Istorijski Institut (indispensable).

JANKOVIĆ, Dragoslav. *O političkim strankama u Srbiji XIX veka.* Belgrade, 1951.

JOVANOVIĆ, Radovan. *Politički odnosi Crne Gora i Srbije, 1860-1878.* Cetinje, 1977.

JOVANOVIĆ, Slobodan. *Druga vlada Miloša i Mihaila, 1858-1868.* Belgrade, 1923.

————. *Ustavobranitelji i njihova vlada 1838-1858.* Belgrade, 1925.

————. *Vlada Milana Obrenovića, 1868-1889.* 2 vols., Belgrade, 1926-27 (classic accounts superbly written).

JOVANOVIĆ, Vladimir. *Za slobodu i narod.* Novi Sad, 1868.

KALLÁY, Benjamin. *Dnevnik Benjamina Kalaja, 1868-1875,* ed. A. Radenić. Belgrade, 1976.

KEĆMANOVIĆ, Ilija. *Ivo Franjo Jukić.* Belgrade, 1963.

KLAPKA, Georg. *Der Nationalkrieg in Ungarn und Siebenbürgen in den Jahren 1848 und 1849.* Leipzig, 1851.

KONEV, Il. *B'lgaro-sr'bskite literaturni vr'zki prez XIX v.* Sofia, 1964.

KONSTANTINOV, Georgi. *Vodji bugarskog narodnog pokreta: Rakovski-Karavelov-Botjev.* Belgrade, 1939.

LEBL, A. *Revolucionarni pokret u Vojvodini 1848-1849 godine.* Novi Sad, 1960.

LHÉRITIER, Michel. *Histoire diplomatique de la Grèce de 1821 à nos jours.* 3 vols., Paris, 1925.

MARINKOVIĆ, Dimitrije. *Uspomene i doživljaji Dimitrija Marinkovića 1846-1869,* ed. D. Stranjaković. Belgrade, 1939. SKA.

MARKOVIĆ, Svetozar. *Srbija na istoku.* Belgrade, 1946.

MIHAILOVIĆ, Stevča. *Memoari Stefana-Stevče Mihailovića,* ed. Ž. Živanović. Belgrade, 1928. SKA, Zbornik za istoriju, jezik i književnost srpskog naroda. Prvo odeljenje. Knj. XVIII.

MILIĆEVIĆ, Jovan. *Jevrem Grujić.* Belgrade, 1964.

MILIĆEVIĆ, Milan Dj. *Kneževina Srbija.* Belgrade, 1876.

————. *Pomenik znamenitih ljudi u srpskog naroda novijega doba.* Belgrade, 1888. 2nd ed. with "Dodatak," Belgrade, 1900.

MILUTINOVIĆ, Kosta. *Štrosmajer i jugoslovensko pitanje.* Novi Sad, 1976.

NENADOVIĆ, M. *Karadjordje.* Belgrade, 18??.

———. *Memoari.* Belgrade, 1893.

NIKOLIĆ, Anastasije. "Opis radnje po predmetu opšteg sporazumljenija za ustanak i ujedinjenje (1860-1868)." Written April 1876. Manuscript in MID Archive, Belgrade.

NOVAK, Viktor. *Vuk i Hrvati.* Belgrade, 1967, SANU.

OSLOBODJENJE Gradova u Srbiji od Turaka, 1862-1867, ed. V. Čubrilović. SANU. Odeljenje društvenih nauka. Belgrade, 1970.

PAVIĆEVIĆ, Branko. *Crna Gora u ratu 1862 godine.* Belgrade, 1963, Istorijski institut.

PAVLOVIĆ, Dragoslav. *Srbija i srpski pokret u Južnoj Ugarskoj 1848 i 1849.* Belgrade, 1904.

PETROVIĆ, Nikola. *Svetozar Miletić.* Belgrade, 1958.

PETROVIĆ, Rade. *Nacionalno pitanje u Dalmaciji u XIX stoljecu (Narodna Stranka i nacionalno pitanje 1860-1880).* Sarajevo, 1968.

PIROĆANAC, Milan S. *Istoriska razmišljanja.* Belgrade, 1897.

———. *Knez Mihailo i zajednička radnja Balkanskih naroda.* Belgrade, 1895.

———. *Nekoliko napomene povodom bezimene brošure "Srpski narodni misao i M. Piroćanac."* Belgrade, 1895.

POLIT-DESANČIĆ, Mihailo. *Recimo koju.* Novi Sad, 1887.

———. *Sve dosadanje besede Dr. Mihail Polit-Desančića.* Novi Sad, 1883.

POPOV, Nil A. *Rossiia i Serbiia... s 1806 po 1856.* 2 vols., Moscow, 1869.

POPOVIĆ, V. *Politika Francuske i Austrije na Balkanu u vreme Napoleona III.* Belgrade, 1925. SKA, Posebno izdanje.

PRODANOVIĆ, Jaša. *Istorija političkih stranaka i struja u Srbiji.* Belgrade, 1947, vol. 1 (no more published).

PRŽIĆ, Ilija. *Spolašnja politika Srbije (1804-1914).* Belgrade, 1939.

RADENIĆ, Andrija. *Iz istorije Srbije i Vojvodine 1834-1914.* Novi Sad-Belgrade, 1973.

REISWITZ, J. A. von. *Belgrad-Berlin, Berlin-Belgrad, 1866-1871.* Munich and Berlin, 1936.

RISTIĆ, Jovan. *Bombardovanje Beograda.* Belgrade, 1872.

———. *Da kažemo još koju.* Belgrade, 1894.

————. *Jedno namesništvo 1868-1872.* Belgrade, 1894.

————. *Još malo svetlosti o našim poslednim ratovima za oslobodjenje i nezavisnost od 1875-1878.* Belgrade, 1898.

————. *Pisma Jovana Ristića Filipu Hristiću od 1870 do 1873 i od 1877 do 1880.* Belgrade, 1931.

————. *Poslednja godina spoljne politike Kneza Mihaila.* Belgrade, 1895.

————. *Prepiska izmedju Knjaza Mihaila Obrenovića III.* Belgrade, 1897.

————. *Spoljašnji odnošaji Srbije Novijega vremena 1848-1872.* 3 vols., Belgrade, 1887-1901.

SIMIĆ, Kosta. *Četrdeset druga.* Belgrade, 18??.

SKERLIĆ, Jovan. *Istorijski pregled srpske štampe, 1791-1911.* Belgrade, 1911.

SLIJEPCEVIĆ, Djoko. *Srpsko-arbanaški odnosi kroz vekove za posebnim osvrtom najnovije vreme.* Munich, 1974.

STAJIĆ, Vasa. *Svetozar Miletić.* Belgrade, 1938.

STIPČEVIĆ, Nikša. *Dva preporoda. Studije o italjansko-srpskim kulturnim i političkim vezama u XIX veka.* Belgrade, 1979.

STOJANČEVIĆ, Vladimir. *Južnoslovenskie narodi u Osmanskom carstvu od Jedrenskog mira 1829. do Pariskog Kongresa 1856. godine.* Belgrade, 1971.

STRANJAKOVIĆ, Dragoslav. "Ilija Garašanin" (1949), unpublished manuscript in Arhiv SANU, No. 14233. (Indispensable source.)

————. *Mihailo i Julija.* Belgrade, 1940.

————. *Vlada Ustavobranitelja, 1842-1853.* Belgrade, 1932. (Very valuable source.)

————. *Vučićeva buna 1842 g.* Belgrade, 1936. SKA, Posebno izdanje 112, Društveni i istoriski spiski, knj. 46.

STRATIMIROVIĆ, Djordje. *Uspomene generala Djordje Stratimirovića.* Vienna-Zagreb, 1913.

ŠIMUNJIĆ. *"Načertanije," Tajni spis srpske nactionalne i vanske politike.* Zagreb, 1944.

TARLE, E. V. *Krymskaia voina.* 2 vols., Moscow-Leningrad, 1950.

TATISHCHEV, S. S. *Vneshniaia politika Imperatora Nikolaia Pervogo.* St. Petersburg, 1887.

THIM, Jozsef. *A Magyarorszagi 1848-49. Iki Szerb Fölkeles Törtenete.* 3 vols., Budapest, 1930-1940 (text in Magyar, but bibliography in vol. I, pp. 447-481 contains numerous items in other languages).

TOSHEV, Andrei. *Balkanskite voini.* Sofia, 1925.

VASIĆ, Ignjat (Prota). *Dnevnik.* Sabac, 1889.

VESELINOVIĆ, Rajko L., ed. *Gradja za istoriju Beograda od 1806 do 1867.* Belgrade, 1965.

VUČKOVIĆ, Vojislav J. *Politička aksija Srbije u južnoslovenskim pokrajinama Habsburške Monarhije, 1859-1874.* Belgrade, 1965. (Extremely important documentary collection from a variety of archives.)

VUJOVIĆ, Dimitrije-Dimo. *Crna Gora i Francuska, 1860-1914.* Cetinje, 1971.

WENDEL, Hermann. *Aus dem südslawischen Risorgimento.* Gotha, 1921.

————. *Bismarck und Serbien im Jahre 1866.* Berlin, 1927.

WERTHEIMER, Eduard von. *Graf Julius Andrassy, sein Leben und seine Zeit.* 3 vols., Stuttgart, 1910-1913.

ŽAČEK, Vaclav. *František Zach.* Prague, 1977.

ŽIVKOVIĆ, Blagoje. *Predaja gradova 1867. godine u ocima savremenika.* Belgrade, 1967.

ŽUJOVIĆ, Mladen. *Beleške.* Belgrade, 1902.

VI. ARTICLES

ALEKSIĆ, Liljana. "Francuski uticaj u spoljašnoj i unutrašnjoj politici Srbije za vreme Krimskog rata (1853-1856)," *Istoriski časopis,* XI (1960), pp. 55-87.

————. "Misija Miloja Lešjanina u Parizu, Londonu i Torinu 1862 godine," *Ist. časopis,* XXI (1974), pp. 125-164.

ALEKŠIĆ-PEJKOVIĆ, L. "Srpska štampa i ratovi za oslobodjenje i ujedinjenje Italiji, 1859-1866," *Ist. časopis,* XX (1973), pp. 251-306.

ALEKSIĆ, L. "Štv je dovelo do stvaranja "Načertanije," *Istoriski pregled,* I (1954), 2, pp. 68 ff.

BATOWSKI, H. "Jedan poljski preteća Balkanske unije. Knez Adam Czartoryski," *Knjiga o Balkanu,* II. Belgrade, 1937.

BERIĆ, Dušan. "Socijalno-politička previranja u Bosni, 1848 godine," *Ist. časopis,* XXV-XXVI (1978-79), pp. 139-150.

BUCAR, F. "Arhiv i muzej knezova Cartoryskih u Krakowu," *Obzor,* LXXIV (1933), no. 55.

ĆOROVIĆ, Vladimir (ed.). "Jedan memorandum Ljudevita Gaja o prilikama u Srbiji iz 1846 godine," *Spomenik SKA,* LXII (1925).

————. "Oko pada Ilije Garašanina u jesen 1867 godine," *Politika,* April 23-26, 1938.

————. "Pobliski srpskoj prošlosti–Knez Nikola prilazi Austriji, 1862-1866," *Politika*, No. 5186, October 1, 1922.

————. "Pregovori o balkanskim savezima," *GNČupića*, XLVII (1938).

————. "Pruska i Srbija 1866 godine," *Politika*, May 1, 1925.

CZAJKOWSKI, Michal. "Zapiski," *Russkaia starina*, 1895-1904.

ĆUBRILOVIĆ, Vaso. "Ilija Garašanin," *Enciklopedija Jugoslavije*, III, p. 428. Zagreb, 1958.

————. "Istorijski osnovi postanku Jugoslavije 1918," *Naučni skup u povodu 50-godisnice raspada Austro-ugarske Monarhije i stvaranje jugoslavenske države*, pp. 59-99 (1969).

DANIĆ, Danilo. "Uticaj garantnih sila na politiku ustavobranitelja," *Pravda* (Belgrade), January 6-9, 1939, p. 51.

DIMITRIJEVIĆ, Stevan. "Stevana Stratimirovića mitropolita karlovačkog plan za oslobodjenje srpskog naroda," *Bogoslovlje*, I (Belgrade, 1926).

DIMITROV, S. A. "Serbiia i krest'ianskoe vosstanie 1850 g. v Bolgarii," *Études Balkaniques*, I 1964) (Sofia), pp. 49-70.

DOSTIAN, I. A. "K voprosu ob anglo-russkom sopernichestve v Serbskom kniazestve v 30-3 gody XIX v.," *Sovetskoe Slavianovedenie*, 1966, No. 66, pp. 17-30.

DURKOVIĆ-JAKŠIĆ, Ljubomir. "Učestvovanije Poljaka u Omer-Pašinom ratovanju u Bosni i Hercegovini 1850-1851 godine," *Ist. časopis, XXI* (1974), pp. 269-276.

————. "Saradnja Jugoslovena sa Poljskim društvima "Ligom Poljskom" i "Slovjanskom Lipom" 1848-1849 godine," *Ist. časopis, XXI* (1974), pp. 261-68.

EKMEČIĆ, Milorad. "Mit o revoluciji i austrijska politika prema Bosni, Hercegovini i Crnoj Gori za vrijeme Krimskog rata 1853-56 godine," *GDIst.BiH*, 1963, pp. 95-165.

————. "Nacionalna politika Srbije prema Bosni i Hercegovini i agrarno pitanje (1844-75)," *GIDBiH*, X (1959), pp. 179-219.

————. "Pokušaji organizovanja ustanka u Bosni i Hercegovini 1860-62 g.," *GIDBiH*, IX (1957), pp. 73-107.

————. "Spoljni faktor u procesu sazrijevanja balkanskih revolucija 1849-1878," *JIC*, III (1964), sv. 3, pp. 3-35.

————. "Srpsko-bugarski odnosi polovinom XIX vijeka (1844-1853)," *Ist. časopis*, XXVII (1980), pp. 141-156.

GARAŠANIN, Ilija. "Spomenica srbske vlade na visoku Portu od godine 1854," *Narodni list*, No. 17, 1878, p. 37.

GAVRILOVIĆ, Slavko. "Pokušaj obaranja Ustavobranitelja 1847 godine," *Ist. časopis,* XXIV (1977), pp. 177-189.

GROSUL, V. Ia. "Pol'skaia politicheskaia emigratsiia na Balkanakh v 40-nachale 50-kh godov XIX v.," *BISbor.,* II (Kishinev, 1970), pp. 23-68.

HANDELSMANN, Marceli. "La politique yougoslave du prince Czartoryski entre 1840-48," *Bull. int. de l'Acad. polonaise des sciences et lettres* (Krakow, 1929), pp. 107-112.

―――. "Polska polityka jugoslowianska w latach 1840-1848," ibid.

HRISTIĆ, Nikola. "Iz memoarskih zabeležaka starog državnika, Nikole Hristića," February 16, 21, and 27, 1940.

"Ilija Garašanin," *Zastava,* September 18, 1870, No. 109 (critical article).

JAKŠIĆ, Grgur. "Jedan sukob izmedju Ilije Garašanina i Milovoje Blaznavca," *Arhiv za Pravne i društvene nauke,* XXXIII (Belgrade, 1938).

―――. "Knez Mihailo i Bosna," *Politika,* April 23-26, 1937.

―――. "Prvi srpski-grčki savez, 1867-68," *Arhiv za pravne i društvene nauke* (1924).

―――. "Sastanak Ilije Garašanina i Louis Napoleon," *Politika,* January 6-9, 1934, p. 9.

―――. "Tragični svršetak Kneza Mihaila," *Politika,* January 6-9, 1937, p. 6 (according to Svetozar and Ilija Garašanin).

JOVANOVIĆ, Slobodan. "Ilija Garašanin," in *Portrety iz istorije književnosti,* Novi Sad, 1963, pp. 79 ff.

―――――. "Spoljašnja politika Ilije Garašanina," *SKG* (1931), pp. 422-431.

KEĆMANOVIĆ, Ilija. "Barišceva afera," *Naučno društvo NR BiH,* Djela, knj. III, odelj. istoiko-filoloskih nauka, knj. 3.

KIRILOVIĆ, Dimitrije. "Ban Jelačić o srpsko-hrvatskom jedinstvu," *Politika,* September 19, 1928.

―――. "Vojvodina i Srbija pre 75 godina," *Politika,* January 6-9, 1937.

LASCARIS, S. Th. "La première alliance entre la Grèce et la Serbia''' âout 1867," *Le Monde Slave,* III, No. 9 (Paris, 1926).

LESHCHILOVSKAIA, I. I. "Ljudevit Gaj," *Sovetskoe slavianovedenie,* 1973, No. 2, pp. 37-43.

LJOTIĆ, Vlada. "Sveto-Andrejska Skupština i odvodjenje Kneza Aleksandru u grad Turcima," *Politika,* July 14, 1925.

LUCERNA, Kamila. "U spomen Matije Bana Dubrovćana," *Ljetopis Jug. Akademije,* (1906-07). Zagreb, 1907, pp. 120-168.

MILIĆEVIĆ, M. B. "Iz svojih uspomena," *GNĆupića,* XVII (1897), pp. 1-71.

MILIĆEVIĆ, Milan Dj. "Iz uspomena," *SKG,* knj. 33, August 16, 1931.

NIKITIN, S. A. "Evropeiskaia diplomatiia i Serbiia v nachale 60-kh godov XIX veka," *Voprosy istorii,* IX (1962), pp. 75-102.

—————. "K voprosu o politicheskoi dvizhenii serbov Voevodiny v 1848 godu," *Uchenye zap. in-ta Slavianovedeniia* (Moscow, 1949), pp. 85-118.

—————. "Russkaia diplomatiia i natsional'noe dvizhenie iuzhnykh slavian 50-70 gg. XIX v.", *Istoriia, fol'klor, iskusstvo slav. narodov. Doklady sov. delegatsii.* V. Mezhdunarodnyi s'ezd slavistov (Moscow, 1963), pp. 159-86.

NOVAK, Viktor. "Kako i zašto nestala prepiska izmedju Kneza Mihaila i Štrosmajera," *Politika,* January 6-9, 1935, p. 13.

—————. "Krsto Kulišić i Dalmatinski pokret 1848," *Politika,* January 6-9, 1937, p. 10.

PEROVIĆ, Radoslav. "Beograd za vreme Vučićeve bune," *GMgradaBeograda,* II (1955).

—————. "Diplomatskii spor o prenosu srpskog oružja 1862 preko Rumunije," *GNČupića*

—————. "Oko 'Načertanije' iz 1844 godine," *Istorijski glasnik,* I (1963), pp. 71-94.

POPOVIĆ, Milivoje. "Borba Srbije za neutralnost u Krimskom ratu," *Politika,* January 6-9, 1940, p. 16.

POPOVIĆ, Vasilj. "Brlić i Garašanin," *Politika,* January 6-9, 1939.

—————. "Meternihovi pogledi o promenama u Srbiji 1842 i 1843 godine," *Prilozi za književnost, jezik, istoriju i folklor,* knj. VII (Belgrade, 1927), pp. 123-129.

RADENIĆ, Andrija. "O problemima periodizacije i ocenijivanja srpskog pokreta u Ugarskoj, 1848-1849," *Ist. časopis,* XXVII (1980), pp. 159-181.

—————. "Svetoandrejska Skupština," *Spomenik SANU,* CXIII (Belgrade, 1964) (important collection of documents with commentary).

—————. "Vojvodjanska štampa prema Namesništvu 1868-1872," *Ist. časopis,* 1956, knj. VI, pp. 65-108.

RISTIĆ, Jovan. "Autobiografija J. Ristića," *Arhivski pregled* (Belgrade), 1967, 1-2.

ROUX, Charles. "La Russie, la France et la question d'Orient apres la guerre de Crimee," *Revue historique,* 1912.

SENKEVICH, I. G. "Russkaia diplomatiia v pervye mesiatsy Kritskogo vosstaniia, 1866-1868 gg.," *BISbor.* (Kishinev, 1968), pp. 76-94.

SETON-WATSON, R. W. "Les relations de l'Autriche-Hongrie et de la Serbie entre 1868 et 1874," *Le Monde Slave*, (1926), I, 211-230, 2, 186-204.

STEFANOVIĆ-VILOVSKI, "Odlomci iz memoara," *Trgovinski glasnik*, 1908, No. 190, 194.

STOJANČEVIĆ, Vladimir. "Razvojni pravci državne politike Kneževine Srbije prema Bugarima u XIX veku (do 1878), *Zbornik za istoriju*, XX (1979), Matica Srpska, Novi Sad, pp. 16 ff.

STRANJAKOVIĆ, Dragoslav. "Arbanija i Srbija u XIX veku," *SKG*, 1937, N.S., knj. II, pp. 624-633.

—————. "Bolesti Ilije Garašanina," *Srpski arhiv za celokupno lekarstvo*, LXXXIV, No. 5 (1936), pp. 683-690.

—————. "Bosanski franjevci u Srbiji, 1843 i 1844," *Pravda*, April 27-30, 1940.

—————. "Buna Srba hrišćana u Bosni (1833), *GNĆupića*, XL (1931).

—————. "Ilija Garašanin i zabrana 'Šumadinke' 1850 g." *Prilozi za književnost, jezik i folklor*, knj. XII, sv. 1 (Belgrade, 1932), pp. 171-174.

—————. "Ilija Garašanin i zabrana Vukovih dela," *Kritika*, god II, knj. 3 (Belgrade, 1931), pp. 198-202.

—————. "Ilija Garašanin, šef političke propagande medju Jugoslovenima 1849-1853," *Politika*, January 6-9, 1936, p. 13.

—————. "Kako je postalo Garašaninovo 'Načertanije,'" *Spomenik SAN*, XCI, pp. 63-115 (important).

—————. "Kako je postalo namesništvo 1868 godine. Borba Blaznavca protiv Ilije Garašanina," *Pravda*, January 6-9, 1939.

—————. "La collaboration des Croates det des Serbes en 1848-1849," *Le Monde Slave*, June 1935.

—————. "Nacionalna politika kneza Miloša," *Politika*, October 10, 1939, p. 10.

—————. "Odnosi izmedju Zagreba i Beograda 1848 godine. Uloga Ljudevita Gaja i Garašanina," *Pravda*, April 23-26, 1938.

—————. "Politička propaganda Srbije, 1844-1858," *GIDuNS*, IX (Novi Sad, 1936), pp. 155-179 (important).

—————. "Svetozar Miletić i Jevrem Grujić," *Zbornik Matice Srpske za društvene nauke*, XIII-XIV (1956), pp. 141-148.

STRANJAKOVIĆ, Dragoslav. "Prvi politički sporazum izmedju Srba i Hrvata 1860 god," *Biblioteka Kulturnog Kluba,* II, br. 1-2 (Belgrade 1941) (remains in manuscript form).

————. "Uticaj poljskih emigranata na stvaranje Garašaninovo 'Načertanije,'" *Pravda,* February 6, 1939, No. 12299.

ŠIDAK, Jaroslav. "Hrvatsko pitanje u Habsburškoj monarhiji," *Historijski pregled,* IX (1963), 2, bilj. 27.

————. "Jugoslavenska ideja u hrvatskoj politici do prvoga svjetskog rata," *Enciklopedija moderna,* 1967, 3-4.

————. "Jugoslovenska ideja u ilirskom pokretu," *JIC,* II, No. 3 (Belgrade, 1963), pp. 31-42.

————. "L'Hôtel Lambert et les Croates," *Annales de l'institut français de Zagreb,* VI-VII (1942-43), pp. 1 ff.

————. "O uredniku i značenju ilirskog 'Branislava,' (1844-45)," *Historijski zbornik,* XIV (1961).

————. "Poljska revolucionarna propaganda u Hrvatskoj prije stotinu godina," *Hrvatsko kolo,* I (1948), pp. 542 ff.

————. "Prilozi historiji stranačkih odnosa u Hrvatskoj uoči 1848," *Historijski zbornik,* XIII (1960), pp. 67 ff.

ŠIŠIĆ, Ferdo. "Knez Mihailo i Bugari," *Politika,* August 8-9, 1937.

————. "Knez Miloš u Zagrebu 1848," *Jugoslavenska njiva,* VIII (1924), pp. 49-53, 139-44, 188-94, 219-30, 265-75, 297-302, 341-46. Interesting.

————. "'Načertanije' Ilije Garašanina u g. 1844," *Novosti,* 1929, No. 357 (Bozični broj.).

————. "Štrosmajerova ideja narodnog ujedinjenja," *Politika,* May 6-13, 1932.

ŠPIRA, Djerdj. "Pokušaji Generala Percela u probleće 1849 da se umire Srbi u Ugarskoj," *Zbornik za istoriju,* XXI (Matica srpska, 1980), pp. 135-148.

THIM, Jozsef. "Uloga Obrenovića za vrijeme (madžarske) revolucije (1848)," *Branik* (Novi Sad), November 23, 1893, No. 150.

TÜRR, Stefan. "Fürst Bismarck und die Ungarn: Reminiszenzen aus dem Jahre 1866," *Deutsche Revue,* XXV, No. 1 (1900), pp. 313 ff.

"Ukaz o penzionisanju Ilije Garašanina i postavljenju Jovana Ristića za ministra spoljnih poslova, 3 novembra 1867 u Beogradu," *Srpske novine,* No. 143, 1867.

VASILJEVIĆ, Jovan H. "Srpski narod i turske reforme (1852-1862)," *Brastvo,* XV (Belgrade, 1921), pp. 146-191.

VUČKOVIĆ, Vojislav. "Knez Miloš i osnovna politička misao sadržana u Garašaninovom 'Načertaniju'," *Jugoslovenska revija za medjunarodno pravo,* IV, No. 1 (1957), pp. 35-44.

————. "Prilog proućavanje postanka 'Načertanija' (1844) i 'Osnovnih misli' (1847)," *Jugoslovenska revija za medjunarodno pravo,* VIII, No. 1 (1961), pp. 49-79.

————. "Učešče Hrvata u pripremi Garašaninovo 'Načertanija'," *Jugoslovenska revija za medjunarodno pravo,* I (1956), pp. 44-58.

————. "Vojvodjansko pitanje u odnosima izmedju Srbije i Madjara od 1859 do 1868," *Zbornik Matice Srpske,* sv. 5, serija društvenih nauka, 1953.

VUKIČEVIĆ, Milenko. "Program spoljne politike Ilija Garašanina na koncu 1844 godine," *Delo* (1906), pp. 321-336 (first publication of "Načertanije").

VUKSAN, Dušan. "Crna Gora i Srbija. Prepiska Vladike Rada sa srpskim vladarima i drugim licima iz Srbije," *Zapisi* (Cetinje), II, 1928; III, Nos. 1-2, pp. 81-91; 3, pp. 168-73.

————. "Nekoliko pisama iz vremena knjaza Danila," *Zapisi* (Cetinje), XIV (1941), 2, pp. 104-107; 3, pp. 160-65.

ZACEK, Vaclav. "Češko i poljsko učešče u postanku Garašaninova 'Načertanija' (1844)," *Historijski zbornik* (1963), XVI, pp. 35-53 (vital).

————. "František Zah o stanju u Srbiji pedesetih godina XIX v.," *Istoriski glasnik,* 1978, 1-2, pp. 121-153.

————. "Uloga Františeka Zacha u Srbiji," *Glas SNU,* CCLXI (Belgrade, 1974), pp. 153-193 (important).

ADDENDA:
KRESTIĆ, Vasilije. "Knez Miloš Obrenović i Djakova Buna," *Glas SANU,* CCLXL, odeljenje istorijskih nauka, knj. 1 (Belgrade, 1974).

————. "Koncepcije Josipa Jurja Štrosmajera o istočnom pitanju," *Istraživanje,* knj. V (Novi Sad, 1975), pp. 347-426.

————. "Srbi u Vojvodini za vreme Bahova apsolutizma (1849-1860)," *Zbornik za istoriju* (Novi Sad), No. 13, 1976, pp. 53-69.

————. "Pisma Antonija Oreškovića Generalu Ištvanu Tiru (1864-1868), *Mešovite gradja.* Istorijski institut (Belgrade), knj. IV (1976), pp. 109-33.

————. "Jugoslovenska politika Josipa Jurja Štrosmajera," *Istoriski glasnik,* I (Belgrade, 1969), pp. 9-30.

INDEX

EAST EUROPEAN MONOGRAPHS

The *East European Monographs* comprise scholarly books on the history and civilization of Eastern Europe. They are published under the editorship of Stephen Fischer-Galati, in the belief that these studies contribute substantially to the knowledge of the area and serve to stimulate scholarship and research.

21. *The Crises of France's East-Central European Diplomacy, 1933–1938.* By Anthony J. Komjathy. 1976.
22. *Polish Politics and National Reform, 1775–1788.* By Daniel Stone. 1976.
23. *The Habsburg Empire in World War I.* Edited by Robert A. Kann, Bela K. Kiraly, and Paula S. Fichtner. 1977.
24. *The Slovenes and Yugoslavism, 1890–1914.* By Carole Rogel. 1977.
25. *German-Hungarian Relations and the Swabian Problem.* By Thomas Spira. 1977.
26. *The Metamorphosis of a Social Class in Hungary During the Reign of Young Franz Joseph.* By Peter I. Hidas. 1977.
27. *Tax Reform in Eighteenth Century Lombardy.* By Daniel M. Klang. 1977.
28. *Tradition versus Revolution: Russia and the Balkans in 1917.* By Robert H. Johnston. 1977.
29. *Winter into Spring: The Czechoslovak Press and the Reform Movement 1963–1968.* By Frank L. Kaplan. 1977.
30. *The Catholic Church and the Soviet Government, 1939–1949.* By Dennis J. Dunn. 1977.
31. *The Hungarian Labor Service System, 1939–1945.* By Randolph L. Braham. 1977.
32. *Consciousness and History: Nationalist Critics of Greek Society 1897–1914.* By Gerasimos Augustinos. 1977.
33. *Emigration in Polish Social and Political Thought, 1870–1914.* By Benjamin P. Murdzek. 1977.
34. *Serbian Poetry and Milutin Bojic.* By Mihailo Dordevic. 1977.
35. *The Baranya Dispute: Diplomacy in the Vortex of Ideologies, 1918–1921.* By Leslie C. Tihany. 1978.
36. *The United States in Prague, 1945–1948.* By Walter Ullmann. 1978.
37. *Rush to the Alps: The Evolution of Vacationing in Switzerland.* By Paul P. Bernard. 1978.
38. *Transportation in Eastern Europe: Empirical Findings.* By Bogdan Mieczkowski. 1978.
39. *The Polish Underground State: A Guide to the Underground, 1939–1945.* By Stefan Korbonski. 1978.
40. *The Hungarian Revolution of 1956 in Retrospect.* Edited by Bela K. Kiraly and Paul Jonas. 1978.
41. *Boleslaw Limanowski (1935–1935): A Study in Socialism and Nationalism.* By Kazimiera Janina Cottam. 1978.
42. *The Lingering Shadow of Nazism: The Austrian Independent Party Movement Since 1945.* By Max E. Riedlsperger. 1978.
43. *The Catholic Church, Dissent and Nationality in Soviet Lithuania.* By V. Stanley Vardys. 1978.
44. *The Development of Parliamentary Government in Serbia.* By Alex N. Dragnich. 1978.
45. *Divide and Conquer: German Efforts to Conclude a Separate Peace, 1914–1918.* By L. L. Farrar, Jr. 1978.
46. *The Prague Slav Congress of 1848.* By Lawrence D. Orton. 1978.
47. *The Nobility and the Making of the Hussite Revolution.* By John M. Klassen. 1978.
48. *The Cultural Limits of Revolutionary Politics: Change and Continuity in Socialist Czechoslovakia.* By David W. Paul. 1979.
49. *On the Border of War and Peace: Polish Intelligence and Diplomacy in 1937–1939 and the Origins of the Ultra Secret.* By Richard A. Woytak. 1979.
50. *Bear and Foxes: The International Relations of the East European States 1965–1969.* By Ronald Haly Linden. 1979.

51. *Czechoslovakia: The Heritage of Ages Past.* Edited by Ivan Volgyes and Hans Brisch. 1979.

52. *Prime Minister Gyula Andrassy's Influence on Habsburg Foreign Policy.* By Janos Decsy. 1979.

53. *Citizens for the Fatherland: Education, Educators, and Pedagogical Ideals in Eighteenth Century Russia.* By J. L. Black. 1979.

54. *A History of the "Proletariat": The Emergence of Marxism in the Kingdom of Poland, 1870–1887.* By Norman M. Naimark. 1979.

55. *The Slovak Autonomy Movement, 1935–1939: A Study in Unrelenting Nationalism.* By Dorothea H. El Mallakh. 1979.

56. *Diplomat in Exile: Francis Pulszky's Political Activities in England, 1849–1860.* By Thomas Kabdebo. 1979.

57. *The German Struggle Against the Yugoslav Guerrillas in World War II: German Counter-Insurgency in Yugoslavia, 1941–1943.* By Paul N. Hehn. 1979.

58. *The Emergence of the Romanian National State.* By Gerald J. Bobango. 1979.

59. *Stewards of the Land: The American Farm School and Modern Greece.* By Brenda L. Marder. 1979.

60. *Roman Dmowski: Party, Tactics, Ideology, 1895–1907.* By Alvin M. Fountain, II. 1980.

61. *International and Domestic Politics in Greece During the Crimean War.* By Jon V. Kofas. 1980.

62. *Fires on the Mountain: The Macedonian Revolutionary Movement and the Kidnapping of Ellen Stone.* By Laura Beth Sherman. 1980.

63. *The Modernization of Agriculture: Rural Transformation in Hungary, 1848–1975.* Edited by Joseph Held. 1980.

64. *Britain and the War for Yugoslavia, 1940–1943.* By Mark C. Wheeler. 1980.

65. *The Turn to the Right: The Ideological Origins and Development of Ukrainian Nationalism, 1919–1929.* By Alexander J. Motyl. 1980.

66. *The Maple Leaf and the White Eagle: Canadian-Polish Relations, 1918–1978.* By Aloysius Balawyder. 1980.

67. *Antecedents of Revolution: Alexander I and the Polish Congress Kingdom, 1815–1825.* By Frank W. Thackeray. 1980.

68. *Blood Libel at Tiszaeszlar.* By Andrew Handler. 1980.

69. *Democratic Centralism in Romania: A Study of Local Communist Politics.* By Daniel N. Nelson. 1980.

70. *The Challenge of Communist Education: A Look at the German Democratic Republic.* By Margrete Siebert Klein. 1980.

71. *The Fortifications and Defense of Constantinople.* By Byron C. P. Tsangadas. 1980.

72. *Balkan Cultural Studies.* By Stavro Skendi. 1980.

73. *Studies in Ethnicity: The East European Experience in America.* Edited by Charles A. Ward, Philip Shashko, and Donald E. Pienkos. 1980.

74. *The Logic of "Normalization:" The Soviet Intervention in Czechoslovakia and the Czechoslovak Response.* By Fred Eidlin. 1980.

75. *Red Cross. Black Eagle: A Biography of Albania's American Schol.* By Joan Fultz Kontos. 1981.

76. *Nationalism in Contemporary Europe.* By Franjo Tudjman. 1981.

77. *Great Power Rivalry at the Turkish Straits: The Montreux Conference and Convention of 1936.* By Anthony R. DeLuca. 1981.

78. *Islam Under the Double Eagle: The Muslims of Bosnia and Hercegovina, 1878–1914.* By Robert J. Donia. 1981.

79. *Five Eleventh Century Hungarian Kings: Their Policies and Their Relations with Rome.* By Z. J. Kosztolnyik. 1981.

80. *Prelude to Appeasement: East European Central Diplomacy in the Early 1930's.* By Lisanne Radice. 1981.

81. *The Soviet Regime in Czechoslovakia.* By Zdenek Krystufek. 1981.

82. *School Strikes in Prussian Poland, 1901–1907: The Struggle Over Bilingual Education.* By John J. Kulczychi. 1981.

83. *Romantic Nationalism and Liberalism: Joachim Lelewel and the Polish National Idea.* By Joan S. Skurnowicz. 1981.

84. *The "Thaw" In Bulgarian Literature.* By Atanas Slavov. 1981.

85. *The Political Thought of Thomas G. Masaryk.* By Roman Szporluk. 1981.

86. *Prussian Poland in the German Empire, 1871–1900.* By Richard Blanke. 1981.

87. *The Mazepists: Ukrainian Separatism in the Early Eighteenth Century.* By Orest Subtelny. 1981.

88. *The Battle for the Marchlands: The Russo-Polish Campaign of 1920.* By Adam Zamoyski. 1981.

89. *Milovan Djilas: A Revolutionary as a Writer.* By Dennis Reinhartz. 1981.

90. *The Second Republic: The Disintegration of Post-Munich Czechoslovakia, October 1938-March 1939.* By Theodore Prochazka, Sr. 1981.

91. *Financial Relations of Greece and the Great Powers, 1832–1862.* By Jon V. Kofas. 1981.

92. *Religion and Politics: Bishop Valerian Trifa and His Times.* By Gerald J. Bobango. 1981.

93. *The Politics of Ethnicity in Eastern Europe.* Edited by George Klein and Milan J. Reban. 1981.

94. *Czech Writers and Politics.* By Alfred French. 1981.

95. *Nation and Ideology: Essays in Honor of Wayne S. Vucinich.* Edited by Ivo Banac, John G. Ackerman, and Roman Szporluk. 1981.

96. *For God and Peter the Great: The Works of Thomas Consett, 1723–1729.* Edited by James Cracraft. 1982.

97. *The Geopolitics of Leninism.* By Stanley W. Page. 1982

98. *Karel Havlicek (1821–1856): A National Liberation Leader of the Czech Renascence.* By Barbara K. Reinfeld. 1982.

99. *Were-Wolf and Vampire in Romania.* By Harry A. Senn. 1982.

100. *Ferdinand I of Austria: The Politics of Dynasticism in the Age of Reformation.* By Paula Sutter Fichtner. 1982

101. *France in Greece During World War I: A Study in the Politics of Power.* By Alexander S. Mitrakos. 1982.

102. *Authoritarian Politics in a Transitional State: Istvan Bethlen and the Unified Party in Hungary, 1919–1926.* By William M. Batkay. 1982.

103. *Romania Between East and West: Historical Essays in Memory of Constantin C. Giurescu.* Edited by Stephen Fischer-Galati, Radu R. Florescu and George R. Ursul. 1982.

104. *War and Society in East Central Europe: From Hunyadi to Rakoczi—War and Society in Late Medieval and Early Modern Hungary.* Edited by János Bak and Béla K. Király. 1982.

105. *Total War and Peace Making: A Case Study on Trianon.* Edited by Béla K. Király, Peter Pastor, and Ivan Sanders. 1982

106. *Army, Aristocracy, and Monarchy: Essays on War, Society, and Government in Austria, 1618–1780.* Edited by Wayne S. Vucinich. 1982.

107. *The First Serbian Uprising, 1804–1813.* Edited by Wayne S. Vucinich. 1982.

108. *Propaganda and Nationalism in Wartime Russia: The Jewish Anti-Fascist Committee in the USSR, 1941-1948.* By Shimon Redich. 1982.

109. *One Step Back, Two Steps Forward: On the Language Policy of the Communist Party of Soviet Union in the National Republics.* By Michael Bruchis. 1982.

110. *Bessarabia and Bukovina: The Soviet-Romanian Territorial Dispute.* by Nicholas Dima. 1982

111. *Greek-Soviet Relations, 1917-1941.* By Andrew L. Zapantis. 1982.

112. *National Minorities in Romania: Change in Transylvania.* By Elemer Illyes. 1982.

113. *Dunarea Noastra: Romania, the Great Powers, and the Danube Question, 1914-1921.* by Richard C. Frucht. 1982.

114. *Continuity and Change in Austrian Socialism: The Eternal Quest for the Third Way.* By Melanie A. Sully. 1982

115. *Catherine II's Greek Prelate: Eugenios Voulgaris in Russia, 1771-1806.* By Stephen K. Batalden. 1982.

116. *The Union of Lublin: Polish Federalism in the Golden Age.* By Harry E. Dembkowski. 1982.

117. *Heritage and Continuity in Eastern Europe: The Transylvanian Legacy in the History of the Romanians.* By Cornelia Bodea and Virgil Candea. 1982.

118. *Contemporary Czech Cinematography: Jiri Menzel and the History of The "Closely Watched Trains".* By Josef Skvorecky. 1982.

119. *East Central Europe in World War I: From Foreign Domination to National Freedom.* By Wiktor Sukiennicki. 1982.

120. *City, Town, and Countryside in the Early Byzantine Era.* Edited by Robert L. Hohlfelder. 1982.

121. *The Byzantine State Finances in the Eighth and Ninth Centuries.* By Warren T. Treadgold. 1982.

122. *East Central European Society and War in Pre-Revolutionary Eighteenth Century.* Edited by Gunther E. Rothenberg, Bela K. Kiraly and Peter F. Sugar. 1982.

123. *Czechoslovak Policy and the Hungarian Minority, 1945-1948.* By Kalman Janics. 1982.

124. *At the Brink of War and Peace: The Tito-Stalin Split in a Historic Perspective.* Edited by Wayne S. Vucinich. 1982.

125. *The Road to Bellapais: The Turkish Cypriot Exodus to Northern Cyprus.* By Pierre Oberling. 1982.

126. *Essays on World War I: Origins and Prisoners of War.* Edited by Peter Pastor and Samuel R. Williamson, Jr. 1983.

127. *Panteleimon Kulish: A Sketch of His Life and Times.* By George S. N. Luckyj. 1983.

128. *Economic Development in the Habsburg Monarchy in the Nineteenth Century: Essays.* Edited by John Komlos. 1983.

129. *Warsaw Between the World Wars: Profile of the Capital City in a Developing Land, 1918-1939.* By Edward D. Wynot, Jr. 1983.

130. *The Lust for Power: Nationalism, Slovakia, and The Communists, 1918-1948.* By Yeshayahu Jelinek. 1983.

131. *The Tsar's Loyal Germans: The Riga German Community: Social Change and the Nationality Question, 1855-1905.* By Anders Henriksson. 1983.

132. *Society in Change: Studies in Honor of Bela K. Kiraly.* Edited by Steven Bela Vardy. 1983.

133. *Authoritariansim in Greece: The Metaxas Regime.* By Jon V. Kofas. 1983.

134. *New Hungarian Peasants: An East Central European Experience with Collectivization.* Edited by Marida Hollos and Bela C. Maday. 1983.

135. *War, Revolution, and Society in Romania: The Road to Independence*. Edited by Ilie Ceausescu. 1983.
136. *The Beginning of Cyrillic Printing, Cracow, 1491: From the Orthodox Past in Poland*. By Szczepan K. Zimmer. 1983.
137. *Effects of World War I. The Class War After the Great War: The Rise of Communist Parties in East Central Europe, 1918-1921*. Edited by Ivo Banac. 1983.
138. *Bulgaria 1878-1918. A History*. By Richard J. Crampton. 1983.
139. *T. G. Masaryk Revisited: A Cirtical Assessment*. By Hanus J. Hajek. 1983.
140. *The Cult of Power: Dictators in the Twentieth Century*. Edited by Joseph Held. 1983.
141. *Economy and Foreign Policy: The Struggle of the Great Powers for Economic Hegemony in the Danube Valley, 1919-1939*. By György Ránki. 1983.
142. *Germany, Russia, and the Balkans: Prelude to the Nazi-Soviet Non-Aggression Pact*. By Marilynn Giroux Hitchens. 1983.
143. Guestworkers in the German Reich: The Poles in Wilhelmian Germany. By Richard Charles Murphy. 1983.
144. *The Latvian Impact on the Bolshevik Revolution*. By Andrew Ezergailis. 1983.
145. *The Rise of Moscow's Power*. By Henryk Paszkiewicz. 1983.
146. *A Question of Empire: Leopold I and the War of the Spanish Succession, 1701-1705*. By Linda and Marsha Frey. 1983.
147. *Effects of World War I. The Uprooted: Hungarian Refugees and Their Impact on Hungarian Domestic Policies, 1918-1921*. By Istvan I. Mocsy. 1983.
148. *Nationalist Integration Through Socialist Planning: An Anthropological Study of a Romanian New Town*. By Steven L. Sampson. 1983.
149. *Decadence of Freedom: Jacques Riviere's Quest of Russian Mentality*. By Jean-Pierre Cap. 1983.
150. *East Central European Society in the Age of Revolutions, 1775-1856*. Edited by Béla K. Király. 1984.
151. *The Crucial Decade: East Central European Society and National Defense, 1859-1870*. Edited by Béla K. Király. 1984.
152. *The First War between Socialist States: The Hungarian Revolution of 1956 and Its Impact*. Edited by Béla K. Király, Barbara Lotze and Nandor Dreisziger. 1984.
153. *Russian Bolshevism and British Labor, 1917-1921*. By Morton H. Cowden. 1984.
154. *Feliks Dzierzynski and the SDKPIL: A Study of the Origins of Polish Communism*. By Robert Blobaum. 1984.
155. *Studies on Kosova*. Edited by Arshi Pipa and Sami Repishti. 1984.
156. *New Horizons in East-West Economic and Business Relations*. Edited by Marvin A. Jackson and James D. Woodson. 1984.
157. *Czech Nationalism in the Nineteenth Century*. By John F. N. Bradley. 1984.
158. *The Theory of the General Strike from the French Revolution to Poland*. By Phil H. Goodstein. 1984.
159. *King Zog and the Struggle for Stability in Albania*. By Bernd J. Fischer. 1984.
160. *Tradition and Avant-Garde: The Arts in Serbian Culture between the Two World Wars*. By Jelena Milojković-Djurić. 1984.
161. *The Megali Idea and the Greek Turkish War of 1897*. By Theodore G. Tatsios. 1984.
162. *The Hungarian Jewish Catastrophe: A Selected and Annotated Bibliography*. By Randolph L. Braham. 1984.
163. *Goli Otok—Island of Death [A Diary in Letters]*. By Venko Markovski. 1984.
164. *Initiation and Initiative: An Exploration of the Life and Ideas of Dimitrije Mitrinovic*. By Andrew Rigby. 1984.
165. *Nations, Nationalities, Peoples: A Study of the Nationality Policies of the Communist Party in Soviet Moldavia*. By Michael Bruchis. 1984.
166. *Frederick I, The Man and His Times*. By Linda and Marsha Frey. 1984.
167. *The Effects of World War I: War Communism in Hungary*. By György Peteri. 1984.

168. *PNA: A Centennial History of the Polish National Alliance of the United States of North America*. By Donald E. Pienkos. 1984.

169. *The Slovenes of Carinthia*. By Thomas M. Barker and Andreas Moritsch. 1984.

170. *The Saga of Kosovo: Focus of Serbian-Albanian Relations*. By Alex N. Dragnich and Slavko Todorovich. 1984.

171. *Germany's International Monetary Policy and the European Monetary System*. By Hugh Kaufmann. 1985.

172. *Kiril and Methodius: Founders of Slavonic Writing*. Edited by Ivan Duichev. 1985.

173. *The United States and the Greek War for Independence, 1821-1828*. By Paul C. Pappas. 1985.

174. *Joseph Eötvös and the Modernization of Hungary, 1840-1870*. By Paul Bödy. 1985.

175. *Jewish Leadership during the Nazi Era: Patterns of Behavior in the Free World*. Edited by Randolph L. Braham. 1985.

176. *The American Mission in the Allied Control Commission for Bulgaria, 1944-1947: History and Transcripts*. Edited by Michael M. Boll. 1985.

177. *The United States, Great Britain, and the Sovietization of Hungary, 1945-1948*. By Stanley M. Max. 1985.

178. *Hunyadi: Legend and Reality*. By Joseph Held. 1985.

179. *Clio's Art in Hungary and in Hungarian-America*. By Steven Bela Vardy. 1985.

180. *Slovakia 1918-1938: Education and the Making of a Nation*. By Owen V. Johnson. 1985.

181. *Ilija Garasanin: Balkan Bismarck*. By David MacKenzie. 1985.

182. *Medieval Buda: A Study of Municipal Government and Jurisdiction in the Kingdom of Hungary*. By Martyn C. Rady. 1985.

183. *Eastern Europe in the Aftermath of Solidarity*. By Adam Bromke. 1985.

184. *Istvan Tisza: The Liberal Vision and Conservative Statecraft of a Magyar Nationalist*. By Gabor Vermes. 1985.